Reinterpreting Russian History

Reinterpreting Russian History

READINGS
860–1860s

Compiled and Edited by

DANIEL H. KAISER
Grinnell College

GARY MARKER
State University of New York at Stony Brook

New York   Oxford
OXFORD UNIVERSITY PRESS
1994

For Joshua, Nina, and Andrew

Oxford University Press

Oxford   New York   Toronto
Delhi   Bombay   Calcutta   Madras   Karachi
Kuala Lumpur   Singapore   Hong Kong   Tokyo
Nairobi   Dar es Salaam   Cape Town
Melbourne   Auckland   Madrid

and associated companies in
Berlin   Ibadan

Published by Oxford University Press, Inc.,
200 Madison Avenue, New York, New York 10016

Oxford is a registered trademark of Oxford University Press

Library of Congress Cataloging-in-Publication Data
Reinterpreting Russian history : readings, 860-1860's / compiled and edited by
Daniel H. Kaiser and Gary Marker.
p.   cm.
ISBN 0-19-507857-8.
ISBN 0-19-507858-6 (pbk.)
1. Russia—History—Sources.   2. Russia—Historiography.
I. Kaiser, Daniel H., 1945-   . II. Marker, Gary, 1948-   .
DK3.R45   1994
947—dc20   92-46294

2 4 6 8 9 7 5 3 1

Printed in the United States of America
on acid-free paper

Contents

LITERATURE

B. Government and Politics in the Eighteenth Century

DOCUMENTS

LITERATURE

C. Government and Politics in the Nineteenth Century

DOCUMENTS

LITERATURE

15. The Imperial Economy   268

DOCUMENTS

Preface

This reader represents the end product of several years of work, and even more years of thinking and discussion with friends and colleagues at numerous colleges and universities. Although one of us teaches at a small liberal arts college and the other teaches at a large state university, we had come to a common conclusion that most of the existing readers, as valuable as they were, were seriously out of date, and in most instances out of print. We decided, therefore, to compose a text that reflected the depth of contemporary scholarship in Russian history as well as the changes in thematic foci that have taken place over the past twenty years.

At the same time, we have chosen to include large numbers of documents in this text, and to integrate them topically with the secondary literature. Documents have proven their effectiveness in a wide variety of classrooms, and there have been several successful readers built around documents alone. We opted for a mix of documents and scholarship as a way of allowing students to see more clearly the connection between the two, and to facilitate their awareness that many issues lend themselves to more than one perspective or interpretation.

The need for hard choices has steered this reader somewhat away from periodizations organized around reigns, and consequently away from issues that focus on specific rulers (e.g., the Petrine ''revolution'' or the constitutionalism of Alexander I). It has also entailed a break with *histoire evenementielle:* foreign policy, reform projects, and specific laws, policies, and collective reactions to them (from palace coups to Cossack and peasant revolts) have received a lower visibility here than they have in most previous endeavors of this sort. We do not wish to minimize the importance of events, and we recognize that most instructors (including the two of us) discuss them at some length in survey courses. Long hours of consultation and deliberation have convinced us, however, that most of our colleagues endeavor to strike a balance between a chronology of events and broader underlying themes and structures, and it is toward establishing that overall balance that this reader is directed.

Even with these seemingly strict guidelines, we have been continuously impressed—and more than once overwhelmed—by the large, not to say unwieldy, volume of important contemporary scholarship that fits our conception of the reader. Many scholars whom we greatly admire, and whose work has received just acclaim, do not appear on these pages, simply because of an embarrassment of riches. Clearly, design and selection are inherently subjective, and we concede that someone else might make different choices. Nevertheless, the essays and documents contained in this volume sustain a very high standard of scholarship and synthesis, and they reflect the state of Russian history as we currently read it.

All of the secondary literature, and most of the documents, have been extensively condensed in order that the overall volume not be too lengthy, and as a way of directing students' eyes to the major issues that the literature raises. We also have eliminated footnotes, and in many cases cut down on the use of Russian-language terminology, either by translating terms or by eliminating them altogether when we concluded that the narratives could be understood without them. Under the best of circumstances transforming texts intended for scholarly audiences into ones that are somewhat more student-friendly is not a scientific endeavor, and we hope that our colleagues will accept the spirit in which we carried out such editing.

In the process of putting this volume together we have benefited from the advice and experience of many colleagues. We wish especially to thank Bill Wagner, Val Kivelson, Matt Schneer, Cathy Potter, and Ann Kleimola for helping us to figure out what would work and what would not. Nicholas Riasanovsky, John Alexander, and Ronald Suny provided valuable suggestions for modifying and rethinking the text. Several other colleagues, including Lewis Siegelbaum, Christine Ruane, Joseph Bradley, and Mary Zirin offered their advice and gave us the benefit of their experience. Julia Vaingurt, Darrin Mendlove, and Olga Barskaya assisted with some of the translations, and Rachel May helped to transform rough translations into readable prose. Lisa Rile helped to enter some of the texts into the computer, and Marshall Poe was helpful in contacting some of the permission holders in Russia. Benjamin Goldsmith and Edward Kasinec— were particularly helpful in finding and reproducing illustrations from the collections of The New York Public Library. Finally, Nancy Lane and Edward Harcourt of Oxford University Press have assisted and advised us at every step, and we wish to express our gratitude to them. Responsibility for the final product rests, of course, upon us, but our work would have been incomparably more difficult without all of their assistance.

Grinnell, Ia.   D. K.
Stony Brook, N. Y.   G. M.
February 1993

List of Illustrations and Tables

Reinterpreting Russian History

I

The East Slavs and
Kievan Rus'

(860s–ca. 1150)

Since antiquity various peoples have occupied the territories of Eastern Europe that came to make up Rus' and the Russian states which succeeded it. But the early history of these peoples is obscure, the product of occasional references by ancient authors who themselves seem not to have been very familiar with the peoples whom they described. Modern archeology has provided more data, confirming the long history of residence in this area. Excavated objects and exhumed remains, however, cannot answer all the questions which historians might put to them.

The rather hazy understanding of the ancient past communicated by antique sources gradually yields to somewhat more precise information which originated in the last centuries of the first millennium of the modern era. First among these improved sources are the chronicles, especially the so-called Primary Chronicle. Although itself only compiled probably early in the twelfth century, the Primary Chronicle preserves in its pages a series of earlier narratives, undoubtedly both oral and written, which describe the earliest history of the Slavs and the other peoples who interacted across the Eastern European Plain. With the rise of Kievan Rus' sometime in the ninth century, still more records appeared to supplement our understanding of state and society in this earliest period open to our view. The increase in available sources does not, however, satisfy all the curiosity of the modern student. Most of the ancient sources are frustratingly terse, sometimes layered with religious and ideological conviction, and worst of all, frequently silent on exactly those

3

questions which today seem of most interest. It is easy to understand, then, why so many basic questions about the earliest past in Rus' remain disputed today.

For a long time, the dominant view asserted that the first state to arise on this territory was indisputably Slavic, borrowing little from the other peoples known to have been resident across Eastern Europe. In its extreme form, this argument alleged that Kievan Rus' was distinctly Russian, the historical predecessor to Muscovite Russia; other Slavs—especially Ukrainians and Belorussians—who shared this territory represented mere variations—linguistic dialects—on the Great Russian tradition which achieved its final form in Moscow. The non-Slavs who also resided in these lands gained scant attention from this interpretation, a reflection of ethnic policies prevalent in modern politics.

Historians impartially investigating the sources cannot, however, accept these generalizations. The available evidence, both literary and archeological, demonstrates unequivocally that the society which came together in the Middle Ages on the territory stretching from the Black Sea to the Baltic was distinctly multi-ethnic. Together with several Slavic tribes, each of which evidently had its own culture and which occupied defined territory within the Eastern European Plain, Finnic and Baltic peoples also played important parts in taming the land, though they left little written testimony to their presence. Furthermore, outsiders also had an impact on state and society. Particularly influential were the Vikings (normally called Varangians in Rus' sources) who took their trading and plundering down the rivers of Eastern Europe just as they had done further west. That these Germanic peoples should have contributed anything positive to early Slavic civilization was an idea especially repugnant to Russian historians who had lived to see German armies cross Russian frontiers more than once, and who in more recent times had heard Germans allege their native superiority to the less able Slavs.

So it was that many Russian historians blanched when they read in the Primary Chronicle a narrative which seemed to indicate that the medieval Slavs had invited the Vikings to establish a state in Rus' so as to end the disorder over which they themselves were powerless. Long were the debates about the reliability of this evidence, and other information which pointed to a Viking presence in Rus'. But it now seems incontrovertible that the Vikings were present in Rus' from an early time. We know from the collection of Viking tales gathered in medieval Iceland by Snorri Sturluson that even on that remote island storytellers remembered Viking exploits in distant Rus'. Additional testimony to Viking activity in Eastern Europe comes from the memorial stones which today still stand all over Scandinavia, a thousand years after the men whom they commemorate had perished somewhere in that territory which came to make up Rus'. Taken together, the evidence demonstrates persuasively that the Vikings played an important part in the economy and society of Rus'. What remains unclear is how far into the political life of Rus' Viking influence extended.

Equally contentious has been the discussion about what kind of state it was that first arose in Rus'. Historians have divided over this matter too, some discerning in Kievan Rus' an ancient monarchic tradition, others alleging that only more recently did monarchs and autocrats abuse the more authentic, more antique democratic traditions of Rus'. As might be expected, the evidence is open to more than one interpretation. Kievan Rus' certainly had princes, and it is they who dominate the extant sources. We read in the chronicles about their making war and peace, about their decisions on law and religion, and much else. And Christian chroniclers, who relayed much of this information to us, were inclined to see in the princes the legitimate voice of God's authority on earth.

There is, however, additional evidence which seems to point to countervailing political institutions. In Kievan Rus', and later even more forcefully in Novgorod in the north, the city assembly (*veche*) seems to have taken a very active part in politics, sometimes even removing princes from their thrones. In Novgorod, the assembly left many traces of its authority, not least in the limitations which it came to impose upon its princes. Other evidence, too, seems to indicate that the princes of Rus' played a small part in the lives of most people of that time. The oldest legal code, the Pravda Russkaia, thought to have been compiled sometime in the eleventh century, makes no provision for the prince's court or any form of judiciary. Instead, the code recognizes blood revenge and a system of self-help which required little aid from the prince's state, whatever that may have meant. From this perspective, then, the earliest state structures in Rus', if monarchic at all, gave plenty of expression to popular participation.

Records detailing the economy of the remote past are frustratingly hard to come by. What we know about these processes comes mainly from archeology rather than from any written sources. All the same, it seems clear that Kievan Rus' depended upon both agriculture and trade. The fertile steppe where Rus' civilization seems to have originated was, except for its flank which was exposed to the nomads who shared the grassland, ideal for agriculture. Rich in humus like the American plains, steppe soil was very productive and relatively easy to farm. But nomad raids proved a serious disincentive to sedentary farming, driving more and more agriculture beyond the forest frontier where the technology of steppe farming had to yield to implements and strategy better suited to forest zones. In this transition important changes occurred, affecting not only the methods of farming, but also the kinds of crops tilled.

Trade was vital to the Rus' economy as far back as the records go. We know, for example, about Rus' trade with the Greeks in the tenth century, a trade which was part of what drew the attention of the Vikings. But trade in Rus' also reached further, coming to include, in addition to various forest products harvested from the north woods, a variety of goods from Western Europe and Asia which passed through the waterways of Eastern Europe on their way to distant markets. Evidence of this commerce survives in many forms, including both foreign coinage and imported goods only recently unearthed by archeologists. Determining the origin and the chronological frequency of these finds permits us to reconstruct the character of trade in early Rus' even in the absence of more conventional documentation.

As the Pravda Russkaia, the chief legal text of the time shows, Rus' society featured many distinctions. Chief among them was the difference between freeman and slave. The law makes clear that slavery and indenture played quite visible roles in Rus' society. The code also distinguishes the privileged from the commoner. Consensus on the origin of this distinction has not yet emerged, but the oldest version of the Pravda Russkaia seems to rank men depending upon their relationship to the prince: the prince's servitors always ranked more highly than someone not associated with the prince. But other distinctions also applied. The Church Statute attributed to Grand Prince Iaroslav distinguishes penalties to be paid by boyars, lesser boyars, "good people," and others. It seems likely that these distinctions originated with birth, but the sources do not confirm this supposition.

Even more difficult to make out is the importance of gender in Kievan Rus'. According to the later, larger version of the Pravda Russkaia, the homicide of a woman earned half the compensation payable for slaying a free man. But the older, short version of the Pravda Russkaia has nothing to say on this score. Other records prove more expansive. The Church Statute of Grand Prince Iaroslav, for example, describes in detail a whole series of offenses against women, including rape, abduction, and forced marriage. The Statute punishes these crimes with fines and monetary compensation. Women who practiced pre-marital and extra-marital sex, however, could expect no protection from this code: the law is absolute in proscribing all women's illicit sexual activity, but proves to be less censorious of men's sexual exploits. Overt anxiety about controlling reproduction and the gender-based distinctions which governed sexuality suggest that both patriarchy and patrilineality dominated social relations. None of this, however, can gainsay the fact that some women in Rus' exercised real power. The challenge comes in appraising the sometimes maddeningly reticent sources.

If patriarchy did dominate early Rus' society, then the arrival of Christianity, itself patriarchal, must have been welcome in many quarters, in spite of the long period when other religions continued to retain the loyalty of the citizens of Rus'. But the Eastern Christianity which St. Vladimir imported sometime around the year 988 had other important influences as well. One cultural ingredient attributed to Christianity finds expression in the narrative about the deaths of Princes Boris and Gleb, whose murders at the hand of their brother Sviatopolk the Primary Chronicle likens to Christ's crucifixion. And, although the Chronicle condemns Sviatopolk for his crimes, it also praises Boris and Gleb for the way that they, like Christ, accepted their deaths. Boris and Gleb were early canonized for their saintly deaths, and the tradition of self-denial gained an enduring place in Russian Orthodoxy. Of course, few people must actually confront their deaths in the way that Boris and Gleb did, but the Orthodox in Rus' came to admire all forms of self-denial, especially mortification of the flesh. These traits gained special attention in the *Life* of St. Theodosius, one of the early heroes of Rus' monasticism. St. Theodosius, in practicing a life of denial and isolation from the world, became a model not for an evangelizing, rationalizing religion, but rather for an internalized, subjective religious experience poorly suited to recruiting new converts. It is unsurprising, then, that Christianity in Rus' should so long remain a minority religion in spite of the official support and financial contributions which the Kievan princes lavished upon it. To be sure, Theodosius's Christianity was not the only variant to prosper in Rus', but it did represent one version of Orthodox Christianity which had a long life in the lands which later became the Russian Empire.

The adoption of Christianity also brought other monuments of culture to Rus'. Chief among these were the ritual objects used in Christian worship: icons and frescoes, liturgical books, psalters, and much else. In the beginning, only the imported clergy could fully utilize all these objects, but over the course of time, more and more citizens of Rus' could paint, write, and read. What is difficult is to know how many people could exercise these abilities. Until recently debates on this subject raged around minuscule written texts, which maintained, for example, that Grand Prince Iaroslav (d. 1054) had had a large library of books. But whether Iaroslav himself could read or write we do not know. And even if Iaroslav could read and write, how many others of his court were able to?

Again modern archeology has provided fascinating new evidence with which to examine these questions. The discovery, first in Novgorod in the 1950s, then later in some other northern towns, of small strips of birch bark onto which people had scratched brief inscriptions, excited a new discussion about literacy in Rus'. Because these texts appeared on rather common materials instead of costly parchment, and inasmuch as their contents were ordinary and everyday, some historians were inclined to think that reading and writing were common in Kievan Rus'. Publication of newly-revealed grafitti from Kievan Rus' seemed to confirm that some form of literacy was widespread. It seems likely, however, that most men and women of the time could not read or write. Their lives took shape against the more mundane tasks of work, the outline of which is only dimly visible in our reconstruction of their crafts.

1

The Multi-Ethnic Peopling of Rus'

One of the enduring characteristics of the various states and societies which arose on the Eastern European Plain was the varied ethnic makeup of the populations which came to inhabit this area. From the first settling of the region fully up into the present day, Slavs shared their home with non-Slavs, especially Finnic and Baltic peoples. But even among the Slavs there were differences which related to their ethnogenesis many centuries in the past. Quite often the dominant ethnicity absorbed and silenced other ethnic groups, a historical feature which has occasionally found reflection in the histories written about Russia. The selections which appear below restore to the narrative some of the peoples who came to fashion Kievan Rus', one of the earliest of the historical states to arise in this part of Europe.

For a long time historians have differed—often heatedly—over the presence of the Vikings in Rus', and the extent of the Viking contribution to Rus' culture. Particularly troubling to some historians has been the assertion, voiced already in Kievan times, that the Slavs, unable to govern themselves, had resorted to inviting foreigners, the Viking Varangians, to fashion a state in Rus'. Whether the Vikings actually played so prominent a part in the politics of Kievan Rus' may well be doubted, but that the Vikings lived and worked in Rus' cannot. Not only do the chronicles record the story of their invitation to rule, but we know from many other sources that Vikings served in the armed retinues of the Kievan princes. Others traded across the Rus' lands, leaving their unmistakably Scandinavian names behind. And even in remote Iceland when Snorri Sturluson gathered together the numerous tales recited over the generations by Vikings and their Icelandic descendants, the exploits of Harald Hardradi at the court of Prince Iaroslav rang out. But if Harald was a short-term visitor who took small part in fashioning the Rus' state or its economy, what impact did other Vikings have? And what of the contributions of other peoples who resided in Rus'?

Archeology provides the best evidence on the multi-ethnic composition of the population of Rus'. The burial complexes of the Upper Volga River basin which I. V. Dubov discusses below are only part of an extensive collection of finds attesting to the presence and activity of many peoples in Rus'. Although archeology cannot detail all the ways in which diverse peoples contributed to the economy and society of Rus', it does confirm the complex makeup of the population in Rus'. Other sources, like the Pravda Russkaia, introduced in the next section, confirm that Vikings and Finns all rubbed shoulders with Slavs, each making a contribution to a distinctly multi-ethnic society.

DOCUMENTS

The Primary Chronicle on the Early Settlers of Rus' (ca. 600–860s)

The Primary Chronicle, or Tale of Bygone Years, is one of our oldest and best sources of information on the early history of Rus'. Probably compiled at the beginning of the twelfth century on the basis of narratives from an earlier time, the Chronicle constitutes a kind of digest or annal of the first, semi-mythical history of Rus'. Although depending upon several sources, the Chronicle as it survives seems to have been written by a monk in a Kievan monastery, and displays a distinctly Christian view of history, beginning with the very arrangement of the text, whose first pages borrow from the biblical Genesis the story of creation. Narratives of a later time seem to derive from folk legends, like the one which describes the early Slavic settlements. But archeological excavations have confirmed the existence of a variety of Slavic (and non-Slavic) settlements across Southeastern and Eastern Europe, confirming in general the picture contained in the Primary Chronicle; distinctly Slavic remains may be dated from at least the sixth century AD.

For many years the Slavs lived beside the Danube, where the Hungarian and Bulgarian lands now lie. From among these Slavs, parties scattered throughout the country and were known by appropriate names, according to the places where they settled. Thus some came and settled by the river Morava, and were named Moravians, while others were called Czechs. Among these same Slavs are included the White Croats, the Serbs, and the Khorutanians. For when the Vlakhs attacked the Danubian Slavs, settled among them, and did them

violence, the latter came and made their homes by the Vistula, and were then called Liakhs. Of these same Liakhs some were called Polianians, some Lutichians, some Mazovians, and still others Pomorians. Certain Slavs settled also on the Dnieper, and were likewise called Polianians. Still others were named Derevlians, because they lived in the forests. Some also lived between the Pripet and the Dvina and were known as Dregovichians. Other tribes resided along the Dvina and were called Polotians on account of a small stream called the Polota, which flows into the Dvina. It was from this same stream that they were named Polotians. The Slavs also dwelt about Lake Ilmen, and were known there by their appropriate name. They built a city which they called Novgorod. Still others had their homes along the Desna, the Sem, and the Sula, and were called Severians. Thus the Slavic race was divided, and its language was known as Slavic.

When the Polianians lived by themselves among the hills, a trade-route connected the Varangians with the Greeks. Starting from Greece, this route proceeds along the Dnieper, above which a portage leads to the Lovat. By following the Lovat, the great lake Ilmen is reached. The river Volkhov flows out of this lake and enters the great lake Nevo. The mouth of this lake opens into the Varangian [Baltic] Sea. Over this sea goes the route to Rome, and on from Rome overseas to Tsargrad [Constantinople]. The Pontus [Black Sea], into which flows the river Dnieper, may be reached from that point. The Dnieper itself rises in the upland forest, and flows southward. The Dvina has its source in this same forest, but flows northward and empties into the Varangian Sea. The Volga rises in this same forest, but flows to the east, and discharges through seventeen mouths into the Caspian Sea. It is possible by this route to the eastward to reach the Bulgars and the Caspians, and thus attain the region of Shem [Asia]. Along the Dvina runs the route to the Varangians, whence one may reach Rome, and go on from there to the race of Ham. But the Dnieper flows through various mouths into the Pontus. This sea, beside which taught St. Andrew, Peter's brother, is called the Russian Sea. . . .

The Derevlians possessed a principality of their own, as did also the Dregovichians, while the Slavs had their own authority in Novgorod, and another principality existed on the Polota, where the Polotians dwell. Beyond them reside the Krivichians, who live at the head waters of the Volga, the Dvina, and the Dnieper, and whose city is Smolensk. It is there that the Krivichians dwell; and beyond them are the Severians. At Beloozero are situated the Ves, and on the lake of Rostov, the Meria, and on Lake Kleshchino the Meria also. Along the river Oka (which flows into the Volga), Muroma, the Cheremisians, and Mordva preserve their native languages. For the Slavic race in Rus' includes only the Polianians, the Derevlians, the people of Novgorod, the Polotians, the Dregovichians, the Severians, and the Buzhians, who live along the river Bug and were later called Volhynians. The following are other tribes which pay tribute to Rus: Chud, Meria, Ves, Muroma, Cheremis, Mordva, Perm, Pechera, Iam, Litva, Zimegola, Kors, Narva, and Liv. These tribes have their own languages and belong to the race of Japheth, which inhabits the lands of the north.

Now while the Slavs dwelt along the Danube, as we have said, there came from among the Scythians, that is, from the Khazars, a people called Bulgars [a Turkic people who preceded the mainly Slavic contemporary Bulgarians], who settled on the Danube, and oppressed the Slavs. Afterward came the White Huns, who inherited the Slavic country. For these Huns first appeared in the reign of the Emperor Heraclius [610–41] who campaigned against Chosroes, the Emperor of Persia. The Avars, who attacked Heraclius the [Byzantine] Emperor and nearly captured him, also lived at this period. They made war upon the Slavs, and harassed the Dulebians, who were themselves Slavs. . . . The Pechenegs came after them; and

the Black Huns passed by Kiev later during the time of Olga.

Thus the Polianians, who belonged to the Slavic race, lived apart, as we have said, and called themselves Polianians. The Derevlians, who are likewise Slavs, lived by themselves and adopted this tribal name. But the Radimichians and the Viatichians sprang from the Liakhs. There were in fact among the Liakhs two brothers, one named Radim and the other Viatko. Radim settled on the Sozh, where the people are known as Radimichians, and Viatko with his family settled on the Oka. The people there were named Viatichians after him. Thus the Polianians, the Derevlians, the Severians, the Radimichians, the Viatichians, and the Croats lived at peace. The Dulebians dwelt along the Bug, where the Volhynians now are found . . .

These Slavic tribes preserved their own customs, the law of their forefathers, and their traditions, each observing their individual usages. For the Polianians retained the mild and peaceful customs of their ancestors, and showed respect for their daughters-in-law and their sisters, as well as for their mothers and fathers. For their mothers-in-law and their brothers-in-law they also entertained great reverence. They observed a fixed marriage custom, under which the groom's brother did not fetch the bride, but she was brought to the bridegroom in the evening, and on the next morning his gifts were presented.

The Derevlians, on the other hand, existed in bestial fashion, and lived like cattle. They killed one another, ate every impure thing, and there was no marriage among them, but instead they seized upon maidens by capture. The Radimichians, the Viatichians, and the Severians had the same customs. They lived in the forest like any wild beast, and ate every unclean thing. They spoke obscenely before their fathers and their daughters-in-law. There were no marriages among them, but simply festivals among the villages. When the people gathered together for games, for dancing, and for all other devilish amusements, the men on these occasions carried off wives for themselves, and each took any woman with whom he had arrived at an understanding. Whenever a death occurred, a feast was held over the corpse, and then a great pyre was constructed, on which the deceased was laid and burned. After the bones were collected, they were placed in a small urn and set upon a post by the roadside, even as the Viatichians do to this day. Such customs were observed by the Krivichians and the other pagans, since they did not know the law of God, but made a law unto themselves. . .

(859). The Varangians from beyond the sea imposed tribute upon the Chuds, the Slavs, the Merians, the Ves, and the Krivichians. But the Khazars imposed it upon the Polianians, the Severians, and the Viatichians, and collected a squirrelskin from each hearth.

(860–862). The tributaries of the Varangians drove them back beyond the sea and, refusing them further tribute, set out to govern themselves. There was no law among them, but tribe rose against tribe. Discord then ensued among them, and they began to war one against another. They said to themselves, "Let us seek a prince who may rule over us, and judge us according to the law." They accordingly went overseas to the Varangian Russes: these particular Varangians were known as Russes, just as some are called Swedes, and others Normans, Angles, and Goths, for they were thus named. The Chuds, the Slavs, and the Krivichians then said to the people of Rus', "Our whole land is great and rich, but there is no order in it. Come to rule and reign over us." They thus selected three brothers, with their kinsfolk, who took with them all the Russes and migrated. The oldest, Rurik, located himself in Novgorod; the second, Sineus, in Beloozero; and the third, Truvor, in Izborsk. On account of these Varangians, the district of Novgorod became known as the land of Rus'. The present inhabitants of Novgorod are descended from the Varangian race, but aforetime they were Slavs.

SOURCE: Samuel H. Cross, "The Russian Primary Chronicle," *Harvard Studies and Notes in Philology and Literature* 12 (1930):137–8, 140–2, 144–5 (excerpted). Transliteration and spelling have been slightly modified.

King Harald's Saga: Harald Hardradi of Norway (ca. 1050)

The Scandinavian sagas recount the tales of Viking adventure throughout the world they knew. Those attributed to Snorri Sturluson (1179–1241) were part of an oral culture which thrived in Iceland in the Middle Ages. One part of the complete cycle of sagas, called the Heimskringla, a history of the kings of Norway, describes the activity of Harald Hardradi ("Hard Ruler") who, as the following account makes clear, was close to power in many parts of Europe, including Rus', where he befriended Iaroslav the Wise (d. 1054). Harald met his death in England in 1066.

Harald Sigurdsson was a half-brother of King Olaf the Saint; they had the same mother. Harald took part in the Battle of Stiklestad where King Olaf was killed. Harald was wounded in that battle, but managed to escape, along with many other fugitives. . . .

Harald travelled east across Jamtland and Halsingland, and from there into Sweden. There he met Earl Rognvald Brusason and many more of King Olaf's men who had escaped from the battle.

Next spring they got some ships, and that summer they sailed east to Russia to the court of King Jaroslav and stayed with him over the winter. . . .

King Jaroslav gave Harald and Earl Rognvald and their men a good welcome. He made Harald and Earl Rognvald Ulfsson's son, Eilif, commanders of his defence forces. . . .

Harald stayed in Russia for several years and travelled widely throughout the East. Then with a large following he set off on an expedition to Greece, and eventually he reached Constantinople . . . As soon as Harald reached Constantinople he presented himself to the Empress and immediately joined her army as a mercenary . . . Soon after Harald joined the army, all the Varangians became very attached

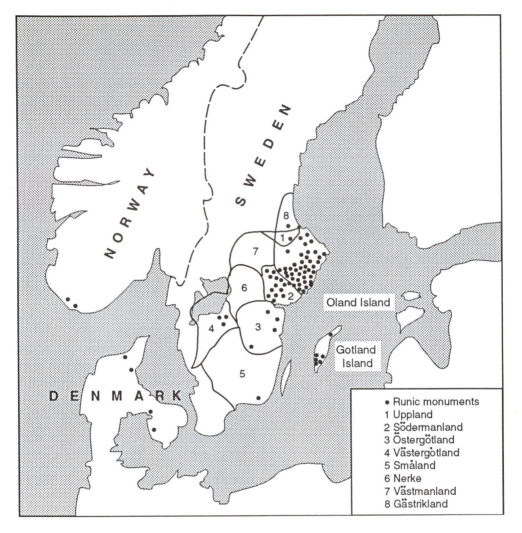

Distribution of Viking stellae containing runic inscriptions mentioning Eastern Europe. Adapted from E. A. Mel'nikova, *Skandinavskie runicheskie nadpisi* (Moscow: Nauka, 1977), p. 34. Reprinted with the permission of E. A. Mel'nikova.

to him, and they fought side by side in battle. Eventually Harald became the acknowledged leader of all the Varangians. . . .

Harald spent several years in Africa and garnered there an immense hoard of money, gold and treasure of all kinds. All the booty he did not require for expenses he used to send by his own reliable messengers to Novgorod into the safe keeping of King Jaroslav. . . .

Harald spent several years on these campaigns, both in the Land of the Saracens and in Sicily. . . . [He] went with his troops to the Holy Land and all the way to Jerusalem; wherever he went in Palestine, all the towns and castles were surrendered to him. . . .

When Harald returned to Constantinople from his expedition to Palestine, he was eager to visit Scandinavia and see his native land again; he had heard that his nephew, Magnus Olafsson, had become king of Norway and Denmark. So Harald now resigned his command with the Byzantine Emperor.

But when Empress Zoe heard about this she was furious, and brought charges against him: she accused him of having defrauded the emperor of treasure which had been won in campaigns under Harald's command.

Empress Zoe had a beautiful young niece called Maria; Harald had asked for her hand in marriage, but the empress had refused. Some Varangians who had been mercenaries in Constantinople brought north the story that according to well-informed people, Empress Zoe had wanted to marry Harald herself, and that this was her real complaint against Harald. . . .

[So] Harald escaped from Constantinople and sailed on to the Black Sea . . . When [he] arrived in Novgorod, King Jaroslav gave him a most cordial welcome. Harald stayed with him over the winter and took into his own keeping all the gold he had previously sent there from Constantinople, valuable treasure of all kinds . . . That winter King Jaroslav gave his daughter Elizabeth in marriage to Harald; the Norwegians call her Ellisif . . . In the spring Harald set off from Novgorod and travelled to the town at Lake Ladoga; there he got some ships and sailed off west in the summer. He first made for Sweden, and landed at Sigtuna.

SOURCE: From Snorri Sturluson's Heimskringla, published in *King Harald's Saga: Harald Hardradi of Norway*. Translated by Magnus Magnusson and Hermann Pálsson (NY: Penguin, 1966), pp. 45–8, 52, 58–60, 63–4. Copyright © Magnus Magnusson and Hermann Pálsson. Reproduced by permission of Penguin Books.

Runic Inscriptions on Viking Stellae in Western Europe (Eleventh Century)

That the Vikings did spend considerable time in the lands of Rus' finds confirmation in another kind of source, the great stone stellae to be found all over Scandinavia (see p. 12). Many of these memorial stones, onto which craftsmen carved runes celebrating the memory of the deceased, mention that the person being remembered had perished in the East, often described as Gardy, the Viking name for Rus'. Other stones mention Novgorod (Holmgard), confirming that the narratives of the Primary Chronicle and Snorri Sturluson had as their basis actual Viking activity in ancient Rus'.

No. 34: Innberga, Södermanland, Sweden; middle of the eleventh century.

Tjodulf, Bui, they established this stone for Farulf, their father. He died in the east in Gardy [Rus'].

No. 48: Turinge kyrka, Södermanland, Sweden; first half of the eleventh century.

Ketill and Björn, they established this stone in memory of Torsteinn, their father, [and] Önund for his brother, and [his] military retainers for Iafni, [and] Ketiley for her spouse. They were brothers there from the best people on earth, and during campaigns they kept their retainers well. He fell in battle in the east in Gardy [Rus'], head of an army, the best of [his] fellow countrymen.

No. 57: Esta, Södermanland, Sweden; first half of the eleventh century.

Ingifast ordered this stone to be carved in memory of Sigvid, his father. He fell in Holmgard [Novgorod], a helmsman with his shipmates.

No. 89: Sjusta, Uppland, Sweden; second half of the eleventh century.

Runa ordered [them] to make [this] monument in memory of Spialbud and for Svein, and for Andvetta, and for Ragnar, his sons, and for Hel'ga; and Sigrid for Spjalbudi her spouse. He died in Holmgard [Novgorod] in the church of [saint] Olaf. Öpir carved the runes.

SOURCE: E. A. Mel'nikova, *Skandinavskie runicheskie nadpisi* (Moscow: Nauka, 1977), pp. 75, 82, 89; translated by Daniel H. Kaiser. Reproduced with the permission of E. A. Mel'nikova.

LITERATURE

I. V. DUBOV

The Ethnic History of Northeastern Rus', in the Ninth to Thirteenth Centuries

Vikings, of course, were not the only non-Slavic people to play a part in fashioning Rus' society. Other peoples, however, have either disappeared as a result of assimilation or demographic disasters, or else they bequeathed us no written record of their earlier history. Archeology has rescued the past of some of these peoples, and the selection which follows concentrates upon Northeast Rus', whose center lay in the upper Volga River valley. I. V. Dubov finds evidence that Finnic peoples—some of whose descendants still live in this area—controlled the region well before the Slavs and Christianity arrived. The Vikings, too, had a presence here, as their burial field at Timerovo near Iaroslavl' demonstrates. Evidently drawn to the area by the prospect of trade with the East, the Scandinavians first reached the Upper Volga River in the ninth century, and had established a small outpost by the following century. Overall, then, Dubov finds evidence of a multi-ethnic population living together along the Volga and its tributaries in the tenth and eleventh centuries.

Although much information is already available on the history of Northeast Rus' in the pre-Mongol period, each year more and more new archeological materials come to light. All the same, many problems of the history of Northeast Rus', most of which were first posed in the last century, remain unresolved. The complexity and intricacy of problems of ethnic history are connected with the fact that the relevant written sources are quite laconic, and ar-cheological complexes cannot always be identified by their ethnic origins.

Let us begin with the Finno-Ugrian ethnic group, the Meria, study of whom began already in the middle of the past century. . . . Until that time the Meria were known only from the scant written sources and from local legends and traditions. First mentioned in the works of Jordanes, an historian of the sixth century, the Meria occasionally figure in Russian chronicles as the people who settled the shores of Lakes Rostov (Nero) and Kleshchino (Pleshcheevo). Under the year 859 the chronicle identifies the Meria as a tribe from whom the Vikings took tribute. Their participation in some of the most important political events in Russia's history also earns mention. For example, the Meria took part when in 882 Oleg

Rune stone (second half of the eleventh century) from Skokloster, Sjusta, Uppland, Sweden. Reprinted by permission of Antikvarisk-Topografiska Arkhivet, Stockholm.

undertook his campaign to establish his authority in Kiev, and in 907 when he went against Byzantium. Especially interesting are the notices about rebellions in the Suzdal' land in 1024 and 1071.

Saints' lives and other sources confirm the existence of a "Chud [Meria] borough" in the city of Rostov Velikii up to the end of the twelfth century. In the 1070s a "stray Chud" killed the Rostov bishop Leontii, who was then canonized. In the fifteenth and sixteenth centuries in Iaroslavl', sources recall not only a Chud population (Meria) which lived here before the coming of the Slavs, but locals also followed various Finno-Ugrian customs: they worshiped a "lord"—a bear, and in the duck they saw the ancestor of the world; they worshiped stones, for example the so-called "blue" stone which lay on the shores of Lake Pleshcheevo. These "demonic teachings" earned cruel persecution from the Orthodox Church, but churchmen were not always strong enough to overcome the influence of ancient pagan traditions.

In the Tale of the Building of the City of Iaroslavl', a rather late source (eighteenth century) which all the same has an ancient basis, one can see especially clearly local Finno-Ugrian cultural roots. In particular the Tale says: "And there was a settlement [in Iaroslavl'] called the Bear's Corner in which the people who lived there were pagans, evil heathen. . . . They worshiped an idol of Volos, the god of livestock." A statue of Volos stood in a complex which included a sanctuary where a sacrificial fire burned and where rituals and sacrifices were carried out. Among local residents the sorcerers, who presided over these ceremonies, enjoyed special honor and respect. The Tale also describes the struggle of Prince Iaroslav with the inhabitants of the Bear's Corner. At first "these people swore by Volos to live in peace with the prince, and to give him tribute, but they did not wish to convert to Christianity." This notice undoubtedly attests to the unyielding opposition to Christianization in this region in the eleventh century. Consequently, when Iaroslav arrived in the Bear's Corner to convert the pagans,

". . .the people released from a barn some dogs and a wild beast to tear the prince to pieces and eat him. But the Lord preserved the blessed prince, and with his own sword he conquered the beast."

This "certain beast" was evidently a bear, which the Meria population of the Upper Volga worshiped. It was kept in a barn in the settlement. One must remember that they fed the bear so as to prepare for its ritual slaughter at the time of the bear holiday. Judging by the Tale, the cult of the bear in Iaroslavl' was combined with the worship of Volos, the livestock god of the Novgorod Slovenes who settled the Upper Volga River basin in the ninth through eleventh centuries.

So one can see both Meria and Slavic elements in the paganism of this region. The last written sources on the Meria come from the end of the eleventh century, after which this tribe disappears from the chronicles, and scholars must employ other sources. The similarity of the names of the Meria and Mari (Cheremiss), the frequent exchange between the letters "a" and "e," and the appearance of the root Mar-Mer in the names of various rivers, lakes, and settlements in the Volga-Oka basin . . . revealed a broad territory inhabited by the Meria in the early Middle Ages, and revealed a direct connection between the Meria of the chronicles and the Mari (Cheremiss).

One point of view holds that the Meria were but one component of the peoples who made up the contemporary Mari. Evidently, the Meria and ancient Mari were related, so that one can speak about the presence in the early Middle Ages of a kind of Finno-Ugrian community here in Northeast Rus'. However there is no basis to identify the Meria with the contemporary Mari. . . . The difference in the fates of these two ethnic groups consisted most of all in the fact that one of them (Meria) was fully assimilated by the Slavs. In connection with this the Meria disappeared from the pages of the chronicles (although one can trace them by archeology for some time), and the other (the Mari) survived and later constituted a nationality.

Archeological monuments of the Meria may

be divided into two chronological layers. The first includes the period from the sixth through the ninth centuries, and seems relatively "pure" from an ethnic point of view; the second, the period from the tenth through the thirteenth centuries, demonstrates that the Meria became one of the constituent elements in old Rus' material and spiritual culture. . . .

From the ninth century across the whole territory of the Volga-Oka River basin the assimilation of the Meria by the Slaviano-Russian settlers who came here from the northwestern lands proceeded swiftly. . . . But not everywhere did the process go quickly and fully. Away from the main paths the old traditions and many local characteristics survived up to the twelfth and thirteenth centuries. . . . But in the Volga area around Kostroma only in the eleventh through thirteenth centuries was the old Rus' populace fashioned as a result of mixing local Meria with the migrants who came here from Iaroslavl' and directly from the Novgorod lands. The process of including the Kostroma region in Old Rus' was completed by the middle of the twelfth century.

During the ninth to thirteenth centuries there was a definite renaissance of ancient tradition in the culture of the Russian populace of the Northeast, archeologically expressed in the materials of burial sites and settlements. . . . This is connected with the fact that the isolation of various groups within this multicultural populace, characteristic of this first stage of Slavic-Russian colonization of the region, alternated with active contacts, with the interpenetration of cultures. Meria elements were organically absorbed by the new ethnic group being formed, and therefore must be examined as an inseparable part of the fusion of the different ethnic traditions in old Rus' culture, in which the Slavic component played a leading role.

The second part of our problem concerns the settlement by the Slavs of the forest zone. In pre-revolutionary historiography the understanding of the formation of Old Rus', and the Great Russian ethnos in the Upper Volga River Basin, was often reduced to a process of settling this territory by Slavs, known in the literature as "colonization." In the works of M. P. Pogodin, S. M. Solov'ev, M. S. Hrushev'skij and others, the formation of the Rus' nationality in the Northeast emerged as a process of uninterrupted colonization of this region by the Slovenes and Krivichians. Kliuchevskii noted that "settlers from various regions of Kievan Rus', having absorbed native Finns, founded here a dense, homogeneous mass . . . which served as the grain of the Great Russian tribe." Solov'ev wrote that "the Slavic tribes gained material and spiritual supremacy over the Finnic tribes, who therefore had to yield to the Slavs." Many historians suggested that the local Finno-Ugrians were quickly assimilated by the arriving Slavic population. This process, they proposed, bore a primarily peaceful character. However there were also other views, according to which "the establishment of the Slavic newcomers, or, to be more precise, the weakening of the Finns under the pressure of Novgorod's influence, did not pass without bloodshed." Similar views were expressed in the works of archeologists and leading historians of the past century. . . .

In our time archeologists have repeatedly returned to these questions. . . . P. N. Tret'iakov has treated the problem of the Slavic settlement of the Volga-Oka River basin most comprehensively. Originally he . . . wrote that "in the second half of the first millennium AD the Upper Volga constituted the outskirts of the Slavic lands. At that time the Krivichians occupied all the upper reaches of the Dnieper River, the upper branches of the Western Dvina and the Valdai Plateau. Along the Volga settlements of Krivichians reached to the mouth of the Kotorosl', around which later rose the city of Iaroslavl'. Here the territory of the Krivichians constituted a wedge into territory occupied by other tribes." Later Tret'iakov proposed a northwest movement of Slavic settlement in the Iaroslavl' region of the Volga, although the basic home of the Krivichians remained for him the southwest. The massive resettlement of the Slavs in the lands of the Meria took place from the end of the eighth to early in the ninth century, which is why, in his opinion, in its first stage the colonizing streams went from the Novgorod lands along the largest water routes . . .

So, in the ninth century on the territory of the Volga-Oka River basin, thinly settled by Finno-Ugrians, the Slavs appeared, either establishing new settlements or inhabiting already established places. The basic means of travel of the Slavs were the rivers emptying into the Volga system; beginning from that time the Volga was transformed from an internal water route of the Finno-Ugrian tribes into a trade route for Novgorodian Slovenes in their movement into the forest lands. Originally the new population was centered in a small region; at any rate, only here, in the Volga-Oka River basin are Slaviano-Rus' antiquities from the ninth century known . . .

Historico-archeological observations coincide with the conclusions of linguists. It emerges that the flow of migrants from the Novgorod lands was heterogeneous in its ethnic composition. They settled mainly along the left-bank of the Volga, "but a few groups of them penetrated and settled in separate regions on the right bank of the Volga, especially on the territory of present-day Iaroslavl' and partly in the Ivanovo region." The migrants brought with them much that was new. In the first place, plow agriculture began to spread, which provoked its own kind of revolution in economics. The Slavs and the Scandinavians who came with them also included this area in the sphere of international trade. The new populace created a series of trade-craft centers, the prototypes of early feudal Rus' towns. Changes also occurred in spiritual culture and ideology. A new burial custom— the burial mound—appeared. Finally, the main material of production became iron, supplanting bone.

In the tenth century the Slavs spread out from this region along the whole Suzdal' steppe all the way to the Kliaz'ma River. At this time the movement from the Iaroslavl' portion of the Volga into Beloozero took place. Of course, this scheme does not exclude the direct penetration of the migrants from Novgo-rod into Beloozero and the southern regions of the Volga-Oka River basin directly from the Upper and Middle Dnieper . . . Chronicle sources do not say anything about when and where the first Slavs appeared in the Volga-Oka River basin. However the fact that the northern Slavic groups (Slovenes and Krivi-chians) figure in the all-Rus' events of the ninth century, together with the Ves' and Meria, suggests that the first waves of Slavic settlers moved into the Northeast in the ninth century. They came here from the regions of settlement of the Slavic tribes already mentioned.

In the eleventh to twelfth centuries in the Volga-Oka River basin the flow of the population from southwest Rus' swelled, and the northwest direction of migration recedes into the background, although the traditional ties were preserved all the way to the seventeenth century.

The settlement by the Slavs of the forest land in various stages also had a definable socio-economic character. Without a doubt this was reflected in the processes of ethnogenesis. So, in the first stage in the ninth century the appearance here of the Slavs was dependent, evidently, most of all on trade and crafts. Thus, the new population appeared first either in centers which occupied a key position along the Volga route, or they created new centers which had analogous significance for trade. The new settlers—Slavs—appeared in the old Meria tribal centers. . . . And inasmuch as the process of the decay of the Finno-Ugrian tribal structure had already gone far, the Slavs, having a higher material and spiritual culture, rather rapidly occupied the dominant position. The phenomenon of the formation of the old Rus' nationality was extraordinarily complicated and many-sided. Here the settlement of the Slavs, the assimilation of the local Finno-Ugrians, and their acculturation all played a role. Of course, it is impossible to reduce this complicated process to any single factor.

Another real problem of the ethnic history of the forest zone is the role of the Scandinavian elements in the life of this region in the early Middle Ages. Scandinavian complexes and separate archeological finds are known from the great number of burial sites in Vladimir and Iaroslavl', in rural and trade-crafts centers, and in cities.

The most deeply studied among the Scandinavian antiquities are those found in the Timerevo complex, where they are broadly represented by burials accomplished according to Scandinavian ritual, and by separate objects of northern origin in the burial site, and by the types of structures and other finds in the settlement. Elements of Norman culture are also visible in the form of Kufic coin hoards discovered here.

One of the first students of the Iaroslavl' necropolis, Tikhomirov, pointed out that the basic mass of graves in Timerevo and the Mikhailov burial grounds near Iaroslavl' belongs to Vikings, and that the burial mound tradition itself was transferred to Iaroslavl' by the Normans. Studies of the Swedish archeologist T. Arne fully developed the view according to which the Volga route at its origin was Viking and that the Iaroslavl' lands along the Volga were a Scandinavian colony.

The studies of Iu. V. Got'e and A. P. Smirnov treated the complexes near Iaroslavl' exclusively as trade centers on the Volga trade route, which is why they connected their rise with the appearance in the Upper Volga of the Scandinavians. Got'e suggested that the "settlement near Iaroslavl' was Slavic ... but within it was a Norman colony, which constituted a staging point midway on the route from the Vikings to the East." J. Brønsted figured that emigrants from Norway founded the "Scandinavian colony" near Iaroslavl'.

The most careful assessment of Scandinavian antiquities in the Iaroslavl' region belongs to V. V. Sedov, who suggests that the areas around Iaroslavl' represented one of "two large concentrations of burial mounds of warrior-retainers in the northeast portion of the East Slavic territory of that time. Both regions were located at key points along the Baltic-Volga water route, connecting the states of Northern and Western Europe with the East."

He also notes a decidedly Scandinavian ethnic component in these graves. Objects of North European origin also have been discovered in the Timerevo settlement.

M. V. Fekhner ... argues against the view which identifies the Iaroslavl' necropolises as burial grounds for Scandinavian trading stations. She says that "a small number of Scandinavian graves in a given cemetery proves only that in the tenth century a small group of Normans, who settled in Iaroslavl' in the tenth century, evidently were already in the eleventh century assimilated by the local population".... Fekhner identifies 4% of the burial complexes in Timerevo as Scandinavian, 30% as Finnic, and 15% as Slavic; it was impossible to determine the ethnic origins of 43% of the complexes. Such calculations, however, provoked doubts, and a new quantitative analysis was undertaken, having discarded those graves whose ethnic origins were unknown. As a result, it appears that in the tenth century 13% of the burial sites belonged to Scandinavians, 75% to Finns, and 12% to Slavs; early in the eleventh century, 3.5% of the burials were Scandinavian, 72.5% Finnic, and 24% Slavic.

Presently in Timerevo more than 30 burial complexes are known, and about 5% of all the excavated burial mounds erected over the course of two centuries belonged to Scandinavians. This percent of course does not reflect the real number of Scandinavians who were here, for many of whom the visit to Timerevo was brief. Besides, under some of the mounds might be buried the wives of the Scandinavians who might have had an entirely different ethnic origin....

Altogether then, we get the following picture. In the ninth century, when the movement of the Slavic population from the Novgorod lands to the Upper Volga began, there came also groups of Scandinavians with their established custom of burial (burial mounds with their characteristic round stone piles). In the tenth century the Scandinavian burial tradition—burial chambers—was preserved. The proportion of things of northern origin significantly increased as a result of the growing role of the Volga route as a trans-European trade artery. Northern traditions also were recorded in the house buildings of Timerevo settlement . . . which included types characteristic of the Scandinavian north. . . . Several types of ceramics discovered at Timerevo also have their roots in Scandinavia, or at least have analogies there. . . . Altogether, however, objects of Scandinavian origin constitute a miserly percent of the total of all finds, and nothing firmly indicating a complete Norman complex has yet been found.

Russo-Scandinavian ties, first made in the ninth century and having reached their apogee in the following century, evidently tailed off in the eleventh century. Finds of northern origin from archeological layers dated to the eleventh century are rare, and do not confirm a broad presence of Scandinavians in the Russian lands. . . .

The newest advances of archeological science in the area of Russo-Scandinavian relations are summarized and analyzed in a series of works recently published. Not long ago D. A. Avdusin [a contemporary archeologist who denies that the Vikings had much influence in Rus'] published an article devoted to this problem. The author practically ignores Scandinavian antiquities found in the Upper Volga, and only in passing mentions materials from the Iaroslavl' burial sites, the Scandinavian components of which were analyzed above. . . .

Avdusin suggests that he is correcting "the distortion" which, in his view archeologists have committed by exaggerating the role of Scandinavians in Rus' and by presenting the Scandinavian finds as more ancient than in fact they are. . . . But the point was not to allege some exclusive Scandinavian role in Rus' or an artificial exaggeration of its significance in the historical processes which took place in the early Middle Ages. On the contrary, the idea was to point out the "fruitful and mutually advantageous character of Russo-Scandinavian interaction." The second reproach of Avdusin is also unacceptable, for no one has ever tried to make the Scandinavian finds older than in fact they were. It is clearly demonstrable that these materials are synchronous with the same finds in Scandinavia

itself, mainly dated objects like fibulas, pendants with the hammers of Thor, swords, etc. . . .

According to Avdusin, the presence of Scandinavians in old Rus' urban centers "may be explained not by their town-building mission, but by their participation in the economic and political life of the old Rus' state." In this way he hopes to show that the Vikings had no relation to the appearance and development of towns in old Rus'. But in his assertions there is an internal contradiction, inasmuch as the rise of towns in Rus' was the result of economic and political development. If in these processes Scandinavians took part, this means that they played a definite role in the establishment of early urban centers, as can be seen from many examples, including Timerevo, which arose as a result of the mastering of the Volga route by the Slavs, together with whom at this early stage in the beginning of the ninth century the Scandinavians also were present. Then in the tenth century the local Finno-Ugrians—the Meria—also appeared in the composition of the population of this important trade-crafts center. Of course, one could not claim that the Scandinavians were the founders of towns in Rus', but one also could not deny fully, as Avdusin does, their participation in the processes of founding towns in the ninth and tenth centuries.

In Avdusin's opinion, Scandinavians participated only in the transcontinental trade. He writes: "A considerable part of the trade in Rus' took place without the Scandinavians, without their participation." By that he evidently meant those regions where Scandinavians had never been. But it is clear that Scandinavian goods came into the medieval heartland of Russia either directly from Scandinavian merchants or through intermediaries, as finds of Scandinavian objects across the extensive territory of old Rus' confirm.

Questions about the ethnic history of Northeast Rus' in the early medieval epoch are far from resolved. However, the role of two main ethnic components—Slavic and Finno-Ugrian—in the process of the formation of the

ancient Russian nationality has in general outline been defined. The character and share of
the Scandinavian contribution to the material
and spiritual culture has been established, but
further research will deepen and make more
concrete our understanding about these complex processes of the development of this area
in the period prior to the coming of the Mongols.

SOURCE: I. V. Dubov, "Spornye voprosy etnicheskoi istorii
Severo-Vostochnoi Rusi IX–XIII vekov," *Voprosy istorii*
(1990) no. 5, pp. 15–27 (excerpted). Translated by Julia
Vaingurt, edited by Daniel H. Kaiser. Reproduced with the
permission of I. V. Dubov.

2

The State Structure of Kievan Rus'

Another thorny issue for historians is the kind of state structure which prevailed in the first centuries of Rus': was it a monarchy or some kind of primitive democracy? For most historians, like the early chroniclers, there was little question: princes governed Rus', and most people were their subjects. This interpretation seemed logical to ancient chroniclers who saw in their Christian princes an earthly representation of the heavenly king. Similarly, most historians who wrote in the heyday of the Russian Empire found it easy to imagine that the tradition which had eventuated in so glorious an autocratic state had had its distant beginnings with the Kievan princes.

However, even in the nineteenth and early twentieth centuries, there was a dissenting voice, arguing that autocracy was only a corruption of another, more deeply democratic tradition which was born in Kievan Rus'. For evidence, they pointed first of all to the ancient city assembly (*veche*) which finds occasional mention in the chronicles. The majority of historians discounted the infrequent allusions to the city assemblies, observing that at most times the Kievan princes seem to have encountered no hindrance at all in the exercise of their will. Besides, formal texts like the Kievan law, the Pravda Russkaia, make no mention of the city assembly, while elaborating upon a long list of the prince's retainers.

But the evidence may be read differently. In the first place, even the chronicles observed that the princes often failed to act like God's agents on earth, more often mimicking instead the king of another realm. Furthermore, the chronicles do tell of occasions when the city assembly chose to replace a prince who had failed to discharge his duties honorably and successfully. And more than once the overthrown prince fled before this expression of lost confidence. Finally, the law code, even if it fails to mention the city assembly, also has little to say about the operation of the state whose personnel it enumerates.

In thinking about the state structure of Kievan Rus', then, one must pay careful attention both to what the surviving sources say, and what they neglect to say.

DOCUMENTS

The Primary Chronicle on Dissension Among the Princes of Rus' (1012–54)

As already noted, the Primary Chronicle, in keeping with its origins, displays a distinctly religious view of the world. Not infrequently, and certainly in the texts which appear here, the chronicler inserted biblical quotations liberally, using them to draw morals for the enlightenment of his readers. One recurring theme in the Primary Chronicle is the explanation for the decline of Rus', which the compiler found in the behavior of the princes of Rus'. The worst of them, like Sviatopolk, desired to rule so desperately that they even murdered their brothers. The best of the princes, by contrast, imitated the behavior of Christ, offering up their lives as innocent sacrifices rather than resisting evil. Boris and Gleb, whose deaths the following selection describes, were early canonized by the Church, and their lives came to represent a peculiar form of Christianity which is visible in the Life of St. Theodosius (below). At the heart of the present selection, however, is the struggle between kinsmen to succeed to the throne in Kiev. In Vladimir's time (980–1015) each of his sons occupied a lesser principality while their father ruled them all from Kiev; the eldest son and heir-apparent, ruled Novgorod. With the death of the Grand Prince, the eldest son should have succeeded him, each younger son moving up the ladder one step. But inasmuch as Prince Vladimir had many sons, conflict between siblings, some of whom could never expect in the normal order of things to succeed to the throne, proved vicious. As a result, Iaroslav, son of Vladimir, who became Grand Prince himself only after the bloodletting described below, at his death urged on his sons a more orderly succession, respecting the eldest as the legitimate heir. But the system did not long last, and these struggles, the Chronicler averred, determined that Rus' would succumb to powers better able to control the distribution of authority.

(1012–1014). When Iaroslav was in Novgorod he paid two thousand grivnas a year as tribute to Kiev, and distributed one thousand to his courtiers in Novgorod. All the viceroys of Novgorod had always paid like sums, but Iaroslav ceased to render this amount to his father. Then Vladimir exclaimed, "Repair the road and build a bridge," for he purposed to attack his son Iaroslav, but he fell ill.

(1015). While Vladimir was desirous of attacking Iaroslav, the latter sent overseas and imported Varangian reinforcements, since he feared his father's advance. But God will not give the devil any satisfaction. For when Vladimir fell ill, Boris was with him at the time. Since the Pechenegs were attacking the Russes, he sent Boris out against them, for he himself was very sick, and of this illness he died on July 15. Now he died at Berestovo, but his death was kept secret, for Sviatopolk was in Kiev. . . .

Sviatopolk settled in Kiev after his father's death, and after calling together all the inhabitants of Kiev, he began to distribute largess among them. They accepted it, but their hearts were not with him, because their brethren were with Boris. When Boris returned with the army, after meeting the Pechenegs, he received the news that his father was dead. He mourned deeply for him, for he was beloved of his father before all the rest.

When he came to the Alta [River], he halted. His father's retainers then urged him to take his place in Kiev on his father's throne, since he had at his disposal the latter's retainers and troops. But Boris protested, "Be it not for me to raise my hand against my elder brother. Now that my father has passed away, let him take the place of my father in my heart." When the soldiery heard these words, they departed from him, and Boris remained with his servants.

But Sviatopolk was filled with lawlessness. Adopting the device of Cain, he sent messages to Boris that he desired to live at peace with him, and would increase the territory he had received from his father. But he plotted against him how he might kill him. So Sviatopolk came by night to Vyshegorod. After secretly summoning to his presence Putsha and the boyars of the town, he inquired of them whether they were wholeheartedly devoted to him. Putsha and the men of Vyshegorod replied, "We are ready to lay down our lives for you." He then commanded them to say nothing to any man, but to go and kill his brother Boris. They straightway promised to execute his order. . . .

These emissaries came to the Alta, and when they approached, they heard the sainted Boris singing vespers. For it was already known to him that they intended to take his life. Then he arose and began to chant, saying, "Oh Lord, how are they increased who come against me! Many are they that rise up against me" (Ps. iii.1). . . . After finishing vespers, he prayed, gazing upon the icon, the image of the Lord, with these words: "Lord Jesus Christ, who in this image has appeared on earth for our salvation, and who, having voluntarily suffered thy hands to be nailed to the Cross, didst endure thy passion for our sins, so help me now to endure my passion. For I accept it not from those who are my enemies, but from the hand of my own brother. Hold it not against him as a sin, oh Lord!"

After offering this prayer, he lay down upon his couch. Then they fell upon him like wild beasts about the tent, and overcame him by piercing him with lances. They also overpowered his servant, who cast himself upon his body. For he was beloved of Boris. He was a servant of Hungarian race, George by name, to whom Boris was greatly attached. . . . They also killed many other servants of Boris. . . . The desperados, after attacking Boris, wrapped him in a canvas, loaded him upon a wagon, and dragged him off, though he was still alive. When the impious Sviatopolk saw that he was still breathing, he sent two Varangians to finish him. When they came and saw that he was still alive, one of them drew his sword and plunged it into his heart. Thus died the blessed Boris, receiving from the hand of Christ our God the crown among the righteous. . . .

The impious Sviatopolk then reflected, "Behold, I have killed Boris; now how can I kill Gleb?" Adopting once more Cain's device, he craftily sent messages to Gleb to the effect that he should come quickly, because his father was very ill and desired his presence. Gleb quickly mounted his horse, and set out with a small company, for he was obedient to his father. When he came to the Volga [River], his horse stumbled in a ditch on the plain, and broke his leg. He arrived at Smolensk, and setting out thence at dawn, he embarked in a boat on the Smyadyn. At this time, Iaroslav received from Predslava the tidings of their father's death, and he sent word to Gleb that he should not set out, because his father was dead, and his brother had been murdered by Sviatopolk. Upon receiving these tidings, Gleb burst into tears, and mourned for his father, but still more deeply for his brother. He wept and prayed with the lament, "Woe is me, oh Lord! It were better for me to die with my brother than to live on in this world. Oh my brother, had I but seen thy angelic countenance, I should have died with thee. Why am I now left alone? . . . If thou hast received affliction from God, pray for me that I may endure the same passion. For it were better for me to dwell with thee than in this deceitful world."

While he was thus praying amid his tears, there suddenly arrived those sent by Sviatopolk for Gleb's destruction. These emissaries seized Gleb's boat, and drew their weapons. The servants of Gleb were terrified, and the impious messenger, Goriaser, gave orders that they should slay Gleb with dispatch. Then Gleb's cook, Torchin by name, seized a knife, and stabbed Gleb. He was offered up as a sacrifice to God like an innocent lamb, a glorious offering amid the perfume of incense, and he received the crown of glory. Entering the heavenly mansions, he beheld his long-desired brother, and rejoiced with him in the joy ineffable which they had attained through their brotherly love. . . .

Now the impious and evil Sviatopolk killed Sviatoslav in the Hungarian mountains, after causing him to be pursued as he fled into Hungary. Then he began to reflect on how he would kill all his brethren, and rule alone in Rus'. . . .

The impious Sviatopolk thus began his reign in Kiev. Assembling the people he began to distribute skins to some and furs to others, and thus dissipated a large sum.

When Iaroslav heard of his father's death, he had many Varangians under his command, and they offered violence to the inhabitants of Novgorod and to their wives. The men of Novgorod then rose and killed the Varangians in their market place. Iaroslav was angry, and departing to Rakom, he took up his abode in the castle. Then he sent messengers to Novgorod with the comment that the death of his retainers was beyond remedy, but at the same time he summoned before him the chief men of the city who had massacred the Varangians, and craftily killed them. The same night news came from Kiev sent by his sister Predslava to the effect that his father was dead, that Sviatopolk had settled in Kiev after killing Boris, and was now endeavoring to compass the death of Gleb, and she warned Iaroslav to be exceedingly on his guard against Sviatopolk. When Iaroslav heard these tidings, he grieved for his father and his retainers.

On the morrow he collected the remnant of the men of Novgorod and regretfully lamented, "Alas for my beloved retainers, whom I yesterday caused to be killed! You would indeed be useful in the present crisis." He wiped away his tears, and informed his subjects in the assembly that his father was dead, and that Sviatopolk had settled in Kiev after killing his brethren. Then the men of Novgorod said, "We can still fight for you, oh Prince, even though our brethren are slain." So Iaroslav collected one thousand Varangians and forty

thousand other soldiers, and marched against Sviatopolk. . . .

(1016). Iaroslav arrived before Kiev, and the brothers stood over against each other on both banks of the Dnieper, but neither party dared attack. They remained thus face to face for three months. Then Sviatopolk's general rode out along the shore and scoffed at the men of Novgorod, shouting, "Why did you come hither with these crooked-shanks, you carpenters? We shall put you to work on our houses." When the men of Novgorod heard this taunt, they declared to Iaroslav, "Tomorrow we will cross over to them, and whoever will not go with us we will kill." Now it was already beginning to freeze. Sviatopolk was stationed between two lakes, and caroused with his retinue the whole night through. Iaroslav on the morrow marshaled his troops, and crossed over toward dawn. His forces disembarked on the shore, and pushed the boats out from the bank. The two armies advanced to the attack, and met upon the field. The carnage was terrible. Because of the lake, the Pechenegs could bring no aid, and Iaroslav's troops drove Sviatopolk with his followers toward it. When the latter went out upon the ice, it broke under them, and Iaroslav began to win the upper hand. Sviatopolk then fled among the Liakhs, while Iaroslav established himself in Kiev upon the throne of his father and grandfather. Iaroslav had then been in Novgorod twenty-eight years. . . . [More dissension among the sons of Vladimir followed, but in 1036] Iaroslav assumed the entire sovereignty, and was the sole ruler in the land of Rus'. . . .

(1054). Iaroslav, Great Prince of Rus', passed away. While he was yet alive, he admonished his sons with these words: "My sons, I am about to quit this world. Love one another, since ye are brothers by one father and mother. If ye dwell in amity with one another, God will dwell among you, and will subject your enemies to you, and ye will live at peace. But if ye dwell in envy and dissension, quarreling with one another, then ye will perish yourselves and bring to ruin the land of your ancestors, which they won at the price of great effort. Wherefore remain rather at peace, brother heeding brother. The throne of Kiev I bequeath to my eldest son, your brother Iziaslav. Heed him as ye have heeded me, that he may take my place among you. To Sviatoslav I give Chernigov, to Vsevolod Pereiaslavl, to Igor the city of Vladimir, and to Viacheslav Smolensk." Thus he divided the cities among them, commanding them not to violate one another's boundaries, not to despoil one another. He laid upon Iziaslav the injunction to aid the party wronged, in case one brother should attack another. Thus he admonished his sons to dwell in amity. . . . The end of Iaroslav's life drew near, and he gave up the ghost on the first Saturday after the feast of St. Theodore (February 19). . . . When they had transported the body, they laid it in a marble sarcophagus in the Church of St. Sophia . . . Iziaslav then took up his abode at Kiev, with Sviatoslav in Chernigov, Vsevolod at Pereiaslavl, Igor in Vladimir, and Viacheslav at Smolensk.

SOURCE: Samuel H. Cross, "The Russian Primary Chronicle," *Harvard Studies and Notes in Philology and Literature* 12 (1930):212, 214–20, 225, 231–2. Transliteration and spelling have been slightly modified.

The Primary Chronicle
on the Rebellion
in Kiev (1068–69)

If in many accounts the Primary Chronicle makes it seem that Rus' was a monarchy over which the princes ruled supreme, other narratives emphasize the authority which the populace exercised irrespective of the prince's will. The following selection relates one such incident. In 1067 Vseslav, Prince of Polotsk, had attacked and captured Novgorod in contravention of the assigned allotment. Consequently, three of his cousins campaigned against Vseslav, and managed by trickery to capture and imprison him in Kiev, where Iziaslav ruled. But when in the following year Iziaslav failed to heed their demands to arm them for a campaign against the Polovtsians— Steppe people who regularly raided Kiev—the citizens of Kiev determined to overthrow the Iziaslav because of his military failures and his lack of resolve. Having liberated Vseslav from prison, the populace then made him prince in Kiev, in the process ravaging the possessions of Iziaslav. Later the citizenry repented of their move, and meeting in assembly, decided to restore Iziaslav to the throne. In so doing, they demonstrated that in Kiev popular sovereignty also had a part to play in organizing the state in Rus'.

———————

(1068). A multitude of those nomads known as the Polovtsians attacked the land of Rus', and Iziaslav, Sviatoslav, and Vsevolod went forth against them as far as the Alta. They joined battle in the dead of night, but since God had let loose the pagans upon us because of our transgressions, the Russian princes fled and the Polovtsians were victorious. . . . When Iziaslav, accompanied by Vsevolod, had fled to Kiev, while Sviatoslav had taken refuge in Chernigov, the men of Kiev who had escaped to their native city held an assembly on the market place and sent the following communication to the Prince: "The Polovtsians have spread over the country. Oh Prince, give us arms and horses, that we may offer them combat once more." Iziaslav, however, paid no heed to this request. Then the people began to murmur against his general Constantine. From the place of assembly, they mounted the hill, but when they arrived before the house of Constantine, they could not find him. They then halted before the house of Briachislav and proposed that they should go and liberate their friends from prison. They then separated into two parties: half of them went to the prison, and half over the bridge. The latter contingent arrived before the Prince's palace, and as Iziaslav was sitting with his retinue in his hall, the crowd below began to shout at him. As the prince and his retainers were watching the crowd from a small window, Tuky, the brother of Chud, called to Iziaslav's attention that the people were aroused, and suggested that he should send men to guard Vseslav. While he was thus speaking, the other half of the crowd approached from the prison, which they had thrown open. The retainers, remarking that the situation had become serious, urged the Prince to send pursuers after Vseslav who should entice him to a window by a ruse and then slay him with the sword. Iziaslav, however, did not heed their advice. The mob then gave a shout and went off to Vseslav's prison. When Iziaslav beheld their action, he fled with Vsevolod from the palace. But on September 15, the people thus haled Vseslav from his dungeon, and set him up in the midst of the prince's palace. They then pillaged the palace, seizing a huge amount of gold and silver, furs, and marten-skins. Iziaslav made his escape to Poland.

While the Polovtsians were ravaging throughout the land of Rus', Sviatoslav was meanwhile at Chernigov. As soon as the pagans raided around Chernigov itself, Sviatoslav collected a small force and sallied out against them to Snovsk. The Polovtsians remarked the approaching troop and marshaled their forces for resistance. When Sviatoslav observed their numbers, he said to his followers, "Let us attack, for it is too late for us to seek succor elsewhere." They spurred up their horses, and though the Polovtsians had twelve thousand men, Sviatoslav won the day with his force of only three thousand. Some of the pagans were killed outright, while others were drowned in the Snov [River] and their prince was captured on November 1. Sviatoslav thus returned victorious to his city. Vseslav was meanwhile ruling in Kiev. . . .

(1069). Reinforced by Boleslav, Iziaslav marched to attack Vseslav, who went forth to meet them, and arrived at Belgorod. But during the night he hid himself from the men of Kiev, and fled from Belgorod to Polotsk. Then the men of Kiev saw on the morrow that their prince had fled, they returned to Kiev, and after calling an assembly, they sent messages to Sviatoslav and Vsevolod saying, "We did wrong in expelling our Prince, and now he leads the Poles against us. Return to your father's city. If you refuse to return, then we have no alternative but to burn our city and depart to Greece." Sviatoslav replied, "We shall communicate with our brother. If he marches upon you with the Poles to destroy you, we shall fight against him, and not allow him to destroy our father's city. If his intentions are peaceful, then he shall approach with a small troop." Then the people of Kiev were pacified.

SOURCE: Samuel H. Cross, "The Russian Primary Chronicle," *Harvard Studies and Notes in Philology and Literature* 12 (1930):235, 237–9 (excerpted). Transliteration and spelling have been slightly modified.

Pravda Russkaia: The Short Redaction (Eleventh Century)

One of the best sources by which to judge the structure of the state in early Rus' is the Pravda Russkaia ("Rus' Justice"), a code of customary law which probably first took shape sometime in the eleventh century. Three basic versions of the Pravda survive: the Short Redaction, reproduced here; the Expanded Redaction, which is about three times the size of the Short Redaction, and probably achieved its final form late in the twelfth or early in the thirteenth century; and the Abbreviated Redaction, the latest version which borrows from both earlier redactions, but also reflects changes which developed in the early Muscovite period. The Short Redaction betrays very little editorial organization, and seems rather to reflect a gradual accumulation of practice. Extremely laconic, the text seems to presume that its readers are familiar with the norms it lays out. Such understatement makes translation difficult, because without adding explanatory terms (here supplied in brackets) the text is almost impenetrable. However, the terse, imprecise character of the text is also suggestive of legal practice. The code itself indicates that little justice in Rus' depended upon a court; judges, bailiffs, and other officials of a judiciary make scant appearance. Instead, the Pravda depicts a self-help system in which state officials played only supplementary roles. Those interested in reading English translations of the other versions of the Pravda Russkaia may consult *The Laws of Rus' (Tenth to Fifteenth Centuries)*,trans., ed. Daniel H. Kaiser (Salt Lake City: Charles Schlacks, Jr., forthcoming).

---

1. If a man kills a man, then a brother may avenge a brother, or a son [may avenge] his father, or a father [his] son, or a brother's son or sister's son [may avenge the death of their uncle]; if there be no one to avenge [the man] then [the offender] is to pay 40 grivnas* for the corpse [lit., for the head]; if [the dead man] be a [Kievan] Rus' man, junior member of the prince's retinue, merchant, bailiff, member of the prince's personal guard, or if [the dead man] be a freedman under the prince's protection or if he be a [Novgorodian?] Slav, then [the killer] is to pay 40 grivnas for his [murder].

2. If someone be beaten so that he bears bruises and is bloody, then he need seek no eyewitness [to confirm his complaint]; if he bears no sign [of the fight], then [let] an eyewitness come forward; if the [complainant] is unable [to produce a witness], then that is the end of the matter; if [the victim] is unable to avenge himself, then he is to take for the offense 3 grivnas, and also payment for the physician.

3. If someone strikes someone with a cudgel, or a rod, or palm of the hand, or cup, or horn or the back of the hand, then [he is to pay] 12

grivnas; if they do not catch him [to return the blow], then he is to pay, and that is the end of the matter.

4. If someone strikes [a man] with a sword, but does not unsheath it, or [if someone strikes a man] with the hilt [of a sword], then [he is to pay the victim] 12 grivnas for the offense.

5. If [someone] strikes [a man's] arm, and the arm falls off or withers, then [the guilty party is to pay] 40 grivnas.

6. If [someone is struck in the leg but] the leg remains whole, and then [the victim] begins to limp, then [let the victim's] children humble [the offender].

7. If someone cuts off a finger, then [he is to pay the victim] 3 grivnas for the offense.

8. And for a mustache, twelve grivnas; for a beard 12 grivnas.

9. If someone unsheaths a sword, but does not strike [anyone], then he pays 1 grivna.

10. If a man either shoves [another] man away from himself or pulls him toward himself, [then he is to pay the victim] 3 grivnas, if [the victim] presents two eyewitnesses; if the man [the victim] is a Viking or [some other] foreign resident, then let him take an oath [to prove his claim].

11. If a slave is hidden either with a Viking or with another foreign resident, and they do not bring [the slave] forward within three days [after the slave's owners announce their loss], and [the slave's owners] learn [the slave's whereabouts], then on the third day [the slave's owners are] to take back their slave, and [receive] 3 grivnas for the offense.

12. If someone rides on someone else's horse, not having asked him [the owner] for permission, then [he] is to provide [the owner] three grivnas.

13. If someone takes another's horse, or weapon, or clothes and [the owner] recognizes [his property] in his own community, then he is to take back his own [property], and [receive] 3 grivnas for the offense.

14. If someone recognizes [his property], he is not to take it back, and ought not say to him [who possesses his property], "This [property]

Editors' Note: The relative values of the monetary units mentioned here are as follows: 1 silver grivna = 4 grivnas of "fur" [presmably borrowed from an original, pre-money economy] = 80 nogatas = 100 rezanas = 200 kunas =196.2 grams of silver. Apparently there were 150 vekshas in a silver grivna; the value of the veveritsa is unknown.

is mine"; instead he ought to say, "Come to a confrontation [to disclose] where you obtained [the property]"; if he [who is asked to appear] does not come, then [he is to provide] a guarantor within five days.

15. If somewhere someone seeks from another person the balance [of money owed him], but that person begins to resist, then he is to appear at an investigation before twelve men; and if he wrongfully did not give [the money] back, then he is [to return] the money [to its rightful owner], and [pay] 3 grivnas for the offense.

16. If someone, having recognized his own [stolen] slave, wishes to take him back, then [the man who acquired the stolen slave] is to lead him to another [man], from whom he purchased [the slave], and that man leads him to another, even to the third [party from whom the slave was acquired]; then say to the third [party], "Give me your own slave [in exchange for the stolen slave], and you seek your own property [i.e., his loss] in the presence of an eyewitness [with the help of the stolen slave]."

17. If a slave strikes a free man, and [then] flees to [his lord's] house, and [his] lord does not give him up [for punishment], then the lord takes his slave, and pays for him 12 grivnas; and if after that somewhere they find him [the slave], then the man [whom the slave struck] may beat him.

18. And if someone breaks a lance, or shield, or destroys clothes, and wishes to keep [the damaged property] for himself, then [the owner] is to take payment for it; and if he has broken it, and if he will return it, then [the one who broke it] is to pay [the owner] money, as much as [the owner] gave for it.

The Pravda established for the Rus' land, when Iziaslav [1054–78], Vsevolod [1076–93], Sviatoslav [1073–76], Kosniachko Pereneg [the Pecheneg?], Mikyfor [Nikifor] the Kievan, and Chiudin Mikula met together.

19. If they kill a steward as an offense, then the killers must pay for him 80 grivnas, and [no other] people [of the community] are respon-

sible; and [for killing] the prince's collector of fines [they are also to pay] 80 grivnas.

20. And if they kill a steward in an assault, or they [the residents of a community] do not seek the murderer, then [the community] in which the corpse lies must pay the bloodwite [payment for murder].

21. And if they kill the steward by the storeroom [while they are engaged in theft], or [while stealing] horses or cattle, or [if they kill the steward while committing] cattle theft, then kill [them] like a dog. And the same regulation obtains for [the homicide] of an overseer.

22. And for [the homicide] of the prince's overseer [pay] 80 grivnas.

23. And for the senior stablemaster [who is murdered] while [he is] with the herds [pay] 80 grivnas, as Iziaslav [1054–78] established when the residents of Dorogobuzh killed his stablemaster.

24. And [for the homicide of] the prince's field supervisor and [for the homicide of] the plowland supervisor [pay] 12 grivnas.

25. And [for the homicide of] the prince's contract laborer pay 5 grivnas.

26. And [for the homicide of] a peasant and [for the homicide of] a male slave [pay] 5 grivnas [each].

27. And [for the homicide of] a slave wet-nurse or male tutor [pay] 12 [grivnas].

28. And for [killing] the prince's horse, if it is branded [the offender is to] pay 3 grivnas, and for a peasant's [horse he pays] two grivnas, for a mare 60 rezanas, for an ox 1 grivna, for a cow 40 rezanas, for a three-year-old [cow] 15 kunas, for a two-year-old [cow]½ grivna, for a calf 5 rezanas, for a lamb 1 nogata, [and] for a ram 1 nogata.

29. And if [someone] abducts another's male or female slave, then [he is to] pay 12 grivnas for the offense to him [who owned the stolen slave].

30. And if a man, bloody and blue with bruises, comes forward [to complain], then he does not need to find a witness [to substantiate his complaint of assault].

31. And if someone steals either a horse or

oxen, or [steals from] the storeroom, and if one man committed the theft [alone], then he is to pay him [the owner of the property] 1 grivna and 30 rezanas; or if there were eighteen [thieves], then [they are to pay the owner] 3 grivnas and 30 rezanas each.

32. And if they set fire to or destroy the prince's beehive, then [they are to] pay 3 grivnas.

33. And if they torture a peasant [of the prince] without the prince's authorization, then [they shall pay] 3 grivnas for the offense; and if [they torture the prince's] steward, overseer or guard, then [they shall pay] 12 grivnas.

34. And if someone plows across a border or [beyond] a border marker carved on a tree, then [he is to pay the owner] 12 grivnas for the offense.

35. And if someone steals a boat, then [he is] to pay [the owner] 30 rezanas for the boat, and a fine of 60 rezanas.

36. And [for the theft of] a dove or a chicken [pay the owner] nine kunas, and for a duck, a goose, a crane, or swan [pay the owner] 30 rezanas; and [pay] a fine of 60 rezanas.

37. And if they steal someone's dog, or hawk, or falcon, then [they are to pay the owner] 3 grivnas for the offense.

38. If they kill a thief at their own home, or at the storeroom or by the barn, then the thief is killed [and there the matter ends]; [but] if they hold him until daylight, then [they are] to conduct him to the prince's residence; but if they kill him, and people have seen [the thief] tied up, then they shall pay for him.

39. If they steal hay, then [they are to pay the owner] 9 kunas; and [thieves are to pay] 9 kunas [for stealing] firewood.

40. If they steal a sheep, or a goat, or a swine, and if there will be ten [men] who stole one sheep, then they shall pay 60 rezanas each as a fine; and the one who captured [the thieves receives] 10 rezanas [as a reward].

41. And from a 1-grivna [fine] 1 kuna goes to the prince's guard, [and] 15 kunas [go to the church] as a tithe; and the prince receives 3 grivnas [sic]; and from 12 grivnas 70 kunas go to the one who captured [the thief], and 2 grivnas [to the church] as a tithe, and [the remainder of the] 10 grivnas [goes] to the prince.

42. This is the schedule of fees paid in connection with the collection of the bloodwite: the bloodwite collector gets seven buckets of malt each week, and also a ram or half a carcass of meat, or two nogatas; and on Wednesday a rezana or cheese; on Friday the same;* and as much bread as he can eat, and millet; and two chickens each day; provide four horses, and feed them as much as they will eat; and 60 grivnas to the bloodwite collector, and 10 rezanas and 12 veveritsas, and 1 grivna in advance; or if [the bloodwite collector arrives] during Lent, then fish are needed; [he is entitled to] take 7 rezanas for fish, a total of 15 kunas each week; and give them [the bloodwite collectors] as much bread as they can eat; and the bloodwite collectors are to gather the bloodwite within a week. This is the regulation of Iaroslav [1019–54].

43. And this is the schedule for the bridge builders: If they have built a bridge, then [they are to take] for their work a nogata, and 1 nogata for each span; if they repair an old bridge with several boards—either three, or four, or five—then the same [payments obtain].

SOURCE: *The Laws of Rus' (Tenth to Fifteenth Centuries).* Translated and edited by Daniel H. Kaiser (Salt Lake City: Charles Schlacks, Jr., forthcoming), pp. 15–19. English translation copyright © 1992 Daniel H. Kaiser.

---

*Editors' note: According to Orthodox canon law, Wednesday and Friday are fast days.

LITERATURE

I. IA. FROIANOV AND
A. IU. DVORNICHENKO
The City-State in Kievan Rus'
(Eleventh–Twelfth Centuries)

Most historians maintain that for much of its history Russia has depended upon some form of monarchy, a condition which they use to help explain the modern totalitarian variations on the state in Russia. However, a dissident tradition has maintained that it was the monarchy itself which was the deviation in Russia's past. To these historians, democracy was the genuine, enduring form of state organization which the Moscow princes, Romanov tsars, and Communist commissars illegally displaced. The work which appears below belongs to this second tradition, and argues that in Kievan Rus', even in the presence of princely administration, it was popular election which determined the organization of the state.

In contemporary historical science a tradition has grown up which depicts the Kievan land as the fulfillment of monarchism in Kievan Rus' in contrast to those cities, such as Polotsk and especially Novgorod, which had a strong city assembly (*veche*).

For example, V. L. Ianin and M. Kh. Aleshkovskii see in the Novgorod Republic something phenomenal, completely unlike the socio-political organization of the old Russian principalities, especially the Kievan principality where the monarchic principle prevailed. P. P. Tolochko writes that the Grand Prince in Kiev was the "supreme chief." True, the city assembly also played a role: "During the reign of a strong Kievan prince the city assembly was an obedient appendage of supreme authority, but during the reign of a weak prince, the pic-

ture was just the opposite. In other words, in Kiev in the eleventh and twelfth centuries both the representative of monarchic authority (the Grand Prince) and the organ of feudal democracy (the city assembly) coexisted, supplementing one another and sometimes coming into open conflict."

In our view the establishment of the rural structure of the Kievan land does not accord with the picture outlined by these scholars. The rise of the *volost'*, the city-state in the middle Dnieper River, followed that same path [of republicanism] which other lands charted. . . .

In the collisions of the clan structure there arose a new Kievan commune which powerfully emerges from the pages of the chronicles, in spite of the fact that the chronicler attempted to elevate the activities of the prince to first place. . . . The princes who ruled in the end of the tenth and early eleventh centuries had to reckon with the growing authority of the city commune, attempting somehow to curry its favor. It is no accident that [in 1015] Sviatopolk hid from the Kievans the death of Prince Vladimir, and, having seated himself on the throne, convoked the Kievans and "began to give them gifts." After the murder of Boris and Gleb, he also "assembled the people, and began to distribute mantles to some and furs to others, and thus dissipated a large sum."

The city commune, which grew stronger over time, had the responsibility for religion. So [in fulfilling religious duties] Prince Vladimir appears on the pages of the chronicle in the company not only of his retainers but also of the people. Together with "the people" he completes pagan sacrifices. And in the performance of the heathen cult the populace took an active role. . . . It is particularly important to emphasize the participation of the "people" of the Kievan commune in the establishment of Christianity in Rus' [see in Chapter 5]. They were present at the gathering called to select a religion, they offered their own voice, and selected "good men and wise" for

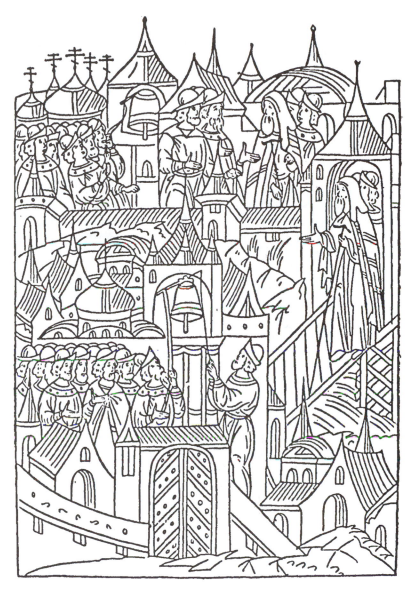

Manuscript miniature (sixteenth century): Ontsyfor Lukin convokes the Novgorod city assembly at St. Sophia's Cathedral and Mayor Fedor Danilovich at Iaroslav's Court. From A. V. Artsikhovskii, *Drevnerusskie miniatiury kak istoricheskii istochnik* (Moscow: MGU, 1944), p. 149.

the journey abroad to "test the faiths." One of the Scandinavian sagas reports that the Russian Prince convoked a popular assembly on the question of a new religion. So in deciding the most important questions, the princes were obliged to reckon with the opinion of the city commune.

Such an attentive attitude toward the city commune becomes more understandable if one takes into account the fact that the commune had its own military organization, largely independent from the prince. These warriors, the city militia, constituted a real military force even in this early period. Indeed, Prince Vladimir went against the Pechenegs [a steppe people with whom Rus' often did battle] in 992 with these warriors. It is curious that in the legend placed in the chronicle under this year, the hero of this battle was not a retainer of the prince, but a youth who came from the common people. In 997 Vladimir could not rescue the citizens of Belgorod because "the Pechenegs were numerous, but he did not have many warriors" from the city militia, and without them it would be impossible to defeat the Pechenegs.

Militia warriors actively took part also in the internecine princely conflicts, which is why [when Sviatopolk plotted against him] the advisors of Boris, Vladimir's son, told him: "You have a retinue and militia warriors. Go to Kiev and occupy the throne of your father." [In 1015] militia warriors also served as a support to Iaroslav in his claims to Kiev, and also to Sviatopolk in fending off Iaroslav's detachments.

So was begun the process of the formation of the local commune in the Kievan land. It is not always possible to trace the entire process, for it sometimes seems quiet, almost latent, hidden from the eyes of the scholar, but at other times bursts through the surface of the historical events, and comes to the attention of chroniclers.

Especially interesting in this respect are the events which took place in Kiev in the years 1068–69, when before us arises the constituted city commune. The primary form of its expression was the city assembly, the gathering of all free residents of Kiev and its surrounding neighborhoods. The indignant Kievans, demanding arms, gathered at the market. It appears from the words of the chronicler that the people who gathered for the assembly themselves took the decision to resume the fight with the Polovtsians, and present the prince with a demand to issue horses and weapons. It is impossible not to see in this an assertion of the independence of the assembly *vis-à-vis* princely authority. In general, the Kievan commune acted as a fully independent organ in the events of 1068–69, placing itself on the same plane as the prince. Instead of the expelled Iziaslav, the Kievan people seated Vseslav on the throne. When the balance of forces seemed on the side of Iziaslav, the commune turned for help to his brothers. This appeal to Sviatoslav and Vsevolod also was the result of a decision by the city assembly.

The question arises, Who were the Kievans who expelled Iziaslav? . . . In our view, one can hardly understand the term "Kievan people" as signifying either townsmen or rural citizens. More likely this term included both the remnants of the Kievan militia, defeated by the nomads, as well as residents of the villages of the Kievan land, who sought shelter behind the walls of the capital city. Having discovered the meaning of the term "Kievan people," we can state a very important detail: participation in the assembly in 1068 involved not only townsmen but also rural residents. This observation permits us correspondingly to discover the meaning of the term "Kievan," by which the sources not infrequently indicated the populace of the Kievan countryside (and not only of Kiev [city]). . . .

[In the events of 1068–69] we see the Kiev city assembly, a genuine people's gathering, in action. At the assembly, participants discussed the situation, expelled one ruler and installed another, negotiated about the continuation of war with the enemy, and dispatched embassies. In the events of 1068–69 the city assembly stands out as the supreme organ of popular rule, higher than that of princely authority. This is why it is impossible to characterize the Kievan state administration of that time as monarchic. Here we observe a state structure based on a republican foundation. . . .

In the chronicle account of the events of 1068–69 there is still one more curious detail which clearly characterized the city commune. Having expelled Iziaslav, the Kievans "plundered the Prince's residence, seizing countless amounts of gold and silver, furs and linen." Exactly this kind of phenomenon we also meet in other lands of Rus'.

There is no reason to qualify this plunder as an act of exclusively class conflict. In ancient societies "the aggregated surplus product, alienated in various forms to the profit of the leader and his subordinates, was seen not only as compensation for fulfilling the socially useful functions of administration, but also as a kind of social fund, the expenditure of which must serve the interests of the whole community."

In light of this information, the internal sense of the Kievan plunder of 1068 (and other similar plunders) becomes understandable. The princes in Rus' survived to a significant degree because of "feeding," a peculiar payment from the free populace for the fulfillment of public service, the origin of which was lost in deep antiquity. All this contributed to the conceptualization of the prince's property as being at least partly public property, which became the basis for the demand which the Kievans made to the prince: give us weapons and horses. The princes in Kievan Rus' had to furnish the people's militia with horses and weapons. So under the years 1068–69 the chronicler reveals a vivid picture of the activity of the Kievan commune.

Chronicle notices from the late eleventh century provide additional detail to this picture. The formation of the Kievan commune was achieved on the path to the democratization of socio-political relations, which is why the princes appealed to the opinion of the commune even in questions of intra-princely affairs. So, for example, in 1096 "Sviatopolk and Volodimer sent to Oleg, saying, 'Come to Kiev, and let us lay before the people of the city the situation of the Rus' land, and let us defend the Rus' land from the pagans.'" Oleg,

"having listened to evil advisers," arrogantly replied: "'I shall not have some bishop, abbot, or peasant judge me.'" This last phrase says much. In the first place, it alludes to the fact that the term "city people" included democratic elements, which is why Oleg compared them to peasants. Secondly, it follows that the prince was invited to Kiev not only for working out a common plan of action against the "pagans," but also for deciding inter-princely disputes, where the "city people," together with the bishops, abbots, and boyars were designated as intermediaries. . . .

The characteristic features of the Kievan local commune come through in the events of 1113 which followed the death of prince Sviatopolk. Scholars are inclined to two versions of these events contained in the ancient sources. According to the Hypatian chronicle, after the death of Sviatopolk "the Kievans, having made peace, sent to Volodimer [Monomakh], saying, 'Come, prince, to the throne of your father and grandfather'; having listened to them, Volodimer wept deeply, and did not go because of his sorrow for his brother. The Kievans then pillaged the residence of Putiatin, the millenarius, then came to the Jews, and pillaged [their homes]; then again the Kievans sent to Volodimer, saying, 'Come, prince, to Kiev; if you do not come, then much more evil will take place, not only to Putiatin's residence, to those of the hundredmen, and the Jews, but also against your sisters-in-law, against the boyars and monasteries, and you will have to answer, prince, if they pillage monasteries.' So Volodimer heeded them, and came to Kiev." The Tale of Boris and Gleb depicts the enthronement of Vladimir Monomakh in Kiev somewhat differently: "Sviatopolk died . . . and there was much mutiny and treason among the people, and also many foul rumors. Then all the people gathered, especially the powerful and well-off men, and having come to a gathering of all the people, they begged Volodimer to come put an end to the treason among the people. And having come [to Kiev] he put down the rebellion and the din among the people.". . .

The text of the Hypatian Chronicle and the

Tale of Boris and Gleb . . . are in principle the same; they simply supplement one another. . . . The information extracted from these sources puts everything in its place. It seems that the "Kievans" (a socially undivided mass of residents of Kiev and the districts adjacent to it), having gathered in assembly, named Vladimir Monomakh as their prince. In the embassy to him the assembly commune dispatched a deputation composed of the "important" and "well-off" men—the boyars. There is no reason to see in this fact evidence that the ordinary populace of Kiev did not have full political authority or were deprived of rights. Similar ambassadorial practice had existed already in tribal society, and continued . . . even after these events, especially in Kiev itself. For now one must emphasize the activity of the Kievan city commune in one of the main questions of internal politics of the region— the appointment of a new prince. Monomakh became the Kievan prince at the wish of the popular assembly, and not at the invitation of the local nobility, as some scholars assert. . . .

The establishment of the principle of electing princes in Kiev, an expression of the principle of the freedom with which the Kievans dealt with their princes, could not help but exert an influence on that same order of electing authorities in other centers. Of course, one ought not exaggerate the degree of this influence, because socio-political institutions in Novgorod came together as a result of internal social development. But at the same time the scholar cannot disregard this influence either. Indeed, the struggle of those cities subordinate to Kiev for independence inevitably engendered a spirit of rivalry which provoked from the local communes a tendency to establish the same structure for which Kiev's commune had gained fame, in that way reaching the same level with it. . . .

The election of princes was the result of a single process, common to all Rus' in the eleventh and twelfth centuries, of formation of city-states, the supreme organ of which was the popular assembly, within whose competence, among other things, came the filling of princely thrones. In Kiev in 1068 this function

of the assembly was still palpable: the Kievans expelled Prince Iziaslav, having selected in his stead Vseslav of Polotsk. . . .

Against the backdrop of the events of 1113 the Kievan commune emerges as a self-sufficient organization, possessing sovereignty, the ability to determine who would rule in Kiev, in spite of the calculations of the Riurikid princes about seniority. So one can say that by the beginning of the twelfth century the establishment of the city-states in Kiev was an accomplished fact. Its future history only strengthens our conclusion. . . .

The sovereignty, the independence of the commune emerges most vividly in the activity of the city assembly. In 1146 Kievan Prince Vsevolod Ol'govich, having returned from a military campaign, "fell seriously ill." The prince, being gravely ill, halted above Vyshgorod, to which he summoned the "Kievans," so as to settle with them the conditions of his successor. One can suppose that the "Kievans" whom the dying prince invited were elected people, messengers from the Kievan assembly. But their agreement to accept Igor' as prince had to be approved at the assembly in Kiev. Therefore they, together with the new "pretender" to the throne, departed for Kiev, where near Ugorskoe [just south of Kiev, near the Caves Monastery] they summoned to assembly all Kievans who "kissed the cross to him [Igor'], saying, 'You are our prince.'"

After the death of Vsevolod a new assembly took place. The successor to Vsevolod, Igor', "convoked all the Kievans on the hill at Iaroslav's court, and they kissed the cross to him." Then the chronicler notes that "all the Kievans" gathered again at the Turov chapel. We shall not explain the reasons for this repeated gathering of the assembly. For now it is more important to establish the social composition of the participants in the assembly. Whom does the chronicler intend under the term "all Kievans?" The key to this question we find in the description of the assembly at the Turov chapel, more exactly in the notice that Prince Sviatoslav, "having come to an agreement" with all the Kievans and "having taken the best men," went to Igor' who waited for him nearby. From this it is clear that those "best men" who swore allegiance to Igor' were only part of the people in attendance at the assembly at the Turov chapel. Consequently, "all the Kievans" in the mouth of the chronicler signifies the mass of townsmen, whose social structure was fairly mixed. The same meaning was contained in the words "all Kievans" when the chronicler talked about the assembly at Iaroslav's court and above Ugorskoe. So, the assemblies above Ugorskoe and at Iaroslav's Court, just as at the Turov chapel, were all popular gatherings, considering and deciding the main problems of socio-political life of the Kievan region.

The assembly meetings which took place later in the reign of Iziaslav were analogous in social composition. Once, for example, in 1147 Iziaslav "convoked the boyars and his retinue and the Kievans, in order to draw the Kievan army into a campaign against Suzdal' and Prince Iurii Dolgorukii. The Kievans, however, did not yield to persuasion. The chronicle in this instance saves us from guessing about the composition of the "Kievans." Boyars and members of the prince's retinue in this case may be specifically excluded, since the chronicler speaks of them separately. There remains the mass of townsmen, giving to the assembly the character of a popular gathering.

In that same year Iziaslav again turned to the Kievan assembly, from whom he requested "warriors" in order to fight Sviatoslavich Vsevolodovich and the descendants of Prince Davyd. According to the testimony of the Laurentian chronicle, to the assembly "came great multitudes of Kievans, and they sat by St. Sophia Cathedral to listen." The Hypatian chronicle says: "All Kievans from the least to the great came to St. Sophia's court, and there convoked an assembly." Both chronicles—the Laurentian and Hypatian—depict a massive meeting of "Kievans," convoked at the request of Prince Iziaslav. This is one of the clearest examples illustrating the popular structure of Kiev's assembly.

Notice about the assembly in 1147 is also remarkable because it reproduces the order of the conduct of assembly meetings. Before us is

no chaotic crowd . . . but an altogether orderly gathering, operating under rules worked out by assembly practice. Those Kievans who came to St. Sophia were seated gradually, awaiting the beginning of the assembly. The prince, Metropolitan, and millenarius directed the session. Ambassadors, in accord with etiquette, greeted in turn the Metropolitan, millenarius, and Kievans. Only then did the Kievans say to them: "Tell us why the prince has sent you." All these details confirm the presence in Kiev of the twelfth century of a more or less developed manner of conducting the assembly. . . .

The central place which the assembly occupied in the socio-political mechanism of the Kievan land in the middle of the twelfth century was determined not only by its social composition, but also by the circle of questions which it decided. The assemblies found within their competence questions touching war and peace and the election of princes. More than that, this competence reached even to the naming of judicio-administrative officials. . . .

We suggest, then, that one consider the assembly and princes in Kiev within the frame of a single socio-political whole, in which the assembly was the supreme organ of authority and the prince the personification of the highest executive authority, accountable, moreover subordinate to, the assembly. The prince, being the head of the commune administration, at the same time represented communal authority, fulfilling various functions. This is why the prince appeared a necessary element of socio-political structure. Just as in other lands, a long absence of the prince was a misfortune for the Kievan land. "Then it was difficult for the Kievans; not a single prince remained in Kiev," notes the chronicler. But this does not mean that the Kievan prince was a monarch nor was his authority monarchic.

In the Kievan land in the eleventh and early twelfth century there took place a process of founding a republic, not a monarchy. A republican structure came together somewhat earlier in Kiev even than in Novgorod, the republican structure of which contemporary historiography undeservedly recognizes as a phenomenal development. Of course, a prince

Manuscript miniature (sixteenth century): The election of the Novgorod Archbishop at the city assembly. From *Drevnerusskie miniatiury kak istoricheskii istochnik* (Moscow: MGU, 1944), p. 147.

of that time had the potential for monarchic authority. But for monarchy to emerge, other social and political conditions were necessary. These conditions arose beyond the limits of the Kievan period of our history.

And what was the fate of Kiev and its land in the second half of the twelfth and early thirteenth centuries? At that time the "Mother of Russian Cities" fell into decline. Of course, this process occurred gradually, hardly noticeable to a contemporary observer.

The former sovereignty and independence of the town commune was preserved, as reflected in the calling of princes. [In 1154] the Kievans summoned Iziaslav Davydovich [to rule in Kiev]: "The Kievans sent [bishop] Demian Kanev'skii for Iziaslav Davydovich''[, the Chronicle reports]. It is clear why Iziaslav, justifying himself before Iurii [Dolgorukii, who laid claim to Kiev], said, "The Kievans enthroned me." The chronicle notice about the calling of Iziaslav is interesting for still one more detail. A bishop appears as a representative of the town commune. Clerical authority, evidently, began more and more to play that same role which it did somewhat later in Novgorod: to be the support of the commune.

After the death of Iurii "the Kievans came to Iziaslav, saying, 'Come reign in Kiev.'" The town commune of Kiev again controlled the Kievan principality. On the other hand, with Iurii himself the matter was much more complicated. This prince, who based himself on the northeastern regions, clearly was not popular in Kiev. Speaking about his enthronement in Kiev, the chronicler notes, "Happy was the entire Rus' land." We have reason, however, not to trust the spirit of this remark. When, after a drinking bout with Petrilo, Iurii departed for a better world, "they [the people] did much evil ... they pillaged his beautiful court and they ransacked another of his courts across the Dnieper ... and they also pillaged the court of his son, Vasil'ko. They killed Suzdalians throughout the town and in the villages, and stole their property." In this pillage we see, as it were, two layers. On the one hand, it is fully associated with the already archaic reallocation of property within the commune. On the other hand, we can also see reflected in it dissatisfaction of the Kievans with Iurii. Iurii, evidently, was confirmed on the throne in Kiev by the forceful support of those very Suzdalians, the fate of whom was so sad after his death. Northeast Rus' imposed their prince on Kiev. In this it is impossible not to see evidence of some weakening of the Kievan city commune.

In 1160 the Kievans accepted Rostislav on the throne. "All people with honor gathered, and he sat on the throne of his father and grandfather." We observe the same practice under the year 1169 when, after the death of Rostislav, "the brothers Volodimir Mstislavich, Riurik and Davyd began to send for Mstislav, and the Kievans sent from themselves the Black Hoods [representatives of the commune]." This means that the traditions of earlier times were preserved. But the anti-Kievan struggle of the developed districts of Rus' and the struggle of the princes for the Kievan throne had achieved their end: they exhausted the strength of Kiev. The capital city became the booty of neighboring city-states. Testimony to this was the weakening of Kiev at the initiative of Andrei Bogoliubskii. The army of enemy city-states devastated the city [of Kiev in 1169]: "While the churches burned, while they killed peasants and tied up others, they took their wives captive, separating them from their husbands by force, and babies sobbed, watching their mothers, and they ravaged estates, and robbed churches of their icons, books, chasubles, and bells, and the Smolensk people, Suzdalians, and people from Chernigov carried it all off."

The plunder of Kiev was a reflection of that process ... of the formation of independent city states, the crystallization of local life. Its reverse was the gradual decline of the capital which lost all its former power ...

After the massacre, the political power of Kiev's community was broken, and could never fully recover from that blow.

SOURCE: I. Ia. Froianov and A. Iu. Dvornichenko, *Gorodagosudarstva Drevnei Rusi* (Leningrad: LGU, [Leningrad State University], 1988), pp. 41–50, 57, 59–64, 75–77 (excerpted). Translated by Julia Vaingurt and Daniel H. Kaiser. Reproduced with the permission of I. Ia. Froianov and A. Iu. Dvornichenko.

3

The Economy in Kievan Rus'

Another long-standing debate among historians of Russia was whether Kievan Rus' was primarily a commercial society headquartered in towns, as Kliuchevskii maintained, or primarily a rural, agricultural society for which towns served only as marketplaces. Nothing so far discovered has finally settled this debate, in part because there is plenty of evidence for both trade and agriculture. The Pravda Russkaia, for example, certainly mentions a market, and the Expanded Pravda pays considerable attention to banking, storage, and other matters related to commerce. At the same time, the Pravda Russkaia also devotes attention to agriculture, reserving special attention for livestock. On the basis of this evidence, then, both trade and farming had their place.

Nevertheless, it now seems that agriculture may have played the more prominent role. As with other long disputed questions, archeology here too has added considerably to the information base with which we can consider the problem. For example, even though the Pravda Russkaia mentions cattle, sheep, and swine among the herded livestock, excavations demonstrate that people in Kievan Rus' consumed all these animals, as well as a good variety of fish and other meats. At the same time, although the Pravda has little to say about grain-farming, archeology has revealed a wide range of grains which formed the backbone of the Kievan diet.

None of this is to say that trade was unimportant. As I. V. Dubov showed above, from a very early time settlements along the Volga depended on trade, and other river settlements doubtless shared in the commerce. But in some areas trade was probably the dominant sector of the economy. Novgorod seems to have been one such place. Well-situated to profit from trade along the Dnieper as well as along the Volga to the East, Novgorod grew rapidly in the Middle Ages until it had become so notable a trading town that it joined in that remarkable northern European trade network, the Hanseatic League.

Archeology has revealed much about the operation of the commercial economy in Novgorod. The range of wares uncovered there testifies to the far-flung connections which the Novgorodian merchants had. Nuts from the Caucasus, amphora from the Mediterranean, cloth from Flanders, and many other items lay buried beneath the damp Novgorod soil until recent excavations brought them back to the surface. In examining and counting these finds, we can gain some insight into the commercial life of this era, and the role that distant disturbances had upon the local economy.

LITERATURE

V. P. LEVASHEVA

Agriculture in Rus'
(Tenth–Thirteenth Centuries)

If in later, imperial Russia bureaucrats and landowners documented carefully the operation of the economy, few written sources survive to tell us how the economy of Kievan Rus' operated. Instead, we must rely in the main on non-verbal materials uncovered by archeologists. In the selection which follows, V. P. Levasheva concentrates upon agriculture, which appears to have played the more important part in the Rus' economy. Vital to understanding this economy is a realization of the difference between southern Rus' (the regions around Kiev), where verdant fields rich with humus opened out onto the steppe, and northern Rus', where dense forests made tillage difficult, and where soil quality was often poor. These two environments demanded different farming strategies and different implements. And these differences, in turn, determined other aspects of agriculture, including the kinds of crops grown and their overall productivity.

In the tenth through thirteenth centuries over the entire territory of Rus' (both in the forest and forest-steppe zones) plow agriculture was the basis of the economy, but the earlier history of its development was not the same in the north and in the south. In the first millennium in the forest zone of Eastern Europe slash-and-burn agriculture prevailed, while in the forest-steppe zone a system employing fallow land dominated.

Slash-and-burn does not require draught power of livestock, inasmuch as fire is all that is necessary to prepare the soil for sowing [see p. 40]; plowing is not necessary. Only a harrow must be employed to loosen the surface layer of soil. Under the fallow system, on the other hand, plowing virgin soil is necessary with the help of the draught power of animals.

On the territory of southern Rus' plow agriculture has very ancient roots. The plow was known there already in the first millennium BC at the time of the Scythians. The Scythian "plow," judging by its depiction on a coin from the second century BC, was a light plow with a base. In the first millennium AD on this same territory they used draught labor to pull implements which had iron blades and shares similar to those of modern plows as archeological finds from the middle and second half of the first millennium confirm.

In the forest zone the most ancient finds of iron blades may be dated only to the second half of the first millennium, when slashburn began to displace plow agriculture. . . . Slash-and-burn ruins the structure of the soil. The cleared plot of land may be planted for two to three years in a row, which under favorable circumstances will bring high yields. But then the soil becomes so exhausted that to restore its fertility it is necessary to allow the plot to "rest."

In such circumstances it was necessary to clear new plots further and further from settlements. This inconvenience led to a transition to forest fallow, under which the period of "rest" was reduced to 10–16 years, but which also required more thorough clearing for sowing. Meantime, the role of fire in forest fallow diminished. Livestock-raising grew in importance, making possible the application of draught labor—in short, all the prerequisites for the transition to plow agriculture . . . Of course, this transition took place gradually. For an extended period both systems coexisted, and slashburn remained an important means of clearing new forest plots for a long time.

Manuscript miniature (1648), depicting slash-and-burn agriculture. From A. V. Artsikhovskii, *Drevnerusskie miniatiury kak istoricheskii istochnik* (Moscow: MGU, 1944), p. 200.

In the south, in both the steppe and forest-steppe zones, the fallow system also required bringing under cultivation more plots by means of labor-consuming plowing of virgin soil (inasmuch as those plots exhausted by sowing had to be rested for several years). Consequently, it too gradually yielded to a system in which the land lay fallow only one year, thereby permitting a longer period when the land was in production. But the new system also required better cultivation of the land.

So, around the year 1000 AD in almost all the Rus' lands two- and three-field plow agriculture was in use.

IMPLEMENTS OF SOIL CULTIVATION

Iron shares, plow blades, and moldboards are all known from excavations of sites dated to the period between the tenth and thirteenth centuries ... From these finds, together with ethnographic data, one can establish the general form of the plow-type implements in Rus' and the means of their use.

The difference between the scratch-plow *(ralo),* heavy plow, and light plow is that both the scratch-plow and light plow only tear up the land, furrow it, and loosen it, whereas the heavy plow cuts off a horizontal layer of earth, pushing it aside and turning it over. . . .

Ethnographic parallels help recreate the picture of how these plows worked [see p. 42]. The scratch-plow remained in use in Ukraine until quite recently. It worked the soil by means of a wooden share, the end of which was either burned hard or equipped with an iron point, the size and form of which recalled ancient Rus' parallels; the share itself was fixed on an angle. . . . Light scratch-plows, used in light soils, had a shorter shaft for harnessing horses; the heavy plow, on the other hand, demanded harnessing several pairs of oxen, although it could, with some difficulty, plow virgin soil. The primitive character of this implement makes one think that farmers worked with the old Rus' scratch-plow in the same way.

Work with the ancient plow, the prototype of the contemporary "Ukrainian plow" and the "saban," followed different courses. It was easier to till virgin soil with them. The blade, attached to the front of the share, makes a vertical cut of the soil; the share itself, placed horizontally on the base of the plow, cut off a layer of the ground horizontally. This layer of soil, rising along the wooden part of the implement or along the moldboard with the motion of the plow, falls off, toppling to one side opposite the blade. But, in pushing a layer of soil to the side, the Ukrainian plow does not break it up, so that after such a plowing a second tilling was necessary with a light plow so as to loosen the soil. This is why archeologists at the Raikovetsk excavation in Zhitomir region found both plow shares and iron plow points in great quantities. Here both the heavy plow and the scratchplow had still another, different function—to rework old plowland, for which it was necessary only to loosen the soil prior to sowing.

In the forest zone the scratch-plow was the first plow-type implement using draught power to appear, sometime in the second half of the first millennium AD, brought there from southern Rus'. Its role was not to raise a layer of virgin soil, but simply to rework old plowland on plots already cleared by slash-and-burn. In this same zone another kind of implement, the light plow, appeared in connection with the transition to plow agriculture. . . .

Until recently opinion on the origin of the light plow was uniform. . . . Scholars figured that at first there was only the one-toothed light plow or the scratch-plow, but then, in order to plow (or, more accurately, to loosen) a broader stretch of land with each pass, farmers moved to a two-toothed plow with two iron plowshares, and then to those with three or more. The appearance of the forked light plow produced a new name, sokha. . . .

Not long ago the archeologist P. N. Tret'iakov and then the ethnographer A. K. Supinskii advanced a different explanation on the origin of the light plow. They figured that the two-toothed light plow derived not from the scratch-plow, but rather from the multi-toothed plow, which in its turn derived from the wooden harrow fashioned from twigs [see p. 42], which, in turn, descended from a more primitive instrument of slash-and-burn agriculture—a tree with its branches lopped off—which harrowed the ashes [left from slash-and-burn]. Multi-toothed light plows (with three, five, and even ten teeth, each with iron shares) until recently could still be found in forest regions. The same could be said for the primitive harrow and all forms of slash-and-burn agriculture which brought new forest plots under cultivation.

This explanation on the origin of the light plow makes sense, and is supported by both archeological material and information from "ancient ethnography"—Russian miniatures and written sources from the middle of the second millennium AD. The antiquity of the three-toothed light plow found confirmation in the discovery in Novgorod in 1954 of three plow shares in layers dated to the eleventh century. The oldest depiction of a Russian light plow is contained in a sixteenth-century miniature from the life of St. Sergei [see p. 43]. Here is visible a three-toothed light plow. The shares have the same form as the multi-toothed plows from nineteenth-century Vologda. The shares are placed on separate, almost vertical mounts, the middle one advanced a bit relative to the others, whereas on the multi-toothed light plows from Vologda and the three-toothed Kostroma plows all the shares are arranged in one row, perpendicular to the furrow. Another, relatively late miniature of the second half of the sixteenth century depicts a two-toothed light plow with one forked beam, placed as steeply as the shares of the three-toothed light plow of the sixteenth century and having the same narrow shares.

Juridical materials describe the pillaging of a village in the Iur'ev district, during which the

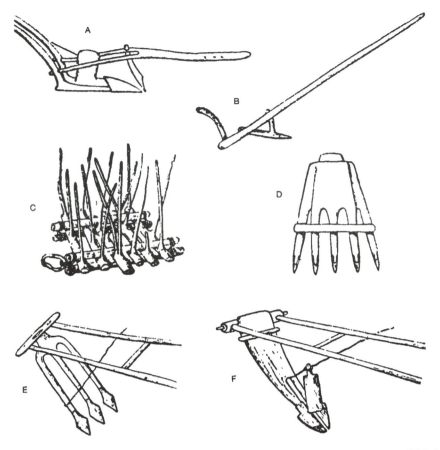

Primitive plow-type implements used in the nineteenth century: (A) Ukrainian and Moldovan heavy plow, (B) Ukrainian scratch-plow, (C) harrow, (D) multiple-toothed light plow, (E) three-toothed light plow, and (F) two-toothed light plow. From V. P. Levasheva, "Sel'skoe khoziaistvo," in *Ocherki po istorii russkoi derevni X–XIII vv.*, Trudy gosudarstvennogo istoricheskogo muzeia 32(1956):24.

raiders seized from several peasants the most valuable implements of that time—plow-shares, axes, etc. The document enumerates several households from which the robbers took two plowshares and from one peasant three. It is doubtful that a single peasant possessed several light plows. More probably each pair of shares was taken from a single light plow, and the three shares stolen from one household all came from the same light plow. That only one peasant had a three-toothed light plow in this village argues that the two-toothed light plow had by that time already displaced the three-toothed plow.

All these examples indicate that the Russian light plow originated in the north, in the forest zone where slash-and-burn preceded plow agriculture, and that the primitive harrow—an instrument of slash-and-burn agriculture—was the prototype of the light plow . . .

If one compares the map of soil types with a map depicting archeological finds of plows, it becomes obvious that across the forest-steppe zone of southern Rus', with its cher-

Manuscript miniature (sixteenth century) depicting a light plow. From A. V. Artsikhovskii, *Drev-nerusskie miniatiury kak istoricheskii istochnik* (Moscow: MGU, 1944), p. 187.

nozem [dark soil, rich in organic matter] and grey podzolic [acidic] soils, implements of a plow type intended for horizontal plowing—scratch-plows with a base and plows with blades—were widespread. The working of heavy chernozem soils also required repeated plowing with the scratch-plow which had no base: finds of plowshares from such scratch-plows are also noted in this region. . . .

In the middle Volga and lower Kama River basins, where the same soils exist, implements of the plow type, and their companions, the scratch-plow, were in use. But in the forest zone of northwest and northeast Rus' in podzolic soils there predominated the local form of draught-animal implements—the light plow. Only a few parts of the heavy plow have

been discovered on the territory of northeast Rus', and they are connected mainly with Ria-zan' and Suzdal', which represent oases of grey podzolic soils with traces of chernozem. That the heavy plow was known in northwest Rus' is confirmed by a miniature from the Radziwill chronicle which was painted not in the south, but in the Smolensk land.

Finds of plow points in northwest and north-east Rus' are also rare. This kind of implement, as with all forms of early plow technology, was brought to the north from southern Rus'. South Russian agricultural technology, devel-oped in conditions of chernozem soils, did not correspond to the natural conditions of the territory of the forest zone with its podzolic, and sometimes stony and boggy soils. Therefore, the scratch-plow, which did not have wide application here, soon was displaced by the light plow.

The dominance of the light plow by no means indicates that agricultural technology in northwestern and northeastern Rus' lagged behind that of southern Rus'. Rather, the specific conditions dictated by clearing and working forest lands explains the choice. To be sure, the heavy plow was known here, but utilized only on appropriate soils. . . .

There is direct evidence for the use of draught-labor plowing in the chronicle under the year 1103: "The peasant began to plow, but the Polovtsians who came shot him with arrows, and took his horse . . ." Here is evidence about plowing with the scratch-plow, using one horse . . .

After tillage of the field by the light plow, additional reworking was necessary with a harrow, just as in our time. The use of the harrow in ancient Rus' is confirmed by an article from the Pravda Russkaia: "If a lord gave [his indentured laborer] a [heavy] plow and harrow . . . [the indentured laborer] who destroyed [his lord's property] is to pay [for it]" [art. 57, Expanded Pravda Russkaia]. One substantive indicator of the existence of the harrow is a discovery from a ninth-century layer of Staraia Ladoga, where a wooden-toothed harrow was unearthed. This was a so-called bow harrow, which was in use up to the nineteenth century in the former Pskov province. These harrows were made out of fir trunks with branches still attached, although they were trimmed to uniform size. The harrow excavated from Staraia Ladoga has teeth significantly shorter than those on the primitive harrow.

Judging by the material from Staraia Ladoga, the second reworking of soil in the northern regions involved the smashing of clods of earth by wooden hammer-crushers, which until recently were still in use in peasant households in Vologda region. This implement was necessary for smashing very large clods which were the result of plowing only with a heavy plow or light plow. Under the slash-and-burn system, no crushing was necessary. Therefore the find in Staraia Ladoga is

clear evidence of the presence of plowland already long under cultivation. . . .

Together with the prevailing system of plow agriculture in the forest zone, slash-and-burn continued to exist, as written sources from the twelfth through the fourteenth centuries confirm, as do miniatures of the seventeenth century, and ethnographic material. In the period before the thirteenth century, slash-and-burn was mainly necessary for opening new forest plots, which could be achieved not by the forces of separate families, but by an entire rural commune.

SOURCE: V. P. Levasheva, "Zemledelie," in *Ocherki po istorii russkoi derevni X–XIII vv.*, Trudy gosudarstvennogo istoricheskogo muzeia, vyp. 32 (Moscow, 1956), pp. 20–27, 34–9 (excerpted). Translated by Julia Vaingurt, edited by Daniel H. Kaiser.

E. A. RYBINA

Novgorod's Amber Trade (Tenth–Fourteenth Centuries)

Agriculture was not, of course, the only ingredient in the Kievan economy. As the activity of the early Vikings demonstrates, trade too played an important part. One item widely traded throughout northern Rus' was amber, whose translucent beauty continues today to attract jewelers. In the selection which follows, E. A. Rybina uses the extensive archeological digs at Novgorod to trace the history of the amber trade in northern Rus'. Novgorod ("New Town") was built in the forests around Lake Ladoga, and therefore depended on wood construction much more than did the older cities of southern Rus'. The damp environment of this area proved conducive to preserving the wooden city, so that when teams of archeologists first began systematic excavations in Novgorod around 1940, they discovered an immense trove of items from the ancient city. New digs were begun at different times in various parts of town (Il'in Street, the Nerev district, etc.), each yielding an astonishing quantity of finds. Almost all the excavated materials may be easily dated using a technique pioneered by Soviet archeologists. Dendrochronology matches tree ring growth patterns revealed in the logs and saplings recovered from the excavations with chronicle notices of specific dates of construction of large structures. Combining this information, archeologists have established a time line stretching back into the 900s and forward into the early fifteenth century. Into this grid E. A. Rybina inserts the finds of amber, in the process revealing a trade dynamic reflective of larger processes of international trade.

Finished and unworked fragments of amber represent one of the most important categories of imports found in the Novgorod excavations. The collection of these objects, gathered during excavations conducted between 1951–1970, now number more than 2000, and that total increases every year. Amber came to Novgorod as raw material for handicraft production, as the numerous finds of unworked, semi-finished, and finished amber products (mainly beads and crosses which have their analogies among Russian antiquities) prove.

The massive character of amber finds makes it possible to identify the dynamics of the importation of amber into Novgorod . . . Over twelve years of work at the Nerev excavation, 734 finished articles and pieces of amber were found, including 370 beads, 112 crosses, 44 rings, 37 other objects, and 171 fragments. By distributing this material by archeological layer, each of which has a precise date, one receives a complete chronological picture of amber delivery to Novgorod [see p. 46].

Separate examples of amber articles appear already in the middle of the tenth century, after which their number grows steadily, reaching the greatest frequency in the middle of the twelfth century. Then a decline in the quantity of amber sets in, all the way to the end of the thirteenth century, the least number of amber articles being collected in layers dated to 1224–99, after which finds of amber again become plentiful, reaching their maximum in the years 1369–1409. Does this distribution represent the reality of amber import or is it accidental? For an answer, we turn to material from other excavations [in Novgorod].

At the Il'in Street excavation, conducted between 1962–67, researchers collected 156 finished amber articles and amber fragments. Unfortunately, no dendrochronological data are yet available for this excavation, so one cannot construct a detailed diagram of chronological frequency of finds. However, preliminary dating of archeological layers by characteristic items which do have a narrowly-defined date makes it possible to group amber objects of the Il'in Street excavation by century, although not with the same precision as at the Nerev excavation. Here, just as at the Nerev excavation, only isolated finds belong to the thirteenth century.

The 1970 Suvorov excavation yielded 139 examples of amber handcraft. Thanks to the presence in the excavation of excellently preserved wooden street pavement, examples of which were subjected to dendrochronological analysis, it proved possible to date not only each layer of pavement, but also those objects found in each archeological layer. The distribution of amber from the Suvorov excavation is analogous to the amber distribution from the Nerev excavation. The quantity of amber finds were most numerous in the middle of the twelfth century, decreasing thereafter with each decade. In layers of the thirteenth century amber practically disappears, reappearing again only in the first quarter of the fourteenth century. True, the general quantity of amber at the Suvorov excavation is several times less than that at the Nerev excavation. But the coincidence of curves on both graphs, reflecting the general trend in Novgorod, suggests that the amber found here is sufficient for conclusions based on a comparison of data.

So, the chronological distribution of amber by archeological layers reflects the actual picture of its import into Novgorod. The interruption in the amber trade in the thirteenth century, which several scholars had noted earlier, now finds persuasive confirmation in this new material.

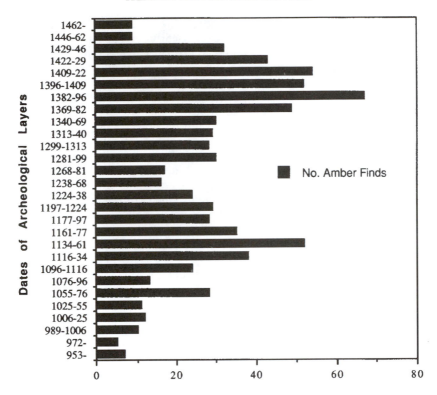

Chronological distribution of amber finds in Novgorod. Adapted from E. A. Rybina, *Arkheologi-cheskie ocherki istorii novgorodskoi torgovli X–XIV vv.* (Moscow: MGU, 1978), pp. 160–61. Reprinted with the permission of E. A. Rybina.

However, prior to explaining the causes of the interruption in the delivery of amber to Novgorod in the thirteenth century, let us turn our attention to . . . other objects of southern origin which reached Novgorod via the Dnieper River. Just as with amber, slate spindles, amphoras, walnuts, and glass articles produced in Kiev are all known in Novgorod from the middle of the tenth century. Gradually expanding in the course of the eleventh century, the frequency of these goods reaches its maximum in the twelfth century, which is also characteristic for imported amber. . . . The decline in the import of other southern goods into Novgorod late in the eleventh, early in the twelfth century, is also characteristic of the import of amber. . . . [S]uch a coincidence cannot be accidental, but must reflect the fact that amber came to Novgorod in the period between the tenth and early thirteenth century from the Dnieper River valley.

Until recently it was thought that the famous amber deposits along the Baltic Sea were the only source of amber for medieval Novgorod and the other Russian lands. For the fourteenth and fifteenth centuries, this conclusion is indisputable, but for the period from the tenth to the thirteenth centuries, the arguments for so categorical an assertion are clearly inadequate, all the more because deposits of amber are also known from South Russia, especially from the Dnieper River basin.

Already ancient authors named Scythia, together with Sicily and the Ligourian Baltic lands, as sources for the extraction of amber used in the ancient world. Pliny the Elder in his *Natural History of Minerals* provides the testimony of one Philemon, who declared that amber was gathered in two places in Scythia, one yielding dark red amber, the other white and wax-colored amber. Herodotus, Tacitus, and Theophrastes also recall Scythian amber. . . .

The archeological literature contains many assertions that the amber found in Eastern Europe was not Baltic in origin, but came rather from the Dnieper River valley. . . . During excavations of medieval Riazan', archeologists discovered in 1926 a workshop which produced amber beads from local red amber. Excavations in Kiev in layers dated to the late eleventh, early twelfth century revealed a similar workshop which held a supply of [local] raw and semi-finished amber averaging 600 grams. . . . Amber excavated from a Bulgarian settlement of the tenth and eleventh centuries also originated from deposits in the Dnieper River region. Finally, scholars assert that many amber beads found in graves in the Northern Caucuses were also of Dnieper origin.

The graph of chronological distribution of amber finds in Novgorod and the evidence introduced above confirms that the amber delivered to Novgorod in the period between the tenth and early thirteenth centuries came from the Dnieper River region.

In this connection, the amber discovered at Lubianitsk excavations in Novgorod is also of interest. Altogether investigators collected here about 1000 pieces of amber and nine finished amber articles. An ancient wooden road discovered at this site made it possible to locate all finds by dated layer, as a result of which it emerged that the overwhelming bulk of amber (about 800 pieces) was concentrated in layers dated to the period between 1190 and 1240. The single source of amber in Novgorod in this time could only be the Dnieper region, since from the beginning of the thirteenth century the Teutonic Order, with which Novgorod was at war during almost the entire thirteenth century, seized the Baltic amber deposits.

Of course the most persuasive proof of the Dnieper origin of the amber found in Novgorod in the pre-Mongol period would be analyses distinguishing the composition of amber originating in the Baltic and Dnieper regions. However, study of the infrared spectra of both types of amber showed that they were identical because both deposits (Baltic and Dnieper) originated from the same amber-bearing strata. . . .

Numerous citations about amber deposits in the Dnieper region and the coincidence between the graphs of amber with graphs of other objects of southern origin which reached Novgorod by the Dnieper River trade route confirm that the amber imported into Novgorod in the tenth through early thirteenth centuries came from the Dnieper River basin, or, more precisely, from Kiev itself. With the invasion of the Mongols, however, the Dnieper River trade route practically ceased to play any kind of role in Novgorod trade, as the distribution of objects of southern origin within Novgorod archeological layers shows. Consequently, after the Mongol invasion, amber, too, ceased to come from the Dnieper region, and its finds in layers of the second half of the thirteenth and fourteenth centuries reflect the import of amber from the Baltic region where its deposits were known already from deep antiquity, and where its reworking continues to the present day.

The remarkable decrease in amber finds in archeological layers of the thirteenth century is also explained by the fact that at that period it was impossible for amber to reach Novgorod from the Baltic region because of the complicated political conditions along the western frontiers of the Novgorod land.

At the beginning of the thirteenth century the German knights began to seize the Baltic lands. The Teutonic Order, the Order of Knights, and then the Livonian Order began their conquest of the Baltic region, having subdued the Letts at the beginning of the century. By 1228 the same fate befell the Esty, closest neighbors of Novgorod, and then in the 1230s there began the conquest of Prussia, which lasted for more than half a century. The aggression of the knights and their attempt to fortify their position in Estonia represented a serious political threat to Novgorod, especially because the Germans not infrequently conducted raids across the frontier into Novgorod lands. The Novgorod Chronicle preserves numerous notices about collisions with the Germans and about campaigns of Novgorodians against the Germans into the area around Lake Peipus. Such notices appear under the years 1212, 1214, 1219, 1223, 1224, 1228, 1234, 1240, 1241. Finally in 1242 there occurred the famous Battle on the Ice which halted the movement of Germans into Rus'. However, even after this defeat the Germans attempted to raid Rus' lands (especially in 1253 when they conducted a raid against the trading quarter of Pskov). Only after the Rakovor battle of 1269 did relations with the Germans stabilize somewhat.

The trade routes which connected Novgorod with the Baltic Coast became particularly dangerous in the thirteenth century. Protection of merchant goods and security of travel on these routes ceased to be guaranteed. Of course, the main cause of the interruption of trade between Novgorod and the Baltic was the state of war which excluded any possibility of trade relations. And inasmuch as the basic region for producing amber in the Baltic (Prussia) was then in the hands of the Teutonic Order, the abrupt reduction in amber finds from thirteenth-century Novgorod becomes understandable.

The Teutonic Order, having seized Prussia, where the greatest quantity of amber was found, and having received from the Pope authorization for the eternal possession of this territory, declared that all reserves of amber were its property. In the thirteenth century the Order established an amber monopoly, according to which the Order received the exclusive right to the income from monopolized quarrying and trade in amber. According to the order of one of the new rulers of these lands, any person caught collecting amber without special permission was executed. There was even a special executioner who carried out all sentences connected with amber offenses. Punishment was severe—for gathering three pounds of amber one could be broken on the wheel. According to the instruction of the Order, the whole coast was covered with gallows so as to frighten smugglers. Residents of coastal villages had to swear not to gather amber, and also not to attempt to buy it up; after dark no one was allowed to walk along the seashore. By special arrangement serfs gathered amber for the Order. Later the collection of amber was transferred to an alliance of German fishermen who received from the Order a pound of salt for each pound of amber they gathered. Consequently, with the occupation of Prussian territory the Teutonic Order became the sole supplier of amber to the Russian lands.

From the beginning of the fourteenth century peaceful relations between Novgorod and the Order were stabilized, so that the delivery of amber could resume. So, from early in the fourteenth century amber once again became abundant in Novgorod, reaching its apogee in the second half of the fourteenth and beginning of the fifteenth centuries.

SOURCE: E. A. Rybina, *Arkheologicheskie ocherki istorii novgorodskoi torgovli X–XIV vv.* (Moscow: MGU [Moscow State University], 1978), pp. 38–41, 43–5, 60–62. Translated by Julia Vaingurt, edited by Daniel H. Kaiser. Reproduced with the permission of E. A. Rybina.

4

Society in Rus'

As attentive readers will already have noticed in the Pravda Russkaia above, Rus' society was most certainly stratified. The law distinguished between freeman and slave, privileged and commoner, and male and female. But exactly what separated all these categories the law does not fully reveal. For example, was privilege purely the consequence of birth, or was it instead the result of honorable service to the prince? Did wealth necessarily improve one's social station? The Pravda Russkaia does not answer these questions, nor does it reconcile the stratification it confirms with the importance it extends to kinship, whose dominance normally recedes in the face of growing stratification.

One way to determine the basic organization of any society is to look at gender and reproduction. Societies preoccupied with descent and kinship also regulate carefully and control access to reproduction. It comes as no surprise that Christian Rus', like other Christian societies, devoted special attention to sexual morality, urging modesty in sexual relations. But, as the Church Statute of Iaroslav indicates, much more than Christian dogma informed formal prescriptions on sexuality. The compilers of the statute also betrayed deep anxieties about maintaining the prevailing values of descent and kinship, worrying about sexual intercourse between kin. Likewise, almost inadvertently the Church Statute opens to view sexual and marital customs of non-Christians in Rus'. In reading the following document, then, one ought consider the functions which these regulations might have had, and what forms of social organization they were intended to sustain.

We do not yet know very much about gender relations in Rus'. The standard, big stories are of course well-known: Princess Ol'ga was very clever; the daughters of Iaroslav the Wise married monarchs from all over Western Europe. But how did gender relations operate at a less lofty level? Until recently, few historians bothered about this question. Gradually, however, more about the operation of gender in Rus' has come to light. We already observed that women in Kievan Rus' seem to have suffered discrimination hardly unique to Rus'. But Natal'ia Pushkareva and Eve Levin argue that, whatever the official limitations, women in Rus' were actually quite influential. Reading their account, one ought consider how their interpretation squares with the available evidence, and also what questions remain to be answered.

49

DOCUMENT

The Statute of Grand Prince Iaroslav (Eleventh Century)

The Statute of Grand Prince Iaroslav [1019–54] claims to come from the son of Prince Vladimir, who Christianized the Rus' land. The Statute was clearly very popular in Rus', inasmuch as about one hundred copies are still extant. No early copies of the statute survive, however: the oldest copy now known comes from the early fifteenth century. But because the internal organization of the Statute, its terse language, and some of its provisions are reminiscent of the Pravda Russkaia, in whose composition Prince Iaroslav had a part, scholars in the main agree that the document probably did originate at about the same time as the Pravda Russkaia. Another statute, this one attributed to Prince Vladimir, also purporting to have originated in Kievan Rus', provided a financial and judicial guarantee to the infant Orthodox Church in Rus'. Iaroslav's Statute seems to develop these themes, detailing specific offenses subject to clerical, rather than secular courts. Marriage, death, fornication, rape, and other matters of special interest to the clergy occupy most of the compiler's attention. One interesting sidelight of these issues is the way that the Statute treats social classes, distinguishing different penalties for offenders from different social orders. Reading these materials carefully, then, can reveal basic attitudes in Rus' toward gender, family organization, and sexual behavior, as well as values about social layering, religion and multiculturalism.

---

1. Lo I, Grand Prince Iaroslav, son of Volodimir [ca. 980–1015], following [the example of] my father's gift, have consulted with Ilarion [1051–54], Metropolitan of Kiev and All Rus', [and] we have compared [readings in the] Greek nomocanon; since a prince, or his boyars, or his judges ought not have jurisdiction over these suits, I have given to the Metropolitan and bishops [jurisdiction over the following]: divorce [cases] in all towns; the customs duty each tenth week [is to go] to the church and the Metropolitan; and his people are not to pay the customs duty anywhere, nor the duty levied on goods entering a town; and I have given [the church the revenue from] the "eighth" [exacted from weighed goods brought into town for trade].

2. If someone abducts a girl [with the aim of marrying her] or rapes her, [and] if she be a boyar's daughter [the offender] is to pay 5 grivnas of gold for her dishonor and 5 grivnas of gold to the Metropolitan; if she be [a daughter] of lesser boyars [the offender is to pay] one grivna of gold, and 1 grivna of gold to the Metropolitan; if [she be a daughter] of the "good people" [the offender is to pay] 2 grivnas of silver for the dishonor, and a ruble to the Metropolitan; and those who help in the abduction are to pay 60 [nogatas] each to the Metropolitan, and the prince punishes them.

3. If someone rapes a boyar's daughter or a boyar's wife, [then he is to pay] five grivnas of gold for the dishonor, and the same amount to the Metropolitan; [if someone rapes the daughter or wife] of lesser boyars [then he is to pay] 1 grivna of gold, and 1 grivna of gold to the Metropolitan; [if someone rapes the daughter or wife] of well-to-do people [he is to pay] 2 rubles, and 2 rubles to the Metropolitan; [if someone rapes the daughter or wife] of common people [he is to pay] 12 grivnas of fur, and 12 grivnas of fur to the Metropolitan, and the prince punishes [him].

4. If a boyar throws out his wife [who is a daughter] of great boyars, [then he is to pay] her 300 grivnas for the dishonor, and 5 grivnas of gold to the Metropolitan; [if the woman be the daughter] of lesser boyars [he is to pay her] 1 grivna of gold, and 1 grivna of gold to

the Metropolitan; [if she be the daughter] of well-to-do people [he is to pay her] 2 rubles, and 2 rubles to the Metropolitan; [if she be the daughter] of common people [he is to pay her] 12 grivnas, and 12 grivnas to the Metropolitan, and the prince punishes [him].

5. If a girl engages in sexual intercourse or becomes pregnant [while she still lives] with her father or mother, or while she is a widow, after having found [her] out, put her in a church house [convent].

6. Likewise if a wife without her husband or [even while living] with her husband becomes pregnant [by some other man], and kills [the child], or throws it to the swine, or drowns [it], having found [her] out, take her into a convent, and what her kinsmen pay to redeem her [goes to the Metropolitan].

7. If a girl who sits [in a convent be the daughter] of great boyars, [they must pay] 5 grivnas of gold to the Metropolitan [to redeem her]; [if she be the daughter] of lesser boyars, [they must pay] the Metropolitan one grivna of gold; if [she be the daughter] of well-to-do people [they must pay] the Metropolitan 2 rubles or 12 grivnas; if [she be the daughter] of common people, [they must pay] the Metropolitan 1 grivna of silver or 1 ruble.

8. If someone prevails upon a girl [to come to him] and he gives her [over] for a group rape, then [exact] from the abductor 1 grivna of silver for the Metropolitan, and from the rapists 60 [nogatas] each, and the prince punishes [them].

9. If a husband has intercourse [with some woman other than] his wife, then the husband is guilty before the Metropolitan, and the prince punishes [him].

10. If a husband marries another woman, still not having been divorced from the old [wife], the husband is guilty before the Metropolitan, and take the young [i.e., more recent] wife into a convent, and he is to [resume] living with the old [i.e., first] wife.

11. If a wife goes from her husband [to marry] another man, or if she has intercourse [with that man] apart from her husband, take that wife into a convent, and [the adulterer is

to pay] the marriage fee to the Metropolitan as a fine.

12. If a wife becomes seriously ill, or is blind, or is ill for a long time, [the husband] is not to abandon her for that.

13. Likewise the wife is not to abandon her husband [if he suffers serious or prolonged illness].

14. If a godfather engages in intercourse with a godmother [he is to pay] the Metropolitan 12 grivnas, and the prescription of penance [will be] according to the law of God.

15. If someone burns a threshing floor, or a house, or anything else, [he is to pay] the Metropolitan 40 grivnas, and they [sic] shall undertake penance, and the prince punishes [him].

16. If someone engages in intercourse with his sister [he is to pay] the Metropolitan 40 grivnas, and [fulfill] the prescription of penance according to the law.

17. If someone marries within close kinship [i.e., within the prohibited degrees of consanguinity], [he is to pay] the Metropolitan 30 or 40 grivnas, and separate them, and let them undertake penance.

18. If someone marries two wives, [he is to pay] the Metropolitan 20 grivnas, and whichever is false [i.e., the second wife], take her into a convent, and [the man] is to keep and maintain the first wife according to the law. If he keeps and treats her badly, punish him.

19. If a man separates from his wife by his own wish, and if there was a church wedding, then they shall give the Metropolitan 12 grivnas. And if they were not married in church [they are to pay] the Metropolitan 6 grivnas.

20. If a Jew or Muslim [takes] a Rus' woman [to marriage], or [if some] other [non-Orthodox] foreigner [takes a Rus' woman], [he is to pay] the Metropolitan 50 grivnas; and take the Rus' woman into a convent.

21. If someone has intercourse with a nun, [he is to pay] the Metropolitan 40 grivnas, and assign [him] penance.

22. If someone copulates with an animal, [he is to pay] the Metropolitan 12 grivnas, and [execute] penance and punishment according to the law.

23. If a father-in-law engages in intercourse with his daughter-in-law, [he is to pay] the Metropolitan 40 grivnas, and they shall take penance according to the law.

24. If someone falls into fornication with two sisters, [he is to pay] the Metropolitan 30 grivnas.

25. If a [stepfather] engages in intercourse with his stepdaughter, [he is to pay] the Metropolitan 12 grivnas.

26. If a husband's brother falls into fornication with his brother's wife, [he is to pay] the Metropolitan 12 grivnas.

27. If someone falls into fornication with his stepmother, [he is to pay] the Metropolitan 12 grivnas.

28. If two brothers engage in intercourse with one woman, [they are to pay] the Metropolitan 30 grivnas; and take the woman into a convent.

29. If a father falls [into fornication] with his daughter, [he is to pay] the Metropolitan 40 grivnas, and they shall take penance according to the law.

30. If a girl does not wish to marry, [and] then the father and mother give her [in marriage] by force, and if the girl causes [harm] to herself, then the father and mother are guilty before the Metropolitan, and they are to pay the losses. Likewise with a young man [who does not wish to marry].

31. If someone calls another man's wife a whore, and if she be a boyar's wife [and the daughter] of great boyars, [then he is to pay] her for the dishonor 5 grivnas of gold, and the Metropolitan 5 grivnas of gold, and the prince punishes [him]; and if she be [the daughter] of lesser boyars, [he is to pay] her 3 grivnas of gold for the dishonor, and 3 grivnas of gold to the Metropolitan; and if she be [the daughter] of townspeople, [he is to pay] her 3 grivnas of silver or a ruble for the dishonor, and the same amount to the Metropolitan; and if she be a farmer's wife [he is to pay] 60 rezanas, and 3 grivnas to the Metropolitan.

32. If someone shaves the hair off someone's head or beard, [he is to pay] the Metropolitan 12 grivnas, and the prince punishes [him].

33. If a man has stolen hemp or flax or any [sort of] grain, or if a woman [has stolen it], [the guilty party is to pay] the Metropolitan 3 grivnas.

34. If a man steals white clothes, and linen and pieces of cloth, [he is to pay] the Metropolitan 3 grivnas. Likewise a woman [is to pay if she has stolen these things].

35. If someone steals the wedding [fee] and betrothal [fee], everything [goes] to the Metropolitan.

36. If the cheese be cut for the sake of a girl [thereby sealing a marriage agreement according to pagan ritual], [those who engage in this ritual are to pay] one grivna for [using] the cheese, and [pay] her [the girl] 3 grivnas for the dishonor, and whatever is lost, [repay] her, and 6 grivnas to the Metropolitan, and the prince punishes [them].

37. If a wife steals from her husband, and he catches her, [she is to pay] three grivnas to the Metropolitan, and her husband punishes her, but for this do not divorce them.

38. If [a wife] steals from a storeroom, treat her in the same way.

39. If a daughter-in-law steals from her father-in-law, they shall carry out the same [procedure] on her.

40. If a woman be a maker of charms, or a witch, or a pagan sorceress, or a maker of potions, then her husband, having caught her [doing these things], punishes her but does not separate from her, and the Metropolitan is [to be paid] 6 grivnas.

41. If two men fight like women, either tearing at the skin [with their nails] or biting, [they are to pay] the Metropolitan 12 grivnas [of fur] or 1 grivna [of gold].

42. If a woman beats her husband, [she is to pay] the Metropolitan 3 grivnas.

43. If two women fight, [exact] from the guilty [party] either 60 rezanas or 6 grivnas.

44. If some man beats another man's wife, [he is to pay] her for the dishonor as the law [prescribes], and 6 grivnas to the Metropolitan.

45. If a son beats his father or mother, let them punish him with the ruler's punishment, and [he stands as] guilty before the Metropol-

itan, [and take] such a youth into a church house [monastery].

46. If a monk, or nun, or priest, or priest's wife, or widow, or the woman who bakes the Eucharist bread, or a sexton falls into fornication, the Metropolitan is to judge them separately from laymen, and [he is] free to condemn them to whatever [he pleases].

47. If a girl wishes to marry, but her father and mother do not allow her [to marry], and she causes [some harm] to herself, the father and mother are guilty before the Metropolitan. Likewise with a youth [whose parents prevented him from marrying].

48. If a priest, or monk, or nun gets drunk at an inappropriate time [e.g., during Lent], [he or she] is guilty before the Metropolitan.

49. If someone sets fire to a house, or threshing floor, or anything else, [he is to pay] the Metropolitan 40 grivnas, and the prince punishes [him].

50. If someone eats pagan food by his own volition, whether it be mare's meat, or bear's meat, or any other forbidden meat, he is guilty before the Metropolitan and [is subject] to punishment [by him].

51. If a priest christens children in the district of another priest, except in an emergency or during [the infant's] illness [which threatens its life], that [priest who] celebrates a christening not in his own district [but in another], he is guilty before the Metropolitan.

52. Do not eat or drink with those who are not baptized or with a foreigner or [with anyone] from our own people if he be not baptized, until he is baptized. And whoever knowingly eats and drinks [with unbaptized persons] will be guilty before the Metropolitan.

53. If someone eats and drinks with those who are excommunicated he will himself be excommunicated.

54. If someone engages in intercourse with a Muslim or Jewish woman, and he does not separate [from her], let him be excommunicated from the Church and from Christians, and [he is to pay] the Metropolitan 12 grivnas.

55. If a monk or nun renounces [his or her] vows, [he or she is to pay] the Metropolitan 40 grivnas.

56. And for these causes divorce a man from his wife.

And this is the first cause. If a wife hears from other people that they plot against the tsar, or against the prince, but she does not tell her husband about this, and later is discovered [to have known about the plot], divorce them.

And this is the second cause. If a man catches his wife with an adulterer or initiates a case against her [on the basis of testimony given] by good witnesses, divorce them.

And this is the third cause. If a woman plots against her own husband with poison or with other people, if she has come to know that [other people] wish to kill or murder her husband, but she says nothing to her husband, and later this comes to light, divorce [them].

And this is the fourth cause. If a wife without her husband's permission goes [around] with other people, or drinks or eats [with them], or sleeps outside his house, and then the husband finds out, divorce [them].

And this is the fifth cause. If a wife without her husband's permission goes to the pagan dances either in the day or at night, and her husband finds out, but she does not obey [his command to stop these activities], divorce her.

And this is the sixth cause. If a wife leads thieves against her husband, orders [them] to rob the house of her husband, or herself robs [him], having stolen [his] goods or [goods] from a church, and gives [the stolen property] to others, for this divorce them.

57. And whatever goes on among monastery people and among church people, and in the monasteries themselves, neither the prince nor his rural judge [is to] interfere in that, and the Metropolitan's lieutenants have jurisdiction over these [matters], and their escheated estates go to the Metropolitan's lieutenant.

58. If someone violates my statute and transgresses my regulation, whether my sons, grandchildren, great-grandchildren, someone from among my kinsmen, or boyars from among the boyar kinsmen of my boyars; if they transgress my ordinances and interfere in the Metropol-

itan's court, and in the church courts which I have given to the Metropolitan and the bishops according to the canons of the Holy Fathers, having judged [them], punish them severely according to the law.

59. If someone shall judge [these cases that are in church jurisdiction], he shall stand with me at Judgment before God, and may the curse of the three hundred and eighteen holy fathers who were in Nicea [AD 325, First Council of Nicea] [and the curse] of all the saints be upon him. Amen.

SOURCE: *The Laws of Rus' (Tenth to Fifteenth Centuries).* Translated and edited by Daniel H. Kaiser (Salt Lake City: Charles Schlacks, Jr., forthcoming), pp. 45–50. English translation copyright © 1992 Daniel H. Kaiser.

LITERATURE

N. L. PUSHKAREVA AND E. LEVIN
Women in Medieval Novgorod from the Eleventh to the Fifteenth Century

As some provisions of the Statute of Grand Prince Iaroslav indicate, women in Kievan Rus' were held to a different standard than were men. Because clerical texts dominate the surviving sources, and because church materials consistently denigrated women and their social rights, it sometimes seems as though women in Rus' suffered severely because of their sex. In the selection reproduced below, Natal'ia Pushkareva and Eve Levin offer a different view. Although acknowledging that many church texts did indeed criticize women, they observe that women nevertheless played important parts in Novgorod society: some were active in politics, others owned and disposed of property, and all women found protection in the law.

With the Christianization of Russia at the end of the tenth century, all familial relations, and, with them, all questions relating to the place and position of women, came under ecclesiastical jurisdiction. Thus, the richest material available on the present question is found in church literature. In this literature, the family's role in society was affirmed in religious terms. Meanwhile, the dicatates of Christian"norms" of behavior, contained in saints' lives and confirmed as criteria for judging morality, permitted control of women's conduct and their life within the family through the use of confessional material. . . .

Most apparent in an initial examination of the didactic literature is the effort of the "spiritual fathers" to divide all representatives of the fair sex into two categories—into "good" and "evil" women. Evidently there were more of the latter, and therefore the clergy focused its main attention on them. While characterizations of the "good woman" in church literary monuments are usually rather laconic, descriptions of the immorality of "evil women" are frequently used as an excuse for setting forth an entire set of instructions on "lustful women and how one should avoid them." Such characterizations of the two types of women were handed on from one church document to another and remained remarkably constant for centuries. . . .

In disseminating the ideal and norms for attitudes toward women as worked out by the church, the didactic literature sought to make people godfearing and law-abiding and to reinforce the hierarchical nature of the primary social nucleus of the family. In this regard, we may note that women were admonished to be "silent," to submit to God and to their husbands, and to refrain from interfering in any sphere except that of the family. "Listen, women, to God's commandments and learn to be silent, so that you will save your soul. In the beginning, God said to Eve: thou art taken from man, and he shall rule over thee. Thou shalt submit to him in silence. . . . Women, do not oppose your husbands, for just as Christ rules over the church, so man rules over his wife." This commandment, like others, threatened that "death and life are in the hands of the tongue," that a "slandering" tongue could even lead to divorce. . . .

An analysis of the church literature shows that what the clergy viewed as "evil" might be regarded not only by us but also by their contemporaries as "good." After all, Marfa Isakova Boretskaia [who at one time was mayor of Novgorod] was considered to be an "evil" woman for her participation in political intrigues directed toward preserving the independence of the feudal republic of Novgorod. Thus, for the church, "evil" women were not only those who strayed from the faith and the norms of Christian behavior; they also included many women who were socially independent and—as secular documents indicate—they were not the exception in medieval Novgorod. . . .

The family and marriage law of the medieval Russian state as a whole and of the republic of Novgorod in particular was the law of a society in which, beginning in the ninth and tenth centuries, a process of feudalization was taking place. In a context of growing social inequality, feudal law, too, based differences in women's rights on their position in society as a whole.

Feudal law gave women from the underprivileged social strata a very modest role in the society. Among three bases for full slavery given in the [Expanded] Russkaia Pravda is the marriage of a free man to a slave woman, without any exceptions. The reverse situation, when a free woman married a male slave and lost her higher social status, is not found in any Novgorod sources, incontrovertible evidence of the fact that marriage was not a reason for enslavement among Novgorodian women. On the contrary, legal documents contain instances of Novgorodian families where the father, sometimes with his son, was a slave, while his "wife and daughters were free." Evidently, a female slave could be the object of her owner's "contract" with a free man if such an agreement offered her the opportunity of being freed. This seems confirmed by a twelfth-century treaty between Novgorod and Gotland in which one of the first articles defended the honor of slave women in relation to foreigners: "Whoever attempts to rape a female slave but does not dishonor her must pay a *grivna* for the wrong done; but if he dishonors her, she will be freed." Since in medieval Novgorod, the moral damage sustained in being dishonored by a foreigner was compensated for by freedom, we may assume that a similar rule extended to other categories of the population as well, including other dependent members of society. The life of a female slave as the subject of the law was valued more than that of a full male slave; her murder was punished by a fine of six *grivny* rather than five. Here the motivation was not humanitarian, but rather protection of the social role she fulfilled. A slave woman's primary role was in reproducing the work force, and when she functioned in this role her life was valued two and one-half times less than that of a craftswoman. . . .

Information in non-normative sources about the societal position of Novgorodian women from the lower social strata is very limited. Among the birchbark documents, for example, we find a reference to a certain Fedos'ia (evidently a peasant woman) who brewed beer. Another poorly preserved document possibly testifies to dependent women engaging in the bleaching and weaving trade. Such fragmentary data, although they suggest that dependent women participated in the economic life of an estate, give practically no information about the value of these women's labor or their rights. . . .

The property rights of women from the dependent classes of Novgorod were also extremely limited. The sole reference to these rights in any legal document is an article [in the Expanded Pravda Russkaia] about inheritance in the peasant family. Here the widow had no right to the legacy, and the possible claimants to a portion included only unmarried daughters. . . .

The position of Novgorodian women of the aristocracy and privileged classes, and their societal rights, are much more fully articulated in the sources. [The Expanded] Russkaia Pravda, the law code for all of Russia, defined the status and the value of the life of a free woman as follows: "If anyone kills a woman, he will be tried as though it were a man; if guilty, then a half-wergeld, twenty *grivny*." There is still some dispute as to how this article should be interpreted: was the life of the woman valued at a half-wergeld, or was her murder punished in that same manner as the murder of a man? Variant copies of the Russkaia Pravda allow different readings of this article. In one Pushkin version, a redaction of the fourteenth century, and the Trinity and second Archeographic versions from the fifteenth century, the word "guilty" is in the masculine, implying that the perpetrator of the crime, if convicted, would pay only half. This reading is flawed, because the second part of the article contradicts the first. However, in other Pushkin versions and in the Obolenskii version, all from the fourteenth century, the word "guilty" is in the feminine, and the article is internally consistent. The full wergeld is paid, except if the woman was "guilty," in which case the fine was halved. There were many occasions when a woman could be at fault, judging by Novgorod documents of the period. Improper conduct included brawling, both between women, and between a woman and a man, not only in disputes within the family. Iaroslav's Statute even distinguished "fighting like a woman" as a special category. A final fact argues in favor of the view that the wergeld was equal for the murder of a man or a woman: since the same fine was paid for the murder of a craftsman or a craftswoman, a tutor or wet-nurse, and even more for the murder of a slave woman than for that of a slave, why should the value of a free woman's life be less than that of a man?

The law of the feudal society of Novgorod defended not only the life but also the honor, dignity, and social freedom of privileged and aristocratic women. In 1016, the chronicle relates, the Novgorodians "slaughtered the Varangians in Poromon's Court" when the latter began to commit excesses in the city and "raped married women." In order to avoid

similar conflicts, those guilty of rape were punished by high monetary fines differentiated according to the social status of the female victims. The development of feudal law is particularly noticeable in this area. Whereas in the Russkaia Pravda (of the eleventh century) the murder of a woman was punished by a fine of forty *grivny* (*kun*—old marten skins), in the Novgorod Treaty of the twelfth century this was the fine for defiling a woman. It is notable that this treaty provides for the same fine for raping a free woman as for killing a Novgorodian man: "If a Novgorodian merchant is killed, the fine is ten silver *grivny*" (one silver *grivna* was equal to four *grivny kun*). Moreover, an offense to a free woman was punished more severely than one to a man: "If someone removes the headdress from another's wife or daughter . . . the fine is six old *grivny* for her shame." . . .

The Novgorodian Charter shows clearly that at that time, in both Novgorod and Pskov, women could themselves participate in judicial duels without any hired substitutes. When women were insulted without cause, the law was on their side. Thus, for example, in birch-bark document No. 415 a certain Fevronia advises, "greetings from Fevronia to Feliks with a complaint. My stepson beat me and drove me out of the house. Direct me to come to town or you come here yourself. I have been beaten. . . ." Incidentally, we should note here that this letter is an example of the fact that many Novgorod women were literate. According to Vladimir's Statute, such cases fell under ecclesiastical jurisdiction, while under Iaroslav's Statute such matters were also punished by the civil authorities. The [Expanded] Russkaia Pravda gave mothers the right not to bequeath their "Portion" to sons who displayed a lack of respect. We may therefore suppose that in this instance, a stepson would not go unpunished if he insulted his stepmother, especially as Fevronia, judging by the document's contents, is addressing a responsible individual (Feliks). . . .

In several cases, a Novgorodian girl was able to make decisions even on questions relating to her marriage. Indeed, in birchbark document No. 377 Mikita addresses his bride directly rather than applying to her parents: "Marry me. I want you, and you want me. Ignato is witness to this. . . ." Iaroslav's Church Statute, which was in effect in Novgorod, prescribed a special fine for parents who forced their daughters to marry. The fact that the female representatives of the privileged strata of Novgorod society were able to decide their own fate indicates that their social position differed somewhat from that of their Western contemporaries, who spent their entire lives as dependents of some male relative, their father or their husband, that is, their legal guardian.

That Novgorod women were independent is confirmed to a great extent as well by the existence of the highly developed institution of female inheritance, characteristic of both Novgorod and other areas of the medieval Russian state. It is well known that the [Expanded] Russkaia Pravda confirmed the widow's primary rights of guardianship and her right to make use of the estate until her children reached maturity. In their wills, aristocratic Novgorodians usually left their wives the largest share of the inheritance, sometimes not even dividing it between wife and children. However, the wife enjoyed the right to use it only until she should remarry; following such remarriage, the land and the widow's portion were divided among the children.

The question may justly be raised as to whether Novgorod women had the right to land only as bequests to guardians, or whether female ownership and disposition of property was in general widespread. In answering this question, let us examine the laws with regard to rights of ownership in effect in Novgorod in the eleventh to fifteenth centuries. According to Russian jurisprudence, the institution of the dowry already existed in the eleventh century. For an unmarried girl, the law [the Expanded Pravda Russkaia] stated, "If there is a sister at home she receives no inheritance, but her brothers give her in marriage, as they are able." A woman who married for the second time was to receive a "portion" "set aside for her by her husband." Many Russian historians of the nineteenth and early twentieth centu-

ries considered the question of the use of the dowry and the "share" to be unresolved. However, references to women's property in marriage are found in various sources even in the early period (before the thirteenth century). Even the early legal documents refer to the possibility in principle of "disputes" "between husband and wife about movable property." The Novgorod Treaty of the thirteenth century confirms that a Novgorodian woman could own such property, stating that a wife could participate in her husband's business ventures or avoid participation in them, vouch for her husband or refuse to do so. Thus, Novgorod law, as distinguished from Russian law overall and the laws of feudal principalities, continued the tendencies toward separation of a wife's property which were first clearly articulated in the medieval Russian treaty with Byzantium. This separation relieved the wife of responsibility for her husband's financial ventures. . . .

In the early period of Novgorodian history, women could only hold movable property. For example, birchbark document No. 228, from the twelfth century, lists debtors, among whom is a certain Iaroshkovaia, or "wife of Iaroshka" (a diminutive of Iaroslav), who owed nine *rezany;* document No. 449, also from the twelfth century also speaks of an unidentified "debtoress." Among the birchbark documents found in the nearby town of Staraia Russa there is a letter of the twelfth century from some Ivan's wife to a debtor named Foma in which she asks that he pay the money owed for salt, threatening to raise the interest charged. An interesting real-life crisis is reflected in document No. 531, from the twelfth century: A certain Anna and her daughter had lent money for interest, and had earned a profit from it. Anna's husband Fedor had not participated in this venture, although it appears that he had previously borrowed the money in question from a certain Konstantin. In this letter, Anna and her daughter asked Anna's brother Kliment to defend them against their angry husband and father. The document demonstrates the relative independence of women in money-lending at that time, as known from the Russian Law and the charter of the feudal republics. It is indisputable testimony to the separation of spouses' property, for the profit from the money Anna lent obviously became her property. Otherwise there would have been no reason for her husband to be upset. . . .

[I]t is only in the fourteenth and fifteenth centuries that we can speak of the acquisition of extensive rights to land by aristocratic Novgorodian women . . . The women of the fifteenth century who owned land include Anna, owner of the village Bykovshchina, Nastas'ia Mikhailovna, who received a complaint from the peasants in her village, and Ul'iana in the recently-unearthed birchbark document No. 580 who received land "in Zdarveia" from her father-in-law and bequeathed it to her sons, and others.

Thus, female ownership of land became a common phenomenon in the legal life of the fourteenth and fifteenth centuries in Novgorod and its environs. The publication of the bulk of the private documents from Novgorod dating to that period permits us to define certain aspects of this transformation. Wives (widows) are most often encountered among those receiving real estate as an inheritance. It was legally possible for daughters to own land ("if there are no sons, the daughters take it . . ."). The operation of this provision can easily be discerned both in other principalities and in Novgorod. Private act No. 156 provides an interesting illustration: the testator has three daughters and a son Vasilii, but nevertheless it is the daughters who receive the property, including a married daughter, Mar'ia. An explanation of this bequest is found in one version of the Novgorodian Statute of Grand Prince Vsevolod on Church Courts and Merchants in a postscript to article 18 establishing a sister's right to receive a share of the estate "equal to her brother's." In bequeathing land to his wife, a husband usually limited her tenure, requiring her to relinquish it if she should remarry (as indicated above). There were probably exceptions to this rule, such as may be observed in neighboring principalities, but no similar documents have survived from Novgo-

rod. This limitation on widows' tenure cannot be construed as a legal disability relative to their sons and husbands. Legal documents from Pskov in the fifteenth century contain a provision to the effect that the husband of a deceased woman may "live off her estate as long as he lives, unless he marries, but if he should marry he can no longer live off it." Thus feudal law, including that of Novgorod, defended the interests of the owner of an estate without regard to his or her sex. . . .

It is clear that relatives on the husband's side played an important role in women's actual participation in economic and other matters. This is not only reflected in the institution of guardianship. For example, when documents were drawn up, as a rule men served as witnesses; it was they who "witnessed the sealing." But did this mean that women were not permitted to serve as witnesses? We do find rare instances, for example, when Abbot Vasilii of the Nikolaevskii Monastery made a purchase "Luker'ia witnessed the sealing," or, in another purchase deed, Matrena served as Melentii's witness. Analogous instances can also be found in documents from the Lithuanian and Polish territories adjacent to Novgorod. Nor are there any concrete prohibitions in this regard in canon law from eleventh-to fifteenth-century Novgorod.

We have examined attitudes toward women as expressed in the ecclesiastical literature of Novgorod and their actual position as reflected in secular sources—law codes, birchbark documents, narrative material, and private land acts. Since religious ideology predominated in the society, ecclesiastical perceptions of woman's place in that society represented the dominant view of her societal role and status. The division of all women into "good" and "evil" wives and the subsequent dichotomy in descriptions of actual historical figures resulted from various factors in the development of social consciousness in medieval Russia, and particularly in Novgorod.

While recognizing that the development of ideology, including church dogma, may be independent to a certain degree, we must take into account the common processes of social development, in this case, of feudalization. These processes influenced to some extent the spread of the ecclesiastical postulate that "a woman is ruled by her husband, the husband by the prince, and the prince by God." Preeminent to ecclesiastical literature was a societal imperative: the reinforcement and justification of the hierarchical nature of the family as the primary social nucleus, and through it that of the society as a whole. . . .

The actual social position of Novgorodian women was not at all what the church imagined. It would be difficult to reconstruct the church's perception of the "average" woman on the basis of the available documents. First of all, because of feudal social stratification, the rights of women from the dependent groups among the population were severely limited. Second, we cannot help but note the overall inequality of Novgorod women in relation to men. The latter were more likely to serve as witnesses in legal disputes or in drawing up documents; and only ten percent of the private land documents testify to women's ownership rights. However, the study of the social position of women through secular and ecclesiastical sources allows us to conclude that the women of Novgorod from all social strata,

including slaves, were formally protected by feudal law. In actuality, many female citizens of the medieval Novgorodian republic could, on their own, defend their honor and property, which they owned independent of their husbands. Whereas in the early stages of the development of the medieval Russian state, the aristocratic women of Novgorod could own only movable property, by the end of the thirteenth or the beginning of the fourteenth century, they were able to hold land, including "patrimony." This right was given legal definition in the fifteenth century. Medieval Russia and Novgorod also possessed the institution of female guardianship, unquestionably an exceptional phenomenon.

The literary sources of medieval Novgorod permit us to perceive societal activities of women from the privileged classes. Women's roles were relatively broad; the forms their activities took varied according to each woman's social position, degree of literacy, and other factors.

SOURCE: N. L. Pushkareva and E. Levin, "Women in Medieval Novgorod from the Eleventh to the Fifteenth Century," *Soviet Studies in History* 23, 4(Spring, 1985):71–87 (excerpted). Some Russian terms have been omitted. Reprinted with the permission of M. E. Sharpe, Inc.

5

Culture and Everyday Life
in Kievan Rus'

The arrival of Christianity in the tenth century meant the construction of cathedrals, churches, and monasteries, each decorated with frescoes and icons, and provided with the bejeweled liturgical books and sacerdotal robes. All this activity, no doubt gradual and building over time, helped sustain the artists and artisans responsible for creating these monuments of culture. Of course, these relics of Christian culture, impressive as they might be, did not exhaust the range of values which Kievan culture contained. But inasmuch as the churchmen who commissioned this work also likely controlled the written word, we have only the faintest sense of popular culture in Kievan Rus'. Christianization, then, plays an important part in any discussion of Kievan culture.

The Primary Chronicle preserves two narratives purporting to describe the decision to Christianize Rus'. There is much between the stories to provoke skepticism, but what is not in question is the conviction of the writers that the coming of Christianity was significant for Rus'. One tale emphasizes the achievements of Greek Christianity at the expense of the other competing religions. For example, when the representatives of Prince Vladimir recounted their visit to Constantinople where they had attended a service in St. Sophia Cathedral, they are reported to have said, "We knew not whether we were in heaven or on earth. For on earth there is no such splendor or such beauty. . . ." The Muslim Bulgars, by contrast, they reproached for their filth and stench. In this telling the aesthetic appeal is primary.

But the narratives of Christianization also point to political motives. We may observe in passing that whatever the enthusiasm of those who reported on Greek ceremonial, Vladimir evidently was not swayed to convert immediately. He seems to have sought other things from Christianization, which may explain why conversion did not follow directly so enthusiastic an account. The reader will note that before adopting Christianity, on first coming to the throne, Vladimir had tried to institutionalize another pantheon, perhaps to unify the multi-ethnic realm over which he aspired to rule. And in the portion of the story which describes the appeal of various religions, Vladimir betrays his political interest in conversion. When inquiring of the Jewish Khazars about why they were cast out of their native land, Vladimir remarks, "If God loved you and your faith, you would not be thus dispersed in foreign lands. Do you expect us to accept that fate also?"

But whatever the motives of the prince in accepting Christianity, the new faith brought with it much which affected both the form and content of art in elite culture. One form of art to develop early was the saint's *Life*. As in the Mediterranean in late antiquity and in medieval

Carved wooden spoon (early twelfth century) excavated at Novgorod. From *Drevnii Novgorod: Prikladnoe iskusstvo i arkheologiia* (Moscow: Iskusstvo, 1985), p. 116. Reprinted courtesy of Iskusstvo Publishers.

Western Europe, the saint's *Life* in Rus' took on certain characteristic formulae. The *Life* of St. Theodosius conforms to these traits. From an early age the boy accepts a destiny which separates him from his coevals, and he must do battle with parents unconvinced of his special calling. Like St. Francis, Theodosius is intent on shedding all possessions, and sharing them with the poor. But the *Life* of Theodosius nevertheless reveals some distinctive characteristics. More like its Mediterranean than its European parallels, the *Life* of Theodosius promotes severe asceticism

Carved bone salt box (tenth century) excavated at Novgorod. From *Drevnii Novgorod: Prikladnoe iskusstvo i arkheologiia* (Moscow: Iskusstvo, 1985), p. 97. Reprinted courtesy of Iskusstvo Publishers.

and isolation which yield a highly individualized, internalized spirituality which coheres with the value system of Orthodoxy. In so doing, the *Life* of St. Theodosius idealized values perhaps better suited to individual than communal religious experience.

Until recently, there was little to be said about popular culture in Rus'. Little evidence of its existence could be found, so that all discussions about culture in Kievan Rus' revolved around the monuments of churchmen and the odd text with secular origins. But here too archeology has changed our impression. The excavations at Novgorod and similar digs elsewhere have brought to life the architecture of everyday life. Housing, implements of labor and warfare, and much else has emerged from these excavations. Most significant of all, perhaps, was the discovery of birchbark charters, strips of bark onto which various brief messages were scratched centuries ago. The charters may not have delivered all the insight which their discovery first promised, because the contents are generally laconic, sometimes interrupted, and usually difficult to inter- pret. All the same, the birchbark charters have opened new questions about literacy and the uses of literacy in Rus'. And together with other texts uncovered in unexpected places they have contributed to a new appraisal of popular culture in Rus'.

Because so many of the implements used in daily life in Kievan Rus' were fashioned from wood, few survive. We have already seen that the plows and harrows in use on the fields of Rus' depended on wood, sometimes in a near natural state. But much else was made from wood as well, as archeological excavation has demonstrated. Whether in Kiev, where subway construction periodically unearths the remains of some ancient house, or Novgorod, where whole teams have been systematically combing excavation sites for years, the wooden houses of that distant time have come partially back to life. In the south, wood was less important, but almost everywhere else timber sheltered the inhabitants of Rus'. Wood also served to contain and serve food, and digs have revealed many examples of these implements (see p. 61). In fact, artisans used wood for toys, chess pieces—almost anything.

Not everything, however, was made from wood. Those who could afford more durable mate- rials acquired them, as the bone salt box reproduced here indicates (p. 61). In addition, bone served for combs, dice, and ornamental eating utensils. Excavations have also revealed many items fashioned out of iron, especially materials related to fishing and hunting. Although many Kievans might not have possessed such durable goods, their existence proves that a prospering artisanry was at work. Exactly how large it was and how widely used their products were cannot yet be determined.

DOCUMENTS

The Christianization of Rus' According to the Primary Chronicle (978–88)

By some scholars' reckoning, nothing in Rus' history was more important than the decision of Prince Vladimir in 988 to accept Christianity from Byzantium. The entrance of Rus' into the cultural world of Eastern Christianity decisively oriented Rus' toward Europe and the West, and away from the steppe, the locus of the other great magnet of Rus' society and culture. The Primary Chronicle, whose description of early Slav society and politics we read above, here relays two narratives which explain Vladimir's decision. One need not accept one or the other as the "true" story of Christianization, since it is clear that even by the time the chronicler compiled this work, different legends had grown up around that momentous decision. The chronicle notices are nonetheless revealing. In the first place, we observe traces of the multicultural milieu which prevailed in Kievan Rus'. The Rus', we learn, worshipped a pantheon of gods which originated in different cultures—some Iranian, others Slavic, still others Scandinavian—to judge only by the names of Khors, Simargl, Dazhbog, and Perun. Also important to these narratives is the motivation behind the decision to convert to Christianity. Both in the story which compares the different religions and in the narrative which relates Vladimir's own conversion we discover that the prince was interested not so much in his eternal welfare as in the prosperity of his earthly principality. So it was that Christianization, just like the cult of Perun before it, came to Rus' through the agency of the state, whose chief, the prince, also endowed and protected the church in the first centuries of its life in Rus' when other religions still held greater sway. There is considerable evidence to indicate that Christianity did not succeed in displacing other religions until as late as the fourteenth century: for example, archeologists at Novgorod have uncovered from the earliest layers many objects indicative of pagan, animistic religions (see p. 64). But objects of Christian identity (such as the amber crosses reproduced on p. 65) begin to outnumber the other cult objects only in layers dated to the fourteenth century or later. These clues indicate that for a very long time Orthodox Christianity remained a religion of the minority, possibly confined only to elite urban culture.

(978–980) . . . Vladimir then began to reign alone in Kiev, and he set up idols on the hill outside the castle with the hall: one of Perun, made of wood with a head of silver and a mouth of gold, and others of Khors, Dazhbog, Stribog, Simargl and Mokosh. The people sacrificed to them, calling them gods, and brought their sons and their daughters to sacrifice them to these devils. They desecrated the earth with their offerings, and the land of Rus' and this hill were defiled with blood. . . .

(986). Vladimir was visited by [Turkic] Bulgarians of Mohammedan faith, who said, "Though you are a wise and prudent prince, you have no religion. Adopt our faith, and revere Mahomet." Vladimir inquired what was the nature of their religion. They replied that they believed in God, and that Mahomet instructed them to practice circumcision, to eat no pork, to drink no wine, and, after death, promised them complete fulfillment of their carnal desires. "Mahomet," they asserted, "will give each man seventy fair women. . . ." They also spoke other false things which out of modesty may not be written down. Vladimir listened to them, for he was fond of women and indulgence, regarding which he heard with pleasure. But circumcision and abstinence from pork and wine were disagreeable to him. "Drinking," said he, "is the joy of the

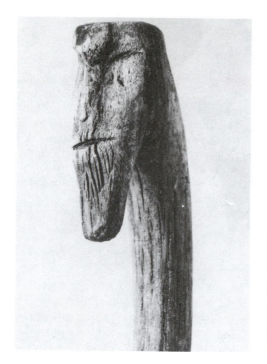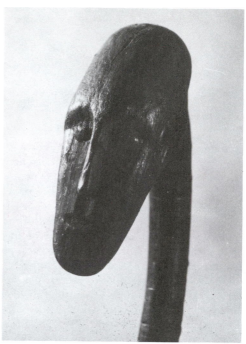

Two wooden household idols (late twelfth, early thirteenth centuries) excavated at Novgorod. From *Drevnii Novgorod: Prikladnoe iskusstvo i arkheologiia* (Moscow: Iskusstvo, 1985), pp. 207, 209. Reprinted courtesy of Iskusstvo Publishers.

Three bronze pagan amulets (all twelfth century). From *Drevnii Novgorod: Prikladnoe iskusstvo i arkheologiia* (Moscow: Iskusstvo, 1985), p. 68. Reprinted courtesy of Iskusstvo Publishers.

Amber crosses (fourteenth century) excavated at Novgorod. From *Drevnii Novgorod: Prikladnoe iskusstvo i arkheologiia* (Moscow: Iskusstvo, 1985), p. 133. Reprinted courtesy of Iskusstvo Publishers.

Russes. We cannot exist without that pleasure."

Then came the Germans, asserting that they were come as emissaries of the Pope. They added, "Thus says the Pope: 'Your country is like our country, but your faith is not as ours. For our faith is the light. We worship God, who has made heaven and earth, the stars, the moon, and every creature, while your gods are only wood.'" Vladimir inquired what their teaching was. They replied, "Fasting according to one's strength. But whatever one eats or drinks is all to the glory of God. . . ." Then Vladimir answered, "Depart hence; our fathers accepted no such principle."

The Jewish Khazars heard of these missions, and came themselves saying, "We have learned that Bulgarians and Christians came hither to instruct you in their faiths. . . . [W]e believe in the one God of Abraham, Isaac, and Jacob." Then Vladimir inquired what their religion was. They replied that its tenets included circumcision, not eating pork or hare,

and observing the Sabbath." The Prince then asked where their native land was, and they replied that it was in Jerusalem. When Vladimir inquired where that was, they made answer, "God was angry at our forefathers, and scattered us among the gentiles on account of our sins. Our land was then given to the Christians." The Prince then demanded, "How can you hope to teach others while you yourselves are cast out and scattered abroad by the hand of God? If God loved you and your faith, you would not be thus dispersed in foreign lands. Do you expect us to accept that fate also?" . . .

(987). Vladimir summoned together his vassals and the city-elders, and said to them, "Behold, the Bulgarians came before me urging me to accept their religion [Islam]. Then came the Germans and praised their own faith [Roman Christianity]; and after them came the Jews. Finally, the Greeks appeared, criticizing all other faiths but commending their own, and they spoke at length, telling the history of the whole world from its beginnings. Their words were artful, and it was wondrous to listen and pleasant to hear them. They preach the existence of another world. 'Whoever adopts our religion and then dies shall arise and live forever. But whosoever embraces another faith, shall be consumed with fire in the next world.' What is your opinion on this subject, and what do you answer?" The vassals and the elders replied, "You know, oh Prince, that no man condemns his own possessions, but praises them instead. If you desire to make certain, you have servants at your disposal. Send them to inquire about the ritual of each and how he worships God."

Their counsel pleased the prince and all the people, so that they chose good and wise men to the number of ten, and directed them to go first among the Bulgarians and inspect their faith. The emissaries went their way, and when they arrived at their destination they beheld the disgraceful actions of the Bulgarians and their worship in the mosque; then they returned to their own country. Vladimir then instructed them to go likewise among the Germans, and examine their faith, and finally to visit the Greeks. They thus went into Germany, and after viewing the German ceremonial, they proceeded to Tsargrad [Constantinople] where they appeared before the Emperor. He inquired on what mission they had come, and they reported to him all that had occurred. When the Emperor heard their words, he rejoiced, and did them great honor on that very day.

On the morrow the Emperor sent a message to the Patriarch to inform him that a Russian delegation had arrived to examine the Greek faith, and directed him to prepare the church and the clergy, and to array himself in his sacerdotal robes, so that the Russes might behold the glory of the God of the Greeks. When the Patriarch received these commands, he bade the clergy assemble, and they performed the customary rites. They burned incense, and the choirs sang hymns. The Emperor accompanied the Russes to the church, and placed them in a wide space, calling their attention to the beauty of the edifice, the chanting, and the offices of the archpriest and the ministry of the deacons, while he explained to them the worship of his God. The Russes were astonished, and in their wonder praised the Greek ceremonial. Then the Emperors Basil and Constantine invited the envoys to their presence, and said, "Go hence to your native country," and thus dismissed them with valuable presents and great honor.

Thus they returned to their own country, and the Prince called together his vassals and the elders. Vladimir then announced the return of the envoys who had been sent out, and suggested that their report be heard. He thus commanded them to speak out before his vassals. The envoys reported, "When we journeyed among the Bulgarians, we beheld how they worship in their temple, called a mosque, while they stand ungirt. The Bulgarian bows, sits down, looks hither and thither like one possessed, and there is no happiness among them, but instead only sorrow and a dreadful stench. Their religion is not good. Then we went among the Germans, and saw them performing many ceremonies in their temples; but we beheld no glory there. Then we went on to Greece, and the Greeks led us to the edifices where they worship their God, and we knew not whether we were in heaven on or earth. For on earth there is no such splendor or such beauty, and we are at a loss how to describe it. We only know that God dwells there among men, and their service is fairer than the ceremonies of other nations...." Vladimir then inquired where they should all accept baptism, and they replied that the decision rested with him.

After a year had passed, in 6496 (988) Vladimir marched with an armed force against Kherson, a Greek city, and the people of Kherson barricaded themselves in. Vladimir halted at the farther side of the city ... [and] besieged the town ... Then a man of Kherson, Anastasius by name, shot into the Russ camp an arrow on which he had written, "There are springs behind you to the east, from which water flows in pipes. Dig down and cut them off." When Vladimir received this information, he raised his eyes to heaven and vowed that if this hope was realized, he would be baptized. He gave orders straightway to dig down above the pipes, and the water-supply was thus cut off. The inhabitants were accordingly overcome by thirst, and surrendered.

Vladimir and his retinue entered the city, and he sent messages to the Emperors Basil and Constantine, saying, "Behold, I have captured your glorious city. I have also heard that you have an unwedded sister. Unless you give her to me to wife, I shall deal with your own city as I have with Kherson." When the Emperors heard this message, they were troubled, and replied, "It is not meet for Christians to give in marriage to pagans. If you are baptized, you shall have her to wife, inherit the kingdom of God, and be our companion in the faith. Unless you do so, however, we cannot give you our sister in marriage." When Vladimir learned their response, he directed the envoys of the Emperors to report to the latter that he was willing to accept baptism, having already given some study to their religion, and that the Greek faith and ritual, as described by the emissaries sent to examine it, had pleased him well. When the Emperors heard this report, they rejoiced, and persuaded their sister Anna to consent to the match. They then requested Vladimir to submit to baptism before they should send their sister to him, but Vladimir desired that the princess should herself bring priests to baptize him. The Emperors complied with this request, and sent forth their sister, accompanied by some dignitaries and priests. Anna, however, departed with reluctance. "It is as if I were setting out to captivity," she lamented; "better were it for me to die here." But her brothers protested, "Through your agency God turns the land of Rus' to repentance, and you will relieve Greece from the danger of grievous war. . . ."

Vladimir was baptized in the Church of St. Basil, which stands at Kherson upon a square in the center of the city, where the Khersonians trade. . . . After his baptism Vladimir took the Princess in marriage. Those who do not know the truth say he was baptized in Kiev, while others assert this event took place in Vasiliev, while still others mention other places. . . .

When the Prince arrived at his capital, he directed that the idols should be overthrown, and that some should be cut to pieces and others burned with fire. He thus ordered that Perun should be bound to a horse's tail and dragged along Borichev to the river. He appointed twelve men to beat the idol with sticks, not because he thought the wood was sensitive, but to affront the demon who had deceived man in this guise. . . . After they had thus dragged the idol along, they cast it into the Dnieper River. . . . Thereafter Vladimir sent heralds throughout the whole city to proclaim that if any inhabitant, rich or poor, did not betake himself to the river, he would risk the Prince's displeasure . . . On the morrow, the Prince went forth to the Dnieper with the priests of the Princess and those from Kherson, and a countless multitude assembled. They all went into the water: some stood up to their necks, others to their breasts, the younger near the bank . . . while the adults waded farther out. The priests stood by and offered prayers. There was joy in heaven and upon earth to behold so many souls saved.

SOURCE: Samuel H. Cross, "The Russian Primary Chronicle," *Harvard Studies and Notes in Philology and Literature* 12 (1930): 178, 180, 183–84, 197–205 (excerpted). Transliteration and spelling have been slightly modified.

The Life of St. Theodosius (Eleventh Century)

The arrival of Christianity in Rus' brought in its train a gradually growing collection of local, Rus' saints. Boris and Gleb, about whose martyrdom in 1068 we read above, were the first local saints, their deaths symbolizing a particular form of piety which came to be highly regarded in Rus' culture. The Primary Chronicle, inserting dialogue into the mouths of these victims of Sviatopolk, alleged that these sons of Vladimir preferred to model their behavior on Christ, who willingly accepted death rather than resist evil. Theodosius, whose *Life* appears below, follows in that same tradition, repeatedly preferring to mortify the flesh, and deny self in order to achieve a purer religious experience. In this quest, he turned his back on all social convention, including the high standing of his own family. Finally, he determined to retreat to an isolated monastic life, helping champion a kind of monasticism (eremitic or hermitic) which, unlike much Western and later Russian monasticism, confined an individual to a cell separated from almost all outside contact. Only in this state, Theodosius believed, might sinful humankind achieve direct communion with God. This particular vision of religion was not unique to Rus', but all the same did play an important part in determining religious values in Rus', and in subsequent Russia.

About fifty *poprishche* [about 30 miles] from Kiev, the capital city, there is a town called Vasyl'kiv. Here the parents of the holy one lived in Christian faith and adorned with every kind of piety. They bore this blessed child, and on the eighth day they brought him to God's priest, as is the custom of Christians, to give the child a name. The priest looked at the child, foresaw within his heart that from his youth he would dedicate himself to God, and named him Feodosii [Theodosius, "gift of God"]. When the child was forty days old, he was baptized. He grew up under his parents' care and God's grace was with him, for from youth the Holy Spirit dwelt in him. . . .

It happened that the blessed one's parents moved to another town, called Kursk, by the prince's order, or rather I should say by God's will, so that the life of this valiant child might shine forth there. . . .

Growing in body and drawn in his soul to the love of God, he would daily go to God's church and listen to the divine Scriptures with the utmost diligence. Moreover, he would not approach other children when they were playing, as young people usually do, but despised their games. His clothes were patched; his parents often urged him to dress himself in fine

clothes and go out to play with other children, but he would not obey them, preferring to be like one of the poor. He also begged his parents to let him study the divine books with one of the teachers. This they did, and he soon learnt all sacred Writ, so that everybody marveled at the child's wisdom and understanding and at the speed with which he learned. Who shall recount the submissiveness and obedience which he showed in his studies, not only towards his teacher, but to all who studied with him?

When the blessed Feodosii was thirteen years old, his father passed away. Henceforth he grew more zealous in his labors, so that he would go out to a village with his slaves to work with the utmost humility. But his mother restrained him from such activity and forbade him to do it, and again begged him to dress in fine clothes and go and play with children his own age. She would say, "By going about this way, you bring disgrace on yourself and your family." But he did not heed her, so that she frequently became furious with him and beat him. For she had a strong, powerful body, like a man; anyone who heard her talking, but could not see her, would have thought she was a man.

Meanwhile this blessed youth was pondering how and by what means he might be saved. Then he heard about the holy places where our Lord walked in the flesh, and wanted to go there and revere them. He prayed to God, "My Lord Jesus Christ, hear my prayer and deem me worthy to go to Thy holy places and revere them." While he was then praying, some pilgrims came to the town. Seeing them, the blessed youth rejoiced and ran and greeted them, kissing them affectionately and asking where they were from and where they were going. They replied, "We are from the holy places and, God willing, we will go back there." The holy one begged them to take him as their traveling companion. They promised to take him and to conduct him to the holy places. When the blessed Feodosii heard their promise, he was filled with joy and went home.

When the pilgrims were about to leave they informed the youth about their departure.

That night he arose, unbeknownst to anyone, and left home secretly, taking nothing with him except the clothes which he was wearing—and they were very shabby. Thus he departed in the wake of the pilgrims. . . .

Three days later his mother learned that he had left with the pilgrims and set off after him, taking along her only [other] son, who was younger than the blessed Feodosii. They pursued him for a considerable distance, overtook them, and seized him. Out of fury and rage his mother took him by the hair, flung him on the ground, and trampled on him with her feet. The pilgrims protested greatly and she let go, but returned home, leading him tied up like some malefactor. She was so possessed by anger that she beat him until her strength gave out. Then she took him into a room, tied him up, shut him in, and departed. The blessed youth accepted all these things with joy and prayed to God about them all.

Two days later his mother came and let him out and gave him something to eat, but as she was still gripped by anger she put irons on his feet and ordered him thus to walk about, taking care lest he run away from her again. He went about like this for many days. Then her heart softened towards him and she began to beg and urge him not to run away from her, since she loved him more than the others and accordingly could not bear to be without him. When he promised that he would not leave her, she removed the irons from his feet and told him to do whatever he wanted. The blessed Feodosii then returned to his former labors and went daily to church.

He saw that often there were no sacramental loaves for the liturgy, because none had been baked. He was very grieved about this, and in his humility he resolved to set himself apart for this task, which he did. So he began to bake loaves and sell them. If there was anything left over cost, he gave it to the poor. With the money he received he bought more grain, ground it with his own hands, and made more loaves. Thus was it God's will, so that pure loaves be brought to His church by a pure and innocent child. This went on for two years or more. All his young companions, prompted by

the enemy, mocked and reproached him on account of this work, but the blessed one gladly accepted all their reproaches and maintained silence.

When the enemy—the hater of good—saw himself vanquished by the humility of this holy child, he did not give up, since he wanted to turn him away from this work. He began to incite his mother to forbid him to go on with this activity. Because she could not bear her son to be in disgrace, she began to speak to him affectionately. "I beg you, my child, give up this work, for you are bringing disgrace on your family. I cannot bear to hear you insulted by everybody because of this work. It is not fitting for you, a child, to do such work." The blessed Feodosii answered her meekly, "Listen, mother, I entreat you! The Lord God Jesus Christ Himself became poor and was humbled, giving us an example, so that we might humble ourselves for His sake. He was reviled and spat upon and beaten and endured all these things for the sake of our salvation. How much more fitting it is for us to endure them so that we might receive Christ. As for this work of mine, listen: When our Lord Jesus Christ sat down for supper with His disciples, He took bread, blessed it and broke it, and gave it to His disciples, saying 'Take and eat, this is my body, broken for you and for many for the remission of sins.' If our Lord called bread His flesh, should I not all the more rejoice that our God has considered me worthy to make his Flesh?" When his mother heard this, she marveled at the child's great wisdom, and from then on left him alone.

The enemy, however, did not desist, but goaded her to forbid her child to show such humility. For a year later, when she again saw him baking loaves and being blackened by soot from the oven, she was greatly distressed and again began to reproach him, now tenderly, now with threats; sometimes she beat him to make him stop doing such work. The blessed youth was very unhappy about this and perplexed as to what he should do. Then he got up at night and secretly left home and went to another town not far away; he lived with the priest and continued his work as usual.

His mother looked for him in her town and was in great distress when she failed to find him. Then many days later she heard where he was living and hurried after him in a great rage. When she came to the aforementioned town she looked for him and found him in the priest's house. She took hold of him, beat him, and dragged him back to her town. After she had brought him home, she locked him up and said, "Henceforth you will not go away from me. Wherever you go, I shall come and find you and tie you up and bring you back to my town." Then the blessed Feodosii prayed to God and daily went to God's church.

He was indeed lowly in heart and submissive towards everyone, so that the governor of the town, seeing that the boy was so meek and submissive, felt a great love towards him and told him to stay by his church. He also gave him some fine clothes in which to go about. The blessed one did this for a few days, as though he was carrying a heavy burden, but then took the clothes off and gave them to the poor; he himself dressed in shabby clothes and thus went about. The governor saw him thus going about and gave him another set of clothes, better than the first, and begged him to wear it. But he took this off too and gave it away; he did this many times. When the judge learned of this he began to love him even more, and marvelled at his humility.

After this the blessed Feodosii went to one of the blacksmiths and told him to make him an iron chain, which he took and girded round his loins, and he went around like this. The iron was tight and cut into his body, but he went on as though this caused him no discomfort.

When many days had passed and a feastday came, his mother began to urge him to dress in fine clothes to serve at table, since all the town's magnates would be dining at the governor's table that day and the blessed Feodosii had been ordered to stand by and serve. This was why his mother had told him to put on fine clothes, especially when she had heard that the governor had arranged for all the town's magnates to dine with him. While he was putting the fine clothes on, being an innocent-minded youth he was not on his guard with her, but she was watching him closely and saw blood on his shirt. She wanted to find out the true state of affairs and realized that the blood was caused by the chain biting into him. She was inflamed with anger against him and got up in a furious temper, tore off his shirt, beat him, and snatched the chains from his loins. The blessed youth got dressed as though he had received no harm and went to serve the diners with the utmost meekness.

Some time later he heard the Lord in the Gospel saying, "Whosoever hath not forsaken his father and mother and followed after me is not worthy of me." . . . Having heard these words, the divinely inspired Feodosii was inflamed with love for God; inspired by zeal towards God, he pondered daily and hourly how and where he could be tonsured [take monastic vows] and hide from his mother. . . .

Then he heard about the blessed Antonij, who was living in a cave. His spirits soared, and he set out for the cave and came to the venerable Antonij. When he saw him he fell down and prostrated himself before him and begged him with tears to accept him. The great Antonij said to him, "My son, do you not see that this cave is a wretched place, narrow and confined? As you are still a child, I think, you will not be able to endure the discomfort of this place." He said this not only to test him, but he also had foreseen with prophetic vision that he would build up that spot and make a glorious monastery to assemble many monks. The divinely-inspired Feodosii answered him meekly, "You see, honored father, that Christ our God, Who cares for all His creatures, whosoever they are, has brought me to your holiness and told me to seek my salvation through you. Therefore, whatever you bid me, I shall do." . . . Then the elder blessed him and commanded the great Nikon to tonsure him, since he was a priest and an experienced monk. He took the blessed Feodosii and tonsured him according to the custom of the holy fathers and dressed him in monastic garments in the

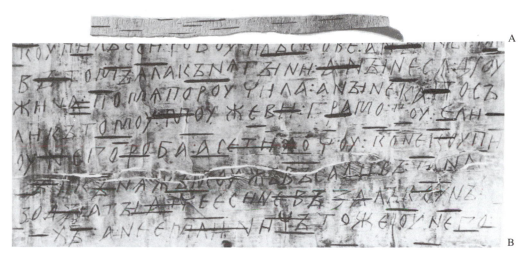

A

B

Two birchbark charters from Novgorod: (A) late twelfth century and (B) early twelfth century. From *Drevnii Novgorod: Prikladnoe iskusstvo i arkheologiia* (Moscow: Iskusstvo, 1985), p. 20. Reprinted courtesy of Iskusstvo Publishers.

year 1032, in the reign of the pious prince Iaroslav Volodimerovich.

Our father Feodosii dedicated himself entirely to God and the venerable Antonij, and henceforth gave himself up to a life of physical austerity: he spent whole nights in vigil, praising God and casting off the heaviness of sleep, striving to subdue his flesh. He also worked with his hands. . . . Thus he humbled himself by self-denial in every way and tormented his body with labors and abstinence, so that the venerable Antonij and the great Nikon marveled at his meekness and submissiveness and at such virtue, steadfastness, and good cheer in a youth.

SOURCE: *The* Paterik *of the Kievan Caves Monastery.* Translated by Muriel Heppell (Cambridge, MA: Harvard Ukrainian Research Institute, 1987), pp. 26–33 (excerpted). Reprinted with the permission of the Harvard Ukrainian Research Institute.

Birchbark Charters From Novgorod (Twelfth Century)

The discovery by Novgorod archeologists (and later by archeologists of several other early towns) of written texts scratched onto birchbark strips has revolutionized our understanding of early Rus' society, as Pushkareva and Levin demonstrated above. About 700 such birchbark charters are now known, preserved for centuries in the damp soil several meters below the surface of today's city streets. Many of the charters survive only as fragments, some containing just a few characters. Others, however, were recovered intact, but because the charters rarely separate characters into words and contain no punctuation, their interpretation is nevertheless sometimes quite difficult (see the illustration above). All the same, the surviving texts depict Novgorodian life in all its variety, including private letters, business notes, and even doodling and practice writing, providing evidence of a rudimentary literacy in medieval Rus' society. The texts which appear here illustrate the kinds of texts preserved on birchbark.

———————

No. 384. Charter No. 384 was found in 1960 during construction work . . . This is the text:

From Stoeneg to Mother. I have given Savva five kunas and a towel, two spoons, two knives, and a deerskin.

Its length is 0.311 meters, its width 0.034 meters . . . The charter may be dated to the twelfth century tentatively; there is no stratigraphy information to confirm the date.

No. 502. Charter No. 502 was found in the Trinity excavations on level 14 . . . at a depth of 2.18 meters. It is a complete letter, fragmented in its upper portion where the tops of the letters of the first line were lost.

From Miroslav to Olisei Grechin. Gavko from Polotsk comes here. Ask him where he is staying. Probably you saw what happened when I seized Ivan, and placed him before witnesses. Tell me how he answers.

Its length is 21.4 cm, its width 3.7 cm. Stratigraphic date is late twelfth century, to which paleographic data also correspond.

No. 509. Charter No. 509 was found in the excavations on Kirov Street . . . at a depth of 6.8 meters. It is a complete document.

Take from Voislav ten kunas principal and five kunas interest. He has given me two kunas in interest. From Nezhiat' take ten kunas and one grivna, and from Budot' take one grivna interest. From Boian take the stipulated six kunas interest in Ozerevo. Give the assistant one kuna for each man.

The charter is 29 cm long, 4.8 cm wide. Stratigraphy dating places it in the second half of the twelfth century. Paleographic indicators confirm this date.

SOURCE: A. V. Artsikhovskii, *Novgorodskie gramoty na bereste (Iz raskopok 1958–61 goda)* (Moscow: AN SSSR, 1963), pp. 84–

6; A. V. Artsikhovskii, V. L. Ianin, *Novgorodskie gramoty na bereste (Iz raskopok 1962–1976 gg.)* (Moscow: Nauka, 1978), pp. 96–7, 104–5. Translated by Daniel H. Kaiser. Reprinted with the permission of V. L. Ianin.

Graffiti from St. Sophia Cathedral, Kiev (Eleventh–Twelfth Centuries)

Another kind of evidence for literacy in Rus' comes from the walls of cathedrals where ancient visitors scratched into the stone various short inscriptions. Over the centuries, during remodelings, the addition of frescoes, and other changes, many ancient graffiti disappeared from view, only to reappear in modern times during restoration work. Most such graffiti, like those reproduced here, are understandably brief, and although some provide evidence with which to identify the writer, the authors of most of these graffiti are doomed to eternal anonymity. All such writing, however, adds to our impression of literacy in Rus'. Still, what one makes of the evidence can vary widely, as Simon Franklin points out below.

———————

No. 10. The inscription is situated in the Apostles' side chapel (southern gallery), on a column with an ancient fresco. . . . It is found at a height of 2.55 meters from the level of an eleventh-century floor. The text reads:

> The month of August on
> the 22nd day died the slave
> of God Luka, the blessed Bishop
> of Belgorod.

. . . Despite the fact that the inscription is furnished with an incomplete date (only the month and day are indicated) which is not characteristic for memorial graffiti, it is easily dated thanks to the remembrance of the Bishop Luka of Belgorod. This name is met in the chronicle under the years 1088 and 1089. . . . Luka is last recalled in the chronicle under the year 1089, and in 1113 Nikita was elevated to the Belgorod cathedra. There are no notices about the death of Luka of Belgorod in the chronicle. He apparently died in the interval between 1089 and 1113. . . .

No. 18. This inscription is found in the central nave of the cathedral, on the second cross-shaped column south of the altar, carved on a fresco depicting Nicholas. [The graffito is found] at a height of 1.1 meters from the level of the eleventh-century floor. The text reads:

> Wrote
> Stavr
> Goro
> dniatin[i]
> ch

["Stavr Gorodniatinich wrote (this)"]. . . . The name Stavr, together with the patronymic Gorodiatinich, appear both in this graffito and in the Testament of Vladimir Monomakh. Therefore it is difficult to doubt that Stavko Gordiatich of the Testament and Stavr Gorodiatinich, recalled in the inscription on the wall of St. Sophia's cathedral, are one and the same historical person, all the more since the name Stavr in antiquity was a real rarity. And so, the text of the inscription concerns a commander of Vsevolod Iaroslavich, Stavr Gorodiatinich, with whom Vladimir Monomakh completed his second campaign to Smolensk [dated to 1068 or 1069–70].

No. 307. In 1972 . . . an interesting inscription of the twelfth century was discovered. The graffito is found in the northern part of the choir loft of the cathedral, on the northern wall. . . . The inscription was spackled over . . . but after removal of the nineteenth-century spackling it was possible to read the following text:

> Volodimiriaia
> [He]re sat the most unfortunate
> daughter-in-law of Andrei, si[s]ter of Oleg
> and Igor' and Vsevolod. [V]anko wrote [this],
> priest of the archbishop. . . .

No. 381. In the apse of the southern chapel of the Kirillov church [also in Kiev] was discovered a significant quantity of various graffiti scratched onto the fresco plaster, which is partially preserved in this place on the south wall. On the wall of the apse several notable, clear old inscriptions are visible, one over another. The upper inscription is written in one long line of 46.5 cm and reads:

+ [Lord] help your slave Martin Semiunov[ich].

. . . Paleographic particulars make it possible to date the graffito to the middle of the twelfth century.

SOURCE: S. A. Vysotskii, *Drevnerusskie nadpisi Sofii Kievskoi XI–XIV vv.*, vyp. 1 (Kiev: Naukova dumka, 1966), pp. 45–47, 56–58; idem, *Kievskie graffiti XI–XVII vv.* (Kiev: Naukova dumka, 1985), pp. 25, 87; translated by Daniel H. Kaiser. Reprinted with the permission of S. A. Vysotskii.

LITERATURE

SIMON FRANKLIN

Literacy in Kievan Rus'

The numerous birchbark charters, the considerable body of reconstructed graffiti and other sources have helped persuade some scholars that many persons in early Rus' were literate. In the selection which appears below, however, Simon Franklin considers this evidence and the problems it presents as we attempt to understand how usual literacy was, and what purposes it served in Rus' culture and society.

With reference to medieval England M. T. Clanchy argues that "the growth in the uses of literacy [between 1066 and 1307] is indicated by, and was perhaps primarily a consequence of, the production and retention of records on an unprecedented scale." That is, rather than view literacy as a step on the road to literature, to learning and high culture, Clanchy stresses the interrelationship between literacy and administrative practice. Writing creates the possibility of documentation; documentation brings more people into contact with the written word (whether or not they themselves possess literate skills); and, in time, as documentation becomes accepted as necessary, as mental habits adjust to it, as reliance upon it increases, so it in turn stimulates further expansion in the uses of literacy . . .

The present study is concerned with "Kievan" Russia, c. 1050–1200. Before the mid-eleventh century direct evidence for literacy in Russia is extremely sparse, and its interpretation is hotly controversial. Some knowledge of writing doubtless existed in the tenth century, a knowledge fostered both by international trade and by the Christian church, whose presence was gradually established over many decades prior to Russia's "official" conversion in the late 980s. But the sources, fragmentary and ambiguous, provide no indication of the extent of this literacy, nor of the language or languages in which it was applied. The regular native use of Slavonic writing is attested only after Russia's official conversion, with the training of clergy and copyists. Even then, however, for over half a century we have to rely mainly on occasional statements in later narrative sources, to which may be added a few seals and some sporadic inscriptions. There seems to be a kind of invisible barrier set in the mid-eleventh century, after which contemporary evidence of literacy in a variety of contexts begins to appear in ever-increasing quantities: the first extant manuscripts, the first birch-bark letters, and a proliferation of seals and inscriptions. One suspects that the pattern of survival is not entirely accidental: hence the starting point of the present survey, c. 1050 . . .

Until fairly recently the extent of lay literacy in Kievan Russia had to be deduced mainly from hints contained in literature and in the colophons of manuscripts. Since the Second World War, however, epigraphers and archeologists have discovered and published a cornucopia of material which brings us into much more direct contact with an incomparably broader range of writing. Through inscriptions on objects in everyday domestic and commercial use, through graffiti in churches, and perhaps most of all through the celebrated birch-bark letters of Novgorod, we are introduced to a world of apparently routine and almost casual literacy far removed from the austerity of manuscripts and literature. As symbols of literacy, ink and parchment make way for the simple stylus . . . and any surface which may conveniently be scratched upon, be it wax, or bark, or the interior wall of a church.

An index of people involved in this literacy during the eleventh and twelfth centuries—owners or makers of objects, senders and recipients of letters, authors or authorizers of inscriptions—now runs to about a thousand named and at least as many anonymous individuals, and the numbers increase year by year. New excavations continually bring to light more objects marked with the names of their owners or makers, objects which range from high-quality silver goblets to plain and humble spindle whorls. Nearly four hundred graffiti from before the thirteenth century have been identified in the cathedrals of St. Sophia in Kiev and Novgorod, as well as several other buildings. Almost six hundred birch-bark letters have now been published: the majority of them have been unearthed in Novgorod, but some have also been found in Staraia Russa, Smolensk, Pskov, and Vitebsk. Roughly one hundred and seventy of these letters can be dated to before c. 1200.

And yet these new sources, despite their relative abundance, are curiously resistant to detailed social analysis. The general impression seems seductively clear, but the all-important particulars can be elusive. . . .

Practically all sections of the urban community are represented in these sources (though not all in equal measure or on equivalent levels). Craftsmen sign their wares; masons and builders scratch marks and initials in the stones of the churches they build. The artists of frescoes in St. Sophia in Novgorod leave a record of their names near their work. An icon painter . . . takes commissions, and jots down plans for his compositions, on scraps of birch bark. Soldiers scratch prayers in church, or send letters in preparation for a campaign. Traders in furs, wax, tin, and lead discuss business, debt collectors plan their tactics, and creditors list their debtors, all on birch bark. Even women occasionally put in an appearance, both in the graffiti and as senders of letters. One birch-bark letter may be from a mayor . . . of Novgorod. The clergy are prominent, not unexpectedly, among the authors of graffiti. As for the birch-bark letters, it used to be thought that this form of communication was used almost exclusively by laymen. The more recent finds, however, make it clear that the impression was mistaken, that the apparently overwhelming predominance of lay letters reflected not the actual social background to birch-bark letters in general, but merely the locations of the excavations. Birch-bark letters could be sent by laymen and clergy alike.

What did all these people write about? The topics seem to be as varied and diverse as the authors. Most writers of the graffiti simply record the fact that they have written a graffito ("X wrote this"), or else they scratch brief prayers such as "Lord (or St. X) help thy servant Y." Yet the graffiti are by no means entirely religious or entirely formulaic and repetitive. They include chronicle-like notes on great events: the deaths of princes, the conclusion of peace, the arrival of dignitaries. There are liturgical quotations, wise sayings, and the lines of what appear to be folk verses and proverbs. Casual doodles and drawings abound. The birch-bark letters, more than any other written source for the period, allow us to glimpse some of the mundane concerns of urban life. For example, before the publication of the letters there was very little evidence on the relationship between legal codes and legal practice. The letters give a wealth of detail about individual cases. The citizens of Novgorod write about the accusations made against them, about witnesses and the procedures of evidence, about fines, and their payment or avoidance; they write of theft, receipt of stolen goods, fraud, slander, and wife-beating. A good deal of correspondence and many private jottings, lists, and memoranda are generated by business. A few letters are purely per-

sonal and domestic: George writes to his parents, "Sell the house and come to Smolensk or Kiev; bread is cheap; if you cannot come, write to me about your health."

Geographical variation is hard to determine. By far the greater part of the extant and known material emanates from Novgorod: not just the birch-bark letters themselves, but also seals, styluses, and indeed the earliest extant or recorded manuscripts. Even the graffiti in St. Sophia in Novgorod are distinctly less "official," more ordinary than their equivalents in Kiev. The obvious and attractive conclusion is that this lay literacy, while not unknown in other Russian cities, was nevertheless particularly widespread in, and characteristic of, Novgorod. Against this one should point out that the conditions in Novgorod have been particularly favorable for the appropriate discoveries: the sodden ground, subsequent building history, and postwar planning policy all work to the advantage of the archeologist. The materials are better preserved, and archeological investigation encounters fewer obstacles, whether natural or man-made. Birch-bark letters have been found only in northern cities: but birch bark was less readily available in the south, where in any case it (or a local substitute) is more likely to have decomposed and less likely to have been excavated. As to other kinds of evidence of literacy, analogous material turns up in all major (and several minor) towns of Kievan Russia. It is less abundant than in Novgorod, but the balance of extant evidence does not necessarily reflect the balance of literacy in the eleventh and twelfth centuries. . . .

Did "authors" write, and did recipients read, or were the technical tasks of correspondence performed by scribes? In a more modern context this question would be of paramount importance, since our basic measure of literacy is the ability (which can be defined on several levels) to read, to write, or to do both. But in a medieval context . . . the criteria can be somewhat different: scribes worked to dictation, and the result was read aloud; a perfectly competent scribe could be "illiteratus"; the author of learned tracts, or the issuer of documents, need never have set quill to parchment. One could participate fully in, and even control, the uses of the written word without actually applying the technical skills oneself. Similarly, the implications of scribal practice are not always plain: a man might be able to read and write, yet still employ a scribe. . . .

Thus if the birch-bark letters were written with the aid of scribes, one should not automatically conclude that the senders were unable to write. But even if the senders did lack the ability to scratch their own letters, they still participated in one of the routine uses of writing and thereby helped to shape the literacy of their time. The modern notion of the illiterate as one who, by virtue of his inability to read and write, remains to an appreciable extent outside literate culture is not properly applicable in this context.

Fortunately the birch-bark letters do not compel us to dwell on such niceties, since the overwhelming majority of them probably were written by their senders, at least during the eleventh and twelfth centuries. . . . The early letters contain no evidence for the use of scribes (except perhaps a couple of cases in which the sender is referred to in the third person); in fact they provide a certain amount of evidence to the contrary. The very nature of the letters, their relative informality, their general brevity, the apparently casual way in which they were treated (they were thrown away to be trodden into the mud), none of this combines very comfortably with the idea of a literacy based on the labor of scribes. Paleographic observations, tentative though they must be, nevertheless point to the same conclusion. In the early period no two letters from different people are in the same hand, while letters from the same person are, so far as can be determined, in the same hand . . .

In other words the senders of the early birch-bark letters were, by and large, literate in the modern sense. The levels of this literacy are not easy to ascertain. . . . The letters are not literary, and much of the spelling would indeed be unacceptably casual in, say, a liturgical text. But this is surely beside the point: the purpose was to convey a written message effectively, not to emulate liturgical or literary norms of presentation. If the letters achieved

their purpose (and there is no reason to doubt that they did) then their writers possessed all the literacy which they needed, rather than half the literacy which they did not need. Their literacy is fully practical, therefore full. Furthermore, it is quite feasible that a man could use casual spelling in his casual correspondence, yet still copy a Gospel or read the Psalter in good Church Slavonic.

Letter writing in Kievan Russia was not restricted to birch bark, or to ordinary urban business. Princes used letters in their dealings with one another, in internal diplomacy. The one surviving and relatively uncontroversial example . . . is a letter from Vladimir Monomakh to Oleg Sviatoslavich, written in 1096. Perilous though it is to generalize from a sample of one, I think it can safely be stated that Vladimir's letter, whatever its remarkable and individual qualities, was not an isolated or unusual phenomenon. Vladimir informs us explicitly both that he writes in response to a letter which he has received from his son Mstislav and that he expects a letter from Oleg in reply.

On an even more elevated plane, there was apparently a certain amount of public, "learned" correspondence: letters from churchmen, but for the ears of princes. Again only one such letter survives, but it, too, provides evidence of the existence of others . . .

The general impression, therefore, is of a quite startlingly widespread, active, lay literacy on practically all levels of (urban) society. Moreover, whether learned or mundane, this was apparently literacy in the modern sense, the ability to read and write, rather than the ability merely to direct the activities of a professional caste of scribes who monopolized the technical skills. In the home, at work, in financial and legal transactions, in diplomacy and negotiation, the use of writing was familiar and habitual . . .

Widespread, routine, vernacular literacy: this is what the sources initially suggest, and in many respects the impression is not unjustified. And yet if one looks at the sources more closely they turn out to be distressingly opaque . . .

For example, inscriptions on spindle whorls

might not in fact indicate the "ordinariness" of literacy; it emerges that the incidence of inscriptions and scratched marks on spindle whorls is quite exceptionally high, that they are far more common than inscriptions on other "ordinary" objects. So perhaps spindle whorls were not "ordinary" at all, and one should look for special reasons why they, rather than other objects, attracted inscriptions. Nor are the birch-bark letters as helpful as one would like. Several prime sites in Novgorod have yielded not a single letter. How does this affect our general conclusions? Furthermore, the numbers of excavated letters can give a false impression of their value as sources, since roughly a quarter of them (40–45 out of about 170 from the early period) are too fragmentary to permit any sensible decipherment.

More disturbingly, our social classifications of the graffito writers and letter senders have to be based almost entirely on guesswork or, at best, on highly tenuous inference. We speak airily of the social range of literacy, of the merchants and the soldiers, the craftsmen and the tax gatherers, the judges and the usurers. We provide such categories; the sources themselves do not. Apart from two priests, Drochka and Mina, no sender of a birch-bark letter (in the eleventh and twelfth centuries) names either his own or his addressee's profession, status, rank, title, occupation, or other badge of social position. The graffiti are slightly more informative: on some 25 occasions (out of about 350) the signatories do indicate their occupation. Together they yield the names of only a dozen laymen. Curiously, with the exception of one "traveling merchant" and one painter (who was not necessarily a layman) all these lay signatories seem to be soldiers or servitors. . . . The sample is too small, and the odd proportions may be wholly fortuitous or else due to circumstances of which we know nothing. So one is forced to produce inferences from the contents of the sources, especially of the birch-bark letters.

However, the contents are, to put it mildly, ambiguous. Most of the early letters are brief— a dozen words or less—and tersely styled (pre-

sumably for recipients who already knew much of the background of which we are ignorant). In addition, most of them are riddled with lacunae. They might refer to a sum of money, to witnesses, or to goods, but such brief hints are scarcely reliable indicators of social context. Even when the letters are detailed and complete they usually leave room for various interpretations. For example, several letters concern debts: they list the names of debtors and the size of the debts, or they deal with how debts are to be collected. On a very few occasions these debts are clearly incurred as a result of borrowing: the letter names the sum borrowed and the interest due. But such letters are exceptional. Normally there are no clear signs to show whether the debts are incurred as a result of usury, fines and penalties, taxation, rent demands, or commerce. Similarly, we may glean from a letter that a certain sum of money is in dispute, but usually we can only guess as to whether the dispute concerns the payment of a debt (of whatever kind) or, say, the allocation of an inheritance. Thus any social classification of the senders must remain vague unless new kinds of evidence can be discovered. And even if one does find the occasional social label, one still has to bear in mind the possibility (indeed, the likelihood) that apparently heterogeneous social categories overlap with one another. Thus although one may speak of letters sent by a landowner, a merchant, a public official, or a soldier, all these may in reality be one and the same person or category of person: a landowner who sells his produce (or buys luxury goods), serves as a judge or tax collector, and joins his prince in time of war. . . .

Yet the letters are not entirely without patterns and regularity. Some significant and recurrent features of the early letters become apparent when they, as a group, are compared to the letters of a later period. Three such features should be mentioned here.

In the first place, as others have noted, the early letters almost all deal with money, while later letters deal more with land. There may be a wide variety of lay contexts (the family, litigation, trade, usury, etc.), but in each context the concern of the lay letter writers, the particular issue that provoked them to resort to the medium of writing, was virtually always money. Even in the most fragmentary letters, in letters which yield no names and no hint of what their senders and recipients might be doing, even here where we can decipher nothing else, we can often piece together the scraps of a word denoting a sum of money.

Secondly, the early letters seem to have circulated within a fairly homogeneous social group comprised of relatively rich people. No letter of the eleventh and twelfth centuries was indubitably written by a subordinate to his social superior. The first two specimens of letters written to the sender's "lord" date from c. 1190–1210: one of these is quite exceptional in that it is written from a woman, Anna, to her "lord and brother," Klimiata. . . . But most were apparently sent from equal to equal. Increasingly in the thirteenth century, and commonly in the fourteenth and fifteenth centuries, letters were sent from (though not necessarily written by) subordinates: from peasants to their lords, from employees to their employers. . . .

Thirdly, the early letters include not a single formal document. It would be tempting to dismiss this apparent lacuna with the claim that birch bark was not a suitable vehicle for formal documentation, that it was by nature appropriate only for casual messages. The claim would be invalid. Again, birch-bark material from later centuries shows that the pattern of the early letters is not accidental. Among the later letters formal documents do appear, and not just sporadically, but commonly: there are wills, petitions, contracts, transcripts of court proceedings, copies of legal documents, and agreements of all kinds. Birch bark was, therefore, a perfectly suitable medium in which to produce documents. . . .

To conclude: the sources for lay literacy in early medieval Russia (chiefly chronicles, graffiti, inscriptions, and birch-bark letters) are abundant, but not as socially informative as they may initially appear: both their exact social provenance and their contents are too frequently vague. Yet even if they do not yield precise social classifications, they do allow one to perceive a fairly regular pattern of social differentiation, and they do not justify some of the broader claims which have been made on their behalf. The upper echelons of society—princes and the (predominantly male) urban rich—commonly (although by no means universally) resorted to the use of writing, and most of those who did so probably possessed the technical skills themselves. Literacy is attested sporadically among certain types of craftsmen and artisans. There is no solid evidence, in the eleventh and twelfth centuries, for literacy among peasants, whether in the reading, writing or commissioning of texts.

Among the literate, however we choose to circumscribe them, some uses of writing were habitual and routine. The most striking feature of this literacy is its apparent casualness: the materials were cheap and disposable, and the messages they carried were mundane and ephemeral. In business, in negotiations, in disputes, writing was a convenience, a means of simple communication to others or a reminder for oneself; it was not the preserve of a mandarin caste, nor did access to writing necessarily require knowledge of a mandarin language. Though the several styles and levels of writing were in various degrees shaped or affected by written conventions, this was vernacular literacy, and the fact that it was vernacular must have contributed in fair measure to the ease with which it was borne, to the casualness with which it was often treated.

SOURCE: Simon Franklin, "Literacy and Documentation in Early Medieval Russia," *Speculum* 60(1985):1–16 (excerpted). All footnotes and some Russian terms have been omitted, and transliteration modified. Reprinted with the permission of the Medieval Academy of America and the author.

II

The Post-Kievan
Experience

(ca. 1150–1497)

By the middle of the twelfth century, Kievan Rus' had slipped into decline. Internecine war between the princes grew more ferocious, while the attacks of successive
waves of steppe nomads continued to sap the vitality of the Rus' economy. At the
same time and in part in response to these developments, the center of gravity in
Rus' seems to have shifted. In the northwest, Novgorod waxed more powerful than
ever, its economy growing stronger as its trade links expanded. In Northeast Rus',
at the headwaters of the Volga River and its tributaries, Vladimir-Suzdal' grew more
powerful, its princes more ambitious. As Froianov and Dvornichenko observed
above, several times the princes of northeast Rus' brought their armies to Kiev, rout-
ing the defenses and rendering considerable damage to the old capital. Meantime,
more and more Slavs made their way out of southern Rus' into the forest zones
where they hoped to escape the plague of war. In Galicia and Volhynia in the southwest, still other factors combined to alter the politics.

The decline of Kiev saw therefore a devolution of power to these various centers.
To become prince in Kiev late in the twelfth century did not have the same real or
symbolic meaning as it had a century or two earlier. Instead, the distant corners of
Rus' each pursued their own solutions to state-building. In Novgorod, where the
city assembly had always been active, democracy seems to have grown stronger,
leading to a unique combination of authority shared between prince and populace.
In Southwest Rus', too, the prince lost authority, but here it was the boyars—local
nobles and descendants of cadet branches of the Riurikid house—who filled the

vacuum, while in the northeast the princes exercised more and more power independent of any competitors.

The separate destinies of the different parts of the old Kievan Rus' state might
have proceeded at their own pace for some time, but there were other powerful,
remote forces also at work. Most notable among these was the successful expansion
of the Mongol Empire. Having spread across much of China and Central Asia in the
first decades of the thirteenth century, the Tatars, as the Rus' sources called them,
stood poised to invade Rus'. A chance encounter in the 1220s frightened but did not
warn the Rus' princes, who to their misfortune ignored the threat. Beginning in 1237
the Mongols broke through the Upper Volga, surprising the princes of northeast Rus'
by entering from the East and by moving so rapidly westward. Taking refuge in
cities, peasants and prince alike hoped for a miracle. Instead they endured sieges
which the Mongols often ended with brutal efficiency, overrunning the mainly
wooden fortifications.

The coup de grace for Kiev itself came in 1240, by which time the Mongol onslaught
was almost spent. The main centers of the Northeast had already been taken and,
more often than not, leveled. Just as the Mongols reached southwest Rus' and just
before they continued on into Hungary, upheaval within the far-flung Tatar state
halted the advance. But Rus' in its entirety was now within the Mongol realm, paying
tribute to powers whose capital was in distant Karakorum. It was a dark period for
Rus', or so the sources maintain. The destruction of so many towns meant the deci-
mation of market places and the centers of craft and culture. Some artisans found
themselves captive, harnessed for service to the Great Khan, while others fled into
the forest wilderness, hoping thereby to escape the worst. Flight also depressed agriculture, which was deprived of markets and sources of agricultural implements.

The impact of the Mongols, however, was not everywhere the same. Novgorod,
for example, chose wisely to submit without resistance, although their famous prince,
Alexander Nevskii, had to persuade the more stubborn Novgorodians that it was in
their interest to avoid open conflict. The result was that even though considerable
Novgorodian income flowed out of Rus', Novgorod nevertheless was able to maintain its economy. Indeed, in some respects its trade increased, leading to new levels
of prosperity which contrasted sharply with the desolation which greeted visitors to
Kiev, Riazan', and other places where Mongol armies had come.

Somewhat paradoxically, the Orthodox Church, too, benefited from the Mongol
conquest. Although the literature which survives from the pens of churchmen is
almost unanimous in condemning the godless pagans, the Mongols nevertheless
practiced a religious tolerance which not only permitted Orthodoxy to survive, but
which also exempted church properties from taxation. Consequently, even though
many churches and monasteries suffered immensely during the original onslaught,
over the long run the Orthodox Church won special status from its overlords, in the
process becoming a very wealthy and powerful institution. One result was that by
the end of this period Orthodoxy had displaced all other religions in Rus', having

overcome its old adversaries. With this victory, the Christian cross began to appear in villages all across the lands of Rus'.

The Tatar Yoke, as the Rus' chronicles invariably label it, formally lasted into the late fifteenth century. But the demise of Tatar domination was already clear by 1380 when the Moscow Grand Prince Dmitrii did battle with the Tatar armies on a field near the Don River. Thereafter Mongol detachments continued to do damage, although less and less often. The disintegration of the immense empire which Chinggis (Genghis) Khan (d. 1237) and his successors had so rapidly constructed meant a diminished pressure on tributary territories like Rus'.

But the ebb of Tatar power did not destroy the impression among observers of the terrible cost of this episode in the history of the East European Plain. Many centuries after the last Tatar soldier fell on Rus' soil, debate still rages about the actual influence of the conquest on Rus' and its successor states. Many historians today maintain that all of Russia's subsequent destiny was at least partially the result of the Mongol Yoke. They claim that the conquest, by severing Russia from Western Europe and the humanizing elements of the Renaissance while simultaneously bringing Muscovy into a realm of brutality, smoothed the way for autocracy and enserfment. By this interpretation, the Mongols brought nothing of use to Rus', and left behind no cultural contribution.

Certainly to some extent the Mongol invasions did separate Rus' from its neighbors further west. But that circumstance need not be seen as negative. One group of historians early in the twentieth century saw in the fusion of Asian and European cultures the source of a unique and powerful synthesis which had generated much energy and innovation in Muscovite culture. A more recent evaluation of the Mongol Yoke has gone further, arguing that the sources on which historians have traditionally depended to appraise the effects of the invaders are themselves intentionally biased, denying the inevitable fruits of frontier symbiosis and cultural interaction. The invective of churchmen must be suspect, given the obvious flowering of church institutions in precisely this period, but what exact impact the Mongol conquest had on Rus' remains an issue of contention.

Even the harshest appraisals of the Mongol Yoke admit that sometime in the fourteenth century, while the burden of taxation and political interference in the Rus' lands was still great, a cultural revival was underway. In the person of Andrei Rublev and his contemporaries, painting reached a new pinnacle and distinguished itself fundamentally from the painting of an earlier time. Likewise, letters also revived; the tradition of local chronicles, interrupted at the time of the invasion, experienced a renewal, and soon other entirely new forms of literature appeared, leading to a considerable flowering by the fifteenth century. If the weight of Mongol dominion was so heavy, how can this cultural revival be explained?

The economy of Rus' likewise experienced a gradual recovery. There can be no doubt that the first consequences of the invasion were disastrous, and required some time to overcome. Particularly in northeast Rus' the recovery was slow in coming.

Agriculture seems to have stagnated at a low level, the product of environment and technology as much as anything else. But Novgorod seems not to have suffered much at all, so that if one looks at the Novgorod Judicial Charter, one is aware of a vital economy where trade, commercial credit, and agriculture all thrived. In fact, as we know from many sources, Novgorod's international trade reached new highs in the fourteenth and early fifteenth century before other, more distant influences brought this expansion back to earth.

Perhaps the most important development in these several centuries was the emergence of Moscow as the new power center in Rus'. Kiev had long ago ceded its place of primacy, and in any case fell to Lithuanian armies just as Moscow's power waxed. Novgorod might well have laid claim to the mantle of leadership, rich as it was. But, as already mentioned, Novgorod's economic well-being collapsed at just the moment when the Moscow princes exercised their ambitions. Furthermore, the Novgorodian political system proved to be more fractious than it might seem from first glance, so that when Novgorod came into direct conflict with Moscow it could not summon unified support for its potentially costly struggle. And in any case, regardless of the problems elsewhere, the Moscow princes certainly must be credited with a visionary—if diabolical—policy of expansion.

By the late fifteenth century, the devolutionary trend observable late in the twelfth century had abated and been reversed. In annexing Novgorod, Tver', Viatka, Pskov and other principalities, Moscow brought within its ambit much of the territory of Kievan Rus'. Moscow accomplished this goal with the firm assistance of the Orthodox Church, whose chief official, the Metropolitan, since the early fourteenth century had cast his lot with Moscow. Sanctioning Muscovite expansionism with divine blessings, the Orthodox Church equipped the Moscow princes with an ideology which also affected the kind of state structure with which they proposed to administer their earthly kingdom.

What happened to ordinary men and women in these momentous years is less easy to make out. It is clear that large numbers of them perished during the conquest, and that the survivors probably suffered a declining standard of living, especially those who tried to till the land in the forests of Northeast Rus'. Their lot began a steep descent in these years, first signaled in the mid-fifteenth century on the heels of a disastrous civil war by temporary limitations on their right to move from lands claimed by secular or clerical landlords. But of the details of their well-being we remain largely uninformed. We know that some of these men and women brought music, stories, and entertainment to remote villages where churchmen could not evict them. And we have discovered some signs of the implements they employed to work the land and clothe their bodies. But little else survives to depict the lives of those unremarked upon by the historical record.

6

State-Building in Post-Kievan Rus'

The fall of Kievan Rus' led to further decentralization, each of the principalities following its own course. From time to time, princes might coordinate their activities, especially their military campaigns, but overall the different principalities developed distinctive characteristics. Northwest Rus', with its economic and political center in Novgorod, seems to have followed the most radical course. In 1136 the Novgorodians overthrew their prince, and established a system which required a new prince to agree to limitations on the exercise of his power. The mayor, archbishop, and other officials who governed the city and its far-flung territories were all subject to election by the city assembly. As Soviet historians have been especially keen to demonstrate over the years, the exercise of this franchise was hardly free from manipulation and domination by elite groups within the city. Still, princely power declined here, as the surviving contracts which Novgorod negotiated with its princes demonstrate.

Elsewhere, princely authority met a different fate. In the southwest as in the northwest, the princes also lost ground, but here elites interfered more openly, ignoring the masses altogether in order to dethrone and install their favorites. In the northeast, in the lands around Vladimir and Suzdal', whose princes helped apply the final humiliation to Kiev, princely power seems to have suffered no restriction whatever. Especially from the fourteenth century, the Moscow princes gained the upper hand over their rivals, and brought to their administration a patrimonial conception of their principality. Or at least so it seems from the surviving sources. When, for example, the Moscow Grand Prince Ivan III finally extinguished Novgorod's independence and carted off the bell which had for centuries summoned Novgorodians to assembly, he was, he said, merely reclaiming his patrimony. We shall have occasion below to reconsider this idea, but most historians of Russia today still maintain that this picture of state-building in Moscow is essentially accurate. The Moscow princes viewed their principality as so much personal property, and in that conception one may find the explanation for the absence of any institutions to check the exercise of absolute power.

One vastly complicating factor in considering the form of the state in these centuries was the arrival of the Mongols toward the middle of the thirteenth century. For centuries, critics of Russian state administration have attributed to the Mongols many ills, chief among them the brutality and absolutism which seemed to emerge in Moscow on the heels of the "Mongol Yoke." The earliest chronicles helped chart the way for this interpretation, blaming the Mongols for almost all deficiencies in Rus' culture and society in the two centuries or so when the Mongols maintained formal control of the Rus' lands. But the surviving evidence indicates that far from everyone suffered at the hands of the conquerors. The Orthodox Church most of all seems to have benefited handsomely from special exemptions which it won from its overlords. Without discounting any of the physical consequences of the invasion itself, it might also be argued that other institutions benefited from the Mongol dominion. Some modern commentators like Charles Halperin urge a reappraisal of the Mongol invasions, discounting the reluctance of witnesses to acknowledge the positive contributions of Mongol politics and culture. Undoubtedly citizens of Rus' found it difficult to acknowledge the benefits which Mongol rule had brought them, but before one revises the usual interpretation, it will be necessary to balance the known losses with evidence of specific Mongol contributions to Rus' government and culture.

DOCUMENTS

Northwest Rus':
The First Treaty of Novgorod
with Tver' Grand Prince Iaroslav
Iaroslavich [ca. 1264–65]

In the centuries that followed the decline of Kiev, Novogorod grew richer and more powerful, even as southern Rus' reeled from the internecine and Mongol wars and while northeastern Rus' remained as yet insignificant. Partly as a result of this circumstance, Novgorod in these years developed a very powerful set of civic institutions which succeeded in imposing upon the prince of Novgorod certain restrictions. To some historians, this development marked Novgorod out as a "merchant republic" whose political institutions better matched the aspirations of its citizens than did the more absolutist forms of government which emerged later in Moscow. One early piece of evidence of that republican sentiment is the series of treaties negotiated between Novgorod and its princes. The selection which follows is typical of the genre which only grew more exact and demanding until the late fifteenth century when Novgorod lost its independence to the Moscow Grand Prince.

———————

Blessings from the Archbishop [of Novgorod], and greetings from the [Novgorod] mayor Mikhail, and from the millenarius Kondrat, and from all the [Novgorod] hundred-men, and from the elders, and from all Novgorod to Prince Iaroslav.

1. To that which your father Iaroslav kissed the cross [i.e., swore], you too are to kiss the cross.

2. Hold Novgorod according to custom, as your father held it.

3. You, prince, are not to violate the treaties [negotiated between Novgorod and its princes].

4. And you are not to deprive a man of his land without [just] cause.

5. And without the mayor you, prince, are not to give out any lands, nor issue any documents [concerning land transactions].

6. And you, prince, are not to hold the Novgorod lands by your men, but hold them with Novgorod men. And take a gift from those lands [to do with as you please].

7. And these are the Novgorod lands [in which you are not to interfere]: Volok with all its districts, and you are to keep an overseer on one half, and a Novgorodian on one half of all the Volok lands. And in Torzhok, prince, you are to keep an overseer on your own part, and a Novgorodian on its [Novgorod's] own part.

8. And Gorodets', prince, [Prince] Dmitrii gave together with Novgorodians to Ivanko, and you, prince, are not to take it back.

9. And these are [also] Novgorod lands: Bezhiche [Bezhetsk], Gorodets, M[ele]chia, Shipino, Egna, Vologda, Zavolots'e [the district beyond Volok], Koloperem, Tre, Perem' [Perm'], Iugra, Pechera. And you are to rule those districts with Novgorodian men; and take a gift from those [lands].

10. And you may kill wild boars no closer than 60 versts [39.6 miles] from the city.

11. And indentured servants, prince, you are not to accept [into your household], nor

[ought] your princess or your boyars [accept indentured servants].

12. Neither you, nor your princess, nor your boyars, nor your servitors are to hold any villages throughout the Novgorod lands; nor are you to establish any [new] settlements throughout the Novgorod lands.

13. And you are not to rule Novgorod from the Suzdal' land, nor give out any lands.

14. And you, prince, may travel to Ozvad in summer to go hunting. But to Rusa you are not to go; you may go [hunting] in Rusa [only] every third winter.

15. And to Ladoga, prince, you may go [hunting] every third summer.

16. And your sturgeon master is to travel in Ladoga according [to the regulations of] the treaty of your father.

17. And your judges are to travel throughout the [Novgorod] lands in summer, beginning on St. Peter's Day [29 June].

18. And those fields which your brother took from Novgorod, you, prince, are to release [back to Novgorod]; what was property of Novgorodians [belongs] to Novgorodians, and what belonged to the prince, then that is the prince's [property].

19. And you, prince, are not entitled to remove [anyone from Novgorodian land to your own estates] in all the Novgorod lands.

20. And your servitors, prince, are to travel [through the Novgorod lands collecting the prince's income] as of old, as happened from the very first.

21. And from a Novgorodian and from a Novotorzhok citizen for the customs tax take two vekshas from [each] cart and from [each] box of hops.

22. And do not send your man beyond Volok, [but rather] send a Novgorodian [on any such mission].

23. Kiss the cross to everything [specified above] in love, without any dissimulation, in justice, in the presence of our emissaries.

SOURCE: *The Laws of Rus' (Tenth to Fifteenth Centuries)*. Translated and edited by Daniel H. Kaiser (Salt Lake City: Charles Schlacks, Jr., forthcoming), pp. 67–8. English translation copyright © 1992 Daniel H. Kaiser.

Southwest Rus':
Extracts from the Galician-Volhynian Chronicle (1240–41)

In Southwest Rus'—present-day Western Ukraine—a different form of government developed in these centuries. Here princely power was also weak, as in Novgorod, but in Southwest Rus' it was the local elites—the boyars—who jockeyed for control of the state, in the process greatly diminishing state authority for their own purposes. The Galycian-Volhynian Chronicle here provides some examples of state authority in Southwest Rus' in the thirteenth century.

―――――――

(1230). A great conspiracy was forming among the godless Galician boyars: With Danilo's nephew [Prince] Oleksander [of Belz, d. ca. 1234] they plotted to kill [Prince] Danilo [d. 1264] and to deliver his land [to the Hungarians]. As [Danilo and Prince Vasilko (d. 1269)] sat in council, [the boyars] wanted to set fire [to the building], but the [all-]merciful Lord implanted in Vasilko's mind the idea to leave [the council]. And he unsheathed his sword and fenced with a subject of the king, while someone else took [down] a shield and feigned battle. When the unfaithful Molibogovich boyars saw this, they were seized by the fear of the Lord. With the words, "Our plot has been crushed" on their lips, they fled like the accursed [Prince] Sviatopolk. They fled, and the princes Danilo and Vasilko still knew nothing [of the intended plot]. Vasilko rode off to Voldimer' and the godless [boyar] Filip summoned Danilo to [his castle] Vishnia, for it was there that the other boyars plotted to murder him with the aid of his nephew Oleksander. When Danilo reached the fields of Branichev, a courier from his [millenarius] Demian came to him with the message: "An evil feast has been prepared for you, for your godless boyar Filip has conspired with your nephew Oleksander to murder you [at Vishnia]. Now that you have heard this, go back and continue to hold the throne of your father.'' When Kosniatin finished, Danilo turned back from the middle of the Dniester [River]. The godless boyars crossed the river at another place, for they did not wish to face him. Upon his return to Halych, Danilo sent a courier to his brother Prince Vasilko instructing him to march [immediately] against Oleksander. Oleksander, however, fled to his co-conspirators in Peremyshl'. Vasilko occupied Belz. He sent his royal groom Ivan to fetch the faithless Molibogovich boyars [from their estates] along the Voldrisa. Ivan Mikhailovich captured 28 of them, but they were spared and not put to death. Once when Danilo was making merry at a feast, one of these godless boyars threw the contents of his goblet in Danilo's face. But Danilo bore the insult, hoping that God would repay them some day.

(1231) Danilo himself called his eighteen faithful retainers and his [millenarius] Demian to council and said to them: "Will you remain true to me that I may set out against my enemies?'' But they cried out: "We remain true to God and to you our master. Go with God's help.'' And [the boyar] Mikula Sotskii [added]: "Master, you cannot eat honey without first killing the bees.'' After praying to God, the Blessed Virgin, and the Lord's Archangel Michael, Danilo hurriedly went forth accompanied by [very] few soldiers. But [the boyar] Miroslav came to his aid with a small retinue. And then all the traitors also flocked to Danilo's side, pretending to be loyal to him, and held council with [Danilo's forces], for bad times had come upon them. Danilo came to Peremyshl but Oleksander fled, not being able to oppose him. In the [ensuing] chase [the boyar] Shelv was mortally wounded. He was a brave man and was buried with great honors. The traitor Volodislav Iur'evich [another boyar], who conspired with them, pursued [Oleksander] to the Sanok [river] and the Hungarian Gates. [But] Oleksander escaped leaving all his property [behind]. And thus he arrived in Hungary and went to Sudislav, [who] was at that time in Hungary. Sud-

islav went to King Andrei and persuaded the Hungarian king [to march against Danilo] and King Andrei advanced (1232) upon Iaroslavl' in the company of his son Bela and his other son Andrei. The boyar David Vyshatich and [the voevoda or commander] Vasilko Gavrilovich barricaded themselves in Iaroslavl', [defending it] in Danilo's name. The Hungarians fought until sunset but the city repulsed them. In the evening [the besieged] held a council [during which] David became frightened because his mother-in-law, the wife of the steward Nezdilo, whom he addressed as mother, was faithful to Sudislav and told him that he would not be able to hold the city. But Vasilko [exhorted] him: "Let us not disgrace our prince. [Their] army cannot take this city,'' for he was a strong and brave man. David, however, would not heed him and was bent on giving up the city. Then Chak came from the Hungarian regiments and reported that they could not defeat them, for they had been badly beaten. Yet despite Vasilko's heated insistence not to surrender the city, David delivered it to [the Hungarians], for fear had paralyzed his heart. He walked out unharmed with all his troops, and the king occupied Iaroslavl', [from which] he then advanced upon Halych. But [the boyar] Klimiata of Golye Gory fled from Prince Danilo to the king, and following his example all the Galician boyars surrendered. . . .

(1241) The Galician boyars called Danilo their prince but ruled the whole country themselves: [the boyar] Dobroslav Sud'ich, a priest's grandson, had occupied the prince's throne and plundered the whole land. [Then] he went to [the town of] Bakota and took all of Poniz'e without the prince's permission, while [the boyar] Grigorii Vasil'evich planned to appropriate the hilly region of Peremyshl'. And because of them there was great unrest and [much] looting in the land. When Danilo learned of this, he sent his *stolnik*, Iakov, to Dobroslav and [the other boyars] complaining bitterly to them: "I am your prince and yet you do not obey my orders. You are ruining the land: I gave no orders to you, Dobroslav, to accommodate the boyars of Chernigov. [I ordered you] to distribute the land to the Galician [boyars] and to give me the salt from Kolomia." And [Dobroslav] replied: "So be it!" During the time that Iakov was with [Dobroslav], Lazor Domazhirets' and Ivor Moliboshits, two lawbreakers who were serfs by birth, [came and] bowed to the very ground to [Dobroslav]. Iakov was surprised and asked for the reason why they had bowed to him. And Dobroslav answered: "I gave them Kolomia." But Iakov said to him: "How could you give it to them without the prince's permission? Great princes have been holding this [town of] Kolomia so that they could pay their soldiers [with the profits from the sale of its salt], and these [men] aren't even worthy of holding Votnino." But he [only] smirked [and] said: "And what can I say [to that]?" When Iakov returned, he related all of this to Danilo. Danilo was greatly saddened and prayed to God for his native land, which was held by these godless [boyars] and ruled by them.

SOURCE: *The Galician-Volynian Chronicle.* Translated by George A. Perfecky (Munich: Wilhelm Fink Verlag, 1973), pp. 38–9, 50 (excerpted). Copyright © 1973 Wilhelm Fink Verlag, München, Germany. Reprinted by permission of the publisher.

Northeast Rus': The Second Testament of Moscow Grand Prince Dmitrii Donskoi (1389)

Dmitrii Donskoi, whose last will and testament appears below, was one of the heroes of early Muscovite history. He came to the throne in 1359 as a mere boy, and only the determined efforts of his guardian, the Metropolitan Aleksei (1354–78), protected him in his youth. But he grew into an able and wily prince. The most famous moment of his reign occurred in 1380, when the Prince headed a Muscovite force at Kulikovo Field near the River Don (from which Dmitrii acquired his nickname, Donskoi), fighting the Mongols to a draw, thereby promising the eventual overthrow of the hated conquerors. His reign also witnessed the continual expansion of Muscovite territory, some estimate of the size of which can be gained from the testament which follows here. One aspect of the testament which has drawn the attention of historians is the way that the Grand Prince conceived of his state. If in Novgorod some form of republic developed, then in Northeast Rus' the princes seem to have viewed their principality primarily as their patrimony, their heritable property, a development which, according to some historians, determined the whole future course of governmental structure in Russia. Dmitrii's testament, like that of Grand Prince Iaroslav introduced above, distributed his holdings among all his sons. This practice—partible inheritance—was common among the Slavs, but on the face of it threatened the integrity of the testator's property. If every generation shared the inheritance, soon no heir would receive much property. Although Dmitrii evidently tried to bequeath a larger share to his eldest son, the practice of partible inheritance promised future difficulties which materialized in civil war early in the fifteenth century. Finally, readers should note the legacy awarded the Grand Prince's widow as a means to appreciate the role of gender in Moscow.

———

In the name of the Father, and of the Son, and of the Holy Ghost, lo I, the sinful poor slave of God, Dmitrii Ivanovich, write [this] testament, being of sound mind. I give [this] arrangement to my sons and to my princess.

I commit my children to my princess. And you, my children, live as one and heed your mother in all things.

And I bequeath my patrimony, Moscow, to my children, to Prince Vasilii, to Prince Iurii, to Prince Andrei, [and] to Prince Petr. And my brother, Prince Vladimir, shall manage his third with which his father, Prince Andrei, blessed him. And my son, Prince Vasilii, I bless with the larger revenue in the city and in the [districts] of my patrimonial principality, [namely] with one half of [my] two shares, and [I bless] my three [other] sons [with] one half, and of the city customs, one half. And of my two shares of the [customs duty], my princess [shall receive] one half and my sons one half. And my princess [shall receive] my two shares of the [customs duty on measured goods]. And in addition to the larger revenue, my son, Prince Vasilii, [shall receive] Vasiltsevo hundred, and the Dobriatin'skoe apiary with the village Dobriatin'skoe. And the beekeepers in the city districts, and the horse [revenue district], and the falconers, and the huntsmen: these my sons shall share equally. And of the enrolled people of my two shares, my sons [shall receive] each a part and shall care for them as one man.

And lo, I give to my son, Prince Vasilii, Kolomna with all its [rural districts] and with its [customs duty], and with its [transit fee], and with its apiary, and with its villages, and with all its customs. . . . The Moscow villages, I give to my son, Prince Vasilii: Mitin [clearing], Malakhov''skoe, Kostiantinov''skoe, the hamlets Zhyroshkiny, Ostrov''skoe, Orinin'skoe, Kopoten'skoe, Khvostov''skoe, [and] Velikii Meadow near the city, beyond the river. And from among the Iur'ev villages I give to my son, Prince Vasilii, my purchase the village Krasnoe, with Elezarov''skoe Provatovo, and the village Vasilev''skoe in Rostov.

And lo, I give to my son, Prince Iurii, Zvenigorod with all its [rural districts], and with its [customs duty], and with its [transit fee], and with its apiary, and with its villages, and with all its customs. . . . And from among the Moscow villages I give to my son, Prince Iurii, the village Mikhalev''skoe and Domantov''skoe, and Khodyn'skii Meadow. And from among the Iur'ev villages to him [shall pass]: my purchase, the village Kuzmydem''ian'skoe, and the [clearing] of the village Krasnoe beyond the Vezka [River], I have given to Kuzmydem''ian'skoe, and the village Bogorodits'skoe in Rostov.

And lo, I give to my son, Prince Andrei, Mozhaisk with all its [rural districts], and with its [customs duty], and with its [transit fee], and with its apiary, and with its villages, and with all its customs, and with its outlying [rural districts] . . . And from among the Moscow villages [I leave] to him: the village Naprud'skoe, and Lutsin'skoe on the Yauza [River], with the mill, Deunin'skoe, Khvostov'skoe in Peremyshl', and Borov''skii Meadow and another opposite [the Monastery of] the Resurrection. And from among the Iur'ev villages [I give] to him the village of Oleksin'skoe on the Peksha [River].

And lo, I give to my son Prince Petr, Dmitrov with all its [rural districts], and with its villages, and with all its customs, and with its [customs duty], and with its [transit fee], and with its apiary. . . . And from among the Moscow [rural districts] [I give] to Prince Petr: Mushkova Gora, Izhvo, Ramenka, [the settlement] Kniazha Ivanova, Vori, Korzenevo, Rogozh, Zagar'e, Vokhna, Selna, Gusletsa, and the burg Sherna. And from among the Moscow villages [I give] to Prince Petr: the village Novoe, [and] Sulishin [churchyard]. And from among the Iur'ev villages [I give] to him my purchase the village Bogoroditskoe on the Bogon [River].

And lo, I give to my son, Prince Ivan: Rameneitse, with its beekeepers and with that which appertained to it, and the village Zverkov''skoe with the [clearing] Sokhon'skii, which has been given up by Prince Vladimir. And Sokhna also [shall pass] to my son, Prince Ivan. And in this [his] patrimonial principality, my son, Prince Ivan, is free; he may give it to whichsoever brother is kind to him.

And lo, I bless my son, Prince Vasilii, with my patrimony, the Grand Princedom.

And my son, Prince Iurii, I bless with my grandfather's purchase, Galich with all its [rural districts], and with its villages, and with all its customs, and with those villages which appertained to Kostroma, Mikul'skoe and Borisov''skoe.

And I bless my son, Prince Andrei, with yet [another] purchase of my grandfather, Beloozero with all its [rural districts], and Vol's-koe with Shagot', and Miloliub''skii Weir, and with the [settlements] that were my children's.

And my son, Prince Peter, I bless with yet [another] purchase of my grandfather, Ugleche Plain and that which appertained to it, and with Toshna and with Siama.

And lo, I give to my princess, from the Grand Principality of my son, Prince Vasilii: Iulka in Pereiaslavl', and Iledam, with Komela in Kostroma, and [from that] which belongs to Prince Iurii in Galich, Sol', and [from that which] belongs to Prince Andrei in Beloozero, Vol'skoe with Shagot', and Miloliub'skii Weir. And from among the Volodimer villages, [I give] to my princess the village On'dreev'skoe, and from among the Pereiaslav villages, the village Dobroe, and that which appertained to them. And from my son's, Prince Vasilii's, patrimonial principality [I give to my princess]: Kanev, Pesochna, and from among the villages, the village Malin'skoe, [and] Lystsevo. And from Prince Iurii's patrimonial principality, [I give to my princess]: Iur'eva [settlement], Sukhodol, with Iet'ia, with Isterva, and with the village On'dreev'skoe, and Kamen'skoe. And from Prince Andrei's patrimonial principality, [I give to my princess]: Vereia, and Chislov, and the village Lutsin'skoe on the Yauza [River], with the mill. And from Prince Petr's patrimonial principality, [I give to my princess]: Izhvo and Siama. And concerning that which I have given to my princess from the patrimonial principality of my son, Prince Vasilii, and from Prince Iurii's, and from Prince Andrei's, and from Prince Petr's [rural districts] and villages, now should God decide something concerning my princess [i.e., should she die], then those [rural districts] and villages in whose patrimonial principality they are, then to him shall they belong.

And lo, I give to my princess: my acquisition Skirmenov''skaia [settlement] with Shepkovo, Smolianye with the [clearing] Mitiaev''skii, and with the apiary, and with the Vyshegorod beekeepers, Kropivna with the Kropivna beekeepers, [and with the Ismeia (beekeepers)], and with the Gordoshevichi [beekeepers], and with the Rud' [beekeepers], Zheleskova [settlement] with its apiary, with Ivan Khorobryi's village, Iskon'skaia [settlement], Kuzov''skaia [settlement], and that which my princess pur-

chased, and that which has appertained to her, this belongs to my princess. And in those places in which [settlement] administrators administered a [settlement] under me, the rural district administrators of my princess shall administer justice in those same places, as it was under me. And concerning the purchase of my princess, Lokhno, now it is hers. And in Kolomna, my acquisition, the [clearing] Samoiletsev with its hamlets, the [clearing] Savel'ev''skii, the village Mikul'skoe, Babyshevo, [and] Oslebiatev''skoe: now these belong to my princess. And concerning her village Repen'skoe and [her] purchase, now these also are hers. . . . And concerning that which Princess Fedosiia gave me, Suda in Beloozero, and Kolashna, and Slobodka, and concerning that with which she blessed my princess, Gorodok and Volochok: Princess Fedosiia shall manage these places during her lifetime, and upon her death [they shall pass] to my princess. And I bless my princess with all these my acquisitions, and in these acquisitions my princess is free: she may give them to one of her sons or she may give them for the memory of her soul. And my children shall not interfere in this. . . .

And if, because of my sins, God takes away one of my sons, then my princess shall divide his patrimonial principality among my sons. That which she gives to one is his, and my children shall not evade her will.

And if God gives me [another] son, then my princess shall also give a share to him, taking portions from each of his older brothers.

And if the patrimony of one of my sons, with which I have blessed him, should be diminished, my princess shall also give a share [to him] from the patrimonial principalities of my [other] sons. And you, my children, obey your mother.

And if, because of my sins, God takes away my son, Prince Vasilii, then the patrimonial principality of Prince Vasilii [shall pass] to my son who follows him, and the patrimonial principality of the latter shall be divided among the others by my princess. And you, my children, obey your mother: that which she gives to one, now that is his. . . .

And if God brings about a change regarding the Horde [i.e., the Golden Horde, the Mongols] [and] my children do not have to give Tartar tribute to the Horde, then the tribute that each of my sons collects in his patrimonial principality shall be his. And concerning that which I have given to my princess—[rural districts] and villages from the patrimonial principalities of my children, and my acquisitions, and [settlements], and villages, and Kholkhol, and Zaiachkov—now that which my princess collects from these [rural districts], [settlements], and villages shall be hers. And my children shall not interfere in this. . . .

And lo, I bless my children. To my oldest son, Prince Vasilii, [I bequeath] the icon [which is] the work of Paramsha, the golden chain which Princess Vasilisa gave me, the great golden belt with precious stones without a strap, the golden belt with a strap [which is] the work of Makar, the shoulder pieces of the grand prince, [and] the Golden Cap.

And to my son, Prince Iurii, [I bequeath] the new golden belt with precious stones [and] pearls [and] without a strap, the golden belt [which is] the work of Shishka, [and] the outer garment embroidered with pearls and precious stones.

And to my son, Prince Andrei, [I bequeath] the suit of golden armor [and] the old golden belt from Novgorod.

And to my son, Prince Petr, [I bequeath] the golden belt decorated in black [and] with precious stones, the golden belt with the moneybag and with ornaments, and [I bequeath him] the shoulder straps and a breastplate.

And to my son, Prince Ivan, [I bequeath] the leather belt with golden studs and two golden bowls, each [weighing] two *grivenka*.

And the gold or silver or other things which remain, no matter what they are, all [shall pass] to my princess.

And concerning my herds that remain, these my princess shall divide with my children, each [receiving] a share.

And any of my treasurers, or any of my secretaries who have managed my income for me, . . . or my [stewards], or anyone who has married these people, none of these are of any concern of my princess or of my children.

And I have committed my children to my princess. And you, my children, heed your mother in all things, and do not go against her will in anything. And if any of my sons does not heed his mother and goes against her will, my blessing shall not be upon him.

And my younger children, brothers of Prince Vasilii, honor and obey your older brother, Prince Vasilii, in the place of me, your father. And my son, Prince Vasilii, shall hold his brother, Prince Iurii, and his younger brothers in brotherliness and without injustice.

And those of my boyars who serve my princess, those boyars, my children, care for as one man.

And may God judge him who violates this testament, and neither God's favor nor my blessing shall be upon him in this life or in the next.

And I have written this testament in the presence of my fathers, in the presence of Abbot Sergii and Abbot Sevastian.

And present [at the writing of this testament] were our boyars Dmitrii Mikhailovich, Timofei Vasil'evich, Ivan Rodivonovich, Semen Vasil'evich, Ivan Fedorovich, Aleksandr Andreevich, Fedor Andreevich, Fedor Andreevich, Ivan Fedorovich, [and] Ivan Andreevich.

And Vnuk wrote [this document].

SOURCE: *The Testaments of the Grand Princes of Moscow.* Translated and edited by Robert Craig Howes (Ithaca: Cornell University Press, 1967), pp. 208–17 (excerpted). Transliteration has been modified, and some words untranslated in the text have been translated by the Editors of this volume. Copyright © 1967 Cornell University. Used by permission of the publisher, Cornell University Press.

The Annexation of Novgorod According to the Moscow Nikonian Chronicle (1471–78)

Few events illustrate better the patrimonial concept of the state than the Muscovite annexation of Novgorod in the 1470s. Part of the fascination in the act is the fact that, at least according to this narrative, the dispute between Novgorod and Moscow Grand Prince Ivan III arose over precisely the question of whether Novgorod was or was not part of Ivan's patrimony. Of course, Novgorod had long imposed upon its princes limitations never experienced by Moscow princes, so that the changes implicit in being recognized as Muscovite patrimony were clear to all. Still, Ivan III won out, mainly due to divine intervention, according to the Moscow chronicler, whose narrative appears below. Emphasizing the threat to Orthodoxy which Novgorod's "treason" represented, the chronicler pictures the Moscow Grand Prince as God's special agent on earth, obliged to protect the only true faith. Moreover, the chronicler imagines that God has sanctioned for Novgorod (and all Muscovy) a particular form of government destined to silence forever the bell which formerly had summoned Novgorodians to assembly where they might decide matters of state.

[1471]. . . . After the death of this perspicacious and most holy bishop Jonas, the people of Novgorod as of old, as was their custom, met in *veche* [city assembly] to select a candidate from among the priest monks to be archbishop. And having selected three of them, they cast lots, and the lot fell to a certain priest-monk by the name of Theophilus, and he was enthroned in the Archbishop's palace. And they sent their envoy, Nikita Larionov, to petition Grand Prince Ivan Vasilievich for safe conduct and that he should kindly request the nominated monk Theophilus to come to Moscow, be consecrated there by his [spiritual father], Metropolitan Philip, to the archbishopric of Great Novgorod and of Pskov, as it used to be in the time of the previous grand princes. The Grand Prince, receiving the petition, did not make any obstacle, treated them honorably and sent them back, agreeing with everything which they had petitioned him for on behalf of all Novgorod; and his answer was the following:

"My patrimony, Great Novgorod, sent you to me to inform me that . . . they have elected

the priest-monk Theophilus, according to the old [way] by casting lots; and you petition that I, Grand Prince, honor this nominated Theophilus and request him to come to me to Moscow and to my spiritual father, Metropolitan Philip, so as to be consecrated to the archbishopric of Novgorod and Pskov without hindrance. And that I do it according to the old tradition as it used to be under my father, Grand Prince Vasilii, and under my grandfather and my great grandfather, and all the grand princes who were before, since we are of the same stock of Vladimir, Great Novgorod and all Russia."

When their envoy, Nikita Larionov, came to them to Novgorod and told them the decision of the Grand Prince, many of the best people who were there, the posadniks [mayors], tysiatskiis [millenariuses], and commoners, as well as their nominated [Archbishop] Theophilus, were very happy about it. Some of them, however, some children of the late posadnik Isaak Boretskii with their mother, Marfa, and with other traitors who were instructed by the devil—because worse than devils were those who tempted the destruction of their land and their own ruin—started shouting during the *veche*, speaking senseless and depraved things: "We do not want to be called his patrimony. We are free people of Great Novgorod and the Grand Prince of Muscovy has caused us many offenses and has perpetrated many injustices; but we will be with Kasimir, King of Poland and Grand Prince of Lithuania."

And so the entire city became restless and they behaved as if drunk. Some wanted the Grand Prince according to the old [ways] and to be with Moscow. Others were for the King and Lithuania.

Thereafter the traitors began to hire poor commoners, members of the *veche*, who were always, according to habit, ready to do that for which they are [paid]; and, coming to the *veche*, they started ringing bells and shouting, "We want to be under the King!" The others answered them, "We want to be under the Grand Prince of Muscovy according to the old [way], as it used to be before!" The hirelings of these traitors started throwing stones at those who were for the Grand Prince and there was such a disturbance among them that they started fighting among themselves, rising up against each other. . . .

Grand Prince Ivan Vasilievich, hearing this—that in his patrimony in Great Novgorod there was a great mutiny—sent them his envoys, saying the following:

"People of Novgorod, your land is my patrimony, and so it was beginning with our grandfathers and forefathers, since the time of Grand Prince Vladimir, who Christianized the Russian land, who was the great-grandson of Rurik, the first grand prince in your land. And from this Rurik up to the present day you have known only one dynasty of grand princes, from the Kievan princes to Grand Prince Dmitrii Iurievich, who was also called [Grand Prince] Vsevolod of [the city of] Vladimir. And from the Grand Prince up to me it was the same lineage. We rule you and we bestow honor on you, and we defend you from everyone and we are free to chastise, in the case you begin to regard us differently than as of old. You have never been under any king [of Poland] or under any grand prince of Lithuania, and it was this way since our land came into being. And now you break away from Christianity and go to the Latins, despite your pledge on the cross. And I, the Grand Prince, apply no force upon you and I do not tax you higher than was done under my father, Grand Prince Vasilii Vasilievich, or under my grandfather or my great-grandfather, or under other grand princes of our lineage. And I intend in future to bestow my good will upon you because you are my patrimony."

Hearing this, the people of Novgorod, their boyars and posadniks, their tysiatskiis and burghers who did not want to break the tradition or their pledge on the cross, were happy about this and wanted to be ruled by the Grand Prince as of old.

His Holiness Philip, Metropolitan of all Russia, sent to them, the people of Novgorod the Great, not one but several admonitions according to holy writ in which he said, "I hear, my sons, that some among you are supporting grave agitation and disorder in your land be-cause they are willing to start a great rebellion and a great schism in the holy church of God, breaking away from Orthodoxy and from the ancient dominion, and want to join the Latins . . . you sons, you must submit to a strong hand of the law-abiding and pious sovereign Grand Prince Ivan Vasilievich of all Russia because you are submitted to him by God. . . ."

But these aforementioned children of Isaak [Boretskii] and their mother, Marfa, with their supporters and their hirelings, became like mad people, like beasts which have no human mind. They did not want to heed the words of the Grand Prince's envoys or of Metropolitan Philip's envoy. . . .

The Grand Prince, hearing this, was very aggrieved, grew sad and thought, . . . "I know not what to do, and I will lay all my hope only on Lord God." He contemplated at length and then announced to his [spiritual] father, Metropolitan Philip, and to his mother, Grand Princess Maria, and to the boyars who were with him, that he wanted to go against Novgorod with an army. Hearing him, they advised him to carry out his thought about the Novgorodians and to rely upon God, in view of the latters' disobedience and betrayal. Thereupon the Grand Prince sent for all his brothers, for all the bishops of his land, for the voevodas [commanders] and all his warriors. . . .

They pondered this at length and finally decided to rely upon Lord God, His Purest Mother, on the power of the honorable and life-giving cross on which the Novgorodians had pledged [their loyalty] before their betrayal. The Grand Prince received a blessing from Metropolitan Philip and from all the bishops of his land, and from the entire Holy Council, and began to arm his forces in order to campaign against them. And thus did his brothers and all the princes, boyars and voevodas, and all his warriors. . . . And so pious Grand Prince Ivan [started campaigning] against those apostates. . . . And they came to a place called Korostin on the shore of Lake Ilmen'.

And there, unexpectedly, a Novgorodian army in boats came against them. Usually in summer the lakes and marshes of the Novgorodian land are greatly flooded, and therefore in summertime horse troops would never have been sent thither by any earlier grand princes. Therefore, living in the fall, winter, and spring obediently, the cunning [Novgorodians] would fearlessly commence their troublemaking in the summer because their land would be protected then by the floods. This time, however, by God's will and for their chastisement and amendment, their land was quite dry since not a drop of rain had come from the sky onto their land over the entire summer, from the month of May till the month of September. And because of the sun's heat, all their land and all their marshes dried out. Such was the grace which was given from above by the Lord to his pious servant, Grand Prince Ivan Vasilievich of all Russia, so that he could subdue his enemies by his strong hand. From all sides and from everywhere his armed forces were advancing through the Novgorodian land without hindrance and could fight unimpeded, chasing cattle everywhere where usually were impassable places and marshes. But this time they were dry.

They [the Novgorodians] left their boats and stealthily approached the [Grand Prince's] camps but the latter became alarmed in time because the sentries of the Grand Prince's voevoda, noticing them, warned their voevodas. The latter took up arms straightaway and went against them, and many Novgorodians were killed, while many were captured by hand. [The Grand Prince's voevodas] ordered those who were captured to cut away each other's noses and lips and send them back to Novgorod; and they took away their armor and either threw them into the water or burned them because they did not need any of them since they had sufficient arms and weapons of their own.

From thence the same day they [the Novgorodians] returned to Rusa, where was another foot army which was more numerous and stronger, and which had come to Lake Ilmen' in boats on the Pola River. But the Grand Prince's voevodas also marched against them and defeated those who arrived.... The Grand Prince's voevodas went to the river She-

lon' and when they started fording it the Novgorodian army approached from the opposite side....

All the Novgorodian posadniks and tysiatskiis and, speaking plainly, the carpenters and potmakers, and those who, since their birth, had never ridden a horse and had never had the intention of raising a hand against the Grand Prince—they were all forced by the traitors to march [against the Grand Prince]. Those who did not want to fight were sacked and beaten, and some among them were thrown into the Volkhov River. They, themselves, claim that there were forty thousand of them in this battle.

The Grand Prince's voevodas, although they had few [troops]—it was said that there were only five thousand of them—and despite the fact that they saw that there were a great many [of the enemy]—did not take fright, however, relying upon Lord God and His Most Pure Mother and on the truth of their sovereign's [cause]. They advanced headlong against them in the manner of roaring lions, crossing this large river—the Novgorodians, themselves, say that there has never been a ford there—but those [warriors of Ivan III], without looking for a ford, crossed and were all alive and healthy. Seeing this, the Novgorodians became confused and hesitant, as if drunk; but those [soldiers of Ivan III] marched against them and started shooting at them, and the [Novgorodians'] horses started rearing and throwing off their soldiers. Soon the Novgorodians began to flee, driven by the wrath of God for their misdeeds and for their betrayal not only of their sovereign but also of Lord God, Himself. The Grand Prince's regiments pursued them, stabbing and chopping them, and those [Novgorodians] ran away, pushing and stomping each other....

A great many of them at that time were killed; they, themselves, claimed that there were twelve thousand men who perished in these battles, and more than two thousand were taken captive by hand. [Among] the prisoners were their posadniks, Vasilii Kazimir, Dmitrii Isaakov Boretskii, Kuzma Grigoriev, Iakov Fedorov, Matvei Selezenev, Vasilii Selezenev, two of Kazimir's nephews—Pavel Teliatev and Kuzma Gruzov—and a multitude of wealthy burghers. . . .

And after this battle the army of the Grand Prince continued to campaign in many towns near Novgorod, up to the German border on the river Narva; and the larger city called Novoe Selo was occupied and burned. . . .

The same month, the twenty-fourth of July, the day of the memory of Holy Martyrs Boris and Gleb, the Grand Prince came to [Staraia] Rusa and commanded that [the following] Novgorodian posadniks should be punished for their treason and for their apostasy with capital punishment: Dmitrii Isakovich Boretskii, Vasilii Selezenev Guba, Eremei Sukhoshchok, and Kiprian Arzubiev.

And he sent many others to Moscow in order to imprison them. . . . The Grand Prince, himself, came on the twenty-seventh of July, a Saturday, to Lake Ilmen at the mouth of the river Shelon', to the place between the shore and Korostyn. . . .

The same day there came to the mouth of the Shelon' River in boats the nominated Archbishop Theophilus with the posadniks, tysiatskiis and other wealthy burghers from all sections of the city. First of all they solicited the Grand Prince's boyars and voevodas, asking them to intercede with the Grand Prince; and that [thereafter] they, together with the boyars themselves, would also intercede with the Grand Prince. The boyars went with them and solicited the Grand Prince's brothers; and [they] . . . petitioned the Grand Prince for them [that is, for the Novgorodians]. And for the sake of his brothers and his boyars, the Grand Prince accepted their entreaty and bestowed mercy upon them, and permitted the nominated Monk Theophilus, posadniks, tysiatskiis, and the others to come to him and appear before his eyes. And they came to the Grand Prince, bowed to the earth because of their crimes and because they had raised their hands against him. [They begged] the sovereign to pardon them, to be merciful toward them, to turn aside his wrath, and to do so not because of their petition but in order to show

his good heart toward those who had sinned, and that he order no more executions, sacking, burning, or capturing. And the Grand Prince became merciful. He showed them his mercy and accepted their solicitation, stilled his wrath and commanded forthwith to stop burning and taking prisoners, and to release those who had been captured. And those who had been sent away and taken off were to be returned. And so [they] entreated the Grand Prince, [providing] him sixteen thousand Novgorodian silver rubles [as indemnity] besides [giving] to the Grand Prince's brothers, to the other princes, to the boyars and voevodas, and to all others who had interceded for them.

And their land was occupied and burned to the sea. . . .

Then the Grand Prince granted the Novgorodians peace, love and mercy, honored their nominated [Bishop] Theophilus and their posadniks, tysiatskiis, and others who came with them, and let them return to their city. He sent with them to Novgorod his boyar, Fedor Davydovich, to bring everyone in Novgorod the Great, from the small to the great, to swear on the cross and to receive silver from them. And they went to Novgorod and did as they were commanded.

On the thirteenth day of the month of August Grand Prince Ivan Vasilievich of Vladimir, Moscow, and Novgorod and all Russia, returned from thence to Moscow with a great victory; and with him were all his brothers, princes, all the voevodas and all their warriors, bringing with them great booty. . . .

In the Year 6985 [1477]. In the month of March Theophilus, the Archbishop of Novgorod, and all Novgorod the Great sent their envoys, *podvoiskii* [bailiff] Nazar and Zakharii, clerk of the *veche*, to Grand Prince Ivan Vasilievich and to his son, Grand Prince Ivan Ivanovich; and addressing him, they called him "*Gospodar'* [Master]." And this never happened before, not since our land came into being. None of the grand princes was called "*Gospodar*" but always "*Gospodin* [Lord]." The same spring on the twenty-fourth of April, a Thursday, the Grand Prince sent his envoys,

Fedor Davydovich and Ivan Borisovich, and with them *diak* [secretary] Vasilii Dalmatov, to Novgorod, to the Archbishop and to all Great Novgorod, to clarify "what manner of government does their patrimony, Great Novgorod, want?" And they [the Novgorodians] began arguing, saying, "We did not send them with it." And they called it a lie . . .

The same month [May] when the Grand Prince's envoy was in Novgorod there was a disturbance in Novgorod; they summoned the *veche* and assembling, took Vasilii Mikiforov and brought him to the *veche*, crying, "You traitor! You went to the Grand Prince and swore to him on the cross against us." And he told them, "I pledged on the cross to the Grand Prince that we want to serve him with truth and good, and [I did not speak against] my lord, Novgorod the Great, or against you, my elders, or my brethren." But they killed him mercilessly. . . . And from that time they became maddened, as if drunk, and spoke all manner [of nonsense] and wanted again [to be under] the King [of Poland].

The Grand Prince learned of this from his envoys and from their posadniks who were faithful to him and who escaped to him [from Novgorod] when the evil dissent arose, as occurred after their first crime and as had occurred before [the battle] of Shelon'; and he bemoaned them greatly [for the killings] and he wept . . .

He started preparing his army against his patrimony, against the Novgorodians who had become apostates and had broken their pledge on the cross, and he did so with the blessing of Metropolitan Gerontius of all Russia and of his entire Sacred Council, of the Archbishop and bishops of the entire clergy, as well as having received the advice and prayers of his mother, his brothers, the boyars, princes, and voevodas. . . .

On the thirtieth of the month of September the Grand Prince sent to Novgorod with a declaration of war a certain Radion Bogomolov, a clerk.

On the ninth day of the month of October, . . . the Grand Prince set out from Moscow to Novgorod in order to chastise them with war for their crimes. . . .

On the twenty-third of October the Grand Prince left Torzhok and moved against Novgorod with the army. . . .

On the eighth of November at [the Church of] the Saviour in Iaglino, the Grand Prince commanded the Novgorodian envoys, Fedor Kalitin and Ivan Markov, who had asked for safe conduct, to appear before him. When they approached him they petitioned him in the name of the Archbishop of Novgorod, Theophilus, and in the name of Novgorod the Great, for safe conduct, calling the Grand Prince their "Sovereign" [*Gosudar*]: "We ask you, our Sovereign, that you grant safe conduct to the Archbishop and to the Novgorodian posadniks so that they might come to petition you and return according to their intentions." The Grand Prince agreed to grant them safe conduct, and gave them his charter of safe conduct. . . .

On Sunday, the twenty-third of November, there came to the Grand Prince, who was in Sytino, the Archbishop of Novgorod, Theophilus, and with him the Novgorodian posadniks . . . and . . . the wealthy burghers . . . and the merchant Iakov Tsarishchev; and all of them petitioned the Grand Prince, and the Archbishop said, "Our lord and sovereign Grand Prince Ivan Vasilievich of all Russia! I, my lord, your prayerful bishop, as well as the archimandrites, abbots, and all the priests of all seven cathedrals of Great Novgorod, we petition you, our sovereign Grand Prince. You, our lord sovereign Grand Prince, have turned your wrath upon your patrimony, Novgorod the Great. Now your sword and fire go through the Novgorodian land and Christian blood is shed. [We ask you] our sovereign lord, to be merciful to your patrimony; stop your sword and extinguish your fire so that Christian blood be no more shed. Grant it us, our sovereign lord! . . . ."

On the twenty-fifth of November, Tuesday, being in Sytino, the Grand Prince commanded that his answer be given to the Archbishop and to the Novgorodian envoys through Prince

Ivan Iurievich, and with the latter were Vasilii and Ivan Borisovich [Obolenskii]. Prince Ivan Iurievich said the following:

"Grand Prince Ivan Vasilievich of all Russia responds thus to you, his prayerful Archbishop, to the posadniks, and to the wealthy burghers. You, our prayerful bishop, and you, posadniks and wealthy burghers, you have petitioned me, the Grand Prince, that I, the Grand Prince, should turn aside my wrath from my patrimony, Novgorod the Great. . . .

[But] you know, yourselves, that you sent to us, the Grand Princes [to Ivan III and his son, Ivan], from our patrimony, from all Great Novgorod, your envoys, the police official Nazar, and the *diak* of the *veche*, Zakhar. They have called us, the Grand Princes, *Gospodar'*. And after having received your message, we, the Grand Princes, sent to you, the Archbishop, and to our patrimony of Novgorod the Great, our boyars. . . . And we commanded them to inquire of you, our prayerful Archbishop, and our patrimony of Novgorod, what manner of government by the Grand Princes you want in our patrimony, Novgorod the Great? And you denied that you sent us your envoys [to call us *Gospodar'*]. And you claimed that we, the Grand Princes, are responsible for using violence against our patrimony, and you not only tried to demonstrate that I, your Sovereign, lied, but you also perpetrated many misdeeds and dishonor upon us, the Grand Princes. And there was much disregard toward us. But we restrained ourselves, awaiting your appeal to us; but you behaved in the most evil way toward us and we could not tolerate this, and we decided to make our anger manifest to you, and decided to campaign with armies against you. . . . [W]e the Grand Princes of Russia, campaigned against you because of your misdeeds.". . . .

After these speeches, Prince Ivan Iurievich said, "The Grand Prince tells you that in the case our patrimony wants to petition us, the Grand Princes and your Sovereign, then you, our patrimony, should know how to petition us, the Grand Princes."

Thereafter the Archbishop, posadniks, and wealthy burghers asked the Grand Prince to furnish them a police official who would conduct them to the city, and the Grand Prince commanded his police official, Runa, to accompany them. . . .

On Friday, the fifth day of December, there came to the Grand Prince from Novgorod Archbishop Theophilus with the posadniks and wealthy burghers, who had already come to him earlier; and at that time he had [present] his brothers, Prince Andrei, Prince Boris, and Prince Andrei the younger. The Archbishop and all those with them earlier petitioned that the Sovereign show his mercy, and they accepted their guilt for having sent Nazar and Zakhar as their envoys to the Grand Prince and that thereafter they had denied it.

The Grand Prince answered, "In that case you, yourselves—the Archbishop and our entire patrimony, Novgorod the Great—accepted your guilt before us, the Grand Princes, and acknowledged having sent them [Zakhar and Nazar] to us with those speeches, and then denied it. And now you, yourselves, witness to this and ask what manner of government there should be in our patrimony of Novgorod. We, the Grand Princes, wanted [there] our own government. In the same manner as we are in Moscow, so we want to be in Novgorod." And the Archbishop with all his posadniks and wealthy burghers again petitioned that the Grand Prince be kind and permit them to return to the city to think about this, and that they use the same safe conduct and that he should give them a term wherein they must return to him. And the Grand Prince allowed them to do so, and commanded them to return to him on the third day, a Sunday. . . .

On the seventh of December there came to the Prince the Archbishop of Novgorod with the aforementioned posadniks and wealthy burghers, and with them five common people from five sections. . . . The Archbishop, wealthy burghers, and commoners petitioned as before that the Sovereign show them mercy and suffer them to hold counsel with his boyars. And the Grand Prince sent to them his boyars Prince Ivan Iurievich, Fedor Davydovich, and Prince Ivan Striga [Obolenskii], and the boyars Vasilii and Ivan Borisovich [Obolenskii]. And the Archbishop took counsel with them together with all his posadniks, wealthy burghers, and commoners.

The first speech was the petition of Iakov Korobov, that the Grand Prince command his namestnik [lieutenant] to execute justice together with the posadniks. Posadnik Feofilat petitioned that the Grand Prince agree that every year he receive from all the districts of Novgorod a tax of half a Novgorodian grivna from every *sokha* [tax unit]. And posadnik Luka petitioned that the Sovereign rule the minor cities of Novgorod through his namestniks, and that justice be administered as of old. Posadnik Iakov Fedorov petitioned that the Grand Prince agree not to move any people from the Novgorodian land; he also petitioned concerning the landholdings and lands of the boyars, that the Sovereign not interfere with them and agree that the people of Moscow not settle on Novgorodian lands. And they all petitioned that "We Novgorodians should not perform military service in the Nizovskaia land [Northeast Rus', the Suzdal' land] on the shore, but serve where the foreign lands adjoin the Novgorodian land. Then we would be glad to defend them, our patrimony, on command of our Sovereign."

The boyars went to the Grand Prince and told him about those speeches, and the Grand Prince sent them the same boyars with an answer, commanding them to say the following: "You, Archbishop, and our patrimony, Great Novgorod, petition us, calling us your Sovereigns, that we kindly show our patrimony what manner of government there should be in our patrimony, in Novgorod the Great. And I, Grand Prince, told you that I want in my patrimony, Novgorod the Great, the same government as we have in the Nizovskaia land, in Moscow. And now you teach me what my government should be. How, then, can it be *my* government?"

The Archbishop, posadniks, and wealthy burghers petitioned and told the boyars the following: "We do not want to teach the Grand Prince how to govern, [but we expect] that our sovereign Grand Princes be kind toward their patrimony, that they show their patrimony,

Novgorod the Great, what manner of government will be in their patrimony because, Sovereign, your patrimony, Great Novgorod, does not know what custom there is in the Nizovskaia land or what sort of government our Sovereigns, the Grand Princes, have in the Nizovskaia land." The boyars went to the Grand Prince and told him this, and the Grand Prince sent them back with an answer, commanding them to speak as follows.

AND PRINCE IVAN IURIEVICH SPOKE

"The Grand Prince says the following to you, his prayerful Archbishop, to you, posadniks, and wealthy burghers, and to the common people: You petition me, the Grand Prince, that I should explain to you what manner of government there should be in our patrimony. And our government and our Grand Princes' government is the following:

"There will be no *veche* bell in our patrimony of Novgorod. There will be no posadniks, and we will conduct our own government.

"And the Grand Prince will govern in his patrimony [Novgorod], and in its environs and in its towns in the same way as in our Nizovskaia land. And all the lands of the Grand Prince which you keep now will be ours.

"You petition me, the Grand Prince, that your people should not be removed from the Novgorodian land, that we should not interfere with the land ownership of the Novgorodian boyars; and we grant you the following: no people will be taken from your land. We will not interfere with your land ownership; and justice in our patrimony of Novgorod will be as of old, in the same way as justice now is in your land. . . ."

On the fourteenth [of December], Sunday, the Archbishop came to the Grand Prince with the posadniks and with the aforementioned, and they petitioned that the Sovereign show mercy to his patrimony and order his boyars to negotiate. And the Grand Prince sent his boyars to negotiate with them. And they petitioned him to delay the suppression of the *ve-*

che, of the bell, and of the posadniks, asking the Sovereign to remove his dislike from his heart and not to move people away or interfere with their land ownership, with their lands and waters, or with their wealth; and that he kindly delay moving the Muscovites to Novgorod; also, [they asked] that he should kindly agree not to send [Novgorodians] into military service in the Nizovskaia land. And the Grand Prince granted them all this. Then they again petitioned that the Sovereign assure his patrimony, Novgorod, that he give [his oath] on the cross [not to take any of these actions]. But the Grand Prince responded, "There will be no oath on the cross by me." And then they petitioned that the boyars give them their oaths on the cross, and the Grand Prince rejected this, too. And then they petitioned that the namestnik who would be with them give his oath on the cross; but he [Ivan III] also did not accept this. Then they asked for safe conduct, but the Grand Prince did not give them even this. . . .

On the twenty-ninth of December the Archbishop, with the aforementioned, again spoke humbly to the Grand Prince's boyars: "The Sovereign bestows nothing on us. He has delayed his oath on the cross. He does not grant us safe conduct. In what way does he demonstrate his good will? And we would like to learn of his good will from his own lips, without being sent away." And the boyars went to the Grand Prince and told him this. And the Grand Prince showed his good will, told them to come to him, and told them, "You, our prayerful Archbishop, as well as you posadniks, wealthy burghers and common people; you petition me, the Grand Prince, in the name of our hereditary domain, Novgorod the Great, that I should deign to turn aside my wrath, that I should not move your people out of the Novgorodian lands, that I should not interfere in land ownership or the wealth of the people, that I should not settle Muscovites, and that justice should be done according to the old way in Novgorod, the same way as justice is now performed in your land. And [you asked] that I should not send you into military service in the Nizovskaia land. And I granted all this to

my hereditary domain [Novgorod], my good will. And so I will do all this." . . .

And they, hearing this, bowed deeply and departed from him. Thereafter, however, the Grand Prince sent after them the boyars, in order to say the following concerning the lands and towns: "I, Grand Prince Ivan Vasilievich of all Russia, say, 'I am sending my boyars to you, my prayerful Archbishop, posadniks and wealthy burghers, concerning the *volosts* [cantons] and towns because we, the Grand Prince, must maintain our government in our hereditary domain, Novgorod the Great, and without this [income] it will not be possible."

The Archbishop, posadniks, and wealthy burghers replied, "We will tell Novgorod, our Sovereign." . . .

On the first of January [1478] the Archbishop with the posadniks and wealthy burghers came to the Grand Prince, offering him the following *volosts*: Velikie Luki and Rzhev; but he did not take them. On the fourth, Sunday, the Archbishop with the aforementioned persons came to the Grand Prince and presented ten *volosts*: four of the Archbishop's; three of the Iur'iev Monastery; one of the Annunciation Monastery in Diemon; the entire Antonovskaia *volost*; and the entire Tubas *volost*. And, also, all the lands in Novotorzhok: the Archbishop's, the monasteries', and the boyars' lands; and all other lands [in Torzhok], whosoever owned them, would be ceded to the Grand Prince. And the Grand Prince did not accept these ten *volosts*. And then they petitioned that the Sovereign, himself, think what he should be given by his hereditary domain and how many *volosts* he wanted to take, and that his hereditary domain [Novgorod] relied upon God and upon him. And the Grand Prince ordered the boyars to tell them, "I want to take half of all the *volosts* of the Archbishop, [half] of [all] the monasteries, and all the lands of Novotorzhok, to whomsoever they belong." And they [the Archbishop and the others] responded, "Sovereign, we will report this to Novgorod."

On the sixth of January, the day of the Baptism of Our Lord, Tuesday, the Archbishop came with the posadniks and wealthy burghers to the Grand Prince, rendered him honor and offered him half of the Archbishop's *volosts* and all the districts in Torzhok [Novotorzhok]: the lands of the Archbishop, of the monasteries, of the boyars, and others, to whomsoever they belonged. And all were ceded to the Grand Prince. And they petitioned [him] concerning the monasteries, that he agree to take half the *volosts* and lands from six monasteries—Iur'iev, the Annunciation, Arkazh, St. Anthony, St. Nicholas near the Nerevskii "end," and St. Nicholas Monastery on Skovorodka—and that the Sovereign should agree not to take the land of other monasteries because those monasteries were poor and had little land. And the Grand Prince told the Archbishop and the posadniks to go to the city and provide the rolls of half of the *volosts* owned by the Archbishop and by the monasteries, and that they should not hide anything: and if they should hide something, it would become the land of the Grand Prince.

On the seventh of January the Archbishop came with the posadniks and wealthy burghers to the Grand Prince, bringing the rolls: half of the Archbishop's *volosts* and the same of those of the monasteries. And the Grand Prince decided not to take half of the Archbishop's districts, and took only ten. . . . And he took all the lands of Novotorzhok, those of the Archbishop, of the monasteries, of the boyars, and whosesoever there were in Torzhok. And from the six above-mentioned monasteries, half of their *volosts*. . . .

On the fifteenth of January, Thursday, the Grand Prince sent to Novgorod his boyars . . . to bring all Novgorod to the oath according to the charter about which the Novgorodians had petitioned the Grand Prince. And the Grand Prince bestowed his grace on Novgorod. The Grand Prince also ordered Prince Ivan Vasilievich [Striga-Obolenskii] to go alone to the [Bishop's] palace as his envoy to the Bishop and to the city of Novgorod [to say that] from this day on there was no longer any *veche* in Novgorod. . . .

On the eighteenth of January, Sunday, all the Novgorodian boyars, junior boyars, and

wealthy burghers petitioned to be accepted into the Grand Prince's service; and having given the oath, they departed from thence. . . .

The first of the month of February, the Sunday of Shrovetide, the Grand Prince commanded that they arrest Mark Pomfiliev, the merchants' *starosta* [elder], and he was arrested in the city. . . .

[On] Monday, the first week of Lent, the Grand Prince commanded that they arrest in Novgorod Marfa Isakova, widow of Novgorodian boyar Boretskii, and her grandson, Vasilii Fedorov, Isaak's son. . . .

On the seventh of February the Grand Prince commanded they send to Moscow the arrested Novgorodians, Marfa Isakovna with her grandson; Ivan Kuzmin Savelkov; Akinf with his son, Roman; Iurii Repekhov; Grigorii Arzubiev; and Mark Pomfiliev. And what they owned he ordered confiscated for his treasury. . . .

On the seventeenth of February, Tuesday, early in the morning, the Grand Prince left Novgorod. . . . After his departure the Grand Prince commanded the *veche* bell to be brought from Novgorod to Moscow; and when it was brought thither it was put in the belfry on the square to ring with the other bells. And since the land of Novgorod the Great and the whole Russian land came into being, there was not such a punishment laid upon them [that is, upon the Novgorodians] either by the Grand Prince or by anyone else.

SOURCE: *The Nikonian Chronicle*, Vol. 5. Edited by Serge A. Zenkovsky. Translated by Serge A. Zenkovsky and Betty Jean Zenkovsky (Princeton: Darwin Press, 1990), pp. 122–9, 131–5, 136–40, 178–86, 188–90, 193–9, 203–7 (excerpted). Copyright © 1989 Serge A. Zenkovsky and Betty Jean Zenkovsky. Reprinted by permission of Darwin Press, Princeton, New Jersey.

The Novgorod Chronicle on the Mongol Invasion (1235–38)

Aside perhaps from Christianization, no event in the pre-modern history of Russia resounds with such authority as the Mongol invasion, which began toward the middle of the thirteenth century and lasted formally until about 1480. In the centuries since, many words have been fashioned to appraise the significance of this happening, and below we shall consider some recent opinions. But to the chroniclers of Rus' the meaning of the Mongol disaster was clear: the Christian God had employed the Tatars to punish Rus' for the folly of its princes who, rather than abiding by the wise advice of Grand Prince Iaroslav (see the selection from the Primary Chronicle in Chapter 2), had instead fought against one another, and had failed to honor one another. The Novgorod Chronicle, for example, from which the following selection is taken, depicts the arrival of the Mongols as an unmitigated disaster, a characterization which ought to be compared with Halperin's interpretation below.

AD 1235. The accursed and all-destroying devil, who from the beginning wished no good to the human race, raised discord among the Russian Princes, that men might not dwell in peace; for this reason too the evil one rejoices in the shedding of Christian blood. Prince Volodimir Rurikovich with the men of Kiev, and Danilo Romanovich with the men of Galich went out against Mikhail Vsevolodich the Red, to Chernigov, and Iziaslav fled to the Polovtsian people, and laid much waste around Chernigov, and burnt villages. And Mikhail came out from Chernigov and having devastated much around Chernigov went away again. And Mikhail having practised deceit on Danilo killed many of the men of Galich, even without number, and Danilo barely escaped. And Volodimir having come back again, he sat in Kiev. And not even thus was there enough of evil, but Iziaslav with the pagan Polovtsian people in great strength, and Mikhail with the men of Chernigov came to Kiev, and took Kiev. And the Polovtsian men having taken Volodimir and his princess led them away to their own country, and did much harm to the people at Kiev. And Mikhail took his seat in Galich, and Iziaslav in Kiev. . . .

AD 1238 . . . That same year foreigners called Tatars came in countless numbers, like locusts into the land of Riazan, and on first coming they halted at the river Nukhla, and took it, and halted in camp there. And thence they sent their emissaries to the princes of Riazan, a sorceress and two men with her, demanding from them one-tenth of everything: of men and princes and horses—of everything one-tenth. And the princes of Riazan, Gyurgi, Ingvor's brother, Oleg, Roman Ingvorevich, and those of Murom and Pronsk, without letting them into their towns, went out to meet them to Voronezh. And the princes said to them: "Only when none of us remain then all will be yours." And thence they let them go to Iurii in Volodimir, and thence they let the Tatars at Voronezh go back to the Nukhla. And the princes of Riazan sent to Iurii of Volodimir asking for help, or himself to come. But Iurii neither went himself nor listened to the request of the princes of Riazan, but he himself wished to make war separately. But it was too late to oppose the wrath of God. . . . And then the pagan foreigners surrounded Riazan and fenced it in with a stockade. And prince Iurii of Riazan, shut himself in the town with his people, but Prince Roman Ingvorovich began to fight against them with his own men. Then Prince Iurii of Volodimir sent Yeremei as *voevoda* with a patrol and joined Roman; and the Tatars surrounded them at Kolomno, and they fought hard and drove them to the ramparts. And there they killed Roman and Yeremei and many fell here with the Prince and with Yeremei. And the men of Moscow ran away having seen nothing. And the Tatars took the town on December 21, and they had advanced against it on the 16th of the same month. They likewise killed the Prince and Princess, and men, women, and children, monks, nuns and priests, some by fire, some by the sword, and violated nuns, priests' wives, good women and girls in the presence of their mothers and sisters. But God saved the Bishop, for he had departed the same moment when the troops invested the town. And who, brethren, would not lament over this, among those of us left alive when they suffered this bitter and violent death? And we, indeed, having seen it, were terrified and wept with sighing day and night over our sins, while we sigh every day and night, taking thought for our possessions and for the hatred of brothers.

But let us return to what lies before us. The pagan and godless Tatars, then, having taken Riazan, went to Volodimir, a host of shedders of Christian blood. And Prince Iurii went out from Volodimir and fled to Iaroslavl, while his son Vsevolod with his mother and the archbishop, and the whole of the province shut themselves in Volodimir. And the lawless Ishmaelites approached the town and surrounded the town in force, and fenced it all round with a fence. And it was in the morning Prince Vsevolod and Archbishop Mitrofan saw that the town must be taken, and entered the Church of the Holy Mother of God and were all shorn into the monastic order ... , the Prince and the Princess, their daughter and daughter-in-law, and good men and women, by Archbishop Mitrofan. And when the lawless ones had already come near and set up battering rams, and took the town and fired it on Friday before Sexagesima Sunday [Second Sunday before Lent], the Prince and Princess, seeing that the town was on fire and that the people were already perishing, some by fire and others by the sword, took refuge in the Church of the Holy Mother of God and shut themselves up in the Sacristy. The pagans breaking down the doors, piled up wood and set fire to the sacred church; and slew all, thus they perished, giving up their souls to God. Others went in pursuit of Prince Iurii to Iaroslavl. And Prince Iurii sent out Dorozh to scout with 3,000 men; and Dorozh came running, and said: "They have already surrounded us, Prince." And the Prince began to muster his forces about him, and behold, the Tatars came up suddenly, and the Prince, without having been able to do anything, fled. And it happened when he reached the river Sit they overtook him and there he ended his life. And God knows how he died; for some say much about him. And Rostov and Suzdal went each its own way. And the accursed ones having come thence took Moscow, Pereiaslavl, Iurev, Dmi-

trov, Volok, and Tver; there also they killed the son of Iaroslav. And thence the lawless ones came and invested Torzhok on the festival of the first Sunday in Lent. They fenced it all round with a fence as they had taken other towns, and here the accursed ones fought with battering rams for two weeks. And the people in the town were exhausted and from Novgorod there was no help for them; but already every man began to be in perplexity and terror. And so the pagans took the town, and slew all from the male sex even to the female, all the priests and the monks, and all stripped and reviled gave up their souls to the Lord in a bitter and a wretched death, on March 5, the day of the commemoration of the holy Martyr Nikon, on Wednesday in Easter week. And there, too, were killed Ivanko the mayor of Novi-torg, Iakim Vlunkovich, Gleb Borisovich, and Mikhailo Moisievich. And the accursed godless ones then pushed on from Torzhok by the road of Seregeri right up to Ignatii's cross, cutting down everybody like grass, to within 100 *versts* [about 66 miles] of Novgorod. God, however, and the great and sacred apostolic cathedral Church of St. Sophia, and St. Kiuril, and the prayers of the holy and orthodox archbishop, of the faithful princes, and of the very reverend monks of the hierarchical assembly, protected Novgorod. And who, brothers, fathers, and children, seeing this, God's infliction on the whole Russian Land, does not lament? God let the pagans on us for our sins.

SOURCE: *The Chronicle of Novgorod, 1016–1471.* Translated by Robert Mitchell, Neville Forbes (Hattiesburg: Academic International Press, 1970), pp. 80–84 (excerpted). Spelling has been modernized, and some Russian terms translated. Reprinted by permission of Academic International Press, PO Box 1111, Gulf Breeze, FL 32562.

Mongol Immunity Charter (Iarlyk) *to Metropolitan Peter (ca. 1313)*

Despite the destruction which evidently accompanied the conquest in the thirteenth century, one apparent beneficiary of the Mongol Yoke, as contemporaries frequently labeled it, was the Orthodox Church. Although many local churches suffered destruction, the central church administration gained recognition as an independent institution. A series of documents, one of which appears in translation below, certified the status of the Orthodox Church in the Rus' lands then under the formal control of the Mongols. It bears repeating that it was precisely in the fourteenth century when Orthodoxy seems finally to have displaced other religions in Rus'. But over and above their increasing spiritual influence, the Orthodox Church also became a very powerful economic agent in Rus', as the enumeration of Church privileges indicates.

By the power and will of the Most High and Eternal God and by the majesty and most merciful word of Uzbek. . . . Let no one offend against the cathedral church in Rus' of Metropolitan Peter or against his people and his churchmen, and let no one take either his movable property, lands or people. Metropolitan Peter recognizes justice, and conducts court, and administers people in justice in everything; and Metropolitan Peter himself alone, or whomever he orders [to appear in his place] hears all cases, including robbery, red-handed theft, and petty theft. And all church servitors submit to and confess to the Metropolitan, according to their first laws and according to our first charters, the grand charters of the first tsars and the khan's tax charters. And no one is to interfere in church affairs or in the metropolitan's business, for they are God's business. If someone does interfere, disobeying our charter and our word, then that person is guilty before God, and brings on himself the wrath from him [God], and execution from us. If the Metropolitan conducts himself justly, remains on the just path and is content, if he administers all church business with a just heart and just thought, and if he judges [justly] and administers [church people rightly], or if whomever he orders in his stead so acts and administers [the Church's business], then let no one interfere in those affairs, neither my children nor any of our princes from our kingdom or any of our lands or any of our uluses [the Mongol term for kin-dominated entities], and let no one at all interfere in church matters or in the Metropolitan's matters, nor in their towns or rural districts, nor in their villages nor in any of their fishing grants, nor in their apiaries, nor in their lands, their uluses, their forests, their gardens, their rural places, their vineyards, mills, wintering places, nor with their horse herds or any of their livestock herds; for the Metropolitan himself, or whomever he shall name in his stead, administers all church property and possessions, their people and their clergy and all their laws, from the oldest of their codes . . . If our tax collectors and customs collectors, tribute collectors, dues gatherers, and enumerators go against these our charters, as our word said and established, that all the cathedral people of the Metropolitan's church ought in no way be offended by anyone, that no one ought offend any of his people and his property, as this immunity charter maintains, [that no one ought offend] the archmandrites [heads of monasteries] and abbots and priests and all the clergy in any way; if they take tribute or anything else, such as customs duty, plowland tax, post tax, transit fees, bridge tolls, war tax [?], fishing tax, or if they order them to collect recruits for our service from our uluses when we wish to go to war, then from the cathedral church and from Metropolitan Peter no one is to take anyone from among their people or from their clergy, and they shall pray to God for us . . . If someone violates church property and the Metropolitan's property, the wrath of God will be on him, and he will not be excused from our great torture by any excuse and he shall die by terrible execution.

SOURCE: *Sbornik dokumentov po istorii SSSR dlia seminarskikh i prakticheskikh zaniatii*, ch. 2: XIV–XV vv (Moscow: Vysshaia shkola, 1971), pp. 184–5. Translated by Daniel H. Kaiser.

LITERATURE

S. F. PLATONOV

Statebuilding in Moscow: The Birth of Autocracy

As already noted, according to one historical tradition, the princes of Moscow had always viewed their principality not so much as a trust to govern as a part of their own personal property, something which they owned rather than ruled. This idea stood in sharp contrast to Novgorodian custom embodied in the thirteenth- and fourteenth-century agreements with their princes, a dissonance which lay at the root of Novgorod's troubles with Ivan III in the 1470s. Indeed, the last will and testament of Moscow Grand Prince Dmitrii Donskoi allots portions of his principality, his patrimony, like so many baubles and coins. Such evidence informs the interpretation of Sergei Platonov, who received his education in the last years of tsarism. Platonov argues that apologists of the Grand Prince imbued him with divine authority which gave the Muscovite tsars an almost messianic right to absolute power.

The Moscow state . . . was formed by the annexation to the princely appanage of Moscow of neighboring appanages in northern Russia and, later, of the Land of Novgorod and the *volost* of the Grand Prince of Lithuania. The Muscovite princes regarded their appanage as a personal possession, just as the owner of an estate looks upon it as his hereditary landholding. When the Great Principality of Vladimir was acquired permanently, the Moscow princes designated it as their hereditary holding. Later, when they demanded that Lithuania yield the old Rus' towns to them, they instructed their envoy to declare that all the lands of Rus' had once been part of their patrimony. In such fashion, the Muscovite princes

expanded the claims of proprietorship from their appanage to the whole country, and staked out claims to possess and control the whole vast state. This view was generally accepted; the people of Moscow always declared that they belonged to the great sovereign because they lived on his lands. When property was sold, the deed read: "I have sold the land of the sovereign and of my possession." The authority of the Moscow princes thus took on the character of the authority of a lord of a manor over its land and people, and was, therefore, complete and very autocratic. The prince was not only the ruler of the country; he was also its owner. In the course of time, when the Moscow princes took the leadership in gathering together and unifying all of northern Russia, they received recognition as the main leaders of all the people and acquired power which was public, democratic, and national in character. To gain public sympathy and mass support, the Moscow princes presented themselves as entitled to pride and power only as representative of the people and of national independence . . . So was created in Moscow a powerful autocracy, patrimonial in origin and national in magnitude.

This took place at a time when other Orthodox governments were moving toward their decline and fall. The awesome Turkish conquerors were encroaching upon the Orthodox East. Having seized the Asiatic provinces of the Byzantine (Greek) Empire, the Turks moved on Europe. At the close of the fourteenth and start of the fifteenth century, they conquered the Balkan Slavs and encircled Constantinople. We have seen how the Greeks, in apprehension of this, had sought far and wide for aid. To no avail, however; no help came, and in 1453 Constantinople fell to the Turks. There then remained in the East only one Orthodox state, only one independent bishopric; all the others were captured by the Godless infidels, as the Turks were called. The Moscow state alone retained its Orthodox prince and an independent metropolitan. They alone stood steadfast and strong, forming a powerful union of the Great Russian tribes, and maintaining the last barrier against the Tatar yoke.

For a long time—since the conversion of the Rus' to Christianity—the notion had been held in Russia that all "Orthodoxy," that is to say, all Orthodox Christians, had for untold centuries been united under the one supreme power of the Greek [Byzantine] Sovereign ("caesar," "tsar") and the Greek Church. Constantinople, seat of the Greek Patriarch and of the tsar, was therefore called Tsargrad by the Russians, and was looked upon as the capital of all "Orthodoxy." When Constantinople and all the eastern states and churches were in the hands of the Turks and were subordinated to them, the Orthodox recognized no other capital than free Moscow. The people of Moscow awoke to this soon after the fall of Constantinople. The Muscovite princes Ivan III [1462–1505] and Vasilii III [1505–33] regarded themselves as the heirs and successors of the Greek tsars. Ivan III married a Greek princess, adopted for himself the Greek coat-of-arms, crowned his grandson Dmitrii "to the Tsardom." He himself, like Vasilii III, sometimes titled himself "Tsar.". . .

The Russian literature of that time shows that the Russians had a great interest in the subject of the relations between Rus' and Byzantium. Proceeding from the theory of the Divine One-ness of the entire Christian world, one of the writers of that period, the Monk Philotheus of Pskov, wrote an epistle to the Grand Prince Vasilii III in which he argued that Ancient Rome had been the original center of the world; after this appeared a new Rome (Nova Roma—Constantinople), and in the most recent time, a Third Rome—Moscow. "Two Romes have fallen," said Philotheus, "but the third stands, and a fourth [there] shall not be." Thus arose the important theory of the universal role of Moscow—the Third Rome.

After Philotheus, other writers expanded on the same theme, calling the Grand Prince of Muscovy the tsar of all "Orthodoxy"; Moscow,

"the new city of Constantinople (i.e., the new Tsargrad)"; and the Russian people, "new Israel," whom God Himself had chosen to lead all the Orthodox. The theory of the transfer of world supremacy from Tsargrad to Moscow having been accepted, it was argued and expounded in every way . . . The legends of unbroken succession [to the Orthodox legacy] gave strength to Muscovite claims such as the following: the state of Moscow is the foremost in all "Orthodoxy"; the Muscovite prince is the Orthodox Tsar; and the Muscovite Church preeminently among the Orthodox churches preserves its independence and purity so that it stands above the older, Eastern Patriarchate.

Adopting this majestic theory, the Muscovite princes raised themselves to great heights. Conscious of their absolute power over their estates and their lands, feeling themselves to be the national leaders of a strong and numerous people, they now sought to play a larger role as tsars of all the Orthodox world. Such mighty and autocratic power seemed to them to be naturally theirs.

SOURCE: S. F. Platonov, "The Transition from Appanages to a Unified Autocracy," in *Readings in Russian History From Ancient Times to the Post-Stalin Era*, 4th ed, Vol. 1 (Syracuse: Syracuse University Press, 1963) pp. 65–8 (excerpted). Reprinted by permission of the publisher.

CHARLES HALPERIN

Interpreting the Mongol Yoke: The Ideology of Silence

If the Novgorod Chronicle claimed that the Mongol conquest had been a singular, unmitigated catastrophe for Rus', others saw the Mongol overlordship differently. For one thing, as noted above, the Orthodox Church received from the Khan a guarantee of immunity—economic and judicial—from Mongol officials. Nevertheless, churchmen like others unrelentingly protested that the "godless Tatars" were responsible for the devastation of Rus'. The surviving narratives are studded with details about gruesome deeds allegedly carried out by the conquerors. In the selection which appears below, however, Charles Halperin argues for a different view. Basing his revision upon similar frontier encounters elsewhere in the world, Halperin finds that, although the Mongols doubtless did significant damage, they also had much positive to offer. The extant sources, however, betray scant recognition of such a contribution. Why? According to Halperin, religious intolerance generated an "ideology of silence" which refused to acknowledge the genuine achievements of the conquerors. Readers should pay special attention to the benefits of Mongol rule which Halperin identifies, and note the sources of information on which he relies.

———————

From the thirteenth to the fifteenth centuries, Russia fell under the sway of the Golden Horde, the successor state on the Volga River of the grand Mongol empire founded by Chinggis [Genghis] Khan. However, the Tatars, as the Mongols are called in the Russian sources, did not move into the Russian forest zone. In order to maintain their pastoral nomadic way of life, they remained in the Pontic and Caspian steppe, where they became assimilated with the indigenous Turkic-speaking nomadic population, the Kipchaks. By the fourteenth century, the shamanist Mongols had converted to Islam, so that Russo-Tatar relations became another variant of Christian-Muslim interaction. The Mongols restructured the social and political order of the steppe, the mainstay of international commerce and nomadism, but they left the political infrastructure of Russia alone because of its lesser importance to their economy and polity. Chinggis had decreed the toleration of all religions in his empire, a practice of most Inner Asian empires; thus even the Muslim Golden Horde did not interfere with the Russian Orthodox Church. As a result of the particular relationship between Russia and the Golden Horde, the Mongols influenced Russia, but the Russians did not influence the Tatars. Therefore . . . in the Russo-Tatar instance, the con-

quered wound up borrowing the institutions of their absentee conquerors.

The Mongol conquest of Russia was enormously destructive, and the economic drain of subsequent raids and taxes was probably an even greater assault. It is hardly surprising that the medieval Russian sources present the Tatars as cruel and evil infidels, either instruments of divine chastisement for Russian sins or henchmen of the Devil, sowing discord among true Christians. Experience justified such invective, although the Mongol assaults had nothing to do with religion. However, there is another side to the story of Russo-Tatar relations.

Considerable evidence demonstrates that despite the stereotyped negative image of the Tatars in the Russian sources, less hostile relations between the two peoples also existed. A number of Russian princes married Tatar princesses . . . [who] converted from shamanism to Russian Orthodox Christianity. The Russians borrowed heavily from Mongol political, military, administrative, and fiscal institutions, for example, the postal service which the Mongols had perfected to carry information and people across the Eurasian continent; the division of the army into the five divisions of advance guard, main regiment, left and right flanks, and rear guard; the Mongol customs tax, tax-collector and seal, and treasury; and Mongol diplomatic etiquette. The Russians showed praiseworthy perspicacity in imitating the institutions in warfare and government which had permitted the Mongols to create and control an empire stretching from the Pacific to the Baltic and Black Seas. The Muscovites did not borrow institutions which did not suit them; for example, the census was too equitable for the Russian aristocracy and the *diwan* system of bureaucracy from Persia bore the taint of Islam. Instead the Russians mostly copied Horde institutions from the all-Mongol empire, preferring Mongol institutions less associated with Islam . . . [I]ntermarriage and institutional borrowing thus finessed the religious obstacle to pragmatic relations, through conversion and selectivity, but neither activity accords well with the depiction of the

Tatars in Russian sources as blood-sucking infidels.

The economic burden which Mongol rule imposed on the Russians was partially offset in two ways. First, Russian princes who participated in joint Russo-Tatar military campaigns shared in the booty. Second, Russians participated in and profited from the expansion of international commerce under the Pax Mongolica. In Russia the Mongols rerouted the fur trade to extract greater revenue; as a result, Muscovite and Ustiug merchants, rather than Novgorodian, reaped the benefits ... Booty and commerce mitigated the economic drain of Mongol rule in Russia.

Presumably, those Russian princes, nobles, officials, merchants, and clerics who dealt frequently with the Horde had the greatest incentive to learn Tatar, the Turkic dialect which became dominant in the Horde. At first, some baptized bilingual Kipchaks served as translators, although this practice did not equal in scope or significance the use of ethnic intermediaries elsewhere on the medieval religious frontier. Some Arabic names and slogans found their way onto bilingual Russian coins ... The fifteenth-century Tverian merchant Afanasii Nikitin so mastered a kind of oriental patois of Turkic, Persian, and Arabic that he unconsciously slipped in and out of it in composing his travelogue about India. Bilingualism must have been more prevalent than our scanty sources admit ...

The Russians acquired an intimate familiarity with the geography, personnel, society, mores, and customs of the Horde ... They had no choice but to acquire such knowledge, since political survival in dealing with the Horde depended on it. The Russians fully mastered Mongol political concepts and ideology. They utilized such Mongol terms as *orda* (horde) and *ulus* (people-state) with ease. Most important, they understood the single overriding political principle upon which the Mongol empire rested, the blood legitimacy of the clan of Chinggis [Genghis] Khan ... The Muscovites may even have modelled their dynastic concept upon that of the Chinggissids.

Despite religious prejudice, the Russians developed a comprehensive, pragmatic expertise and even ideological fluency in Horde affairs.

That the Mongols did not influence Russian high culture was attributable to Russian religious practice, and not to a sense of the superiority of Russian culture to that of the "barbarian" nomads. Horde culture cannot be called inferior; Sarai, the Horde capital, with its aquaducts, caravansaries, *medresses* (religious schools), mosques, and foreign merchants' quarters, rivalled any medieval Russian city. The Golden Horde enjoyed a respectable Muslim religious culture, which is precisely why the Russians could not borrow from it. The Russians did not seek better ways to build a mosque or comment upon the Koran. The high culture of the Horde was untouchable, religiously tabu, to the Russians. Texts of oriental literature which reached Russia before or during the Mongol period had already been sanitized, i.e., Christianized, and it is doubtful that the Russians even knew of their infidel origin. As elsewhere on the medieval religious frontier, those areas of life closest to religion, such as the Russian high culture, most resisted infidel influence.

The Muscovites could not discard all elements of pragmatic relations with the Mongols after the overthrow of the "Tatar Yoke" in 1480. Muscovy still had to deal with the successor states of the Golden Horde; annexation of Kazan' and Astrakhan' waited until the 1550s, and of the Crimea, which became a vassal of the Ottomans, until the late eighteenth century. Chinggisids continued to enjoy high status in sixteenth-century Muscovy, the by then Russian postal service served neither pork nor alcohol to Muslims, and a Muslim could swear an oath on a Koran kept in the Kremlin ... Muslim envoys prayed daily to Allah in the capital of the Orthodox Christian empire of Muscovy. However, the growing social and political pressures of Russian centralization generated tensions which found their outlet in religious and ethnic antagonism and demands for homogeneity. A virulently anti-Muslim sentiment arose in the militant wing of the Russian Orthodox Church, which produced an aggressive missionary policy in annexed Kazan' ... During the seventeenth century, Russian involvement with the steppe in general declined and Russian need for steppe expertise greatly diminished. Therefore, Russia's need for pragmatic relations with the Mongols outlasted Mongol sovereignty by about a century, after which the pressures of prejudice reasserted themselves with new and greater potency.

No medieval Russian source of the Mongol period comments on the Russian familiarity with the steppe, or explains why Russians cultivated such knowledge of the infidel. Russian Orthodox Christian canon law frowned upon socializing with the infidels, but Russian priests could accompany the nomadic Horde to provide for the religious needs of Russian faithful; why Russians joined in nomadic journeys with the Horde went unmentioned. Only the Mongol name betrays the Horde origin of Mongol institutions borrowed by the Muscovites. No medieval Russian merchant had a kind word to say about steppe merchants, and the chronicles treated intermarriage gingerly. A chronicle would criticize a rival Russian prince for employing Tatar military auxiliaries or assistance, but if the chronicler's princely patron relied upon Horde military or political allies, this policy escaped critique. . . . [T]he Russians did not permit their pragmatic relations with the Tatars to soften the religiously hostile portrayal of the infidels in the medieval Russian sources. Silence shrouded cooperation; value judgments concerning Tatars dwelt only on Tatar evil. No medieval Russian writer articulated an ideology for coexistence with the Tatars. . . .

Thus the medieval religious frontier suffered a precarious existence. It functioned during the interim between the initial conquest and the development of power sufficient to allow the sentiments of the conquered to be disregarded, and also in situations where neither side in the struggle had the ability to eliminate the other. The transience of the frontier derived from its intrinsic instability. . . .

The demands of religious prejudice prevented the formulation or articulation of any medieval theories genuinely equivalent to modern concepts of peaceful coexistence or détente. One might admire, intermarry with, trade with, even borrow intellectual skills from, the infidel, but never concede the legitimacy of his religion. To admit the legitimacy of the religion of the enemy would have automatically called into question the insistence upon the exclusive religious superiority of one's own. Since religion subsumed under it one's conception of the political and social order—one's way of life—such ideological tolerance would have undermined the social, political, and cultural foundations of one's own society and polity. For this reason, exchange at the intellectual level, inextricably tied to religion, became even more difficult to achieve.

By and large, therefore, medieval frontier societies preferred to deal with the contradiction between the ideal and real, between prejudice and pragmatism, with ideologically motivated silence.

SOURCE: Charles J. Halperin, "The Ideology of Silence: Prejudice and Pragmatism on the Medieval Religious Frontier," *Comparative Studies in Society and History* 27 (1984): 459–66 (excerpted). Footnotes and some Russian terms have been omitted. Reprinted by permission of Cambridge University Press.

7

Economy and Society in
Post-Kievan Rus'

If the outlines of social organization and the dimensions of the economy are difficult to make out in Kievan Rus', the task is somewhat easier in the period which followed Kiev's decline. The Expanded Pravda Russkaia, probably completed sometime late in the twelfth or early in the thirteenth century, documents economic change, including an entire set of regulations on interest and commercial loans. The same code features special sections on slavery, indentured labor, and inheritance, laying out in bold relief many characteristics of society and economy.

But among legal texts of the era, probably the Novgorod Judicial Charter stands out as an index to economic and social change. As noted below, the text which survives derives from a relatively late time, and in any case is incomplete. Still, the Novgorod Judicial Charter contains a fascinating portrait of the economy and society which came to prevail in northwest Rus'. Many aspects of the code deserve careful attention, but for present purposes the reader ought note what the law tells us about social differentiation, about the legal standing of women, and about the role of documentation in judicial hearings. Likewise, one may compare the extant sections of the Charter with the Pravda Russkaia to determine what changes in the economy the law registers. In the same vein, comparing the Pravda with the Novgorod Judicial Charter reveals a significant change in judicial procedure which later Muscovite court cases reinforce. Although not all peasant litigants were up to the new demands, Muscovite litigation like that in Novgorod, came to depend increasingly upon written proofs, a change which significantly altered the conduct of litigation.

The economy in these years, however, had to cope with some especially heavy strains, chief among which was the Mongol conquest. To determine the exact cost of the invasion is not possible, but we need nevertheless to understand the general consequences. A. M. Sakharov reminds us that the Mongol armies struck primarily at cities, and in so doing they destroyed the basic infrastructure of the economy—buildings, workshops, markets, housing stock—as well as decimating and scattering the population. The initial consequence, then, whatever the subsequent result, was a severe blow to productivity. But to Sakharov, even more telling was the indirect consequence of the invasions and destructions. By impoverishing the population at the conquest, and later demanding payment of large taxes, the Mongols helped set the stage for an entirely new form of social and economic organization. In this environment of want, in the absence of urban crafts and capital accumulation, agriculture resumed its status as the unrivaled basis of the economy. But, in contrast to the earlier period when agriculture had also been dominant, now the raping of the countryside demanded that individual peasants seek protection, so grave was the financial disaster. And protection came increasingly in the form of great lords—monastic institutions as often as secular lords—who strove to chain their labor supply to the land they tilled. If Sakharov is to be believed, the Mongol conquest was of considerably more import than most historians have assumed.

But, as we have had occasion several times before to note, the economy in northwest Rus' enjoyed considerable prosperity, even in the very years when the Mongol conquest devastated other parts of Rus'. Much of Novgorod's prosperity revolved around trade which sometimes reached remote points indeed. The amber trade which E. A. Rybina discussed is one example of Novgorod's distant commerce, but another, even more profitable trade concerned fur which merchant and peasant alike harvested from the great forests of northern Rus'. For many years this was a most lucrative enterprise, but its collapse, coinciding with political pressure from Moscow, proved the last blow to Novgorodian independence.

DOCUMENTS

The Novgorod Judicial Charter (Late Fifteenth Century)

The Novgorod Judicial Charter survives only in a fragment and only from its revision after the Moscow conquest which the Nikonian Chronicle related above. As a result, the Charter contains many provisions which extend to the Grand Prince substantial latitude in deciding certain kinds of litigation. At the same time, however, the Novgorod Judicial Charter, even in this late and fragmentary form, reveals much about the authority which the Novgorod archbishop and mayor had exercised in the years before their collision with Ivan III. The Charter also details court procedure, demonstrating considerable innovation since the days of the Pravda Russkaia. Finally, and perhaps most interestingly, the Novgorod Judicial Charter reveals some contours of the local economy. One finds here ample evidence of merchant activity, and also indication that by the fifteenth century, at any rate, the courts did a lively business in litigation over land, indicating that land ownership was well-developed in Novgorod.

ON COURT[S] AND ON SURETY [DEPOSITS?] FOR THOSE WHO COMMIT ASSAULT AND ROBBERY

Having conferred with [our] lords the grand princes, Grand Prince of All Rus' Ivan Vasilievich [III (1440–1506)], and his son, Grand Prince Ivan Ivanovich [1458–90] of All Rus', and according to the blessing of the hieromonk Feofil [Theophilus] who was named to the archbishopric of Novgorod the Great and Pskov, so [then] the mayors of Novgorod, and the Novgorod millenariuses, and boyars, and ranking men, and merchants, and taxpaying townsmen, all five boroughs [of Novgorod], [and] all Lord Novgorod the Great at assembly in Iaroslav's court decided:

1. Hieromonk Feofil, who was appointed to the archbishopric of Novgorod the Great and Pskov, is to conduct his own court, the church court, according to the canons of the Holy Fathers [of the Church], [and] according to the Nomocanon; and he is to judge everyone equally, whether boyar, [a man of] middling means, or a poor man [lit., a young man].

2. And the mayor is to conduct his own court [together] with the Grand Prince's lieutenant according to custom; and without the Grand

Prince's lieutenant the mayor is not to conclude [judging] any case.

3. And the Grand Prince's lieutenants and overseers are to conduct their own judicial review according to custom.

4. And the millenarius is to conduct his own court.

4a. And they [the judges named above] are [all] to conduct [their courts] justly, according to [the oath to which they swore by] kissing the cross.

5. And at court [there should be no more than] two men. If someone selects someone [else to represent him in court], then he must allow him [his representative] to conduct the case.

5a. And [no one] is to remove the mayor and millenarius and the archbishop's lieutenant and their judges from [their] court[s].

6. And a complainant is not to slander a defendant, nor the mayor, nor the millenarius, nor the archbishop's lieutenant, nor any other judges, nor judges to whom the case was referred for decision. And if someone slanders the mayor, or the millenarius, or the archbishop's lieutenant, or other judges, or the judge to whom the case was referred for decision, or [if] a complainant [slanders] a defendant at court, or at the referral [hearing], or at the [dueling] field, then the Grand Prince and Novgorod the Great are to take from the guilty party for the slander 50 rubles [if he be] a boyar, 20 rubles [if he be] a man of middling means, and 10 rubles [if he be] a poor man; and the defendant is to take [his] losses [from the slanderer].

7. If someone is involved in a suit over land, [whether it be one] village, or two, or more, or fewer: until the hearing he is not to enter the land, nor send his own people [to that land]; rather, concerning the [question of ownership of the] land, he is to call [the other claimant] to court. If [he] wins [the suit] about the land, then he is to take from the judge a charter [certifying his right to] the land, and [he is to collect his] losses from the defendant; and from the land the judge is to take no fee.

8. And from [each] ruble [penalty prescribed by a] court, the archbishop, and his lieutenant, and the steward for [affixing] the seal take 1 grivna [= 10%], and from [each] ruble [penalty prescribed for a decision] without a [full] court hearing [because one litigant did not appear at court], the archbishop and his lieutenant and the steward are to take 3 dengas [= 1.5%] for [issuing] the charter [about the land]. And the mayor and millenarius and their judges and [any] other judges are to take from [each] ruble [penalty prescribed by] a court 7 dengas [= 3.5%], and from [each] ruble [penalty prescribed for a decision] without a [full] court hearing 3 dengas [= 1.5%].

9. The mayor, and millenarius, and archbishop's mayor,* and their judges, and [any] other judges are to complete their cases within a month; they are not to drag out cases beyond that term.

10. If someone in a suit about land accuses someone of assault or robbery: then first decide [the charges] of assault and robbery; and [then] decide the case about the land. If they convict someone of assault and robbery, then the Grand Prince and Novgorod the Great are to take from the guilty party: 50 rubles from a boyar, 20 rubles from a man of middling means, and 10 rubles from a poor man; and the [other] litigant is to take [his] losses [from the convicted man]; and [then hold] a hearing about the land. If there is no hearing in Novgorod [about the land], then [there shall be at least] a hearing on [the charges of] assault and robbery.

11. And if some complainant suddenly wishes to initiate a suit over assault or robbery and land, then the defendant is to answer him; and if he wins [the suit] over land and assault and robbery, then the judge is to give him a charter [certifying the results of the suit] over land, assault and robbery.

12. If someone wins a suit against someone over land and takes a judgment charter [certifying his victory], then he is to go to his own land according to the judgment charter, and he is to possess that land; and [he is to pay] no fine for that.

*Editor's note: Probably an error; should be archbishop's lieutenant.

13. If a complainant summons a defendant in some suit, and presses his own case [against the defendant], and if the defendant [has his own] suit against the [original] complainant; then the [second] litigant is to summon the [original] complainant [over his suit], and [so] try one and the same case [for both litigants simultaneously]; but do not accept other summonses against him in some other case, [and] do not instigate Novgorodians [against him], [but conduct the case] without deception in accordance with [the oath you swore when you] kissed the cross, until those cases [specified above] are resolved.

14. If someone initiates some suit against someone, without having kissed the cross to this charter, then, having kissed the cross, the one may begin the suit; and if a defendant [arrives to answer the charges] without having kissed the cross to this charter, then he is to answer [only after] he has kissed the cross [to be faithful to the provisions of this document]; if he does not kiss the cross, then he loses [the case].

15. If a defendant in some suit presents himself at court, and the complainant will not have kissed the cross [to be faithful] to this charter, then the complainant is to kiss the cross alone, and the defendant in his place answers [the charge]; but [if] he does not kiss the cross, then he loses [the case].

16. If someone has a complaint against a widow of a great [man] or [a man] of middling means, and if she has a son, then her son is to kiss the cross [both] for himself and his mother; if the son does not kiss the cross for his mother, then [his] mother is to kiss the cross for herself in [her] home in the presence of the plaintiff and the Novgorod bailiffs.

17. And a boyar and a man of middling means, and merchant are to kiss the cross [in suits] both over their own land and [their] wives' [land].

18. If they summon a boyar or man of middling means or merchant to his land, or to [his] wife's land, then he [himself] is to answer [them] or send a representative in his place and in [his] wife's [place], [and] kiss the cross on that.

19. And the representative [whom the de-fendant nominated] and a character witness are to kiss the cross at the hearing.

20. And those judges to whom [a case] was referred [for final decision] shall complete the case [and issue a decision].

21. If judges refer [the case] to [other] judges [for review and final decision], then the judge [of the original hearing] is to order his secretary to write a record of the hearing; and the referring judges are to affix their seals to this copy [of the trial record].

22. And there shall not be a character witness to testify against a character witness. And neither is a resident of Pskov nor a full slave to serve as character witness [against a free Novgorodian]. But a slave may act as witness [only] against [another] slave.

23. If some [litigant together] with some other [litigant] refers to [the same] character witness, then the deputy is to take his fees for 100 versts [= 66 miles] according to custom, and the bailiffs and the archbishop's bailiffs and the town criers and the men who deliv-ered the summonses [all are to take] 4 grivnas for 100 versts. If some litigant refers to a wit-ness [who is] more than 100 versts [from Nov-gorod], and if the other litigant wants to refer to that same witness: then [they may both] re-fer to him [and the bailiffs shall summon him]; if the other litigant does not wish to refer [to a witness who is] more than 100 versts [from Novgorod], then he is to present his own witness at court; and he will have three weeks to deliver the witness for [every] 100 versts [from Novgorod that the witness lives]; and the loser [in the case] is to provide the deputy's fees for 100 versts.

24. If someone goes to court with someone about land, [and] then requests a postpone-ment [to obtain additional] evidence, or [to summon] co-owners [of the land in question], then give him one postponement [of] three weeks for [every] 100 versts [he needs to travel to locate the additional evidence or co-own-ers]; but if [the evidence or co-owners] are fur-ther or closer [than 100 versts], then [set the postponement] according to this allowance [i.e., 3 weeks for every 100 versts]; and he [the litigant who requests the postponement] is to refer by name under oath to the co-owner with

whom the evidence is stored; and he is to obtain the agreement of the other litigant; and the mayor is to affix his seal to the postponement charter. And there is to be no other postponement. And a grivna [fee] is to be collected for the postponement. Likewise, all other judges are to award a postponement according to the same [principle]. And if a litigant does not obtain a postponement [charter] with [the appropriate] seal, then the judge, before whom the case was being heard, is to declare him to have lost the case; and do not wait [to decide the case] for the postponement term. And [judges are to handle] postponement [requests] in [all] other cases according to custom.

25. And people of good repute are to be in attendance in the overseer's quarters [for a trial], one person for each bailiff from [each litigating] side; and [furthermore] they are to judge [cases] justly, having kissed the cross to this charter.

26. And the referral [hearing] is to take place in the archbishop's quarters, and at the referral [hearing] there should sit in court from each borough one boyar and one man of middling means, and [any] other persons [who attended the original] hearing, together with bailiffs; and no one else shall be [in attendance] at the referral [hearing]. And the referral judges shall hold hearings three times a week, on Monday, Wednesday, and Friday. If some referral judge does not hold a hearing on that day [sic], then take [as a fine] 2 rubles [if he be] a boyar, and 1 ruble [if he be] a man of middling means. And the referral judges are to take no bribe from the referral hearing, nor are they to befriend [a litigant] by any deception at the referral hearing, in accordance with [the oath they swore when they] kissed the cross. And if someone is to conduct a referral hearing, then he is to kiss the cross to this charter once and for all.

27. And the mayor and millenarius and the archbishop's lieutenant and their judges and all other judges are to kiss the cross [to swear that they] will judge justly.

28. And [judges are to] complete cases on land [disputes] within two months, and [they are] not to delay [such cases] more than two months. Just as soon as the official responsible for establishing the border comes [to court] from the border [measurement], then the same mayor is to complete the case in another two months, and [he] is not to delay [the case any] longer. If some mayor, having sent the border inspector [on a case], then [himself] leaves town for an extended period without having finished the case, then the Grand Princes and Novgorod the Great [will exact as a fine] 50 rubles from that mayor, and the litigant takes [his own] losses [from him]; if a millenarius or an archbishop's lieutenant goes out of town for an extended period without having completed a case, then the Grand Princes and Novgorod the Great are to take 50 rubles [from him as a fine], and the litigant takes [his own] losses [from them].

29. If a judge does not complete a case over land within two months, then the litigant is to take bailiffs from Novgorod the Great against him [the judge], and he [the judge] is to finish that case in the presence of those bailiffs. If the referral judges do not return [the case] to the judge within [the specified] two months, then [that] judge is to go with the litigant to Novgorod the Great, and [he is to take] bailiffs against the referral judges, [and] then the referral judges are to return that case to the [original] judge in the presence of the bailiffs, and the judge is to complete that case for the litigant in the presence of those same bailiffs.

30. If litigants request a postponement from some judge and [they receive] postponement [charters] with [the judge's] seals, and [then] that judge is replaced, and someone [else] will be the judge in his place, then those litigants are to appear before those judges [sic] and present their postponement [charters] for that postponement, and that judge is to judge that case and complete [it].

31. If one litigant appears before the judge at the time specified [in the postponement charter], and places his postponement charter [before the judge], but the other [litigant] does not appear, then the judge is to issue against him a [judgment] charter, and [the judge is to] attach the postponement charter to that [judgment charter], but he is not to summon him [again].

32. If a representative be in someone's place [and he] received a postponement, but before [the expiration] of that postponement the replacement died, then at the [expiration of the] postponement the litigant himself must appear [in court] or [he must nominate] some other representative [to appear in his place]; if he himself does not appear or if he does not nominate another representative [to appear in court in his place], then he loses the case.

33. If someone wins [against] someone [a case] over theft in the presence of physical evidence, or assault, or robbery, or homicide, or slavery, or over a dueling charter, then the judges are to take 4 grivnas for a judgment charter [at the conclusion of litigation], and 2 grivnas for [issuing a decision that did not require litigation].

34. If someone takes a judgment charter against someone, and he [who lost the case wants to negotiate] something with the judge or plaintiff, then he is to [complete] negotiation with them [within] a month; [but] if he does not begin to negotiate in that month, then take bailiffs from the [Novgorod] assembly against him, and [he] is to seize him in the town or village with those bailiffs; if he begins to hide from the bailiffs, then all Novgorod the Great is to punish him.

35. If a character witness implicates someone, then [the litigant] has two weeks to present [the witness to refute the charge]; if in those [two weeks the litigant] does not summon the witness, then summon the litigant; if the litigant hides the witness, then his testimony is not acceptable [lit., then that testimony is not testimony], and award the decision to the other litigant. If someone [who is accused of a crime] does not begin to summon a witness or litigant in those two weeks, then issue against him a judgment charter according to that testimony.

36. If someone goes to court with a man [slave?] of the archbishop, or a boyar's [man], or a [man who serves] a man of middling means, or a merchant's [man], or a monastery's [man], or a [man] of a [Novgorod] borough, or [Novgorod] street over [a charge of] theft, assault, robbery, arson, homicide, [or] slavery, and whoever [of such plaintiffs] will

kiss the cross to this document, that his word is just, and give his hand [guarantee? provide surety?] according to his oath, that that [accused] man is a thief and robber or arsonist or murderer or slave, then in whatever district the archbishop's lieutenant or overseer is, then they are to present that man at court; if the overseer is a boyar's [man] or [overseer] of a man of middling means, or of a merchant or monastery, or from a [Novgorod] borough or street, then [they] likewise are to present [the accused] at court; and [they] are to take three weeks for [each] 100 versts [that they have to travel in order to apprehend and present the accused at court]; and [if the accused] is nearer or further [than 100 versts from Novgorod, they are to calculate the time allotted them] according to this formula; and [they are] not to employ force against them [to bring the accused] to court, and whoever exercised [unnecessary] force will stand accused.

37. If they win a case against someone, and he is given away [as a slave to the winner] in a [judgment] charter, then he is not to live in the district of that [former] lord; but if he [indeed] lives in the district of that [former] lord, and they prove that, [then his new] lord takes his losses [from the losing side]. If the [man] flees to some other district, then the [new] lord is to return him to the plaintiff; and neither he [the lord] nor his people are to send him into another district, [and] they [are to] kiss the cross [to that effect]; regarding any other matters, then the litigants are to settle [them] themselves. [If] someone under oath denies that that man is with him, and gives his hand [guarantee? provides surety?] on that, but they prove that the man [in fact] is in his district, then the lord is to restore the losses to that [plaintiff]. If [the man] flees to some lord in another district, [then that] lord is to present him at court according to [the oath he swore by] kissing the cross. If someone does not present [such a fugitive], then seize his deposit [the guarantee that he left] according to the Novgorod [Judicial] Charter.

38. If someone accuses a man [who serves] the archbishop, a boyar, a man of middling means, a merchant, a monastery, [Novgorod] borough or street, and he himself will not kiss

the cross to this charter, then he himself is to settle [the matter] with the defendant by his own evidence, without [the assistance] of [his] lord.

39. If someone pledges to [appear] at court at some [certain] day, then after the pledge do not send to him a summons; but if the judge does not hold a hearing on that day, then when the judge holds the hearing, [send] him a summons; if he does not see the summons, and begins to hide, then send a summons to his residence three times, and the crier is to shout out [his summons]; and if [after that] he [still] does not appear at court, then issue against him a promissory charter, but the ex-action [specified in the charter] is not to be more than 3 dengas.

40. If they bring a bailiff to a village, and they begin to beat him, then issue to his [the bail-iff's] nephew or friend in place of a summons a charter [certifying a decision against those who beat the bailiff, even though no trial was held].

41. If someone summons someone to a vil-lage by a bailiff or courtier, then give him two weeks for [each] 100 versts [to effect the sum-mons], and if [the object of the summons is] further or nearer [than 100 versts], then use that formula [to calculate the time allowed to summon the man].

42. From a [Novgorod] borough, or street, or hundred, or row, litigants are to go [to court] in pairs, and no other [person] is to go to court or to the investigation [to provide] help. If there is a slander from a [Novgorod] borough, or street, or hundred, or row, then the Grand Princes and Novgorod the Great are to exact from those two men according to the Novgorod Char.*

SOURCE: *The Laws of Rus' (Tenth to Fifteenth Centuries)*. Trans-lated and edited by Daniel H. Kaiser (Salt Lake City: Charles Schlacks, Jr., forthcoming), pp. 79–86. English translation copyright © 1992 Daniel H. Kaiser.

Editor's note: The charter is interrupted here, and no more survives; presumably the entire text was much longer, approximating in length the Pskov Judicial Charter.

A Muscovite Judgment Charter (ca. 1463)

Muscovite law codes—the *Sudebniki* of 1497 and 1550—make special provision for the con-duct of trials before the Grand Prince's rep-resentatives. These hearings left much to the discretion of the litigants, who were obliged to provide their own evidence, whether it be writ-ten documentation, oral testimony, or some form of "God's Justice" (lots, trials, or even judicial duel—although it seems that litigants were more often expected to offer to under-take these extremes rather than actually un-dergo them). The judge in these proceedings took a relatively passive and inactive part, re-stricting himself to inquiring (almost formu-laically) of the litigants what evidence they had to substantiate their claims. The hearing rec-ord then seems to have travelled routinely to a court of higher instance (normally the Grand Prince himself), where the matter was decided. Quite a number of these trial records have survived, the earliest coming from the fif-teenth century. The example which appears below is typical in many respects, revealing at work both the traditional forms of testimony and the more abstruse, less familiar forms of written evidence. In this way, Muscovite judg-ment charters relay not only a judicial deci-sion, but also hint at the values and procedures which prevailed in Muscovite society.

JUDGE IAKOV SHACHEVAL'TSEV
TO THE AUTHORITIES OF THE SIMONOV
MONASTERY . . . FOR THE DESERTED VILLAGES
KUZEMKINO AND DERNKOVO . . .

On instructions of Grand Prince Ivan Vasil'ev-ich, and in accordance with the Grand Prince's charter, Iakov Shacheval'sev [sic] tried this case, standing on the land [of] the deserted village[s] Kuzemkino Tsechetkino, and Dern-kovo. Kornilko and Ivashko were in litigation with the Simonov monasterial supervisor Nikita, and with the Bylovo [village] estate manager Misailo.

Thus spoke Kornilko and Ivashko: "Sire, those deserted village[s] Kuzemkino and Dernkovo have been the Grand Prince's taxpaying cantonal land since olden time. And now, Sire, those [monasterial] elders, from their Bylovo village, are ploughing this [Grand Princely] land, we know not why."

And the judge ordered the elders, Nikita the supervisor and Misailo: "Answer!"

And Mikita the supervisor and Misailo spoke thus: "Sire, those deserted village[s] Kuzemkino and Dernkovo are the monastery's land, our [land]; Timofei Dybin, Sire, willed us those deserted lands of Kuzemkino and Strynevo, for the house of the Immaculate [Mother of God], to the Simonov [monastery], in accordance with Grand Princess Sof'ia's charter; that, Sire, was almost thirty years ago. And, Sire, Vasilei Mikhailovich Morozov willed Dernkovo to the monastery, likewise almost thirty years ago—our monastery has its fourth archimandrite [since then]. And, Sire, those lands were registered for us. And since those archimandrites, Sire, a fifth estate manager [has been employed] in our village Bylovo. And, Sire, our estate managers have ploughed those lands for the monastery. And all this time, Sire, we have heard no formal protest from anyone about these lands."

And Kornilko spoke thus: "Sire, Timofei Dybin gave them his land. And we, Sire, are not trespassing on that land of theirs."

And the elders, Mikita the supervisor and Misailo, placed [before the judge] the Grand Princess's charter.

And the judge examined the charter, and in the charter [the following was] written:

Lo I, Grand Princess Sof'ia, have bestowed my favor on Timofei Dybin, [and] have permitted him to give the Dybinskie deserted lands to the house of the Immaculate [Mother of God] at the Simonov [monastery].

And the judge asked Kornilko and Ivashko: "Where then do ye yourselves live, [and] how long then has it been since the elders began to plough these deserted lands?"

And Kornilko and Ivashko spoke thus: "We live, Sire, here with them near Iakov Podubitsyn's gully. And they came riding [here from their village] and began to plough the deserted lands—Sire, about fifteen years ago."

And the judge asked Kornilko and Ivashko: "Why did ye, living with them in the same place, near the gully, say nothing to them from that time until now?"

And Kornilko and Ivashko spoke thus: "We, Sire, were not [then] concerned with the land."

And the judge asked Kornilko and Ivashko: "Who then are your witnesses for these lands Kuzemkino and Dernkovo, [to testify] that this land has been the Grand Prince's cantonal land since olden times?"

And Kornilko and Ivashko spoke thus: "Sire, for this we have [as] witnesses the old fiftyman Lazar' Koporulin, and the old tenman Ivashko Lyko, and Iakov Podubitsyn, and Kostia Bobichev, and Makar—to them is it known, Sire, that this has been the Grand Prince's land from olden times."

And the judge asked the Simonov [monastery] elders: "Have ye any witnesses [to testify] that this deserted land is Kuzemkino Dybinskoe, and Dernkovo, and [that] this Kuzemkino has gone since olden times with that Dybinskaia land [for cadastral purposes], and [that] Dernkovo belonged to Vasilei Mikhailovich Morozov?"

And the supervisor Mikita and Misailo spoke thus: "For this, Sire, we have the longtime residents Fedor Lokot' the cantonal man, and Olfer Malygin, and Volodia Stanip'ian, and Vantei—to them, Sire, is it known that this deserted land Kuzemkino has gone with the Dybinskaia land; and that is solely Dybinskaia land, Sire. And, Sire, Vasilei Mikhailovich [Morozov] gave us that Dernkovo for the monastery."

And the judge ordered both litigants to present their witnesses on the land. And both litigants presented [their] witnesses on the land.

And the judge asked Kornilko's and Ivashko's witnesses, the old fiftyman Lazar' and the old tenman Ivashko Lyko, and Iakov Podubitsyn, and Kostia and Makar: "Tell [us], brothers, as is right before God, whose is that land?"

And Lazar' spoke thus: "I, Sire, remember back fifteen years before Edigei's raid [a Tartar attack into central Muscovy in 1408]: at that time Kuzemka Chechetka lived on that land, and on the other [land] lived Dernko—and those are the Grand Prince's cantonal deserted lands—and, Sire, [they] paid tribute [to the Grand Prince] and went with us in [the payment of] all levies. And, Sire, my father was then the fiftyman in those same lands. And, Sire, when my father died, then, Sire, after Edigei's raid I was the fiftyman in the same lands for eight years."

And Iakov Podubitsyn, and Lyko the tenman, and Kostia, and Makar spoke thus: "It is known to us, Sire, that that has been the Grand Prince's cantonal land since olden times."

And the judge asked the elders' witnesses Fedor, and Olfer, and Volodia and Vantei: "Tell [us], brothers, as is right, whose land is that?"

And Fedor spoke thus: "I, Sire, remember back twenty years before Edigei's raid, and, Sire, that is boyar-held land. And, Sire, Grigorei Dybin lived on the Strynevskaia land. And after that, Sire, it became Timofei Dybin's land. And, Sire, this land where we are standing has been since olden times solely boyar-held Dybinskaia land. And, Sire, Vasilei Mikhailovich [Morozov] willed that Dernkovo [land] to the Simonov monastery, and, Sire, that too is boyar-held land, and has gone with this village of Bylovo [for cadastral purposes]."

And Alfer, and Volodia, and Vantei spoke thus: "We, Sire, know that land—it has been boyar-held land since olden times; that, Sire, was Timofei Dybin's land, and, Sire, it went with Strynevo [for cadastral purposes]. And that, Sire, is Dernkovo; Vasilei Mikhailovich [Morozov] willed that land to the monastery, and, Sire, it too [was] boyar-held land. And, Sire, we have been ploughing that land for the monastery for almost thirty years."

And the judge spoke thus to both [sets of] witnesses: "What evidence do ye have in support of your [various] claims? [For] thou, La-

zar, with [thy] comrades, dost call it cantonal taxheld land, and not tax-paying [land]."

And Lazar' and [his] comrades spoke thus: "Sire, thou shalt award us a judicial duel for the Grand Prince's land, and we, Sire, shall go to the [dueling] field with the monastery's witnesses."

And the elders—Mikita the supervisor and Misailo, spoke thus: "Sire, the house of the Immaculate [Mother of God]—the Simonov monastery—is [on] the sovereign Grand Prince's [land], and, Sire, the monastery's lands are both God's and the Grand Prince's. And, Sire, we shall order our witnesses not to go to the [dueling] field. And thou thyself hast heard, Sire judge, what Kornilko and Ivashko are saying before thee: that we have ploughed that land for fifteen years. And, Sire, we have ploughed this land for almost thirty years. And those lands have all been cleared (of conflicting claims) by Grand Prince Vasilei Vasil'evich's charter of grant. And those lands were given [to the monastery] during the tenure of archimandrite Iona and archimandrite Ivan. And here, Sire, is that charter."

And the judge examined the charter; and in the charter [the following was] written:

For the mercy of the holy Mother of God, [and for] her pious dormition, lo I, Grand Prince Vasilei Vasil'evich, have bestowed my favor upon archimandrite Gerontii and the brethren of my Simonov monastery, for the house of the holy Mother of God. [I affirm] that they had charters of grant to the monastery from my grandfather, Grand Prince Dmitrei Ivanovich, and from my father, Grand Prince Vasilei Dmitrievich, and from me, Grand Prince Vasilei Vasil'evich—and those charters burned up in the city. Likewise whoever gave something to them for the monastery, lands and waters, and meadows, and forests, and any appurtenances whatever, and whatever they themselves (the monasterial authorities) purchased from anyone—all those charters of purchase and donation perished in the fire. And whatever went with the monastery prior to that fire, during the tenure of archimandrite Iona and archimandrite Ivan—whatever lands and waters, and meadows and any other appurtenances whatever, anything at all— all that shall go with the monastery in the same way as it went before. And no one shall trespass on their [lands] in any matter. And [this] charter was issued in the year six thousand nine hundred and fifty-six (1448) on the fourth day of January.

And in Grand Prince Ivan Vasil'evich's charter the same was written, word for word.

And the judge agreed to refer this matter to [his] lord the Grand Prince. And placing both litigants before the Grand Prince, he presented the records from his court [before him].

And the Grand Prince, examining the trial records, [and] having heard the trial [record read aloud], ordered the judge Iakov Shacheval'tsev to give judgment in favor of Mikita the supervisor and Misailo, [for themselves] and in place of archimandrite Antonii, and he ordered [him] to give judgment against Kornilko and Ivashko; and he ordered [the judge] to award the land—the deserted village[s] Kuzemkino and Dernkovo—to the archimandrite and the brethren.

And when Iakov the judge, placing both litigants before the Grand Prince, told [the

Grand Prince] about the proceedings in his court, the [following] boyars were present with the Grand Prince: Prince Dmitrei Ivanovich, and Volodimer Grigor'evich, and the Grand Prince's secretaries Fedor Semenovich and Oleksei Poluekhtovich.

And at the trial on the land were: Fedor Levskoi the hundredman, and Vasilei Eufim'ev, and Ivan Kulepanov, and Iakov Pasynkov, and Semen Stolbov, and Ruka the counted man.

And on the original trial report is a black seal.

SOURCE: *Russian Private Law XIV-XVII Centuries.* Translated and edited by H. W. Dewey and A. M. Kleimola, Michigan Slavic Materials, no. 9 (Ann Arbor: Department of Slavic Languages and Literatures, University of Michigan, 1973), pp. 63–66. Transliteration and spelling have been slightly modified, and some Russian terms have been omitted. Reprinted by permission of Michigan Slavic Publications, Department of Slavic Languages and Literatures, University of Michigan.

LITERATURE

ANN M. KLEIMOLA
Justice in Medieval Russia

Judgment charters confirm that the judicial system had undergone considerable development since the codes of Kievan Rus', which had made no provision for this kind of litigation. At the same time, however, there was in the adjudication much which owed its origin to distant times and irrational proofs, not unlike those which had governed dispute settlement in ancient Rus'. Here Ann Kleimola describes court process as the judgment charters depict it, demonstrating both the innovation and tradition inherent in early Muscovite practice.

Testimony of witnesses was the form of evidence most frequently used in the trials recorded in the judgment charters. The majority

of these documents dealt with land disputes, and here the witnesses called upon to testify most often belonged to the category known as *starozhil'tsy* (longtime residents of the area) or *dobrye liudi* ("good men," probably because they were reputable members of the community). The testimony of the longtime residents usually followed a standard pattern. Before stating the facts, the men indicated the period of years for which they had knowledge of local events, generally beginning with the eldest, although a strict precedence based on age was not always followed. A 1490 document provides a good illustration. The plaintiff, when asked why he called the land the monastery's, replied: "This is known, Sire, to [our] good men, the longtime residents Timokha Denisov, and Senka Veraksin, and Levon Nos, and Fedko Savelov, and Ivashko Medved', and Foka." All these men then appeared before the judge to testify. Timokha Denisov said: "I, Sire, remember seventy-five years that this Shishkinskoe deserted village is monasterial land of the Verznevskoe village." Senka Ver-aksin spoke next: "I, Sire, remember seventy years that it is monasterial land." Levon followed: "I, Sire, remember sixty-five years, and that deserted village is monasterial land." Fedko Savelov said: "I, Sire, remember sixty years, and that is monasterial land." Ivashko Medved' and Foka concluded the testimony: "And we, Sire, remember fifty years, [and] that deserted village Shishkinskoe is the Simonov Monastery's land and goes with their Verznevskoe village [for cadastral purposes]."...

The longtime residents served as "experts" on the land in question, testifying about its status (e.g., whether it was the Grand Prince's, a secular landholder's, monastery's, or the metropolitan's), how long it had been in the holder's possession, or had been part of a particular village, hamlet, or canton, who had plowed or mowed it in which years, or what the boundaries were. The testimony of such longtime residents would carry greater weight than that of newcomers to the area, and a litigant's case undoubtedly appeared stronger if his witnesses were actually old. One plaintiff, in fact, challenged a witness for the other side on the basis of age: "Sire, [his] witnesses testified before thee that Prince Ivan (the defendant) has been plowing that land, the deserted village Zelenevo, for thirty years; and, Sire, his witness Gridka Alekseev is not thirty years old." It must be kept in mind that the longtime residents, although called upon as experts, were not impartial; each litigant named his own witnesses, men he thought would support him, and he might include members of his own family.

Memory was the basis for all testimony of longtime residents in land cases. As we have seen, these men usually testified that they remembered for a specific number of years. There are even some instances of witnesses claiming to remember for ninety or one hundred years. While one is inclined to doubt the precision of their figures, particularly in the case of witnesses claiming to remember for such long periods of time, their relative chronology may have been roughly accurate. Vas-

iuk, a longtime resident who declared that he remembered for one hundred years, was probably the oldest man around, while his comrades Karpik and Petiunia, who remembered for seventy-five years, knew they were about the same age, and the two younger witnesses, who remembered for sixty and forty years, knew they were of a completely different generation. Witnesses tended to give their own ages in round numbers, yet would state that an event happened seventeen or even forty-nine ... years before. In no case is the year given by date. Usually there is just the simple statement that the witness remembers for so many years, or that the event occurred so many years before....

Witnesses usually testified on the basis of their own knowledge. ... Other witnesses, less frequently, testified about what their fathers had told them. For example, Mitiuk Kostin said:

Sire, I heard from my father that that was the deserted village Popkovo, and Popko lived here, and he gave that deserted village to Biser, and Biser gave the village Biserovo and the deserted village Popkovo to the metropolitan Fotei [to provide for prayers] for his soul, and [that was] about fifty years ago.

In another case the witness Gridia testified:

Sire, my father Malakh lived in Pereboro, and, Sire, I went with my father to those deserted lands to gather mushrooms, and, Sire, my father told me that those deserted lands Mikhailovskoe and Bliznino [were] the metropolitan's lands, and it has been twenty-five years, Sire, since my father told me, and, Sire, it is thirty-five years since my birth....

Many of the judgment charters recorded cases which involved boundary questions. Each party might claim that the land lay within his territory, or one might accuse the other of crossing the boundary, or incorporating land which did not belong to him. Since more effective surveying techniques had not come into use in Muscovy, boundary demarcations consisted of marks (crosses or notches ...) on trees, pits or holes ... dug in the ground, and various physical features of the landscape—rivers, streams, swamps, lakes, sand bars, duck snares, weirs, gullies, ravines, fences, paths, roads, rocks, stumps, and all manner of trees, such as gnarled oaks, three birches growing from one root, three pines in a cluster, shrubs, and trees which were crooked, bent over, split, cracked, twisted, charred, dried out, or without tops. Cases were tried on the disputed land, and often the judge was treated to an extensive tour of the neighborhood.

Boundary descriptions themselves were of two types, either very general or very specific. The land in question may be described as the area "where the plow has gone, where the axe has gone, where the scythe has gone," "where Vasilii's plow and scythe have gone, where the axe has gone." The specific descriptions, on the other hand, are very specific indeed and vary from case to case. Testimony concerning boundary divisions often concluded with an offer from the litigant or his witnesses to lead the judge along the boundary: "and come, Sire, we shall show thee the boundary, up to what point the land of the Kozlovo manorial village [goes]." "Sires, ride after us, we shall show you the boundaries between the Grand Prince's lands and the metropolitan's lands." Sometimes first one litigant, and then the other, led the judge along the "true boundaries." On other occasions, each litigant's witnesses acted as guides. Sometimes one of the litigants led the judge, as did the witnesses for the opponents. In yet other instances, each litigant, and then his witnesses, led the judge around the boundaries. It was imperative in such situations that a litigant and his witnesses know the boundaries and that witnesses point out exactly the same markers as their principal. . . .

Written records took second place. Litigants presented several different types of documents to support their claims: many had charters of grant, usually from the Grand Prince but occasionally from another landholder; some offered title-confirming charters; others presented purchase deeds. Still other documents could help prove title to disputed land. . .

Presentation of written proof gave rise to other problems. Some litigants, for various reasons, could not produce documents which would have supported their case. For example,

in a trial which took place between 1462 and 1470 the defendant, monk Semen of the Simonov Monastery, explained that the monastery had formerly possessed such proof of title: "Sire, we had purchase deeds and donation charters for those lands and deserted areas, but they burned up in the Suzdal' fire." Fire was the reason most commonly cited in explaining loss of documents. The defendant in a mid-fifteenth-century trial declared that he had his father's purchase deed for the land, and offered to produce it if the judge would give him a postponement. When he returned to the land on the designated date, however, he did not bring the document: "Sire, my purchase deed has burned up." The judgment charter is abbreviated, and there is no more information. Perhaps the defendant had been trying to bluff, hoping that no one would ask to see his purchase deed, and then fell back upon loss of the document in a fire to explain his failure to bring it. On the other hand, he could easily have been telling the truth; fires were not an uncommon event in Muscovite Russia . . .

[I]lliterate members of society apparently had great faith in the power of anything written, regardless of what it said. In explaining their presentation of a redemption charter, litigants declared that their father had had a purchase deed for part of the land in question, but the "bondsmen Levsha Tregub and Maksimko ran away from our father, and, Sire, those bondsmen stole that purchase deed for Bliznino, thinking [it was] their bondage document." These men apparently believed that removing the written record would aid them in attaining liberty. Others, however, upon being confronted with documents disproving their claims, expressed complete skepticism as to the accuracy of the evidence. When defendants in one case produced a judgment charter previously issued against the plaintiffs' father in an earlier trial over the disputed lands, the judge asked the plaintiffs whether they accepted the document. They replied: "Why should we accept [that]? Whatever they wanted for themselves, they wrote down.". . .

In addition to the evidence presented in witnesses' testimony and documents, cases could be decided upon the basis of other forms of proof. These methods of settling the issue, which could be suggested by the litigants or their witnesses, or decreed by the judge, can be termed collectively "God's justice."

The pagan custom of swearing by the earth continued to be used occasionally up to the nineteenth century. During boundary demarcations men walked around the borders of land which they claimed, and throughout the procedure carried a piece of turf . . . on their heads. In theory, if they did not show the true boundaries, the earth would strike them dead. The church, however, opposed this heathen survival, demanding that an icon be substituted, so that the symbol of the Mother of God would replace that of Mother Earth. A judgment charter issued between 1494 and 1499 refers to use of this procedure, walking with an icon to mark off the "true" boundaries, during an earlier boundary division. The defendant's witnesses, in the course of the trial, led the judge along the same markings and pits where "the Simonov [Monastery's] witnesses, with icon, had measured off [the land] for Ivan Bitiagovskoi" several years before. . . .

[A]nother form of "God's justice" was an oath taken upon kissing the cross; it was used for religious, political-administrative, and judicial purposes. Some judgment charters record instances where witnesses were asked to testify "after kissing the Grand Prince's cross." In a 1499 case, the defendants admitted that they did not know the boundaries of their land and agreed to accept whatever dividing line the plaintiff's longtime residents would point out. The judge then ordered the peasant witnesses to carry out their task: "Upon kissing the Grand Prince's cross, lead [us], brothers, in God's truth, where ye know that the boundary of the Metropolitan's land with the Ezhov land has been since olden times, since both litigants have placed themselves on your souls.". . .

While cross-kissing could be used as an independent form of proof, the judgment charters mention it most frequently in connection with a third form of "God's justice," the judicial duel. . . . Litigants (or more often their witnesses) could offer to fight a duel with the opposition in an attempt to counter the other side's evidence. Some requested a judicial duel after declaring that their opponents had not pointed out the true boundaries. In a judgment charter of 1499/1500, after witnesses for both sides had testified and each group had shown the judge the boundaries, the plaintiff's longtime residents declared:

Sire, those longtime residents of the Grand Prince, Petrushka Koshelev and his comrades, led thee incorrectly about the Archangel [Cathedral's] land of the Plotniche village; and, Sire, that deserted village Opraksino is Archangel [Cathedral land], that deserted village across [which] they led thee. Sire, give us God's justice with them, and, having kissed the cross, we shall go to the [dueling] field to fight.

In other cases, one side asserted that the opposition's witnesses had lied. For example, longtime residents testifying on behalf of the peasant Kur'ian, defendant in a 1499/1500 case, declared: "Sires, the monastery's witnesses Kuzemka and Kondratik have given false testimony; give us God's justice with them; after a week's fast and after kissing the cross, we shall go with them to the field to fight.". . .

In the fifteenth-century judgment charters, the judicial duel seems to be a matter of much talk and very little action. . . . A few judgment charters record cases in which the judge decreed a judicial duel, but we do not find a complete description of the event. Something always interfered with carrying out the procedure. A judgment charter issued between 1464 and 1482 provides an example, and also illustrates the use of representation in judicial duels. The Grand Prince's beekeepers had brought suit against a certain Ostafii, charging that he was depriving them of fishing rights. After the plaintiffs' witnesses had testified, Ostafii declared that they had testified against him wrongly ("not according to his deeds"). He would send his man, who would kiss the cross in the matter to support Ostafii, to fight a judicial duel to prove that the plaintiffs had no rights to the lakes. The plaintiffs agreed that, after kissing the cross, they would likewise send one person, selected from among them, to the dueling field, and the Grand Prince ordered a judicial duel. When both sides appeared at the field on the designated date, the plaintiffs declared that if four of Ostafii's servants would kiss the cross, after swearing that the plaintiffs had been given no fishing rights, they, the plaintiffs, were ready to concede. Ostafii agreed, and at the designated time, St. Peter's Day, Ostafii presented his men and, by kissing the cross, they settled the matter. . . .

In general, Muscovite courts of the fifteenth and sixteenth centuries viewed a lawsuit as a form of supervised verbal contest between the two parties. On the whole, responsibility for conduct of the case and presentation of evidence lay with the litigants themselves. When a plaintiff brought charges, the defendant answered the accusation as best he could. Each party in turn then presented whatever support he had for his claim, the prevailing maxim being "the more the better."

Documentary evidence constituted the first step in the chain of proof. Those litigants who possessed documents, or claimed to have them, or declared that they had formerly had such records, generally mentioned them first, before calling for the testimony of witnesses. Next the parties named their witnesses, usually longtime residents when land litigation was the issue; these men testified after the court had examined the documents. A litigant might bring in further evidence after this, calling for an examination of the Grand Prince's record books or an inquest of "good men" or even the testimony of witnesses not mentioned earlier. Most judgment charters, however, record only the testimony of witnesses named by the parties at the outset.

Some litigants had—or claimed to have—documents but no witnesses. In a large number of cases, however, a litigant had no documents (or even assertions that he had formerly possessed them), and relied upon testimony of witnesses alone to support his claims. The ju-

dicial duel ritual—except in those cases when combat was the only proof offered—came after documents and testimony had been introduced, and, as we have noted, was often the last step before *doklad* [referral to higher court for decision]. On the whole litigants played the active role in courtroom procedure, determining the course of the trial by the evidence which they presented. With the exception of requests for an examination of the Grand Prince's land records or in situations where the original document was in the archives or in the possession of one of the Grand Prince's officials, the parties were responsible for producing their documents and placing them before the court. When calling for the testimony of witnesses, the litigants themselves more often than not brought these men to court. Presentation of their case was not a responsibility which litigants could afford to take lightly. As we have seen, many litigants sent a representative to court on their behalf (such as a peasant hundredman, a monasterial elder, or a literate slave) who had previous experience in such legal matters.

Judges tended to limit themselves to an essentially supervisory role, ensuring each party an opportunity to counter evidence produced by the opposition with proof of his own. The judges seem to have considered it their basic function, during the trial itself, to listen to whatever support the litigants might wish to offer for their claims. The court's primary objective was to collect as much evidence as possible. Documents and testimony were usually accepted as presented. Even when a judge had seemingly reliable evidence before him, such as official documents, he nevertheless tried to get additional "new" evidence. The court willingly agreed to conduct inquests, when one of the parties so desired, and, except at the time designated for a judicial duel, was very lenient in granting postponements to allow parties time to produce witnesses or documents. In fact, on some occasions judges showed admirable patience, particularly in the matter of viewing the boundaries of disputed land. It must have been a very time-consuming, and rather tedious, process, when first each litigant and then his witnesses in turn led the judge from one tree to another, down ravines and across swamps. As a rule litigants received every opportunity to present whatever proof they could muster.

Yet many judges apparently felt that the court's responsibility ended there; while it was their task to examine all information offered for their consideration, the litigants were responsible for producing the evidence. In most cases the judges were content to ask the usual—and obvious—questions. If a litigant mentioned a document and did not place it before the judge, he asked where it was; then, if the man produced it, the judge examined the record and proceeded with the hearing. If witnesses were named, he questioned them. If not, the judge usually asked the parties whether anyone knew the facts and could support the claims advanced. If the plaintiff merely stated his accusations and the defendant denied them, the judge asked each man why the land in question was his, what proof—documents or witnesses sometimes specified—he could produce.

The judge's questions generally were directed toward giving each litigant an opportunity to present his side of the question to the fullest extent possible. The judge himself rarely engaged in any form of interrogation or cross-examination. When longtime residents testified, for example, they told what they knew without any interruption. Most questions about documents arose when the record did not name the disputed land specifically or did not include a precise boundary description. Yet many such documents were accepted by the court at face value. Most judges apparently operated on the assumption that the proper decision would make itself evident during the course of the trial. One litigant might challenge the other's documents or witnesses and be able to provide overwhelming support for his contention, or testimony on one side would contain contradictions or inconsistencies, or one party would eventually confess. At any rate, many judges apparently felt that it was their job only to hear the case and then render a decision based upon the overall strength of each side's argument and the specific evidence stated in the trial record. Of course, if all else failed, the issue could be referred to God or the Grand Prince for final decision.

Thus many judges confined themselves to a relatively passive role throughout the trial. The burden of proof rested with the litigants.

SOURCE: Ann M. Kleimola, *"Justice in Medieval Russia: Muscovite Judgment Charters* (Pravye Gramoty) *of the Fifteenth and Sixteenth Centuries," Transactions of the American Philosophical Society,* 65, 6 (October, 1975): 35–8, 46–7, 52, 58–60, 62–3, 74–5 (excerpted). Reprinted by permission of the American Philosophical Society.

JANET MARTIN
The Decline of Novgorod's Fur Trade Network

As already noted, Novgorod had from an early time developed direct contact with remote, international markets. Indeed, in the Middle Ages Novgorod became the easternmost outpost of the Hanseatic League, bringing European merchants and European goods to Russia. Trade with Europe also gave Novgorod the opportunity to export its most abundant commodity, fur. Possessing immense tracts of land in the northern forests, Novgorod was peculiarly well-situated to supply a whole range of furs to distant consumers. Although exotic furs are perhaps best known as Russian, the Novgorodians had developed in the late Middle Ages a lively trade in squirrel, whose output reached London and Paris. In the fifteenth century, however, when Novgorod came under increasing political pressure from the Moscow princes, Novgorod also confronted more distant economic frustrations, leading to a collapse of the fur trade. The combination of Muscovite politics and changing European markets proved doubly debilitating for Novgorod, as Janet Martin here shows.

During the second half of the fifteenth century Novgorod's fur trade network disintegrated. Its role as a fur mart and export center declined; and its carefully constructed squirrel supply system crumbled. A variety of factors interfered with the Novgorodian market. One was Novgorod's relations with the Hanseatic League. Commercial relations between the Germans and Novgorodians had been tenuous throughout the thirteenth and fourteenth centuries. The two groups engaged in numerous disputes that, in extreme situations, involved arrest, death, and/or the confiscation of property of one party by the other. In such cases the Hansa would ban trade with Novgorod, while Novgorod might temporarily close Peterhof [headquarters for Hansa merchants].

In the fifteenth century such disputes became more severe and had longer-lasting effects. In conjunction with a war between Novgorod and the Livonian Knights in the 1440s, the Hansa blockaded Novgorod; this time the Hansa also abandoned Peterhof for six years (1443–48). Twenty years later the visiting German merchants were arrested and Peterhof again remained closed for an extended period. During that episode the Hansa transferred its merchant quarters from Novgorod to Narva for four years.

The effects of these politically induced disruptions combined with several economic factors to undermine the centrality and value of Novgorod's fur trade. One factor . . . was the Hansa's increasing reluctance to export silver to Novgorod. Its attitude developed as production in central Europe's silver mines diminished in the late fourteenth and early fifteenth centuries. The cumulative effect of the Hansa's exhortations to ban silver export was to reduce the amount of silver reaching Novgorod; even the silver that continued to be received was likely to be less pure than in preceding decades.

A second factor that affected Novgorod's fur trade from the mid-fifteenth century was the change in patterns of foreign fur consumption. The very success of the squirrel trade had resulted in the fifteenth century in a drop in the price of squirrel pelts abroad. Members of the lower classes were more easily able to purchase squirrel fur; upper class consumers in England, Burgundy and other northern European centers responded by favoring luxury fur—sable, fox, and marten. Novgorod, which had specialized in the production of northern gray squirrel, was not equipped, especially in the context of a weak market structure, to adjust to the changing demand.

At this time the role of two of the major contributing groups in the supply system—the boyars and the government treasury—radically declined. Some of the boyars . . . divested themselves of their northern fur-producing estates. Others . . . converted their rents in the fifteenth century from fur into cash; they thereby transferred the burden of selling squirrel in an uncertain market onto their peasant tenants. Only a few Novgorodian boyars tried to adapt to the new demand; to do so, they attempted to gain control over northeastern lands beyond the Dvina river that provided sable and ermine. By this time, however, these territories belonged to Moscow, and the Novgorodian attempts to recapture them were unsuccessful. The net result of all these actions was the withdrawal of the Novgorodian boyars from the fur supply system.

The Novgorod city government's ability to procure its fur supplies also declined after the middle of the fifteenth century. By 1462 Novgorod had ceded extensive holdings in its fur hinterland as well as important points along its northern fur supply routes to the Muscovite grand prince. . . . These territories were all peasant lands, which had been subject to Novgorodian taxes. Their loss meant a decrease in tax revenue for Novgorod, specifically a decrease in fur revenue. . . .

By the time Ivan III annexed Novgorod the latter's fur trade network was already in disarray. Ivan's policies intensified a trend that was well under way. After annexing Novgorod, he confiscated the privately owned estates of its boyars and many ecclesiastical institutions. He also assumed title to the remaining peasant holdings among Novgorod's northern territories, and thereby took over Novgorod's remaining fur resource areas. On the confiscated estates the Muscovite government restructured the rents. Grain and cash became the sole acceptable forms of payment; rent in squirrel fur was eliminated. By the mid-sixteenth century fur taxes paid by the peasants to the government had undergone a similar conversion to cash.

Even as he dismantled the squirrel supply system, Ivan also undermined Novgorod's ability to develop a luxury fur trade by evicting Novgorod's chief merchants and replacing them with Muscovite tradesmen. By the end of the century all that remained were, on the one hand, small supplies of squirrel fur in the hands of individual peasants, some of whom did opt to sell their pelts for cash. On the other hand, there were supplies of luxury fur, which Muscovite merchants purchased from Swedes, Finns, Karelians, and Laplanders in the northwestern Russian lands on the Swedish border.

Finally, the Hansa-Novgorod disputes in the mid-fifteenth century had provided the Livonian towns with an opportunity to gain a commercial advantage over Novgorod. The fact that the Hanseatic League was itself disintegrating contributed to this circumstance. The League was losing command of the Baltic seaways. The Livonian towns further undermined the League's cohesiveness by extending their own dominance over Peterhof and conducting their own policy there, at times in direct defiance of Lübeck [headquarters of the Hanseatic League].

As a result, by the third quarter of the fifteenth century the Russian-European trade was already shifting away from Novgorod to the Livonian towns, which became the major centers of exchange. Novgorodian and, increasingly, Pskovian merchants brought their goods to Reval and Dorpat. They sold them to local merchants as well as to Hansa merchants from the other towns, and, despite the League's prohibitions, to non-Hanseatic merchants, such as the Dutch, who also frequented those towns.

When Muscovy annexed Novgorod, its policies further reduced Novgorod's ability to function as a fur market. Ivan III ordered the construction of Ivangorod in 1492, and two years later closed the Hanseatic trading compound . . . in Novgorod. Pskov, Narva, and Vyborg and ultimately Ivangorod subsequently played increasingly important roles in the Russian export trade to northwestern Europe.

[But] Novgorod never fully recovered its position as the major fur center of the Russian lands.

SOURCE: Janet Martin, *Treasure of the Land of Darkness: The Fur Trade and Its Significance for Medieval Russia* (Cambridge: Cambridge University Press, 1986), pp. 81–4 (excerpted). Reprinted by permission of Cambridge University Press and the author.

A. M. SAKHAROV
The Mongol Yoke and Socioeconomic Change

Accounts of late Rus' are nearly unanimous in blaming the Mongols for devastating the economy, and A. M. Sakharov, whose essay appears below, is no exception. However, there is here something new as well. Sakharov, in presenting a Marxist interpretation of economic development, lays special emphasis upon the decline of cities which the Tatars wasted. In destroying Rus' cities, he claims, the Mongols undermined "progressive" economic forces and simultaneously aided the more reactionary "feudal" forces. Sakharov, who detects some signs of economic recovery in the fourteenth century, observes as well the explosion of conditional landholding, with its concomitant enserfment of free peasants who, having been ruined by the Mongol invasion and occupation, found it necessary to take refuge in this dependent status. From this perspective, then, the Mongol invasion had extremely far-reaching consequences which long outlived the thirteenth-century military and economic disasters. In undermining urban economies and stimulating the creation of a group of landlords whose service the state purchased with land grants and peasant enserfment, the Mongol conquest directly influenced the most basic social and political institutions of subsequent Russian history.

———————

One of the most serious consequences of the invasion and yoke was the pronounced weakening of the Russian towns, a considerable proportion of which existed under comparatively unfavorable conditions even without the foreign yoke ... [The] Mongol-Tatars not only destroyed towns but also took skillful urban craftsmen into captivity. After the Mongol-Tatar invasion commodity production and commodity circulation were undermined at their very roots. The process of accumulation of money—that mighty weapon with which the townsfolk of certain countries of Western Europe fundamentally undermined the old political system of feudal fragmentation in the fifteenth century—went at an excruciatingly slow pace in Rus'. When by approximately the mid-fourteenth century, urban life began to undergo a revival, the economic development of the cities was strongly undermined by the constant pumping out of funds to pay tribute to the Golden Horde. Novgorod and Pskov, not touched by the Mongol-Tatar ravages, found themselves in comparatively favorable circumstances, but enormous sums of money were regularly exacted from these cities both for payment to the Horde and to meet the expenditures of the Moscow grand prince and metropolitan. All this occurred at the time when a stream of gold and precious things flowed from distant overseas countries into many cities of Western Europe on the sea lanes. The rate of development of the Russian towns was greatly slowed by comparison to those of certain countries of Western Europe: England, Flanders, Holland, northern France, and others. . . .

While the towns found themselves in very difficult conditions, farming and pastoral pursuits, which were comparatively uncomplicated, recovered with comparative rapidity. This was furthered by a considerable increase in population density in the confluence of the Oka and Volga rivers, to which masses of peo-

ple fled in the hope of gaining in the forests at least relative security against the terrible raids of the nomads. True, in this respect the Mongol-Tatar invasion brought nothing fundamentally new: the process of movement of masses of people from the fertile but defenseless steppe and forest-steppe of the south into the wooded regions of the north with their fertile ploughlands had begun long since. Names on the geographical map are testimony to this movement: towns named Trubezh, Pereiaslavl, Vladimir, Starodub, Galich, and others are to be found both in the south and the north. When they arrived at new places, migrants gave them the names with which they were already familiar. After the Mongol-Tatar invasion the shift of masses of people to northeastern Rus' merely took on a new scale. This is the proper explanation for the comparatively rapid economic advance of the Oka-Volga interfluence . . .

This territory was brought to life by the stubborn labor of the peasants—both the "old settlers" and the "incomers," as the sources call them. Forests were cleared to make new lands, wastelands were ploughed, hamlets in clearings, settlements, villages arose, and craft industries developed: beaver-dam exploitation, wild-hive honey-gathering, fishing, hunting. With the passage of time land ceased to be freely available, and the old descriptive formula for the bounds of holdings "where the scythe, plough, and axe had passed," came ever more frequently to be replaced by exact topographic descriptions of boundaries, and disputes over land became more frequent. The flow of peasant colonization began to head even farther to the north and northeast, beyond the Volga. Here too new lands were ploughed, salt resources were mastered, as were rivers and lakes rich in fish, and the forests overflowing with fur animals. Walrus ivory—"fish tooth"—was hunted at the shores of the "Frozen Sea." The second half of the fourteenth century saw a clear economic rise of the Russian lands. It manifested itself not only in an increase in the area of worked lands but also in a certain improvement in the techniques for working them. It would appear that by the end of the fifteenth century the three-field system of agriculture gained greater prevalence. Along with farming, stock-raising and hunting occupations there was a development of crafts serving the needs of agriculture, for example the smelting of iron from bog ores and the production of various metal wares. Water mills began to make their appearance as early as the mid-fourteenth century in large farms. On the whole, the economy continued to maintain its subsistence character typical of the middle ages, although market trade increased noticeably in the second half of the fifteenth century. A tendency for monetary rent to spread made its appearance in the Novgorod country at that time.

The upsurge of productive forces in the sphere of farming and the craft industries increased the value of land and intensified the interest of the ruling class in it. The fourteenth and fifteenth centuries came to be a time of intensive growth of feudal landholding and farming in northeastern Rus', occurring primarily by seizure of peasant lands. Clerical feudal lords came to be the great landlords of that time. As [one recent scholar has noted], "starting with the second half of the fourteenth century, the old eremitic monasteries, which played no independent economic role, were replaced by monasteries of a new type, comprising feudal patrimonies with diversified economic undertakings, based principally on the labor of feudally dependent peasants.". . .

The growth of feudal landed property was not only quantitative. The spread of a new kind of feudal property—conditional land tenure—was an important phenomenon of the fourteenth and fifteenth centuries. In order to assure the opening to agriculture of their extensive possessions and at the same time acquire military and other servitors, great feudal lords would turn over part of their lands to such people. For having land placed at their disposal, these *deti boiarskie* or *dvoriane* (from the word *dvor*) were required to serve the owner of the land and provide for all his requirements from exploitation of the land made over to their use. This kind of conditional land tenure began to appear on the lands of the grand prince, the metropolitan, and other major feudal lords. The grand-princely authorities had a particular interest in increasing the number of their military servitors, for the latter were their social base. The struggle with external enemies also called forth an acute need for military strength. However, much land was needed for the nobility, for the potentials of the grand-princely authority were quite limited so long as feudal fragmentation existed. The need for supplies of land determined the princes' striving to expand to the maximum the territories under their authority, to subject other lands and principalities and, thus, to unify the country under their rule.

On the other hand, the interests of the ruling class as a whole demanded the same thing. The growth of feudal land tenure was indissolubly associated with bringing the peasantry into the sphere of serf exploitation. Under conditions of the Mongol-Tatar yoke, the ruination of the people took on a mass character. The constant invasions by the enemy hordes, and the need to pay tribute to the Horde, and the internal migration, taken together, undermined peasant farming, which was unstable enough at the level of the productive forces then existing. The great mass of the people, particularly on newly opened lands, was compelled to seek material support from rich holders of land, and to take loans of money and tools, or to settle on the lands of the feudal lords safeguarded by the privileges of immunities and special benefits which the grand-princely authority granted specifically to attract a population. A considerable number of people found themselves in bondage to usurers that included monasteries and secular feudal lords. Peasant debtors were required to work off their loans and interests for the feudal lords. Thus, in the final analysis, the Mongol-Tatar yoke with its associated ruination and migration of masses of the peasantry, facilitated the offensive of the feudal lords against the peasants.

SOURCE: A. M. Sakharov, "Rus' and Its Culture, Thirteenth to Fifteenth Centuries," *Soviet Studies in History* 18, 3 (Winter 1979–80: 26–32 (excerpted). Reprinted by permission of M. E. Sharpe, Inc.

8

Culture and Everyday Life
in Post-Kievan Rus'

Although much scholarship has focused upon the Mongol invasion and some other areas of post-Kievan Rus', culture in these centuries has drawn less attention. A partial explanation for this inattention may be the invasion itself, which evidently dramatically affected the output of works of elite culture, including written sources on which historical scholarship has traditionally depended. The difficulties of sorting out the changing and complex politics of the era when rival principalities followed independent courses also complicates the historian's task. In some ways, then, the history of culture in the thirteenth, fourteenth, and fifteenth centuries remains underdeveloped.

But as some of the works already introduced demonstrate, these centuries witnessed some remarkable developments. It is clear, for example, that new and sophisticated understandings of the law emerged in this era, as the Novgorod Judicial Charter admirably demonstrates. Increasing reliance upon written proofs and the establishment of an archive in which to house official documents testify to a rationalization of the law. Bureaucratic specialization within the judiciary furthered this process, bringing more dispute resolution within the control of the state. There is unambiguous evidence, then, of cultural change.

In other respects, however, detecting cultural change seems more difficult. Almost until the mid-fourteenth century, literature practically disappears, and even when it emerges, the new works seem slavish copies, dead to innovation. Art and architecture too fall quiet. How to explain this apparent vacuum?

It may be, as A. M. Sakharov argues, that the Mongol occupation really is to blame. Sakharov, a portion of whose work we read above, here continues his appraisal of the Mongol Yoke, focusing attention upon the devastation of the centers of elite culture—the cities. With their destruction, he argues, artists and artisans alike suffered. Not only did the Mongol armies destroy town walls and urban structures, but what was worse, craftsmen who survived confronted lost markets, while artists lost their patrons. In this respect, then, the invasion was highly traumatic for Rus' culture. Everything connected with elite culture suffered, and this undermining of the cultural infrastructure explains the apparent gap in the sources.

All the same, Sakharov finds evidence for a cultural renewal as early as the fourteenth century, when the Moscow principality helped sponsor a new flowering of Rus' culture. Perhaps the highest expression of this efflorescence was Andrei Rublev, arguably the most accomplished painter of this era. Born about mid-way through the Mongol Yoke, Rublev helped pioneer whole new perspectives on painting. Having completed his most famous work some fifty years before the Moscow princes formally overthrew the Mongol domination, the great painter managed then to help nurture an artistic revival irrespective of whatever alien cultural influences the Mongols may have exerted. But Mikhail Alpatov, who here attempts to appraise the significance of Rublev's art, argues that the importance of Andrei Rublev far transcends the history of Rus', equalling the great humanistic art of better known artists at work in Western Europe.

These essays, of course, concentrate upon elite culture, but for most residents of the Rus' lands in these centuries, it was not the work of chroniclers or icon painters which articulated their cultural values. They celebrated more readily the antics of the minstrels who brought music, acting, and animal acts to village squares. Although we cannot hope ever to rescue the lyrics of their performances, the minstrels almost surely brought satire, romance, and other genres to their audiences, and presented their material in a lexicon readily appreciated and understood by peasants.

But official culture, especially as represented by churchmen, condemned the minstrels. In assaults reminiscent of similar scenes enacted in Western Europe, churchmen vilified the minstrels for the carnival values which they evidently brought to their performances. Dancing with animals, cavorting behind masks, and singing bawdy songs, Rus' minstrels caricatured the world around them. Doubtless these performances delighted village audiences, but they also threatened the social order over which churchmen and officials presided. And, by controlling the written record, these representatives of elite culture succeeded in the main in preventing the minstrels from bequeathing these performances to subsequent generations.

DOCUMENTS

Evidence for Literacy: Novgorod Birchbark Charters (ca. 1220–30s)

Among the most interesting finds excavated at Novgorod are two pieces of birchbark which resemble primers (see facing page), teaching devices known to elementary education for hundreds of years afterward. One text identifies and lists the letters of the alphabet, and the other features the alphabet and basic combinations of letters. Especially arresting is the fact that one of these very clearly belonged to a boy named Onfim, who not only put his name on the birchbark, but also left us his drawing of a horse and its rider (perhaps Onfim himself) spearing some imaginary opponent. The nature of the formal text, together with Onfim's apparently spontaneous doodling, has suggested to some that literacy in Novgorod may have been quite high, and that students may actually have undertaken formal

instruction in reading and writing (from which Onfim was distracted to depict his own imaginary conquests). This claim seems extravagant without further evidence, but these elementary primers do pose interesting questions about the teaching of reading and writing in Rus'.

———————

No. 200. . . . This piece of birchbark contains mainly a drawing. A horseman stabs an enemy with a spear. Along the figure of the horseman to the right is a signature in little letters: Onfime. In the right upper corner is written the beginning of the alphabet:

А Б В Г Д Е Ж
З З И I К

Its length is 0.1 meters, its width 0.07 meters. [Dated to 1220s–1230s.]

No. 201. Judging by the hand, Charter 201

Birchbark charter No. 200 (early thirteenth century): Onfim's writing exercises. From V. L. Ianin, *Ia poslal tebe berestu. . .* (Moscow: MGU, 1965), p. 53.

Birchbark charter No. 201 (early thirteenth century). From A. V. Artsikhovskii, V. I. Borkovskii, *Novgorodskie gramoty na bereste (Iz raskopok 1956–1957 gg.)* (Moscow: AN SSSR, 1963), p. 22.

does not belong to the author of the preceding [similar] charter. Again we have a school exercise, an alphabet and syllables:

А Б : В Г : Д Е : Ж Ѕ :
З И : I К : Л М :
Н О : П Р : С Т : У Ф :
Х Ш : Ц Ч : Ш Щ :
Ъ Ы : Ь Ѣ : У Ю :
Ж Я : Б А : В А : Г А
Д А : Ж А : З А : К А
Л А : М А : Н А : П А
Р А : С А : Т А : Ф А : Х
Ц А : Ч А : Ш А : Щ А :

Its length is 0.085 meters, its width 0.075 meters. [Dated to 1220s–30s.]

SOURCE: A. V. Artsikhovskii and V. I. Borkovskii, *Novgorodskie gramoty na bereste (Iz raskopok 1956–1957 gg.)* (Moscow: AN SSSR, 1963), pp. 20–22. Translated by Daniel H. Kaiser.

The Last Will and Testament of Patrikei Stroev (Late Fourteen–Early Fifteenth Centuries)

The testament of Patrikei Stroev (1392–1427) is one of the oldest extant wills to have originated from a secular hand in Muscovy. But much of the style and substance of this testament very soon became standard form by which to prepare for death. Later Muscovite testaments often proved to be more detailed, not only in enumerating greater properties but also in elaborating upon sentiments about death. There is little of that here, but Stroev does provide a thorough review of his property, giving us insight into the economy of individual freeholders in early Muscovy.

———————

In the name of the Father, Son, and Holy Ghost. Lo, I, Patrikei, slave of God, departing this world [and] being of sound mind, do write this testament, from whom to take [what is owed me] and to whom to give [what I owe]. Take from Panuta a ruble; for a half-ruble have him mow the hay, and for the other half-ruble take two rams. Take from Panuta's brother, Onisim, a half-ruble; for that [money] have him do the mowing. Take from Ermak Ogofonov a half-ruble and two sheep. Take from Foka and Panetelek a half-ruble and a sheep. Take from Ustinka in [the village of] Okhotino a half-ruble and a pig carcass. Take from Iakusha, son-in-law to the priest Ofonasii, seven grivnas. And give two rubles to Fegnost. Give a half-ruble to Vasiian Ondronov. Give four rubles to my brother Kosten. Give four grivnas to one Klim in Moscow.

I have given to my two sons, Big Doronka and Fetka, the year-old bay, and to Doronka [another] bay mare and the mixed-color cow, the brown ox, and another black [ox]. To my wife [with] my children [I give] the light brown stallion with a black mane and tail, and the blue mare, two cows, one black the other brown, and the ginger ox. And they are to cast lots for my grain, whether [they get] the rye or the spring wheat. And they are each to take half of the rye which they just sowed.

And I direct my brother Kosten to sell two horses to pay my debts—the raven-black stallion and the chestnut mare.

And for the remembrance of my soul I have given to the Holy Trinity monastery the village of Ignat'evskoe and three beehives.

And I have entrusted to my brother Kosten [the care of] my wife and my children, and the collection and payment of my debts. And [while I composed this testament] my confessor, Abbot Nikon, sat by my head. And present [to hear the testament were]: Ivan Beklemishev, Klim Danilov, Klim Molotilo, and Piantel'i. Vasuk, son of the priest Ivan, wrote this testament. And all the witnesses imprinted [on this testament] a seal of a cross.

On the reverse: According to the testament of my brother, who ordered me to sell two horses and pay his debts, I sold them and paid the debt: to Parfenii I gave three rubles, [and] retrieved the borrowed silver; to Fegnast, the abbot's son, I paid two rubles, [and] to Kas'ian I paid a ruble. From Ermak I took a half-ruble

Leather shoe (fourteenth century). From *Drevnii Novgorod: Prikladnoe iskusstvo i arkheologiia* (Moscow: Iskusstvo, 1985), p. 153. Reprinted courtesy of Iskusstvo Publishers.

and paid it to Vas'ian the elder, and [I gave] two sheep to the Ondronov son. From Foka and Panteleika I took a half-ruble.

SOURCE: *Akty sotsial'no-ekonomicheskoi istorii Severo-Vostochnoi Rusi kontsa XIV-nachala XVI v.*, Vol. 1, no. 11 (Moscow: AN SSSR, 1952). Translated by Daniel H. Kaiser.

Minstrels in Rus':
An Immunity Charter
(1470)

Because so much of elite culture opposed them, Rus' minstrels have left behind little evidence of their activity: no direct descriptions survive, and no narratives from the minstrels themselves. Instead, we have the words of their critics, and some other materials—both verbal and pictorial—with which to reconstruct their place in Rus' culture. Evidently the minstrels played stringed instruments (*gusli*) to accompany their songs, and some very ancient instruments of this type have been unearthed in Novgorod (see p. 132). The Novgorod digs

also uncovered a superb leather mask, almost certainly also part of the minstrel's tools (see p. 134). Manuscript illustrations show them as jugglers and animal tamers, and clearly they were also musicians. But their activity was not welcome everywhere. Some landlords sought special immunity from the minstrels, but away from the centers of elite culture the minstrels evidently found a ready welcome. Indeed, surviving village inventories from around the year 1500 list minstrels just as they might some priest or smith, indicating not only a tolerance for such entertainers but also a recognition of their social station and value.

DMITROV PRINCE IURII VASIL'EVICH
TO ABBOT SPIRIDON OF THE
TRINITY-ST. SERGIUS MONASTERY

Lo I, Prince Iur'i Vasil'evich, have granted to the abbot of the Trinity Monastery, Spiridon, and to all the brothers of the St. Sergius Monastery, or to whoever will be abbot at that monastery, [the following:] that my princes, mili-

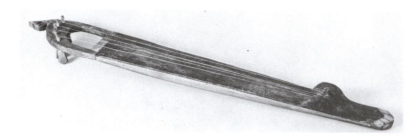

A

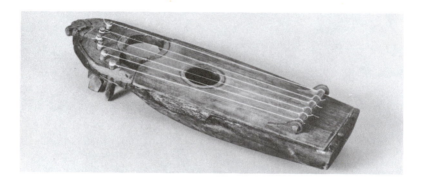

B

Five-stringed (mid-eleventh century) (A) and six-stringed (early twelfth century) (B) gusli. From *Drevnii Novgorod: Prikladnoe iskusstvo i arkheologiia* (Moscow: Iskusstvo, 1985), p. 28. Reprinted courtesy of Iskusstvo Publishers.

tary commanders, servitors, and all impost collectors, kennel keepers, fishermen, beaver-men shall not be placed in their villages in Inobozhskii canton, namely, Ozerskoe, Zhol-tikovo and Abramovskoe, with all their settle-ments, neither shall they collect maintenance provisions, cart obligations, except when someone is in pursuit with my post-horse char-ter. Likewise no minstrels shall play among them in their villages.

If someone in violation of this my charter takes from them [fees or provisions] or if someone offends against them, he shall re-ceive punishment from me.

This charter was given in the year 6978 [=1470] on the 14th day of January.

On the reverse: Prince Iurii Vasil'evich.

SOURCE: *Akty sotsial'no-ekonomicheskoi istorii Severo-Vostochnoi Rusi XIV-nachala XVI v.*, vol. 1 no. 393 (Moscow: AN SSSR, 1952). Translated by Daniel H. Kaiser.

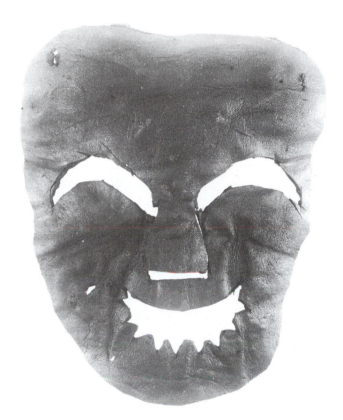

Leather minstrel's mask (second half of the thirteenth century). From *Drevnii Novgorod: Prikladnoe iskusstvo i arkheologiia* (Moscow: Iskusstvo, 1985), p. 30. Reprinted courtesy of Iskusstvo Publishers.

LITERATURE

RUSSELL ZGUTA

Russian Minstrels:
A Modern View

Historians of Russia, long having concentrated upon questions of state administration and economy, have perhaps too often overlooked the history of popular culture. Difficult to reconstruct in any case, given the ephemeral character of much of its expression, popular culture has seemed to generations of histori-ans relatively unimportant. But for persons who lived in remote villages in late medieval Rus' (and most people of the era lived in these circumstances), the visit of a minstrel was almost certainly of more moment than any edict or monument of elite culture. In the selection which appears below, Russell Zguta traces the history and activity of these entertainers, introducing such scant evidence as we have to circumscribe their role in Rus' culture.

Upon leaving the strife-torn Kievan lands in the twelfth and early thirteenth centuries, the *skomorokhi* [minstrels] proceeded in two directions: directly north toward Novgorod and northeast toward Vladimir-Suzdal. In both areas they left indelible traces of their early settlement and widespread activity by giving their name to numerous villages and hamlets. . . . Their primary objective . . . was Novgorod and Pskov. . . . At no time . . . were secular music and entertainment proscribed in Novgorod until Aleksei's universal ban on the *skomorokhi* in 1648. . .

The migration and resettlement of the Russian minstrels in the north were completed by the late thirteenth and early fourteenth centuries. Evidence for this can be found in the series of initials, or miniature letter-figures, from Pskov, Novgorod, and Riazan, which art historians have identified as depicting *skomorokhi*. The earliest of these initials dates from the late thirteenth or early fourteenth century and is found in a Pskovian Psalter. . . . The initial in question is an Old Slavonic **T** depicting a standing *skomorokh* dressed in a knee-length tunic and playing a five-string triangular-*gusli*. . . .

The earliest of the Novgorod initials date from 1323 and are found in the . . . collection of Sunday Gospels [see p. 135]. . . . Two are in the form of the Old Slavonic letter **P** and four in the form of **B**. Of these six, two are animal tamers in the act of giving a performance; the animals they are handling are stylized dogs. The other four can be described as actors; one is sitting, another standing, and two are crouched on one knee, holding an axe and a cane respectively. All are wearing costumes . . . described as the standard attire of the *skomorokhi*. . . . In addition, several of the figures are wearing elaborate headdress.

In another group of Novgorod letter-figure initials, taken from a 1355 edition of the [Sunday Gospels], two actors and a juggler are represented, both in the form of the letter **B**. A third version of the [Sunday Gospels], dating from 1358, contains an initial **P** depicting a musician playing an oval, nine-string *gusli* (us-

ing a feather as a plectrum) and simultaneously dancing. Above and to the left of the letter-figure are inscribed the words *gudi gorazdo* ("play skillfully"), probably added by someone other than the copyist-artist by way of marginalia.

Perhaps the most interesting of the Novgorod initials are two from the mid-fourteenth century, one of which appears in a Psalter, the other in a Sluzhebnik, or Liturgicon. Both are in the form of the letter Д and depict flamboyantly dressed musicians [p. 135]. The Psalter *skomorokh* plays the oval *gusli* and is pictured in a squatting position, as if engaged in a dance. . . . Without a doubt, these two miniatures provide us with the most accurate visual description of early Russian minstrels to be found anywhere. Among the miniatures from Riazan [is one]. . . from the 1544 edition of the [Sunday Gospels]. . . . The letter Ч is represented by a *skomorokh*-juggler [see p. 135].

The thematic inspiration [for these illustrations] was provided by the *skomorokhi* themselves, who, as these miniatures clearly show, were not only widely dispersed throughout the north and northeast by this time, but were evidently also so well known that the illuminators could use them as easily identifiable models. With their flamboyant, colorful costumes and versatility of repertoire (the initials show them as musicians, dancers, actors, jugglers, and animal tamers), they offered the artist a wide range of possibilities, enabling him to execute any letter in the Old Slavonic alphabet in singularly eloquent fashion.

Finally, the thoroughly nonsecular nature of the manuscripts in which these miniatures appear (that is, Psalters and Liturgicons) might lead one to conclude that the Russian minstrels found conditions in the north far more favorable to the professional development than those in the south, where no such miniatures of *skomorokhi* have been found. . . .

With the sole exception of the *Zlatoust*, a late fourteenth-century translation of sermons and other didactic literature from the Greek Fathers, there are no further written references

Five manuscript initials depicting (A) a minstrel playing the Psalter (mid-fourteenth century), (B, C) taming animals (1323), (D) dancing (1358), and (E) juggling (1544). Reprinted courtesy of Russell Zguta.

to the *skomorokhi* until the second half of the fifteenth century. In the *Zlatoust* the *skomorokhi* are condemned, along with a host of other worldly amusements, for preparing the road to perdition for themselves and their listeners. It appears that, though the minstrels had found greater tolerance in the north, the church's official attitude toward them, particularly in the Muscovite lands, had changed little.

Their reputation and popularity continued to grow nonetheless. . . .

Revealing in this regard is a clause in a charter, or letters patent . . . , granted by Prince Iurii Vasil'evich of Dmitrov in 1470 to the Trinity-Saint Sergius Monastery (located some forty-eight miles north of Moscow). Here the *skomorokhi* are specifically forbidden to entertain in the villages and hamlets belonging to the monastery. Allowing for the ecclesiastical status of the petitioner, it is nonetheless significant that the first reference to *skomorokhi* in Muscovite sources is a negative one. Similar charters granted to both ecclesiastical and non-ecclesiastical petitioners in the early sixteenth century also evince varying degrees of antipathy toward the *skomorokhi*: in some they are forbidden to set foot in specified towns, villages, and hamlets; in others they are allowed to enter provided they refrain from loud

or boisterous entertainment. Thus, while the civil authorities may not have shared the Muscovite clergy's traditional contempt for the *skomorokhi*, they were willing to grant certain communities the right not to be entertained against their will. The tolerant atmosphere that enabled the Russian minstrels to flourish in the northwest evidently did not prevail in the northeast. . . .

Sixteenth-century sources confirm the Muscovite church's virulent opposition to the *skomorokhi*. Maksim Grek, the controversial Greek scholar-translator living and writing in Moscow in the 1520s, addressed himself at length to the subject in one of his "Instructions". . . . He begins by stating that the *skomorokhi* have learned their trade from Satan himself and by virtue of this are already cursed and damned. . . . He lashes out at their sinful abuse of animals such as bears, whom they train to dance and engage in other Satanic games to the accompaniment of various musical instruments, and finally, he links them to witchcraft, which compounds their pernicious influence among the people. . . .

So the Muscovite *skomorokhi*, faced with relentless hostility from the ecclesiastical authorities, found it not only necessary for professional reasons (in order to reach a wider audience), but also expedient for personal reasons (to elude the authorities) to take to the road. . . .

Upon examining the cadastres, census books, and customs duty records, it becomes clear that many of the *skomorokhi* were well integrated into the economic structure of sixteenth- and seventeenth-century Russia. They could be found in the city and in the country, as taxpayers and with tax-exempt status. Some of them were relatively well to do, others eked out an existence as members of the lower taxpaying class . . . , while still others were poor, landless peasants . . . , or even serfs, not infrequently living off the church as paupers. Some were engaged in business and commerce, and a few were involved in small industry. There were also *skomorokhi* who doubled as professional soldiers. . . . Women were not excluded from their professional ranks, and there is at least one recorded instance of a *skomorokh*'s son who became a priest. . . .

In the course of their long history one musical instrument—the *gusli*—became a trademark of the *skomorokhi*. The term *gusli* itself is quite broad in meaning. Among the Eastern Slavs it ultimately acquired the meaning of "horizontal harp." In the early Russian sources it was used to denote strings and the sound that they made; a musical instrument in general; and a stringed musical instrument, as distinct from a percussion or wind instrument. . . . Not until the first half of the sixteenth century did *gusli* acquire the meaning it has today. Evidence . . . suggests that the *gusli* the early *skomorokh* carried was probably a small, light instrument of maple wood, resembling a four-sided horizontal harp. It had three or more strings of woven horse hair and was always played with the hand or fingers, never a bow. Prior to the eighteenth century it was used primarily to provide accompaniment for the singer. . . .

By the thirteenth century the oval or half-moon *gusli*-psaltery had become popular among the Eastern Slavs, especially in the northwest. This instrument, though frequently thought of as a variant of the traditional *gusli*, did not derive from it but was probably bor-

rowed by the northern Slavs from the Balto-Finns. . . .

As the oval *gusli*-psaltery was gaining in popularity, a triangular version of the instrument also came into vogue; late thirteenth- and early fourteenth-century miniatures from Pskov and Novgorod bear this out. Like its oval counterpart, the triangular *gusli*-psaltery was probably of Balto-Finnic origin.

The *skomorokhi* began very early to favor the versatile *gusli*-psaltery, both oval and triangular, over the traditional four-sided version; in fact, this is the instrument depicted in all of the extant illustrations of *skomorokhi* playing the *gusli*. . . . Its popularity can be explained by the simple fact that the traditional *gusli* . . . must be played in a sitting position, with the instrument resting on one's lap or on a table. The *gusli*-psaltery, on the other hand, can be played either sitting or standing (with the instrument propped up against one's chest), giving the performer much greater freedom of movement and even enabling him to dance while playing. The miniature from the 1358 collection of Sunday Gospels and another one from a fourteenth-century Novgorod Liturgicon show how this can be done. . . .

The other stringed instrument with which the *skomorokhi* are frequently identified is the *gudok*. . . . This instrument, which resembles the modern cello, made its appearance very early in Russia, apparently imported from central Asia. Onion-shaped, with three strings, the *gudok* was held in a vertical position and played with a bow. Two of its strings were tuned in unison; the third, a fifth higher.

During the sixteenth century, and perhaps even earlier, the *skomorokhi* are known to have used several other instruments: the *domra*, which eventually gave birth to the modern Russian *balalaika*, the drum, the fiddle, the flute, and the horn. None of these, however, approached the *gusli* and *gudok* in popularity. With the exception of the *domra*, they seem to have been used primarily to provide musical accompaniment for dancing.

SOURCE: Russell Zguta, *Russian Minstrels: A History of the Skomorokhi* (Philadelphia: University of Pennsylvania Press,

1978), pp. 23–7, 30–2, 37, 105–7 (excerpted). Reprinted by permission of Russell Zguta.

A. M. SAKHAROV
The Mongols and Cultural Change

Some historians have determined that whatever the economic and political consequences of the Mongol invasion, the cultural consequences were far more significant. Cut off from Western Europe by the Mongols and oriented instead toward Asia and nomadic culture, Rus' developed independent of the great humanizing influences embedded in the Renaissance and Reformation. Others go further, and observe that economic consequences—like the destruction of Rus' cities—determined certain cultural costs as well, destroying objects of cultural value (books, buildings, etc.), robbing Rus' of its most accomplished artisans, and simultaneously depriving artists of their patrons. In the selection reproduced here, A. M. Sakharov makes this point, observing that the Mongols failed to introduce any cultural innovations in their place. All the same, Sakharov detects a cultural revival in the fourteenth century which coincided with the gradual rise of the Moscow principality.

The extermination and exiling into captivity of masses of craftsmen undermined the very foundation of material culture, craftsmanship, which in the middle ages rested upon manual tools and involved many years of practice to develop the required skills for mastering the trade . . . Slate spindles and cornelian beads, glass bracelets and amphora-pots disappeared; the art of making enamel with ultra-fine partitions was lost forever; polychrome building tiles disappeared, and filigree and stamping of metal disappeared for a century and a half.

Russian architecture, which achieved such astonishing perfection and grandeur in the pre-Mongol period, suffered severely from the invasion. Masonry construction ceased entirely for half a century for lack of the material means and of master builders. The resumption of building with masonry at the end of the thirteenth century was accompanied by the loss of many devices of construction technique that had previously been used. In the fourteenth and fifteenth centuries, Moscow builders returned to building walls of trimmed stone alone, whereas as early as the first half of the thirteenth century the architects of Vladimir-Suzdal' were able to combine stone and brick, dense limestone and limestone tuff. The remarkable art of carving whitewashed stone, which made twelfth- and thirteenth-century structures so decorative, disappeared. Many devices of building technique were lost, and structures recently erected or just being built collapsed on more than one occasion (as occurred, for example, with the new Uspenskii Cathedral in Moscow in 1474).

A vast number of artifacts of the written word perished in the course of repeated invasions. The chronicle names only a few instances of the loss of collections of books, but from these one can picture how seriously Russian writings suffered from the onslaughts of the Mongol-Tatars. In 1382, when the Muscovites beat off a sudden attack by Tokhtamysh, the townsfolk and inhabitants of the nearby villages brought their books to stone churches to protect them against fire, and these books were so numerous that they filled the interiors of the Kremlin cathedrals to their roofs. All these riches were lost when Tokhtamysh succeeded in breaking into the city by treachery. It is no accident that many of the surviving monuments of the literature of ancient Rus' reached us via Novgorod, which was not destroyed by the Mongol-Tatars. The discovery at the end of the eighteenth century of the only copy of *The Lay of the Host of Igor* is clear evidence of what works of ancient Rus' literature might have disappeared forever during the invasions of the Mongol-Tatars and to what a degree, in probable consequence, our notions of ancient Rus' culture of the pre-Mongol period have been impoverished.

The damage done to literature by the Mongol-Tatar invasion was not limited solely to destruction of written legacies: the very character of works of literature changed. The writing of chronicles declined for a period, as manifested, in the words of D. S. Likhachev, "above all in total cessation of the maintaining of chronicles in a number of towns which were either entirely wiped from the face of the earth, like Staraia Riazan, or devastated and culturally bled white, as in the case of Vladimir, Chernigov, and Kiev." But even in those centers where chronicling activity suffered less destruction, "the writing of chronicles nonetheless became narrower, paler, laconic, and lacking . . . that broad Russia-wide horizon characteristic of the Russian chronicles of the eleventh and twelfth centuries."

Both painting and applied arts suffered decline after the Mongol-Tatar onslaught. . . . Wherever the Mongol-Tatar conquerors went in Asia and Europe they brought death, destruction, and the downfall of culture. Nor did the fact that the conquerors made use, in their destruction, of improved means of military equipment and devices of troop organization borrowed from China and the Arabs, convert their destructive role in the conquered territories into the organization of any higher culture. The Mongol-Tatar invasion was a terrible calamity for Russian culture: that is an indisputable historical fact. . . .

It may be taken as established that the second half of the fourteenth century marked the beginning of a new upsurge of Russian culture, determined by the successes of economic development and the major triumph over the conquerors at the historic Battle of Kulikovo [1380].

Reborn and developing Russian culture retained its national character in full. The Mongol-Tatars enriched it with nothing whatever, and their influence was quite insignificant in practice. A small number of Eastern words that entered the Russian language via the Mongol-Tatars (*bazaar*, *magazin* [store], *cherdak* [garret], *altyn* [monetary unit], *sunduk* [chest], *zenit* [zenith], *kaftan*, *tiufak* [mattress], etc.), some motifs in applied arts, in the clothing of the feudal elite—this essentially is the totality of the Mongol-Tatar influence upon Russian culture. The opinion held by some scholars to the effect that certain negative customs such as the sequestration of women came to Rus' with the Mongol-Tatars, as did a "spoiling of morals," have long since been cast in doubt . . . [I]t must not be forgotten that both in Rus' itself as in all countries in the Middle Ages, there was much that was dark and savage from the standpoint of present-day notions of manners and morals, and was determined by the times, the epoch . . .

Neither in legislation, nor in social thought, nor in literature, nor in painting is it possible to observe anything borrowed from the Mongol-Tatars. The most reliable indicator in this respect is the evaluation of the Mongol-Tatar invasion and yoke by the people themselves. Everything we know of oral folklore of the fourteenth and fifteenth centuries testifies unequivocally and categorically to the sharply negative evaluation the people gave to the Mongol-Tatar invasion and yoke. . . .

A number of stages in the process of cultural history in Rus' from the latter half of the thirteenth to the end of the fifteenth centuries can be identified, corresponding to stages of general historical development.

The first stage (from the Mongol-Tatar invasion approximately to the middle of the fourteenth century) is characterized by a notable decline in various spheres of material and intellectual culture. However, at the same time, the first signs of the beginning of a rebirth are to be seen as early as the end of the thirteenth century. In Tver, Novgorod, and later in Moscow, stonemasonry was revived and new centers of chronicle-writing appeared (Moscow and Tver). There was a general change in the geography of cultural centers, with the former centers of culture—Vladimir, Suzdal', and Rostov—retreating into the background. This was related to the change in the relationship of political forces in Rus', and also with the shattering of the towns by the Mongol-Tatars. In this period Russian culture's external connections proved to be almost totally interrupted. Only Novgorod and Pskov retained communication with the countries of the West. Those two cities have a special place in the history of Russian culture in the thirteenth to fifteenth centuries. Having survived the Mongol-Tatar pogrom and established the political structure of feudal republics, they reached the apex of their economic and cultural development in the period in question. Here the traditions of old Rus' literature, architecture, and painting were preserved and continued. Culture acquired noticeable democratic features. Novgorod and Pskov were major centers of the European culture of their time. This is persuasively testified to by the results of the work of Soviet archeologists during recent decades, including the finding, in 1951, of the celebrated birch-bark documents.

The second stage (approximately from the mid-fourteenth to the mid-fifteenth centuries) was that of the economic rise of Rus', the strengthening of local governmental structures, the upsurge of Moscow, Tver, Novgorod, Nizhnii Novgorod, and Riazan as large and powerful economic and political centers. . . . This period saw the rise of Russian culture, and it was also the period when the idea of the unity of the Russian land and some highly distinctive local features appeared. Andrei Rublev and Theophanes the Greek, so great and dissimilar from each other; the *Words of Praise of the Monk Foma*; the chronicle tale about Prince Mikhail Iaroslavich and the contrasting chronicling done in Moscow, which persistently advanced the idea that Moscow had been divinely chosen and that the descendants of Kalita had the right to the political direction of the Russian lands; the flourishing of the distinctive architecture of Novgorod and Pskov—all these and many other phenomena of Russian culture bore distinctive testimony . . . to the fact that it was unquestionably on the rise . . .

This was the period when the isolation of Russian culture, brought about by the Mongol-Tatars, began to be broken down, and connections with Bulgarian and Serbian cultures were established. While coming under South Slavic influence, Russian literature, however, retained its national character to the full and was noticeably enriched by virtue of that influence

both as art and, in part, in the realm of ideas. Elements of the psychological made an appearance in literature, and then grew stronger . . . Anticlerical "heretic" currents arose, and bold rationalist thinking made its appearance in embryonic form. Novgorod, Pskov, and Tver, where these heresies spread, were in open contact with the culture of the West. Russian social thought sought on the whole—still within the framework of the religious worldview—to interpret and connect the past and present of the Russian land. All these are the characteristic features of that distinctive stage in the development of Russian culture that D. S. Likhachev [the leading contemporary scholar of early Russian culture] called the "Pre-Renaissance."

The new stage in the process of cultural history pertains to the second half of the fifteenth century and continues into the beginning of the sixteenth century. This was the time of the unification of the Russian lands with all its consequences, both progressive and conservative. The interpenetration of local cultures intensified. Master builders from Pskov made an appearance in Moscow and local chronicles followed events in Moscow with great care. Having become the country's center of government, Moscow became the center of the culture of the Russian nationality then taking shape. . . . Connections with the countries of the West were further expanded and intensified, but cultural contact with them was blocked by the Church with its stubborn struggle against "Latinism," and everything new and foreign. The Russian "Pre-Renaissance" was not succeeded by an actual Renaissance, and this is primarily due to the features of the socioeconomic basis of the unitary Russian state, which had risen and developed on the foundation of feudalism and serfdom. The lag and weakness of the towns was particularly strongly felt in the fate of Russian culture. . . .

Thus, the fourteenth and fifteenth centuries were a time of reestablishment and upsurge of the culture of the Russian lands after the terrible Mongol-Tatar devastation, and of the beginning of the shaping of the culture of the Russian (Great-Russian) nationality. It was precisely during that period that it was enriched by such very major achievements as the painting of Rublev and Dionysius, which were the apex of the development of the culture of Rus' and rested upon its entire multiform advance. . . .

SOURCE: A. M. Sakharov, "Rus' and Its Culture in the Thirteenth to Fifteenth Centuries," *Soviet Studies in History*, 18, 3(Winter 1979–80): 37–46 (excerpted). Reprinted by permission of M. E. Sharpe, Inc.

MIKHAIL ALPATOV
The Historical Significance of Andrei Rublev

Perhaps the best proof for those who contend that a cultural revival did occur in the fourteenth century is the work of Andrei Rublev (ca. 1370–ca. 1430). Probably first a monk at the Trinity St. Sergius Monastery, Rublev later joined the Andronnikov Monastery in Moscow. By early in the fifteenth century, he had become an acknowledged master, painting icons and frescoes for some of the most important and beautiful new churches of his time. Sometimes compared to the Italian painter Giotto, Rublev brought to his painting a similarly deeply humanistic sensibility and an ethereal palette which contrasted sharply with the more severe, spare painting of an earlier time (see p. 141). In the selection reproduced here, Mikhail Alpatov ascribes even more importance to Rublev, observing that Rublev lived in an era of great inequality, a time of regimentation of art, both of which limitations he destroyed with his brush.

In old Rus' people infrequently praised a great artist. All the same, the name of Rublev was surrounded by general recognition and honor. It became almost a common noun by which to signify a genuine artist . . . People did not find in the works of Rublev depictions of their contemporaries, or of contemporary events, especially battle victories of the Rus' army. Nevertheless, people discerned in his works an incomparable charm which can characterize only the works of genius. They were proud of Rublev, they valued his masterpieces, and they rejoiced in the fact that they possessed them, and through him they communed with the highest artistic creation. By his art Rublev elevated humankind.

Remembering the difficult time when Rublev lived and worked, one cannot help but be amazed by the fact that he succeeded in creating such an accomplished art. In his rise and later in his death there was a kind of historical regularity. The struggle with the Mongols who had invaded from the East . . . demanded from the Russian people enormous exertion of physical and moral strength. And the art of this time gave birth to this moral upsurge. . . .

The Russian people went to battle [against the Mongols in 1380] under the banner of [Prince] Dimitrii [Donskoi] in order to break the force of the Mongols, and no one could have foreseen then that Moscow would become the stronghold of autocracy, that the people would exchange the Tatar yoke for enserfment, that both in the life of the church and in that of the state the police regime would triumph, the tsar's authorities would subordinate art to themselves, would thrust on artists their own program, and reduce their role to being simply illustrators. . . . And if in art something lively and poetic was preserved, then it was in spite of what the authorities did. This whole time, until the complete disappearance of old Russian painting under Peter, there was not one master equal to Rublev or Dionysii.

One must ask why the art of Rublev did not become the beginning of prolonged development. It was the result of a brief opening in the historical tragedy of the nation. Rublev used this brief period of creative liberty to express in the creations of his genius the most memorable representations of the world, of humankind, and of beauty, and to express his dreams and ideals. Later artistic geniuses of Russia could only guess at this fleeting dream.

Rublev lived at a time when Russian society

Icon of "The Prophet Elijah" (late fourteenth century). From V. N. Lazarev, *Novgorodskaia ikonopis'* (Moscow: Iskusstvo, 1976), plate 25. Reprinted courtesy of Iskusstvo Publishers.

was strictly subordinated to an order which claimed the right to control everything, including art. The inequality which prevailed between the highest and lowest layers of society burdened many people of that time. But the founder of the Trinity monastery, St. Sergei himself, lived like an ordinary peasant his whole working life. His contemporaries often remarked that all people, both the highest-ranking and the most simple, were children of Adam.

Every great artist of that time was obliged to work to the orders of the social elite. The patrons of Rublev were the Grand Prince Vasilii Dmitrievich, the father superior of the Trinity Monastery, Nikon, and perhaps Prince Iurii of Zvenigorod. Only these people possessed the means to finance the creation of significant and sizable monuments of art. And this inevitably led to the fact that art became a privilege of the social elite.

One can imagine that a peasant, educated in the "primitive" letters of the Russian North, would wonder at the absence in Rublev's "Trinity" of Patriarch Abraham and Sarah [see p. 143]. He might be troubled by the fact that in Rublev's "Last Judgment" the sound of the angels' trumpets did not provoke fear

"Old Testament Trinity" from the Novgorod Quadripartite icon (fourteenth–fifteenth centuries). From V. N. Lazarev, *Novgorodskaia ikonopis'* (Moscow: Iskusstvo, 1976), plate 34. Reprinted courtesy of Iskusstvo Publishers.

among those being resurrected from the dead, as popular religious poetry of the time suggested. On the other hand, for Rublev and for people of his circle, the crudeness, the wild fanaticism in the icons of peasant masters alienated them. In fact, most icons which then existed in Rus', especially icons which were deeply revered, were not Rublev-like in character or spirit.

Indeed, between Rublev and the Novgorod school there were wide differences. The "Trinity" icon of the so-called "Quadripartite Icon" from the Church of St. John in Novgorod depicts a mighty divinity in the company of associates wholly submissive to his will. In the Novgorod icon there is no trace of "triple harmony" of the world; rather hierarchy prevails here, expressed in a pyramidal composition, the subordination of the lesser to the greater. Only clear, brilliant coloring deprives the icon of the fearful force of an idol. . . .

The icons and frescoes of Rublev were intended to beautify churches. The themes of his painting are borrowed from Scripture, and in that way silently took part in the Orthodox liturgy. Of course, Rublev served his art because he believed deeply, and this faith overflowed from him, and inspired him in his creative

"Old Testament Trinity" icon by Andrei Rublev (ca. 1411). From V. N. Lazarev, *Moskovskaia shkola ikonopisi* (Moscow: Iskusstvo, 1980), plate 35. Reprinted courtesy of Iskusstvo Publishers.

achievement. But this does not exhaust the explanation of that which came from his hands. In his art Rublev served the Church, but he also always remained an artist, an artistic genius. Many other ordinary masters, like Rublev, recognized the dogmas of the church and scrupulously observed its rituals. But only he had that which distinguishes him from the ordinary icon-painter—great insight, penetration into the world of the human spirit. His art is like an inspired song, like an exciting vision, like prophecy. He had revealed to him the truth, the fate of humankind, its good and beauty. Therefore the value of Rublev does not lie in the fact that by his brush or the colors

he gave to it he expressed that which previously the fathers of the church had put into words. Rublev expressed in his painting things which no one else before him had ever expressed—or had ever even thought. Each of his icons is a triumphant hymn, a psalm of praise, a prayer. There are no words, no texts or even lyrics which could duplicate that which even now conquers us in the works of Rublev. . . .

The majority of the contemporaries of Rublev submissively, almost mechanically "copied" iconographic canons. Rublev, however, attempted to reach the truth; in the visible forms of reality he surmised the secrets of the creation of the world, and therefore in the teaching of the Pseudo-Dionysius [neo-Platonist philosopher] he must have been drawn to the conviction that one learns the invisible through the visible, that created beauty is but a reflection of an uncreated beauty, that a heavenly light falls on our earthly things. . . . Rublev could give to icon painting a deep philosophical meaning, inasmuch as he felt that each subject had, beyond its direct meaning, another, allegorical meaning. . . . He did not attempt a precise reproduction of the subject, but contented himself with a "rough similarity," metaphors which help one understand the connection of phenomena. . . .

Most of all there is in Rublev a vitality of understanding of the organic structure of forms, in the communication of the movement of the human figure. . . . In the works of Rublev the tempo is slower, and correspondingly in its contours there is more fluidity and smoothness. . . .

The completeness, the subordination of its parts, is a characteristic quality of the painting of Rublev. In his works one never notices a deformation, an excessive stretching of proportions. He is content to lighten the forms, and lightly he narrows the body extremities. This is noticeable already in his early works, and remained later, and forever distinguishes the works created by Rublev's own hand from the works of his students, who exaggerated figures, and so deprived them of organic integrity. Medieval masters rather often depicted as larger that which was more important. . . . Rublev acted differently. In his "Savior" from the Zvenigorod iconostasis [see p. 145] the outline of the face, especially the eyes, nose, and lips, are considerably decreased in comparison with the rather large figure. Furthermore, its aspect becomes more spiritualized, more refined, narrower.

In the painting of Rublev there is a feminine softness. But the precise definition of forms gives his figures force and firmness. The art of Rublev at bottom is very lyrical, but this is not a modern lyricism in which a person in search of a refuge is saved from the surrounding world. The lyricism of Rublev is a sympathy of the artist for what is personal, and this sympathy is raised to a level of a general human norm. This is why Rublev, like a monumentalist, escaped the cold ceremony which frequently attaches to the works of Byzantine masters.

Rublev was not only an artist, poet and thinker, but he was also a painter, a master of colors. . . . The palette of Rublev startles not so much by the wealth of colors (in this respect Dionysii outdoes him), but by the abundance of different color registers. . . . Color possesses for Rublev a great force, even in half-tones, but it is never dense, never too heavy. . . . Rublev shied away from high light which falls on colors. Color itself emits light in his hand; colors are arranged according to the force of their own light, giving an impression of lightness which dominates his paintings and does not admit any gloominess. In Rublev's world, colors and light breathe lightly and freely.

The colors of Rublev are beautiful, tender, and noble. They never clang, but rather sing. They seem like the expression of something more elevated than they themselves. They open to our eyes something unseen, and draw us to them. The symbol of color, about which thinkers have spoken, does not have decisive significance. Over its conditional language prevails something more generally understood. Pure colors and light express a spiritual beauty. This is the promise, a presentiment of heavenly bliss. . . .

In order to determine the historical place of Rublev one must remember that his younger contemporary was Jan van Eyck, that the "Trinity" of Rublev is also a masterpiece, like the remarkable Ghent altarpiece, "Adoration of the Lamb," done somewhat later. The Dutch masterpiece wins one over most of all by its broad scope of the real world, by its loving appreciation and reproduction of the smallest details in combination with the deep symbolic sense of the whole. The masterpiece of Rublev, on the contrary, conquers one by its ability to express much in a small, laconic allegory embracing the whole world. This attests to Rublev's attachment to ancient tradition. . . .

"Savior" icon by Andrei Rublev (1410–20). From V. N. Lazarev, *Moskovskaia shkola ikonopisi* (Moscow: Iskusstvo, 1980), plate 31. Reprinted courtesy of Iskusstvo Publishers.

Sometimes people call Rublev the "Russian Fra Angelico," since they were both artist-monks, overcoming medieval asceticism and both brought to art faint notes of humanity. They have compared Rublev with other masters of the fourteenth and fifteenth centuries, like Simon Martin, Brederlam, and Meister Frank. But in distinction from these other masters, Rublev was not an artist of a transitional epoch. Traces of duplicity, artistic eclecticism were deeply alien to him. Rublev marks not a turning point in the development of Russian art, but one of its most remarkable peaks. This is why his art entrances by its wholeness and accomplishment, why with all the relativity of similar designations Rublev may justly be named the "Russian Rafael."

SOURCE: M. Alpatov, *Andrei Rublev* (Moscow: Izobrazi-tel'noe iskusstvo, 1972), pp. 129–40 (excerpted). Translated by Daniel H. Kaiser.

III

The Muscovite
Centralized State

(1497–1689)

The years which separated the compilation of the 1497 law code from the full accession to power of Peter the Great were filled with happenings important not only to
this era, but to much of subsequent Russian history. The expansion of the Moscow
Grand Principality, graphically illustrated in the account of the annexation of Novgorod, continued, first swallowing nearby principalities, then in the sixteenth century
reaching out to German lands along the Baltic and Turkic lands along the upper and
lower Volga River valley. The grandest acquisition of all, perhaps, was Siberia to
which the first ambassadors of Muscovite power came late in the sixteenth century.
Still later, Muscovy yielded, then reconquered territory along its western and northwestern borders, bringing in one of the greatest prizes in mid-century when Ukraine
cast its lot with Muscovy. Most of the territorial expansion did not come easy, and
therefore war did much damage to the economic and social fabric of Muscovite
society in these years. But undeniably the territory of the state grew.

It is ironic that just as the Muscovite state embraced more and more territory,
calamities of unparalleled dimension struck the Muscovite economy and society.
Some were man-made, others sprang from impersonal, uncontrollable forces. To the
first category belongs the disastrous experiment in governmental dualism which Ivan
IV invented. The *oprichnina*, he called it, a state "apart," warring on the remnant of
state administration he had deserted. No comprehensive appraisal of the cost of this
experiment will ever be possible, but that it wreaked havoc upon the land can provoke no doubt. Indeed, in a fit of remorse Ivan himself had his scribes identify by

name more than 4,900 persons whose deaths he had effected. How many more went unnamed and unremembered we can only guess.

To many who lived in the last years of the sixteenth century, new disasters came from sources more remote than the tsar. Plague and famine combined to devastate much of Muscovy in the last decades of the century, precisely when Ivan was trying to fight a war with the Germans. To the blind fury of disease and weather the sovereign added the calculating and ruinous hand of the tax collector, whose surtax on the victims of earlier disasters helped empty many villages and abandon tilled fields to weeds and trees. This combination of factors helped weaken the Muscovite economy and enervate its society on the eve of one of the greatest cataclysms ever experienced in Russia.

The years between the death in 1598 of the Tsar Fedor Ivanovich, the last living member of the Riurikid dynasty, and the enthronement of Mikhail Romanov in 1613 came to be remembered in Russia as the "Time of Troubles." A horrible concatenation of political pretenders, economic disaster, and social disorder, this tumultuous era also brought foreign invasion and native rebellion. All these phenomena, though relatively short-lived, nevertheless interacted with historical processes of longer duration. The constitution of the old Muscovite state came under attack, while much of society underwent deep change. Slavery, for example, which had been known since Kievan times, seems to have undergone a fundamental transformation in these years. Whereas foreign captives had long served to replenish the supply of unfree labor, in these disastrous years increasing numbers of Muscovites sold themselves into slavery, evidently hoping thereby to claim from their masters at least food and shelter. Serfdom, whose first stages had been written into Muscovite history more than a hundred years earlier, in these years began to take on a permanence which the law only finally recognized in 1649.

Historians, viewing the disassembling of the Muscovite state at the hands of foreigners and natives alike, sometimes have wondered at the result. Was this not the time to effect some fundamental change in the structure of the state? Was this not the ideal time to guarantee that never again would any arbitrary exercise of power devastate the land? Perhaps some Muscovite activists sympathized with this view, and this may explain how a teenage Mikhail Romanov secured the throne in 1613. In fact, the body which selected the new tsar, the so-called Assembly of the Land (zemskii sobor), did seem to share power with the sovereign in the first, troubled years after Mikhail's accession. But nothing constitutional or institutional, nothing reminiscent of the old Novgorodian contracts negotiated with the princes who ruled there, altered the construction of state power. Though no new tyranny resulted, the edifice of autocracy—whether mere façade or not—rapidly reappeared, and that may yet prove the most inexplicable development of the period.

The expansion of the Muscovite boundaries promised an economic boom. Although Ivan IV eventually lost his war to gain access to the Baltic, the aim was to establish a direct connection to European trade which was then limited to contacts along the White Sea; control of the Volga similarly opened to Muscovy the riches of Central Asia, and the trade which passed through Russia to Europe. Siberia had its own treasures to contribute to Muscovite coffers. By the seventeenth century, some of these hopes had been realized. But the sixteenth century proved less accommodating to dreams of enrichment. Epidemic disease and a string of unfavorable harvests after mid-century brought instead annual dearth and the resulting depopulation of the central Moscow lands. It was this sad prelude which ushered in the Time of Troubles. Only later, once the military and political instability had subsided, did the economy return to normal, maintaining considerable stability for much of the seventeenth century.

The rebound from the calamities of late sixteenth- and early seventeenth-century Muscovy proved to be unexpectedly quick. Already by the 1660s, the Muscovite sovereign was able to field a mainly modern, salaried army which defeated one of the better armies in Europe. Muscovite culture also experienced a revival. Whole genres of literature and painting totally unknown to earlier generations of Muscovites emerged in full flower in the seventeenth century. Individualism and its accompanying humanism displaced an abstract idealism which had long reigned in elite culture. Abandoning unalloyed didacticism, the arts also came to celebrate individuals and their foibles, bringing entertainment as well as enlightenment into elite culture. Learning, though still not organized or distributed as it became in later Russia, nevertheless experienced growth in this century, contributing perhaps to that inevitably small audience able to read and appreciate the new literature.

For most citizens of Muscovy, however, their concerns were little distinguished from those of their ancestors. The construction and provisioning of families, reproduction, birth and death—these basic issues emerge from the more abundant documentation more clearly than they do for earlier times, providing us with a deeper appreciation of the world of early modern Russia.

9

The State Structure
of Muscovite Russia

With the annexation of Novgorod, in the 1470s, then additional principalities toward the end of the fifteenth and early in the sixteenth centuries, Moscow became the unquestioned capital of the East Slavic lands. Of course, the Lithuanian (later Polish-Lithuanian) state occupied many of the original lands of Kievan Rus', and periodically that frontier altered as a consequence of the latest outbreak of hostilities. But Moscow had at least triumphed among most of the central and eastern principalities.

There were many important consequences of this outcome, but perhaps none so significant as the fact that Moscow's own form of state administration came to prevail throughout these lands. As we have already seen, the Moscow Grand Princes came to style their lands their "patrimony," and inasmuch as some of the principalities came into the Grand Prince's hands either through conquest or purchase, the characterization had much to commend it. However, in the opinion of some historians, that patrimonial view of the state helped guarantee that no institutions arose which might rival the exercise of power by the Grand Prince.

No reign confirms historians in that view better than that of Ivan IV ("The Terrible") (1533–84). Succeeding to the throne as a boy, and inheriting a state whose borders his father and grandfather had helped stretch greatly, Ivan had to weather some difficult moments before 1547, when at his formal coronation he adopted the title "Tsar" (Caesar). This was not altogether an innovation; as we have seen above, apologists in the reigns of both his father and grandfather had attempted to appropriate for the Moscow Grand Princes claim to the imperial legacy.

But Ivan's reign has come to symbolize the wantonness of unrestricted power. Although, as Robert Crummey points out below, for most of the first years of his rule Muscovy witnessed a blizzard of reform, Ivan himself changed course abruptly. Whether by virtue of a bizarre, devious policy or by consequence of some kind of mental disorder, Ivan determined sometime late in 1564 that he could not trust those officials on whom he had previously counted for administering the state. He therefore demanded and received the right to establish two separate administrations: one ruled as before by the traditional boyar elite and bureaucratic staff, and another special administration into which he would invite special servitors. This oprichnina came to control an immense portion of the former territory of Muscovy, and seems to have terrorized much of the rest. Ivan cast his lot with this second administration, going so far at one point as to install someone else as tsar over the other administration (*zemshchina*), giving Muscovy an oddly dual state structure. The oprichnina collapsed within a decade, but its record all the same has served critics of Russian absolutism as evidence of a long tradition of abusive government.

Skeptical voices, however, dismiss the charge. Russia had to *appear* to be an autocracy, says one historian, in order to be able to maintain a society and government which actually depended upon cooperation rather than submission. Nancy Kollmann, for example, looks backward from the sixteenth century in order to trace the pattern of elite participation in government. Throughout even the worst of times, she says, the Grand Prince and boyars cooperated, because only in this way could they both protect their mutual interests. Violence was in fact rare, and whenever violence was necessary, it came with the agreement of the boyars, not in contravention of their wishes. Consensus rather than conflict characterized Muscovite politics.

Robert Crummey, in assessing the entire reign of Ivan IV, strikes a compromise. Identifying a raft of reform legislation enacted early, Crummey finds here evidence of a state which, if it acted arbitrarily, nevertheless acted in the interests of its citizens. The establishment of law, the enactment of local administration—this and much more attests to the interest of the tsar in governing with his subjects. But the later stages of Ivan's reign do not evidence this same purpose, and must, Crummey asserts, be consigned to the sovereign's serious personality disorder. The oprichnina, then, cannot serve as evidence of an autocratic state, whatever other evidence may sustain that interpretation.

DOCUMENT

A Foreigner Describes the Oprichnina of Tsar Ivan the Terrible (1565–70)

For those who contend that Muscovy early developed an autocratic political tradition, no ruler serves as better proof of the contention than Ivan IV (1533–84), and no aspect of Ivan's reign better demonstrates the consequences of such politics than the *oprichnina*. Although it lasted less than a decade (1565–72), the *oprichnina* was nevertheless a time of arbitrary terror when the minions of the tsar, clothed in black and bearing special symbols of their authority, exercised almost unrestrained authority in Muscovy. Among those who served the tsar in this way was a foreigner, Heinrich von Staden. Born probably sometime in the early 1540s in Westphalia, Staden had come to Muscovy to accept service. Finding employment in Muscovy disappointing, he composed an account of his experience to persuade the German Emperor Rudolf II to invade Muscovy. Nothing came of these plans, but Staden's narrative remains an interesting

description of a tumultuous era in Muscovite history.

———

Ivan Vasilievich [Ivan IV], Grand Prince of all Russia, . . . chose from his own and foreign nations a hand-picked order, thus creating the *oprichnina* and the *zemshchina*.

The oprichnina was [composed of] his people; the zemshchina, of the ordinary people. The Grand Prince thus began to inspect one city and region after another. And those who, according to the military muster rolls, had not served [the Grand Prince's] forefathers by fighting the enemy with their [estates] were deprived of their estates, which were given to those in the oprichnina.

The princes and boyars who were taken into the oprichnina were ranked not according to riches but according to birth. They then took an oath not to have anything to do with the *zemskie* people or form any friendships with them. Those in the oprichnina also had to wear black clothes and hats; and in their quivers, where they put their arrows, they carried some kind of brushes or brooms tied on the ends of sticks. The *oprichniki* were recognized in this way.

Because of insurrection [in Moscow in December 1564], the Grand Prince left Moscow for Aleksandrova Sloboda, a two-day trip. He placed guards in this sloboda, and had any nobles that he wanted called to him from Moscow and other cities.

The Grand Prince sent an order to the zemskie people saying that they must judge justly: "... Judge justly, ours [the oprichniki] shall not be in the wrong." Because of this order, the zemskie people became despondent. A person from the oprichnina could accuse someone from the zemshchina of owing him a sum of money. And even if the oprichnik had never known nor seen the accused from the zemshchina, the latter had to pay him immediately or he was publicly beaten in the marketplace with knouts or cudgels every day until he paid. No one was spared in this, neither clerics nor laymen. The oprichniki did a number of indescribable things to the zemskie people to get all their money and property. . . .

The Grand Prince arrived in Moscow from Aleksandrova Sloboda and murdered one of the chief men of the zemshchina, Ivan Petrovich Cheliadnin. In the Grand Prince's absence from Moscow, this man was the chief boyar and judge. He willingly helped the poor people find justice quickly, and for a number of years he was governor and commander in Livonia—at Dorpat and at Polotsk. . . .

Prince Andrei Kurbskii was governor and commander after him. When [Kurbskii] became aware of the oprichnina business, he rode off to King Sigismund August in Poland, leaving behind his wife and children. In his place came the boyar Mikhail Morozov. . . .

Afterward [Cheliadnin] was summoned to Moscow. In Moscow he was killed and thrown into a filthy pit near the Neglinna river. The Grand Prince then went with his oprichniki and burned all the [estates] in the country belonging to this Ivan Petrovich. The villages were burned with their churches and everything that was in them, icons and church ornaments. Women and girls were stripped na-

ked and forced in that state to catch chickens in the fields. The oprichniki caused great misery in the country, and many people were secretly murdered.

This was too much for the zemskie people. They began to confer, and they decided to elect as grand prince Vladimir Andreevich [Staritskii]. . . .

Prince Vladimir Andreevich [Staritskii] revealed the compact to the Grand Prince, and revealed everything that the zemskie people had planned and prepared. The Grand Prince . . . returned by post road to Aleksandrova Sloboda, and had someone write down [the names of] those zemskie leaders whom he wanted slaughtered, killed, and executed first. . . .

The Grand Prince continued to have one [zemskii] leader after another seized and killed as it came into his head, one this way, another that way.

Metropolitan Philip could remain silent about this business no longer, and spoke affably to the Grand Prince saying that he ought to live and rule as his forefathers had. The good metropolitan fell into disgrace with these words, and he had to live in very large iron chains until he died. The Grand Prince then chose a metropolitan according to his wishes.

After that the Grand Prince set out from Aleksandrova Sloboda with all his oprichniki. Every city, road, monastery from the sloboda to Livonia was occupied by oprichnina guards, as though it were done because of plague, so that one city or monastery could learn of nothing from another.

The oprichniki came to the *iam*—or post station—at Chernaia and began to plunder. The places where the Grand Prince spent the night were set afire and were burned down the next morning.

All those who came from Moscow to the guard post and wanted to go to the camp of [Ivan's] own hand-picked people, whether they were princes or boyars or their servants, were seized by the guards, bound, and immediately killed. Some were stripped naked in front of the Grand Prince and rolled around in the snow until they died. The same thing happened to those who wanted to leave the camp for Moscow and were caught by the guards.

The Grand Prince then arrived at the city of Tver and had everything plundered, even churches and monasteries. And he had all the prisoners killed, likewise his own people who had befriended or married foreigners. All the bodies had their legs cut off, because of the ice, and were then stuck under the ice of the Volga River. The same occurred in the city of Torzhok. Neither church nor monastery was spared here.

The Grand Prince arrived again outside the city of Great Novgorod. He settled down three furlongs from the city and sent in an army commander with his retinue. He was to spy and reconnoiter. The rumor was that the Grand Prince wanted to march to Livonia. Then the Grand Prince moved into Great Novgorod, into the bishop's palace, and took everything belonging to the bishop. He took the largest bells and whatever he wanted from the churches. The Grand Prince thus left the city alone. He ordered the merchants to buy and sell and to ask a just price from his soldiers, the oprichniki. Every day he arose and moved to another monastery. He indulged his wantonness and had monks tortured, and many of them were killed. There are three hundred monasteries inside and outside the city and not one of these was spared. Then the pillage of the city began. . . .

This distress and misery continued in the city for six weeks without interruption [in January and February 1570]. Every shop and room where money or property were thought to be was sealed. Every day the Grand Prince could also be found in the torture chamber in person. Nothing might remain in the monasteries and the city. Everything that the soldiers could not carry off was thrown into the water or burned. If one of the zemskie people retrieved anything from the water, he was hanged. . . .

The oprichniki ransacked the entire countryside and all the cities and villages of the zemshchina, although the Grand Prince had not given them permission to do that. They drew up instructions themselves, as though the Grand Prince had ordered them to kill this or that merchant or noble—if he was thought to have money—along with his wife and children, and to take his money and property to the Grand Prince's Treasury. In the zemshchina, they thus committed many murders and assassinations, which are beyond description. . . .

When the oprichniki had tortured Russia— the entire zemshchina—according to their will and pleasure so that even the Grand Prince realized it was enough, the oprichniki still had not sated themselves with the money and property of the zemskie people. If one of the zemskie people brought a suit for a thousand rubles, he would accept a hundred rubles or less, but give a receipt [to the oprichniki] for the full amount. All the petitions were set aside together with the records and receipts. [The oprichniki] had sworn to maintain no friendships with the zemskie people and to have nothing to do with them; but then the Grand Prince turned the tables and had all petitions accepted. And when the oprichniki were indebted for a thousand and had a receipt, but had not fully paid, these oprichniki had to pay the zemskie people again. The oprichniki did not at all like this situation. . . .

Then the Grand Prince began to wipe out all the chief people of the oprichnina. Prince Afanasii Viazemskii died in chains in the town of Gorodets. Aleksei [Basmanov] and his son [Fedor], with whom the Grand Prince indulged in lewdness, were killed. Maliuta Skuratov was shot near Weissenstein [Paide] in Livonia. He was the pick of the bunch, and according to the Grand Prince's order, he was remembered in church. Prince Mikhail, the son of the Grand Prince's brother-in-law from the Circassian land, was chopped to death by the harquebusiers [musketeers] with axes or halberds [weapons combining the virtues of the spear and the battle axe]. Prince Vasilii Temkin was drowned. Ivan Saburov was murdered. Peter Seisse was hanged from his own court gate opposite the bedroom. Prince Andrei Ovtsyn was hanged in the Arbatskaia street of the oprichnina. A living sheep was hung next to him [an *ovtsa* is a sheep, thus the murderers played a prank on his name]. The marshal Bulat wanted to marry his sister to the Grand Prince. He was killed and his sister was raped by five hundred harquebusiers. The captain of the harquebusiers, Kuraka Unkovskii, was killed and stuck under the ice. In the previous year [name unclear] was eaten by dogs at the Karinskii guard post of Aleksandrova Sloboda. Grigorii Griaznoi was killed and his son Nikita was burned alive. His brother Vasilii was captured by the Crimean Tatars. The scribe and clerk Posnik Suvorov was killed at the Land Chancellery. Osip Il'in was shamefully executed in the Court Chancellery.

All the chief men of the oprichnina and zemshchina and all those who were to be killed were first publicly whipped in the marketplace until they signed over all their money and property, if they had any, to the Treasury of the Grand Prince. Those who had no money and property were killed in front of churches, in the street, or in their homes, whether asleep or awake, and were thrown into the street. The cause of the death, and whether it was legal or not, was written on a note, which was then pinned to the clothes of the corpse. The body had to lie in the street day and night as a warning to the people.

SOURCE: Heinrich von Staden, *The Land and Government of Muscovy: A Sixteenth-Century Account.* Translated and edited by Thomas Esper (Stanford: Stanford University Press, 1967), pp. 18–21, 24–7, 33–6, (excerpted). Footnotes have been omitted and some Russian terms have been translated. Copyright © 1967 by the Board of Trustees of Leland Stanford Junior University. Reprinted by permission of the publishers, Stanford University Press.

LITERATURE

NANCY SHIELDS KOLLMANN
The Façade of Autocracy

Whatever the violence of the *oprichnina*, some historians are skeptical of claims about Muscovite autocracy. Here Nancy Kollmann points out that from an early time, the service elite—the boyars and the *okol'nichie*, the second highest rank in Muscovite society—themselves were deeply involved in the process of governing. That the Muscovite state appeared to outsiders to be autocratic was in part a strategem of the boyars, who understood that only this apparent monolith could maintain the intricate politics of marriage and consensus in which they all took part. In reading texts of the era, then, Kollmann maintains, we must be cautious to discount assertions about the tsar's unlimited power. These sources are the understandable product of an entire complex of ceremony and assertion designed to present a façade of autocracy.

The [Muscovite] court was immensely successful in concealing the dynamism of its politics from the outside world and in convincing foreigners that Muscovy was ruled literally by an autocrat. Sigismund von Herberstein, an envoy of the Hapsburg court in the early sixteenth century, declared: "In the sway which he [the tsar] holds over his people, he surpasses all the monarchs of the whole world." It comes as some surprise that the ideology and public ceremony of court politics diverged so radically from the reality that we have seen. There was constant sparring of ambitious men at court, yet Muscovite ideology denies that political interaction occurred. The sovereign is depicted as a literal autocrat; neither the boyars nor other individuals or social groups share authority with him. To some extent this political ideology developed from the theocratic vision of the churchmen who wrote chronicles, but it should not be dismissed for that reason. Not only churchmen promoted the façade of autocracy—the boyars themselves accepted it, which suggests that it was grounded in political reality.

The sovereign was routinely described in chronicles and other ideological writings as the sole decision maker, regardless of his age or abilities. . . . Ceremony was an especially effective communicator of this ideology. . . .

In these ceremonies and in written sources, Muscovite political interaction was presented as essentially moral and personal; thus it was denied what might be called public or constitutional legitimacy. Authors of written sources, lacking a term for the collectivity of the boyars, referred to them by name or simply as "the boyars." What modern observers would consider political relationships the sources referred to as personal ties: political conflict and ambition were explained by loyalty, friendship, and kinship. The political realm was depicted as being ruled over by the sovereign alone; therefore, court politics was not characterized by pluralism, conflict, or compromise—all of which are fundamental to politics as generally understood. In ideology Muscovite politics had no dynamism; the state was a harmonious family, each member obediently playing his role in the community of God on earth.

The sovereign was at the center of a theocratic vision of government: court ceremony presented him as separate from and superior to the boyars. When he held audiences, he was seated on a throne raised above the level where the boyars sat; he was surrounded by splendid bodyguards who were regally garbed in white and carried ceremonial axes. The sovereign's omnipotence was demonstrated by the immensity and splendor of his entourage. On festive occasions, the sovereign flaunted jewel-encrusted golden drinking cups, crowns, orbs, and scepters; sovereign and boyars alike were decked out in jewel-encrusted robes. . . . Even when (or perhaps especially when) the sovereign was incompetent and the boyars were managing the state, court ceremony maintained the fiction that Moscow was ruled by its sovereign. . . .

Political disgrace reinforced the centrality of the sovereign; exile from the presence of the sovereign was the symbolic expression of such disgrace, which also included more tangible punishment, such as incarceration and confis-

cation of wealth. Unfortunates were said to have been deprived of the sight of the tsar's "bright eyes." The boyars were portrayed as passive and weak, implying that they recognized and accepted their subservience. . . . Foreign travelers expressed dismay at what they perceived as the humiliation of the great men of the realm, who called themselves "slaves" and prostrated themselves before the sovereign. Olearius noted: "In addressing the Tsar the magnates must unashamedly not only write their names in the diminutive form, but also call themselves slaves, and they are treated as such." Although these descriptions are inconsistent with reality, they evidence a concern for controlling the potentially powerful and ambitious boyars. . . .

In this ideological view of Muscovite politics, boyars were given legitimacy as advisers, reflecting in some measure their real power. Just as the metropolitan oversaw moral and religious matters, the boyars oversaw secular affairs. These men thus acted as liaisons between the grand prince and his people. That boyars had a traditional right to rule jointly with the sovereign is reflected in contemporary illustrations of court ceremony, where the tsar is depicted associating with his boyars, not dominating over them. It is also shown in descriptions of the grand prince's attitude of comradely loyalty toward his boyars. Vasilii III, for example, entreated his boyars to defend his kingdom and his minor son after his death as follows: "I . . . am your born sovereign, and you are my eternal boyars; and you, brothers, stand firm so that my son may be made the sovereign of the state and so that there may be justice in the land."

Through the prism of an idealized ideology, these sources reveal the court's desire that politics be conducted in unanimity without strife. In addresses to the "Hundred Chapters" Church Council attributed to Ivan IV, the sovereign pleaded with the boyars to forget their "prior disputes" and be reconciled. He urged his prelates, boyars, and all his advisers to "help me, assist me, all of you together and in unanimity" in accomplishing the work of the council. . . .

The ubiquity of the theme of harmony and unanimity compels us to take it seriously as a principle of Muscovite politics. It is not consistent with the reality of court politics, which was marked by dissension, but it hints at limits on such fractious disputes. One such constraint was expressed ideologically by the assertion that all boyars were equal—equal in subservience to the sovereign, equal in their degree of access to him, equal in status and power. Implicit in their equality was harmony: the boyars should not disrupt their unity by contentiousness. Unanimity was the implicit way for boyars to prevent and resolve political conflicts. The expectation of rule by unanimity, or consensus, constrained individual boyars, regardless of their personal eminence. Boyars could not rule or aspire to rule. In keeping with the ideology's emphasis on affinitive relations in politics, boyar ambition that caused strife was regarded as a moral defect, not as an unavoidable part of political interaction. . . .

It was the constant threat of instability—resulting from foreign wars, a fragile economy whose functioning was in part dependent upon a hostile climate, the administration of a large state by a small bureaucracy, and the boyars' ambitions for power—that gave rise to such a conservative set of values. The ideology expressed the deepest concerns of Muscovy's political actors; a façade of autocracy was necessary to prevent chaos. The primary purpose of the ideology of autocracy described here was to impose limits on the boyars' political competition. In theory, designation of the sovereign as the only legitimate political figure prevented boyars' competition from threatening the state's stability. Boyars fought to gain a greater share of power but not to replace the sovereign. They sought higher status but did not attempt to prevent others from seeking it. But in 1598, when the dynasty died out, boyar factions ignored all limits on competition and struggled to become sovereign. The result was the state of anarchy that Muscovy's ideology and political controls had been specifically designed to prevent. Typically, however, boyars were guided by this ideology and thus stabilized their potentially volatile political system.

MECHANISMS TO MAINTAIN STABILITY

At most times, relative stability was ensured because all boyars had some degree of power. In the early seventeenth century, a descendant of Prince Ivan Mikhailovich Vorotynskii suggested this when he complained that a share of power was being denied to him and his family: "We experienced disgrace, but a role in government was never taken from us." All boyars had a right to consult with the grand prince, but in practice the inner circle met with him more frequently. All boyars lived in or around the Kremlin; they attended court daily and consulted with the grand prince and with each other frequently. They served in the field as military commanders or as vicegerents, but preferred service in the sovereign's retinue, either participating in a campaign or based in the Kremlin. In those assignments boyars could maintain the personal contacts that ensured rule by consensus and that also frequently led to advantageous marriages. The involvement of all boyars facilitated attainment of the ideal of harmony at court; because of the real disparities of power and the resulting constant state of tension, consensus among them was required to maintain stability.

Consensus between the grand prince and the boyars is evident in the distribution of power at court. The boyars in the inner circle had more power than the others, but they never succeeded in totally monopolizing power (although that would seem a logical goal). . . . [C]onferral of boyar or okol'nichii rank threatened to disturb the balance of power and therefore required the approval of the men already holding those ranks. The boyars and the grand prince sometimes delayed and at other times permitted accessions to boyar and okol'nichii rank. During times of political turmoil, few new appointments were made. However, the resolution of political crises (for example, those of the mid-fifteenth century and those occurring in 1499, 1525, and the 1530s and 1540s) was followed by a cathartic redistribution of power and numerous promotions.

The integration of new families into the boyar elite also required consensus. The logic of court politics would seem to have encouraged exclusivity. As some clans became more powerful, they expelled their rivals from politics. The inner-circle families, being more powerful, might be expected to choose not to tolerate less powerful boyars at court. . . . [But] the number of clans whose men held boyar or okol'nichii rank gradually increased from the fourteenth to the sixteenth centuries. Boyars consented to the sovereign's desire to add to their numbers. . . .

Consensus politics was clearly in evidence when the members of the court took action against one of their number, as when the boyars and the sovereign agreed to bring disgrace [on someone]. . . . There are numerous references between the fourteenth and sixteenth centuries to boyars having their property confiscated or being exiled, forcibly tonsured, or even executed. . . . [T]heir allies and kinsmen apparently consented, if perhaps grudgingly. When boyar families did seek revenge, political crisis was the result; the mid-fifteenth-century dynastic war and the struggles that occurred during the youth of Ivan IV are examples. These episodes of violence were, however, rare. . . .

Even when he had secured the agreement of his boyars for the punishment of one of them, the grand prince sought to limit the degree of violence inflicted. Men who were imprisoned, for example, often died in captivity, but the punishment initially aroused less animosity among boyars because the possibility of release remained open. Several imprisoned servitors are recorded as having been freed—evidence of the relative moderation of this punishment. Other types of punishment—prohibition of marriage, exile from Moscow, forcible tonsure—all stopped short of the violence that would probably have provoked interfamily vendettas. Execution was used only when the offense was serious and the court was united behind the decision. . . .

The rarity of, and the adverse reaction to, unsanctioned violence among boyars suggests that it violated political norms. In 1356, Aleksei Petrovich Khvost was killed by rivals who then fled Moscow to escape vengeance. The public outrage was so great and the murder so unusual that chronicles and genealogical books kept it in the public memory for generations. . . . Furthermore, when an execution was carried out without the prior consent of the boyars, the aggrieved family took revenge, which often precipitated further conflict. The fifteenth-century dynastic war is an example of the cost of such violence and illustrates the Kremlin court's determination to avoid it. . . .

Consensus between boyars and the grand prince was perceived as necessary to avoid violence and preserve stability. Recalcitrance and excessive ambition among boyars posed threats to that stability. Such threats were caused by at least two circumstances. First, there was an inequitable balance of power among boyars, even though all had some degree of power and shared in the benefits of rule. Second, the ties of kinship and alliance that united the boyars imposed retributive obligations. To help avoid violence, the court relied on numerous norms and customs. Tradition prohibited murder and the use of extreme violence against individuals in the event of conflict. When murder was resorted to, it was frequently accompanied by another execution intended to reduce tensions rather than to escalate them. Metropolitans offered to mediate and grand princes offered to negotiate in an attempt to avert the violence that could erupt in such an ambitious community.

THE GRAND PRINCE AND PRIMOGENITURE

The grand prince and the boyars also maintained stability by attempting to prevent disputes that might lead to a political crisis, such as disputes over sovereign succession. They strove to ensure that collateral kinsmen of the ruler would not be regarded as legitimate contenders, and in so doing they developed a system of succession that was so predictable that boyars' families could focus marriage strategies on winning a match with the heir to the throne. To boyar families, dynastic succession by primogeniture was preferable to collateral succession, because collateral succession meant that boyar families could not have enjoyed hereditary status: each grand prince's boyars would have been replaced by the boyar elite from the new heir's appanage. Maintenance of succession by primogeniture in the grand-princely family was therefore crucial to the stability of the political system. . . .

Boyar clans benefitted from the stability created by grand-princely succession by primogeniture, and the Daniilovichi [heirs to the founder of the Moscow principality, Daniil] benefitted from the paucity of heirs in that they avoided divisive disputes over succession such as those that had weakened the dynasties of Tver' and other principalities. Like some of their early medieval West European counterparts, the Muscovite dynasty and boyars found succession by primogeniture to be useful in their drive for internal stability and for regional power. . . .

The ultimate irony was that as a result of this strong suspicion of collateral kinsmen, the Daniilovich dynasty died out in 1598 for lack of collateral lines. Thus Muscovy's future was to be determined by Ivan IV's progeny. Ivan, approaching the end of his life in the early 1580s, had three living sons. The eldest, Ivan Ivanovich, was killed, perhaps at the tsar's own hand, in 1581; the youngest, Dmitrii of Uglich, died in suspicious circumstances in 1591. This left only the feebleminded Fedor Ivanovich, who succeeded Ivan as tsar in 1584. When Fedor died in 1598, he left no sons or daughters. The price of the stability so highly valued by grand princes and boyars was the Time of Troubles.

SOURCE: Nancy Shields Kollmann, *Kinship and Politics: The Making of the Muscovite Political System, 1345–1547* (Stanford: Stanford University Press, 1987), pp. 146–53, 155–6, 158–9 (excerpted). Footnotes have been omitted, and some Russian terms have been translated. Copyright © 1987 by the Board of Trustees of the Leland Stanford Junior University. Reprinted by permission of the publishers, Stanford University Press.

ROBERT O. CRUMMEY

Ivan IV: Reformer or Tyrant?

Despite the excesses which characterized the second part of his reign, the rule of Ivan IV nevertheless also offers some evidence for his reformist intentions. As Robert Crummey here points out, neither the tsar nor his associates bequeathed us a plan of reform. All the same, the long reign of Ivan included a vast array of programmatic change which significantly altered the operations of government, justifying in Crummey's view the label of "reform." Some institutions with a long life in Muscovite government, such as the chancelleries and the Assembly of the Land, originated in Ivan's reign. Unlike some apologists of Ivan IV, however, Crummey is unwilling to credit the *oprichnina* with any rational end. In his view, only the deranged capacities of the tsar can account for the violence and irrationality of this epoch.

———————

[Ivan IV and his advisers] left behind few programmatic statements of their intentions as reformers. The very word "reform" would probably have rung strangely in their ears. Nevertheless, a regime that stages the first coronation of the ruler with an imperial title, issues a new law code, and conducts a comprehensive review of the state of the church intends to inspect and, if necessary, repair the institutional and ideological foundations of society. Moreover, there seems to have been a widespread perception within the ruling elite that changes had to be made. Reform began during the "boyar rule" of Ivan's childhood and continued through Ivan's life-threatening illness in 1553 to about 1560. Finally, the reforms to a considerable extent form a coherent pattern in that many of the government's measures are clearly interrelated.

The concrete objectives of Ivan and his advisers in making reforms, judging by their actions, were primarily to bring consistency and order to the church and royal courts, strengthen the army, and make the royal administration more efficient and less corrupt. Within these broad rubrics, we can distinguish several general types of reform measures.

First, in the early 1550s, Ivan's government made a number of detailed technical reforms that might be characterized as "housekeeping" in state and church. In putting its house in order, Ivan's government issued a new law code (*sudebnik*) in 1550. The act of promulgating a legal codex symbolized the regime's determination to assert its authority over its subjects by systematizing legal norms and procedures. . . .

In a similar vein, the *Stoglav* ("Hundred Chapters") church council of 1551 was the centerpiece of a campaign, supported by the tsar's government, to bring greater order and discipline to the liturgical and moral life and administration of the Eastern Orthodox church and to set limits to its acquisition of lands.

Second, in mobilizing for an all-out assault on Kazan', Ivan's government gave highest priority to strengthening the army. In no sense did its reforms involve a systematic restructuring of the tsar's forces; they consisted instead of piecemeal attacks on specific problems. . . . In preparation for the assault on Kazan', Ivan's government created a new military force with concentrated firepower that complemented the noble cavalry. In 1550, Ivan IV ordered the formation of six companies of musketeers (*strel'tsy*), who fought primarily on foot with the latest firearms. In a certain sense, these units amounted to a small standing army since the men served throughout the year and received a salary from the royal treasury. . . .

At about the same time, Ivan's government attempted to provide lands near Moscow for one thousand military servitors. The idea behind the proposal was reasonable enough. Estates near the capital were at a premium since they allowed a servitor to live on his lands within easy ride of Moscow or alternately in the city, provisioned by his nearby peasants. Whether Ivan's officials were actually able to find enough land suitable for distribution under these conditions is a subject of intense de-

bate among historians. Whatever its concrete achievements, the government's motive was clear—to strengthen the upper echelons of the service nobility.

The "decree on service" in 1556 set norms for the nobles' military obligations. According to its provisions, the owner of any estate—whether held on hereditary or *pomest'e* (conditional on service) tenure—had to appear for muster himself and bring with him one fully equipped cavalryman for every one hundred *chetverti* (about four hundred acres) of good land which he owned. As with so many of Ivan's reforms, the measure gave concrete expression to a well-established assumption—that all members of the traditional warrior caste of Muscovy were obligated to fight for the sovereign when summoned.

In short, the military reforms addressed specific problems of the army. Judging by the army's performance in battle, the results were mixed. Kazan' and other eastern outposts fell to Ivan's troops, but after decades of alternating victories, setbacks, and stalemates, the Muscovite armies that invaded Livonia suffered bitter defeat. The social implications of the reforms were also ambivalent; they made clear the government's concern for the well-being of the noble cavalrymen who made up most of the army while simultaneously telling them bluntly that they had to serve at its convenience.

Third, in Ivan's early adult years, the central administration grew and assumed more distinct organizational forms. Since the fifteenth century, a small number of officials had served at the Muscovite court in essentially non-military functions; however, according to a number of historians, not until the 1550s did the proto-bureaucratic chanceries (*prikazy*) take shape. Certainly, a number of the most important chanceries in the bureaucratic system of the seventeenth century . . . were already in place in Ivan's lifetime. These administrative offices, consisting of a director and his staff of clerks, kept increasingly elaborate records of the government's most important activities and thus considerably increased its control over the country and its resources, above all the tsar's military servitors and the estates that supported them.

Last, and perhaps most significant of all, was the reform of the local administration of justice and tax collection. Banditry flourished in many parts of the country in sixteenth-century Muscovy, and the governors (*namestniki*) sent out from Moscow were unable or unwilling to put an end to it. The urgency of the problem must have been obvious, since the government took the first steps to deal with it in 1539 in the midst of the political struggles of Ivan's minority. Beginning in that year, the royal government issued charters to the population of particular districts, . . . instructing them to select elders . . . who were to be responsible for assembling posses and on their own authority arresting and hanging highwaymen and other notorious characters. Rather than reporting to the provincial governor, the district elders were to be accountable directly to the appropriate officials in Moscow.

These ruthlessly simple arrangements worked above all to the advantage of the royal administration in the capital. Its officials undoubtedly increased their ability to supervise the administration of justice in the provinces since the district elders were strictly accountable to them. The reform placed the elders in an ambivalent position. On the one hand, they gained sweeping powers to deal with troublemakers and were presumably happy to have the central administration's support in doing so. At the same time, as their oath of office made clear, their responsibilities were onerous. For their part, the great nobles of the court who served as provincial governors can hardly have regretted losing functions that brought them little but trouble.

Ivan's government clearly saw the advantages of the new system for, over the next decades, it introduced district elders to more and more areas of the country. The idea that the royal government would function more effectively if it made local elites responsible for their own fate produced an even more sweeping reform of the local administration within a few years. In the mid-1550s, a series of decrees created a new group of officials (the *zemskie starosty*), drawn primarily from the merchants and prosperous peasants, to serve as tax collectors. . . .

Once again, apparent decentralization served to increase the effectiveness of the central bureaucracy. Unlike the old governors, the local merchants or peasants who received the onerous job of collecting taxes from their fellow citizens had little to gain from cheating the royal exchequer under whose supervision they functioned. . . .

Parallel with the new system of local administration were new modes of establishing national priorities with the support of social elites. In Ivan's reign, as before, the tsar and his inner circle of boyars constituted the nerve center of the government. In the first years of his majority—beginning in 1549 according to one version—he and his advisers summoned assemblies of his leading subjects, known in later generations as the *zemskii sobor* or "assembly of the land," to gain their support for governmental policy. Over the course of the next century, the zemskii sobor met at irregular intervals, when summoned by the tsar. Its composition was equally unpredictable. Sometimes it consisted only of the boyars and the leaders of the church; on other occasions, the government reached out to include members of the lesser nobility who happened to be in Moscow and perhaps even merchants and artisans from the capital.

Even though at the height of its development this institution bore a rough resemblance to the parliaments or national estates of the monarchies of western Europe, it would be a mistake to view it as an embryonic representative institution. With rare exceptions in the early seventeenth century . . . the zemskii sobor served not as the authentic voice of Muscovy's leading citizens but as a means by which the government mobilized the support of its leading servitors. Even the most widely representative zemskii sobor of Ivan's reign, the assembly of 1566, did not meet to decide whether to continue the war with Poland; instead, it was called to lend its support to decisions that the tsar and his advisers had already made.

As a result of Ivan's reforms, the so-called middle classes of Muscovite society—the provincial nobles and merchants—undeniably played a more prominent role in public life than before. At the same time, it would be a mistake to see their participation in the zemskii sobor and the local administration as the germ of representative government. The modern word which is most applicable to these institutional arrangements of the mid-sixteenth century is "mobilization." Nobles and merchants were invited to support the government and work for it, not to help it make basic decisions about the future development of government and society. Participation had its price.

For these reasons, it is misleading to look to Ivan's reforms for signs of political modernization or convergence with emerging western European patterns of representative government or civil rights. The institutional scope, legal implications, and social impact of the reforms of the 1540s and 1550s were quite limited. Although a veritable golden age in comparison with the horrors to come, the reform period of the reign was a time of freedom only in the most relative sense. The creation of institutions of political mobilization went hand in hand with the increasingly rigid codification of ecclesiastical ideology and the repression of religious dissenters.

However we interpret the period of reforms, the oprichnina (1565–72) represents something dramatically different. Where it fits in a discussion of political reform is not easy to determine. The narrative sources describing the dramatic scenes Ivan IV staged in the first weeks of 1565 demonstrate that he intended to make radical changes in his mode of governing. Nevertheless, the word "reform" seems a singularly inappropriate characterization of the oprichnina for at least two reasons. The tsar's statements and gestures—and his subsequent actions—showed that he intended to make not gradual but sudden and dramatic changes in the body politic. Moreover, the

changes he made can scarcely be interpreted as steps to improve the administration of the realm or better the lot of downtrodden groups in society. . . .

From the beginning, Ivan made clear that, in order to escape from the clutches of the boyars and chancery officials and the leaders of the church whom he collectively accused of treason, he intended to create for himself a separate administration, court, and army. To support himself and the men who would serve in these new institutions, the tsar took direct personal control of substantial areas of the country, selected primarily for their promise as sources of tax revenues. In the oprichnina lands in central Muscovy, Ivan undertook a review of the nobility. Those who satisfied him of their loyalty joined his private army; those who failed the test had their lands confiscated and were forced to find new estates outside of the oprichnina's boundaries.

Oddly enough, Ivan arranged for the Boyar Council to administer the *zemshchina* (the areas of the country outside of his private principality) and report to him only the most important matters of state. Thus, Muscovy suddenly found itself with two administrations, two armies, and two separate groups of territories, one ruled directly by Ivan IV and the other by the aristocrats of his old court.

The oprichnina's most notorious feature was a reign of terror designed to purge those whom Ivan regarded as his enemies. On a number of occasions during the course of the seven-year experiment, groups of prominent courtiers and officials were executed on charges of treason, often with bloodcurdling brutality. Many times the victims were not only men of prominence but also their more obscure male kin and, on some occasions, their retainers and servants.

The roster of Ivan's victims included prominent aristocratic courtiers—both princes and non-titled servitors—leading chancery officials; Metropolitan Filipp, the head of the church; other prominent clergy; and Vladimir Andreevich of Staritsa, head of the only cadet branch of the ruling dynasty. Most startling of the victims was an entire city—Novgorod—which oprichnina troops occupied and sacked with great loss of life after Ivan accused its population of treasonous negotiations with the Poles. Finally, as students of more recent reigns of terror have come to expect, the oprichnina devoured its own leaders; Ivan's most prominent advisers and officials mounted the scaffold in their turn. . . .

If the oprichnina cannot be viewed as "reform," even by the most elastic use of that word, was it a "counterreform"? Use of the latter term is justified only if we regard the reforms of the 1550s as steps toward political modernization in a Western sense. Moreover, "counterreform" implies that the reforms were reversed or that the oprichnina was directed against the middle classes of Muscovite society who presumably benefited from the earlier changes. Most recent historians would accept the general proposition that, in the oprichnina, the tsar and his inner circle of advisers were aiming at the same goal they had pursued earlier—more effective control over the population and lands of the realm. In addition, the new institutions created in the reform period continued to do their work. The district elders functioned well into the seventeenth century, and the zemskii sobor went on meeting intermittently. Indeed, the liveliest assembly of the sixteenth century took place in 1566 in the midst of the oprichnina.

The social impact of Ivan's experiment was extremely ambiguous. Some lesser nobles suffered death or loss of their lands, while others thrived. The experience of the merchants was equally complex. At one extreme, Ivan favored the wealthy northern regions with their merchant and peasant population by including them in his private principality. On the other, he ravaged Novgorod, the wealthiest trading city of his realm, and executed many of its people.

These observations in no way undermine the common sense judgment that there was a world of difference between the reforms of the 1550s and the oprichnina. The differences lie, however, not so much in the objectives of royal policy or their social implications as in the im-

patience and brutality with which the oprichnina regime pursued them and in the devastating consequences of its actions.

The indiscriminate and often sadistic methods of the oprichnina regime appear to reflect more than anything else the complex and troubled personality of its leader, Ivan IV. A number of historians have suggested that Ivan suffered from paranoia in the oprichnina years. Some of his actions during the period, including his request for a guarantee of political asylum in England, dramatically testify to his exaggerated concern for his own safety. At times, burdened by his fears and chronic illness, he seems to have been obsessed with the need to escape from the dangers of leadership in one way or another.

To put it bluntly, the meaning of the oprichnina is to be sought above all in the realm of psychology. Ivan IV created the oprichnina to keep himself and his realm safe from enemies, real and imagined. Individual paranoia begot social pathology; the tsar's desperate search for security destroyed his subjects' confidence in the order and predictability of life. Years of absurd denunciations, sudden arrests, and horrifying executions left Muscovite society numb and made Ivan IV the terrible and awe-inspiring figure of literature and legend.

However real the substance of Ivan's fears, the social, economic, and political results of the oprichnina were a genuine disaster. Although it did not revolutionize social relations in Muscovy or destroy the princely aristocracy or any other social group, it killed off a wide variety of Russians, ranging from aristocrats to the poorest artisans, peasants, and domestics. One can easily imagine the demoralization and shock of those who survived the whirlwind. Moreover, the oprichnina's operations contributed to the economic decline and social dislocation of much of Muscovy, particularly the Novgorodian lands. The sack of the great trading city contributed significantly to its rapid decline into a run-of-the-mill provincial town. The depredations of Ivan's bodyguards, combined with natural disasters and rising taxes to feed the war in Livonia, forced thousands of peasants to flee from their ancestral homes to the remote forests, the open steppe, or the estates of the wealthiest landlords who could offer them minimal protection and support. Their action, in turn, forced the government to set legal limits on their movement in order to protect the interests of the poorer service nobles and the royal treasury. The enserfment of the peasantry was in sight.

As a program of political reform or enforced social change—if it was ever intended as such—the oprichnina was a dismal failure.

SOURCE: Robert O. Crummey, "Reform Under Ivan IV: Gradualism and Terror," in *Reform in Russia and the U.S.S.R.* Edited by Robert O. Crummey (Urbana: University of Illinois Press, 1989), pp. 13–22 (excerpted). Footnotes have been omitted. Reprinted by permission of the publisher.

10

The Economy of Muscovite Russia

Given the extended (and growing) frontiers of Muscovy, it would probably be more accurate to talk about the economies rather than the economy of Muscovy. The remote reaches of Siberia had its own economy, just as the north, abutting the Arctic Ocean, had its own. Even within the central Moscow lands, traces of difference remained, especially in principalities only recently joined to Moscow. But increasingly the various economies of Muscovy came together, sharing in the bounty and plague of the entire state. It is difficult to chart this process in detail, in part because so much economic activity continued to take place outside the watchful eyes of state officials.

Certainly, however, agriculture remained vital everywhere. Even in the forested north where fishing and other occupations took center stage, farming supplied basic grains. Agriculture in the central Moscow lands had not changed greatly since the Slavs first settled here. Of course, more forest had been cleared over the years, but the quality of the soil and farming technology worked together to keep productivity relatively low. With the acquisition of Kazan' and Astrakhan in mid-century, Moscow brought under its control whole new territories which included relatively unpopulated fertile alluvial valleys. These newly won lands became attractive to farmers in central Muscovy when tax-collectors and plague decimated households. As E. I. Kolycheva shows in the selection reproduced below, both these disasters came increasingly to the doors of Muscovite farmers in the sixteenth century, leading to severe depopulation, first along the borderlands, and then right into the heart of Muscovy. By century's end the situation had reached disastrous proportions, helping provoke a desperate famine and economic depression whose very name (Time of Troubles) continues to resonate through Russian history.

Of course, the economy of Muscovy cannot be told in terms of the sixteenth century alone, nor in terms of agriculture alone. Over the course of the sixteenth and seventeenth centuries international trade came to play an increasingly important part. But trade was highly centralized, operating mainly through a series of privileges granted to foreigners by the sovereigns, who in turn exercised near monopoly control. By the late seventeenth century, even this truism failed to hold: new enterprises arose, and a body of Muscovite entrepreneurs emerged, building fortunes which some of them used to adopt entirely new (and largely foreign) lifestyles.

But these developments seem not to have had a decisive impact upon the overall economy, whose basic indices changed little over the course of the century. Except for one immense inflationary period in the 1660s, generated by the government's attempt to debase the coinage, the seventeenth-century economy remained rather stable in contrast to the much more volatile sixteenth-century economy. Furthermore, if the seventeenth century witnessed the closing stages of the economic changes of the previous century, then the crises of the sixteenth century were decisive in reshaping the society of pre-Petrine Russia.

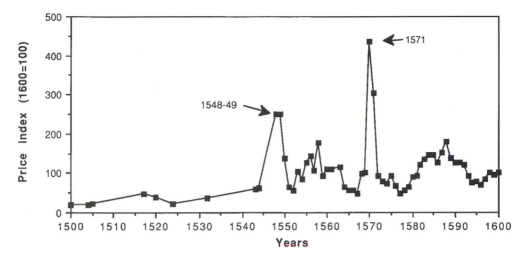

Price index for grains in sixteenth-century Muscovy. From A. G. Man'kov, *Tseny i ikh dvizhenie v Russkom gosudarstve XVI veka* (Moscow–Leningrad: AN SSSR, 1951), p. 33.

LITERATURE

E. I. KOLYCHEVA

The Economic Crisis in Sixteenth-Century Russia

In addition to the political whirlwind which appeared in the form of the *oprichnina*, Muscovites also suffered through a series of other disasters in the second half of the sixteenth century. As E. I. Kolycheva here shows, the first blows were isolated, afflicting distant parts of the growing Muscovite state. Gradually, however, the disasters—both epidemiological and climatic—settled upon much of Muscovy, including the center, leading to sharp population declines. The resulting impact upon the economy was traumatic: depopulated villages meant not only diminished acreage under cultivation (and a resulting fall in foodstuff production) but also a decreased tax base. Several times in the second half of the century (especially in the 1570s and 1580s) Muscovites had to endure immense spikes in the price of

bread (see above). Unfortunately, the government worsened the situation. Unable to tolerate falling tax revenue, the tsar resorted to raising taxes, leading in turn to further depopulation, as taxpayers who remained fit and productive fled to more distant territories in hopes of avoiding tax collectors. By late in the century the economy was in a shambles, obliging the government to find some means of guaranteeing the stability of both the labor supply upon which estate owners depended and the tax base upon which the government itself depended.

LOCAL CRISES ALONG THE BORDERS OF RUSSIA IN THE 1550s–1560s

Among the many signs of a crisis in the 1570s–80s, two stand out: the sharp decrease in population and the enormous quantity of deserted land, which, in turn, caused changes in the whole socio-economic life of the country, influencing all spheres of public life. The crises were the result of a number of unfavorable factors, both ecological (epidemics, bad harvests and so on) and socio-political (wars, ruinous state taxes, raids from nomads and so on), against a background of inadequate production. The economic crisis affected different regions and social types of landowning differently. And it had its peaks and valleys.

In the 1550s–60s some Russian districts (mostly on the outskirts of Russia) had an extremely unstable equilibrium because of the abandonment of plowland and the population decline following on bad harvests, epidemics, the raids of nomads, and the Livonian War. The Northwest suffered especially severely; in some districts there the population by the middle of the sixteenth century had declined 12–17% compared to 1500. There were also considerable areas of fallow land. However, the percentage of abandoned plowland did not greatly exceed the percent of population decline. The local chronicles and Novgorod's cadasters [landholding records compiled for tax purposes] provide abundant information on the frequently dramatic situations in the North and Northwest in the 1550s. "In the year 7058 [1549–50] [the lands] became vacant. Peasants died from starvation." The Solovetsk chronicler describes the tragedy in Novgorod and Staraia Rus' in 1552: "A deadly epidemic came to Novgorod the Great. In August it was especially severe from St. Semen's Day [September 1] to St. Nicholas Day [December 1]. Many churches were without any services for a long time. Altogether in Novgorod and Staraia Rus' 279,594 perished. It came to an end after November 20, 1552."

The epidemic also came to Pskov: in 1551/52 "there was a great outbreak of plague in the city of Pskov and in the surrounding districts from Thursday October 7, and in seven days they buried 4,800 people; later over the course of one month and 3 days, until November 9, they buried another 2,700 people in a new burial plot. . . . Many common people died at that time, and in the city one heard an

inconsolable wailing. . . . And over the course of a year they buried 25,000, and no one knows how many lay [unburied] in pits."

Conditions in the North were also not propitious: "Bread was expensive along the Dvina River . . . and many people died from hunger, and they placed as many as 200 or 300 of the dead in one pit.". . . In 1557/58 and 1558/59 the famine raged in Ustiug: "for two yars there was famine in Ustiug, and people ate fir-tree [needles?], grass, and carrion. And many people died."

Things were also tense in the southern districts, which had suffered from the uninterrupted raids of steppe nomads. So in 1553 43% of the Riazan' properties of the Bogoslovskii monastery "were deserted because of Tatar raids.". . . The eastern districts which bordered on the Kazan khanate were just as vulnerable. Besides that, in 1550/51 epidemics began here too: "the military governors have written from Sviazhsk [to say] that a wasting disease accompanied by marks [buboes?] has come to people, and they die." Consequently, the epidemic of 1551/52 was not a local affair, and did not strike just the Northwest, but affected even the eastern borderlands of Russia, and perhaps also several central districts. . . .

The unfavorable economic situation, to which harvest failures and epidemics contributed, continued in the second half of the 1550s and into the 1560s in the North, Northwest, and West. In 1556 in Kholmogory "there was no grain, and in the fall one could buy in the Dvina land a chetvert' of grain for 22 altyns." In the following year the famine afflicted "all Muscovite towns and the whole land," because strong rains and early frosts destroyed the grain.

In these very years (1556–58) there was a tremendous explosion of bread prices in Kholmogory, Vologda, and Volokolamsk. . . . The situation became more complicated with the outbreak of the Livonian War. The subsequent years, in which local outbreaks of epidemics alternated with bad harvests against the background of war, further deepened the economic "depression" along the borderlands. In

1560 in Pskov "grain did not germinate." Within two years "it was rainy for the haying season and during harvest. . . . And rye germinated poorly . . . the spring wheat was good, but because of the rain there was not enough rye and spring wheat." At the end of 1563 again there was "rain until Christmas (until 25 December), but there was no snow. From 9 December till 9 January people could not travel on the roads, and in the city everything was expensive, and bread was expensive: 11 altyns for rye." Further the Pskov chronicler reports that there had been no such weather for 90 years. In 1565 "in Pskov and in its surrounding districts worms ate the cabbage," and the same thing happened to turnips. The chronicle asserts that nothing similar had happened within memory. The year 1565/66 was also a famine year for Novgorod. . . .

In the 1560s in the Northwest, just as earlier, the centers of epidemic continued to be active. In 1566 "an epidemic appeared in Shelonskaia District of Novgorod the Great" and in adjacent areas. Sixteen years later officials conducting an inventory named as the cause of the destruction, as a kind of turning point, the events of 1565/66: "These villages became deserted even before the Lithuanian war because of a terrible epidemic and from a harvest failure in the year 7074 [1565–66]." Consequently, the coincidence of epidemics and harvest failures led to a sharp demographic decline. . . .

So, over the period of the 1550s–60s along the borderlands of the country, crisis situations developed under the influence of climatic and geographic factors (failed harvests, epidemics) or because of socio-political causes (war, devastating raids from neighboring peoples, growth of taxes), leading to a drop in population and the abandonment of plowland. But these crises bore a distinctly local character, and did not exert any substantial influence on the economy of the state as a whole. . . .

This same period (1550s–60s) was rather favorable for the development of the economy in the greater Moscow region, the center of the Russian state. Judging by the surviving cadasters, in spite of the occasional household and isolated waste land, there is no evidence of a significant abandonment in rural localities. The same may be said of the towns. Even Serpukhov, where the Russian armies regularly gathered before a counterattack against the Tatars, gave the impression in 1552 of being a thriving town. It had 623 households in which 800 families lived, and only 21 households (little more than 3%) seemed deserted. True, there were 122 empty courtyards, but there were no houses on them, which attests to the fact that the "abandonment" had happened long ago. A significant part of the "abandonment" took place in the settlements formerly located around the town which, by the middle of the sixteenth century, had lost their significance, having been seriously depopulated and having been attached to the tax base of the commercial district within the town. Furthermore, the complete absence of abandoned shops and warehouses also testifies to the flourishing condition of the town.

So one can say with confidence that in spite of the Livonian War, which began in 1558, until the early 1560s there was no sign of a decline in the central regions of the country. Indeed, quite the contrary, this decade was a time of rapid growth of the population and an increase in the land under cultivation. . . .

In the beginning of the 1560s the position in the West worsened in connection with repeated harvest failures which stimulated a steady stream of people to head for the southern regions. In 1560/61 "there was a bad famine in Mozhaisk and also in Volok and in many other towns. Many people departed from Mozhaisk and Volok for Riazan', Meschera, and to the towns of the lower Volga, like Nizhnii Novgorod." . . .

In the 1560s signs of abandonment also began to be noticed in Kostroma district, in the northeast part of the Moscow region. The preceding harvest failures which had afflicted the north of the country could now touch even Kostroma. In 1561/62 . . . fallow land in the possessions of the Simonov monastery constituted no less than 40%. . . .

The introduction of the oprichnina with its "repartitioning" of lands and the military failures in the Livonian war further shook the economy of the country. In addition to causes already mentioned, famine years also played a negative role. According to the Solovetsk chronicler in 1567/68 "there was a great famine in Rus'. They bought a chetvert' of rye in Moscow for 1.5 rubles." An alarming symptom was the tendency to abandon lands even in the central districts of the country. In May, 1569 in the Tver' district estates of the Staritsa Uspenskii monastery a third of the villages were abandoned, and in Kashin and Staritskii districts up to half of the villages were deserted. . . .

So, by the beginning of the 1570s as a result of the combination of unfavorable socio-political and climatic-geographic factors, the economy of Russia was seriously weakened. The borderlands of the state were enduring repeated crisis situations: a large quantity of plowland had been left to go wild, population had dropped, and normal production in agriculture was disrupted. At the end of the 1560s even in the central districts signs of abandonment had appeared. The country stood on the eve of a general crisis. If any sufficiently large calamity were to break out while Russia fought a war on a large part of its territory, it would damage decisively the state economy, and would be difficult to reverse. Such a blow came at the very beginning of the 1570s.

THE CRISIS OF THE 1570s–1590s

The beginning of the 1570s was a time of the strongest shocks for the country. An "evil epidemic" roared through the whole territory of the "Russian Land" like a devastating tornado, accompanied in several regions by harvest failure and famine. This was one of the most terrible epidemics of the Middle Ages, of the sort which arise only once in a century and which leave in their wake almost totally depopulated towns and villages, provoking a "depression" in the economy. In both historical and medical literature, these events are reflected only dimly: the area affected by the

"plague," its chronological limits, or scale of its consequences are not known. Also unclear is the epidemiology of the epidemic. Most likely it was plague.

The chronicles of that time unanimously mark the appearance of this vast disaster. "In that same year [7079 = 1570–71] and in the next year, there was plague in Moscow and in all the Russian towns; and in the preceding year there was plague and famine," says the Piskarev chronicler. Other chronicles, including local ones, second his report. "In that same year of 7078 there was a severe plague throughout all the Russian land, and the sovereign then lived in his own settlement, in Aleksandrov settlement [outside Moscow]." "In Moscow and in all the Russian land the famine was severe." In the Volokolamsk chronicle we read under the year 7078: "That same winter there was a dearth in Moscow, and in Tver', and in Volotsk . . .," and under the following year it is noted, "The plague was very hard." The scales of disaster which afflicted the country were so great that they could not but affect contemporaries and foreigners. Heinrich Staden devoted a colorful description to the events of the early 1570s: "There was then a great famine: for a crust of bread a man would kill another. . . . The all-powerful God also sent to this land a great plague. And to whatever house the plague came, whether to a mighty house or to a simple household, they immediately boarded it up; and whoever died in it there they also buried him. . . . The plague grew stronger, and then in the fields around Moscow great pits were dug, and corpses were thrown there without markers— 200, 300, 400, or 500 in one heap." Further, "many settlements and monasteries were completely emptied from this plague.". . .

Toward the middle of the sixteenth century there was already considerable experience in dealing with epidemics. Households where the ill lay were boarded up, and not even priests were admitted under the threat of being set afire. Streets, roads, and centers of the infection were closed off "with fences and regular guards." The dead they buried not in a cem-

etery, but outside the city in specially designated places. All the same, the epidemic
spread to new regions. Even after several years,
long-time residents named the plague as the
main cause of the depopulation of villages,
hamlets, and cities. . . . There is no doubt but
that all the central and northern districts suffered from epidemics. In several of them
which lay to the north and northwest of Moscow famine accompanied the plague. . . . It is
possible that the famine accompanied the
plague in all the central, northern, and northwest districts: in 1568–72 the prices of bread,
rye, oats, and barley all rose. But because of
the disproportionate number of victims afflicted by epidemic, in the minds of contemporaries hunger took second place to the "evil
plague."

Together with natural-geographic disasters
there were also unfavorable socio-political
phenomena: in May of 1571 a devastating raid
of Tatars against Moscow took place. Seeking
refuge from the enemy, a "multitude" of people from nearby areas fled to the capital. Most
of them ("they were without number") perished in the fires in Moscow started by the Tatars. Staden colorfully describes this disaster,
pointing out that an enormous number of people suffered from the smoke, and could not
find salvation even in the river. The fire of
1571 was so devastating that almost 30 years
later people still recalled it. The official code
of Tsar Fedor Ivanovich of 1597 identifies the
fire of 1571 as the main cause for the absence
of documents on slaves ("all the old documents perished in the Moscow fire of 1571 and
in other fires"). The Tatars inflicted a significant loss also on other towns and localities:
Tula, Serpukhov, Kashira, Riazan and parts of
Ruzsk district. Villages and hamlets belonging
to the Serpukhov Vysotskii monastery "were
burned and conquered." Only 18% of the
households remained inhabited in 1571/72;
70% (more than 303 households) had burned
down, and 12% stood empty. Their owners
were killed or taken into captivity. Plowland
occupied only 11% of all arable, and more
than 3412 chetverti were grown over. Among

the properties of the Riazan Bogoslovskii monastery, 32% of the houses were still populated,
and 43% of the plowland had gone wild "because of the coming of the Crimean tsar in
1571". . . .

The consequences of unfavorable factors affected the towns, with their dense populations,
most of all. Some of them for a time altogether
disappeared from the ranks of trade-crafts centers. By 1573 in Murom 83% of all households
in the commercial district were abandoned because of the plague, and the majority of shops
did not function. Kashira stood empty: the
commercial district was burned, and trading
enterprises (104 shops and 315 households)
were burned, as was the fortress. In Kolomna
in 1578 there were only 12 tax-paying households. The inventory-takers, having come to
Kolomna, discovered in the commercial districts clear signs of decay and desolation. In
the households of prince Vladimir Andreevich
and Ivan Bel'skii "all the mansions are de-
crepit," "the mansions and fences have rotted
and collapsed." Things were not much better
at the sovereign's own court, where the "gates
fell apart, the plank fence has collapsed." Several monastery cells were vacant, the monastery gates and walls "rotted," "collapsed". . . .

The number of inhabitants and the amount
of cultivated land also decreased in rural localities. In Vasil'tsevo canton, which adjoined
the Moscow commercial district, no more than
20% of all arable on hereditary estates was being plowed, and even less—12%—on service
estates. The same sad picture held for monastic and episcopal properties: 15% and 11% respectively.

It is significant that a very small amount of
fallow had gone wild, "was grown over by forest," and most of that only on empty waste
land, and very little on monastic properties.
Consequently, the destruction of the Moscow
area had occurred recently. . . .

Toward 1573/74 the epidemic abated, famine receded into memory, and the oprichnina
was officially abolished, but the abandonment
not only did not cease, but continued to gain
in tempo. In the possessions of the Riazan Bo-

goslovskii monastery in 1572/73 empty households represented 32% of the whole, fallow land 43%. In 1574/75 80% of the households were deserted, and 88% of the land was fallow. In the estate of I. Iu. Griaznyi in Bezhetskii Verkh in 1573/74 more than 70% of the land was fallow.... According to the survey of 1576/77 plowland had decreased by 300%... and represented only 9.6% of the entire arable. A still more precipitous decline is noticeable in service estates in the Moscow district, where in 1573/74, taking into account escheated estates, plowland represented 7%, and in 1576/78 only 1.8% of arable. The average percent of abandonment in service estates reached 98.2%. Therefore there is reason to think that in the 1570s in the Moscow district the service estate economy as a system ceased to exist....

So, in the 1570s there were two large centers of crisis: the Northwest and the Center of the Moscow region. Several districts adjacent to the southern frontier of the Moscow region were also rather seriously affected. And if the destruction of the Pskov-Novgorod region lasted for a rather long "preparatory" period (harvest failures, epidemics of the 1550s–1560s), then the desolation of the Moscow district reached a critical point in a relatively brief period of time. The rates of decrease in plowland outstripped (sometimes by a lot) the number of deserted settlements and households.... [T]he decline in population was accompanied by the disappearance of the majority of small settlements.

Why after the end of the epidemics did the abandonment not only not abate, but continue to increase? Epidemics changed the sex and age structure of the population, created a large number of incomplete and childless families, and destroyed the kinship and neighbor bonds in the village, and in that way led to the deformation of the commune. An incomplete family, partially or wholly deprived of male adult hands and help from neighbors, was not in a position to plow a plot the same size as it had formerly tilled. Those who were younger and stronger, unburdened by children, departed for other areas, beyond the borders of the district. The disruption (as a result, mainly, of the epidemic) of normal productive population led to the fact that the economic crisis proved irreversible for some time. To demographic factors were added (and to some degree preceded them) unfavorable socio-political conditions. Military failures in the Livonian War, a sharp decrease in the able-bodied population and in agricultural production obliged the government regularly to increase the tax burden. Furthermore, in the 1560s scribes included in the tax unit not only inhabited but even deserted plowland. It is clear how destructive this policy became in the first stages of abandonment. The higher the proportion of fallow in a tax unit (namely in those settlements where the abandonment of plowland had occurred), the crueler the yoke of taxes became for the remaining population; it hastened their destruction, ruined their ability to produce. And although the government no later than 1573 changed the principles of taxation, separating deserted units from inhabited ones, the inventory always lagged behind the rapidly developing process of abandonment. Petitions of those years are filled with complaints about how "peasants incur losses and big fines," "and landlords take taxes from inhabited households to cover empty ones."...

In 1583 the Livonian War ended, but the economic crisis not only did not end, but deepened, encompassing new regions and new social layers of the peasantry (including peasants who, because of their landlords' immunities, had earlier escaped the worst consequences).

In the 1580s there were four centers of crisis: the Northwest, the Center, the Middle Volga, and Vologda district. The cadaster compiled by Timofei Khlopov in 1584/85 and depicting part of the Moscow cantons, survives.... Out of 109,000 chetverti inventoried by Khlopov, service lands accounted for about 35.8%; 22% was in the hands of secular landlords, and 42.2% was owned by monasteries, the Metropolitan, and the Suzdal bishop. And almost all this land was fallow. Plowland occupied no more than 13.4% of all arable. True, this is higher than in the Novgorod region, where inhabited plots in the 1580s accounted for only 5.6%. But all the same, 13.4% of all the arable is expressive testimony to the destruction, the decline of agriculture around the capital. . . .

The southern districts of the country in the 1570s, judging by the cadasters of Kolomenskoe and Kashira, still had very high levels of abandonment. Tula district was inventoried in the same years as Moscow, and the level of abandonment in Tula hardly differed from that in Moscow. . . .

So, in the 1580s the crisis in one or another degree encompassed the whole territory of the country. Indeed, in some regions of the North, West and East, the trend toward abandonment was growing in comparison with the 1570s. The level of fallow lands was very high. During the period 1582–92 bread grew very dear, one of the causes of which was, perhaps, the decline in the amount of land under cultivation.

It is usual to count the 1590s as a turning point, when the country began to emerge from a crisis . . . [but] the restoration of the economy in the Moscow district proceeded slowly. In the 1590s this region, as before, remained devastated. Those districts adjoining Moscow from the north and northwest were little better-off. In Dmitrov, Pereiaslavl'-Zalesskii, Suzdal', Starodub-Riapolovskii, Vladimir, and Murom fallow land accounted for almost 60% of arable, and sometimes more. In this circumstance in several regions a "declining" dynamic of development (in comparison with the 1570s) took hold. . . .

The northern and northeastern borderlands of the Moscow region distributed along the Volga, were in a more favorable position, fallow land accounting for about a quarter of all arable. But it took more than a decade to overcome the consequences of the crisis and to reach the level which agriculture had achieved in the 1560s. . . .

The abandonment which characterized the central districts and the outflow of population from there led to a rapid colonization of the Volga River basin and the southern borderlands of the country. . . . In the Kama River ba-

sin too new lands rapidly came under cultivation along the banks of the Kama, Belaia, Viatka, Chusova rivers. In Slobodskii district along the Viatka River fallow land was practically non-existent. . . .

From everything mentioned it is clear that toward the end of the sixteenth century the country had not emerged from the crisis. Some improvement was expressed in the incorporation of a relatively small part of fallow land into the system of crop rotation. As before great masses of arable remained out of production or was worked temporarily, "as a brief incursion," without observance of the basic rules of fallow-field agriculture. The overwhelming part of abandoned lands succumbed to forest, which in turn made more difficult the process of cultivating fallow fields. A deep disruption in the conditions of production was present. Population in the central regions did not reach the pre-crisis level. Trade in all cities withered, so that Russia began the seventeenth century—which itself began with a harvest failure—with a much-weakened economy.

The crisis of the 1570s–90s revealed the weakness, the instability of socio-economic structures and relations. Ecological cataclysms (famine, epidemics) during the Livonian war led to a sharp increase in exploitation of the peasants, an increase not only in natural rents, but also in money rent. The growth of state taxes strengthened the market part of the agricultural production without basic changes in its technical base. The peasantry, in conditions of land-based taxation and growing exploitation, was obliged to violate rules for the most effective use of land. As a result, the economic crisis revealed the insolvency and the viciousness of the principles of land-based taxation which acted like a brake on the path of restoring agriculture.

SOURCE: E. I. Kolycheva, *Agrarnyi stroi Rossii XVI veka* (Moscow: Nauka, 1987), pp. 172–83, 187–9, 195, 198–201 (excerpted). Translated by Julia Vaingurt and Daniel H. Kaiser. Reprinted by permission of E. I. Kolycheva.

11

Muscovite Society

Anyone obliged to read the detailed provisions of the 1649 *Ulozhenie* (Law Code) which protected individual honor would be struck at the pronounced layering of Muscovite society. Everyone occupied a rank expressable in terms of cash remuneration. Leading families commissioned the compilation of genealogies to prove their ancient rank, and government bureaux oversaw a complex system which defined one's place in society (*mestnichestvo*): no one need serve in an inferior position to someone who ranked lower than him on the official scale. In addition, as the records abundantly demonstrate, Muscovite servitors engaged in frequent litigation over real and imagined insults to their honor, each one redeemable by payment of a specified sum. Humbler citizens, too, occupied a definite place in the social order, and especially after 1649 these ranks were permanent. How this came to be is a long story, and cannot be told in full here. But some stages in the process stand out especially clearly.

It sometimes comes as a surprise to students of Russian history that in addition to serfdom, Russia also had slavery. Even more surprising, perhaps, is that this slavery was not the result of conquest or the purchase of foreigners, but rather represented in the main self-sale. What drove people to sell themselves into slavery? No doubt countless motives urged these men and women to auction off their liberty. But for many, the answer can be found in the dearth which Kolycheva documents above. Faced with rising obligations and diminishing income, the able came to view slavery as a potential escape from their dilemma, seeking in a slavemaster regular shelter and food. So it was that slavery, known since at least the time of the Pravda Russkaia, should endure in Russia formally into the reign of Peter the Great. But the last great burst of enslavement came early in the seventeenth century, when Muscovy lived through the national trauma described as the Time of Troubles.

Serfdom proved more important to Russia's subsequent history. Finally solidified in the seventeenth-century Law Code, enserfment had had its origins two hundred years earlier. The first stages had been relatively harmless, delaying peasant movement till the end of harvest, but not preventing it altogether. By late in the sixteenth century, however, the situation was considerably different. The reasons for restricting peasant movement had not changed, but the position of farming peasants was desperate, as Kolycheva noted above. Reacting to massive rural depopulation, the government interceded once again to preserve dwindling labor supplies for landlords, this time imposing temporary prohibitions against peasant movement. As often happens, what was once "temporary" in fact continued long beyond anyone's imagination, culminating in the general provision of the 1649 Law Code permanently enserfing all peasants to the lords with whom they were listed in tax registers.

At the apex of Muscovite society were the boyars. Neither a pure aristocracy nor simply a service elite, the boyars of Muscovy had to defend their status on both counts, distinguishing them from their Western European and even Ottoman counterparts. The ambiguity of their position helped inspire multiple strategies by which to sustain their position. According to Robert Crummey, the boyars built patronage networks as a form of protection, but perhaps just as important was the erection of ties through marriage. In this strategy women played an especially marked role, securing clan alliances against the whims of the sovereign or the machinations of their enemies. Nancy Kollmann reminds us that in this political function we may find the explanation behind the practice among the Muscovite elite of secluding their women. Important players in the politics of alliance, women—especially unmarried ones—functioned not only as the pledge of politics, but also as behindstage operators.

Much else might be said about Muscovite society. Perhaps most obvious, given the gigantic territorial additions which took place in the period, is the multi-ethnic composition of the Muscovite population. The absorption of peoples who were neither Slav nor Christian (not to say Orthodox) was, of course, nothing new for states which governed populations on this territory. But the magnitude of the problem continued to grow as the Muscovite state extended its borders. Still in this era the law (both secular and canonical) discriminated against those who were not Orthodox, obliging formal conversion among all those who wished to advance along the social and political hierarchy of Muscovite Rus'.

DOCUMENTS

Documents Recording Self-Sale into Slavery (1595–1603)

The disasters which Kolycheva chronicled above helped pave the way for a particularly grim period in Muscovite history, "The Time of Troubles," variously dated between the years 1584 and 1619. This era of dearth (including an especially severe famine between 1601–1603) dramatically worsened the position of Muscovy's lowest social orders. One indication of this deepening crisis was the increasing frequency with which free men (and women) sold themselves into slavery. Ostensibly, the favored form of slavery—limited service contract slavery—was only temporary: an individual borrowed a sum of money and promised to repay it within one year. In the meantime, the borrower served as slave to the creditor in exchange for the interest. Upon repaying the principal, the borrower would regain his or her free status. In fact, however, these contracts seem to have led instead to permanent slavery. For the contract also stipulated that if the borrower could not repay the principal at the specified date, the creditor

had the right to convert the borrower into a hereditary slave. The seasonal distribution of slavery contracts (see p. 174), the great bulk of which originated in the last years of the sixteenth and first years of the seventeenth century, indicates that individuals may have entered slavery precisely with a view to becoming permanently enslaved, seeing in slavery a form of social welfare by which the impoverished gained food, shelter, and protection in a time of great scarcity. As the century wore on, especially once the new dynasty was enthroned and war concluded, the Muscovite economy stabilized. Price indices for the seventeenth century show (see p. 175) that only twice (both after mid-century) did disaster strike again: once in the early 1660s when the government debased the coinage, leading to runaway inflation, and again in the early 1670s when rebellion affected trade and agricultural production. Some of the stimulus for self-sale accordingly disappeared. The government, for its part, set about to restrict access to slavery, culminating in its formal abolition early in the eighteenth century.

———————————

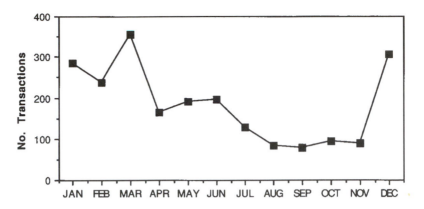

Seasonal distribution of slavery transactions in Muscovy. Adapted from Richard Hellie, *Slavery in Russia 1450–1725* (Chicago: University of Chicago Press, 1982), p. 334. Used with the permission of The University of Chicago Press.

On October 9th [1595] the scribes doing business on the public square of the St. Sofiia side [of Novgorod], Kirilko the son of Ivan Tryznov and Ondrei Dmitriev and Grisha the son of Vasilei Ushakov, brought to State Secretary Dmitrei Aliab'ev for registration a limited service slavery contract on Grisha the son of Eremeev, nicknamed Tormoshko, and they brought that Grisha to the state secretary for the registration with themselves, and they said: "Having come, Sir, to us on the public square, that Grisha ordered us to write on himself a limited service slavery contract in the sum of 10 Moscow rubles, and he is going to serve in the household of Pervoi, the son of Ivan Onichkov; and we, sir, at this, Grisha's, order wrote a contract on him, Grisha, called Tormoshko," and they placed before the state secretary that limited service slavery contract, and in the contract is written: "Be it known that I Grigorei the son of Eremei, called Tormoshko, have borrowed from Pervoi the son of Ivan Onichkov the sum of 10 Moscow rubles from the day of the holy Apostle Iakov Alfeev [October 9] for the period of a year to the same day, and for the interest I, Grigorei, shall serve my lord Pervoi every day in the household; and when the monies come due on the specified date, I, Grigorei, on the same basis shall serve him

every day in his household for the interest. Present as witnesses were Kirilo son of Ivan Tryznov and Ondrei Dmitriev, and the contract was written by Grisha the son of Vasilei Ushakov, on October 9, 1595." And State Secretary Dmitrei Aliab'ev, having heard that limited service slavery contract, asked Grisha: "Did you order the contract scribe of the public square scribes and that witness to write the limited service slavery contract on yourself for the sum of 10 Moscow rubles, and did you take the sum of 10 Moscow rubles from Pervoi son of Ivan Onichkov, and are you going to serve in his household for the interest, and heretofore have you served anyone else?" And Grisha Eremeev, called Tormoshko, said: "That is, sir, the limited service slavery contract that I ordered the contract scribe of the public square clerks and the witness to write on myself in the sum of 10 Moscow rubles and I have borrowed the money, 10 Moscow rubles, from Pervoi Nichkov, and for the interest I am going to serve him in the household, and heretofore I served voluntarily the middle service class cavalry archer Grigorei Gordeev of Derevskaia Piatina [one of the provincial districts of Novgorod], and Grigorei, sir, died in Moscow about five years ago. After Grigorei's death his wife Ogaf'ia and his son Roman manumitted

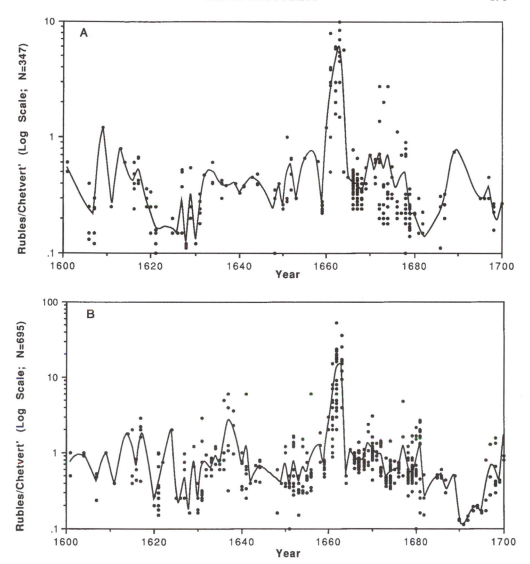

Price indexes for (A) oats and (B) rye in seventeenth-century Muscovy. Graphs prepared from unpublished material supplied by Richard Hellie, and printed with his permission.

me and, sir, gave me a manumission document.'' The slave's stature is average, he is about 50 years old, his hair is going gray, he has a long nose, a sharp face, and a long beard. The state secretary Dmitrei Aliab'ev ordered that limited service slavery contract, having been copied into the permanent record books, returned to Pervoi Onichkov and he ordered the contract clerk of the public square scribes and the witness to affix their signatures to the record books, and he ordered the fees for that limited service slavery [contract] collected from Pervoi Onichkov by the sovereign Tsar's decree at the rate of one altyn per ruble. The fee of 10 altyns for the 10 rubles from that limited service slavery contract was collected from Pervoi Onichkov, and the contract was returned to Pervoi Onichkov. The contract clerk Grisha signed this copy. The witness Ondrusha signed this note. The witness Kirilko son of Ivan Tryznov signed this contract note.

Be it known that I, Ignatii son of Martem'ian, my wife, Matrena the daughter of Ignatei, and my children, a daughter Orinka and a son Aleksei, have borrowed from Afanasei son of Andrei Eremeev the sum of two Moscow rubles from the day of the Holy Apostle Jacob the brother of the Lord in the flesh and until the same date a year hence, and for the interest we shall serve every day in the household; and when the date for the repayment of the principal lapses, we shall serve our lord on the same bases in the household. The Nikola secretary of Peredol'skii district Lazor Semenov witnessed this. The *zemskoi* clerk Zhdanko Gavrilov wrote the contract, April 30, 1603. The contract was entered in the books, and the fees collected.

—The witness Lazarko affixed his hand.

—In the interrogation the borrower Ignat said: "I was born, sir, in the household of Afanasei Eremeev." In stature he is an average man, his complexion is ruddy, hair blond (literally—white), eyes grey, about 30 years old; his wife Matrenka is of average stature, swarthy complexion, grey eyes, about 30 years old; the daughter Orinka is seven years old, has brown hair, grey eyes; the son Oleshka is three years old, has blond hair, and grey eyes.

SOURCE: *Readings for Introduction to Russian Civilization*. Edited by Richard Hellie (Chicago: University of Chicago, 1977), pp. 16–17, 20. Reprinted by permission of Richard Hellie.

Grigorii Kotoshikhin on Boyar Weddings (ca. 1666)

If, as Nancy Kollmann maintained above, boyars used marriages as a means to shore up their social standing, we can easily understand why they might attend carefully to the selection of spouses for themselves and their children. Much was at stake. However, as the following account makes clear, weddings in Muscovy also reflected more general cultural values which transcended boyar politics. In the selection which follows, we learn the outlines of wedding ritual which in general obtained for tsar and commoner alike. Muscovite marriage ritual emphasized the reproductive role of women, the participation of large kin groups in marriage, and the transfer of property via marriage. Grigorii Kotoshikhin (b. ca. 1630), author of this account, had served for a time as a clerk in the Muscovite Foreign Affairs Chancellery. He had, however, compromised himself in the 1660s by selling confidential information to the Swedes. Fearing for his safety, Kotoshikhin fled Muscovy in 1664, taking refuge first in Poland and the following year in Stockholm. The Swedes, who had gone to war with the Muscovites earlier in the century, were deeply interested in what Kotoshikhin knew, and with some encouragement, Kotoshikhin set to paper his observations on Muscovy. The resulting book was quite successful, but the author did not prosper. In 1667 Kotoshikhin was condemned to death for having murdered his landlord in a drunken brawl.

———

3. And if a boyar or closest man decides to marry himself or his son or brother or nephew, or to give his daughter or sister or niece in marriage, after having determined among one another who has a [marriageable] bride, he sends his friends, male or female, to the father or mother or brother of that bride to say that they have been sent with orders to speak and

inquire if he wishes to give his daughter, or someone else, in marriage to that man himself or to another person [in the family], and what dowry that girl would bring in clothing and money and *votchiny* [landed estates] and household servitors. And if he wishes to give his daughter, or someone else, in marriage, he says in answer to those words that he would be glad to give the girl in marriage but must discuss it with his wife and relatives, and after discussing it will give them a reply as soon as possible; but if he does not want to give her in marriage, knowing that [the suitor] is a drunkard or crazy, or knowing that he has some other bad quality, then he will refuse those men, [saying] that he cannot give her in marriage to such a person, or will refuse on some pretext.

And if he decides to give her in marriage to him, and his wife and relatives give their consent, he prepares an itemized list of the dowry that he will give to the girl—money and silver and other vessels and clothing and *votchiny* and household servitors—and sends it to those people who had come to him from the bridegroom, and those people turn it over to the bridegroom; but the daughter or whoever the girl may be is not told and does not know until she is married. And if that bridegroom is satisfied with that bride as far as her dowry is concerned, he sends the same people to the bride's father and mother to ask that the bride be shown to him; and when those people who have been sent arrive and begin to speak about this, the father or mother of the bride says that they would be glad to show their daughter, only not to the bridegroom himself but to his father or mother or sister or some female relatives whom the bridegroom himself trusts. And the suitor accordingly sends his mother or sister to look at [the bride] on the appointed day. And the father and mother of the bride prepare for that day and array the bride in good clothes and call relatives to come as guests and seat the bride at the table; and when the observer arrives she is greeted with honor and seated at the table beside the bride; and while sitting at the table during dinner that person who has been sent to look dis-

cusses various matters with the bride so as to ascertain her intelligence and her manner of speech, and scrutinizes her face and eyes and features so as to tell the bridegroom upon return what she is like. . . . And if that observer does not favor the bride, she tells the bridegroom that he should give up the match, for she has found her to be stupid or ugly or weak-eyed or lame, or unable to speak properly; and that bridegroom abandons that bride and gives up any match with her; but if the observer favors the bride and tells the bridegroom that she is good and clever and not deficient in speech or anything else, then that bridegroom sends the original [emissaries] back to the bride's father and mother [to say] that he has taken a liking to the bride and wishes to conclude an agreement and draw up a contract with them that he will marry her on an appointed day and that they will likewise give her to him in marriage on the same day. And the father and mother of that bride request the bridegroom, through those people whom he has sent, to come to them for the agreement, with a few people whom he trusts in such matters, either before or after dinner on a specified day; and they indicate the day on which he is to come, and prepare for that day. And when that day arrives the bridegroom arrays himself and sets out, with his father or with relatives or with close friends, to see the bride's father and mother; and upon their arrival they are met and greeted with due honor by the bride's father and relatives, and all enter the house and sit down as ceremony requires; and after being seated a while the father or another relative says on behalf of the bridegroom that they have come to do what is good, as requested; and the master of the house answers that he is glad that they have come and wishes to conclude an agreement with them. And both sides begin to discuss the various aspects of the wedding and set a date for the wedding which will allow everyone enough time for the preparations—a week or a month or half a year or a year or more; and they all begin to sign their names and the names of witnesses, and the bride's name, to the contract, and write down that [the bridegroom] must, according to the agreement, take that bride on the duly appointed day, without alteration, and that [the bride's father] must give her to him in marriage on the same day, without alteration; and a pledge is inserted in the contract between them: that if [the bridegroom] does not take the girl on the appointed day, or if [the father] does not give the girl in marriage on that day, the offending party must pay 1000 or 5000 or 10,000 rubles in money, whatever is written in the contract. And having paid the visit and after eating and drinking they return home, and the bride is not shown to him and the bride does not see him, the bridegroom; but her mother or married sister or some married female relatives come out at the time to present the bridegroom with a handkerchief from the bride.

4. And if, following this agreement, the bridegroom learns of the bride . . . that she is not chaste in her maidenhood or is deaf or dumb or crippled, and learns or is told something bad about her, and that man refuses to take that bride to himself, then the bride's father or mother petitions the patriarch about this, that he did not take that bride on the due date according to the agreement and the pledge, and does not wish to, and has thus dishonored her. Or else, if the bride's father and mother, upon learning that the bridegroom is a drunkard or a gambler or disfigured, or upon learning something else that is bad, fail to give her in marriage to him and refuse to do so, then the bridegroom likewise petitions the patriarch about this. And the patriarch orders the matter to be investigated, and on the basis of the investigation and the pledges in the contract the offending party is made to pay the amount of the pledge written into the contract, which is given to the injured bridegroom or bride; and after that he is free to marry as he wishes, and the bride is free to be given in marriage as she wishes.

5. And if both parties carry out their contracts and prepare for the wedding on the appointed day, the bridegroom invites to his wedding relatives and friends from outside the family to be members of the wedding party and seated boyars and boyar women . . . ; and likewise on the day of the wedding banquets are prepared in the homes of the bridegroom and the bride, and when word is sent that the time has come for the bridegroom to go to the bride, they set forth as ceremony requires: first the bread-bearer, bearing bread on trays; then—in summer riding on horseback and in winter on sleighs—the priest with a cross, followed by the boyars and the *tysiatskii* [master of ceremonies] and the bridegroom. And upon arriving at the bride's home they enter the house, as ceremony requires, and the father of the bride and the guests greet them with honor. . . . And when the time comes for them to go to the wedding, the *druzhki* [groomsmen] ask the bride's father and mother to bless the bridegroom and bride as they leave for the wedding, and they bless them with words, and on their departure the father and mother bless the bridegroom and bride with icons, and then, taking their daughter by the hand, give her into the hands of the bridegroom. And then the wedding party and the priest and the bridegroom together with the bride, taking her by the hand, leave the house, and the father and mother and guests accompany them into the courtyard . . . and they go forth from the courtyard to the church where they are to be wed. . . . And following the wedding the entire train accompanies the bridegroom to his home, and sends word to the father of the bridegroom that they have been wed in good health. And when they arrive at the bridegroom's house, the bridegroom's father and mother and the guests greet them, and the father and mother—his real parents or sponsors—bless the bridegroom and the bride with icons and present bread and salt, and then [all] seat themselves at the table and begin to eat, according to ceremony; and at that time the bride's head is unveiled. And following the third course the *druzhki* ask the father and mother to give the newlyweds their blessing to retire, and they give them their blessing; and after dismissing and accompanying them they return and begin eating and drinking as before; and after the bridegroom and bride have come to the apartments where they are to sleep, the *druzhki*

remove the bridegroom's clothes and the *svakhi*—the bride's, and after putting them to bed return to the table. And when an hour by the clock has gone by, the father and mother and *tysiatskii* send a *druzhka* to inquire of the health of the bride and bridegroom; and the bridegroom says that they are in good health, and then the females, the boyar women, enter the apartments and congratulate them and drink toasts to their health; and at that time the *tysiatskii* sends a *druzhka* to the bride's father and mother to tell them that the bridegroom and bride are in good health. . . .

6. And on the following morning the bridegroom and bride go each to a separate bathhouse. And then the bridegroom pays visits with a *druzhka* to invite guests, both his and the bride's, to his house for dinner. And after coming to the bride's father and mother, he salutes them for having cared for their daughter while she was growing up and for giving her away in marriage in purity and good health; and after inviting the guests he returns home. But if the bride entered into marriage with him not having preserved her virginity, then he reproaches them, the father and mother, in private. And when the guests have all gathered at his house, the newly-wedded bride presents gifts to the members of the wedding party. . . . And when the bridegroom returns home, he begins to eat and drink with all the guests, and after eating the father and mother and guests bless the bride and bridegroom with icons and present whatever gifts they have; and after eating and drinking they disperse to their homes. And on the third day the bridegroom and bride and guests come to the house of the bride's mother and father, with all their guests, for dinner; and after dinner the bride's father and mother and guests likewise present gifts to the bridegroom and bride, and after eating and drinking they depart for their homes; and no further festivities take place. . . .

In the same manner whosoever gives his widowed or maiden daughter or sister or niece in marriage, the wedding ceremonies and festivities are similar to this in every way. . . .

9. In the same manner marriage agreements and weddings and ceremonies among *stol'niki*

and *striapchie* and *dvoriane* [three ranks of the service elite] and men of other ranks are similar to what has been described above; and everyone tries to arrange the marriage in the most splendid and worthy fashion, as his means permit. . . .

Likewise among trading men and peasants the marriage agreements and ceremonies are arranged in the same manner in every respect; except that there is a difference in arrangements and garments as compared with the ceremonies among the nobility, depending upon what each can provide.

SOURCE: Benjamin Phillip Uroff, "Grigorii Karpovich Kotoshikhin, *On Russia in the Reign of Alexis Mikhailovich*: An Annotated Translation," Ph.D. diss., Columbia University, 1970, pp. 268–78 (excerpted). Translations of some Russian terms have been added. Reprinted by permission of Benjamin Phillip Uroff.

A Marriage Contract (1668)

As Kotoshikhin's narrative makes clear, perhaps the most important part of negotiating a wedding was the sealing of a marriage contract which defined the timing of the wedding as well as the property destined to accompany the bride into marriage. The marriage contract which follows here, though shorter than some and coming from families of more modest wealth than those whom Kotoshikhin described, is nevertheless typical in many respects: the agreement is not between the prospective spouses, but between their respective parents; the bride's dowry includes icons, clothing, and a dowry slave; and the contract provides a monetary penalty for default, an indication of the social risk involved. Besides the length, this contract is unusual in another respect as well: signed and negotiated by a widow, the agreement illustrates that whatever their other liabilities in society, women—especially widows—often had to shoulder a full range of responsibilities which certainly included negotiating legally-binding contracts (even if someone else had to sign the document in her behalf).

Lo, I, the widow Varvara, daughter of Flor and wife of Mikita Pravoselkov, have issued this memorandum to him, to Ivan, son of Spiridon Vorontsov. In the present 176th year [= 1668] I, Varvara, have agreed [to give] my daughter in marriage to him, Ivan's son, Iev. And I bless my daughter with the mercy of God: [icons] of the Dormition of the Most Holy Mother of God, and of Nicholas the Miracleworker; and dowry clothes: a silk coat and twin earrings; and I [also] give for the dowry my slave Mikitka Oseev, [who is] unmarried. And I, Varvara, am to give my daughter to him, Ivan's son, [to be married] on the day of the Dormition of the Most Holy Mother of God [= 15 August]; and if I, Varvara, at that assigned date do not give

my daughter [to be married], then I, Varvara, am to give my daughter [to be married] at another date, on Mikhailov Day [= 30 September] in the 177th year [= 1668; according to the calendar then in use the new year began on 1 September]. And if I, Varvara, on these two dates which are written in this memorandum [do not give] my daughter Paraskov'ia to [be married] to Ivan's son Iev, then Ivan is to take from me according to this memorandum 100 rubles. And Kharlampii Grigor'ev, priest of the Nativity Church in the settlement of Olfer'evo in Arzamass district, wrote this memorandum, at her [Varvara's] order, 5 May 7176 [= 1668]. To this agreement memorandum Makarii, son of Pavl Levin, affixed his hand, in place of the widow Varvara, [former] wife of Nikita Pravoselkov, at her order.

SOURCE: *Materialy istoricheskie i iuridicheskie raiona byvshago prikaza kazanskago Dvortsa*, Vol. 1: *Arkhiv kniazia F. I. Baiusheva.*, Edited by N. P. Zagoskin (Kazan', 1882), p. 229 (No. 195); translated in Daniel H. Kaiser, "Databanks for a History of the Family in Early Modern Russia," in *Databases in the Humanities and Social Sciences 1985.* Edited by Thomas F. Moberg (Osprey, FL: Paradigm Press, 1987), p. 207. Reprinted by permission of Joseph Raben.

LITERATURE

RICHARD HELLIE

Law and the Enserfment of the Russian Peasantry

Besides the growth of slavery, late sixteenth-century and early seventeenth-century Muscovy also witnessed the final enserfment of the Russian peasantry. Probably no other social institution—including slavery—proved so important to Russia's long-term development as serfdom, so the question about the origin of serfdom has long attracted the attention of historians. By some accounts, the peasants of Muscovy fell into serfdom as a consequence of a growing impoverishment which led in turn to increasing financial dependence upon their

lords. In this scenario, the economic catastrophes of the late sixteenth century play an especially prominent role, and the state plays only a supporting part. Others attribute to the state a much more influential role. By their calculation, the Muscovite state decreed limitations on peasant movement, a process which began in separate decrees in the fifteenth century, and culminated in the 1649 Law Code (Ulozhenie). According to this interpretation, the Muscovite state enacted these statutes in order to guarantee the survival of its main source of military power, the class of servitors from whom the state demanded service in exchange for conditional land tenure. In the selection below, Richard Hellie concentrates upon this second view and the role that the

1649 code played in enacting serfdom. But it is important to note, as Hellie does elsewhere, that a series of earlier regulations had limited peasant movement. The first restrictions, issued as favors to individual landlords, appeared in the mid-fifteenth century, and prohibited peasant transfers except at the end of the harvest season. This regulation was generalized to all peasants by the law codes of 1497 and 1550. Then late in the sixteenth century, in the midst of the crises which Kolycheva described above, new regulations appeared, this time prohibiting all movement temporarily. These so-called "forbidden years" had as their aim to preserve on estates such peasants as remained. There then followed many statutes governing the period during which fugitive peasants might be legally recovered. In general, the government provided longer and longer times for landlords to retrieve their former peasants. Finally, the 1649 Ulozhenie decreed that peasants were forever attached to the lands to which the tax registers had fixed them. There was for these peasants no hope of ever acquiring their freedom, except if the state should intervene and change the law defining their status.

The question has been raised as to how important the *Ulozhenie* [Law Code] of 1649 really was in the history of serfdom in Russia. . . .

The information now available indicates that the *Ulozhenie* was indeed a profound development in the history of the peasantry, "the greatest legal act directed toward the final enserfment of the peasants." The institution of serfdom codified in the *Ulozhenie* was the basis of the institution which was repealed in 1861. . . .

Prior to the *Ulozhenie* the government, lords, and peasants all tended to believe that agriculture could be a free, voluntary, and even temporary occupation. After 1649 this view quickly passed away. The peasantry became a rigidly stratified caste. Prior to the new law code, some peasant settlement contracts with lords viewed the repeal by Boris of the right to

move on St. George's Day as temporary . . . but this phrase no longer was written after that time. Peasants caught by a census-taker knew they could not move legally of their own volition, and those not yet registered on a parcel of land knew their only hope of avoiding enserfment was to keep moving—which some of them did.

The *Ulozhenie* proved to have a deleterious effect on peasant trade and industry when peasants were banned from engaging in what were deemed "urban occupations." Many wealthy peasants were ruined financially when they were forced by the law code to sell their enterprises for very little. This in turn curtailed economic differentiation among the peasantry, as the various legal restrictions combined with the communal system of mutual responsibility for the paying of taxes and dues and for rendering obligations to enforce a greater degree of equality among bound peasants in the countryside. The claim also has been advanced that serfdom hindered the development of peasant handicraft and agricultural technique, neither of which was "backward" by world standards until Russian initiative was stifled by the new social and political conditions. The binding of the peasants unquestionably had a harmful effect on the development of urban industry, as the curtailment of migration to towns created an "unnatural" shortage of labor there.

The year 1649 also proved to be a watershed for the middle service class. . . . [B]inding the peasants permanently to the land did little or nothing to improve the ability of the middle service class to render service. Having sought and achieved a panacea, the middle service class realized full well that it was wanting and tried other tactics to attempt to cope with problems. Never again was ink put to paper to demand the repeal of the limitations on the right to recover fugitive peasants. After the *Ulozhenie* the demand shifted to attempts to get the law enforced, but even more important became the issue of a cash salary to supplement or replace inadequate incomes derived from peasant serfs.

The *Ulozhenie* also had a great impact on the

return of fugitive peasants. The circle of relatives to be returned with a fugitive head of a family was widened. Lords submitted a mass of petitions on peasants whose labor they had assumed was lost to them forever. The state's police powers (and accompanying inhumanity and violence) were injected into the issue as never before. The result was that tens of thousands of fugitives were returned, thousands right after the promulgation of the law code, even more later. . . . The massive returning of peasants from the rich frontier lands to the poorer plots whence they had come delayed the development of these lands. This was hardly desirable from the treasury's point of view because the peasants could have been expected to pay more taxes from the better frontier lands at a time when the government was relying increasingly on direct taxes to support the army.

The landlord class was not slow to react to the new condition of the peasant prescribed by the 1649 law code. The law allowed no way for the peasant to escape, a situation analogous to the period after the introduction of the Forbidden Years. As in the reign of Fedor Ivanovich, so in the 1650s at least some lords decided to take advantage of the peasant's disability by increasing the level of exploitation. This was done either by raising the rent . . . or adding to the corvée obligations. . . .

The most noticeable impact of the enserfment was on the settlement contracts between lord and peasant. Prior to the *Ulozhenie* a peasant usually received a two- or three-year exemption from paying dues (and often taxes as well) from the lord on whose land he settled, but these exemptions diminished rapidly and then disappeared after 1649. Also, lords sometimes subsidized peasants who settled on their lands (to induce settlement and to help put an economy into production), and prior to the *Ulozhenie* some of these loans (in cash or in kind) were repaid by peasants hoping to move. After 1649 there is not extant even one such repayment, for the peasant knew he could not leave his lord legally and so made no effort to repay such loans. . . .

It is also probable that the definitive binding of the peasant weakened the commune and lessened its jurisdiction. Until 1649 much punishment was left in the hands of the commune; perhaps the lord gave orders not to the individual peasant but only to the commune. Prior to 1649 the lord could evict unruly peasants from his lands, but after the promulgation of the new law code some lords (owners of estates, not holders of service lands) legally could "manumit" undesired peasants. The tendency was for the lord to punish (or torture) the serf himself corporally, or else fine the now weakened commune for its members' offenses. . . .

The enserfment of the peasantry also created a sharp distinction between "state" . . . peasants and "seignorial" peasants. A minor difference had existed prior to 1649, but this was greatly accentuated by the *Ulozhenie*. State peasants were bound to the land and their taxpaying status, but seignorial peasants were obliged to work for lords, with many of the consequences discussed above. Seignorial peasants, in the labor-short economy, became part of the value of an estate and in essence were sold along with it. In the eighteenth century the difference became all the more noticeable. The seignorial peasants were essentially converted into slaves who also paid taxes, while the state peasants' position was much envied because they retained a considerable degree of human dignity. The immediate cause of the lamentable status of the seignorial peasantry can be traced to the abasement enforced by the 1649 law code. . . .

Peasants comprised about 90 percent of the Russian population. Nearly three-quarters of the total population was finally enserfed by the *Ulozhenie*, which established permanent and hereditary serfdom based on the land cadastres and censuses. This was the conclusion of the process begun over two centuries earlier during the civil war in the reign of Vasilii III. No one would want to romanticize the condition of the peasant, whose life was indubitably hard, brutal, and short throughout the period under review, but the decline in his legal and social status is unquestionable. The government never seems to have been enthusiastic about limiting the peasant's right to move, but rather responded to different pressure groups. Large monasteries were the first pressure group, then the middle service class took up the issue. After the Time of Troubles monasteries renewed the pressure, and the middle service class finally brought it to a climax. At first the peasant lost the right to move, then the right to call his person his own. . . .

The government, consisting of the great prince-tsar, noble magnates, and a few lesser but still powerful adviser-officials, functioned for two purposes: for what might be termed the preservation of the monarch's patrimony against external and internal threats, and for the personal aggrandizement of the individuals who happened to be the sovereign's favorites. The restriction of the peasantry's mobility never seems to have operated much to the advancement of the personal well-being of the magnates, who profitted more from a system of at least semifree labor which they could recruit and retain with comparative ease. In this context the grants to selected monastic institutions must be viewed simply as favors to friends in the church establishment.

Another motivation behind the enserfment of the peasantry was the realization that the conservation of the realm (or the preservation of the fruits of holding a government post) required an adequately supported army. At times of economic dislocation the only means of satisfying the needs of the army, the backbone of which was the middle service class cavalry, seemed to be to limit the movement of the primary producers capable of rendering this support. This understanding was based on an unwillingness to reduce the army to a size the country could afford. Any reduction was impossible, for it would have forced the admission that Russia was indefensible or that its military aspirations were too grandiose. Since neither of these admissions was possible, reducing the size of the army was impossible. The only solution was to cut off shrinkage of support of the army by curtailing peasant removal from the lands of the middle service class to the estates of the magnates and the frontiers. This was effected by binding the peasantry to the land. However, the well-being of the army was not always the primary motive. The government in the 1590s and in 1649 curtailed peasant freedom to garner middle service class support in moments of political crisis.

SOURCE: Richard Hellie, *Enserfment and Military Change in Muscovy* (Chicago: University of Chicago Press, 1971), pp. 141–7 (excerpted). Reprinted by permission of the publisher.

ROBERT O. CRUMMEY
The Boyars of Muscovy: A Modern View

Opposite the peasants on the social spectrum stood the boyars. The boyars had long held the confidence of the Moscow princes, but the exact contours of their relationship are difficult to make out. It appears as though at some point the highest-ranking boyars formed a body whose advice the sovereign regularly sought (although the evidence on this point is not undisputed). This Duma, as historians have come to call the assembly of boyars, certainly brought its participants high rank, whether or not they actually influenced much policy. And just as certainly, over time duma rank came to depend less and less on birth. As Robert Crummey points out in the book from which this selection is drawn, the boyars of seventeenth-century Muscovy were at one and the same time both an hereditary aristocracy and a service elite whose position depended upon their military and bureaucratic achievements. Their status, therefore, was always somewhat perilous, obliging the boyars forever to seek further means of preserving their standing. This somewhat unusual circumstance invites comparison with aristocracies elsewhere.

Secure in their position as servitors, [Boyar] Duma members had good cause to worry about the dynamics of seventeenth-century court politics. Political life revolved around

Men of different ranks in seventeenth-century Muscovite society: boyar or state counselor, prince, hundredman or captain, *gost'* (elite merchant), merchant, petty nobleman, boyar's servitor, boyar's servitor', musketeer, Kalmyk Tatar, and Astrakhan Tatar. From *Al'bom Meierbergera: Vidy i bytovye kartiny Rossii XVII veka* (St. Petersburg, 1903), p. 23.

personal contacts—above all with the ruler and his most influential advisers. The tsar's favor could make a man powerful and rich, his disfavor could destroy him.

In such a capricious world, Duma members sought security wherever they could. Family ties did much to give coherence to men's lives. Boyar clans, especially the aristocratic inner core of the group, retained a sharp sense of their heritage and standing in society and, within them, each man knew his place. At the same time, neither his ancestry nor his genealogical standing within his family guaranteed a man high office or insured him against a disastrous fall. In addition, numerous marriages connected the core group of families to one another and to the throne. This social elite was exclusive, but open enough to change gradually by receiving new individuals and families which had risen through outstanding service or through royal favor. At the same time, marriage alliances alone could not save Duma members from the hazards of changing political fortune. Rather, marriage ties were a form of insurance; boyar clans pursued a defensive strategy of marriage alliances, forging links with the widest possible variety of potential allies or clients.

Members of the boyar elite also sought safety in informal political groupings. Patronage relationships were ubiquitous in the upper strata of Muscovite society in the seventeenth century. Fragmentary evidence suggests that some men had a particular patron or group of clients. At the same time, men and women, particularly those in trouble, maintained contact with as wide a circle of acquaintances as possible, in hopes of finding among them a powerful protector. Court factions or parties were more visible but affected far fewer men. In the seventeenth century, they tended to be very small and short-lived and took shape around men rather than around ideas or political programs. For the most part, the members of the great aristocratic clans avoided them, for they were a poor risk. If the faction's leader won the struggle for power, his followers would gather the spoils; conversely, however, if he

fell, they might well share in the catastrophe. Most men found it wiser to stay uncommitted.

In the economic sphere, the members of the boyar elite had little reason for concern. The leading families of Russia retained a secure grip on their lands and even increased their holdings. To be sure, like later generations of Russian nobles, the boyars took their estates for granted and did little to make them more productive. Moreover, in spite of extensive holdings of land and large collections of family heirlooms and hoarded goods, they often suffered from an embarrassing shortage of ready cash. Nevertheless, by the standards of their time and society, most members of the boyar elite remained wealthy, and, as far as we know, even the least favored among them were comfortably well-off. To my knowledge, no boyar families fell into bankruptcy in our period. Only political disgrace could cause a man to lose his lands.

The boyars enjoyed a material life of solid comfort and security. In their Moscow houses and new country retreats, surrounded by numerous servants and retainers, they lacked nothing. Reassuring rituals governed the social events and ceremonies at court, and the practice of Eastern Orthodoxy provided emotional stability in life and consolation in the face of death. On the surface, at least, they were content with tried and true patterns of life.

In short, in the seventeenth century, most Duma members thrived. They worked and lived in an apparently orderly world. Beneath the comfortable façade, however, there were signs of insecurity and tension. Like most men, they found death profoundly unsettling and took great pains to ensure the repose of their souls and those of their loved ones. They worried about the attitude of the rulers of this world as well. As servitors of the crown, they owed their power and standing to the favor of the tsar and his advisers. Indeed, as the seventeenth century passed, favoritism came increasingly to dominate political life. Capriciousness and unpredictability became the order of the day, although not to the extent that they had dominated nobles' lives in the terrifying time of Ivan IV. In addition, popular revolts regularly reminded them that, as government officials and landlords, they could expect to bear the brunt of the profound bitterness of the enserfed lower orders of society. Popular mythology cast them in the role of the wicked advisers from whom the well-meaning tsar had to be saved. Dependent on the crown for the rank and service assignments that brought power, economic prosperity, and social standing, and threatened from below, they had no choice but to do whatever the ruler required. . . .

Where does the boyar elite of seventeenth-century Russia fit on the spectrum of elite groups of the world in which they lived? With whom should we compare them?. . .

[T]he Ottoman Empire appears remarkably similar to Muscovy in many ways. Both were absolute monarchies whose rulers claimed all land as their own and all citizens as their servants. In each, lavish ceremony surrounded and imprisoned the monarch, whose court became the center of political life. In more concrete respects as well, Ottoman institutions closely resembled Russian. In both, the core of the army consisted of cavalrymen who received lands and their revenues on conditional tenure in return for service. Then, when lightly armed cavalry alone proved inadequate to meet the demands of the age of gunpowder, each government created an auxiliary force of musketeers. . . .

These striking parallels between the Ottoman and Muscovite systems, however, do not extend to the group with which we are concerned. The sultans applied the principle that all men were their slaves far more rigorously than did their Russian counterparts. At the core of the Ottoman system were officials who were literally slaves. . . . The resulting elite derived its power entirely from service, past and present. Its members, then, bore some resemblance to the powerful chancery officials of Muscovite and early imperial Russia, but none at all to the high court nobility. . . .

At the other end of Europe, the aristocracy or peers of England and France shared many—utterly different—characteristics with the high nobility of Russia. Before proceeding with our comparison, we should note that the peerage in these western countries and the boyar elite in Russia are not precisely equivalent. The members of the Boyar Duma were a larger and more variegated group than the peers and included some men whose family background and career made them roughly similar to nobles of the robe or new nobles in France.

The great nobles of Russia and of western Europe were the products of very different historical traditions. In the late fifteenth and early sixteenth centuries, when Russian aristocrats already served the princes of Moscow, their counterparts in England and France enjoyed great wealth and power independent of the crown. In the West, "overmighty subjects" lived in fortified castles on large estates defended by their own private armies. Moreover, when they deigned to serve the king, the great nobles enjoyed a virtual monopoly on seats in the royal council, important military commands, and governorships of the provinces. They regarded the monarch as the first among equals and opposed any significant increase in his power by any means at their disposal, including rebellion.

By the late seventeenth century, the position of the aristocracy in England and France had changed dramatically. Indeed, the historical development of Russia and the West converged, making their position very similar to that of their Muscovite brethren. In the intervening century and beyond, the policies of the Tudors and early Stuarts in England and of Richelieu and Louis XIV in France had slowly but surely reduced the local strongholds of the great. Private armies and fortified castles had disappeared, and aristocratic families kept only enough retainers to maintain the style to which they had become accustomed. Moreover, the rulers of both countries lured the aristocracy to their glittering and expensive courts. There they received financial rewards, social recognition, and direct access to the king's person and favor. In return they gave up their freedom of action and, in the most extreme case, suffered the genteel humiliation of daily life in Versailles. . . .

Despite these superficial similarities, the western European aristocrat faced very different conditions from those of his Russian counterpart. The French or English nobleman did not have to serve, the Russian had no choice. . . .

The aristocrats of western Europe enjoyed other advantages as well. In practice, their rulers had less effective control over their actions than the tsars had over their Russian counterparts. An English or French grandee might behave disgracefully or flaunt royal ordinances with impunity; an obstreperous Russian faced speedy punishment. On the positive side, western nobles had a better opportunity than Russians to present their views to the king and his ministers. In particular, the House of Lords gave the English aristocracy real power to shape royal legislation. In comparison, representation in the sporadic meetings of the national estates gave the high nobles of France and Russia little opportunity to express corporate grievances or to shape their collective destiny. Last, but not least, many western aristocrats received an incomparably better education than their Russian cousins. . . .

Unlike their fellows [elsewhere in Europe], the Russians had little power in the regions from which they had originally come. In this regard, the contrast with England, France, Prussia, and in particular, Poland, could not be more striking. In addition, the Russian high nobles were imprisoned in a system of universal service to an absolute ruler like the Ottoman. It was precisely this combination of landownership, family solidarity, compulsory state service, and the lack of regional power and corporate rights that made the Muscovite high nobility of the seventeenth century unique.

SOURCE: Robert O. Crummey, *Aristocrats and Servitors: The Boyar Elite in Russia, 1613–1689* (Princeton: Princeton University Press, 1983), pp. 166–71, 174 (excerpted). Footnotes have been omitted. Copyright © 1983 by Princeton University Press. Reprinted by permission of Princeton University Press.

NANCY SHIELDS KOLLMANN
The Seclusion of Elite Muscovite Women

One aspect of life in Muscovy which most fascinated foreign visitors was the practice of secluding women in elite families. Because only elite women experienced this ritual isolation, Nancy Kollmann concludes that the practice had political aims, permitting the great families to construct alliances to secure their positions at court. Seclusion had the advantage of protecting women from casual alliances which might complicate their parents' plans. Finally, even if this system objectified and demeaned females, Kollmann points out that seclusion all the same gave women considerable power. Both as brides and mothers Muscovite women played important parts in the games of power: they were central to the reproductive success of their own families, and could later help arrange new marriages designed to further their families' fortunes. Besides, in addition to their usual public obligations these women also wielded considerable influence through their own gender-specific networks, working behind the scenes to advance the careers of their husbands and sons.

———————————

One of the most remarkable features of Muscovite society was that the elite secluded its women. The wives and daughters of princes and boyars lived in quarters separate from men, did not mix socially with men, and were shrouded by curtains or closed carriages in their rare public appearances. Admittedly, all women in Muscovy, regardless of social class, suffered from constricted public roles and misogynistic attitudes. But only in the elite, as far as we can tell, were Muscovite women confined so completely and their public lives limited so severely. . . .

Women of different ranks in seventeenth-century Muscovite society: wife of a boyar or prince, wife of a townsman or merchant, unmarried townswoman, petty nobleman's wife (dressed for winter), Muscovite child, Muscovite unmarried maiden, nobleman's wife, ordinary maiden, and Votiak Tatar woman. From *Al'bom Meierbergera: Vidy i bytovye kartiny Rossii XVII veka* (St. Petersburg, 1903), p. 24.

Elite women's position in Muscovy had several characteristics. For one thing, men and women lived separately. Jacques Margeret, a mercenary of early seventeenth-century Moscow, noted: "Russian women are held under close supervision and have their living quarters separate from that of their husbands." Women and their children lived in high levels or distant wings of Muscovite houses and in the grand-princely palace.... Women were attended by female servants, and at home did not ordinarily socialize with men. [Grigorii] Kotoshikhin [whose account of boyar weddings appears in this same section] noted: "And [a] host's wife and the wives of [his] guests never eat with the men except at weddings, unless the guests are the most close relatives and no outsiders are present. Then they eat together." Travellers related that a host's wife rarely appeared to greet a male guest; such an exception was considered a sign of great respect.

Separate living quarters themselves are not unusual in the medieval period: elite women in medieval Frankish society lived in separate quarters, as do some Middle Eastern women today. A second characteristic of Muscovite elite women's position is similarly not unique: Muscovite women in the elite and in all strata were subject to marriage arrangements made by their parents. This custom is encountered widely in medieval and early modern European history, and in many other societies. A third aspect was that elite Muscovite women could not hold power independent of their husband. This too is not unique to Moscow, but the degree to which it was practiced there was. In European and Byzantine history, for example, instances are recorded of women assuming the throne in the absence of male heirs; in Frankish Europe women were also crowned along with their husbands and they entertained political entourages. In Muscovy, on the other hand, women were given public responsibility only when their husbands died and their sons were too young to inherit, and even then it was titular. In such a case royal widows were made regents, although they most

likely remained figureheads through whom the established court factions continued to rule.

The only public power that women [in Muscovy] held was that of property ownership. Women owned their dowries, although their husbands managed the dowry property. Widows in the elite with children were allowed to disperse property on behalf of their deceased husbands and their children. Women could also hold responsibility on their own as founders and administrators of convents. But secular women enjoyed no such administrative or cultural authority.

Elite women were studiously excluded from public life. Women in Muscovy had no access to male political entourages. They had no fiscal resources: they did not control the budget of their household, and thus lost a basis that medieval Frankish queens used to build independent political position....

The most extreme characteristic of female seclusion in the Muscovite elite was its physical control over women's lives. Peasant and town women moved in public relatively freely, but elite women rarely appeared in public, usually only to visit kinsmen or attend church....

The treatment of women in the elite in Muscovy, then, resembled in many ways the restricted status of women in other comparable societies, but it subordinated women's public life to their husband's status and limited their public freedom of movement to a far greater extreme than in other classes in Muscovy and in elite classes in the medieval West. Although Muscovite women had some property rights and were allowed freedom of activity if shorn in a convent, seclusion barred them from public life. This suggests that seclusion had political implications, since the elite whose women were secluded constituted the economic and political leadership of the state....

If we examine the Muscovite elite, we see readily some of the characteristics that in other societies correlated with strict control over women. We see, for example, that the family unit, the clan, was fundamental in political organization. This is illustrated in military organization: in the Book of a Thousand from 1550 [which identified 1000 select military servitors] some military units were organized by clan. . . . The clan's primacy in elite society is also illustrated by the keeping of genealogical books at court: these compendia meticulously recorded the male membership of Muscovite clans. Clan importance in the elite is also illustrated by the right that male members of a clan had to repurchase family land sold by a kinsman. We see also that the honor of the clan was jealously guarded in the Muscovite elite. Members of clans avidly sued to protect family honor in [precedence] litigations and in suits over injured honor.

We also see that the elite used marriage alliances to further family strategies, as best it could, given that marriage in a monogamous Christian society was a somewhat inflexible device. Muscovite sources devote a great deal of attention to marriage within the political elite. For example, the lists of attendants at royal weddings were considered so important that, from 1500, they were preserved and were later included in the official military service books. Similarly, Kotoshikhin devoted the first chapter of his analysis of the Muscovite political system to the tsar's wedding ceremony, and paid considerable attention to the favors bestowed on the tsar's in-laws. . . .

Boyar families similarly used marriage to make alliances, and those alliances were stepping stones to political power. Boyars at court were often intermarried. For example, in the 1490s, the leading boyars included Prince Ivan Iur'evich Patrikeev, his son Vasilii and his son-in-law Semen Ivanovich Riapolovskii. . . . A decade later the ruling circle included boyars Ivan and Vasilii Andreevich Cheliadnin and Prince Vasilii Vasil'evich Obolenskii; Agrafena, the niece of Prince Vasilii Obolenskii, married Vasilii Cheliadnin and later became the nurse of Ivan IV. . . . Recent studies on court politics from the fifteenth to the eighteenth centuries have shown that marriage and kin alliances remained a key factor in political position at court.

Muscovite cultural values about women resembled those of other societies that secluded women: women were subordinated to men and their sexuality was distrusted. Misogynistic essays by Byzantine and Russian authors enjoyed wide circulation amongst the Russian Orthodox. Men and women in Russian Orthodoxy as in other societies practiced rituals of impurity that expressed this value system: washing after sexual intercourse, observing a period of purification after childbirth, avoiding women during menstruation.

As in other societies that secluded women, Muscovite elite society used marriage alliances to control the political landscape. Limitation of marriage could be used to prevent alliances in the elite from becoming so complex that the political network they formed became hopelessly entangled. . . . The seclusion of women could then be used to limit marriage alliances. This gives us some clue about why the seclusion of women and control over their marriages may have intensified in [the seventeenth] century, as some sources suggest. Despite the paucity of sources, it would appear that the public appearances of elite women in the seventeenth century were more strictly regulated than in the fifteenth and sixteenth centuries. The trappings of seclusion—veiling in public and limitation of public appearances—would appear to have increased in this period. One might also point out that the royal family significantly strengthened its control over its female members in the seventeenth century. While through the reign of Boris Godunov [1598–1605] daughters in the ruling clan were married off for political alliances, in the seventeenth century the many Romanov daughters languished in the court unmarried. Such practices simplified succession claims and decreased the political networks that the Romanov tsars were involved in and to which they were obligated. The political utility in this was probably considerable. Whether boyars' families in the seventeenth century followed such a pattern has not yet been examined, but foreign travellers' accounts and Kotoshikhin's testimony show that seclusion was widely practiced in the elite in this century.

The evidence of the royal family's seclusion of women suggests how closely linked this practice was with the proper functioning of a political system that heavily emphasized kin and marriage alliances. In this light one might suggest that the seclusion of elite women developed in Muscovy to serve the needs of the developing royal autocracy and boyar elite. Its origins then could be found sometime in the gradual evolution of this political system from its founding in the fourteenth century. Control over women may well have intensified as patrimonial clans tried to maintain control of their political fortunes in the expanding elite of the seventeenth century.

Since elite women's lives in Muscovy were so strictly controlled and diverted from the primary activities of their class, i.e., politics, can we speak at all of a political role for Muscovite elite women? Muscovite women did have a role in the political order, one that they did not control directly but which was crucial for the functioning of the elite. Women were essential as links between groups. By their presence in their husband's family, women symbolized the personal links that held political life together. More importantly, in their associations with other women in the elite, they carried information, were involved in marriage making, and they helped smooth the tensions that arose in intermarried clans.

We know that women associated with other women in their separate quarters at home: boyars' wives and female relations visited one another. Elite women also met each other in the female quarters of the Kremlin. Women in the sovereign's kinship network lived here. . . . The wives of some of the most important boyars lived in the royal palace or in palaces adjacent to the tsar's home in the Kremlin. . . . Others lived at home but served the tsaritsa or visited her. Women in the elite may not have mixed with male political leaders, but they were exposed to many networks in Kremlin politics in these settings.

In their courts and quarters Muscovite elite women could learn information to pass on to their husbands. Anthropologists studying societies that seclude women frequently comment that women's networks can greatly influence men's actions, despite the strictures and prejudices that militate against women openly participating in public affairs.

Similarly, in their associations with other women, boyars' widows, wives, and daughters could physically represent their family's political network, even when their husbands had died. Women in such positions, then, would keep the continuity of their clan in politics as the men of its next generation grew older. . . .

Women could also lobby with other boyars' wives for their husband's favor or for the favor of the tsar, most notably in hopes of arranging a marriage alliance with a powerful family. We know from foreign travellers' accounts that elite mothers and daughters were involved in their kin group's marriage strategies. They interviewed prospective bridal candidates and discussed the choice with male kinsmen. . . .

Some anthropologists maintain that the intensity of strictures over women is proportionate to the real degree of influence they wield over men, whether publicly acknowledged or not. Scholars such as Mary Douglas argue that separation of sexes and misogynistic attitudes, especially concerning sexual activity, express male society's fear of the power women possess by their sexuality and by their communications with other women. In such societies married women have behind-the-scenes family influence. By the same token, older widows and old women in general frequently have high social esteem, ritual roles and matriarchal power, because they are freed of the ability to pollute the family line or impugn its honor through sexual indiscretion.

One need not accept Douglas's interpretation of the underlying attitudes in societies that seclude women to note that in Muscovite elite society widows were accorded public respect and, at least in the report of Sigmund von Herberstein, contemporaries were aware of the women's potential to affront family honor. Herberstein commented: "The women are rarely allowed to go to church and much less often to visit friends, unless they have grown so old as to be beyond attention and suspicion." Similarly, dowagers had honored places at court, widows controlled property and, interestingly enough, the Church prescribed that only widows over forty or fifty years of age were allowed to bake communion loaves for churches.

Women's roles in Muscovite politics and society, then, were not publicly acknowledged, but women were nevertheless significant. Their seclusion enhanced their value as brides and mothers, and their ability to forge bonds between families allowed kin groups to function as units in political life. Their friendships with other women gave them the opportunity to influence marriage making and to supplement male communication networks. Women, however secluded, were integrated into the life of the elite.

SOURCE: Nancy Shields Kollmann, ''The Seclusion of Elite Muscovite Women,''*Russian History* 10, part 2(1983) : 170–86 (excerpted). Footnotes have been omitted, and some Russian terms have been translated. Reprinted by permission of Charles Schlacks, Jr.

12

Muscovite Culture

Muscovite culture (and Rus' culture generally) had long celebrated ideal types. By their very nature, hagiography and icon painting were disposed to focus upon the ethereal. Consequently, no subject of literature or art represented any particular human being, complete with physical and psychological shortcomings. St. Theodosius, for example, a portion of whose *Life* we read above, was beyond all reproach, making it difficult for any less angelic person to identify with him. By the same token, icon-painters strove to idealize and generalize the images with which they represented the saints whose images they painted. Literature and the visual arts both idealized their subjects.

But in the seventeenth century Muscovite culture, in part under the influence of artistic developments in Western Europe, discovered and celebrated the individual. The first expressions of this innovation may seem to a modern reader hardly distinguishable from their predecessors. In the *Life* of Iuliania Osor'ina, for example, the reader confronts a woman whose spiritual determination was every bit the equal of Theodosius's: never raising a harsh word even to serfs who murdered her own son, she was a model of self-abnegation, fitting exactly the pattern laid down in the *Lives* of Boris and Gleb, Theodosius, and many others.

At the same time, however, the biography of Iuliania marks off a new era. In the first place, the author of the piece is her son whose own identity, like that of his mother, is known. And this biographer provides much specific information about his mother, information which, though not unflattering, does not serve to advance the spiritual aims of the *Life*. Written sometime around 1630 or so, the *Life* of Iuliania, then, belongs to a growing body of literature which aspired to depict rather than spiritualize reality. By the end of the century, the arts carried this impulse much further. One discovers literature with no spiritual content whatever, a literature intended to amuse, poke fun at social and political institutions, and much else besides.

The visual arts made a similar transition. Already in the sixteenth century, icon-painters had fallen under the influence of a baroque love of ornamentation, surrounding their icons with intricate patterns, whether simply detailed ligatures or bands of miniature scenes drawn from the *Life* of the saint whom they depicted. Seventeenth-century artists extended this development. Painters like Simon Ushakov cast entire icons in abstract patterns, and populated icons like "The Tree of the Russian State" with historical personages. Later still, secular portraiture emerged, fully desacralizing the art form, and commemorating not idealized saints, but fully human individuals whose earthly wealth and power earned them a place on canvas.

Discussion about individualism and its importance to culture begs the question, however: Who in fact could read this literature or enjoy this art? To be sure, only a thin layer of Muscovite society was equipped—financially and educationally—to appreciate fully these developments. But how thin was that layer? Many historians have attempted to reply to that question, but Gary Marker has plotted a fresh path to examining levels of literacy in Muscovy. Still difficult to make out with certainty, the extent of literacy in Muscovy nevertheless appears to have been slight indeed: somewhere between 3–10% for rudimentary literacy, and probably 1–2% for higher levels.

In this context, then, popular culture continued to function primarily in oral forms, which means that very little of it has survived uncorrupted to the present. Therefore, to get a good fix on developments in village culture will remain difficult. But careful reading of the monuments of elite culture may nevertheless betray traces of popular culture and its values, interacting with and affecting elite Muscovite culture.

DOCUMENT

The Life of Iuliania Osor'ina (Late Sixteenth–Early Seventeenth Centuries)

The *Life* of Iuliania Osor'ina (also known as the *Tale of Iuliania Lazareva*) represents considerable interest for the historian of Muscovy. In the first place, the text is one of the first pieces of biography to appear in Russia. Written by one of her sons, Druzhina Osor'in, sometime in the 1620s or 1630s, the *Life* of Iuliania merges traditional features of a saint's life with specific events in the life of a real woman from Murom. We learn, for example, details about Iuliania's marriage, the social status and occupation of her husband, the physical location of her home, the exact times of her life, and much more. In this way, Iuliania's *Life* approaches biography, introducing and praising individuals as no literary monument had in the past. At the same time, the *Life* celebrates a particular vision of Christianity which goes back at least as far as St. Theodosius. Like the founder of the Kievan Caves Monastery (see Chapter 5), Iuliania repeatedly denies herself, refusing food and sleep, accepting all correction in humility, and even punishing her body with trials. Her mind fully set in another world, she has accepted the challenge of Christ to deny self, and thereby gain eternal bliss. Thirdly, it bears emphasizing that the subject of this biography is a woman. To be sure, some women had earlier achieved fame and recognition in literature and folklore: one need only think of Princess Ol'ga. But Iuliania is no princess; her daily pursuits are in the main quite ordinary. All the same, this rather usual woman is not secreted away from the world, but is active in it, wielding considerable authority and independence, especially but not exclusively during her husband's lengthy absences on business.

———

In the days of the pious Tsar and Great Prince Ivan Vasilievich of all Russia [1533–84], there was at his imperial court a good and charitable man by the name of Iustin Nediurev, a housekeeper by rank. He had a wife named Stefanida, equally devout and compassionate, daughter of a certain Grigorii Lukin from the city of Murom. They led a pious and virtuous life, had several sons and daughters, and possessed considerable wealth and many serfs. To them was born this blessed Iuliania.

Her mother died when she was six years of age, and Iuliania was taken to the lands of Murom by her grandmother, who raised her in piety for six years. When the grandmother died, Iuliania's aunt, Natalia, wife of Putila Arapov, took, at the grandmother's behest, the young girl to her house. As the blessed Iuliania had loved God and the Holy Virgin since her very youth, she respected and honored her aunt and her aunt's daughters. She was humble and obedient, assiduous in prayer and fasting. Because of her fasting, she was much berated by her aunt and ridiculed by her cousins, who said: "O insane one! Why dost thou exhaust thy flesh and so ruin thy beauty, while thou art so young?" They urged her to take food and drink every morning, but she did not yield to them; rather she withdrew in silence, even though she accepted everything with gratitude and was obedient to all. She also refrained from laughter and games, as from her very childhood she was meek, silent, and obedient, and never rude or haughty. Although frequently urged by her companions to take part in games and frivolous songs, she did not comply, pretending confusion in order to conceal her virtues. Instead, she applied herself with great diligence to spinning and hoop embroidery, working late into the night. She also did all the sewing for orphans and ailing widows in the village, and supplied the sick and needy with all kinds of goods. Everyone admired her wisdom and devotion. . . .

When she was in her sixteenth year she was given in marriage to a virtuous and wealthy man, named Georgii Osor'in. They were married by a priest, Potapy, in the church of the righteous Lazar, in her husband's estate. This priest instructed them in the law of God according to the rules of the Holy Fathers, and she carefully listened to the teaching and instructions, carrying them out in her deeds. Her parents-in-law were still alive and, when they saw her of mature age and accomplished in virtue, they commanded her to take charge of the whole household. She humbly obeyed them in all things, never contradicting them, but respecting them and fulfilling all their orders without fail, so that all marveled at her. Many people tested Iuliania in conversation and she gave a seemly and reasonable reply to every question, so that all wondered at her good sense, and glorified God. She prayed much every evening, and made one hundred and more genuflections. Upon arising each morning, she did the same, together with her husband. When her husband would be away in the tsar's service in Astrakhan for a year or two, and sometimes even for three years, she went without sleep all night, praying or working, weaving or embroidering. She would sell her work and give the price to the poor or for the

building of churches; she gave many alms in secret by night. During the day she managed the household and cared for widows and orphans as a true mother, ministering to them with her own hands and giving them to drink and to eat. She provided the serfs, both men and women, with food and clothing, and assigned them work according to their strength. She called no one a rude name, nor did she command anyone to pour water while she washed her hands, or to take off her shoes, but did all this herself. She instructed and corrected foolish serfs with meekness and humility, taking the blame upon herself and denouncing no one, but placing all her hopes in God and the Holy Virgin. She called for help upon the great wonder-worker Nicholas, and he assisted her. . . .

In a short time, for our sins God's wrath fell upon the Russian land, and a great famine occurred, and many starved to death. Iuliania gave many alms in secret; she began to accept food from her mother-in-law for morning and midday meals, and gave all to the poor and hungry. So her mother-in-law said to her: "How comes it that thou hast changed thy custom? When there was an abundance of bread, I was not able to make thee eat early and midday meals, and now, when there is a dearth of food, thou eatest!" Wishing to keep her secret, Iuliania answered: "When I did not bear children, I did not want to eat, but when I started to bear them I grew weak and I cannot eat my fill. Not only in the daytime, but many times in the night as well I am hungry, but I am ashamed to ask." The mother-in-law was glad to hear it, and sent her enough food not only in the daytime but also at night, for in their house there was an abundance of bread and of everything. However, while receiving food from her mother-in-law, Iuliania did not partake of it herself, but gave all to the poor. . . .

In a short time, there was a severe pestilence among the people and many died from the plague. Many locked their doors so that those who were afflicted would not enter their homes; and they would not even touch the garments of the ill. Yet secretly away from her parents-in-law, Iuliania healed many of the afflicted, washing them in the bathhouse with her own hands; she prayed to God for their recovery, and if they died she prayed for their salvation, hired men to bury them, and ordered the forty days' prayer. When her parents-in-law, after having been tonsured, died in extreme old age, Iuliania buried them with honor: she gave many alms in their memory, and ordered many forty days' prayers. She also had the Mass celebrated for them and had meals served at her house for the priests, monks, and beggars every day during the forty days, and sent alms to the prisons. At that time her husband was serving for three years in Astrakhan, and she spent a great part of their wealth in almsgiving, not only in those days, but throughout these years, honoring the memory of her dead parents-in-law.

Having thus lived with her husband for many years in great virtue, according to God's commandments, Iuliania gave birth to sons and daughters. The devil, who hateth all good, sought to cause her strife, arousing frequent discord among the children and serfs. Reasoning sensibly and wisely, Iuliania restrained them all, but the devil provoked a serf to slay the eldest son; then another son was killed in the service. Although she grieved, it was for their souls, and not because of their deaths. And she honored them with memorial Masses, prayers, and almsgiving. Then Iuliania begged her husband to give her leave to go to a nunnery. He did not let her go, but they agreed to live together yet have no bodily intercourse. She continued to prepare his bed as usual, yet she herself, after long evening prayers, would lie down on the stove without any bedding. She lay on firewood with the sharp edges against her body, and she put iron keys under her ribs, and on these she took little sleep until her serfs fell asleep. Then she would rise to pray throughout the night, until daylight, when she went to church for work for matins and Mass. She occupied herself diligently with handiwork and managed her house in a manner pleasing to God. She provided her serfs with sufficient food, and appointed each of them a task according to their strength. She cared for

widows and orphans, and helped the poor in all things.

Ten years after their bodily separation, Iuliania's husband passed away, and she buried him reverently, honoring him with memorial Masses, prayers, the forty-day services, and alms. From then on, she rejected even more all worldly things that she might better care for her soul and emulate the holy women of old and, in this way, to please God. She prayed and fasted, went every day to church, gave unending alms, so that oftentimes not a silver coin remained in her house and she had to borrow in order to give alms to the poor. When winter came, Iuliania borrowed silver from her children for warm clothing, but gave even this money to the poor and she herself passed the winter without any warm clothes. She wore her shoes over bare feet, using nutshells and sharp potsherds instead of inner soles so as to mortify the flesh. . . .

Iuliania lived as a widow for nine years and showed great goodness to everyone. She gave away much property as alms, retaining only the essential for home needs; she rationed food year after year and gave all surplus to the needy. She lived even until the reign of Tsar Boris [1598–1605]. At that time [1601–1603] there was a great famine in the whole land of Russia—such that, in dire need, many partook of unclean meats and of human flesh, and untold numbers starved to death. In Iuliania's house there was great scarcity of food and of all necessary supplies, for the sown spring rye never sprouted, and both horses and cattle died. She implored her children and servants that they in no way touch anything belonging to others, nor steal, and whatever cattle and clothes and vessels were left, she sold for rye to feed the servants. She also gave considerable alms, for even in destitution she did not discontinue her customary charity, but let no one asking for help go away empty-handed. She herself came to extreme need, and not a grain was left in her house; yet she was not alarmed but placed all hope in God.

That year Iuliania moved to another village, called Vochnevo, in the confines of Nizhnii Novgorod. . . .

As her righteous passing drew near, Iuliania became ill on the 26th day of December and stayed abed for six days. In daytime she prayed as she lay in bed, and at night she arose to pray to God, standing without assistance and supported by no one, for, as she said: "Even from the sick God demands prayer." At daybreak on the 2nd day of January, she summoned her confessor and received the last rites. Then, sitting up, she summoned her children and serfs and instructed them in love, prayer, charity, and in the other virtues. She added to this also: "Since my youth and with all my heart I have desired to take monastic vows, but because of my sins and wretchedness this was not granted to me. I was not worthy, being a wretched and lowly sinner, God willing it so; glory be to his righteous judgment." She commanded that a censer be prepared, that incense be put in it; she kissed all those present and bade them peace and forgiveness. She lay down, crossed herself thrice, and, having wound the beads around her arm, she spake her last, saying:

"Praise God in all things! Into thy hands, O Lord, I commend my spirit. Amen!" And she surrendered her soul into the hands of God, whom she had loved since her youth. And all saw a golden halo around her head, such as is painted around the heads of the saints on icons. Having washed her, they laid her out in a storeroom, and that night they saw there light and burning candles, and a strong fragrance wafted from that storeroom. Having put her into an oaken coffin, they took her back to the confines of Murom, and buried her beside her husband at the wall of the church of the righteous Lazar, in the village of Lazarevo, which was three miles from the city. And this came to pass in the year 7112 (1604), on the 10th day of January. . . .

SOURCE: *Medieval Russia's Epics, Chronicles and Tales*. Revised edition, edited and translated by Serge A. Zenkovsky (New York: E. P. Dutton, 1974), pp. 391–8 (excerpted). Russian transliteration has been modified. Copyright © 1963, 1974, renewed 1991 by Serge A. Zenkovsky. Used by permission of the publisher, Dutton, an imprint of New American Library, a division of Penguin Books USA Inc.

LITERATURE

D. S. LIKHACHEV
Individualism in Muscovite Literature

The *Life* of Iuliania, especially when contrasted with the *Life* of Theodosius, illustrates a dramatic change in Muscovite cultural values, a subject which Dmitrii Likhachev here explores in detail. Increasingly in seventeenth-century Muscovy, one finds evidence not only of exceptional, elevated types, but also of more ordinary individuals with whose circumstances even the most impoverished person might identify. Those interested in pursuing this idea might enjoy reading some other works of seventeenth-century writers: the "Life of Archpriest Avvakum," "The Tale of Frol Skobeev," "Shemiaka's Justice," and "The Tale of Savva Grudtsyn," all of which are readily available in

English translation. A similar process was underway in art. If in the past, art had been exclusively religious and painting no more than icons, then in the seventeenth century much changed. In the first place, icon-painting itself underwent substantial innovation. Masters like Simon Ushakov and Semen Spiridonov brought to their icons both a baroque affection for ornament as well as an interest in real history. In his "Tree of the Russian State" (page 198), for example, Ushakov ornaments a traditional icon subject—the Mother of God—with actual Moscow places and persons—the Moscow Kremlin, the Assumption Cathedral, and figures of Tsars and great churchmen. Spiridonov casts "Nicholas the Miracleworker" (page 199) in a quite traditional pose, but surrounds him with a dizzying array of ligature and miniatures drawn from the Saint's *Life*. Both artists, then, contribute

Simon Ushakov, "The Tree of the Russian State" (1668). From V. G. Briusova, *Russkaia zhivopis'*
17 veka (Moscow: Iskusstvo, 1984), plate 17. Reprinted courtesy of Iskusstvo Publishers.

to an increasing appreciation for individuals,
in the process abandoning the more constrict-
ing and formulaic genres of an earlier time.
Even more illustrative of these changes, however, is the appearance of the first secular por-

traits. Orthodoxy had long maintained that
artists executing religious painting had the obligation not to humanize the subjects of icons,
but rather to conform to stylized patterns
which would permit the viewer to enter a

Semen Spiridonov, "Nicholas the Miracle-Worker with Scenes from his Life" (ca. 1682). From V. G. Briusova, *Russkaia zhivopis' 17 veka* (Moscow: Iskusstvo, 1984), plate 77. Reprinted courtesy of Iskusstvo Publishers.

deeper reality through the icon. Ushakov and Spiridonov already had undermined this perspective, but the secular portrait artists of the seventeenth century went much further. The subjects of their paintings are not angels, nor even saints. People such as V. G. Liutkin and G. P. Godunov (see pages 200, 201) earned commemoration for no reason other than their social standing or their wealth. Liutkin and Godunov both achieved the rank of *stol'nik*

Portrait of V. G. Liutkin (1697). From E. S. Ovchinnikova, *Portret v russkom iskusstve XVII veka* (Moscow: Iskusstvo, 1955), tabl. XXV. Reprinted courtesy of Iskusstvo Publishers.

sometime in the last quarter of the seventeenth century. And what stares out from these canvases is no idealized, heavenly visage but rather the determined faces of real men of affairs in Muscovy. Godunov posed for his portrait in December 1686 when he was not yet 23 years of age; an unknown artist painted Liutkin sometime before 1697.

THE CRISIS OF MEDIEVAL IDEALIZATION IN THE GENRE OF SAINTS' LIVES

Idealization was one of the means of artistic generalization in the Middle Ages. The writer imposed upon the characters he created (a state or church activist, saint) his own representations about how such a person *ought* to be, and these representations about what *ought*

Portrait of G. P. Godunov (1686). From E. S. Ovchinnikova, *Portret v russkom iskusstve XVII veka* (Moscow: Iskusstvo, 1955), tabl. XXI. Reprinted courtesy of Iskusstvo Publishers.

to be he identified with what *was*. This was a unique expression of the medieval preference for deduction over induction: the writer attempted to deduce everything which existed from general truths instead of generalizing from experience.

This tendency toward artistic deduction, toward a reduction of life's phenomena under a single normative ideal, was especially forceful in the literature of saints' lives. . . .

The discovery of the complexity of a human character, the revelation of good and evil traces in the same person, led to the destruc-

tion of medieval idealization. But this process moved at an uneven pace in various genres. First idealization was destroyed in historical works. But idealization remained in saints' lives and could not fully disappear there because of specific, purely church requirements which attached to this genre.

However, the new phenomena which accompanied the discovery of character invaded even this genre in the seventeenth century: an interest in the ordinary person, in daily life, in the concrete historical circumstance, etc. Idealization in saint's lives continued, of course, but it was accomplished on a new soil, soil which to a significant degree was simplified and less elevated. The normative ideal itself, which was advanced in this idealization, seemed different, less complex and by no means elevated over everyday life. . . .

[I]n the "Tale About Iuliania Osor'ina" the "typical person," the "average personality," is idealized. Everything in the fate of Iuliania Osor'ina is simple and usual. But she is also a "saint," and her "life" ends with a description of her posthumous miracles, also quite ordinary and undistinguished.

To judge by outward signs Iuliania was not a remarkable woman: she was born into the family of a servitor; like everyone else at that time she married early—at age 16; her husband was also ordinary, a military servitor. Iuliania bears him children, conducts her household with the help of numerous slaves. Her family—husband, father-in-law, mother-in-law and children—surround her. As a result, not only does she not succeed in achieving her secret wish to become a nun, but for a long time she cannot even visit church.

But the idealization of her character proceeds by other means, far from the usual stereotypes of saints' lives. She is idealized in her domestic competence, in her relations to her servants, whom she never calls by diminutive names and never forces to bring water for washing her hands or to untie her boots, but whom she always treats with kindness and thoughtfulness, even punishing them "with humility and gentleness."

She is also idealized in her relations to the parents of her husband, to whom she is subordinated. She obeys her husband, although he prohibits her from entering a convent. Her father-in-law and mother-in-law entrust to her administration of the entire household, having realized that she was "full of goodness and wisdom." In spite of this, she quietly deceives them, although with honorable intentions. Likewise, all does not pass without conflict—one of the slaves kills her eldest son.

Spinning and lace-work are equated in her life with exploits of piety. Her night-time work

is equated with evening prayer. . . . But the combination of a church ideal with secular affairs could not be lasting. An assiduous housewife, she not only declined to think about taking the veil—she simply did not have time to go to church, for which she earned the censure of her parish priest. The priest was obliged to remind her about her duty as a parishioner, and to add to the persuasiveness retailed for her a story about a miracle—a voice from the icon of the Mother of God came to him, saying, "Go, say to the blessed Iuliania, 'Why don't you go to church to pray . . .?' "

So Iuliania is a saint in her domestic service to the members of her household and to those who come to her home. The combination of church idealization with ordinary life inescapably led to the destruction of her idealization. Church ideals stood in contradiction with ordinary life. Life was varied, the ideals uniform, and accommodation of one to the other led to a complication and destruction of church idealization.

However, despite all the internal contradictions observable . . . in the ideal image of Iuliania, the representation of Iuliania Osor'ina was clear and attractive. Evidently this may be explained by the details of everyday life which gave this image special persuasiveness. . . .

THE DISCOVERY OF THE VALUE OF THE HUMAN PERSONALITY IN DEMOCRATIC LITERATURE OF THE SEVENTEENTH CENTURY

. . . Among the works belonging to seventeenth-century democratic literature are "The Tale about Ersha Ershovich," "The Tale about Shemiaka's Justice," "A Primer about the Naked and Poor Man," . . . [and] "Misery-Luckless Plight." This literature circulated among the common people: among craftsmen, petty traders, lower clergy, and even among peasants, etc. It stands in contrast to official literature, the literature of the ruling class, which in part continued the old traditions.

Democratic literature was opposed to the feudal class; this literature underlined the injustice which prevailed in the world, and reflected dissatisfaction with reality, with the social orders. The alliance with the prevailing milieu, so characteristic of persons of the preceding era, was destroyed in this literature. Dissatisfaction with their fate, their position, their surroundings—this is a new characteristic, unknown to the preceding period. This in turn was connected with a tendency to satire and parody, dominating characteristics of democratic literature. Indeed, these satiric genres become the basis of democratic literature in the seventeenth century.

For democratic literature of this era, several characteristics predominate: the conflict between a person and his surroundings, complaints against his fate, an appeal to social orders, and sometimes a lack of confidence in oneself, entreaty, fright, fear before the world, a sense of personal defenselessness, ... the theme of death, suicide and the first attempts to oppose this fate, to correct injustice.

Democratic literature of the seventeenth century also developed a special style of depicting a person: a style sharply lowered, an everyday style, asserting the right of every man to social sympathy.

Conflict with one's surroundings, with the wealthy and high-ranking, with their "pure" literature demanded emphatic simplicity, an absence of literary artifice, deliberate vulgarity. The stylistic structure of the depiction of reality is demolished by numerous parodies. Everything is parodied—even church liturgies. Democratic literature tends toward a complete unmasking and uncovering of all the ulcers of reality. And coarseness helps here—coarseness in everything: coarseness of a new literary language, partly colloquial, partly taken from ordinary business documents, coarseness of the world being depicted, coarseness of eroticism, and a corroding irony in relation to everything in the world, including oneself. On this basis a new stylistic unity arises, a unity which at first glance seems to have no unity whatsoever.

A person depicted in the works of democratic literature does not occupy any official position, or else his position is very low and trivial. This is simply a suffering person, suffering from hunger, cold, from social injustice, from the fact that no one ever bends their head to him [as a mark of deference]. As a result, our new hero is surrounded by burning sympathy from both the author and reader. His situation is exactly the same as any of his readers. He is not elevated before the reader by any official position, by any special role in historical events, nor even by any moral elevation. He is deprived of everything which distinguished and elevated all actors in preceding literary development. This human is in no way idealized—quite the contrary!

If in all the preceding medieval styles of depiction the central character in some way stood above his readers, representing to some degree an abstract personage wandering in his own special space which the reader could not penetrate, then now the hero appears fully his equal, and sometimes even beneath the reader, provoking not admiration but pity and condescension.

This new type of personage is deprived of all posing and haloes. The simplification of the hero is brought to the limits of the possible: he is naked or, if dressed, then in "a tavernkeeper's coat" or some other wretched garment with bast ties.

He is hungry, he has nothing to eat, and "no one gives him anything," no one invites him as a guest. Not even his kinsmen recognize him, and he is expelled by his friends. He is depicted in the most unfavorable positions. Even complaints against the most disgusting illnesses, against a dirty latrine, are relayed from the first person, without embarrassing the author. Naturalistic details fashion this personality into someone completely fallen, poor, almost distorted. This person shuffles aimlessly along the earth, depicted just as it is without any coloring. But it is remarkable that even in this manner of depicting a person there emerges a consciousness of the value of the human person in and of itself: naked, hungry, bare-footed, sinful, without any hopes for the future, without any signs of any kind of position in society.

Look on this person, suggest the authors of these works. Look how difficult it is for him on this earth. He is lost among the poverty of some and the wealth of others. Today he is rich, tomorrow poor; today he got himself some money, tomorrow he spent it. He wanders from house to house, is fed by charity from time to time, stuck in drunkenness, he plays with dice. He is powerless to take hold of himself, to enter on the path of salvation. All the same, he is deserving of our sympathy. . . .

The work of Avvakum has a close connection with the general tendencies of justification of the human personality, so characteristic of democratic literature. The only difference is that in the works of Avvakum this justification is experienced with great force and is conveyed with incomparable precision.

The justification of a person in the work of Avvakum, and more generally in democratic literature, is combined with a simplification of artistic form, with a tendency toward simplicity, and a rejection of traditional means of idealization of a person.

Avvakum proclaimed the value of feeling, spontaneity, the internal spiritual life of a person with exceptional passion. Sympathy or anger, abuse or kindness—everything hurries to pour out from his pen. "To strike one's soul before God"—this is the single thing toward which he aims. No compositional balance, no shades of "weaving of words" in depicting the individual, no "pretty speech" so characteristic of old Rus' didactic literature—nothing which would shy away from excessively burning feeling about everything which concerns a person and his internal life. Often in Avvakum's work church rhetoric does not affect the depiction of a person. None of the writers of the Russian Middle Ages wrote about human feelings as Avvakum did. He grieves, is sad, cries, fights, regrets, wonders, etc. In his speech there are regular remarks about the moods he is experiencing: "Oh, woe is me!" "such sadness," "pity me. . . ." And he himself, and those about whom he writes, sigh and cry: ". . . the dear ones, looking at us, began to cry, and we for them. . . ." Avvakum notes in detail all the external signs of feelings: "my

heart grew cold and my feet trembled." He also describes in detail bows, gestures, and prayers. . . . [In other words,] he attempts to attract to himself the sympathy of readers; complaining about his sufferings and sorrows, he asks forgiveness for his sins, describes his own weaknesses, including even the most ordinary of them.

One should not think that this justification of a person concerns only Avvakum himself. Even his enemies, even those who torture him are depicted with sympathy for their human sufferings. Grasp the meaning only in a remarkable picture of the sufferings of Avvakum on Sparrow Hills: "Then the tsar sent a sergeant with musketeers, and they conducted me to Sparrow Hills; there I found the priest Lazar' and the elder Epifanii, cursed and tonsured, as I had been earlier. They placed us in different houses; all the time 20 musketeers, the sergeant, the hundred-man—they all stood guard over us, ministered to us, and at night sat around the fire, and even conducted us to the building to shit. Christ, have mercy on them! these good musketeers. . . . They were all kind, obliging. . . . These unfortunates drank till they were drunk and cursed their mothers, but all the same they were the equal of the martyrs. . . ."

Sympathy for one's torturers was completely incompatible with the medieval modes of depicting an individual in the eleventh to sixteenth centuries. This sympathy became possible thanks to the fact that the psychology of the depicted persons penetrated the author's conception. Each man for Avvakum was no abstract personage, but a living, familiar person like himself. Avvakum knows well those about whom he writes. They are surrounded by very specific everyday concerns and phenomena. He knows that his torturers are only fulfilling their musketeer jobs, and therefore he cannot get angry with them.

We already saw that the depiction of a person was placed in an ordinary surrounding in other works of Russian literature of the seventeenth century—"The Life of Iuliania Osor'ina," "The Tale about Martha and Mariia." In democratic literature the ordinary surrounding is especially effectively described in the "Tale about Ersha Ershovich," the "Tale about Shemiaka's Justice, . . ." [and other similar works]. In all these works everyday concerns serve to simplify a person, breaking down the medieval idealization. But in distinction from these other works, the attachment to ordinary matters reaches exceptional force with Avvakum. He cannot present his personages outside their everyday circumstance. . . .

In the works of Avvakum, in the special style he worked out, which might be named the style of pathetic simplification of a man, the literature of Old Rus' again rose to the monumentalism of a former art, to the level of "world-wide," universal art, but on a completely different basis. [In this work] the power of a person resides in himself, regardless of any official position; the power of a person, deprived of everything, tossed into a pit in the ground, a person whose tongue they cut out and from whom they eliminated any possibility of writing and communicating with the outside world, whose body decomposes and whom lice devour, whom they threaten with the most terrible tortures and death by fire—this power emerges in the works of Avvakum with staggering force and completely eclipses the external power of official position of a landlord, after which so many Russian historical works of the eleventh to sixteenth centuries strove.

The discovery of the value of the human personality in and of itself represented not only a literary style of depiction. It was also a discovery of the value of the author's person. Hence, the appearance of a new type of professional writer, a consciousness of the value of the author's text, the appearance of the idea of the author's property which would not admit of simple borrowings of texts from predecessors, and the abolition of mere compilation as the principal creative activity. From this discovery of the value of the human personality also comes the interest in autobiography, which becomes characteristic of the seventeenth century. . . .

In representational arts the discovery of the human personality emerged altogether differently: portraits appear, lineal perspective de-

velops, envisioning a single, individual point of view for a depiction; illustrations for the works of democratic literature, depicting an "average" man, giving birth to a whole new genre, popular prints [*lubki*].

SOURCE: D. S. Likhachev, *Chelovek v literature Drevnei Rusi* (Moscow: Nauka, 1970), pp. 104–6, 136–8, 141–3, 145–6 (excerpted). Translated by Daniel H. Kaiser.

GARY MARKER
Literacy and Literacy Texts in Muscovy

Several times in this book we have discussed literacy, both how one might appraise it and what level of literacy might have existed in Rus'. In the selection below, Gary Marker returns to this subject. As with the earlier periods, it remains difficult to know just how literate Muscovy was since we have no standard data from the time which measured any kind of literacy. Furthermore, inasmuch as school was still rare, we have not even indirect evidence about what students might have absorbed. Consequently, Marker turns to another kind of evidence, the printings of books which served as textbooks for elementary literacy. Evidently, Muscovites learned to read using primers, abecedaria (alphabet-type books resembling primers), breviaries (books containing the normal church liturgy), and psalters. In examining the printing history of these books, Marker reveals at the same time much about Muscovite pedagogy and its results.

For well over a century scholars . . . have inquired into the level of literacy in pre-Petrine Russia with mixed success at best. The problem is well known. The array of sources upon which historians of other cultures typically rely to estimate levels of literacy—parish records, wills, service records, and tax lists—either do not exist for pre-Petrine Russia or do not provide the

Miniature from *Life of St. Anthony of Siisk:* Andrei learning to write (1648). From *Drevnerusskaia miniatiura v Gosudarstvennom istoricheskom muzee*, vyp. 7: *Zhitiinaia povest' ob Antonii Siiskom* (Moscow: Izobrazitel'noe iskusstvo, 1983). Reprinted courtesy of Izobrazitel'noe Iskusstvo Publishers.

volume of data necessary for computing literacy in a statistically meaningful way.

As a substitute for "hard data" Russian historians have succeeded in gathering a sampling of sources, some of which, such as collective petitions and military service lists, do lend themselves to counting. Most of the relevant sources, however, such as travelers' accounts and observations in the laws or in church documents, are discursive and thus defy quantification. These "qualitative" records can be put to good use.... For Russia, however, notwithstanding the flurry of recent research on Muscovite printing and education, no one has ventured an overall synthesis of the evidence since Aleksei I. Sobolevskii [late nine-teenth-century scholar of Russian language and literature] published his remarkable and still respected essay ... nearly a century ago. Sobolevskii ... concluded that literacy—defined as the ability to sign one's name—in mid-seventeenth-century Muscovy ran to 75 percent or more among landlords, 50 percent among urban dwellers, and 15 percent among the peasantry. Sobolevskii, in fact, maintained that these high percentages of literacy set a watermark in Russia that was not approached again for several generations.

This classic study has provided powerful ammunition for the optimists in the ensuing discussion of Muscovite culture.... Yet, as Carol Stevens has recently remarked, Sobolevskii's methods were primitive at best and his sources were far too episodic to allow for such sweeping conclusions. In her own study of Belgorod officers, Stevens calculated a Russian-language literacy rate—again by counting signatures—that ranged between 17 percent and 50 percent....

A more skeptical view maintains that Muscovy was characterized by a near absence of literacy and a correspondingly low level of genuine learning and education. The proponents of this line cite a familiar roster of derogatory contemporary observations, such as the scathing comments by the archbishop of Novgorod, Gennadi, ... the dismissive accounts of foreigners, all to the effect that few members of any group in Muscovite society knew how to read. Surely the preponderance of contemporary commentary supports this pessimistic gloss as do the generally low levels of printing and the absence of any formal system of primary education. The overall documentary base for this view of literacy, however, is considerably weaker than Sobolevskii's, and the argument ultimately turns on an interpolative logic by suggesting that Muscovy could not possibly have been very literate or else it would have generated more books and schools. In essence, no smoke, no fire.

An intriguing variation of the pessimistic view was put forward by the noted pre-revolutionary church historian Evgenii Golubinskii who maintained ... that Muscovy was likely strong on literacy but weak on genuine learning. . . . This distinction anticipates that between intermediate or semiliteracy (the mechanical or ritual reading of certain familiar texts over and over again) and full literacy (the ability to read and understand new texts as well as the ability to write) that contemporary historians have developed in studying literacy patterns in societies for which documentation is more abundant. Golubinskii's hypothesis also points to a research strategy that shifts the focus away from counting signatures and concentrates instead on reading or learning to read. Since we are extremely unlikely ever to accumulate sufficient documentation to give a statistically meaningful description of the extent of Muscovite literacy or of its sociological characteristics, examining the educational process from the perspective of literacy may be the best substitute available. . . .

Recent archival research has generated a good deal of new information with which it is now possible to compose a reasonably detailed—if not absolutely complete—publishing history of those books upon which we can test several of the more time-honored propositions and from which a somewhat clearer picture of the possibilities for literacy in Muscovite society ought to emerge. In particular, we can now reconstruct in some detail the frequency with which printed educational tracts appeared, their formats, and their print runs. . . .

Muscovy, scholars agree, lacked any formal system of primary education, private, church-based, or state sponsored. Although it is usually presumed that most studying occurred in churches or monasteries under the tutelage of an individual church man or a member of his family, the teaching of literacy probably took place in an unstructured and largely unregulated way. Virtually no first-hand descriptions of how such teachers actually conducted their instruction exist, but detailed accounts do record the universally accepted method of instruction at the time—the primer system. . . .

The primer system had prevailed with some variations throughout Europe . . . for a very long time. Typically, it emphasized reading

rather than writing, in particular, reading selected devotional texts over and over again until their contents were learned by heart. Instruction regularly began with a primer, hornbook, or abecedarium from which one learned to recognize the alphabet, sounds, and syllables and to read some specific pieces of prose (usually, but not exclusively, prayers), proceeded to the breviary . . . , and concluded with a teaching psalter. It is generally agreed that the pupils who used these books were required to have access to individual copies of the texts. Such an aggressive and intensive pedagogy led to the primers being literally

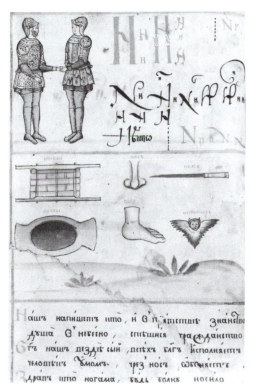

The letter "N" from a 1693 primer. From *Drevnerusskaia miniatiura v Gosudarstvennom istoricheskom muzee*, vyp. 3: *Nauka i prosveshchenie* (Moscow: Izobrazitel'noe iskusstvo, 1980). Reprinted courtesy of Izobrazitel'noe Iskusstvo Publishers.

"read to pieces," . . . thereby giving individual copies such brief lives that hardly any of them have survived, a plausible inference if one assumes that the prescribed system was actually followed. . . .

We can reasonably infer from these circumstances that the rate at which these books were reprinted, along with the sizes of their press runs, if measured over time, ought to reflect the changing rates at which children were learning to read.

Those students who successfully completed this initial three-text course—a process that seems to have taken two or three years—should have been able to read and recite the basic devotional prayers and the Book of Psalms. Historians of western literacy sometimes refer to this common pattern of being able to read but not write as a kind of intermediate literacy. Whether students whose sole exposure to the written language was so rote-centered and ritualized were expected to read and understand unfamiliar texts or whether they were capable of performing this skill that we normally associate with literacy is not clear. Such trained incapacities . . . seem to have been compounded in Muscovy by the particularly cumbersome letter-sound technique . . . that predominated. . . . [S]tudents wasted countless hours learning the letters according to their names . . . rather than according to how they actually sounded in words. . . . Thus, although Muscovy employed the universally recognized method, the instructors applied it in a way that reinforced its rote and recitative aspects and minimized its comprehensive features. Golubinskii's literacy-without-enlightenment formula, thus, may accurately describe the state of knowledge of the beneficiaries of this education.

Of equal significance is the likelihood that students who had completed the teaching psalter had not yet begun to learn to write. Only at a higher level of schooling, when pupils studied the Acts of the Apostles, the Gospels, and sometimes the entire New Testament, was writing meant to be introduced. Clearly, those students who progressed to this higher level possessed full-fledged literacy and could be expected to use the language with facility. How often, then, did students actually follow this progression, or, to put the question in the context of publishing history, how frequently were these various texts reprinted and in what quantities? . . .

The chancellery of the Holy Synod conducted a[n] . . . inventory in 1777 as part of a general effort to reexamine its entire printing system. At that time church archivists were able to go back to 1621 and produce a nearly complete checklist of publications that had been produced in the Moscow printing office . . . in the seventeenth century and the Moscow Synod press in the eighteenth. Their inventory includes formats and press runs for the entire period between 1621 and 1777, with the exception of the years 1622–1625, 1629–1634, and 1639, for which no records have survived. . . .

Moscow's [printing office] had, by the 1650s become the dominant eastern Slavic publishing house, outproducing in terms of volume all of the other presses in the region combined. An examination of its activities, therefore, helps chart the circulation of literacy texts for the whole of the Russian- (or, more precisely, Slavic-) reading population.

Regardless of whether one measures total printings or total copies, the publication of the three categories of literacy texts was decidedly unequal [see table, p. 209]. The [printing office] was printing approximately 6,164 primers . . . annually during this period, but only 2,442 breviaries and 1,586 teaching psalters. In other words, there were two and a half primers for each breviary and about four primers for each teaching psalter, a pattern quite different from what most previous scholarship has supposed.

These figures would seem to point to a sharp decline in the number of children proceeding from one text to the next. If that is so, only about a quarter of those who initiated study of the written language (who might be termed recipients of rudimentary literacy) actually learned to read for understanding or to write. Alternatively, one might speculate that the number of students remained approximately constant through the course of instruction, but that their use of the books varied in such a way as to permit a larger number of readers

Aggregate Press Runs and Printings of Literacy Books Published [by the Printing Office] 1651–1707

Years	Primers, Abecedaria		Breviaries		Teaching Psalters	
	Copies	Printings	Copies	Printings	Copies	Printings
1651–60	14,400	6	10,800	9	4,800	4
1661–70	50,400	7	20,400	4	10,800	4
1671–80	66,000	9	24,000	4	16,800	5
1681–90	94,700	24	39,600	11	21,600	7
1691–1700	91,200	6	31,200	6	25,200	6
1701–7	40,800	6	24,000	6	12,000	3
Totals	357,500	58	150,000	40	91,200	29

to work from breviaries and psalters than from primers.

Since multiple copies of most of the editions of breviaries and psalters have survived, no one has maintained that these books were read to pieces. . . . Paradoxically, then, one might well conclude that individual breviaries and psalters were used less often and intensively than individual primers were. The sources and literature, however, suggest that students were expected to read them intensively and repeatedly until memorization was achieved, a circumstance that would suggest individual copies for students and brief life spans for circulating copies.

These conflicting observations may be reconciled by recognizing that most of the extant seventeenth-century copies have survived because they found their way into libraries and repositories rather than continuing to circulate. Surviving library inventories reinforce the idea that monastic and ecclesiastic libraries tended to keep individual copies of discrete printings of breviaries and psalters . . . in their permanent collections, that they had a lesser attachment to the full primers . . . , and that they displayed little or no interest in keeping abecedaria, which may have been considered as nothing more than workbooks. As a consequence, survival of a given copy may have had more to do with the survival of an entire collection than with the manner in which circulating copies were used. Whether breviaries and psalters were read to pieces or not, indi-

vidual copies probably did not circulate more widely than primers. The publication ratio, therefore, would seem to provide a reasonably accurate reflection of the extent to which children who began with the primer during the second half of the seventeenth century continued on to the other books. If that is so, most students began and ended their studies with the primer.

The full significance of these figures, however, rests on the degree to which they inform our understanding of possible changes in literacy patterns over an extended period of time. . . .

Unfortunately, the data for the first half of the [seventeenth] century are considerably less complete than those for the second. Practically speaking, the inventory is of no use for the first quarter of the century. . . .

During the second quarter of the seventeenth century (the years 1626–28, 1635–1638, and 1640–1649), 8,400 copies of primers and abecedaria were printed in the [printing office] in 2 printings. 25,368 breviaries were printed in 17 runs, and 14,120 teaching psalters in 10 printings. These figures point to a very different pattern of publishing from that evident in the second half of the century; the relationship between primers and the other two texts is clearly askew. This change can be explained in a number of ways: the missing years might have been crucial for the publishing of primers, Muscovy may have been depending on other sources for its primers at this

Publication of Primers and Teaching Psalters
[in the Printing Office] by Decade, 1651–1707

Year	Primers a year (ave. no.)	Psalters to Primers (%)
1651–60	1440	33
1661–70	5040	21
1671–80	6600	25
1681–90	8390	26
1691–1700	9470	23
1701–7	5829	29
Average for whole period	6167	26

time, or the primer system before the late 1640s may have depended in some measure on primary texts other than primers.

No evidence whatsoever suggests that the [printing office] printed primers of any sort before 1647, when the first listing for an abecedarium appears on the inventory.... It seems highly doubtful, therefore, that the missing years from the 1620s and 1630s would reveal anything different.The second hypothesis is more promising, but it too raises serious problems. The ratio of four primers to each teaching psalter remained approximately constant over a long period of time as did the prescribed teaching methods [see table above]. The constant ratio of primers to psalters would seem to provide a plausible basis from which to extrapolate a hypothetical figure for primers of approximately 3,300 a year gathered from multiple sources for use by the recipients of [printing office] breviaries and teaching psalters during the second quarter of the seventeenth century. The available sources, however, give little indication that such abundant alternative sources existed. Burtsev published at least two primers in Moscow during the 1630s and Ukrainian and Baltic monastic presses published possibly eight others.... There is no indication that any other Slavic primers were published during this period of time. The pressruns for the primers from outside the [printing office] are not known, but they would have to have been enormous to

have provided the tens of thousands of copies that would have been needed. It is equally implausible to believe that a sufficient number of manuscript primers were available to make up the difference.

The evidence, therefore, points to the third hypothesis and a shift in pedagogical activity in the late 1640s. Before that time Muscovy seems to have employed a variant of the primer system that allowed for the use of other texts. Alternatively, the number of people who began the course of instruction could have been many times smaller than it was to become, but those who began may have been far more likely to continue on to the breviary than were the initiates of the second half of the century. Either way, Muscovy seems to have embarked on a major redirection of primary education ... in the late 1640s to bring itself somewhat more into conformity with the model of the primer system and, within that, to make the printed primer the new foundation of its endeavor....

Let us recall, at this point, that at the primer level students could not write. In order to become scribes, pupils would have to have studied at least the breviaries and psalters and quite possibly the next level of texts as well. In marked contrast to primers, Muscovite breviaries and teaching psalters came out quite regularly throughout the century, annually or very nearly so in the case of the breviaries, and about once every other year in the case of the psalters. Comparing the total volume of texts between the first and second halves of the seventeenth century reveals a significant increase of nearly 70 percent for breviaries and more than 90 percent for teaching psalters [see table, p. 211, top]. Such increases are quite modest in comparison to the explosive growth of primers, and they fall considerably short of adding up to a literacy revolution; nevertheless, they give a clear indication that the number of people being exposed to literacy texts beyond the primer was growing rapidly.

Beyond the manifest absolute increase, the ratio of breviaries to psalters also changed, albeit modestly. In the second quarter of the century the [printing office] printed only 56

*Annual Averages of [Printing Office] Breviaries
and Teaching Psalters*

Text	Copies Printed a Year (ave. no.)	
	1626–49*	1650–1707
Breviaries	1492	2442
Teaching Psalters	831	1586

*Excluding years for which no information is available.

percent as many psalters as breviaries; during the second half of the century that figure grew to 65 percent, a change that suggests a higher "graduation" rate as the century proceeded. A decade-by-decade check of the second half of the century [see table below], however, reveals no discernible new trends and indicates that the ratio of about six teaching psalters for every ten breviaries was a well-established long-term pattern. . . .

This analysis leads to clear and straightforward conclusions. The rate at which the [printing office], and to a lesser degree the other publishing houses, supplied children with literacy texts grew significantly and consistently during the last half of the seventeenth century. After decades during which the primer apparently was employed only intermittently, it be-

came the predominant teaching text by the late 1640s, and, by the 1690s, more than 9,000 [printing office] primers a year, mostly abecedaria, and perhaps another thousand primers from other sources were available in the east Slavic world. At this time Muscovy placed unprecedented emphasis on teaching the rudiments of reading.

By contrast, the increase in the production of breviaries and psalters, although substantial, was a good deal more modest. The percentage of students who started with the primer and passed through the curriculum to the teaching psalter, moreover, remained at about 25 percent throughout the second half of the century. Comparing the relevant pressrun figures to . . . figures on Muscovy's population . . . yields the following, admittedly crude, proportions: one primer printed per annum for every 1,700 people as compared to one teaching psalter for every 6,600 people. We simply do not know enough about the distribution of this population to give a more precise rendering of the percentage of children from various social or occupational groups who might have had access to a primer, and thus to rudimentary literacy, in the late seventeenth century. Even using the most uniformly and wildly optimistic assumptions of the sizes of the appropriate subgroups in the population and the dissemination and effectiveness of primers, we would still arrive at rudimentary literacy rates

Average Annual Printing of Breviaries and Psalters [by the Printing Office] 1626–1707

Years	Breviaries	Psalters	Psalters to Breviaries (%)
1626–50*	1492	831	56
1651–60	1080	480	44
1661–70	2040	1080	53
1671–80	2400	1680	70
1681–90	3960	2160	55
1691–1700	3120	2520	81
1701–7	3429	1714	50
Average for whole period	2224	1412	64

*Excluding the years for which no information is available.

that were well below 10 percent for the entire population. Similarly optimistic assumptions regarding the circulation of psalters and the frequency with which psalter users could write would yield an intermediate literacy rate of only about 3 percent. Less generous, but more plausible, assumptions obviously yield figures considerably lower than these—about 3 percent to 5 percent for rudimentary literacy and about 1 percent or 2 percent for intermediate literacy.

These numbers, it must be emphasized, represent little more than guesswork, intended to provide only crude estimates for what might be termed the plausible range within which aggregate literacy lay in the late seventeenth century. Access to books, moreover, was decidedly unequal, and boys who were not from peasant families had a much higher chance of being given the opportunity to learn to read than did the majority of the population. Even keeping all of this in mind, Sobolevskii's sense of Muscovite literacy seems unsupportable. Indeed, in the wake of these estimates even Golubinskii's more modest assessment seems unduly optimistic. In the last analysis, late Muscovy, even with its apparently sharp improvement in literacy, would seem by any comparative measure to have been a profoundly illiterate society in which reading was the privilege of a few and writing the domain of a tiny minority.

SOURCE: Gary Marker, "Literacy and Literacy Texts in Muscovy: A Reconsideration," *Slavic Review* 49(1990): 74–85, 88–9 (excerpted). Footnotes have been eliminated, and some Russian terms have been translated into English. Reprinted by permission of the American Association for the Advancement of Slavic Studies.

13

Everyday Life in Muscovy

The texture of everyday life in Muscovy is somewhat easier to make out than it is for earlier periods. For one thing, an expanding number of foreigners entered Muscovy, particularly after the opening of trade with the Dutch and English in the sixteenth century. Quite a few of these visitors returned home, put pen to paper, and described what they had seen and heard. Later, when foreigners entered the service of the tsar, still more perspectives on Muscovy came into print. All the while, diplomatic missions regularly journeyed to Moscow, their personnel carefully eyeing the mysterious world around them. Still today their reports make fascinating reading. And if woven into these narratives are fradulent reports and second-hand gossip, there is also much of value which no Muscovite commentator would have thought to record. Foreigners, for example, have supplied us with detailed accounts of the many rituals and routines of everyday life in Muscovy. Somewhat surprising is that an artist accompanied one of these delegations. His drawings provide our best glimpse into the clothing styles which distinguished the various orders of Muscovy.

Records from the seventeenth-century Muscovites themselves are, however, still rare. The tradition of diary- or journal-keeping seems not to have taken hold in Russia until the late eighteenth century. But we do possess some personal correspondence which reveals quite unself-consciously basic values of the time. As the earlier discussion about literacy will have made clear, none of this correspondence comes from the lowest social orders; not possessing literacy, they also lacked the means to document their own past. But their lives nevertheless sometimes made it onto paper. One place which proved especially attentive to the foibles of Muscovy's lowest orders was the church court, whose judges heard allegations of domestic abuse, sexual misconduct, and dogmatic misadventures. Although the great bulk of these records have evidently perished, the survivors paint a vivid picture of ordinary life in seventeenth-century Muscovy.

DOCUMENTS

Letters to stol'nik Andrei Il'ich Bezobrazov from his Wife (1687)

Andrei Il'ich Bezobrazov came from an ancient, ranking Moscow family. Born about 1621, Bezobrazov held various responsibilities in his career, and by 1647/48 had become a *stol'nik*, the third-highest rank in Muscovite ser-

vice society. A veteran of Lithuanian and German campaigns, by the 1680s (when he was already in his sixties) he had come to spend most of his time on his Borovsk estate, Spasskoe, although he had a fine house in Moscow to which he might repair. Several times in his career when he faced undesirable appointments Bezobrazov complained of infirmities, presumably stemming from his military service; in particular he received medical help for his ailing legs, all of which might help explain his wife's frequent inquiries after his health. Bezobrazov's first wife, Irina Grigor'evna Anichkova, died in 1660. His second wife, who authored the letters which appear below, was Agaf'ia (nicknamed Ogashka) Vasil'evna Shetneva. Her letters, written in February, 1687, combine a formal regard for her husband with a touching solicitude for his appetites, comforts, and health. More to the point, with her husband remote from the capital, Agaf'ia Vasil'evna played a central part in the conduct of her husband's financial and political interests, as the letters also make clear. Bezobrazov himself became involved in political intrigue which led to his execution early in 1690; though his wife did not share his punishment, she shared his guilt, and was imprisoned in a convent in Tikhvin.

––––––––––

To my lord Andrei Il'ich your little wife Ogashka petitions. May you be healthy for many years, my lord, and may God preserve you. And be it known to you, lord, that in your home in Moscow as of February 9th, everything, thank God, is fine. State secretary Vasilii Grigor'evich [Semenov] dispatched to you in Borovsk by horse post a clerk, Alistarkh Kuzmin, from the Military Affairs chancellery, lord; and I sent with the clerk a household slave, Fedka Krivushin, in a horse-driven cart, and with him, with Fedka, I sent you a fresh sturgeon, a large pike, two fresh bream, a tench [a fresh water fish] and four salted whitefish. And this fish [the pike?] Vasilii Grigor'evich sent to me. And I, in turn, sent the fresh pike to you, lord. And with him, with Fedka, I also sent in a bast basket raisins and dried figs (and millet) which remained sealed in the sacks after you [left?]; and I also sent with him, with Fedka, two copies from purchase deeds; please affix to these copies your signature, and send them to Moscow without delay; and with Fedka I also sent a document from Kromskaia village, but no one has appeared from Nizhnii [Novgorod] or from Vologda. The Iazykovs

brought a petition to the Patriarchal Military Affairs chancellery about the estates of Mikhail Khomiakov-Iazykov, and we also wish to bring [a petition]. I sent to Vasilii Grigor'evich a request that he order examined a genealogical chart of Mikhail Khomiakov-Iazykov [to determine] whether there are kinsmen in the same generation [with a claim to the property]. Vasilii Grigor'evich said, "I shall order that copied out this very hour." And Ivan Kobiakov said that there is no signature on the genealogical chart of Mikhail Khomiakov-Iazykov; and when they shall copy out the generations in the genealogical chart of the Iazykovs and [the entry on] Mikhail Khomiakov-Iazykov, then, lord, I shall immediately send you news. Please, lord Andrei Il'ich, order Fed'ka Krivushin to bring the letter from Borovsk to Spasskoe without delay, and in the letter to the estate steward is written [an instruction] about malt. If, lord, you will not take for yourself in Borovsk the small cucumbers from Spasskoe, then please have the steward send them on to me. The musketeers, lord, who accompanied the treasury to Borovsk, brought [me] letters from you. Then to you, my lord, I make many petitions. Kislianskoi has not sent anything. And about the boyar [Vasilii Vasil'evich Golitsyn; see below], lord, there is no word on how he will leave Moscow or along which road. And Vasilii Grigor'evich has refused the petition of Ivan Kharlamov.

To my lord Andrei Il'ich your little wife Ogashka petitions. May you be in good health for many years, my lord, and may God preserve you. And in your home [in Moscow], lord, as of February 11 everything, thank God, is fine. Your serf, Ortiushka Ivanov, came to me in Moscow and brought to me a letter from you, and I released him. And I sent to you, lord, with this letter a list from Aleksei Torshilov of the things he purchased with your money at Samara, [namely] fish—how much he gave for a fish, and what they gave in consideration of which fish; and a clerk's document [I also sent you]. According to your, my lord's, order I gave a bucket of wine to Sava Nekrasov. Be so good, my lord, as to send [back to me] the copies from the signed purchase documents [see above]. As of this date, there is still no decree on the estate of Mikhail Khomiakov-Iazykov; I shall notify you what happens in the future. And regarding the campaign of the boyar [V. V. Golitsyn], I ordered slaves of Prince Vasilii Vasil'evich to find out [his route], and when they genuinely find out [his route], on that very day I shall write you [the details], lord. There is as yet no order for Afonasii Shchelkunov to receive an abstract [from a deed or other document confirming ownership of land]; they could hardly refuse him, lord. Lord Andrei Il'ich, will you write me about whether you would like some milk-mushrooms and dried mushrooms? I would be glad to send some to you. Lord Andrei Il'ich, please order that slave about whom I spoke to you, [the one] who was in your service with Borovsk elder Grigorii, tell him that he should serve with me [here in Moscow]. According to your order, lord, I sent to the clerk Iakov Gavrilov a *chetvert'* of rye flour. As of today's date still no carts from Vologda or from Nizhnii [Novgorod] have appeared. I also sent to you, lord, pressed caviar in a tub and a bucket of saffron milk-cap mushrooms; both the caviar and milk-caps are sealed shut. And that which you wrote, lord, namely ordering Vasilii Grigor'evich to petition against the governors of Maloiaroslavets and Vereia and Borisov, that they do not send army people to you, nor any ink, paper or candles, Vasiliii Grigor'evich said that there is no directive [ordering the governors to do] that; and you, lord, when you came to Borovsk, did not send such directives to Moscow. And Ivan Priklonskoi wrote me to ask for money, but there is nowhere for me to get money. Then to you my lord I petition much.

To my lord Andrei Il'ich your little wife Ogashka petitions. May you, my lord, be healthy for many years and may God preserve you. Please, lord, order [someone] to write me about your many-yeared health; I always wish to hear about your health. Be it known to you, lord, that here in Moscow in your home on the 14th of February everything, thank God, is well. I sent to you, my lord, with the Borovsk dragoons, [namely] with Larion Mal'tsov and with Foma, a charter of the great sovereigns, an instruction to the dragoons, and a land abstract of Afonasii Shchelkunov; and, lord, Vasilii Grigor'evich refused that abstract of Afonasii Shchelkunov, and ordered him to mine [for land?] in [another] place. And with them [the dragoons] I also sent you, lord, a list of cities to which boyar Prince Vasilii Vasil'evich Golitsyn is to go on service, and he departs on Tuesday in the third week [of Lent?]; Ivan Petrovich Odintsov wrote the route in your house by his own hand. And the Kashin peasants did not bring the ice, and the Nizhgorod and Vologda peasants still have not appeared with the carts. Be so good, lord, as to send a list with Prokhov Shenshin of monies, what he took from you and what remains for him to pay up, for he says that he is entitled still to 14 rubles, and that in that [loan] document is written how much money has been given him and how much remains to be paid. Grigorii Bronshchikov has still not come to Moscow. Then to you, my lord, I make many petitions!

To my lord Andrei Il'ich your little wife Ogashka petitions. Be healthy for many years, my lord, and may God preserve you, and to me, lord, be so kind as to order sent to me [word] on your many-yeared health; for I would like to hear about your many-yeared health, to God be the praise. Be it known to you, lord, that in your home in Moscow everything is fine, thank God, on this 16th day of February. And in the Land Grant chancellery there is still no decree for anyone about the Mikhailov estates of Ivanovich Khomiakov-Iazykov, and the Iazykovs, Evdokim Iazykov with his brother, brought to the case in the Land Grant chancellery a genealogy chart. The purchase deeds are still not written. No one has yet appeared from Nizhnii [Novgorod] or from Vologda. And in the Patriarchal Military Affairs [chancellery], lord, the charter is all ready: a scribe has been ordered to go to the Mikhailov estates; he was ordered to go to examine and describe in the presence of petitioners the property in those estates and [the

property in the holdings] of the Nativity monastery in Vladimir. [Tell me] whom you wish
to send, lord, so that [I will know] how many
should stand [in your stead for that inventory].
Please, lord Andrei Il'ich, order Kuzma Kho-
mutov to send a bast mat of salt from Spasskoe;
for here, lord, there is nothing with which to
salt meat or fish, and I borrowed 10 puds [each
pud equals about 36 lbs] of salt from Fedor
Il'ich. As you directed in your letter, lord, I
sent nut butter to Vasilii Grigor'evich and Fedorov Levont'evich [Shaklovityi, with whom
Bezobrazov was implicated in 1690]. Then to
you, my lord, I make many petitions. To Fedor
Levont'evich a daughter, Anna, was born, and
I went to her for the birth, and brought gold;
and I borrowed [money?] from Gavrila Romanov.

SOURCE: A. A. Vostokov, "Perepiska stol'nika A. I. Bezobra-
zova 1687 goda," *Chteniia obshchestva istorii i drevnostei rossi-
iskikh pri Moskovskom universitete* 1888, kn. 1, otd. III, pp. 8–
16. Translated by Daniel H. Kaiser.

Adam Olearius on Food and Dining (1630s)

Adam Olearius took part in two embassies to
Muscovy on behalf of the Duke of Holstein;
the first departed Germany late in 1633 and
lasted until 1635, the second beginning almost
immediately with Persia as a destination, but
with stops in Muscovy along the way. The delegation returned home in 1639, and Olearius
soon thereafter set to work recording what he
had seen. The first edition of his account appeared in 1647. In the selection reproduced
here, Olearius turns his eye to Muscovite diet,
providing a mixture of keen observation and
undisguised disgust at manners different from
his own.

The domestic arrangements of the Russians
vary according to their station. Generally they
live meagerly and spend little on their homes.
The magnates and the rich merchants, it is

true, now live in costly palaces. These were
built only in the last thirty years, however, and
before that they too lived in wretched dwellings. The majority, and especially the common
people, live on extremely little. Their houses
are shoddy and cheap, and the interiors have
few furnishings and utensils. Most have not
more than three or four earthen pots and as
many clay and wooden dishes. Few pewter and
even fewer silver dishes, let alone cups for
vodka or mead, are seen. These people are not
in the habit of expending much effort on
cleaning and polishing their vessels. Even the
Grand Prince's pewter and silver plate, with
which the ambassadors were entertained, was
black and repulsive, as were some of our lazy
hosts' tankards, which had not been washed
for a year or more. None of the houses,
whether rich or poor, display vessels as ornaments; the walls are bare, except in the houses
of the wealthy, where they are hung with mats
and some ikons. Very few people have feather
beds, in lieu of which they lie on benches covered with cushions, straw, mats, or their
clothes; in winter they sleep on flat-topped
stoves, like bake-ovens, as the non-German
people in Livonia do. Side by side lie men,
women, and children, as well as servants, both
male and female. In some places, we found
chickens and pigs under the benches and
stoves.

They are not accustomed to tender dishes
and dainty morsels. Their daily food consists
of groats, beets, cabbages, cucumbers, and
fresh or salt fish. In Moscow, they use coarse
salt fish, which sometimes stinks because they
are thrifty with the salt. Nevertheless, they like
to eat it. One can detect a fish market by the
odor well before he sees or comes upon it. Because of their excellent pastures, they have
good lamb, veal, and pork, but they spend little
on meat; for their religion prescribes as many
fast days as meat-eating days, and therefore
they have become used to coarse and wretched
food. They know how to prepare so many
dishes of fish, pastry, and vegetables that one
may forget about meat. As I have already mentioned, on one fast day the Tsar granted us 40
such dishes. They have a special kind of pastry,

A lord and his servant at dinner (1648). From *Drevnerusskaia miniatiura*, vyp. 2 (Moscow: Izo-brazitel'noe iskusstvo, 1973). Reprinted cour-tesy of Izobrazitel'noe Iskusstvo Publishers.

much eaten in Butterweek [*Maslenitsa*, "Car-nival" which immediately precedes Lent], which they call a *pirog*. It is like a pie, or more exactly, a fritter, though somewhat longer; it is filled with minced fish or meat and onion, and is baked in butter, or during fasts, in vegetable oil. The taste is not unpleasant. Everyone treats a guest with these, if he means to receive him well.

They have a very common food which they call *ikra*, made of the roe of large fish, espe-cially sturgeon and whitefish. They expel the roe from the membrane in which it is con-tained, salt it, and after it has stood for six to eight days, mix it with pepper and finely chopped onions. Some also add vinegar and country butter before serving it. It is not a bad dish. If one pours a bit of lemon juice over it, instead of vinegar, it gives a good appetite, and has a restorative effect. Ikra is salted on the Volga, chiefly at Astrakhan. Some of it is dried

in the sun. They fill hundreds of barrels with it and then send it to other countries, espe-cially to Italy, where it is considered a delicacy and is called *caviaro*. Certain people lease the trade from the Grand Prince for a certain sum of money.

The Russians prepare a special dish when they have a hangover or feel uncomfortable. They cut cold baked lamb into small pieces, like cubes, but thinner and broader, mix them with peppers and cucumbers similarly cut, and pour over them a mixture of equal parts of vinegar and cucumber juice. They eat this with a spoon, and afterwards a drink tastes good again. They generally prepare their food with garlic and onions, so all their rooms and houses, including the sumptuous chambers of the Grand Prince's palace in the Kremlin, give off an odor offensive to us Germans. So do the Russians themselves (as one notices in speak-ing to them), and all the places they frequent even a little.

The drink of the common people is *kvas*—comparable to weak beer or small beer—and also beer, mead, and vodka. Every dinner must begin with vodka, and in the course of the meal other drinks are served as well. In addi-tion to good beer, the tables of the magnates offer Spanish, Rhenish, and French wines, var-ious kinds of mead, and double vodka. They have good beer, which the Germans in partic-ular know how to brew and preserve, doing so in the spring. They prepare ice-cellers, in the bottom of which they place snow and ice, and above that a row of kegs; then another layer of snow, and again kegs, and so forth. Over the top they lay straw and boards, since the cellar has no roof. Thus they can bring one keg after another into use, and they may have fresh and delicious beer throughout the summer—which is quite hot. They import wine by way of Archangel. The Russians, who prefer vodka, do not like wine as well as the Germans do. . . .

SOURCE: *The Travels of Olearius in Seventeenth-Century Russia.* Translated and edited by Samuel H. Baron (Stanford: Stan-ford University Press, 1967), pp. 155–7. Copyright © by the Board of Trustees of the Leland Stanford Junior University. Reprinted by permission of the publishers, Stanford Uni-versity Press.

LITERATURE

EVE LEVIN
Sexuality in Muscovy

Foreigners like Olearius offered some generalizations about sexuality in Muscovy, but their reports on private life seem often to have depended on hearsay rather than any direct observation. First-hand evidence on such matters is understandably hard to come by. Much that concerned sexual behavior never found its way onto paper, and such things as did—records of litigation, for example—often fell victim to fire. However, some court records did survive, and here Eve Levin summarizes several seventeenth-century cases which came before ecclesiastical courts in Ustiug in northern Muscovy. Though not always complete, the extant records nevertheless reveal a good deal both about sexual practices and the attitudes of church courts toward women.

The strictures in canon and secular law against rape did not prevent occurrences. Indeed, certain aspects of medieval Slavic society promoted the sexual abuse of women, despite condemnations of it by clerical authorities. Literary texts, and actual court records of rape cases (from seventeenth-century Russia) illuminate the social context in which rapes took place. . . .

[In 1632] the widow Mariia Mikhailova doch' Trufanova petitioned Metropolitan Varlaam of Rostov, Iaroslavl', and Ustiug, accusing Andrushka Kolokolnitsyn, nicknamed Parniug, of raping her. The attack occurred in the evening, after Mariia returned home from a visit with her brother. Andrushka Parniug ripped the lock from her door, forced his way into the house, raped Mariia, and robbed her. Then he ran off. By filing an official complaint, Mariia could enlist the assistance of the authorities in locating Parniug and returning him to the scene to face charges—a necessary first step in gaining compensation. . . .

In theory and practice, the burden of proof was on the accused, as the case of Tanka Ivanova doch' Zybova [1695] illustrates. Tanka had been married, but her husband had abandoned her more than three years earlier. Since that time, Tanka had lived with her parents at a saltworks owned by the priest Aleksei. When her pregnancy became obvious, she first accused the priest's Cossack boarder, Aleshka Lukiianov syn Zhigulev, of raping her during Lent. After the rape, she stated, she had slept with him willingly. Aleshka had since run away and could not be located. Three days after making this initial accusation, Tanka changed her story. Now she accused the priest Aleksei of raping her while he was drunk. Three weeks after that (the delay was due to the birth of the baby), Tanka again changed her testimony, accusing a neighbor youth, Timoshka, of raping her also on a separate occasion. The priest Aleksei denied raping Tanka, and named the absent Aleshka as the father of the child. Timoshka similarly denied raping Tanka. Tanka then admitted the truth, that no rape had occurred at all. She had slept with Aleshka willingly and had become pregnant by him. Her spurious accusations of rape were motivated by a desire to find an excuse for her illicit pregnancy and, if possible, to force someone to support her child. She had accused the priest because, after learning of the extramarital affair, he had told Aleshka to leave. The accusation against Timoshka was also revenge; Timoshka had made fun of Tanka, teasing her about Aleshka's vanishing act. Ultimately the court waived the fines against Tanka for illegitimate birth, ordered her flogged for perjury, and sent her home. Tanka's contradictory statements were obviously false, but the behavior of the court is noteworthy: each accusation was given due consideration, as though Tanka were a reliable plaintiff. Because it was considered to be defiling to the victim, rape had to be treated as a serious offense, and one not difficult to prove.

A [1640] petition by a bailiff of the ecclesiastical court of Ustiug, Matvei Lobanov, gives insight into the treatment of rapists after conviction. After the court collected any fine or compensation for the victim and inflicted any corporal punishment, the convict was returned to the community. Long prison sentences were not usually handed down in seventeenth-century Russia, because of the expense of incarcerating malfeasants. Instead, the criminal was placed on a sort of parole: his relatives had to swear *poruka* [surety] for him, guaranteeing his future conduct. Lobanov's duty was to collect the *poruka* documents from the convicted rapist Kozma Terent'ev syn Zhilin and to enforce the other terms of the parole. Kozma was forbidden to leave Ustiug, and he was forbidden to marry without the consent of the court. However, Kozma's aunt and cousins refused to cooperate with Lobanov, beat him up, and helped Kozma to flee from the authorities. . . . The court's prohibition of marriage for Kozma . . . reveals an understanding that rapists are dangerous to all women, and that a wife would not be safe in Kozma's household. Further, it reveals that medieval Russians did not believe that rape occurred because the rapist could not find alternative licit sexual outlets.

Perhaps because the plaintiff was readily believed, several of the surviving rape cases were settled out of court. For example, Fevronia Stefanova doch' petitioned Archbishop Aleksandr of Ustiug on July 12, 1686, accusing Danilo Ivanov Malkov and his friend Grigorii of robbing her house, threatening her with death, and raping her. Danilo and Grigorii denied all charges, but Fevroniia produced responsible witnesses. The accused then hastened to settle out of court in the hope of avoiding a judgment against them. Thus on July 16—only four days after the original charge was filed—Fevroniia and the defendants petitioned together to have the case dropped. The erstwhile defendants were left to pay the court costs, as well as whatever Fevroniia extracted as a condition for dropping

the suit. A similar case in the same year was sent to secular authorities, as it concerned soldiers in a border region. Ofimitsa Ivanova doch' Aleshka zhena Artem'eva accused the soldier Grigorii Shchetkin of ripping her dress and forcing oral sex on her. Grigorii countered with an accusation of slander. As the testimony against him increased, Grigorii tried to get Ofimitsa to drop charges in exchange for a half-measure of grain. At first she refused. Ultimately he must have offered her sufficient compensation, because the two petitioned together that the charges be dropped. . . .

The Orthodox Church railed against intoxication, considering it to be an intensifying factor in any crime. A woman who was raped while she was drunk shared responsibility for her victimization. A man who committed rape while he was under the influence of alcohol was condemned as much for drunkenness as for his other crimes; it was overindulgence in liquor that led him into evil. . . .

[According to a case from the 1650s] an unknown woman was found in Dmitrovskaia village, badly beaten and raped. The villagers denied any complicity in the crime. A few identified the woman as a stranger named Tanka, who came from the Streltsy (infantry) garrison nearby. Several reported that they had seen her lying drunk in the street. Suspicion immediately fell on the soldiers who were being quartered in the village. One of these soldiers, Pronka Vysotskii, known by the nickname Shilo, claimed to have seen two drummers, Sofonko and Senka, beating the woman, pulling a wattle fence over her, and walking on top. In his first statement, Pronka Shilo accused a soldier, Savost'ka, of participating, but then credited him with driving the two drummers away. All three of those implicated in Shilo's testimony denied involvement, but their statements conflicted. In order to resolve the conflicts, the court ordered all those implicated, including Pronka Shilo, to undergo torture by hot iron. Under torture, the ranks of the implicated grew to include others, including a soldier, Vaska, and Pronka Shilo's landlord, Eremka Andreev. Meanwhile, the woman had recovered consciousness, named Shilo as her attacker, and died. Investigators sent by the court uncovered additional evidence. First, the nurses who cared for the dying woman reported that her anus was bruised, an indication of rape. Second, the woman was identified definitively. She was the wife of a soldier, and had been publicly flogged for adultery in the past. Third, Pronka Shilo's original testimony against Sofonko and Senka was discredited when an investigator reported that the scene of the crime was not visible from Pronka's yard, and the fence in question was overgrown with grass and had obviously not been moved. Under torture, little by little the truth came out. Pronka Shilo had found Tanka drunk and had had sex with her, along with Savost'ka and Vaska. All three claimed that Tanka had been willing. Later that day, Tanka went to Pronka Shilo's lodging to protest. The landlord, Eremka Andreev, refused to let her in, and kicked her down. Pronka then dragged her out of the house, raped her again, and beat her with a birch rod.

The medieval Russian system of trial did not require conviction on a specific charge. In this case, it was clear that a crime had been committed: the woman was dead, and the three soldiers had had illicit sex with her. Although the victim was hardly a credit to society, the court could not ignore the offense against her. Pronka, Savost'ka, and Vaska were imprisoned for ten months and then returned to their regiments. Shilo, the most culpable, was flogged before his release. Ultimately, it was more important to state authorities to get service out of the soldiers than to punish them for insult and injury to an adulterous woman.

The case of Pronka Shilo and the popular attitudes toward rape suggest that medieval Slavic society had a high level of tolerance for violence against women. . . . Russian sources confirm that husbands beat their wives and daughters; but there were limits to this violence. . . .

The church granted the husband the right to chastise his wife when she committed some wrong, but undue violence was not encouraged. In the sixteenth-century manual on housekeeping, *Domostroi*, husbands were ad-

monished not to use wooden or iron rods on their wives, or to beat them about the face, ears, or abdomen, lest they cause blindness, deafness, paralysis, toothache, or miscarriage. Wives were to be beaten only in private, without anger, for a "great offense," such as disobedience or inattention. The existence of such instructions suggests that men could not be counted on to show restraint. The legal restrictions on wife-beating were considerably weaker. A husband did not have to show just cause to beat his wife. She could protest the treatment only if it were "evil" . . . or endangered her life. Under those circumstances, she was entitled to a divorce. A husband who injured his pregnant wife and caused her to miscarry was guilty of a sin, but the wife received no compensation and was not freed from the marriage. A woman could obtain a divorce if her husband threatened her economic well-being by building up massive debts, selling himself and her into slavery, or being a habitual drunkard. If the husband both committed adultery and beat his wife, she could divorce him after a warning. Neither adultery nor wife-beating alone constituted sufficient cause.

Despite this legal limitation on the wife's right to seek release from an abusive husband, surviving ecclesiastical court records indicate that women indeed did petition successfully for divorce on grounds of physical abuse. In this way, the provision in canon law to permit divorce in cases of marital rape was extended to nonsexual types of [assault].

[In 1687] a woman, Irinka, and her father, Grishka Filipov Popov, petitioned against her husband, Vedenii, and his father, Arist Kondratov. Irinka's right arm had been so injured by her husband's beatings that she could no longer work. Fearing for her life, Grishka took his daughter home. Irinka wanted to become a nun, and demanded that her husband and father-in-law buy her a cell and provide a pension. At first Arist denied beating Irinka at all; Vedenii said that he had only "instructed her because of her disobedience." Irinka's injuries, they claimed, were the result of an act of God, not their maltreatment. Neighbors testified on Irinka's behalf that she had been a chaste wife and a hard worker, and that the beating had not been warranted. Faced with this evidence, Vedenii and Arist settled out of court. It was arranged that Irinka would live apart from her husband with "good people" who would care for her injuries. Vedenii would provide her with an annual income of a measure of rye, half a measure each of millet and oats, a *pud* of salt, and four altyns for clothing. . . .

The [1683] case of Annitsa Alekseeva doch' is most notable in regard to the court's protection of women from severe domestic violence. Annitsa's husband, Vaska Kychkin, first petitioned Metropolitan Pavel of Siberia for a divorce on the grounds of her adultery; he caught her with her lover. The metropolitan, finding Vaska's evidence incontrovertible, was prepared to grant his request, but Annitsa testified that she had been living apart from Vaska for almost a year because she feared that he would murder her. Thus the metropolitan had to decide between two grounds for divorce: the wife's adultery and the husband's attempted murder. He chose the latter, indicating his view that wife abuse was the more significant and serious offense. . . .

The husband who was condemned in a divorce action did not always accept the court's ruling with equanimity, as the [1632] petition by the nun Evpraksiia attests. She appealed to Archimandrite Lavrentii of Ustiug to protect her from her former husband, Semen Kondrat'ev syn Vologzhanin. Clearly Semen was outraged by the criticism of his conduct which Evpraksiia's divorce implied. He came to the convent where she was residing, attacked Evpraksiia with a knife, and injured her severely. Although Evpraksiia did not mention forced sex, she did term her husband's attack *nasil'stvo* [rape, assault]. Semen also took her valuables; one purpose of the petition was to recover them. Two laywomen who lived in the convent abetted Semen in his attack on Evpraksiia, feeling him to be in the right. Another nun, Domnika, witnessed the crime, and ran to the metropolitan's court for help. The metropolitan's bailiffs came, took Semen's knife, and expelled him. Evpraksiia then took

refuge with her daughter and son-in-law and his father, fearing that Semen would come to the convent to attack her again. Semen found her anyway and threatened her protectors. In this case, the formulaic warnings about a life-or-death situation may well have been accurate.

Some victims of wife-beating abandoned their husbands without a formal divorce. A [1632] petition to Metropolitan Varlaam by Kuzma Ivanov syn Popov describes such a situation. Kuzma charged that his stepdaughter Aleksandra Evsiv'eva doch' Kyzemkina suffered from such ill treatment at the hands of her husband and father-in-law that she ran away. At the time he filed the complaint, Kuzma had not located his stepdaughter. Cases of runaway wives are not uncommon in the records of seventeenth-century Russian ecclesiastical courts.

It is clear that medieval Slavic society simultaneously censured rape in its legal and ecclesiastical norms and sanctioned attitudes and structures that justified it. While both ecclesiastical and secular authorities deplored the social disruption caused by rape, physical violence, and insult to women, the protection of women in subordinate positions was accorded lower priority than the preservation of the social order. For that reason, an attack on a woman of a lower class or of poor reputation was punished less severely than an attack on an aristocratic woman. It was more important to social stability to retain masters' authority over their slaves than to uphold slave women's chastity. Women were supposed to defer to their husbands and accept chastisement unless it was exceptionally brutal and unprovoked. In order to escape from an abusive marriage, de facto if not de jure a wife needed the support of her natal family. When a woman did not conduct herself in a manner appropriate to her place in society—if she insulted men, for instance, or got drunk—rape was popularly considered appropriate retaliation.

In the ecclesiastical view, rape served as evidence of evil active in the world: the uncontrolled expression of lust, which threatened the purity and ultimately the salvation of the community. Secular society regarded rape as a crime of violence, the ultimate insult against a woman and her family in a society that valued honor highly. The victim of rape might be blameless, but she was still defiled as a consequence of engaging in illicit sex, and . . . was treated as a repentant sinner. But on balance rape law and its prosecution in the courts worked to the victim's advantage. The penalties, if the victim was blameless, were substantial. The victim's prior sexual conduct, while an issue, did not imply automatic consent. The court did not assume the woman's complicity; on the contrary, the veracity of the woman's testimony was accepted until the overwhelming weight of the evidence indicated otherwise. Consequently, women could use false accusations of rape to manipulate and pressure men.

Despite the strong position of women before the law in the case of rape, in general women's autonomy was sharply constrained. Women did not appear freely in public, did not participate openly in the institutions of political power, and did not choose their own husbands. Despite women's important economic role in the family, they were socially and often physically subject to their husbands. Women had recourse against rapists because rape constituted an insult to the family's honor and a violation of public morality. A woman whose family "deserved" insult, in return for an insult given or resistance in time of war, lost her right to protection. A woman who herself violated public morality by drunkenness or adultery lost any claim to popular sympathy. Medieval Slavs accepted the use of violence by superiors against inferiors and lawbreakers; this was the natural order of a sinful world. In these societies, as in any other that authorizes violence and subordinates women to men, rapes were bound to occur.

SOURCE: Eve Levin, *Sex and Society in the World of the Orthodox Slavs, 900–1700* (Ithaca, NY: Cornell University Press, 1989), pp. 231–41, 245–6 (excerpted). Footnotes have been omitted, and transliteration modified. Copyright © 1989 Cornell University Press. Reprinted by permission of the publisher, Cornell University Press.

IV

The Imperial Period:
From Peter the Great
Through the Great Reforms

(1689–1860s)

Those of us who study the past for a living tend to devote a good deal of time to thinking about where to draw the lines separating one era of history from the next. Often these musings take on an odd tone of abstractness, since it is typically the scholarly observer who decides what constitutes a significant historical transition and what does not. Continuity and change, like beauty, are almost always in the eye of the beholder.

Occasionally the historian's job is simplified—if just a bit—by a past generation's conviction that it was creating or living in the midst of something new. Even then, it is our task to decipher what contemporaries had in mind when they employed this language, and whether their understanding of newness and discontinuity conforms to our own. But at least when historical witnesses speak of renewal or rebirth we have the modest reassurance that we are not being completely arbitrary or subjective.

For Russian history, the shift from the tsardom of seventeenth-century Muscovy to the Russian Empire of the eighteenth century constitutes just such a transition, which the powers that be loudly and insistently characterized as a renewal, virtually from scratch, of the life of their native land. Their descendants, whether they basked in the light of living in a great European empire, chafed at the oppressiveness of being a subject of the last serf-holding autocracy, or bemoaned the loss of a more spiritual past, all concurred that the passing of Muscovy into the Russian Empire had fundamentally changed the course of Russian history.

Most modern historians would qualify that judgment as being too extravagant, and a few, such as Gregory Freeze in his discussion of Russia's estate system, reject it completely. But there remains a broad scholarly consensus that the advent of the Russian Empire marked a major transition that inaugurated a new era, the imperial period, which continued in one form or another until the revolutions of 1917. Although we, too, would impose quite a few broad qualifications, we concur that the beginning of the eighteenth century marked a new period in the history of the Russian state and society.

We have attempted in Part IV to convey through our choice of topics and materials some of the dualisms that are emblematic of imperial Russian history: state and society, Russia vs. Europe, stability vs. reform, faith vs. secularity, capital vs. countryside. The themes raised in earlier sections, the focus on society, economics, politics, culture, and everyday life, are also continued here, but in a slightly different format that devotes more space to specific social groups.

Technically speaking, the empire was proclaimed only in 1721 in recognition of the Treaty of Nystadt which marked Russia's victory over Sweden at the end of the lengthy and destructive Northern War. This victory, luxuriantly celebrated in St. Petersburg with parades, odes, proclamations, and fireworks, brought Russia triumphantly into the mainstream of European politics as the major northeastern power. Conventional periodization, however, argues that the entirety of the reign of Peter the Great (1689–1725) belongs in the new era since it was Peter who was so instrumental in constructing the imperial edifice. Peter's reign initiated a series of sweeping and ambitious reforms that had an immense impact on governmental structures, state service, education, and culture, and on the lives led by the various service classes.

Symbolized by the building of the new capital of St. Petersburg, Peter's "Window on the West," and inscribed in his ambitious—and ambiguous—service law of 1722, "The Table of Ranks," the new "universal service state" transformed its service and aristocratic elites into full-time state servitors, well-bred European gentlemen, and absentee landlords. Although devoted to their religious faith, Russia's eighteenth-century rulers were determined to make the imperial state a secular one in which religion and the Orthodox church occupied a decidedly secondary position. It abolished the powerful Patriarchate of the Orthodox Church and replaced it in 1721 with the Holy Synod, a branch of the government answerable to the emperor. Over time the state seized the extensive lands of Russia's monasteries, and it harnessed the parish clergy to act as local record-keepers and readers of the law. Over the century and a half that separated Muscovy and the Great Reforms, these and other institutions evolved so far away from their Muscovite past that those who worked within them could hardly believe how different they were from their ancestors.

Still, we would do well to resist the temptation of becoming so dazzled by the dizzying pace of reform during the "Petrine Revolution" and beyond that we lose sight of the many features of Russian society standing outside of the state's boundless will to organize and reform. Life for some groups changed almost beyond recognition, but in many ways Russian subjects in the eighteenth and first half of the nineteenth centuries lived not all that differently from their sixteenth- and seventeenth-century forebears. Russia remained as a landlord–peasant society in which a small number of privileged and titled servitors owned land that was worked by multitudes of unfree peasants. As before, authority in Russian society was organized along sharply patriarchal lines. The government maintained—indeed reinforced—its autocratic character with an emperor who was as much the sovereign as the Muscovite tsars had been, but without having to deal with a zemskii sobor (the periodic summoning of representatives of Muscovite society to discuss and sanction state policies) or a boyar duma, both of which had gone out of existence in the seventeenth century.

Within the new capital of St. Petersburg, the informal networks of aristocratic families, which Nancy Shields Kollman and Robert Crummey discussed in earlier sections, continued to wield immense influence in defending the interests of their clans and its clients. Outside of the capital, in spite of numerous palliative reforms, governmental institutions remained understaffed, primitive, and far removed from one another. Most eighteenth-century Russian subjects saw governmental officials only a few times in their lives, and then usually under disagreeable circumstances.

Just how effectively the state intervened in the everyday lives of most people, or in the calculations made in various corners of the society concerning life, work, family, and survival, remain open questions in the historical literature. On the one hand, the state surely did an aggressive and generally effective job of collecting taxes, gathering recruits for the military draft, and putting down disturbances. It also established definitive limits beyond which community autonomy could not go. To give an obvious example, the serfs did not have the choice of becoming free on their own, even if they rarely saw a governmental official or a landlord. Moreover, service, and cosmopolitan life more generally, underwent a radical transformation in the imperial period, almost all of which had its origins in governmental policy.

On the other hand, Arcadius Kahan reminds us of a basic truth when he observes, "For the overwhelming majority of the inhabitants of . . . Russia, the rhythm of life was determined not by the wars or reforms of Peter the Great, nor by anything his successors managed to accomplish or failed to do, but by the conditions of the agricultural cycle of plowing, planting, and harvesting the Russian fields." As we read through these selections we might want to ask ourselves how these two truths could coexist in one society.

14

The State and Political Structure
of Imperial Russia

The principle of service had become an essential feature of rulership already in Kievan Rus' and Muscovy. The Muscovite law codes of the late fifteenth, sixteenth, and seventeenth centuries had made service to the tsar compulsory for serving men, even for those who held patrimonial (*votchina*) estates instead of land gained as part of a life-tenure service contract (*pomest'e*). During the eighteenth and nineteenth centuries, the principle of service remained as a fundamental feature of the relationship between ruler and ruled, but it underwent a number of radical revisions.

Although we have chosen not to dwell in this text on the age-old issue of whether Peter the Great was a "revolutionary" tsar, Peter's immense impact on Russia's service system is simply undeniable. Certainly many—perhaps most—of his policies had their roots in changes that began long before he came to power. But the basic framework for the new imperial service state unquestionably took shape while Peter sat on the throne. Wisely or not, Peter abolished the old chanceries (*Prikazy*) of professional but non-noble administrators, and he replaced them with administrative colleges run by nobles via a principle of collective administration. He accepted the passing of the old and immensely confusing system of precedence (*mestnichestvo*) and endeavored to replace it with a system of his own (which, alas, turned out to be no less confusing). He accelerated the professionalization of the armed services by introducing a draft, various service academies for prospective officers, and by expanding the number of standing regiments.

During Peter's reign service became a full-time, expensive, and nominally lifelong responsibility carried out in Moscow or the new capital of St. Petersburg. Where Kievan and Muscovite serving men served the person of the grand prince or tsar, their descendants in the imperial period served the impersonal state. This shift to *state* service was embodied in legislation that was designed to systematize his reforms, most notably the Table of Ranks of 1722. In the process he abolished most of the dozens of grades and titles, such as "boyar," and "boyar's children," that had defined the Russian service elite, and he replaced them with the simple model of hereditary and lifetime nobility. Peter had convinced himself that he was engaged in creating something brand new, and with the assistance of an unceasing barrage of sermons, celebrations, speeches, fireworks displays, and the like, he convinced others that Russia was now reborn as an imperial state.

The administrative framework and system of taxation that Peter crystallized was more or less in place by the time of his death in 1725, and in spite of a short-term backlash among certain elements of the nobility, especially during the decade of the 1730s, Peter the Great's new imperial model of the state was never seriously threatened over the ensuing two centuries of Russian history. Indeed, it is remarkable to see how quickly the population adapted to Peter's system, to trace how Peter's reputation soared among the population after his death, and to witness the many ways in which the imperial state prospered. Tax revenues continued to expand, the number of servitors grew several times over, and the institutions that grew up to produce educated and capable serving men seemed to satisfy the needs of the state. As a military power the Russian Empire emerged as a formidable force on land and sea, and, notwithstanding some spectacular losses on the battlefield, it ultimately proved victorious in every war it fought until its defeat during the Crimean War of the 1850s. In a world in which governments equated winning wars with defending the nation and keeping it free, such a remarkable string of victories served to nourish the legitimacy of Russian absolutism over several generations.

Thus, from the perspective of state-building, the imperial state was, all things considered, a major success. Russia was stable, strong, and large, and the right of its emperors to govern their domain met very few challenges. How such a high degree of stability was maintained, and at what costs, will be the subject of several of the selections in this chapter. How, for example did the state keep the nobility from mounting any serious challenges to its authority when, as before, the state relied upon the nobility to run the armed forces and bureaucracy, and to keep the countryside quiet?

Still, government and politics did undergo innumerable changes between Peter the Great and the Great Reforms, and most of these reflected the government's perpetual worry over of its own vulnerability. Most people lived in the countryside, and for them government was often ad hoc, far away, and arbitrary. Periodic cossack-led popular rebellions continued through the eighteenth century, culminating in the massive Pugachev revolt of the early 1770s. These revealed just how ungoverned the countryside really was, and the central government found itself in need of new legislative and administrative measures to remedy the situation. Moreover, the Table of Ranks and the college system never worked as intended, in large measure because family networks among the service nobility kept subverting them to their own advantage. Therefore, they too required constant legislative fine tuning to bring them back to their original purpose of creating a noble-based, educated, and professional service corps. Perhaps the most confusing episode in this *pas de deux* between state and nobility occurred in 1762 when the emperor, Peter III, issued a law freeing the nobility from compulsory service.

In the nineteenth century, the college system was finally abandoned in favor of state ministries headed by a single minister, the system employed in most European states then and now. The reign of Alexander I (1801–25) witnessed several unrequited flirtations with constitutionalism on the part of the emperor, but only Poland and Finland came to be ruled through a written constitution. For the rest of the Russian empire the movement toward bureaucratic expansion and centralization of authority remained in force through the reign of Nicholas I (1825–55). Interestingly, this more hierarchical style of governing arose alongside a growing professionalization of the administrative cadre, and their divorce from the immediate interests of the nobility. As we shall see in Section C of this chapter, it was the conservative and repressive rule of Nicholas I that gave rise to the corps of progressive men of state for whom major reform in pursuit of openness, justice, freedom, and civic participation became a top priority.

A. The Imperial Service State

DOCUMENTS

The Table of Ranks of All Grades: Military, Administrative, and Court . . . (January 24, 1722)

This important statute, issued near the end of Peter the Great's reign, embodied Peter's striving to establish an alternative to the old system of *mestnichestvo*, or precedence, that had been abolished forty years earlier. The terms of the law expressed new definitions of nobility and opened up new avenues of achieving it. Most important, the Table formally introduced the principle of merit in affixing rank, status, and to a certain extent nobility.

The Table of Ranks never quite worked as Peter had intended, and it raised enormous unanticipated confusions in deciding the relative weight of merit and lineage in establishing noble identity. The following passages constitute an abbreviated version of the complete Table. Subsequent legislation from the eighteenth and nineteenth centuries, moreover, modified the Table and even adjusted the grades at which nobility could be gained. But the Table itself remained in force as a basic service text for nearly two centuries.

———————

To the Table of Ranks enumerated [here] we add the following points, which explain how one is obliged to act within each rank: . . .

3. Those who demand honors higher than their own ranks, or themselves occupy such a position, must pay a fine of two-month's pay for each infraction. But if he is serving without a salary, then he is obliged to pay a fine equiv-

alent to the salaries of those who occupy the same grade and are currently on salary. . . .

7. All wives shall have ranks according to the grades of their husbands, and when they behave in a contrary manner then they shall pay a fine comparable to what their husbands would pay for such an infraction.

8. Although We [already] allow . . . free entry in public assembly in the vicinity of the Court to the sons of Princes, Counts, Barons, the most distinguished Nobles and servitors of the most distinguished rank of the Russian State ahead of others of lower ranks, We of our own will wish to see that they be distinguished from others in all circumstances as befits their dignity. However, We shall proffer no rank to those who have rendered no service to Us and the fatherland, or who have received testimony to their character. . . .

11. All servitors, Russian and foreign, who occupy the first eight ranks, or who have in fact done so: their legitimate children and descendants in perpetuity are to be granted equal honors to the best Nobility of yore in all their dignity and advantages, although they might be of a lower kind and have never previously been elevated to Noble status or granted a coat of arms by a Crowned Head. . . .

13. Since grades in civil administration have not previously been decreed, and no one, or few people, had been honored for it . . ., [and since] necessity now demands [that they receive] higher grades: for this reason [it is ordered] to take suitable people even if they have no grade at all. But since this will be insulting to people [who are] in military service, who have devoted many years to such harsh service, and who see people with no service receiving an equal or higher grade: for this reason he who is granted a grade must serve for

	Military Grades		
Class	Navy	Army	Civil Grades
1	Admiral-General	Generalissimus; Field Marshal	Chancellor or High Privy Councillor
2	Admiral	General of: Artillery, Cavalry, & Infantry	High Privy Councillor
3	Vice-Admiral	Lieutenant-General	Privy Councillor; Procurator General
4	Rear Admiral	Major General	High State Councillor; Presidents of the Colleges
5	Commodore-Captain	Brigadier	State Councillor
6	Captain, First Rank	Colonel	Councillor in the Colleges; Chief Judges of Guberniia Courts
7	Captain, Second Rank	Lieutenant Colonel	Councillors in the Upper Courts
8	Fleet Lieutenant-Captain; Captain Third Rank	Major	Assessors (Vice Councillor) of the Colleges
9	Fleet Lieutenant; Artillery Lieutenant-Captain	Captain	Titular Councillor
10	Artillery Lieutenant	Staff Captain	College Secretary
11	—	—	Senate Secretary
12	Ensign; Warrant Officer	Lieutenant	Guberniia Secretary
13	Artillery Constable	Second Lieutenant	Senate Registrar
14	—	Ensign	College Registrar

several years in order to achieve the appropriate rank. . . .

15. Whoever has served in military grades up to the level of commissioned officer but is not a Nobleman shall, upon achieving the above-mentioned grade, become a Nobleman himself, as do his children who are born during his service as a Commissioned officer. However, if he has no children during that time, but he had some previously, and the father so petitions, then Nobility shall be granted to one son only, for whom the father shall make a request. The offspring of those who hold other grades, in both civil and court service, whose Ranks are not from the Nobility, shall not become Nobles.

18. Those who have been dismissed from service for committing grave crimes shall be punished in public on an open square, even if they are only stripped or tortured, they shall be deprived of their rightful title and rank.

SOURCE: *Polnoe sobranie zakonov rossiiskoi imperii* Vol. VI, No. 3890, pp. 486–93 (excerpted). Translated by Gary Marker.

Manifesto Freeing the Nobility from Compulsory Service (1762)

Peter III had been on the Russian throne for only six months in 1762 when he was assassinated in a Palace coup engineered by the Izmailovskii regiment on behalf of his wife, Catherine. His brief reign nevertheless produced several important pieces of legislation, none more remarkable than this one. From the day it was proclaimed, the Manifesto on Noble Service generated controversy and confusion, and, to this day, historians have been unable to reach a consensus, either about the reasoning behind the law or about its consequences. Did the metropolitan nobility want to be freed from the requirement to serve? If so, did they actually leave service once given the opportunity? Alternatively, did the autocracy want to free itself from a noble stranglehold over the service system? And if so, did this manifesto achieve the desired result?

In his everlasting glory, the most wise monarch, gracious sovereign, Our grandfather Peter the Great, the Emperor of All Russia, was obliged to bear such a [heavy] burden and [carry out] so many labors solely for the well being and benefit of his fatherland, while [at the same time] uplifting Russia to a complete understanding of military, civil, and political affairs. To all of this the whole of Europe, and also a large part of the world, bears true witness.

But this renewal required, above all, inculcating and showing the nobility, as the leading member in the state, how great are the advantages of [living under] an enlightened power in the welfare of humanity as against the innumerable peoples who are mired in the depths of ignorance. Then, at that very time, extreme circumstances obliged [him], as a symbol of his kindness, to order the Russian nobility to engage in military and civil service; and, above and beyond that, to educate their offspring in the various free sciences, and also in a number of useful arts, [all of] which sent them to European states. For that very same reason, he established various schools in Russia itself in order to achieve the desired fruits with all due speed.

It is true that such establishments initially seemed burdensome and unbearable to the nobility—depriving them of rest, taking them away from their homes, continuing against their wishes military and other forms of service, and inscribing their children in the [ranks]. Some nobles concealed themselves, subjecting themselves not just to fines, but even the deprivation of their property, for neglecting their own well being and that of their descendants. . . .

And therefore, taking these circumstances into consideration, by the authority bestowed upon Us from on high, in Our highest Imperial mercy, from this time forward unto eternity and to all generations to come, We grant to the entire Russian hereditary nobility their freedom and liberty. They may continue to serve either in Our empire or in other European powers allied to us, with the following stipulations.

1. All nobles who are currently in various branches of service may continue to serve as long as they wish and as long as their circumstances permit them. However, during campaigns or for a period beginning three months prior to them, military servitors dare not request retirement or leave from service. But at [a campaign's] conclusion, whether it be within or outside of the [borders of] the state, those who are in military service may request of their commanding officers release from service or retirement, and they may expect a resolution. Those who occupy the first eight ranks in each of Our branches of service [are released] by Our own supreme confirmation, and other ranks shall receive their disposition from the departments to which they belong. . . .

4. Whoever is in retirement from our service and wishes to depart for other European states

"The Mounted Grenadier," woodcut from the mid-eighteenth century, depicting a Russian officer after having undergone the full Europeanization of the Petrine reforms. The text, in the old Muscovite script, speaks of the grenadier "faithfully serving his fatherland." The face and bearing have a striking resemblance to the comtemporary image of Peter the Great.

is to receive the appropriate passport from Our College of Foreign Affairs without difficulty, with the stipulation that, when necessity requires it, those nobles who find themselves abroad are to return to the fatherland. When the appropriate announcement is made on this matter, then in that instance every nobleman shall with all deliberate speed execute our will, under penalty of sequestering his property.

5. Those Russian nobles who choose to continue their service in other European countries may, upon returning to their own fatherland, fill vacant positions in Our service according to their wishes and abilities. . . .

8. Those nobles who are currently serving as soldiers and other lower grades below commissioned officer . . . may not retire with the exception of those who have maintained their service for more than twelve years.

9. But as We decree this Our most merciful arrangement on behalf of the whole of the hereditary nobility for all time as a fundamental and unalterable law, then, in conclusion of this, We by Our Imperial word most solemnly declare that We will maintain this to be sacred and unbreakable forever more. . . . Our lawful descendants may not annul this in any way, for the preservation of this, Our legal ruling, shall stand as an unwavering support of the sovereign all-Russian throne.

We nevertheless hope that the whole of the hereditary Russian nobility, having felt something of Our generosity toward them and their descendants, will be moved by their own most loyal faithfulness and zeal not to abandon or hide themselves from service, but to enter into it eagerly and willingly, and to continue in it honorably and without disgrace to the utmost extent possible. And it is no less important that they educate their children in appropriate subjects with diligence and enthusiasm.

Since there are those who have had no service anywhere, but have simply passed all their time in idleness and inactivity, and have not instructed their children in these useful subjects in the interest of the fatherland, and thereby have not been mindful of the general good, We order all Our truly loyal and true sons of the fatherland to scorn and demean them; and further they shall not be tolerated at Our court or at public gatherings and celebrations.

SOURCE: *Polnoe sobranie zakonov rossiiskoi imperii*, No. 11,444, pp. 912–15, February 18, 1762 (excerpted). Translated by Gary Marker.

LITERATURE

HELJU BENNETT
Russia's System of Ranks and Orders

By the latter half of the seventeenth century, much of the old method of inscription, especially the arcane system of precedence (*mestnichestvo*), had lost its monopoly over defining the world of service, even if, as Robert Crummey demonstrated, the old aristocratic families remained as a durable force. The Table of Ranks constituted a first step in reconstructing the service system, the mechanism of ranking (denoted in the laws by the term "*chin*"), and the definition of status on a new basis. Helju Bennett's essay analyzes the most important features of the Table and its place in the overall evolution of the Russian state. She suggests that it was one part of a much larger agenda to organize the whole of Russian society into a series of legally constituted categories of people, or *sosloviia*.

Peter the Great promulgated a law in 1722 which is usually referred to as the Table of Ranks. Scholars have long considered it important, recognizing, for instance, that with its promulgation the status of the Russian upper classes, the structure of the Imperial bureaucracy, and even the ideas of merit and service inherited from the Muscovite past were changed. . . . The fundamental meaning of the Table of Ranks, as well as its consequences, can be better understood, I think, when it is viewed in the context of an evolving, complex, and peculiarly Russian institution, the *chin* system, or system of rank ordering and niche assignment. . . .

I

Peter promulgated the Table of Ranks law some quarter of a century after his journeys abroad and after he had already effected important changes in methods of recruiting the army and collecting taxes, in the curriculum taught in schools, and in the organization of government institutions and social classes. . . .

Imperial architecture: photograph of the arch of the General Staff Building, St. Petersburg, overlooking Palace Square.

"The Listing of offices, and what ranks any office is to have, and which offices are equal to which, and what grade (rank) any official is to have, and who among officials at one particular level of office list, according to seniority, is entitled to be promoted to higher offices" must be considered against this background. . . .

What is important about the rank ordering of offices is that it brought most of the functions and activities of the state into a formal, definable, and quantifiable relationship to the Emperor, who in Russian tradition was the source of all law. Further, by assigning all state offices to a relatively limited range of fourteen levels, the Table of Ranks made easily understandable the relationship of all offices to every other office. Offices at levels 1 and 2, for instance, could clearly be seen to be better than lower-level offices; their numbers immediately indicated their proximity to the Emperor. And the rank ordering provided a system of earned rewards, where appointment to each level in the ascending scale or ladder was the predictable result of duties performed in a prescribed way. This is indicated by the fact that Peter required that neophytes in state service first hold offices at lower levels.

Obviously, top-level offices could not remain vacant until officials had qualified by a process of step by step promotion. Peter in fact did not observe the stipulation that promotion to each level of office was a reward for service in a lower level; he did, however, try to salvage the orderliness of the system by allowing direct appointments to high offices in cases of necessity and then on the condition that officials so appointed remain in their offices for a specified time. He also provided for appointments to high offices of men who had served in the government before the ranking of offices established by the Table of Ranks, using their records or time spent in state service as justification.

One aspect of the rewards accruing to the ranking of offices was the grading of persons . . . which gave social prerogatives and honor. Since in Peter's time a [grade] could be obtained in a number of ways—for instance, by birth (as was the case for princes of the blood), by time spent in office, or because of skills or actions valued by the Emperor—it did not need to correspond to the level of office one had. . . .

The social preference and legal rights that eventually became dependent on possessions of *chin* were spelled out in the Table of Ranks, and thus the Table of Ranks law itself constituted a kind of charter of prerogatives of *chin* possessors or graded men. It provided that men with grades, their wives and their unmarried daughters were to have "precedence rights," i.e., rights to the most deference and the best seats on all "public occasions," which included, according to the law, "gatherings in churches, at the mass, at court ceremonials, ambassadorial audiences . . . and similar public gatherings." Where persons were to stand and sit on such public occasions was determined by their official grades and the length of time the grade had been possessed. The kind of clothing one could wear on these occasions was also dictated by grade. . . .

The most important reward of *chin* . . . stated that men who had earned *ober* officer's grade in the military service and grade 8 and above in the civil service were to be considered nobles. . . . This meant that they were exempted from the labor burdens and taxes that were levied upon the lower social strata. This reward of grade also had consequences for the children. The child born after the father had attained the grade of ennoblement shared the newly attained legal status of his father, while the child born before could share the family's new legal status only if the Emperor granted him access to it in response to a petition by the father. Even so, the father could petition on behalf of one non-noble son. The men who received grades 9 and lower in the civil service were entitled to the prerogatives of noble status, but their rights could not be passed on to their children. The category of these men was that of non-heritable nobility, a status usually translated as "personal" nobility. . . .

The *chin* system was created, I think, to solve problems that developed when Peter attempted to undertake the diversity of tasks or work done in western countries in a more "backward," institutionally less complex and less wealthy Russia. The institutions that Peter created could be considered "western" or modern from the point of view of a French or German observer of the day. From the Russian point of view the work that these institutions organized simply constituted new obligations that society had to fulfill. Peter did not simply define the tasks that Russia as a contemporary state had to fulfill but assigned them to arbitrarily chosen social groups. Indeed, this way of getting work done in Russia was ancient, so that what Peter did in the end was merely to re-form and rearrange, but not abolish the old system. . . .

When Peter began to govern in his own right, Russia was already a "service state," in which the most important social groups were obligated to render labor and services . . . to the autocracy. The practical result of this was the construction of a system legally compartmentalizing individuals, the *soslovija* . . . system, in which human beings were organized into groups to perform various functions. The group in which an individual happened to belong determined the kind of work, or in lieu of that, taxes or dues, that he rendered the state and defined the limits of his autonomy and choices of activities. . . . In Russian legal codes . . . some categories of this system were referred to as *chiny*, whose meanings of place in a rank ordering system and grade in a personal niche assignment system we have been discussing. This system of assigning persons to categories or levels by birth or tradition, or compulsorily ascribing roles to persons, was a taxation system for a backward land, one which made predictable the delivery of manpower and goods for military purposes to the autocratic state. . . . (I)n Peter's day the system of compulsory subordination of persons and groups to state service was not completed. Some groups were assigned their "roles" by birth and tradition, while other groups in society were still "free," i.e., had a degree of freedom to choose between alternative social roles. . . . If any group could be considered fully bound in Peter's day it was the peasantry. It was bound to the land by the tradition of serfdom, to the authority of the lord by ownership, and to other members of the peasant community by the institution of the *mir* [peasant commune]. . . .

Compared to the peasantry, the categories of merchants, priests, and various townsmen in the stratified social structures were more "free." The roles they were assigned—carrying out the tasks of trading, praying, informing, etc.—were not strictly hereditary, and the institutions that supervised their performance were relatively flexible and even "self- administered". . . But though these groups were relatively free, the fact remains that their tasks were supervised, i.e., their obligations were institutionalized. If members of these groups in the middle failed to fulfill their tasks, their goods and livelihood could be forfeited. Furthermore, they could be made to bear the burdens of the peasantry, namely, recruitment into the army and payment of poll taxes. . . .

The nobility was the least subordinated social group before Peter's day. Its service could

be fulfilled seasonally, and the *pomestie* [non-inheritable land grants] system of rewarding a noble's work for the state with land could be considered a *quid pro quo* or contractual arrangement. Moreover, what supervisory institutions there were exercised minimal control. . . . But this was a condition that Peter changed radically. Having founded a permanent army and civil service, he demanded lifelong service from the nobility, a burden inevitably resisted. To make the nobility conform was a problem that he tried to solve in different ways. . . . But, most consistently, he resorted to beating and branding to enforce the nobility's compliance. These methods did not get the desired results.

The use of physical coercion not only increased the need for manpower —beatings required beaters—but also disabled the men who were to serve. . . . To escape the paradoxical results that the large scale use of violence would have produced and yet to still "force" the nobility to serve, to make it volunteer for "hard and dangerous work" for which he could not hope to pay adequately, was the problem that Peter . . . solved . . . by instituting the rank ordering of offices and grading of persons. . . .

The practical effect of . . . a provision for ennoblement [through one's own service] was that the socially unfixed or 'free-floating' groups found a category in the *soslovija* system by climbing the rungs of state offices or earning grades and that in the end no group remained "outside" of the large ascription system. . . . For most people . . . it was the *soslovie* into which one was born, or inherited status, that prescribed one's role. In fact, it was usually expressly forbidden to leave it at will. Rarely could a nobleman become a priest, or a priest become a nobleman, or a merchant undertake a nobleman's functions. It was impossible, in particular, for a peasant to gain a "permit" to leave his burdened estate and assume a place in the social categories through which he could gain access to noble status. In sum, only those who had been assigned to the functions of the nobility either by virtue of *soslovie* status or by direct Imperial action could undertake the work through which noble status could be earned. . . .

The fundamental impact of the *chin* system on Russia's further development derives from the way it extended the power of the autocrat. While an assignment of status by niche existed in Muscovite times, it was a niche that one had a right to, determined by service and heredity; now the "right to place" was imprinted upon the entire nobility by virtue of office and grade earned, i.e., one's right to a niche or a place in the world came from the autocrat. By arrogating to the state not only the power to rank offices and to assign any state function to a level on a chart, but also the power to render each individual his due by assigning him a "grade," Peter really extended the state's authority to deal with matters of deciding claims of social usefulness and indirectly estimating personal worth. In making use of the state's power to regulate social distance between people, he extended the state's power regulating human behavior, even in such matters as dress, one aspect of an area of conduct that elsewhere was increasingly enforced by mores and rules of etiquette and habits of politeness. . . .

The behavioral restrictions and terms of competition prescribed by the *chin* system, accepted for whatever reason by the nobility, eventually became so assimilated by it that those who behaved in consonance with the rules did not seem to think of them as emanating from laws; grades that determined not only official and government-related prerogatives but also norms of private acceptability became thought of as categories in which the world worked. As early as the eighteenth century, Russian authors began to use a vocabulary derived from the *chin* system . . . to describe individuals and social relationships. . . . [In] "The Nose" by Nikolay Gogol, written about the middle of the nineteenth century . . . [the] hero . . . is a Collegial Assessor who arrives in St. Petersburg from the Caucasus in order to find a new post equal to his "grade." Gogol's explicit labeling of his character immediately alerts the reader familiar with *chin* lore that he is an official in the civil service who acquired

his *chin* by serving in an area of the empire where promotion was easy, requiring little or no education. That he is a snob and social climber is evident from the fact that he insists on using a military title rather than the equivalent title in the civilian hierarchy; the military title gives him social precedence over those who possess the civilian title. The plot turns on the hero's nose running away and assuming the accoutrements and prerogatives of an official ranked higher than it. The nose makes social and official calls in official regalia, claims service in branches of government inaccessible to the Collegial Assessor or major (as he prefers to call himself), and snubs its owner. There are many references to the *chin* code: "place," things not "fitting ranked offices," honor to be yielded to rank, remarks that while "personal insult might be forgiven, insults to rank cannot be," etc. The story can be considered a satire on the *chin* system, and, as such, one can say that Gogol's "message" is that a chunk of mindless flesh if dressed in the uniform of an official could go about without people noticing that it is not human. In more philosophical terms, the story can be seen as an imaginative speculation on the power of symbols to affect human behavior, and indeed shows that symbolizing can endow insensate things with life. . . .

II

The second period of the evolution of *chin* began with Catherine the Great's promulgation of the Charter of Nobility in 1785. . . . Fundamentally, the Charter recognized the "honor and inviolability" of the nobility. . . . In effect, the nobleman could no longer be dis-nobled or demoted to another *soslovie*, nor could he be beaten. . . . He could not be arbitrarily exiled or have his properties confiscated. If accused of a crime, he had a right to predictable treatment in law, a kind of due process, and he had to be tried in a court of his peers. Besides these rights of personal inviolability, he gained some other personal rights, such as the right to passports . . . and the right to choose his profession. The Russian nobleman also was granted some civil rights, for example, a right to private property. . . . A new political right, after a fashion, was the right to "assemble," to form corporate bodies or associations that were empowered to deal with *soslovie* problems. . . . The Russian nobility was granted explicitly and clearly a "right to service" and a "right to *chin*.". . . As far as the nobility was concerned, the obligation to serve was finally completely abrogated; serving became instead a kind of a "reward," and the autocrat in 1785 showed special honor to the nobility by reserving to it the "right" to serve. Since the rewards for service remained grades and the social prerogatives attached to them, grades became quite naturally the preserve of the nobility, i.e., grades became the nobility's *soslovie* rights. This was a change indeed; the burdens of the nobility of 1722 had evolved by 1785 into its perquisites and privileges.

Such a radical restructuring of the nobility's rights implied a fundamental change for the whole *soslovija* structure. For practical purposes, one level or category of the Russian *soslovija* was no longer subject to the laws governing the others. The nobility had no obligations, while the remaining categories were stratified, as before, according to the quantity and degree of difficulty of the obligations imposed on them. . . . The nobility also had rights while the other *soslovija* did not. . . .

At the very time that the autocrat granted a Charter to the nobility, it issued what amounted to partial charters to several other *soslovija*. In the Charter of Towns (1785), the autocrat gave, for example, the [merchantry] and some artists and academicians some "nobles' rights". . . . Most importantly for our purposes, some categories were also given a "right to government service" and a "right to *chin*.". . . The extension of "rights" to new levels of society changed the very principles by which Russian society was stratified, and hence its structure. In the years from 1785 to 1830 Russian society became more complex since some groups were stratified on the basis of obligations, others on the basis of rights (the no-

bility), and yet others on the basis of some exemptions as well as some rights. . . .

From our vantage point, it is possible to see that during the period from 1785 to 1861 the interaction of *chin* laws with *soslovija* laws made it difficult, even impossible, for some individuals to survive as "human beings." In so far as *chin* laws increased human problems and social conflict, they were more than obsolete, they were decadent. More ominous for the state was the fact that by routinizing social mobility, *chin* began to dissolve the *soslovija* order itself by continually increasing the number of subcategories within *soslovija* and the number of men within the subcategories. The *soslovija* order, however, was still fundamental to life in Russia and had to be maintained because it made predictable the supply of goods, human beings, and administrative talent to the autocracy.

SOURCE: Helju Aulik Bennett, "Evolution of the Meanings of Chin: An Introduction to the Russian Institution of Rank Ordering and Niche Assignment from the Time of Peter the Great's Table of Ranks to the Bolshevik Revolution," *California Slavic Studies* X (1977):1–35 (excerpted). Reprinted by Permission of the University of California Press.

GREGORY FREEZE

The Soslovie *(Estate) Paradigm and Russian Social History*

Most scholars are in agreement with Helju Bennett's premise that imperial Russian society, both by law and by practice, came to be divided into a series of *soslovia* which defined the privileges and obligations of all subjects of the Emperor on the basis of their membership in a specific estate. In this provocative essay Gregory Freeze puts forth a very different point of view by suggesting that *soslovia* were not the principal defining categories of social groups, either for the state or for the society during the century and a half between Peter the Great and the Great Reforms. Although his challenge to the accepted view has not been widely embraced, he has at least forced us to recognize that the organization and legal categories of Russia's population may have been much more fluid and complex than we think.

In a series of lectures delivered nearly a century ago, Vasilii O. Kliuchevskii, the dean of prerevolutionary Russian historians, complained that scholars had studied particular groups in Russia but not the larger social structure. Since then historians have written many more studies of specific groups but have yet to reconsider traditional assumptions and ideas about prerevolutionary Russian society that still pervade the historiography. . . .

At the core of prerevolutionary historiography is a cluster of ideas about Russia's peculiar system of "estates" (*sosloviia*; in the singular, *soslovie*) and their development in the eighteenth and nineteenth centuries. The traditional conception of the social structure posited the existence of four main estates (nobility, clergy, townspeople, and peasantry)—a model not unlike the formal structure of medieval Europe. Such a simple system, which seemed logical enough in preindustrial Russia, enjoyed widespread acceptance in both scholarly and popular writings. To quote one historian-journalist, writing in 1859, "Every estate has its own role in the state: the clergy pray, the nobles serve in war and peace, the peasants plow and feed the people, and the merchants are the means that provide each with what it needs." The idea of four estates was, moreover, explicitly recognized in Russian law—above all, in the *Digest of Laws* published in 1832, the first new law code in Russia in nearly two centuries. But broader popularization of the concept of four estates did not come until somewhat later, chiefly through the "state school" of Russian historiography, which emerged in the mid-nineteenth century and formulated many of the basic conceptions that have dominated the field ever since. Most striking here is the notion that Russian estates

developed very differently from their nominal peers in the West: they appeared much later (in the eighteenth century—just as estates were dissolving in Western Europe) and represented not a medieval legacy but a social order consciously established by the all-powerful state. . . .

This essay seeks to reexamine the *soslovie* paradigm—first, by investigating the conception and development of the term *soslovie* and, second, by studying its application to Russian social history. It will be argued here that the modern notion of *soslovie* arose only in the early nineteenth century, that the estate system was dynamic and still actively developing (not disintegrating) in the nineteenth century, and that the resilience of this social order contravenes the customary assumption of an inexorable transition from estate to class in postreform and revolutionary Russia. . . .

Pre-Petrine Russia knew neither *soslovie* (in the sense of estate) nor its equivalent, for the social structure consisted of numerous, small groups and lacked collective terms for legal aggregation. The complicated social terminology of Muscovite Russia is highly suggestive of its social complexity. One lexicon for the period records nearly five hundred separate social categories to denote different ranks and statuses. . . . The most prominent and distinct social category was the *chin* (rank), but it applied only to the privileged service classes, not the rest of society, and, significantly enough, even the privileged classes lacked a collective name. Splintered into a plethora of categories, hierarchically ranked by a system of precedence (*mestnichestvo*), the military and service classes hardly represented a cohesive, unified social stratum. . . .

This "orderless order" changed substantially between the late seventeenth and early nineteenth centuries, generating significant alterations in terminology and conceptualization. The traditional *chin*, to be sure, did not suddenly disappear. Rather, it initially acquired broader meaning (to encompass larger social categories) and remained the term most often used until the 1760s, even recurring sporadically thereafter. But *chin* plainly did not suffice to express the notion of larger estates, partly because of its traditional restriction to ecclesiastical and secular service classes, partly because of its newer usage in the Petrine Table of Ranks, and partly because it denoted specifically the male servitor but not his dependants. . . .

By the last quarter of the eighteenth century, however, the traditional meaning of *chin*, or of newer concoctions, was superseded by two terms that were used in formal law for the duration of the imperial period: *sostoianie* and *zvanie*. Although both these words remained current and could even be employed interchangeably, *sostoianie* became the more prominent term. At first it needed to connote little more than "condition" or "status," with no legal attribution to a particular group, but eventually it came to denote "legal status group" and to refer to any social category, privileged or otherwise. The word's predominance persisted, especially in formal governmental usage, where it remained the basic legal term until the end of the *ancien regime*.

But, even as *sostoianie* acquired predominance in formal law, it had to compete with *soslovie*, a term far more pregnant in semantic potential and significance. The etymology and lexical history of this word provide significant information on the history of social structure and thought in prerevolutionary Russia. Although the meaning of its root has been the subject of some disagreement, the word initially connoted nothing more than "gathering" or "assembly," a social collectivity with no hint of formal organization. It was in this vague sense of assembly that the term appeared until the last third of the eighteenth century. Toward the end of that century, however, it developed a more abstract connotation, referring not merely to "assembly" in the narrower sense but also to "organized society" or "community." Over the next several decades the connotation of "community" broadened, so that *soslovie* acquired the supplementary meaning of "society" in the sense of a formal social organization with a distinct body of members.

That additional meaning led to a semantic breakthrough in the first decade of the nineteenth century, when the term also came to denote "constituted body" and "legal estate." *Soslovie*, to mean a "constituted body," was applied literally to formal governmental institutions—for example, to the Senate and even to the quasi-parliamentary institutions proposed by Mikhail M. Speranskii, who combined the notions of "assembly" and "constituted body" in an effort to describe what he wanted to create. Concomitantly, *soslovie* also appeared, in unofficial usage, in the sense of a legal, formally constituted estate. . . .

This usage of *soslovie* applied most accurately to townspeople and the nobility, who in fact possessed such status and organization after the 1785 Catherinean reforms. But usage steadily broadened, and by the 1820s *soslovie* could be applied to all social groups, not only the four main estates but also other distinctive social categories. By 1847 *soslovie* as a term for a legal estate had appeared in an Academy of Sciences dictionary, which defined the word as "a category of people with a specific occupation, distinguished from others by their special rights and obligations." Although rarely used in formal law, *soslovie* had nonetheless entered the vocabulary of educated people by the 1840s and 1850s, chiefly through the influence of the state school, which superimposed on the conception of a legal estate its own special views on state and social development.

But the term continued to acquire new connotations—in particular, an overtone of "caste," which emphasized the endogamous and cultural separateness that significantly deepened differences in legal status. Indeed, by the 1860s, when Vladimir I. Dal' composed his classic dictionary of the Russian language, he felt obliged to include "caste" as one of the defining words in his entry on *soslovie*. That additional connotation, distinctly pejorative, emerged in the very midst of the Great Reforms, when state and society sought to regenerate Russia and to eliminate all that impeded its growth and development. As the reformers made their comparisons between Russia and Western Europe, it is hardly surprising that they cast a critical eye on hereditary *sosloviia.* As they sought the gradual dismantlement of this social order, *soslovie* reached the final stage in its semantic development, becoming the primary descriptive term for the social system in late imperial Russia. . . .

[T]he lexical history of *soslovie* suggests that some traditional assumptions about the state's role need to be reconsidered. As the amorphous and shifting development of legal terminology shows, the state's social policy and thought were essentially unsystemic before the early nineteenth century. The reasons for this are many, from the extra-legal status of serfs to the burden of a traditional idiom, but the main point is that the state did not articulate, or seek to establish, a "four-estate model" in the eighteenth century. . . . Although some measures (from the poll tax to the creation of constituted bodies) had the effect of rigidifying social categories, these should not be elevated—as historians have traditionally done— into a conception of a deliberate, systematic policy to create a Western order of estates in Russia.

[T]he changes in terminology [also] suggest a different conceptualization of the social structure of prereform Russia, that is, Russia before the Great Reforms of the 1860s. The *soslovie* system—whether defined as legal, social, or cultural psychological—was maturing, not dissolving, in the first half of the nineteenth century. As the lexical history indicates, consciousness of social categories changed substantially between 1775 and 1850—from an individual (*chin*) to a group (estate) identity, from strictly legal definitions to cultural and caste dimensions. Whatever the viability of Catherinean corporate bodies, social groups were acquiring sharper legal and cultural definition—that is, the *sosloviia* were becoming more, not less, distinct as the Great Reforms approached. In that important sense the first half of the nineteenth century witnessed a fundamental process of estate formation, not breakdown, as historians have assumed. . . .

Let us turn now from terminology to the social structure of prereform Russia. At issue are two traditional propositions in the historiography—the existence of a four-estate paradigm and the predominant role of the state in creating "artificial" estates.

As a descriptive model, the four-estate paradigm is manifestly deficient. The primary juridical division in prereform Russian society was not by estates but by a different social and legal demarcation—those members of the society who were required to pay the poll tax and those who were not. For all the refinements in the *Digest of Laws* among various status groups, it was the poll tax registry that created the great chasm between privileged and unprivileged Russians. In a direct, literal sense, social policy focused not on formation of estates but on determining which group would be inscribed in the poll tax registry and which not. The tax itself was less important than inclusion in the registry, because that entailed a demeaning juridical status (including liability to corporal punishment), significant disabilities (for example, limitations on travel), and onerous burdens (in particular, recruit levies). . . . Lasting until the military and poll tax reforms of 1874–87, the bifurcation created by the poll tax registry provided the basis for two profoundly separate social hierarchies. More important still, by stressing the aggregation of ranks into estates in the eighteenth century, the traditional historiography has obscured the fundamental continuity between the Muscovite and imperial social structures, for the poll tax division was at bottom a redefined version of the earlier Muscovite bifurcation of the population into service- and tax-bearing segments. . . .

There is a still more fundamental problem with the four-estate paradigm: neither in the eighteenth nor in the nineteenth century did the *sosloviia* as conventionally identified comprise a simple hierarchy of four estates, not even in strictly legal terms. On the contrary, they formed an enormously complex congeries of social categories with numerous, distinct subcategories. . . . The *Digest of Laws* hinted at the underlying complexity, when it had to resort to the phrases "rural inhabitants" and "urban inhabitants" to designate the peasantry and townspeople, who, both legally and socially, actually comprised a variety of distinct, hereditary *sosloviia* in their own right. In the case of peasants, for example, the category of "rural inhabitant" subsumed state peasants, crown peasants, serfs, economic peasants (that is, peasants under the administration of a government office called the Economic College), and a host of other smaller hereditary groups such as single homesteaders, state peasants assigned to factory labor, possessionary (factory) serfs, and tributary . . . peasants. . . .

Moreover, these groups differed not only in status but also in their defining principle and social physiognomy. Thus, some groups denoted by law and popular idiom as *sosloviia* were not even hereditary; instead, they acquired the status through personal choice, individual achievement, or in recognition of economic success. Still more extraordinary were the professional groups formed in the first half of the nineteenth century, which had corporate status but were only feebly linked by heredity. Finally, while all *sosloviia* exhibited considerable variations in the economic and occupational profiles of their members, the smaller groups, for example, Cossacks, soldiers, Jews, and other minorities, actually constituted subsocieties rather than strata. . . .

It was this social dynamic, tolerated and even abetted by the state, that no doubt produced the amorphousness, plasticity, and complexity in the *soslovie* system. In that sense historians should not exaggerate the regressiveness of the prereform social order; though superficially resembling the Western estate system, the *soslovie* structure was far more differentiated and fluid than a rigid "four-estate" paradigm would allow. . . . Expressed more baldly, the *soslovie* structure proved adaptable to the exigencies of social and economic development; a multivariate structure permitted specialization and occupational professionalization, yet within a formal system of hereditary estates. . . .

A second traditional argument—that Russian *sosloviia* were artificial creations of the state and doomed to impotence—also requires qualification. The formation of specific categories did not, first of all, rest solely with the state; however important its policies might have been in legitimizing or reinforcing such social orders, the *ancien regime* with its notoriously "underdeveloped bureaucracy" was incapable of engineering, legislating, and managing a social system. More important, particular social groups—at least those with any semblance of legal or economic privilege—sought to reinforce their separateness as distinct social categories. . . .

It is also necessary to modify the corollary that *sosloviia* were "weak" artifacts without authority, cohesion, or self-awareness, created by the state at its own whim. . . . (A)s became clear during the Great Reforms, the disinclination of social groups to collaborate with the state voluntarily was no measure of their capacity to function as corporate bodies; rather it was a means of evasion and noncompliance. But even before that confrontation between state and *sosloviia* in the 1860s, the structure of *soslovie* relations with the state can hardly be reduced to a simple matter of "bureaucratic stifling of the living forces of the nation". . . . [T]he interaction between state bureau and estate worked in both directions: the former not only exercised influence over the latter but also articulated the group's special interests. The Russian *soslovie*, in contrast to Western estates, may have lacked autonomous social organization, but its close ties to the state provided a legal and serviceable substitute— indeed, one that meshed well with the bureaucratic structure of the traditional regime. . . .

SOURCE: Gregory Freeze, "The *Soslovie* (Estate) Paradigm and Russian Social History," *American Historical Review* 91, 1 (February, 1986):11–25 (excerpted). Republished by permission of the author.

B. Government and Politics in the Eighteenth Century

DOCUMENTS

The Statute on Provincial Administration (1775)

Although Russia was an absolutist state, few full-time institutions of civil authority existed in the provinces. Peter the Great had made a modest attempt to establish provincial standing government when he divided Russia into eight enormous regions, or *gubernii*, in 1708. Still, that reform left most of the countryside acutely under-governed in comparison to nearly all other European states. More than half a century later, Catherine the Great learned just how dangerous it was to have such a primitive standing authority when the Pugachev revolt raged out of control in much of the south for months on end until the armed forces were called in to suppress it.

The Statute on Provincial Administration represents Catherine's plan to redress this structural problem by enumerating, on paper at least, an elaborate and full-time network of paid provincial offices. While the end product came nowhere near establishing all of these new administrative bodies (there simply were not enough provincial servitors to go around), the law did succeed in creating a much more significant administrative presence in the provinces than had been there before. At the very least, this statute offers a vivid legislative blueprint of Catherine's ideal of an involved, bureaucratically rational, and socially concerned provincial government.

A MODEL PLAN OF THE STAFF
FOR EACH PROVINCIAL CAPITAL

1. So that the provinces can be administered in an orderly fashion, each one is expected to have [a population] between 300,000 and 400,000 souls.

2. In the absence of Her Imperial Majesty, each province shall be administered by a commander in chief.

3. Each province shall have a chief administrator, or governor.

4. Each province shall have a provincial administration.

5. The commander in chief, . . . the governor, and two councillors shall preside over the provincial administration.

6. Each province shall establish a criminal court. . . .

8. Each province shall establish a civil court. . . .

11. Each province shall establish an office to oversee households and state revenues. . . .

13. Each province shall establish an upper land court, and those provinces that cover a wide territory may establish more than one. . . .

15. Where necessity requires it, the province shall be subdivided into regions. . . .

16. Provinces and regions are to be subdivided into districts and counties.

17. Each district, or county, should contain from 20,000 to 30,000 souls.

18. In each district . . . a district court shall be established. . . .

20. Within each district court shall be established an office called the Noble Wardship.

21. The district marshal of the nobility, the district judge, and his assistants shall preside over the Noble Wardship.

22. Each district . . . shall establish a lower land court.

23. In the lower land court presides the land officer, or captain, and two or three assistants. . . .

24. In each district there shall be one bookkeeper, one legal land surveyor, one doctor,

one medic, two assistant medics and two apprentice medics.

25. Every town that is lacking a commander shall have a town police official, and the provincial capital shall have a chief of police. . . .

34. In each province there shall exist under the watch of the commander in chief, . . . on behalf of peasant freeholders and others, . . . one court for every 10,000 to 30,000 souls called the lower justice of the peace.

38. Each province shall have . . . a Bureau of Public Welfare.

39. The Bureau of Public Welfare is to be chaired by the governor himself, assisted by two of the assistants from the upper land court, two from the provincial magistrate's office, and two from the upper justice of the peace office. . . .

ON GRADES

47. . . .The governor . . . shall be considered to have a ranking of four [on the Table of Ranks]. . . .

48. . . .The vice-governor, chief of police, chairman of the criminal court, chairman of the civil court, . . . shall be considered to have a rank of five. . . .

[Articles 49 through 57 delineate the rankings down to rank 14 for most of the other offices. Article 58 lists those petty offices that are granted no ranking at all.]

THE ORDER OF APPOINTMENTS

59. Commander in chief, governor, vice governor, chief of police are appointed by Her Imperial Majesty. . . .

[Articles 60 through 62 identify other important offices which are filled by the Governing Senate.]

64. The district marshal of the nobility is elected by the nobility every three years by ballot. . . .

66. The district . . . judge and land captain are elected by the nobility every three years and recommended by the governor. . . . In those districts which have no nobles, or very few of them, the land captain is determined by the provincial administration from among the local petty officials. . . .

72. In cities and towns the mayors and town officials are elected by ballot every three years by urban society. Elders and judges in the conscience courts are elected in the same manner. . . .

81. The provincial commander in chief is empowered . . . to maintain a strict and precise oversight over all those offices that are answerable to him, specifically: the criminal court, the civil court, the treasury and everything under it, the chief of police, town police officials, land surveyors, Bureau of Public Welfare, conscience court [see article 395 below], and all those in the province who are charged with enforcing the law. . . .

ON THE RESPONSIBILITIES
OF THE PROVINCIAL ADMINISTRATION

94. The commander in chief is the chairman of the administration. Alongside of him presides the governor and two councillors. . . .

95. The administration of the province is [understood to be] that office which administers the entire province in Her Majesty's name. . . .

173. The upper land court shall hear all appeals from the district courts, the noble wardships, and the lower land courts; complaints and lawsuits from and against the nobility, both civil and criminal, relating to their patrimonies, privileges, wills, property inheritance, and rights to inheritance. . . . It also shall hear all appeals concerning the *raznochintsy* [miscellaneous urban groups, such as clerks and teachers, who fit into no other *sosloviia*] from the district and lower land courts. . . .

209. Each upper land court shall house an office to be known as the Noble Wardship for noble widows and children. . . .

214. The Noble Wardship does not on its own become involved in the affairs of widows and orphans, but it takes on these cases upon receiving a petition or a report from the district marshal of the nobility, or from close relatives, or from the child's guardians. . . .

225. On police matters . . . or those relating to bridges and roads the lower land court functions directly under the authority of the provincial administration. . . .

229. The lower land court shall see to it that no one is sheltering runaways in the district. . . .

380. The Bureaus of Public Welfare shall oversee and safeguard the establishment of . . . (1) public schools; (2) foundling homes for the welfare and upbringing of male and female orphans. . . ; (3) hospitals; (4) almshouses for the wretched, crippled, and aged of both sexes who cannot subsist on their own . . . ; (5) special homes for the incurably ill. . . ; (6) mad houses; (7) work houses for both sexes; (8) poor houses for both sexes. . . .

393. The Bureau of Public Welfare shall convene for one session a year lasting from January 8 until Holy Week. . . .

395. Since the personal security of every loyal subject is quite precious to the Monarch's philanthropic heart, and in order to extend a helping hand to those who are suffering, sometimes more because of an unfortunate misadventure, or as a victim of overburdened circumstances . . ., we order the establishment of a conscience court . . . in every province.

SOURCE: *Polnoe sobranie zakonov rossiiskoi imperii* 20, 14,392 (November 7, 1775) (excerpted). Translated by Gary Marker.

The Charter to the Nobility (1785)

Historians characterize the post-Petrine nobility and its evolving relationship to the state, governmental service, and political authority in varying ways. For some, the relationship revolved around a lengthy, and ultimately successful, struggle for freedom from state service and toward a definition of nobility that emphasized heredity, privilege, and authority in the countryside. For others, the process had more to do with the state struggling to allow the Table of Ranks to function as intended without it being choked by incompetent noble status-seekers crowding out more capable people. All, however, agree that the 1785 Charter to the Nobility, in which Catherine the Great

enumerated the specific rights and privileges of Russia's elites, was the legal culmination of this process.

——————

The Russian Nobility always has been, is now, and with God's help will forever be, particularly distinguished by qualities brilliantly [suited] for command. This is evidenced irrefutably by the very successes that have led the Russian Empire to its current pinnacle of majesty, power and glory.

And how could it be otherwise, when that most notable and well-born Russian Nobility, entering into military or civil service, passes through all the ranks of command, and from its youth in the lowest [ranks] acquaints itself with the fundamentals of service, becomes accustomed to burdens, and to bearing them firmly and patiently? And by learning obedience it prepares itself for higher command; for there cannot be in all the world a good commander who in his time did not become accustomed to obeying. The highest ranks are attained by those celebrated individuals within the Russian Nobility who distinguish themselves through service, or bravery, or fidelity, or skill. [They are also attained] by those who, remaining patiently obedient, through firmness of spirit diligently surmount difficulties and [the passage of] time itself, increasing by experience their knowledge and abilities in areas pertaining to their calling.

Russia has become accustomed since ancient times to seeing service, fidelity, zeal, and industry of every sort abundantly rewarded, decorated with honors and preferred by distinctions at all times from the Throne of Our ancestors. Ancient testimony thereto is to be found in the most ancient generations of the families of Our faithful, loyal Russian Nobility which, prepared at any hour to throw themselves into the struggle for Faith and fatherland, and to bear every burden in the service that is so essential to the Empire and the Monarch, with their blood and their life then acquired service holdings from which they procured their sustenance. And, augmenting their services, they received as a reward from the Autocratic power their service landholdings as hereditary estates in perpetual tenure. . . .

To you, O deservedly distinguished by military orders of victory, We address Our words! We praise you, O descendants worthy of your ancestors! They were the foundation of Russia's greatness; you have solidified the power and glory of the fatherland by six years of uninterrupted victories in Europe, Asia, and Africa; on dry land in Moldavia, Bessarabia, Wallachia . . . and along the great course of the Danube. . . .

With the new gains and the expansion of Our Empire, now that We everywhere enjoy complete domestic and external tranquility, We increasingly direct our attention to the ceaseless task of providing Our faithful subjects with firm and stable enactments in all the requisite areas of civil administration, for greater prosperity and order in times to come. And to that end We have seen fit, first of all, to extend Our solicitude to Our faithful and loyal Russian Nobility, being mindful of its aforementioned services, ardor, zeal, and unswerving fidelity to the Autocrats of All the Russias. . . . We do in keeping with Our Imperial will and pleasure vouchsafe, declare, ordain, and confirm for the recollection of future generations, the following articles, for the benefit of the Russian Nobility, Our service and the Empire, immutably and for all time to come.

CONCERNING THE
PERSONAL PRIVILEGES OF NOBLES

1. The title of Nobility is a consequence of the quality and virtue of men who in times past commanded, distinguished themselves by [their] services, whereby, transforming itself into dignity, they acquired for their posterity the designation of well-born.

2. It is not only beneficial to the Empire and the Throne but also just that the respected station of the well-born Nobility be preserved and confirmed immutably and inviolate. And to that end the well-born Nobility's dignity, as it was in times past and is presently, shall henceforth and forever be inalienable, inheritable and hereditary for those honorable family lines that enjoy it, and therefore:

3. A Nobleman imparts his noble dignity to his wife.

4. A Nobleman transmits his well-born noble dignity to his children by inheritance.

5. A Nobleman or Noblewoman shall not be deprived of noble dignity unless they deprive themselves thereof by a crime irreconcilable with the principles of noble dignity. . . .

7. But inasmuch as noble dignity may not be taken away except for a crime; and as marriage is honorable and instituted by God's law: therefore a well-born Noblewoman who marries a non-noble shall not be deprived of her station; but she does not impart nobility to her husband and children.

8. A well-born [nobleman] shall not be deprived of noble dignity without trial. . . .

12. A well-born [nobleman] shall not be tried except by his peers. . . .

15. Corporal punishment shall not extend to the well-born [nobleman]. . . .

17. We confirm that the well-born Russian Nobility is to enjoy freedom and liberty [now and] in future generations for all time to come. . . .

19. We confirm to well-born [nobles] permission to enter into the service of other European powers allied with Us, and to travel abroad.

20. But inasmuch as the well-born noble title and dignity have in times past been, are presently, and shall henceforth be acquired by service and industry beneficial to the Empire and throne . . . therefore at any time when the Russian Autocracy has want of him . . . each well-born Nobleman is obligated at the first summons of the Autocratic Power to spare neither labor nor even life itself in State service. . . .

22. A well-born [nobleman] has the authority and freedom to give away, or to bequeath, or to confer either as dowry or as a maintenance allotment, or to transfer or to sell to whomever he deems fit, any estate he is the first to acquire; but an inherited estate may be disposed of only in the manner prescribed by law.

23. In the event of his conviction of even the most serious crime, the inherited estate of a well-born [nobleman] shall be passed on to his legal heir or heirs. . . .

26. The right of well-born [nobles] to purchase villages is confirmed.

27. The right of well-born [nobles] to sell wholesale whatever is grown in their villages or produced by handicraft . . . is confirmed.

28. Well-born [nobles] are permitted to maintain factories and [other] industrial works in their villages.

29. Well-born [nobles] are permitted to establish trading settlements on their hereditary estates, and to hold markets and fairs at them. . . .

30. The right of well-born [nobles] to own or to build or to purchase houses in towns and to maintain handicraft industries is confirmed. . . .

35. The manor house in the village is to be free from quartering.

36. A well-born [nobleman] is to be personally exempt from personal taxes.

CONCERNING THE ASSEMBLY
OF NOBLES, THE ESTABLISHMENT OF
THE NOBLE CORPORATION IN THE PROVINCE,
AND CONCERNING THE BENEFITS OF THE
NOBLE CORPORATION

37. We grant Our faithful Nobles permission to assemble in that province in which they maintain their residency, to form a noble corporation in each lieutenancy, and to avail themselves of the rights, benefits, distinctions, and privileges set forth below.

38. The Nobility assembles in the province every three years in the winter time, at the summons and with the permission of the Governor-General or Governor, both for the elections entrusted to the Nobility and for hearing the proposals of the Governor-General or Governor. . . .

47. The Assembly of the Nobility is permitted to submit representations to the Governor-General or Governor regarding its corporate needs and interests. . . .

49. The Assembly of the Nobility is forbidden to make regulations contrary to the laws, or demands in violation of legislation. . . .

55. The personal crime of a Nobleman shall not be held against the Nobility as a whole. . . .

60. . . . [T]he County Marshal of the Nobility presides over the Noble Wardship Office, and the County Judge and his Assessors serve as members. . . .

66. . . . (F)or the recollection by future generations, We once more command that a heraldry book of the Nobility be compiled in every province, in which the Nobility of that province is to be inscribed, so that each well-born Noble family line be particularly enabled thereby to perpetuate its dignity and title hereditarily, from generation to generation, uninterruptedly, immutably and safely, from father to son, to grandson, to great-grandson, and to legitimate posterity, as long as God deigns to grant it issue.

SOURCE: David Griffiths and George E. Munro (Trans. and eds), *Catherine II's Charters of 1785 to the Nobility and the Towns* (Bakersfield, California: Charles Schlacks, Jr., 1991), pp. 2–8, 11, 15, (excerpted). Reprinted by permission of the editors and publisher.

LITERATURE

MARC RAEFF
The Well-Ordered Police State

In this selection Marc Raeff maintains that eighteenth-century Russian government was primarily concerned with order, orderliness,

and institutional control, in pursuit of which it adapted a model of rulership ("the well-ordered police state") that had been developed for the small German states of Central Europe. This concept of a state constructed on rules and regulations with which it endeavors to police society was, he suggests, transferred to Russian soil by Peter the Great, but, in the process, its very meaning underwent a substantial change. We might ask whether, in Raeff's opinion, the Russian state did, or could effectively involve itself in regulating so sprawling and disorderly a realm as Russian society.

Peter the Great did have an overall goal and a general conception of what he wanted to accomplish, or he had one at any rate after about 1701, following his return from his first trip to Western Europe and after overcoming the critical situation created by his defeat at Narva. He himself stated his goal on a number of occasions, and there is no reason not to take him seriously, the more so that the sum total of his measures did amount to a coherent and sustained effort to achieve a specific purpose. Peter wanted to modernize, to Europeanize Russia's establishment. He obviously did not care to Europeanize the peasantry and common people, for he believed that they would eventually follow, provided the upper classes of society performed their leadership functions well. This also implied the westernization, or making over on a European model, of the administration, the military, the court, and the elite's culture. . . . Peter wanted for Russia an elite composed of individuals capable of playing an active role in transforming society—not slaves . . . but loyal servants of the emperor and of the fatherland whose central concerns were to be the nation's welfare, prosperity, and progress.

Finally, the reign reflected Peter's own personality—his impatience, driving energy, and ruthlessness. Indeed, the transformations introduced by the tsar-reformer were rushed through, brooking no opposition; any attempt at resistance was pitilessly crushed. Peter rode roughshod over his people, the country, even his family, disregarding difficulties and resistances and quite unmindful of the high price paid by the population. The furious tempo of his reign created the impression of relentless hurry and impatience, as if centuries of Western European experience had to be crammed into the twenty-five years of the reign. . . .

The Muscovite administration had developed regular chancery procedures quite early, but they were cumbersome and largely oral, adapted to the semipatriarchal and personal regimen of the Kremlin. Nor was the administrative apparatus very extensive; since the clerical personnel was quite small, the main clerks . . . participated in deciding policies as well as in administering them. This situation changed drastically in Peter's times. He introduced and firmly rooted Western chancery techniques, with their emphasis on the written document. As a matter of fact, this approach was initiated quite early in his reign when he decreed that henceforth all documents were to be kept in book fashion rather than in scrolls (where each paper was stitched to the top of the next following). . . .

In short, government was to be completely separated from the population's life pattern; administration had to partake of the aura of the arcane possessed by the sovereign ruler. Naturally this meant a great increase in the technical tasks of writing and keeping the papers needed for administration, so that more personnel were needed. At the same time the role of the copyist or clerk diminished as his task became more mechanical and routinized, and the gap separating the staff of responsible officials from the scriveners who performed mechanical tasks grew wider. . . .

These procedural innovations were not merely due to Peter's copying of Western models and to his desire to have a more efficient administrative apparatus to perform the traditional governmental functions of the Muscovite state. Had this been the case, fewer and less costly changes would have sufficed. The more important reason is that in Europe, and now in Russia, the very conception of the function of government and administration had undergone a basic change. . . . Put very simply, . . . Peter attempted to turn the imperial government into an agency for the direction and organization of a dynamic, production-oriented society. No longer was the task of government to be the passive care of internal and external safety; it was to be that of aggressive promotion of all the country's potential, social as well as material. . . .

Peter . . . acted on the assumption that all of his innovations would be resented and resisted. This was one of the main reasons why we do not find in Peter's acts anything that might be considered the equivalent of a police ordinance, in the sense of a set of laws or decrees endeavoring to produce a new pattern of behavior in the operation of existing aspects of public, economic, and social life. In Russia we have the direct command that introduces and orders something altogether new under threat of dire punishment. Old patterns of behavior were forbidden outright, without any suggestion of alternative paths, while new ways were commanded without regard to whether the presuppositions existed for them or not. Little wonder that so much of this kind of legislation of Peter's proved stillborn. . . .

Since Muscovy possessed no lawyers and academics who could readily provide technical competence and leadership, the Petrine government had to create cadres of its own entirely out of the traditional service class. To this end Peter imposed an educational requirement on all young servitors, a requirement that eventually became the main criterion for membership in the establishment. All male members of the younger generation of the service class were forced to go to school (or study on their own and pass an examination) before being granted full legal rights (for example, the right to marry) and admitted to regular service. This requirement was new and burdensome, for there were few schools or other educational institutions; moreover, the knowledge that had to be acquired was outside the traditional religious instruction that had been provided in Muscovy. Modern, service-oriented knowledge had to be imparted by force; all efforts at evading it were severely punished. Yet in spite of the fierce resistance it encountered and the obvious difficulty in acquiring education, within a generation or so the Petrine policy had taken hold; the young noble henceforth acquired the minimum of instruction that prepared him for the effective service

in either the military or civilian branches. Even more remarkable, the notion that education was desirable and the criterion for belonging to the elite had taken hold among the nobility; education became the single most significant factor affecting admission to and recognition of membership in the elite class of the empire. . . .

The pattern of compulsion imposed on the nobility was extended to others as Peter I tried to enroll various groups of the population in the productive and modernizing endeavors of the state. In good cameralist fashion, Peter was convinced of the necessity of developing manufactures and trade to the maximum possible extent. He believed that the towns were the main source of strength and support of the Western European states' power and material wealth. . . . Conscious of the backwardness and inadequacy of the Russian merchants and entrepreneurs, Peter tried to organize them along European lines, so as to increase their material contribution and make it more effective. But again he resorted to the only methods he knew: state service and compulsion. . . .

What were then the results of Peter's turbulent reign?

The consciousness of rapid change on the part of the emperor and his aides as well as on the part of the population was very intense. The reign had an almost revolutionary character, largely because of the drive, forcefulness, speed, and ruthlessness with which the changes were pursued. Naturally the resistance was almost equally great and violent. The transformations wrought by the well-ordered police state in the West had been extensive and had required determined efforts over a long period. Peter's changes had been even greater, and they appeared to have rained down like some tropical downpour. Moreover, in the West the changes had been gradual and had been adjusted to special conditions or to incorporate newly acquired insights. Peter's actions were not only more impetuous but seemed capricious as well, since he easily gave up measures that did not bring the expected results as rapidly as he had hoped. He produced a sharp break, sharper than anywhere in the West, in the psychological outlook and makeup of Russian society. On the one hand, the government—that is, the ruling elites—assimilated the goals, purposes, and also the new practices and values of the rationally constructivist state. . . . The people, on the other hand, all those who were not part of the elites—not only the peasantry but also urban classes, the clergy, and the non-Russians—were baffled and dispirited, and they reacted by sulkily withdrawing. The purpose of the changes were incomprehensible to them, and the new practices were unfamiliar and seemed to result only in harsher treatment and heavier burdens. It was therefore preferable to escape direct contact with all novelties. The psychological rift and consequent withdrawal made it even more difficult for the government to identify individuals and groups whom it could co-opt and to whom authority could be delegated to promote the aims of the tsar.

This situation reinforced the government's propensity toward limiting its purview to the central establishment—quite the opposite of the European well-ordered police state, which aimed at extending to the local level the policies and purposes of the central institutions. Instead of diffusing the new social and political conceptions and practices, the Russian government concentrated them at the center among a tiny minority of the population, the elites in the capitals. As a result, the government's impact was limited to a very narrow circle, and the huge state establishment seemed to float in mid-air, unconnected to the population and country at large. . . .

A major reason for this weakness of the state and government was the very amorphousness of Russian society. It allowed the government neither to act effectively on society nor to draw on society to delegate responsibility for implementing its policies. A genuine division of social labor was precluded as well, since peasants and nobles engaged in activities that in the West were traditionally the function of urban classes and merchants. In their turn, merchants and townspeople engaged in the same enterprises as nobles and peasants. Such overlapping would have been of little consequence

in a more open, dynamic, and productive society, but in Russia the absence of functional division of labor was a function of poverty, inadequacy of human resources, and of the weak condition of estates and corporate bodies. . . .

The difficulties and dissonances of the Petrine heritage, the intellectual development of the elites, and the individual qualities of Catherine II enabled the latter to approach the implementation of the well-ordered police state in a new and more sophisticated manner. Her contribution was to recognize that . . . [it] needed a structured, westernized type of society in order to operate. Catherine's government did not go all the way and grant the autonomy and self-government that the Western intermediate bodies had come to enjoy. It is also arguable that the social structure needed for the well-ordered police state never materialized in Russia; the concrete cameralist policies had to be imposed by a bureaucracy, which precluded their having the necessary impact on the modernization of the country. Yet with respect to the cultural life of the elites, Catherine did lay the foundation of a civil society that was to be the seedbed for Russia's cultural explosion in the nineteenth century, at the same time bringing into the open the tensions and conflicts that resulted from the limitations imposed by the autocracy on creative social initiative.

In central and Western Europe the well-ordered police state initiated a trend that not only brought about great material and cultural progress but also stimulated and strengthened individual initiative, enterprise, and rational or critical constructivist features of intellectual life. This dynamism could not be restrained, in the long run, by the leading strings of government authority and officialdom. A clash was hard to avoid. A civil society had come into existence, and because the . . . [state] had made use of (even strengthened) basic social institutions, the clash was a purely political one. Once the barriers of bureaucracy and monarchy had been broken down (or a compromise had been reached), once the authoritarian political systems that had initiated the well-ordered police state and modernity had been removed, society was still there, and its members could go on being productively active on their own account. This was not to be the case in Russia. The state remained in command and retained the initiative until the end of the nineteenth century, for there was no comprehensively structured society either to defer to or challenge it. When the imperial autocracy was eventually challenged, it was by the only kind of civil society that had been allowed to develop—namely, one based on cultural and ideological criteria incorporated by intelligentsia. When the challenge proved successful, the political system virtually collapsed, and the social void became visible to all. A well-organized minority of the cultural elite, the radical intelligentsia, moved in to fill it and organize it in its own way.

SOURCE: Marc Raeff, *The Well-Ordered Police State. Social and Institutional Change Through Law in the Germanies and Russia, 1600–1800* (New Haven: Yale University Press, 1983), Part Three: "The Russian Experience," pp. 198–9, 202–208, 210–11, 217, 249–50 (excerpted). Reprinted by permission of Yale University Press.

ISABEL DE MADARIAGA

Catherine the Great, an Enlightened Autocrat

No one takes issue with the proposition that the Russian state was absolutist in the sense that the monarch's formal authority was supreme, and that the monarch's right as the law giver was unchallenged. Nevertheless, absolutism lent itself to a wide variety of understandings and governmental practices. In this selection, Isabel de Madariaga, one of the foremost authorities on the reign of Catherine the Great, makes a determined case for Catherine as an absolute ruler who nevertheless maintained a consistent adherence to the principles of human progress and enlightenment. How does her interpretation compare to "the well-ordered police state?"

When Catherine seized the throne in 1762, Russia was an absolute monarchy, placed at the despotic end of the spectrum which extended through the Prussia of Frederick II to the France of Louis XV. There were no institutional limitations on the power of the ruler, who was even entitled to name his, or more often her, successor. There were no constituted bodies or 'estates', no 'intermediate powers' of the kind that existed elsewhere in Europe. As head of the executive the sovereign exercised authority through a series of functional colleges headed by boards under presidents, whose work was co-ordinated by an appointed administrative Senate of some twenty or thirty people. This misleadingly-named body had no legislative powers, which were lodged entirely in the ruler. . . .

In the years before she seized the throne, Catherine had occupied herself with systematic reading of political literature. . . . Throughout her life she continued in a completely pragmatic and empirical way to borrow ideas from authors who struck her as modern, sensible and rational. She worked systematically and very hard, with a small number of chosen advisers, and in the case of major administrative reforms, she tried them out on a small scale before introducing them throughout the empire. Most of her senior servants remained with her for decades, strengthening the impression of stability of her government, in spite of occasional changes of direction. She was also very attentive to manifestations of public opinion.

Catherine set out her political theory in the famous *Nakaz*, or Instruction, which she wrote for the Legislative Commission, summoned in 1767 to draft a code of laws for Russia. . . . What was novel about Catherine's experiment is that, only five years after her *coup d'etat*, she felt sufficiently confident to embark upon the kind of large-scale consultation advocated by Diderot in the *Encyclopedie* (article *representants*), by calling together representatives of all the free estates of the realm, government bodies, and non-Russian peoples, to examine the chaotic state of Russian law, and to draft a new code. Over 500 deputies were elected, each bringing with him an 'instruction' from his electors setting out local grievances, and the whole enterprise was managed with considerable pomp and publicity. Such a public consultation had not been held for more than a hundred years in Russia, and was not to be made again until the meeting of the first Duma in 1906.

It has been pointed out by Catherine's critics that the serfs were not represented. This is of course correct, but it has to be seen in the context of contemporary theories of representation. In Ancien Regime institutions it was not individual opinion, but corporate interests which were represented, and in no country at that time were peasants represented in diets or estates except in Sweden. . . . Thus, in Russia, serfs were held to be represented by their landowners, while state peasants sent deputies to the Commission. The Commission thus did not reflect individual opinion, let alone party opinion. . . .

The clearest evidence of the influence of both Enlightenment and cameralist thought on Catherine is provided by the Instruction she wrote in 1765–68 to guide the Commission in its labours. In it she analyzed the government and society of Russia as she thought it ought to be, and expounded the general direction she wished to follow. Her principle source was Montesquieu's *L'esprit des lois*, from which some 294 out of 526 articles were almost literally copied. She has been accused not only of plagiarism (to which she freely admitted), but of distorting Montesquieu's views, in that she applied to Russia (which he regarded as a despotism) the maxims which he applied to a 'moderate' monarchy; that she located the limitations on absolutism . . . in the bureaucracy and not in social groups such as the nobility, and that she rejected the doctrine of the 'separation of powers'. This judgment is partly true. Considering the low regard in which despotism was held, Catherine naturally rejected its application to Russia, and preferred to argue that the ruler of Russia must be absolute in view of the size of the country. She justified her argument by postulating the existence in Russia of fundamental laws and the acceptance

of a decree of self-limitation in the ruler's use of absolute power. . . .

The Instruction was not a code of law, nor did it have any legal validity. But it exercised a considerable influence on the intellectual climate of Russia in the eighteenth century and even in the nineteenth, since it opened the way to public discussion of many public issues which had never previously been openly debated. Though its circulation seems originally to have been limited to officials, the Instruction was nevertheless freely available to the public from the beginning, since it was advertised as for sale in the Senate bookshop for 50 kopecks as early as 1768. Though its natural law principles, which paid scant regard to Russian positive law, led to its having but slight influence on subsequent Russian legislation, the Instruction had a beneficent influence on Russian practice, particularly in the field of penal law, when it was frequently quoted in favour of moderation and the reduction of penalties. . . .

The Statute of Local Administration of 1775, many of whose provisions lasted until 1864, some until 1917, was not simply the continuation of policies adumbrated in previous reigns. It represents a quite novel amalgamation of earlier Russian attempts to solve the problem with the doctrines of Catherine's Instruction, particularly those derived from Montesquieu, and a substantial dose of cameralism. . . .

The reform of 1775 was based on a number of specific principles, namely the multiplication of administrative centres in the provinces, and the corresponding transfer of functions from the centre to the localities; the separation of functions previously combined in one instance; the establishment of specific institutions for the free estates of the empire, and some degree of corporate organisation of these free estates to enable them to participate in the election of representatives forming part of local administrative institutions.

By the division of the vast *guberniyi* of Russia into smaller units, subdivided into districts of some 30,000 inhabitants, the various judicial instances were multiplied and brought much closer to the people, and a number of settlements of varying size, some extremely small, were raised to the status of towns. The separation of functions took quite elaborate forms: general administration, including what would today be regarded as welfare and was then grouped under the general heading of police, was entrusted to the governor, assisted by a board of appointed councillors, and a Board of Social Welfare, on which sat elected representatives of the various free estates. Financial administration including the collection of taxes and the administration of the state peasants became the responsibility of the deputy governor. . . .

The participation of representatives of social groups in local government institutions, except in the administration of finance which remained firmly in government hands, was provided for by election at the lower levels, by appointment at the higher levels. A rudimentary corporate structure of the nobles and the towns was laid down in the Statute, to organize the elections: the nobles of a district met to elect a marshal, who became the lynchpin of the subsequent establishment of local noble assemblies. The towns elected a town chief, who in turn became the centre for the future development of urban corporate organisation. In these institutions we have pale shadows of Montesquieu's *'pouvoirs intermediaires'*.

The Statute of 1775 was introduced only gradually throughout the Empire. Even so there were serious difficulties in implementing a policy which was in so many ways designed for a more advanced society than Russia. It did not take account of the enormous variation in type of population (serf or state peasant); of the presence of resident noble landowners; of the size of towns and the presence of enough educated merchants and townsmen to fill elective posts; of economic potential, communications, racial homogeneity, and the need for a considerable infrastructure of surveyors, doctors, teachers, clerks, etc. Nevertheless the new institutions did bring life to provincial towns, where energetic governors proceeded to erect new stone buildings, set up schools, hospitals, inoculation centres, to open libraries, patronise the theatre, give balls and enliven social

and intellectual life, and encourage manifestations of local initiative in the field of social welfare.

But in spite of the increased services available to the local inhabitants, both urban and rural, and the presence of some conscientious and honourable officials, there is little doubt that Russian local administration continued to be inefficient, corrupt, and often brutal. In spite of new attitudes of mind inculcated into the elite, the mental outlook of centuries could not be changed overnight. The habits of servility to superiors and bullying inferiors were deeply ingrained, the notion of public service as a vocation and not a burden or a means of enriching still limited to the most enlightened. Even more difficult, because so alien to the Russian tradition, was the attempt to introduce the concept of legality in the judicial process. The total absence of legal training (the first professor of Russian law was appointed only in 1768) helps to account for the failure to grasp the first principles of the rule of law among even governors, whose experience was often entirely military. The efforts of the government to provide better trained officials only began to have results in the nineteenth century. . . .

If the new system of local administration was to work at all, it had to draw on the voluntary participation of elected representatives of the free estates. Catherine therefore considered it necessary in the two Charters of 1785, to the Nobility and to the Towns, to enumerate and enact the basic civic, property, status and corporate rights of these estates, and to define their membership. From now on, nobles could not be deprived of rank, honour, property or life without trial by their peers. The noble's immunity from corporal punishment and personal taxation was confirmed. Noble land was freed from any state restrictions on its exploitation, and the noble's right to buy land with serfs was expressly stated, as was his right to set up manufacturing enterprises, to leave Russian service, to travel and to serve abroad. The Charter extended the corporate rights granted in 1775, authorising the nobles in each *guberniya* to meet every three years to elect their marshal, who acted as the head of the local corporate nobility. A register of the nobles was introduced on a *guberniya* basis: the nobles were divided into six groups according to their origin, though all equal in rights, and the register was to be kept in the office of the local noble assembly. To some extent the decision as to who was a noble was thus placed in the hands of the nobles themselves. The corporate nobility was also allowed to 'make representations' to the Senate or directly to the Empress on local needs. It was this right which was used by the noble assemblies, for example in Tver, in the period leading up to the emancipation of the serfs in 1861.

The Charter to the Towns granted the same kind of personal property and civil rights to the townspeople, though corporal punishment was banned only for the wealthiest groups, namely rich merchants and entrepreneurs, and for a new category of 'distinguished citizens', mainly professional people. The Charter of 1785 also provided the towns with an elaborate system of local administration, in which elected officials took part, an extension to the towns of the provisions of the Statute of 1775. . . .

Concern with education was central to enlightenment thought, whether in absolutist Prussia and Austria, or in the Polish gentry republic. . . . The moving spirit behind [Catherine's] educational reform was Joseph II who in the course of his visit to Russia in 1780, informed her of the policy pursued in the Habsburg lands after the expulsion of the Jesuits. . . . Catherine's Statute of National Education of 1786 set up a comprehensive system of high schools and junior schools, free, secular, co-educational, open to all classes including serfs if they had the permission of their masters. A centrally-devised curriculum was imposed, teaching aids and textbooks were produced including elaborate regulations on the duties of teachers and a textbook setting out the moral and political principles to be inculcated into the pupils, designed to produce dutiful and obedient citizens.

There was inevitably a considerable discrepancy between an ambitious plan and a more modest achievement. The Boards of Social Welfare, charged with setting up and running the schools had neither the funds nor the staff. There was an enormous shortage of qualified teachers, and though they were not ill-paid compared to other public servants, and though they were given positions in the Table of Ranks, with the possibility of rising to hereditary nobility after twenty-two years service (the ladder by means of which Lenin's father rose to noble rank) the teachers were too uncouth, and the members of the Boards of Social Welfare too inexperienced to be widely successful. Moreover the education provided was still too sophisticated to respond to the basic needs of Russian townspeople, who did not demand more than the three Rs and the ability to read devotional works.

Nowhere was Catherine more truly a daughter of the Enlightenment than in her patronage of arts and letters. St. Petersburg became one of the most beautiful European cities, once the banks of the Neva were clothed in granite and the canals spanned by elegant bridges. Less visible to the general public was Catherine's private sponsorship of a wide programme of translations into Russian which she subsidised to the tune of 5000 roubles a year. In fifteen years the Translation Society formed by her was responsible for the publication of 112 translations, thus giving employment to many noble and non-noble intellectuals. The works included the best that France could offer, selections from the *Encyclopedie*, Montesquieu's *L'Esprit des Lois*, works by Corneille, Racine, Voltaire, Mably (translated by Alexander Radishchev), and many of Rousseau's writings, though not the *Social Contract*. . . .

By 1790 Catherine woke up to the dangers implicit in unrestricted publications, not only of masonic obscurantism but of revolutionary ideas. Until 1789, and well into 1790, Russians had been surprisingly well-informed about events in the United States and France. Novikov had published, in a supplement to the *Moscow Gazette*, a series of articles praising George Washington as the 'founder of a republic which will probably be the refuge of freedom, exiled from Europe by luxury and depravity'.

The French 'Declaration of the Rights of Man' of 1789 was published in No. 74 of the *St. Petersburg Gazette* in that same year. There were graphic descriptions of peasants burning chateaux in France, of the invasion of the French royal family's apartments in Versailles, reports of the debates in the National Assembly. French Revolutionary pamphlets, leaflets and periodicals were on sale in Russian bookshops. . . .

By 1790 even the advertisements of books for sale had to be submitted to the police, and in 1791, the Academy of Science was given directives on what foreign news to publish in order to eliminate items about Russia, and to present news from France in a hostile light. Finally, in September 1796 Catherine withdrew the freedom she had once granted, and set up formal censorship of imported and locally printed books. . . .

Catherine II has on the whole been harshly treated by historians, . . . [and many] have totally rejected her claim to be counted among the enlightened despots. The somewhat disparaging portrayal of her personality and her reign now current is based on a number of issues which have been differently viewed at different times. These include the murder of her husband, her numerous lovers, the charge that she did nothing to put the 'liberal' maxims of her Instruction into effect, and that they were designed by a consummate hypocrite to throw dust in the eyes of the *philosophes* in Paris; that in her reign serfdom was both intensified and extended; that she brought unnecessary wars on Russia and that she partitioned Poland. . . .

It is necessary to refine the precise meaning of the concept of Enlightenment in the context of Catherinian reform. Like her contemporaries, she believed that it was desirable to maximise and hold on to state power in order to achieve reforms necessary for the welfare of the people. . . . The style of government, the language in which policies were explained, reflected the values of the Enlightenment. The classical paternalism of the 'police' state was disguised in the language of 'progress'. This is particularly noticeable in the series of edicts of

the years 1775–86 which laid down the basic parameters of a uniform administration and uniform rights throughout the empire, with scant regard to historical tradition. The language of the Enlightenment is also used to support the domination of the state over the church coupled with religious toleration in practice, if not in law. Catherine asserted her right to regulate Catholic, Protestant and Moslem religious organization, including the appointment of Catholic bishops, while the Jews were not only granted religious toleration but more extensive civil rights than anywhere in Europe at the time. The educational programme was totally secular, and priests were not allowed to teach in state schools. The regulation of health and hygiene and the provision of inoculation centres and hospitals belongs more to the world of cameralism, as does the whole undercurrent of the control of national resources, improvement of communications, the land survey, efforts to improve agriculture (including the introduction of the potato with instructions on how to cook it), the freeing of manufacture from state shackles, but the language is still that of the Enlightenment.

If one is to sum up, it is time that Catherine as a ruler should be re-evaluated. She was a rational human being; she worked hard, with well-chosen advisers, whom she trusted and who stayed in their posts for decades, not one of whom was ever sent into exile even when he was dismissed. She did not go about in snuff-stained coats like Frederick the Great, or shabby uniforms like Joseph II, and her court outdid theirs in brilliance and extravagance. In private life she preferred simplicity; she lit her own fire and made her own coffee in the morning, because she disliked being waited on, and her private parties at the Hermitage were remarkable for the ease and informality which prevailed. But in public and on state occasions she still believed in using the magic of monarchy, regarding the court as a necessary mechanism of government, a means of holding the allegiance of those who hoped to win power, fortune and favour, and of impressing the illiterate multitudes. She travelled extensively in her wide domains, attempting to acquaint herself with conditions.

Perhaps her main service to Russia was that she created a framework for government and society, more civilised, more tolerant, more free than ever before or after. But she did not find it possible to improve the lot of the private serfs, and it is this contrast between the freer and more orderly life of the upper classes, and even to some extent of the state peasants, and the unreformed state of private serfdom, which produces the impression that the situation of the serfs worsened during her reign. Yet they evidently benefitted too from the increase in agricultural production, the growing domestic market, the development of craft industries, and even sometimes from facilities for education and promotion.

The difficulty about making a final assessment, or embarking on a political or sociological interpretation of Catherine's reign, is that though we know a great deal about the laws she enacted, we know so little about how they actually worked in practice. Was torture really no longer used? Was corporal punishment never inflicted in state schools? What sort of justice did the new courts dispense? Were the guarantees of property, life and honour observed? Were the rich and the powerful able to bend the law in their favor? Was Catherine merely the willing tool of a rapacious nobility, or did she, as she believed, preside over an autonomous state? In view of the present state of research we must suspend judgement for the time being. Experience suggests that practice lagged far behind the theory, and many of Catherine's reforms were distorted in her reign already, and certainly in that of her son Paul, so that their ultimate import is hard to grasp. Nevertheless, in what she attempted to do, and in her style of government, she belongs clearly in the tradition of those who governed in what they believed to be the interests of the people and who go by the name of enlightened despots.

SOURCE: Isabel de Madariaga, "Catherine the Great," in H. M. Scott (ed.), *Enlightened Absolutism: Reform and Reformers in Later Eighteenth-Century Europe* (Ann Arbor: University of Michigan Press, 1990), pp. 289–311 (excerpted). Republished by permission of the author.

C. Government and Politics in the Nineteenth Century

Historians have never managed to agree on whether Peter the Great's system of governing colleges functioned very well. The most common point of view maintains that they constituted a cumbersome and inefficient model of doing business, and, by the late eighteenth century, they had evolved toward the principle of having one person in charge at each college. If so, the establishment of ministries, based explicitly on the idea of there existing ministers of state, constituted a logical reform. In any case, they certainly reinforced the tendency toward centralization that had been apparent for a long time. Some historians believe that the new ministries made government even more hierarchical and further removed from the voices of its subjects. Others have suggested that the ministries, unlike the colleges, cultivated a new attitude among upper servitors, men who now came to identify themselves as professionals and as overseers of the entire society, rather than primarily as representatives of a privileged group of landowners.

Subsequent reorganizations from the reign of Alexander I (1801–25) and Nicholas I (1825–55) continued, and even accelerated, this trend. As you read the documents below pay attention to the law's sense of the obligations, rights, and function of government, and try to understand what Russia's rulers were hoping to achieve by changing governmental structures. Has their sense of the role of the state changed at all since the eighteenth century?

DOCUMENTS

The Statute Establishing State Ministries (1802)

London: Yale University Press, 1972), pp. 483–84. Reprinted by permission of Yale University Press.

We have thought it fit to divide governmental affairs, according to their natural connections, into several parts and, for their most successful operation, to entrust them to the jurisdiction of our selected ministers after establishing the main principles by which they shall be guided in the accomplishment of everything their office shall demand of them and of that which we expect from their loyalty, efforts, and devotion to the general welfare. To the Governing Senate, whose duties and basic powers we have confirmed by our decree of this date, we assign the authority, most important and fitting for this high institution, to oversee the activities of the ministers in all subdivisions entrusted to their administration and, after duly comparing and coordinating these activities with the laws of the state and with the reports received by the Senate directly from lower administrative offices, to state its own conclusions and to submit them to us in reports. . . .

Accordingly the following clauses will serve to designate all these departments in their natural interrelation, as well as all matters pertaining to them and the main duties of the ministers to whose administration we entrust them.

1. The administration of the affairs of the government is divided into eight departments, each of which, comprising those areas which by their nature belong to it, constitutes a separate ministry and is under the direct control of a minister to be named by us today or whom we shall deem fit to name later.

These departments are the following: (1) of the Army; (2) of the Navy; (3) of Foreign Affairs; . . . (4) of Justice; (5) of Internal Affairs; (6) of Finance; (7) of Commerce, and (8) of Public Education.

SOURCE: George Vernadsky et al., *A Source Book for Russian History from Early Times to 1917*, Vol. 2 (New Haven, CT, and

An Edict Defining the Responsibilities of the Ministries (1810)

The basic reason for this modification is to introduce a more equal division of state affairs and more uniformity in their execution, and to simplify and make easier their functioning in order that the limits of authority and responsibility may be precisely defined and that thereby the executive branch . . . may obtain more means for the speedy and precise execution of the laws. . . .

1. The executive affairs of the state are [to be] divided into five main categories:
   a. Foreign relations
   b. Maintenance of defense
   c. State economy
   d. Maintenance of civil and criminal courts
   e. Maintenance of internal security. . . .
3. State affairs are thereby, divided as follows:
   a. Foreign relations: Ministry of Foreign Affairs
   b. Defense: Ministry of War; Ministry of the Navy
   c. State economy: Ministry of Internal Affairs; Ministry of Public Education; Ministry of Finance; the State Treasury; Department of Control of State Accounts; Central Administrative Agency for Transportation
   d. The courts: Ministry of Justice
   e. Internal Security: [formerly within the Ministry of Internal Affairs] . . . the former post of Policemaster-General is to be reestablished under the title minister of police. . . .
6. The main object of the Ministry of Internal Affairs is to encourage and foster the expansion of agriculture and industry. In conse-

quence, the following categories of affairs belong within the jurisdiction of this ministry:

a. Affairs concerning the encouragement of agriculture and colonization, resettlement within the country, and those various branches of the economy pertaining to this question.

b. Factories

c. Internal trade

d. The mails

e. Public buildings

SOURCE: George Vernadsky et al. (see p. 256) Vol. 2, pp. 494–5. Reprinted by permission of Yale University Press.

An Edict Creating the Third Section of His Majesty's Own Chancery (1826)

The matters to occupy this Third Section of my own chancery shall be as follows:

1. All instructions and announcements of the higher police on all matters.

2. Intelligence concerning the number of various sects and schismatic groups existing within the state.

3. Information concerning the discovery of counterfeit banknotes, coins, stamps, documents, and so on. . . .

4. Detailed intelligence concerning all persons under police surveillance, as well as all orders bearing on this matter.

5. The exile and placement of suspicious and harmful persons.

6. Supervision and economic management of all places of internment where state criminals are kept.

7. All edicts and instructions concerning foreigners residing in Russia, arriving within its borders, and leaving it.

8. Reports on all events, without exception.

9. Statistical information relevant to the police. . . .

SOURCE: Vernadsky (see p. 256) Vol. 2, p. 533. Reprinted by permission of Yale University Press.

LITERATURE

W. BRUCE LINCOLN
The Genesis of an 'Enlightened' Bureaucracy (1825–56)

For generations we have tended to describe the Russian bureaucracy as a blind, if woefully inefficient and corrupt, instrument of imperial authority. Alternatively, state service has been portrayed as a haven for status seeking and human pettiness, the notoriously mean spirited characters made famous by Gogol and Dostoevsky. In this essay, Bruce Lincoln attempts to modify this picture by arguing that these undeniable forces of corruption and inertia were obliged to compete with an emerging spirit of professionalism and reform whose source he links to the influx of new "enlightened bureaucrats" who came to prominence within the state ministries at the end of Nicholas I's reign.

I

One of the critical issues confronting the Russian Emperor after the Napoleonic wars was the question of how his Empire could meet the challenge of the rapidly industrializing nations of western Europe. Faced with the fact that Russia's serf-based social and economic order had begun to fall behind the West as the countries of western Europe entered the age of the

Imperial architecture: arch of the General Staff Building as imagined in the early nineteenth century. From an 1822 lithograph in *Pushkinskii Peterburg* (Leningrad, 1972).

Industrial Revolution, Nicholas was acutely aware that reforms were necessary, but at the same time he had to deal with an aristocracy which insisted upon preserving its traditional way of life and a bureaucracy which stubbornly resisted change and innovation and made it virtually impossible for the Emperor to make his will felt outside the capital. In the provinces, and even in St. Petersburg itself, administration had come to mean the movement of papers from one desk to another, and during the second quarter of the nineteenth century, the quantity of useless and meaningless paperwork increased at a dramatic rate. To take one example, a provincial governor, in addition to his other duties, was expected to sign and process the impossible quantity of over 100,000 documents in the course of a year, according to one estimate, and as a result, the backlog of decrees that were either ignored or simply not acted upon reached proportions estimated to be as high as 3,300,000 by 1842. The Russian

state was becoming suffocated by a blanket of paperwork so dense that simply to keep these papers moving from one governmental bureau to another occupied the full-time energies of countless numbers of officials.

Another striking characteristic of Russia's bureaucratic machine as it emerged in the century after Peter I's death was that it simply could not provide the autocrat with the information which he needed in order to undertake desirable efforts at reform and change. Time and again the Ministries of State Domains and Interior were forced to send out officials on special fact-finding missions when the established procedures for transmitting information from the provinces and districts to the central government did not function as they should. . . .

Gathering such vital information was complex indeed. Officials who were sent from the central government . . . first had to be trained to think in far less restricted terms than was common in the central bureaucracy during the second quarter of the nineteenth century and, in many cases, no matter how carefully they were chosen, these officials were not able to break sufficiently with the pedantry and formalism that had been instilled in them by years of service. As a result, major issues often were lost sight of, and the few progressive bureaucrats ... often were deluged by reports so trivial as to be virtually worthless.

This problem of excessive formalism in the bureaucracy was one which should not be underestimated. It seemed that the goal of each administrative department was not to solve a particular problem but to complete the proper paperwork relating to it. The success of an official often was measured by how quickly documents could be drawn up in his offices and passed on to the next, and government bureaux were filled with numerous petty scribes whose task it was simply to copy one document after another. The mass of the bureaucracy had no conception of the ultimate purpose of the documents they copied, nor did they care. For them, successful performance of their duties simply meant keeping the growing mountain of papers moving. ...

Because of its incompetence and poor training, and because its senior officials usually placed their aristocratic group interests ahead of those of the state, the Imperial Russian bureaucracy gave the impression of a colossus lumbering clumsily in the wrong direction. In an effort to turn it around, or at least to control its path to some degree, Nicholas I sought to create a personal machinery of government staffed by a select group of bureaucrats loyal to their ruler's, rather than their class's, interests. In a sense, Nicholas undertook to recreate the Petrine model of a service class within the gross and incompetent bureaucracy which Peter's initial efforts had spawned. He therefore expanded His Majesty's Own Chancery, the one portion of the state administrative machinery that was immediately responsible to the Emperor himself. ...

In all sections of His Majesty's Own Chancery, Nicholas attempted to establish a new type of bureaucratic order. Section heads reported directly to him and, most important, he staffed at least the upper-level positions in these sections with men far different from the usual aristocrat-bureaucrats who filled the senior positions in most state ministries.

II

In his effort to repeat Peter I's attempt to create a new service class (this time a service bureaucracy rather than a service nobility) Nicholas I had fewer options available and was more bound by the social order in Russia than had been his predecessor. While Peter I had been able to turn to the lesser nobility, men whose elevation to prominence had led them to defend the new order, no similar course of action was open to Nicholas; great and small nobles alike were united in insisting that the existing economic and social order be preserved. The Emperor sought to breach this common front of opposition ... by turning to the Baltic nobility and to the officer corps of the army. But on the fundamental question of serfdom, which formed the economic base for their way of life, even these more loyal servants of the Emperor could not break with the interests of their class. Even Count Kiselev, whom Nicholas regarded as his "Chief of Staff for Peasant Affairs," sought to deal with the peasant question within the framework of the serf system. Time and again Kiselev emphasized that the solution to the peasant problem should be sought in a clear definition of the obligations that the gentry and the serfs owed to each other and in giving the peasants the full protection of the law to guard them from abuses by their masters.

Nicholas I had shown considerable insight in perceiving that the way to break the impasse in the confrontation between autocrat and aristocracy over reform was to create a new service bureaucracy which served the Emperor and accepted his definition of state goals. What was needed was to produce a cadre of men within the state administration as Peter I had done who owed their entire position to their service achievements and who no longer regarded the interests of the aristocracy as their own. But because he was bound by the traditional relationship between nobles and ruler, which had evolved during the course of the previous century, Nicholas did not look beyond the most loyal segments of the aristocracy in his efforts to create a service bureaucracy. When finally faced with the ultimate refusal of all segments of the nobility to accept his demands for change on the serf issue, he allowed his efforts to falter.

Yet just such a group of men who owed their entire social and economic position to their success in the state service had begun to appear, though from their relatively secondary positions in the bureaucracy they remained for the moment obscured from the monarch's view. Throughout the second quarter of the century, men from impoverished noble families entered the state service not simply to fulfill what they regarded as their service function as nobles but to earn their daily bread. Having neither estates nor serfs, these men did not see the existing society and economy as something to be defended and they came to see efficient and loyal service to their Emperor and to state goals as he defined them as being the guiding purpose of their lives. One such official, A. P. Zablockij-Desiatovskij, recalled the attitudes of these men, as they had evolved by the late 1850s, in the following way:

Their ideal was the introduction of legality into all spheres of life . . . Along the path to attaining this ideal, they had two guideposts: work and a sense of duty. In work they saw not only the means without which it is impossible to improve one's position legitimately, . . . but also a necessary requirement for the full enjoyment of life. In their fulfillment of their duty they saw a basic law of morality.

These men ultimately became what we might label 'enlightened' bureaucrats: officials who not only believed in progress but who also shared the social conscience of the *intelligencija*. By the 1850s there were circles of such 'enlightened' bureaucrats in several of the central state ministries, though they were not always well-known to each other. Perhaps the most significant for our purposes (though the point is arguable depending upon where one's interests lie) was the group of 'enlightened'

bureaucrats which developed in the Ministries of State Domains and Interior, several of whom emerged in the late 1850s to play a vital part in drafting the Emancipation of 1861. . . .

During their early years in state service, in the late 1830s and 1840s, these progressive young men, who were to become 'enlightened' bureaucrats, were involved in some of the major reform projects of Nicholas I's reign. [Some] . . . helped to prepare Count P. D. Kiselev's reforms in the administration of the state peasants, . . . [while others] carried out extensive studies of urban conditions in the Russian Empire and were instrumental in drafting the Municipal Reform of 1846 in St. Petersburg. Within the Russian Empire at the time, when statistical data on all aspects of local life and state economy was in acutely short supply in the bureaucracy, these men (and we have mentioned only the most prominent here) were among the foremost authorities on local conditions.

But although they possessed some of the practical knowledge and experience required to plan and to implement reforms, these men had not yet developed a view of change that was sufficiently broad and encompassed the far-reaching reforms which the Empire so badly needed. Most important, during the early and mid-1840s, they still viewed the question of reform as an administrative matter and, like their superiors . . . , they believed that Russia's difficulties could be solved by improvements in the Empire's administrative apparatus. For them, at the time, the ideal to be attained was a well-ordered, finely-tuned machinery of government that would function efficiently and well, guaranteeing the rights of each class within the existing system and eliminating, or at least reducing, the crippling formalistic procedures which made reform work in the bureaucracy so difficult.

To go beyond considering reform as a purely administrative matter, a broader view which regarded change as something which would involve all of society and on which public opinion must be consulted—in brief, a view such as was current among the circles of the Russian *intelligencija* at the time, was needed.

Yet while the *intelligencija*, by virtue of its education and activities, was able to think in broad terms about change, its members lacked the practical ability needed to initiate reforms in a bureaucratic state system. What was needed if change in Russia were to come through legitimate means, was for the moderate *intelligencija* and progressive bureaucrats to combine their abilities and talents to produce an 'enlightened' bureaucracy: a group of men with a knowledge of Russian conditions and practical experience in planning and implementing reforms, who also saw the question of change in other terms than simply improvements in the state administrative machinery. But here too Nicholas I's policies seemed to mitigate against the emergence of such a progressive bureaucrat-moderate *intelligencija* amalgam. From the time of the Decembrist revolt, because he feared all independent expression of opinion as bearing the seeds of disorder, the Emperor had sought to isolate the *intelligencija* from reform work and from participation in state administration as long as it persisted in wide-ranging discussions of intellectual issues and refused to fit itself into the acceptable bureaucratic mold.

Thus, the progressive bureaucrats and the moderate *intelligencija* were isolated from each other not only because one group served the state and the other did not, but also because of their different world views. . . . Only in the 1840s did these intellectuals begin to emerge from their ivory towers and make an attempt to come to grips with the real problems of life in Russia once again.

Practical application of the moderate *intelligencija's* renewed interest in the problems confronting Russia was facilitated in the mid- and late 1840s in a rather unexpected way by the Minister of Interior L. A. Perovskij. In his efforts to improve the quality of the officials in his Ministry, Perovskij had become well aware of the shortcomings of the state policy which led to the exile of many brilliant young men for violating ambiguous and stifling censorship regulations, and continually urged the Emperor to end this drain on the Empire's short supply of able men. When the policy itself continued and, after 1848, intensified, Perovskij was able to have the sentence of exile lifted in a few cases. And it was in the Ministry of Interior that some of Russia's more moderate intellectuals found a haven during the last years of Nicholas I's reign when the increasing pressures from a capricious censorship and increased police surveillance made life for such men difficult. . . .

One result of the moderate intellectuals' entrance into state service was that in the late 1840s and early 1850s they and the progressive bureaucrats began to discuss reform questions together. The meetings which these men had in their day to day service activities undoubtedly provided them with one means of exchanging ideas, but more important was their association in circles outside the Ministries. . . . Miljutin had learned how to guide reform measures through recalcitrant bureaucratic offices including the State Council itself, and was regarded as one of the most able men in the capital in this respect. The moderate *intelligencija* thus began to consider that such men had something significant to offer in terms of their practical experience in the bureaucracy and during the late 1840s and early 1850s, for example, Miljutin, Zablockij-Desjatovskij, and several other progressive young officials became frequent visitors at evening gatherings of N. I. Nadezhdin's and I. I. Panaev's circles. . . .

At the same time, the progressive bureaucrats began to invite members of the moderate *intelligencija*, particularly those whom they knew in the service, to evening discussions where criticism of the formalism and incompetence of the bureaucracy was a central issue. More important, it was at evening gatherings of this type that the progressive bureaucrats began to broaden their views of change, both by discussion with their new associates, and by reading the works of advanced western European social thinkers. . . . But because Miljutin and his friends were searching neither for a new philosophical system nor for a new mold in which to remake Russian society, they passed over the political content of these writings and, it would seem, simply took from them a view of reform as something in which public opinion should play a part because of the impact that change would have upon society as a whole. In a word, the progressive bureaucrats came to share the social conscience of the moderate *intelligencija*.

The interchange of views between progressive bureaucrats and the *intelligencija* produced what we might now call an 'enlightened' bureaucracy in Russia. Further contact between the two groups took place in the early and mid-1850s at the salon of Grand Duchess Elena Pavlovna, the wife of Nicholas I's younger brother Grand Duke Michail Pavlovic. Unlike most of the Imperial family, the Grand Duchess was fully aware of the intellectual ferment in Russia and was deeply interested in the question of reform. Both Perovskij and Kiselev were among her intimate circle and she followed their work in the Ministries of Interior and State Domains with a great deal of interest. After the death of her husband in 1849, the Grand Duchess transformed her salon from one which had been composed almost entirely of men and women closely associated with the Court, to one in which a broad spectrum of Russian intellectuals and progressive bureaucrats were invited. Conversation flowed freely at her salon and, most important, sensitive reform questions, which could not be discussed either in the press or in official circles, were often the topic of conversation. . . .

At this point one should perhaps attempt to draw some conclusions about the emergence of the 'enlightened' bureaucracy in the Ministries of Interior and State Domains on the eve of Alexander II's accession. These men . . . had little stake in the old social and economic order and . . . they owed their social and material position to their success in state service. Further, their knowledge of local conditions in Russia was among the most comprehensive in the Empire, though it still was far from being adequate for preparing reforms of such magnitude as those which came in the 1860s. Throughout the last years of the reign of Nicholas I, these men continued to increase their knowledge of local conditions. For those in

Miljutin's department in the Ministry of Interior this meant a more comprehensive knowledge about conditions in Russia's cities and towns, and a growing understanding of economic and trade conditions in the Empire, while for the Ministry of State Domains . . . their work brought an increased knowledge of rural conditions. There was yet another way in which these men broadened their knowledge of Russian conditions and this was by utilizing the Imperial Russian Geographical Society where they seized control in the years from 1850–1857 and turned the society's resources from explorations of the uncharted frontier regions of the Empire to studies of local conditions in European Russia. Finally, and perhaps most important, as a result of their broad associations with the *intelligencija* in the 1850s, these 'enlightened' bureaucrats had expanded their view of change significantly. No longer did they think of change as embodying only alterations in the administrative apparatus of the state, but they had developed a social conscience.

The culmination of the work of the 'enlightened' bureaucrats . . . came in the Editing Commission of 1859–1860 . . . [in which they] formed a solid front against all opponents of emancipation. . . . United in the view that serfdom was impeding Russia's social and economic development, they were willing to subordinate differences of opinion on less important questions to the common cause of planning the reform which they all agreed was a vital necessity. Faced with bitter opposition from much of the Court, from most of the bureaucracy, and from many of the Russian nobility, they were determined to present a united front in support of the type of emancipation which they believed was in the best interests of the Russian state and society.

SOURCE: W. Bruce Lincoln, "The Genesis of an 'Enlightened' Bureaucracy in Russia, 1825–1856," *Jahrbücher für Geschichte Osteuropas*, new series 20 (1972), pp. 321–30 (excerpted). Reprinted by permission of the author and the journal.

WALTER M. PINTNER

The Russian Higher Civil Service on the Eve of the Great Reforms

In explaining the appearance of "new men" in the service bureaucracy of Nicholas I, Bruce Lincoln placed great weight on personal and subjective qualities: the independence of these loyal servitors from the landed nobility and their sympathy for the ideas of the moderate intelligentsia. Walter Pintner's study of the service and educational records of hundreds of governmental servitors, by contrast, directs our attention to their social and educational background as the keys to understanding what distinguished them from their predecessors.

After the defeat of revolutionary France under Napoleon Russian official policy was generally conservative, in the literal meaning of the word. Its aim was to preserve the existing order. Many of the problems facing Russian society were recognized, but with few exceptions the dangers and difficulties of trying to solve them were considered too great to justify the attempt. In the aftermath of the Crimean War, however, the balance of expected gains and risks shifted and the state undertook a series of important changes, including the emancipation of the serfs, that have been known ever since as the "Great Reforms." Because the reforms were elaborated and administered by the state, not extracted from it by some external force, the question arises as to how the status quo regime that Nicholas I (1825–1855) bequeathed to his successor, Alexander II (1855–81), came to have at its disposal a cadre of officials both capable and willing to undertake the sweeping changes in Russian institutions that were involved in these "Great Reforms."

As at least a partial answer to this problem, the aim of this essay is to examine the social

background, and particularly the training and career experience, of the leading Russian officials on the eve of the reforms. The civil service was not a static body in the first half of the century despite the conservative character of the regime; on the contrary, it underwent important changes that help to explain its ability to meet the new requirements of the state in the post-Crimean decades. . . .

Imperial statutes did not establish explicit requirements for high officials, in terms of social origin, landholding, education, or type of career experience. In theory at least all high officials could have been wealthy nobles from old families educated by French tutors, or they could have been men of humble birth without property who rose through the ranks by dint of merit and seniority, after formal education in some public or ecclesiastical institution. These extreme types, as well as others, existed from the highest levels on down. The important question is in what proportion and in what kinds of positions were they to be found? Who was in charge of what in the mid-nineteenth century? And does the distribution of officials of varying background make the ability of the state to initiate and carry out reform easier to understand. . . .

If [the Russian civil service] was not "professional" in the sense of having specialized training, competence, and high standards of ethics, it clearly was a distinct occupational group, separate from the other segments of mid-nineteenth-century Russian society: the full-time noble landlords, career military men, priests, merchants, artisans, or peasants. However, what was true of the civil service as a whole need not necessarily hold for those at the highest levels of authority who comprised an insignificant proportion of the total number of men employed, yet who were primarily responsible for policy making and the supervision of government activity. . . .

The most widespread characteristics among the higher civil servants is certainly membership in the hereditary nobility; 77 percent were members of that estate by birth. . . . The apparent homogeneity, even disregarding the small admixture of commoners, may be misleading. A hereditary noble in the late eighteenth and early nineteenth century, when the fathers of our officials were forming their families, might be one of many types. He could stem from an old family tracing its service to the state back for generations. Such a man might be rich in serfs, have few, or possibly none at all. But the father might also be a civil or military official who had gained hereditary noble status through a successful career, or he could be the son of such a man. . . .

Noble status by birth was close to being a prerequisite for a career that ended at the top. Wealth clearly was not. The detailed information on property holdings, the only important form of independent wealth, in the service records is expressed in terms of numbers of serfs; it includes parental as well as the officials' own holdings, and is broken down according to method of acquisition, either inherited, or acquired through gift or purchase.

Independent wealth could presumably have facilitated a service career in many ways, and conversely, a successful career might have been a way to gain landed property and independent means through Imperial favor, purchase, or marriage to an heiress. Two striking conclusions emerge, however, from the actual data. a) Forty-three percent of the high officials had no serfs, inherited or acquired, in their family (husband, wife, or parents), but 19 percent were very wealthy and had over 1,000 serfs (38 percent had over 200 and could therefore be considered significant landholders). Thus the high officials included both a very large landless group and a smaller but significant group with substantial or even great estates. b) It is equally clear that success in service was not normally accompanied by the acquisition of landed property. Fifty-nine percent of the high officials were from families entirely without inherited serfs, while 18 percent had inherited over 500. . . . Of the 59 percent without inherited serfs (205 men), only 2 percent (4 men) acquired 500 or more serfs, while 84 percent (173 men) remained entirely serfless despite their highly successful careers. . . . The relatively few officials who did acquire large numbers of serfs tended to be those already deeply involved in rural landholding. Twenty-three men acquired over 500 serfs through purchase or gift, and 14 of these (61 percent) already had that many.

Furthermore, marriage rarely blended the interests of the successful bureaucrat and the landed nobility. In many societies the theme of the poor boy who makes good and marries the heiress (or makes good by marrying the heiress) is a familiar one. Romance, however, seems to have had little impact on bureaucratic serfholding in Russia. Of the 205 officials with no inherited serfs in the families, only two married women with over 500 serfs. Wealth evidently was attracted to wealth, for of the 62 men with over 500 serfs already in the family, 18 (29 percent) married women with a comparable inheritance. . . . Socially, the high officials with landed wealth apparently remained apart and marriage tended to reinforce ties to the land rather than enable the successful career bureaucrat to establish himself in the countryside and presumably, the social circles of the landed nobility. Successful service was the route to power, prestige, and a generous salary and expense allowance, but it did not increase the official's economic or social autonomy from the state by permitting him to acquire independent wealth based on land and serfs. It is safe to assume that most of the officials with no serfs whatever in their family were the sons, grandsons, or great-grandsons of men who rose to hereditary noble status via the table of ranks.

Differences in education and career experience were as important as those in serfholding among the higher civil servants. It was precisely in the decades prior to the "Great Reforms" that the Russian civil service began to shift from primary reliance on "in-service" training for high officials to formal education prior to the beginning of a bureaucratic career. Some such training had been purely nominal, as in the case of the young nobleman registered in a guards regiment shortly after his birth. Other paths to high office came to include serious academic instruction in institutions such as the Imperial Corps of Pages, the Lycee at Tsarskoe Selo, or the universities.

One of three basic patterns can be used to describe the careers of virtually all of the high officials studied: (a) "court-elite," (b) "standard-military," and (c) "bureaucratic-technical." The court-elite pattern was reserved for the privileged few and entailed education or early experience, real or nominal, in some special institution associated with the Imperial Court, such as the Corps of Pages, His Imperial Majesty's Own Suite, the Preobrazhensky or Izmailovsky regiments, or the "junker" training program in the Ministry of Foreign Affairs. Many of these men bore famous old aristocratic names and usually they were educated at home by tutors before entering one of these exclusive organizations. Formal education in the sense of institutions of higher learning such as a university or technical institute was definitely not part of the court-elite pattern of training. Prince Alexander Mikhailovich Urussov, for example, noted on his personal file, with typical aristocratic contempt, that he had been "educated at home and never attended any kind of educational institutions." Most, but not all, of the officials with court-connected careers had large family estates.

The second common career pattern for high civil officials was simply regular military service with education either at home, in the Cadet Corps, or in a technical military school such as the Institute of Transport Engineers, followed by a career in military service and eventual transfer to an important administrative post or a largely honorific appointment as a member of the Senate.

The third, and most significant, of the three routes to high position is the bureaucratic-technical. Of the three, it suggests most strongly the emergence of bureaucracy in the Weberian sense of an organization based on specialized expertise with promotion according to some combination of merit and seniority, rather than ascribed status, wealth, or family influence. Formal education in a university, technical institute, or the Lycee at Tsarskoe Selo enabled the graduate to enter civil service well up the table of ranks, a crucially important advantage because subsequent promotion depended largely on seniority. A mere handful of officials with only elementary or secondary education managed to work their way to the top through the civil service ranks.

The idea that education and state service were closely related was certainly not new in mid-nineteenth century Russia. Throughout the eighteenth century secondary and even primary education were regarded as both a means of achieving a successful service career and as an actual part of the career itself. Service records in the 1790s did not specifically call for information on education, but many officials began their career summary with the phrase, "I entered service in the—school." As preparation for a civil career in the eighteenth century emphasis was given to what can be called "work and study" programs. Young nobles (starting at age twelve) were placed in an office and given special training courses in conjunction with their work. The trainees were given the title "Collegial junker" and many achieved high positions in later years. On the whole, however, the system was not considered successful. Instruction took second place to the work of each office and no single agency could devote sufficient resources to develop an adequate educational program for a handful of boys. It was only in the early nineteenth century, with the expansion of Moscow University, the establishment of several new universities, the Lycee at Tsarskoe Selo, and the Imperial Law Academy, that the Russian system of higher education began to produce a substantial number of graduates qualified for civil service, and by the middle of the century many had reached high positions. . . .

Men with any given career experience were concentrated in particular agencies. Immediately around the Tsar there was a high proportion of officials with the court-elite background. Elsewhere, in the operating agencies, the graduates of the universities and other institutions predominated. . . . Not only were the court-elite members of the State Council wealthy and the products of privileged educational institutions, but they were entered on the service rosters early in life. The average . . . age on entering the service was eleven, and five entrants were five years old or less. . . .

If the type of background and training that characterized the State Council had also been true of other important agencies, one could conclude that Russia was governed by a small hereditary clique of wealthy landowners that surrounded the Tsar. The situation, however, was quite different in other departments of the government. The Senate was one of the most prestigious, if not actually powerful, agencies in the Imperial administration and the senators were men with long and successful careers. Nevertheless the proportion with court-elite careers is much lower than in the State Council. Of a total of fifty-two Senators, twenty (42 percent) had the court-elite background, twenty-one (41 percent) a regular military career, and nine (17 percent) bureaucratic-technical training and career.

In the ministries, where policy was actually implemented, the importance of the career bureaucrat with higher education was even greater. At the Ministry of the Interior (Department of General Affairs), and in the Chancellery of the Ministry of Finance, about 60 percent of the top officials had the bureaucratic-technical career background and only 16 percent had any obvious court connections.

The wealthy aristocrats without formal education held the top positions, while the more formally trained bureaucrats at a slightly lower level were in charge of the actual operations. But this division of labor was not really the result of differences in training but rather was almost certainly a matter of age. The men around Nicholas in the last years of his reign were elderly and their careers had begun before the major expansion of higher education in the early nineteenth century was well underway. In the State Council, for example, 70 percent had entered the service prior to 1810. What was happening under Nicholas I, despite all that is usually said about his penchant for military men, was that graduates of the universities and the Lycee were replacing an older generation trained at home and on the job in the "junker" program, or in the elite army regiments. . . .

The new form of preparation for service certainly did not eliminate the wealthy and well-connected young nobleman from service, but it did mean that his youthful experiences were markedly different from those of the older generation. No longer did a boy enter civil service in his mid-teens, in fact directly from the hands of a tutor, although perhaps nominally enrolled in an elite regiment for several years. Education in a university or the Lycée meant that the entrant was usually about twenty when first embarked on his career. By then the future official had been exposed to a wider variety of academic subjects than in the past and, in the universities, to a student body of far more diverse social origin than he would ever have met under the old system. Greater emphasis on formal higher education, of course, did not mean that the new bureaucrats were necessarily more inclined to be "liberal" than their predecessors; quite the contrary could be the case. It did, however, tend to place the landed and the landless, and even the noble and the non-noble, on a more equal footing in service, in a system that made the level of entrance the crucial factor in an entire career. Another factor working in the same direction was the substantial increase in the size of the civil service in the reign of Nicholas I, which must have tended to reduce the proportion of landed nobles in the bureaucracy.

On the eve of the Great Reforms the Russian higher civil service was feeling the full effects of the expansion of higher education that began early in the nineteenth century. The adjustment apparently continued throughout the reigns of Alexander II (1856–1881) and reached its culmination under Alexander III (1881–1894). In the last years of Nicholas I old men, usually large landowners, trained in the old way, still filled the State Council, but in the operating departments, in the working levels of the Senate, and even in His Majesty's Own Chancellery, the university-trained career official predominated—almost always a hereditary noble, but usually without meaningful ties to the land. There had always been many men without serfs in government, but the new pattern of training gave them a better chance for success than they had ever had before. For the landless career official the interests of the state and its agencies, whatever they were decreed to be by the Tsar, could only be paramount. The Russian bureaucratic system had many faults and they have been frequently noted both by scholars and novelists. Much was lacking in the training provided, even in the universities and the Lycée. But in a society where alternative employment opportunities for an educated man were few, the system did produce a cadre of officials who, if neither highly efficient, or even honest in many cases, were devoted and loyal. How could they be anything else? They had nowhere else to go.

SOURCE: Walter M. Pintner, "The Russian Higher Civil Service on the Eve of the Great Reforms," *Journal of Social History* 8: (Summer, 1978) 55–65 (excerpted). Reprinted by permission of the editors of the *Journal of Social History*.

15

The Imperial Economy

Long before the eighteenth century Russia had developed into a landlord–peasant economy, with the vast majority of the population and economic activity situated in the countryside and engaged in agriculture. This fundamental fact of life remained for the most part unchanged during most of the Imperial period. Unlike much of Western and Central Europe, Russia did not undergo a major industrial or urban expansion in the late eighteenth and early nineteenth centuries. Most physical work was performed, as before, on the land and by servile labor. By contrast, serfdom had all but disappeared from most of the rest of Europe by the end of the eighteenth century.

This sense of primordiality, of the seemingly unchanging character of a rural economy that was governed by nature and by roles fixed generations earlier, rather than by politics or individual will, is vividly evoked by Arcadius Kahan's month-by-month description of the seasonality of farm life. At first glance the photographs and illustrations of peasant life scattered throughout Part IV also appear to reflect the unwavering rootedness of peasants to the soil. A second look, however, hints at a more fluid and complex peasant world. Notice the diversity of implements between the rough-hewn handmade ones and the more uniform machine-produced ones. The fact that the peasants held both farm implements and handicraft tools might indicate a diversification of the rural economy beyond farming alone. Both men and women are pictured with instruments of work, indicating that labor was a shared, if gender-divided, responsibility. The clothing that the peasants wear is mostly handmade, but some articles, such as the tall felt hat, may have come from a factory. Perhaps peasant life may not have been so simple or isolated after all.

The charts on trade and production, especially those that describe a robust trade which managed to send a wide variety of agricultural and horticultural commodities from the Russian countryside to foreign markets, reinforce the idea that the village economy was connected to larger, worldwide economic forces. Kahan's discussion of markets and Boris Mironov's analysis of the price revolution suggest that the rural economy underwent marked changes in the imperial period and that it was profoundly affected by forces, such as international trade and inflation, that peasants never saw and about which they knew very little. Are these competing images (unchanging vs. dynamic, local vs. worldwide) of the peasant economy contradictory, or are they perhaps merely different, but equally valid, approaches to understanding rural life?

DOCUMENTS

Charts and Tables on Economic Development

1. COMPOSITION OF FOREIGN TRADE, 1653–1804: RAW MATERIALS VS. MANUFACTURED GOODS (%)

	1653	1710	1725	1762	1802–4
Exported goods					
Raw Materials:	93.7	55.1	27.0	49.3	77.6
Manufactured goods:	2.5	44.5	72.2	50.3	14.0
Other goods:	3.8	0.4	0.8	0.4	8.4
Total	100.0	100.0	100.0	100.0	100.0
Imported Goods					
Raw Materials:	—	3.7	9.3	5.5	25.7
Manufactured goods:	—	96.3	90.7	94.5	70.5
Other goods:	—	—	—	—	3.8
Total	100.0	100.0	100.0	100.0	100.0

SOURCE: Adapted from Table 1 in B. N. Mironov, "Vliianie revoliutsii tsen v Rossii XVIII veka na ee ekonomicheskoe i sotsial'no-politicheskoe razvitie," *Istoriia SSSR* 1 (1991), p. 87. Reprinted by permission of the author.

2. RUSSIA'S PRIMARY EXPORTS IN THE EIGHTEENTH CENTURY (%)

Category of goods	1710	1725	1750	1769	1802–5
Agricultural products	92.1	51.5	53.1	63.0	72.0
Hemp and hemp yarn	34.4	16.3	28.2	18.8	17.5
Flax and hemp yarn	3.3	3.5	2.7	11.3	10.8
Hempseed and linseed oil, hempseed and linseed	0.3	1.1	1.6	3.5	3.6
Grain, flour, groats	2.9	—	—	16.9	20.2
Tallow	11.4	2.6	6.7	5.0	14.7
Leather, cattle, meat	39.8	28.0	13.9	7.5	5.3
Manufactured and forest products	7.9	48.5	46.9	37.0	27.9
Furs and skins	3.7	5.3	1.3	4.5	7.2
Iron	—	1.1	15.1	9.8	5.7
Textiles	3.7	36.3	16.5	13.0	6.6
Other goods	0.5	5.8	14.0	9.7	8.4
Total	100.0	100.0	100.0	100.0	100.0
Value of Export (in millions of rubles)	1.4	2.	4.4	14.5	65.5

SOURCE: Mironov (see above) Table 2, p. 89.

3. INDEX OF PRICES FOR PRINCIPAL EXPORT GOODS IN THE EIGHTEENTH CENTURY (in grams of silver)

	1711–20	1731–40	1751–60	1771–80	1781–90	1796–1801
Grain	149	190	208	320	480	564
Hemp	113	148	170	210	210	433
Flax	116	157	182	222	235	386
Hempseed	135	196	192	323	410	507
and linseed,	92	139	154	200	237	255
leather and hides	99	84	95	116	—	202
Goods from Forests	—	—	—	—	—	249
Iron	91	125	139	180	214	230
Textiles	100	125	161	216	350	366

Note: 1701–10 = 100.
SOURCE: Adapted From Mironov (see p. 269) Table 3, p. 89.

4. INCOME RECEIVED BY PRIVATE LANDLORDS FROM THEIR SERFS DURING THE EIGHTEENTH CENTURY

The number of landlords' peasants (in thousands of male souls)

Year	Total	Total on corvée	Total on quitrent
1701–10	2915	1312	1603
1711–20	3111	1400	1711
1721–30	3325	1496	1829
1731–40	3558	1672	1886
1741–50	3807	1827	1980
1751–60	4143	2072	2071
1761–70	4515	2348	2167
1771–80	4862	2625	2237
1781–90	5236	2932	2304
1791–1800	5617	3146	2471

Landlords' net annual profit per male soul (in kopecks)

Year	Profit from Corvée	Profit from Quitrent
1701–10	36 k.	40 k.
1711–20	67	50
1721–30	88	70
1731–40	91	90
1741–50	116	120
1751–60	108	160

(continued)

Year	Profit from Corvée	Profit from Quitrent
1761–70	163	300
1771–80	221	450
1781–90	750	600
1791–1800	1000	750

Note: Data based on the territory of Russia as it stood at the beginning of the eighteenth century.
SOURCE: Adapted from Mironov, Table 7, p. 95.

5. LAND RESOURCES IN THE EIGHTEENTH CENTURY

Year	Total (in hectares)	% Plowland	% Meadows	% Forests
1696	405,091,000	7.89	16.56	52.68
1725	418,219,000	10.01	15.85	51.16
1763	423,128,000	12.73	14.96	48.66
1796	485,465,000	16.76	15.79	44.76

SOURCE: Adapted from Arcadius Kahan, *The Plow the Hammer and the Knout. An Economic History of Eighteenth-Century Russia* (Chicago: University of Chicago Press, 1985). Copyright © 1985 by the University of Chicago Press. Table 2.1, p. 46. This and all subsequent charts from Kahan in this section are reprinted by permission of the publisher.

6. OUTPUT/SEED RATIOS FOR THE MAJOR GRAINS

Grain	1710s	1730s	1750s	1770s	1790s
Rye	2.9	3.2	3.7	4.2	3.1
Wheat	3.9	3.9	3.3	4.3	3.0
Oats	2.7	3.3	3.5	4.8	3.6
Barley	3.9	4.0	4.3	4.2	3.1

SOURCE: Adapted from Kahan (see above) Table 2.2, p. 49.

7. URBAN POPULATION IN THE EIGHTEENTH CENTURY
(by census years)

Year	Urban Population
1721	1,240,000
1744	1,260,000
1762	1,520,000
1783	2,080,000
1795	3,040,000

SOURCE: Adapted from Kahan (see above) Table 2.9, p. 58.

8. ESTIMATED GRAIN CONSUMPTION OF THE URBAN POPULATION
(in chetverts)

Decade	Grain Consumption
1720s	2,480,000
1740s	2,520,000
1760s	3,040,000
1780s	4,160,000
1790s (2nd half)	6,080,000

SOURCE: Adapted from Kahan (see above) Table 2.10, p. 58.

9. YEARLY AVERAGE GRAIN EXPORTS BY DECADES (in chetverts)

Decade	Wheat	Rye	Oats	Barley	Other
1711–20	94,388	88,024	4,879	1,485	—
1731–40	121,261	103,798	5,190	12,147	126
1751–60	36,965	34,600	452	1,663	210
1771–80	499,670	360,150	100,463	23,825	12,716
1791–99	337,282	172,982	187,165	49,754	12,022

SOURCE: Adapted from Kahan (see p. 271) Table 2.11, p. 59.

10. GROWTH OF FAIRS IN RUSSIA

Decade	Urban	Rural	Total
1750s	244	383	627
1760s	487	1,143	1,630
1790s	864	3,180	4,044

Note: Data for the entire territory of the Russian Empire.
SOURCE: Adapted from Kahan (see p. 271) Table 5.1, p. 269.

11. SETTLEMENTS WITH BAZAARS, AND MARKET DAYS PER WEEK

Decades	No. of Settlements with Bazaars			Total No. of Market Days per Week		
	Urban	Rural	Total	Urban	Rural	Total
1750s	209	165	374	398	177	575
1760s	278	193	471	428	209	637
1790s	513	570	1,083	722	608	1,330

Note: Kahan here has taken the number of days per week that each market was open, and then added them up to produce these totals.
SOURCE: Kahan (see p. 271), Table 5.6, p. 272.

LITERATURE

ARCADIUS KAHAN
The Character of the Russian Economy

Historians sometimes fall into the bad habit of forcing whole areas of Russian history into the seductive metaphor of "backwardness." Nowhere has this propensity been more marked than in studies of the economy and economic institutions. The late Arcadius Kahan's work marked a refreshing alternative to that tendency. He, too, sees that central features of Russia's economic order were less productive and less efficiently-organized than were many other national economies. But, in these selections, he gives equal weight to other perspectives: the ecological circumstances (weather, soil, water, etc.) within which production had to proceed; the robust development of trade and markets, domestic and foreign; and the pace of economic life for the peasantry.

THE AGRICULTURAL CYCLE AND NATURAL CALAMITIES

For the overwhelming majority of the inhabitants of eighteenth-century Russia, the rhythm of life was determined not by the wars or reforms of Peter the Great, nor by anything his successors managed to accomplish or failed to do, but by the conditions of the agricultural cycle of plowing, planting, and harvesting the Russian fields. The sustenance of the vast majority of Russians depended less upon the level of rents, the burden of government taxation, or profits derived in domestic or foreign trade than upon the work of nature. Of paramount importance was the size of the harvest, the ratio of harvested grain to the seed planted (the output-seed ratio). The major calamities of the century were not necessarily the occasional defeats of the Russian armies or the failures of

Russian diplomacy, but the famines that frequented the Russian countryside.

The reason for the harmful influence of droughts and frosts upon the Russian food supply lay in the low output-seed ratio of grains even during years of normal weather conditions. With an output-seed ratio of 3.0–3.5:1 for grains during normal weather conditions and grain reserves of not more than one year's consumption, any single year of adverse weather put rural households in a precarious situation as far as food supply was concerned. Repetitive bad weather conditions, severe winters, excessive rainfall, or droughts that affected the yields of both spring and winter grains produced a famine if they lasted for two consecutive years. The exhaustion of grain reserves followed the decline of the available current grain supply. This was accompanied by a decline of commercial output, a rise in grain prices, and privation of various degrees.

The first half of the eighteenth century was abundantly endowed with adverse weather, the impact of which was seriously felt by the agricultural sector and the population at large. The low population growth during this period cannot be attributed solely to the conditions of the food supply, but it is an additional indicator of the effects of the frequent failures of the grain yields during this period. . . .

During the second half of the century bad weather conditions that influenced yields were less frequent and apparently of shorter duration. Their effect was less severe and did not lead to famines covering most of the territory of Russia. The growth of the planted area, particularly in the blacksoil steppe zone, had the effect of dispersing the population. Although the steppe zone was susceptible to droughts, there was more of a compensating substitution effect between the nonblacksoil and the blacksoil zones which resulted in spreading and diminishing the risks of famine. . . .

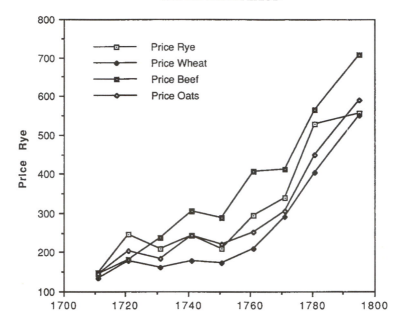

Data from an eighteenth-century "price index."

THE AGRICULTURAL ROUTINE

One of the most vivid descriptions of the activities of the agricultural labor force was provided by Vasilii Levshin, a Tula landowner and member of the Free Economic Society. It conveys the routine of agricultural labor in its seasonal sequence and is arranged by calendar months. Although the timing of the various activities is determined to a major extent by the geographical position of the Tula guberniia [province] in the central region of Russia, both the sequence and variety were typical for most of the agricultural regions of the country and are worth reproducing in full.

January. Continuation of grain threshing and hemp processing. Transportation of hay from meadows. Transportation of grain for sale. Hiring out for day labor in the city. At home the remaining men are making ropes and weaving bast sandals, while the women are spinning and taking care of their sheep, which are giving birth to their young ones.

February. Continuation of the previous activities. The ones who are leaving for work out- side the villages are getting their passports and by the end of February are leaving for work. Preparation of a reserve of flour for the time of the thaw (when the snow melts and the roads are impassable) and for the summer.

March. Besides the above-mentioned activities, men are repairing their carts and agricultural implements for the coming field-work season. Repair of roofs, cleaning off the snow, and spreading straw on the floors of the farm buildings, inspecting the bee-hives and cleaning the hives by the end of March. Women are weaving their cloth and linen and continue to do it through April. They take care of the hens laying eggs and keep the hens on the nests.

April. Repair of wattle fences. Threshing of grain for spring seed. Plowing the soil for spring grains begins. By the end of the month, planting of wheat, peas, and early oats. The women and children take the cattle out to feed on pasture. They continue weaving and caring for the poultry and the new-borns. Dyeing of the yarn, planting of cabbage plants, and row plantings of the seeds of garden vegetables.

May. Planting of oats, hemp, flax, millet, and part of the barley. Plowing of the gardens. Women take care of the poultry, are finishing their weaving, and begin to bleach their linen. Collecting of birch leaves for dyeing. Pasturing on the meadows being prohibited, they move the cattle to the fallow land strip. In the garden various kinds of vegetables are planted and the cabbage is replanted.

June. Planting of buckwheat and the rest of the barley. Transportation of manure to the fallow-field strips, and by the middle of the month, plowing up all of them. By the end of the month, planting of turnips and preparation for hay cutting. Women finish the bleaching of linen. Shearing of sheep, weeding of the spring grains and from the 24th, collecting of dyeing-herbs. The agriculturalists look after the bee hives. Men and women gathering and preparing bast and bark.

July. Beginning of hay mowing, gathering of the hay. From the middle of the month, second plowing and harrowing of the fallow strip. Women begin to harvest rye and weed the flax. Beehiving is continuing. The hungry cattle begin to rest after being moved to the harvested meadows.

August. Threshing of grain for seed, planting of winter grain. Harvesting of barley and wheat, cutting of oats and buckwheat, and gathering of the grains from the fields. Gathering of mushrooms and nuts. The cattle move to the rye fields. Second shearing of sheep.

September. Taking out the honey. Finishing the gathering of harvested grains from the fields. In some places, finishing the planting to winter grains. Women collecting the hemp, men threshing it and putting it into water. Threshing of grains begins. New construction and finishing of construction as well as repair of roofs begun earlier. Youngsters gather firewood in nearby small woods. Harvesting of flax and putting it in prepared places for retting. Digging up of turnips. The cattle enjoy having all the fields to themselves.

October. Taking the hemp out of water, drying and processing it. In some places, plowing of the harvested rye fields for the next spring grains and spring wheat. Spreading manure on the fields. Repair and rebuilding of dwellings continues, as well as gathering of firewood. The carders are carding the wool and the women begin spinning. The village tailors leave to find work. Preparation of the beehives for the winter. Hunters are hunting hares and grouse.

November. The main threshing. Beginning of transportation of firewood prepared for the winter and summer. Completion of hemp processing. Women begin spinning hemp and continue throughout the entire winter. They put the pigs on feeding, and with the arrival of strong frosts, or the beginning of winter, they slaughter the geese and ducks from the fields for sale. Major hunting of rabbits. Discontinue the pasturing of cattle in the fields. Repair the sleighs.

December. Threshing. Finish transporting firewood. Send out grain caravans. Leaving for the steppe for harvested grain and to trade in various goods. The ones who left for outside work return home. Slaughtering of the fattened pigs, sometimes of the fowl that were not slaughtered toward the end of November. The superfluous workers leave the household for the city for day labor. Trap-hunting of wolves and hares, partridges and grouse. In the evenings, the men are weaving bast sandals and making ropes and other home implements. . . .

MARKET FORMATION

The formation of markets in eighteenth-century Russia was a process that depended upon the purchasing power of consumers and upon the extent of production destined for sale rather than for consumption by the producers. It thus depended upon the exchange of goods produced by various social groups, often located at a considerable distance from one another, and their ability to benefit from this reciprocal demand. The exchange occurred predominantly in local meeting places—markets or fairs—in which producers and consumers, but more often middlemen and consumers, conducted their business. . . .

A presumption arises: grain markets were

primarily local, they consisted of relatively small areas producing a grain surplus that could be transported cheaply to urban-type settlements, to alcohol distilleries, or to any party in the vicinity demanding grain. On the basis of such a presumption, one must assume that the production of marketable grain, demanded locally or within a short radius, grew only very slowly, and certainly no faster than the nonagricultural population of that microregion.

We know that this was not the case all over Russia in the seventeenth and eighteenth century. . . . There were already major regional markets for grain in the seventeenth century. They were capable of supplying the city of Moscow, exports to Arkhangel'sk and Sweden, and the demands of Siberian settlements and fur hunters. It was during the eighteenth century, however, that both the expansion and the integration of local markets into major regional markets took place. . . .

The oldest and most extensive mega-region for marketed rye was the territory along the Volga River and its major tributaries. The Volga was the major artery of Russian domestic trade for bulk commodities such as grain and it was the main route connecting the local markets of this vast region. The new agricultural lands were settled and opened up for commercial traffic along the Volga during the eighteenth century. . . .

Another distinct market region can be observed in the first half of the eighteenth century, the Northern Dvina River basin, north of the Volga region. This region reached, in the west, the settlements on the Karelian border and, in the east, via the Northern Urals, the area of northwest Siberia. Arkhangel'sk was its port outlet. This region had a much more limited supply capacity than did the Volga region, and probably a higher degree of grain marketability. The price level was high, reaching that of the north-western extremity of the Volga mega-region. That in part reflected the foreign demand for Russian grain. The price differentials prevailing in the northern region were strongly affected by the transportation costs from the supply areas to the ones which were clearly grain-consuming ones. . . .

Market formation can be attributed to the general expansion of the economy, the growth of the urban population, the foreign trade in grains, and the beginnings of specialization in agriculture. Moreover, serf-owners were increasingly participating in the marketing of their estates' crops, which coincided with the expansion into the blacksoil areas and the rise of grain prices. Holding back the process, on the other hand, was the very slow rate of transportation improvements, the fact that the urban share of the total population was small, the slow rise in the domestic and foreign demand for marketable grain, and the poorly developed apparatus for collecting the marketable surplus.

The role of the state in this process remains to be noted. As with other areas of governmental interference in the economy of eighteenth-century Russia, there were credit and debit entries. On the credit side were the construction of a few canals, improvement of some waterways, and the distribution of state purchases of grain for the armed forces, which tended to minimize price differentials (and perhaps save the government some expense in transporting the grain). On the debit side of the ledger were internal tolls (until 1754), the prohibition against exports during periods of high prices, an inability to set up sufficient reserves to cope with the impact of famines. The government's introduction of free trade in grains in the 1760s removed a major obstacle and uncertainty in the grain market, and contributed to the more rapid development of the grain market. . . .

INTERNAL TRADE

The old dictum by Adam Smith that "the division of labor depends upon the extent of the market" is of crucial importance for an understanding of the structure of the eighteenth-century Russian economy. The closest indicator of the extent of the market in any country is the volume of internal trade. This was particularly true for the period before the dramatic expansion of Russia's foreign trade. . . .

The shift from home-produced goods to goods produced by rural or urban specialized producers was one of the chief sources of the market expansion. This process proceeded along a number of lines. One of them was the expansion of intrarural trade, which was one of two types. One involved an exchange of goods within single villages or between adjacent villages in particular micro-regions. The other type was between distant rural areas, involving goods produced by the rural population, but it was carried on by specialized traders and could be considered as an intervillage trade. Very little of both types of trade was recorded by the fiscal authorities or even described by observers. It is clear, however, that any shifts away from home-produced goods toward specialized production leading to a marketable surplus of either agricultural products or rural crafts found their way in the first instance exactly into those two types of markets, ones that left almost no trace.

A parallel movement of an increasing volume of goods can be observed in the exchange between the countryside and the towns. This movement of goods was predicated upon an increasing differentiation of production between the two as well as upon the development of regional specialization. This trade differed from the intravillage and intervillage trade which, although extensive, consisted of very numerous small transactions with a large component of barter . . . The town-country trade was based on money transactions. . . .

To understand this growth of longer-distance, intervillage and village-town trade (both of which were varieties of interregional trade), one must recall the pattern of industrial growth and specialization in Russia. Specialized production of hemp and flax, tallow and leather in particular agricultural regions was one of the features of this process. Another feature was the development of cottage-type, small-scale, rural enterprises that specialized in primary processing and the subsequent production of consumer goods; wool and hides, flax and hemp were used, yarn and linen, cloth and agricultural tools were made—all activities absorbing an inordinate volume of labor. . . .

The backbone of the goods distribution system in eighteenth-century Russia was made up of periodic *fairs* located in a number of urban and rural settlements. They constituted the institutional arrangement for most of the wholesale trade and a substantial portion of the retail trade. *Bazaars* for markets with appointed market days during the week were another institutional arrangement in which some wholesale trade and much of the retail trade was conducted. Two additional arrangements that facilitated the supply of goods to consumers were stationary trade in stores and stalls, especially in the major cities, and the itinerant trade of peddlers in the countryside. These last two types of trading institutions were less developed than might be expected.

The most interesting feature of the two major institutions of trade, the fairs and the bazaars, was their simultaneous service as wholesale and retail channels and as centers of selling as well as the buying of goods. They combined the sale of imported goods with the mobilization of Russian goods for export abroad. The fairs are a good example of the mosaic of internal trade. . . . [O]ne discovers not only the faster growth of the number of fairs located in rural areas, but also the growth of the number of fairs per rural settlement, something that indicates the growing scope and intensity of rural trade. . . .

The majority of fairs during the 1790s were small ones with a trade turnover of less than 10,000 rubles. There were 2,202 such fairs or 69.7 percent of the total 3,195. In the middle range were 590, or 18.7 percent of the fairs, with a turnover of from 11,000 to 100,000 rubles. The large ones, 367 or 11.6 percent, had a turnover of over 100,000 rubles. . . .

The fairs attracted sellers and buyers from beyond the county in which they were located. In fact, only 278 of all of the fairs were exclusively county fairs. About one-third of all fairs attracted participants from counties located within a particular province . . . ; 638 fairs attracted participants from the counties of adjacent provinces and 558 from adjacent districts and, therefore, should be considered regional fairs. Seventy-six fairs attracted participants from various regions and from abroad,

"Merchants Loading Bags of Wheat for Winter Transport." From *Souvenirs de S. Peterbourg: Costumes russes* (St. Petersburg, 1825), Plate 8. Reprinted courtesy of The New York Public Library, Slavic and Baltic Division.

which made them trans-national in scope. An interesting feature of the fairs was their relatively short duration.... Only 5 percent of fairs on which there are data lasted more than a week....

The fairs presented a broad and varied panorama of goods-exchange. They were differentiated in size and some degree of specialization appeared. The smaller fairs were connected to the middle-sized ones, the middle-sized ones to the larger ones.... It would be ... correct to view the fairs as a well-functioning network fed by two streams of commodity flows. One stream moved from the wholesalers dealing in manufactured goods and imports and got thinner as it moved from the major to the minor fairs. The other stream flowed in the opposite direction and supplied agricultural goods and raw materials for domestic and export use. The second stream grew and swelled as it moved from the local to

the regional and national fairs.... Their timing reminds one of a train schedule in which the main trunk lines are synchronized and the feeder lines are then adjusted in their schedules to the trunk lines. Although the government decreed the schedules of fairs in the eighteenth century, unquestionably they developed gradually, organically, and were based on the proved behavior of sellers and buyers, rather than on the whims of bureaucrats....

Besides the fairs, the so-called *bazaar* or market was the second important institutional arrangement of internal trade. These were markets that operated during certain days of the week in places especially designated for transactions between buyers and sellers of goods.... During the 1760s and 1770s Fridays and Sundays were the most popular market days and accounted for 30 and 18 percent of all the market days, respectively.

Retail trade prevailed in the bazaars, which

An urban bazaar in the early nineteenth century. From *Pushkinskii Peterburg* (Leningrad, 1972).

served as loci for the sale and purchase of food-stuffs and handicrafts by urban and rural craftsmen. Merchants of the second corporation purchased the agricultural surplus at the bazaars to resell to the wholesalers at the fairs. Sales of grains, vegetables, livestock products, and domestically manufactured goods, produced to meet peasant demand, dominated the bazaar trade.

That trade, far more than the fair trade, was affected by seasonal fluctuations. Its peaks were during the early autumn and middle winter months. It declined precipitously during the seasons of heavy agricultural work. It was attuned to the rhythm of agricultural work and life. It was affected by the life-style of the smaller cities and towns in which the urban population made its purchases of foodstuffs in season, at lower prices and in large quantities. . . .

It is almost impossible to estimate the number of participants in the bazaar trade, or even the number of sellers in those markets. Since neither the peasants bringing their products to the market (surprisingly, much grain was sold in such markets) nor the craftsmen selling their wares had to pay any fees, data for their turnover do not exist. It is known, however, that the bazaar market trade, not the fairs, was the domain of the second corporation merchants. Their number was relatively small: the best estimate for the years 1764–66 is about 13,200 men. In general, however, there is no information on how many active, steady participants there were in the bazaar trade nor what the trade turnover was at that institution for goods distribution. . . .

Still another form of goods distribution was the itinerant trade in the Russian countryside. During the eighteenth century the bearers of this trade were primarily the merchants of the smaller provincial towns and their agents, for whom several bazaars and infrequent rural fairs provided insufficient income. What started for some of those merchants as an auxiliary activity later became full-time. The economic rationale for the itinerant trade was the opportunity to bring directly to the villages goods for the peasants' household needs and to obtain some of the agricultural surplus that the peasants decided to sell or barter, but were not because of the costs involved. By saving the peasants both time and transportation costs, those merchants justified obtaining an appropriate price differential on the traded goods. The transactions involved both cash and barter, and less often, credit arrangements. . . .

The itinerant merchants, recruited from the small towns and rural areas, traveled in wagons with their small wares or walked with their boxes as peddlers. . . . It supplemented the other institutional forms of internal trade. It reached the female members of peasant households and helped to bring into the market the rural goods which were the domain of female labor but, because of their small volume, otherwise would have remained outside the market sphere. . . .

The last form of institutionalized trade was the stationary retail trade in stores, continuously operating trading establishments. During the period under consideration, such establishments were located almost exclusively in urban centers, predominantly in the large cities. . . . Already in the seventeenth century Moscow had approximately 4,000 trading establishments. Kazan' had about 850 stores by the end of the eighteenth century, while Simbirsk had only 223. . . .

There were other institutional arrangements of goods distribution besides those discussed above. A sizable part of the internal trade was carried on by the government. Examples are the sale of alcoholic beverages through the government ale houses (*kabaki*) and the sale of salt, another state monopoly.

SOURCE: Arcadius Kahan, *The Plow, The Hammer and the Knout: An Economic History of Eighteenth-Century Russia* (Chicago: University of Chicago Press, 1985), Chapter 2: "Agriculture," pp. 46–48, 50–52; and Chapter 5: "Internal Trade," pp. 267–82 (all excerpted). Copyright © 1985 by the University of Chicago Press. Republished by permission of the publisher.

B. N. MIRONOV
The Price Revolution of the Eighteenth Century

From 1700 through the Great Reforms Russia's economy remained, as before, one that was organized fundamentally around relations between noble landlords and unfree peasants. Still, argues Boris Mironov, within this stable structure eighteenth-century Russia witnessed an extraordinary "price revolution" whose bearing on the long-term social and political character of Russian society, serfdom, urban developments, and the well-being of the "bourgeoisie" was far reaching, and, on the whole, tragic.

By world standards Russia experienced a phenomenal rise in prices during the eighteenth century. The prices for grain, . . . increased 6.3 times, the prices for other agricultural goods 5.5 times, the prices for domestically-produced industrial goods 4 times, and the overall index of real prices rose 5 times during the 18th century. We may say that a real price revolution took place in this century, as prices rose considerably more than during the time of the so-called price revolution of 16th- and 17th-century Europe. This price revolution was brought about by a levelling-off of the enormous (almost 10-fold) difference between prices in Russia and those in West-European countries which had prevailed at the end of the 17th century. This difference was eliminated due to the immense growth in the volume of foreign trade which rose during the course of the 18th century 26.5 times (in constant currency), from 2.6 million gold rubles . . . to 68.1 million rubles. A second factor was an increase in the money supply by 7.4 times (in silver) per head of the population due to the issue of money. A third factor was the domestic production of gold and silver.

This article will cast some light upon the consequences of this price revolution, which were both deep and serious. . . . The Russian price revolution, which continued with a few interruptions throughout the whole of the 18th century, constitutes a crucial, although not the sole factor, for all of Russia's economic developments in the 18th century; and it was an important, although—once again—not determining, factor in social and political developments. . . .

RUSSIA'S ENTRY INTO THE INTERNATIONAL DIVISION OF LABOR

During the price revolution and under its influence, Russia became a part of the international division of labor as a supplier of agricultural products and as an importer of industrial goods. . . . The structure of export indicates that in the second half of the 17th century . . . raw materials composed the lion's share (94%) of the export; in the first quarter of the eighteenth century under the influence of Peter I's export policies, the share of finished products in the export trade began to grow, and reached 72% by 1725. However, during the ensuing years the significance of manufactured goods began to decline, and by the beginning of the 19th century they constituted only about 14% of the export. Correspondingly, the proportion of raw materials fell from 94% to 27% between 1653 and 1725; but after that it began to increase, reaching 78% in 1802–1805.

The changing composition of export after 1725 [was related to] the doubling of prices for agricultural goods everywhere, whereas those for manufactured goods (judging by Moscow prices) grew approximately 1.5 times. During the 1710s Russia acquired its most important Baltic ports, Riga, Revel, Narva, and a new one—St. Petersburg, was built. All this cre-

ated favorable conditions for an increase in the export of raw materials from Russia in the second quarter of the eighteenth century. . . . [T]he second and final stage of the price revolution, that began in 1760, . . . came to an end at the beginning of the 19th century, by which time the prices for agricultural goods had risen approximately 2.7–3 times, and the prices for manufactured goods (judging by Moscow prices) approximately 1.7 times. Russia had [also] acquired and built new ports, this time on the Black Sea. Still another factor which provided a substantial stimulus was the liberalization of customs legislation, which declared freedom of trade.

The factors indicated above stimulated the export of all Russian goods, but especially of raw materials. First, in light of the scissoring of prices in favor of agricultural and handicraft goods; secondly, because of the non-competitiveness of Russian goods on the European market, and the high return brought by its raw materials; thirdly, because of Russia's large capacity to produce grain, flax, hemp, fish, furs and other agricultural and handicraft goods, the country possessed colossal land resources and unexploited arable land (let us recall that the average population density in the European part of Russia was 3.5 souls per square km. in 1719 and 7.2 in 1795, a figure that is approximately ten times lower than in Great Britain). Finally, the export of agricultural goods brought significant revenue to the State (from customs duty and from raising the general tax rate of the peasantry) as well as to the landlords, the peasantry, and the merchantry, which required hardly any substantial capital investment or painful restructuring of the agrarian economy. . . .

[B]y the end of the 18th century, [grain products] headed the list of exported goods—more than 20% of the value of the whole export trade, whereas at the beginning of the 18th century they had made up less than 3%, in 1758–1760 1%. In 1796–1805, compared to 1701–1761, the export of grain products increased 32 times by weight, 47 times by cost, 27 times by value per head of the population. In 1801–1805, . . . the export of grain had reached 12.8 million poods per year—a level which was maintained during the ensuing forty years of the nineteenth century. One fifth of all marketable grain was exported in 1796–1805. . . .

THE INFLUENCE
OF THE PRICE REVOLUTION ON
TOWN DEVELOPMENT

The migration of the peasantry into towns was slow during the 18th century and it diminished during the course of the second half of the century. . . . In certain years (for example 1779–1783) the migration balance was even negative, which meant that the peasantry was re-emigrating to the villages.

This situation, paradoxical at first glance, was explained by perceptive contemporaries by the rise in grain prices. . . . For example, in the responses of the local administration to the government's inquiry of 1767, the governor of Astrakhan noted the interconnection between the rise in prices and the pace of migration: "A peasant who [in the past] wished to sustain himself by doing some other work which he found more profitable, left his plowland because of the extremely low prices for grain and took on various jobs in town. So many peasants emigrated that the balance between grain growers and grain consumers has been lost. Now just the opposite occurs, as these high prices have obliged many town dwellers—raznochintsy and merchants of moderate means—to take up farming, deeming it more profitable than continuing to sell their wares on very little capital."

The contraction in peasant migration to the towns led to a decrease in the share of the urban population . . . from 12% in 1742—the first date available for calculation—and to 8.2 % in 1801. . . . Moreover, the industrial and commercial functions of towns went backward in their development. . . . An indication of this is the change in the distribution of industry between town and countryside during the eighteenth century in favor of the countryside. In 1725 78% of the enterprises . . . engaged in large-scale manufacturing, and 86% of the labor force . . . were concentrated in the

towns. . . . Between 1775 and 1778, i.e., 50 years later, industry had grown noticeably in quantitative and qualitative terms. Now, however, [only] 60% of all enterprises . . . and 57% of the labor force . . . were located in the towns. During the last quarter of the 18th century this tendency intensified and in 1803–1804 58% of the industrial enterprises . . . and 55% of workers . . . were concentrated in the towns. . . .

The success of rural manufacturing was due partly to the peasants, but to an even greater extent to the enterprise of the nobility, which had strengthened in the course of the 18th century. If in the first quarter of the 18th century only two of 40 private factories (5%) belonged to the nobility, then by 1773–1766 out of 328 (20%) of the factories . . . , and in 1813–1814, 520 out of 1018 (more than 50%) enterprises with more than 15 workers belonged to the nobility. . . . The nobility was especially successful in the production of fabrics, stationary, potash, glass and metal, in which it owned correspondingly 66%, 61%, 66% and 55% of all enterprises. But the distillation of spirits was the nobility's most successful field, thanks to the monopoly which it had held since 1754.

The development of urban trade was substantially impeded by competition from rural commercial centers, which developed faster due to the active support of the nobility. Between 1750 and 1800 the number of fairs grew 3.5 times in the towns, 8.3 times in villages, and the number of bazaar days grew correspondingly by 1.8 and 3.4 times. . . . The role of the nobility in developing trade in the village was manifested by the fact that most of the new village fairs were held on the property of landlords. . . .

We should also bear in mind that the mobilization of agricultural production within the internal market . . . was conducted by the landlords themselves, their stewards or the peasantry. As a consequence, a considerable portion of the income from the export of grain and other raw materials went not to the merchantry, but to the nobility, which spent this money without any benefit to the town, and used it almost exclusively for the purchase of the imported goods, predominantly for luxury items. The social parasitism of the landowners caused the money that they received, with rare exceptions, not to go into circulation, which would have increased wealth, but to be squandered recklessly. . . .

The accelerated growth in prices for agricultural goods in comparison to industrial goods, and the general lagging of increases in wages behind the rise of prices adversely affected the living standard of town-dwellers who engaged in industry and handicrafts. This caused a strong desire on the part of town dwellers not to loosen their ties with agriculture and to hold onto their garden plots, their cattle, and even their plow land. Over a long period of time this state of affairs facilitated not only the preservation of the agrarian features of Russian towns, but also contributed to the development of a peculiar type of rural town. According to my calculations, in the 1760s about 60% of the towns were rural—i.e. the basic activity of their inhabitants was the cultivation of land; only 2% engaged in commerce, 4% in industry and 31% mixed, the rest consisting of administrative and military personnel. . . .

THE PRICE REVOLUTION, TAXES AND RENT

The price revolution adversely affected the conditions of the towns, the situation of the traders and craftsmen, but it was one of the most important causes for the success of the noble landlords. The landlords profited twice: first, on account of the redistribution between the treasury to the landlords of the surplus product created by serf labor, in favor of the landlords. In the 17th and the beginning of the 18th century the state had been the principal exploiter of the peasantry, as state taxes exceeded rent. Beginning in the second quarter of the eighteenth century the situation began to change, which can be clearly seen by examining the poll tax—the most important direct tax on the peasantry. Between 1725 and 1794 the poll tax remained unchanged at 70 kopecks per male soul. In 1795 it increased to 1 ruble, and from 1798 it rose to 1.26 rubles, at a time when the nominal prices for agricul-

tural goods had increased about 4.2 times. The landlords took advantage of this disparity, which was due to the scissoring between tax increases and price rises, by increasing the peasants' duty. The additional income which then had accrued to the landlords between 1725 and 1800 amounted to an enormous sum—about 122 million nominal, or 109 million silver, rubles, and between 1763 and 1800 the treasury lost on average more than 7% of its revenue per annum from the state budget. . . .

If we distribute the rise in income during the years 1710 to 1800 among the factors proportionately according to the index of their growth, we can see that because of the rise in prices landlords received 504 million rubles— 75.2% from the general increase in income of 670 million rubles; 83 million rubles (12.4%) owing to the rise in the number of serfs and another 83 million rubles (1.4%)—owing to the growth of corvée.

Between 1711 and 1800 the landlords received a slightly smaller, but still rather significant, addition to their income from quitrent peasants of 527 million rubles: 415 million rubles or 79% of which came from the rise in prices; 85 million rubles (16%) of which derived from the growth of quitrent (in permanent prices); and, 27 million rubles (5%) because of the increase in the number of peasants on quitrent. . . .

Thus the extra income from the rise in agricultural prices brought the landlords 919 million rubles (504 + 415) from corvee and quitrent, of which 122 million rubles (13% of the total) was given as a "gift," by the government thanks to the decrease in direct taxation.

The state, crown, and other categories of non-landlords' peasants, as well as the various tax-paying urban estates, also gained thanks to the scissoring between the rise in taxes and the rise in prices. So, during the years 1724–1794 the collective burden of payments of state peasants increased 3.5 times, of crown peasants 5.4 times, and of the townsmen remained unchanged, at a time when the nominal price of grain increased 5.7 times, and the prices for handicraft and industrial goods rose 4.7 times. Since the taxpaying population of the country increased 2.4 times during the period 1725–1795, the state could at least partly compensate for the loss in revenue from the taxes. . . .

SOCIAL AND POLITICAL CONSEQUENCES OF THE PRICE REVOLUTION

The enormous rise in prices for agricultural goods at a time when they were in great demand both within the country (from the population in the non-blacksoil provinces, the new capital, and the army) and abroad stimulated the production of agricultural commodities based on serfdom. . . . Corvée increased 2.5 times, and real quitrent 1.35 times. A landlord's peasant had been transformed practically into his property, and, at the lord's whim, the serf could be condemned to penal servitude, impressed into military service, moved to a different locality, sold, or torn away from his family. It is symptomatic that the peasants' obligations to the landlord grew particularly intense in the second half of the 18th century when the economic conjuncture was especially favorable for agriculture. All this illustrates the close link between serfdom and the price revolution.

However, it is impossible not to notice another side to the development of the serf economy: the enterprise of the nobility both in the agricultural sphere and in industrial production. By striving to take advantage of the favorable conjuncture and to increase their income, the landlords extended their holdings, intensified the colonization movement, and stimulated the development of commodity production and of commodity-money relations. . . .

A favorable economic situation, the opportunity to make more money in the agricultural business by exploiting the serfs rather than by employment in state service, stimulated a desire among noble landlords to change from being an estate of service to being a landed one. They began to pursue their freedom from compulsory service, and after achieving it in 1762, they settled down in great numbers on the land and became agricultural proprietors. . . .

The 18th century, particularly its second half, was characterized by the reinforcement of the social and political positions of the nobility, for whom it surely was a golden age. Their economic successes, the millions of rubles which they gained from the price revolution all made this state of affairs possible. The Law of 1762 freeing the nobility from compulsory service, and the Charter to the Nobility of 1785, could well have remained empty declarations if the class proclaimed as a ruling estate had lacked a strong material base created by its increased income, because poverty and political supremacy are incompatible. But as usually occurs in an estate-based, non-democratic society, the elevation of one class's role takes place at the expense of all other classes. "After Peter," as V. O. Kliuchevskii writes, "the nobility in its totality is freed from obligatory service, and with its new rights becomes a ruling estate which takes into its hands the administration and the national economy." By contrast, "urban self-government, which was put under the supervision of the governor-nobleman developed slowly and functioned poorly.". . .

What was left for the more enterprising members of the bourgeoisie to do? Become noblemen as quickly as possible. And, in fact, the ennoblement of the elite ranks of the bourgeoisie can be observed in the 18th century. . . . The bourgeoisie was losing its best representatives, and that aggravated the economic and social position of the bourgeoisie itself and of urban society. Thus, along with the reinforcement of the nobility's position, there occurred a corresponding decline of the Russian bourgeoisie and the relative weakening of the economic and social importance of the town. All this had far-reaching political consequences: on the one hand, the reinforcement of absolutism, cementing the power of the nobility, and, on the other hand, bourgeois loyalty turning into servility and an inability to establish an alternative force to the nobility and autocracy. Let us suggest that the price revolution of the 18th century did not play the final role in this process, so tragic for Russian political history.

We should also note the cultural aspect of the 18th-century price revolution. The nobility spent the enormous sums of money that it earned from the price revolution on travelling abroad, education, and the acquisition of western goods, all of which facilitated the westernization of its ways of life and its mentality. Meanwhile the bulk of the Russian people, above all the peasantry which composed more than 90% of the population of the country, remained faithful to the traditional culture. As a result, the social and economic differentiation between the upper and lower classes, which had been in existence before the 18th century, was aggravated by a cultural stratification that was more serious and difficult to overcome than the social and economic separation.

The price revolution in Russia in the 18th century had multi-faceted and contradictory consequences. On the one hand, it facilitated the reinforcement of the serf system, the development of the agrarian sector of the economy, at the expense of industry. It impeded the progress of the towns, as commercial and industrial centers; it reinforced the significance of the nobility and thus contributed to the preservation of the noble-monarchical sociopolitical structure of the society. Without sufficient stimuli and conditions for economic prosperity, or even for its own numerical growth, the Russian bourgeoisie of necessity consolidated itself into an economically and politically weak class which was incapable of waging a decisive struggle for its own civil and political rights. It became prone to conformism and to blatant servility before the ruling class and before the pro-noble government. On the other hand, the price revolution stimulated the development of commodity-money relations, favored progress in foreign trade, and expanded the growth of economic and cultural contacts with West European countries. Similar consequences of the price revolution can also be observed in other countries of Southeastern, Eastern and Central Europe during the 16th and 17th centuries.

SOURCE: B. N. Mironov, "The Influence of The Price Revolution in Eighteenth-Century Russia On Economic and Socio-Political Developments." Originally published as: "Vliianie revoliutsii tsen v Rossii XVIII veka na ee ekonomicheskoe i sotsial'no-politicheskoe razvitie," *Istoriia SSSR* (1991) No. 1, pp. 86–99 (excerpted). Translated by Olga Barskaya and Gary Marker

ELISE KIMMERLING WIRTSCHAFTER
Provisioning the Russian Army

Normally, one thinks of the economy as involving the settled, or civilian population, rather than soldiers. Yet the Russian army dominated the lives of hundreds of thousands of soldiers and their dependents, and, as Elise Kimmerling Wirtschafter explains, provisioning them was an enormous economic enterprise that in turn had a significant impact on the ongoing social and economic life of Russian society.

———————

From the reign of Peter the Great, the regimental economy was tied to a centralized system of supply. However inadequately, the government assumed responsibility for feeding and supplying the troops. Legislation defined monthly rations of meal and groats, and the government established magazines [storehouses] to store provisions. New state factories began producing weapons, ammunition, and cloth for uniforms. Finally, Peter's administrative reforms created central offices with local representatives to guarantee supplies for his standing army. The Commissariat *Prikaz* was responsible for pay, clothing, ammunition, and equipment, while the Provisioning *Prikaz* provided food and forage or the funds to purchase them. Peter's reforms clearly established the role of the central government in supplying the army and also the role of the regiment as an organizing principle in the military economy. . . . As in so many areas of Russian life, the basic Petrine institutions survived until the Great Reforms and beyond.

Despite the government's active role in supplying the army, soldiers still depended upon the surrounding countryside to satisfy most of their material needs. The state supplied bread (or paid for it) and money for meat and salt, while local society was obliged to provide quarters, heat, lighting, and pasture for the horses. Ideally, merchants and noblemen would donate supplies, and residents would "offer" to feed the soldiers they housed without compensation, if not voluntarily, then at the behest of the village or military authorities. When the goods were not forthcoming from local citizens, the military authorities concluded contracts for the purchase of supplies at prices fixed by the state. The state also provided the troops with equipment: the goods received in kind included ammunition, saddles, riding appurtenances, hats, cloth for uniforms, and leather. For other necessary items, such as cooking and storage utensils, the troops received money. The regiment's supplies thus included a combination of money and goods received in kind from private and state sources.

Legislation defined the norm of pay, provisions, and supplies for the individual soldiers. In about 1800 each soldier received 68-1/2 pounds of meal and 7-1/2 pounds of groats a month. In addition, every man received 72 copecks for meat and 24 copecks for salt each year—amounts included in the musketeer's yearly pay of 9 roubles 50 copecks. According to a law of 1808, the authorities also deducted fees to purchase medicines and support hospitals. . . . The daily diet . . . included meat, though the law did permit substitutes like fish, peas, potatoes, or cucumbers. The official military history of Nicholas I's reign claimed that under Alexander I the only soldiers who regularly received meat and vodka were combat ranks in the Guards (37 pounds of meat per year) and troops in the Crimea and Kherson (78 pounds of meat and 156 cups of vodka per year). . . .

Clearly, during the reign of Nicholas I, the government made some effort to improve the soldier's diet by prescribing meat rations more precisely. For, as the *Soldiers' Handbook* noted,

a sick soldier cannot fulfil his service duties and is simply "an unnecessary burden" on the army. Consequently, the government "takes all possible measures to preserve the health of the soldier and constantly concerns itself with his allowance, quarters, food, clothing, and equipment." It is unclear, however, whether the law required meat for all soldiers. Legislation from the reign of Nicholas I suggests this was not the case before 1842. . . . According to the official military history of Nicholas I's reign, in 1826 only about 122,000 soldiers enjoyed meat as a regular part of their diet, whereas by 1850 this number had increased to 1,036,815.

From the standpoint of nutrition and health, the reign of Nicholas I might have brought unprecedented benefits. Regular supplies of meat certainly would have represented a substantial improvement in the diet of the common soldier. If this legislation were actually implemented and meat supplies were available, it could indicate advances in the diet of the civilian population as well. For the government did not provide the meat required to meet these allocations. Instead it distributed funds, so that the actual purchase of meat was the responsibility of the company commander. In reality, the legislated norms would have affected only troops living in barracks. Most soldiers spent the better part of the year quartered among civilians who fed their charges with no regard for military regulations. Those quartered in poor areas, gathered in camp, or residing in close quarters . . . ate "from the common pot" . . . and so were entitled to meat rations. There is no question that some soldiers enjoyed meat as part of their diet. Thus, in 1856 soldiers at the Aland fortifications bought meat locally, though they complained that the meat lasted one week, instead of the two required, because half of it was spoiled. In general, given the character of the quartering system, it is impossible to know how many soldiers actually received meat rations on a regular basis. . . . Clearly, the distribution of supplies in the regimental economy reflected the traditional patterns of Russian administration:

bureaucratic centralization and regulation coupled with local underinstitutionalization and discretionary authority.

II

Once a regiment obtained its legally allotted supplies and funds, the regimental commander distributed them through the company or squadron. Each company in turn was divided into four sections . . . or artels . . . administered by a non-commissioned officer. And each section also contained five groups of ten soldiers supervised by a lance-corporal . . . and one or two older, more experienced soldiers of 'good morality'. . . . The group of ten was a command sub-unit for quartering, training, and enforcing discipline. Along with the company and artel, it served as the centre of the soldier's daily life. The limited information on the artel suggests that its main purpose was to control the common resources of the soldiers in the interests of economic security. . . .

The very existence of the artel implied some degree of popular participation in regulating the company economy. Some sources claim that the lower ranks elected both the company and section head for a six-month period. Memoirs confirm this practice, though P. Nazarov, who in the 1820s served five years as a section provisioner, tried to avoid the responsibility, which he described as "highly dangerous". In contrast, the official centennial history of the War Ministry admitted that despite the legal prescriptions, company commanders usually appointed the head. According to this source, company commanders controlled the activities of the artel to ensure proper use of the funds for provisions and for the purchase and maintenance of horses and vehicles. Like the noble serf-master, the company commander exercised tutelage or 'guardianship' over his subordinates.

The organization of a company's funds also suggest limited popular control over the artel. The 1838 Code of Military Regulations identified three types of soldiers' monies . . . : artel, economic, and personal. . . . Artel funds consisted of deductions from the soldiers' pay (up to one third) and munitions money, earnings from outside labour, and monetary awards granted by the emperor for training, inspections, parades, and manoeuvres. Awards received from the emperor augmented the artel fund only if they were not needed for provisions. . . .

In each company all the artel funds comprised a general artel sum that was the direct property of the lower ranks, so that each soldier possessed his own share. The general artel sum was divided into four sub-artels . . . which served as the basis for calculating the artel monies. The law permitted an infantry company to keep 180 silver roubles in its artel. Commanders were supposed to send any additional money to a bank to earn interest. The law treated the artel funds as the property of the lower ranks, clearly stating that they be used for the soldiers' personal needs and not for any extraneous expenditures, such as clothing or the repair of equipment. The artel thus functioned as a financial entity, partly controlled by the soldiers. Still, there were legal restrictions on the soldiers, since the corps commander could reallocate artel funds for provisioning. Moreover, until retirement, when the soldier received his artel funds in hand, the lower ranks could spend these monies only with the permission of the regimental commander. All company funds were kept in the regimental safe . . . , and the company commander handled deposits and withdrawals in the presence of the chief. The only cash received directly by the lower ranks was their pay and munitions money . . ., but only if their artel fund contained the minimum required by law. . . .

In addition to enhancing the economic security of the lower ranks, the artel and other company funds provided an irresistible enticement for venal commanders. Officers repeatedly used the soldiers' monies for illicit personal gain. Still, through their artel, soldiers exercised some control over the company economy. Although soldiers enjoyed limited access to their artel monies before retirement, commanders at least theoretically had to account for the funds to the satisfaction of their men. Thus records of courts martial reveal repeated disputes between soldiers and officers over the use of artel funds, soldiers' pay, and munitions money. Commanders could also profit at their subordinates' expense by buying provisions or supplies of inferior quality and pocketing the extra money. This too was risky, as soldiers and recruits alike complained of receiving cut rations. . . . Soldiers may not have been entirely innocent in matters of economic gain, but they clearly lacked the opportunities of greedy superiors. So along with soldiers' complaints submitted at official inspections, the structure and, indeed, the very existence of the artel provided a potential check on the corruption of commanders. Corruption was clearly widespread, but there was always some possibility, however remote, that it would not go unpunished.

III

Like the artel, the system of quartering revealed the importance of the company in the soldier's daily life. According to a law of 1806, regiments gathered in the spring and summer for training, while divisions and corps gathered for six weeks during this period. For the remaining six to eight months of the year, soldiers lived in private homes. A single regiment might be scattered among several villages, so that it was impossible to preserve the regiment as a unified social unit. As late as 1860, only about 28 percent of the troops were quartered in barracks and state buildings. Since the obligation to quarter a soldier included feeding him, the legally defined rations had little meaning, except when the troops lived in barracks or gathered in camp. Commanders sometimes distributed supplies in kind, but the soldier usually ate what his host was willing or able to share, regardless of the funds available for purchasing provisions. In the spring when peasant supplies were low, the soldier might receive only bread and water. So hunger was at times a factor, as indeed it was for all the labouring elements of society. . . .

Legislation from the reign of Nicholas I reflected the diverse local conditions. In 1842, for example, the troops of the Caucasus Corps received funds in gold coins, assignats, and deposit notes. But according to the corps commander, these units were quartered with local natives who did not understand the Russian monetary system and always demanded payment in silver. As a result, the soldiers had to change the money they received for silver with a few usurers who arbitrarily fixed the rate of exchange at inordinate percentages. Whenever the local Russian authorities tried to investigate these speculators, they refused to change money, claiming they had no silver. Although the soldiers were supposed to avoid these problems by changing their money at local state treasuries, this was difficult to do, because of a general shortage of silver. . . .

High prices and local poverty distinguished other areas where troops quartered. Because of high prices in Odessa, troops from the Fifth Infantry Corps were 'in extreme difficulty as regards provisioning the men, for they not only had spent their economic funds, but even had used significant sums for the regimental and soldiers' artel monies'. In response, an imperial ukaz [decree or edict] of 1847 granted these units additional funds for provisions. Similarly, from October 1849 until April 1850 the lower ranks of [one] regiment, stationed in the town of Ostrog, used 78 roubles from their artel to purchase wood for cooking and baking. Due to the absolute poverty of the townspeople, the soldiers ate 'from the pot', but the local community had also refused to provide wood. So an imperial ukaz instructed the community to return the 78 silver roubles and also supply wood, for the law prohibited the use of soldiers' funds to buy wood and clothing. In 1851 the government confirmed the right to receive wood for all troops eating 'from the pot', noting that this measure was especially needed in the Caucasus. Unfortunately for the army, the border regions which required larger concentrations of troops were also sometimes the most impoverished and so least capable of meeting military needs. According to one historian, soldiers in Lithuania and Bessarabia experienced unusual hardships. Clearly, the system of quartering integrated the soldier into local society and made him dependent upon local conditions—conditions that fluctuated with the economic, geographical, and cultural diversity of the Russian Empire.

The system of quartering distinguished Russia sharply from the other military powers of Europe. By the nineteenth century, most troops in Austria, France, and England lived in barracks concentrated in cities. The poverty of urban life in Russia partly accounted for this difference, but the real problem lay in the chronic gap between the government's policies and its available resources, in this instance caused by the large size of the army and the geographical peculiarities of the vast Russian land. In contrast to Prussia, where peasant soldiers lived and served in their native cantons, Russian soldiers were completely cut off from their families, but continued to live in civilian society. The Russian government clearly felt that a peasant became a loyal servant of the state only after removal from his home environment, though it could not afford to isolate him in military barracks. Quartering arrangements thus had important implications for the relationship between military and civilian society. For the army, the relationship was one of dependence—a dependence, however, that the central government mediated to the advantage of the military. For the soldier this dependence was more immediate, especially when he received his daily bread from local inhabitants. At the same time, civilians were obliged to feed the soldiers as part of society's service to the state, and so the soldier was identified with the state. The quartering system thus reflected not only the power of the absolutist state, but also the difficulty of making society's resources available for governmental purposes. The government's inability to house and feed its army without extensive reliance on peasant society obviously created tension between uninvited soldiers and their frequently overburdened hosts. But the absence of barracks could also serve as a source of fraternization and integration, giving civilians an understanding of military service and reminding soldiers of a former, perhaps not too distant peasant life. This direct and continual contact between military and civilian society could only increase awareness and keep memories alive. For the system of quartering took the soldier out of his military environment, separating him from the regiment that claimed his loyalties and defined his role as a fighter. So despite the lengthy term of service and the recruit's forced break with his family, the line between military and civilian society remained blurred throughout this period.

SOURCE: Elise Kimmerling Wirtschafter, "The Lower Ranks in the Peacetime Regimental Economy of the Russian Army, 1796–1855," *Slavonic and East European Review* 64, 1 (January 1986): 41–52 (excerpted). Republished by permission of the editors of *Slavonic and East European Review*. Several Russian terms have been omitted or rendered in English.

16

Society: The Lower And Middling Estates of Imperial Russia

As we discovered in the previous section, Russia's social system can be divided in several alternative ways: legal estates, tax paying vs. non-taxpaying, free vs. unfree, privileged vs. unprivileged, urban vs. rural. Regardless of how and where we draw the line, there is no doubt that this was a stratified society in which a very few people lived in wealth and privilege, and the vast majority did not. About nine out of every ten Russian subjects was a peasant, and most of the rest of the population was divided among the poor and middling urban groups (artisans, clerks, merchants, small traders), and the parish—or "white"—clergy.

Those segments of this society who might plausibly be considered privileged, i.e, those who had titles, considerable wealth, high status, extensive education, or freedom from direct taxes, constituted less than 3 percent of the total. Many were hereditary nobles who held numerous legal privileges (freedom from service, the right to own serfs, freedom from direct taxation, exemption from corporal punishment, etc.). But a large proportion of these, were far from well-to-do, largely as a consequence of Russia's system of partible inheritance which granted each of the heirs a portion of the estate. Over a few generations what had once been a sizable property had been subdivided so often that its owners, for all practical purposes, amounted to little more than independent farmers. Except for their freedom from the soul tax, their lives had rather little in commom with the cosmopolitan service nobility described in the section on state and society, and instead in some ways resembled the experiences of the more humble social groups that are discussed in this chapter.

The Russian state's voracious appetite for capable officers and administrators expanded the number of educated and titled servitors many times over between Peter the Great and the Reform era. But, because population growth was also robust (from about 11 million at the beginning of the eighteenth century to just under 60 million in 1858), this expansion had only a very modest impact on the ratio of privileged and unprivileged, or between peasants and everyone else. This chapter, then, is devoted to the unprivileged majority: peasants, townsfolk, and parish clergy, with particular attention paid to the ways in which these populations interacted among themselves and with the government.

The great majority of Russian peasants were born, lived, and died in a state of bondage, mostly as landlords' peasants (serfs), state peasants (those living on land owned by the state), crown peasants (those who lived on land owned by the Romanov family), and prior to 1762 monastic peasants (those who lived on monastic land and owed their dues to monasteries). (After 1762 the state took over all of the land held by monasteries, and it reclassified the peasants living on them as a special category of state peasants dubbed 'economic peasants' after the College of the Economy which oversaw their land.) There were some free peasant householders, but not very many. Therefore, this chapter pays special attention to the meaning and character of bondage and its bearing on peasant life.

Merchants, clergy, artisans, clerks, and the urban poor (the latter three were generally grouped into a single, socially imprecise legal category known as "the petty urban estate," or *meshchanstvo* in Russian), by contrast, were legally free but generally unprivileged. Unlike the peasants, these groups did not live within well-organized communities, and they consequently had a difficult time in defining their collective interests or in establishing organizations to defend them. However, because they were free and unprivileged, the imperial Russian state made considerable demands upon them to help administer and sustain Russian society, but without affording them opportunities to defend their collective interests or to play an active role in setting policy. Merchants and artisans, for example, were organized into a series of so-called "tax guilds" through which the state regulated them and defined their responsibilities and privileges. A few were exempted from direct taxes, and others were granted a handful of other privileges and symbols of status, such as the right to ride around in carriages. But unlike their counterparts in most of the rest of eighteenth-century Europe, they were forbidden from organizing craft guilds or merchants' corporations through which they might have asserted some controls over their trades. Thus their freedom and independence were fragile assets, easily lost or overwhelmed by the force of law and custom. The passages from Ivan Pososhkov's, *Book of Poverty and Wealth* and the selections on the merchantry by Wallace Daniel and Alfred Rieber very much reflect this perpetual struggle against marginality and insecurity.

We should make one final observation about these categories before turning to the selections. The social categories employed by Russian law, whether based upon occupation, service obligations, or heredity, focused preeminently on adult males. Indeed, most of the periodic census revisions did not even count the female population until the very end of the nineteenth century. This one-sided focus on men permeates the documents and, to a somewhat lesser extent, the scholarship. As we shall see, once attention shifts from legal categories to communities and households, women and children magically reappear as important subjects. But, in the end, we remain heavily dependent on the deep, if often unstated, gender biases of our documents, especially for the townsfolk and clergy, whose female members lamentably remain all but invisible to the categories of service, taxation, and paid labor through which they have tended to be described.

A. The Peasantry and the Countryside

By the beginning of the eighteenth century more than nine out of ten Russians were peasants, and nearly all of them lived under a state of legal bondage, either to a landlord (private and institutional) or to the state. Approximately half of the Russian peasantry was legally enserfed, a status which meant, among other things, that they lived and worked on land owned by a private landlord. The wealthier landlords tended to be absentee (i.e., they did not live on their estates) and to entrust the management of their estates to bailiffs (*burmistry*). Most absentee landlords appear not to have intervened extensively in estate management or in the everyday lives of peasants, but they certainly had the right to, and some chose to exercise these discretionary rights of patriarchy quite extensively. (See the comments on this subject in Stephen Hoch's essay in this section.)

For some nobles, this engagement from afar involved drawing up elaborate plans for transforming their properties into model estates, run according to principles of "rational" farming and even civic participation, as dictated by the highest ideals of the Enlightenment. One recent scholar has argued that these model plans actually touched a large number of peasant communities, and thereby had a bearing on the lives of a significant number of peasants. Although that conclusion seems a bit extravagant, these plans nevertheless reveal a great deal about relations of authority between landlords and peasants, at least as imagined by paternalists, both enlightened and less so.

DOCUMENTS

A. Landlords' Instructions on Estate Administration (Late Eighteenth Century)

INSTRUCTIONS OF I. I. SHUVALOV

CONCERNING THE BAILIFF

The bailiff must be chosen for his post with the prior approval of the commune and with my consent; he will be fully entrusted by me to administer the entire estate and to administer justice to the peasants without prejudice or oppression, and he must give a good account of himself in all respects before me.

CONCERNING THE DEPUTY

The Deputy, who is at the same time the bursar, must be elected yearly by the peasants and must be a worthy man, so that he can assist the bailiff in administration. . . .

CONCERNING THE ELDER

The elder must likewise be chosen yearly by the bailiff together with the peasants; he must be a man who can assist the bailiff in the collection of my money on the estate without arrears, and upon collecting it he must hand it over to the bailiff in full.

CONCERNING THE CLERKS

There should be two clerks, selected by the bailiff; they should be accurate in keeping records and not be drunkards; they must attend to every document and must keep accurate accounts in the proper manner. And they must be obedient in all matters to the bailiff, as their superior. . . .

CONCERNING THE PEASANT REPRESENTATIVES

There must be one peasant representative from every small hamlet, and two from a large hamlet, or as many as are assigned by the commune. They must gather in the administration office at the order of the bailiff whenever any matters are being judged or sentences passed, instead of always burdening the people by calling them all together. . . .

CONCERNING THE CHURCH ELDER

The church elder must be chosen by the commune; he must be a man of good conduct. He is entrusted with the church money, of which he must keep a record and give an account to the administration of the estate and to the commune. This money must then be used for decorating the church, and the church elder will be entrusted with looking after the granary, the receipt of grain, and its disbursement to the poor; each year he must send me accurate information about all these things: the church money as well as the condition of the granary.

CONCERNING THE EQUAL DISTRIBUTION OF LAND

The land must be distributed so that one village will not have an excess of land while another has too little; in order that each village can pay taxes on it without falling into arrears. . . .

CONCERNING FUGITIVE PEASANTS

Fugitive and passportless peasants must not be kept anywhere on my estate under any circumstances; and if such should be found with any [of my peasants], the latter must answer for it himself in the proper place, without expecting any help from me.

CONCERNING THOSE WHO ABSENT THEMSELVES WITHOUT PERMISSION

A peasant who absents himself without the permission of the bailiff and goes to the city without having a pass from him is to be fined in money, depending on the amount of property he has. . . . In issuing passes the bailiff should oppress no one, lest the trader should lose his profit and the nontrader his benefits.

CONCERNING UNMARRIED GIRLS

Girls who have reached the age of twenty should not be kept at home by their fathers but should be given away in marriage, without waiting for me to force them into a marriage which would run counter to the will of the father and of the bride.

INSTRUCTIONS OF V. G. ORLOV

CONCERNING THE BAILIFF, HIS ASSISTANT AND THEIR DUTIES

1. Chief authority on the estate belongs to the bailiff; therefore all peasants must be in complete obedience to him. . . .

4. In all the more important affairs, the bailiff should counsel with the deputies and other worthy peasants, and if necessary, with the entire commune. . . .

15. Guilty persons should be punished . . . with rods and cudgels, but not with whips. . . .

17. The bailiff is not to be replaced without my consent. . . .

19. The bailiff receives his salary from the commune; its amount depends upon the commune's wishes. . . .

CONCERNING QUITRENT

8. To assist the poor and weak the following practice is to be observed: an appropriate number of souls shall be removed from the family, but in no case should land be taken away on account of the removal of souls. . .

CONCERNING THE COLLECTION OF MONEY FOR COMMUNAL EXPENSES AND THE RATIONAL UTILIZATION OF THE SAME

1. There are necessary and extraordinary expenses. The will of the commune shall decide when the money should be collected for these expenses and how much should be collected. The commune should draw up resolutions for these collections, to which all must consent. . . .

CONCERNING PERMISSION TO GIVE MAIDENS AND WIDOWS AWAY TO OUTSIDERS IN MARRIAGE, AND CONCERNING THOSE WHO DO NOT MARRY. . .

5. It is highly necessary for all girls of marriageable age and bachelors who have achieved manhood to enter into marriage. This is an act pleasing to God; it safeguards morality and wards off many vices. . . .

6. When a girl reaches the age of twenty, the eldest in the family should give her away in marriage. . . .

7. If upon the expiration of the allotted time the girl is not married, penalties should be exacted yearly: twenty-five rubles from a household of moderate means and fifty rubles from a wealthy family; the poor, who are unable to pay, should be punished at the discretion of the authorities.

9. Bachelors twenty-five years of age and older who are not yet married should be dealt

A peasant man and woman dressed for travel, early nineteenth century. From a collection of Russian postcards, "Narodnye kostiumy."

with in the same way as unmarried girls . . . Widows are likewise subject to this rule.

INSTRUCTIONS OF A. T. BOLOTOV

8. . . .The reasons for which villages are reduced to a bad state and to impoverishment are of three types: the first is by their master or by his own administration of them: as, for example, if the inhabitants are burdened with excessive labor, heavy requisitions, numerous cartage duties, and other such things; or similarly when the administration of the estate is disorderly and ruinous. . . .

75. . . .For the most part the rule is followed that the peasant should plow as much as he has for his own use. Therefore that amount of land the peasants are able to cultivate with their own labor and harvest in the proper manner ought to be divided in half: one half

should go to the peasant and the other half to the master. Nothing can be easier and more suitable for the peasant.

SOURCE: George Vernadsky, et al. (eds.), *A Source Book For Russian History From Early Times to 1917.* Vol. 2: *Peter the Great to Nicholas I* (New Haven and London: Yale University Press, 1972), pp. 444–49. These documents and those that immediately follow which are excerpted from Vernadsky are reprinted by permission of Yale University Press.

An Imperial Edict Forbidding Sunday Labor by Serfs (1797)

We proclaim to all our loyal subjects. The law of God given to us in the Ten Commandments teaches us to devote the seventh day of the week to him. Therefore, on this day, made famous by the triumph of the Christian faith and on which we were honored to receive the holy anointing and were crowned tsar on the throne of our forefathers, we deem it our duty before our Maker and the Bearer of all blessings to confirm that this law must be observed, exactly and without fail, throughout our empire, and we command one and all to see that no one under any pretext dares to force serfs to work on Sundays; all the more so because for agricultural production the six remaining days in the week, which are in general equally distributed between serfs' labor for themselves and their labor due the landlords, should with good management be sufficient to satisfy all economic needs.

SOURCE: Vernadsky (see p. 294) Vol. 2, p. 474.

Moskovskie vedomosti, Newspaper Advertisements Listing Serfs for Sale (1797)

For sale: a waiter, 25 years old, with his wife and a minor son. A very good weaver; can also shave and draw blood. The wife can look after the mistress and is capable of any work. Also for sale in the same place: a . . . carriage, not much used, of the best workmanship. . . .

At house no. 352, 4th block, 6th ward, there are for sale: a good hairdresser for men and women; height above average, of fairly good figure, also useful as a valet for the bedroom, waiter, or footman, 27 years old; his wife, 24 years old, a laundress and needlewoman, with a daughter over 2 years old; both of good conduct. Lowest price for the lot, 1,000 rubles.

For sale: 3 horses: 2 bay stallions, 4 years old, of English breed, well matched, of good size; and a dark bay gelding, 3 years old, also of English breed. They can be seen, and inquiry made about the price, at house no. 260, block

1, ward 8. In the same house there is for sale a musician who plays the bassoon and is beginning to sing in a bass voice. Very well trained in reading and writing. 15 years old.

SOURCE: Vernadsky (see p. 294) Vol. 2, p. 476.

A Speech by Emperor Nicholas I on Serfdom (1842)

There is no question that serfdom in its present state in our country is an evil, palpable and obvious to everyone. However, to attack it now would be, of course, an even more disastrous evil. Emperor Alexander I, of blessed memory, who had intended at the beginning of his reign to grant freedom to the serfs, later, himself, abandoned this idea as still entirely premature and impossible to fulfill. His majesty, likewise, will never venture to do it, feeling that the time when it can be undertaken is still quite distant, any thought of it at the present period would merely be a criminal infringement upon the public peace and welfare of the state. . . . But we must not conceal from ourselves the fact that current ideas are not the same as those that existed previously, and it is clear to every reasonable observer that the present situation cannot last *forever*. The most important reasons for this change in ideas and the ever more frequent unrest in recent times must be attributed in the main: first, to the imprudence of the landowners themselves, who give their serfs more education than is appropriate for their status, thereby developing in them a new range of ideas and making their position still more burdensome; and, second, to the fact that certain landowners—although, thank God, only a small minority of them— employ their power evilly, forgetting their noble duty. And the marshals of the nobility, as many of them have reported to His Majesty, can find no way of halting these abuses under the law, which places virtually no restrictions upon the power of the landowners. . . . There must be no emancipation, but it is necessary to open a path to another, transitional state,

Popular handicrafts: *(left)* salt dish in the shape of a duck, Vologda Province, early nineteenth century; (right) poultry carrier made of birch bark, Vologda Province, nineteenth century. From *Russkoe narodnoe iskusstvo* (Leningrad, 1959), Table 4.

linking with it the inviolable preservation of patrimonial ownership of the land.

SOURCE: George Vernadsky et. al. (see p. 294) Vol. 2, pp. 552–3.

A Report From the Ministry of Internal Affairs on Serf Disorders (1847)

The disorders on the estates of landlords were more persistent and serious than those of preceding years, although the number of instances was somewhat smaller. In 1845 insub-ordination occurred on twenty-six estates, in 1846, on twenty-five, and in 1847, on twenty-three estates in sixteen guberniias. The causes of these disorders were: oppression of the peasants and overburdening them with work on the part of the owners ... but the main reason for the insubordination among the peasants of the landlords was the desire for freedom. ... The aspiration to acquire freedom, aroused by various absurd rumors, resulted in persistent insubordination and violence among the peasants of the landlords on fifteen estates and prompted more than 11,000 peasants to flee.

SOURCE: George Vernadsky et al. (see p. 294) Vol. 2, p. 561.

LITERATURE

STEVEN L. HOCH
The Peasant Commune

Since the early nineteenth century numerous Russian writers have found special significance in the peasant commune, whose imagined virtues they hoped would permit Russia to emerge from its current sorry state directly into a state of freedom, equality, and spiritual wholeness. Here Stephen Hoch presents a less partisan and more systematic reconstruction of the inner workings of the commune, based primarily upon his examination of estate records. His view paints a considerably less ideal picture of the "real world" of the peasantry, but one that reveals the sophistication and complexity of peasant social life far more vividly than the idyllic images of nineteenth-century Romantics.

That the commune (mir) should be viewed as an institution reflecting intergenerational conflict in Russian peasant society would certainly come as a shock to Herzen, Haxthausen, and those Slavophiles and others who saw it as an indigenous form of socialism. But the commune played a central role in maintaining a patriarchal authority. Yet this was far from its only function. The commune was also one of the key forces holding this little society together. In most instances the patriarchs tried to represent the interests of all the serfs, and obviously not all conflicts were between generations. In addition, the commune addressed the estate management and especially the local government authorities with a collective voice and organization, and this gave the peasants substantial autonomy. In fact the commune provided a social cohesiveness that the household could not give. Patriarchy within the family may well have been inimicable to the young, but patriarchy within the commune often served the common good. While these elders did support individual heads of household in dealing with recalcitrant family members, the patriarchs, who embodied communal wisdom, experience, interests, and action, did much to bind the peasants. . . .

The functions and powers of the Petrovskoe commune were extensive. Besides distributing tiaglo [family teams engaged in field work] obligations and peasant allotments, it assessed, collected, and paid taxes and other money dues, determined many communal expenditures, and petitioned the central estate office in Moscow with its grievances and concerns. The commune also administered justice by adjudicating disputes, conducting investigations, disciplining its members, and providing internal police supervision as required by law. In addition, it elected peasant functionaries, oversaw household divisions, determined who would be recruited into military service, maintained work discipline, fixed the order of field labor (though much was well established by custom) and natural dues, cultivated the communal arable land to provide emergency grain reserves, gave some assistance to the needy, and saw to many of the needs of the parish church and clergy. The commune dealt with numerous local officials, bribing them when necessary and providing them or military troops with transport, food, and billeting.

Before beginning an in-depth discussion of the commune's functions, it would be useful to describe in broad quantitative terms the major age-specific status or generational differences at Petrovskoe to see how they relate to the mir and its role in serf society. First, almost half of the estate population consisted of children under 17. Rarely did serfs marry or carry estate labor obligations before this age. Children worked from a very early age, and they lived in their natal household, unless it underwent division, even if orphaned. All matters of upbringing were handled within each peasant household. There is little evidence that either the estate or the commune interfered in head-of-household or parent/child relationships until the assuming of corvee [labor services to the landlord] obligations became a concern or unless it was necessary to find orphans a foster home and establish their property rights. The only exception was for household serfs, especially boys, who usually began learning a skill or craft between ages 10 and 12, the estate seeing to their training.

At the other end of the age spectrum were the heads of household. They and their spouses constituted approximately 17 to 19 percent of the total population and, for males, roughly one-quarter of all tiaglos. It is to this group that many of the advantages in this little society accrued. All heads of household participated in village assemblies directly and in estate assemblies indirectly through their representatives. Approximately 40 percent of the male heads of households were no longer assigned full corvée obligations by virtue of their age. Moreover, from the remaining group came all the serf functionaries on the estate, the serf manager, village heads, overseers, drivers, and possibly serf police agents. In 1837, in the only archival listing of these persons, there were forty such serfs on the Petrovskoe estate, slightly more than one-fifth of all working heads of household, and these peasant functionaries enjoyed a variety of work privileges.

About one-third of the estate population fell between the children and the elders. This middle group carried three-quarters of all field-work obligations. From the time of their arranged marriage until their ascension to head of household, a period of rarely less than ten years and of fifteen to twenty-five years for most, these serfs worked but were accorded no privileges on the estate, in the commune, or within their own household. Males who failed to conform to required norms were sent into the army or, in extreme cases, exiled to Siberia. For young adults, flight was the only refuge from submission and exploitation, an alternative that rarely succeeded.

Recruitment, household division, and the maintenance of work discipline gave rise to in-

tergenerational conflict in the exercise of communal authority. And in all matters, those who worked but were not heads of households were excluded from decision making. Yet the generational split in the commune was not so clear as in the household. While this gathering of old men sought to preserve its interests, its fate was tied to that of the young. Moreover, the problems of poverty and social deviance were not simply generational. Therefore a more subtle view of authority is needed for the commune, and its more complex purposes require appreciation. . . .

Maintaining grain reserves in case of crop failure was required by law. In 1820 a document on land usage at Petrovskoe notes that each tiaglo worked an additional half desiatina of land in the spring fields beyond the normal peasant allotment and demesne obligation. It is likely that the grain from this land went for the communal reserves. Similar documents for 1834 and 1849, years after major crop failures, show clearly that the serfs worked a total of 320 extra statutory desiatinas (864 acres) to replenish the emergency stores. Moreover, each year the commune was required to report to the local authorities in Borisoglebsk on the size of the harvest and the status of the reserves.

Assistance to individuals came primarily as land that had been plowed and sowed by the commune. Harvesting, carting, drying, winnowing, and sifting the grain, however, were the responsibility of the needy themselves. It was extremely rare for the estate to relieve adults capable of working from tiaglo responsibilities. In 1837, the only year for which there is such detailed information, out of 715.5 tiaglos on the Petrovskoe estate, 25.5 were exempted from corvée entirely. Most of these, however, had been freed from their labor obligations because their homesteads had burned down in May. Fewer than 1 percent of all tiaglos were exempted that year for reasons of poverty. Similarly, more than thirty years of financial records for the Petrovskoe commune reveal only a handful of exemptions from taxes and money dues approved by the village assemblies because of poverty. . . .

The commune spent most of its funds to pay soul [a poll tax on each adult male], road, bridge, postal, and local taxes and dues to cover the costs of recruitment. All together these averaged 88 percent of total revenues, leaving the commune little to spend for other purposes . . . Moreover, because the commune paid in . . . paper money it had to pay a premium . . . on the money it owed the state. Until the monetary situation was stabilized with the reforms of the late 1830s, the premium fluctuated from eight to eighteen kopecks per ruble, in effect increasing taxes by that percentage. In addition, contact with government officials frequently meant additional payments. Paying taxes in Borisoglebsk always involved gifts of money to the . . . treasurer, . . . clerk, . . . petty officials, . . . and . . . notary. If the district . . . assessor happened to be in the office, he too did not depart empty-handed. In 1820–21 the Petrovskoe commune gave a total of forty-five rubles to officials for accepting its two annual tax payments; by 1838–39 the amount had risen to over one hundred rubles, these bureaucrats not losing in the decline in the value of paper money. During the intervening years, no tax payment was ever made without being accompanied by such gifts. . . .

Quite distinct from these were the bribes. The most common were attempts to prevent inquests into sudden or accidental deaths. In some instances the commune and the estate hoped to cover up the facts of the case, but more often they simply wished to avoid costly and prolonged legal proceedings, which would take up valuable work time. The documents of the Petrovskoe commune are candid. On occasion it bribed the parish priests, who were legally required to report all incidents in which a person had died before receiving the sacraments. . . .

It was cheaper to bribe village priests than local government authorities, but nevertheless most accidental deaths were covered up. Some included peasants outside the estate as victims or witnesses and could not easily be concealed. Also, local officials derived a considerable portion of their income from conducting inquests, and presumably they would have been suspicious of any village or estate that did not report what was considered to be a normal number of cases.

Upon the discovery of a corpse or the occurrence of a death from other than natural causes, the elected police agent of the appropriate village of the estate would inform the district court and have a report sent to the nobility's court assessor requesting an investigation. This petition usually cost no more that two rubles, though it could reach as high as thirteen. The court assessor generally came to the estate promptly, often within a few days, accompanied by a clerk or two, two soldiers, and on occasion the district doctor. Rarely would a second visit to the estate be needed, and it was unusual for witnesses to be summoned subsequently to Borisoglebsk [the district capital] to give further testimony. The was because at every inquest the commune paid the assessor and his assistants to avoid such developments. Sixty-three rubles were "given as a gift to Borisoglebsk district court assessor Sotsyperov in the examination of a dead body . . . , in order to prevent any further troubles." When assessor Spitsyn came to Petrovskoe to investigate both a drowning and the death of a serf in the apiary, wine, fruit liquor, and food were provided at communal expense. In addition, Spitsyn was given over twenty-eight rubles "so as not to conduct any further investigation.". . .

In Russia, peasants were required to fulfill state corvée obligations, essentially repairing roads and bridges. At times the commune of Petrovskoe was able to convert this into a money payment, but often it had to supply the laborers demanded. The officials who assigned the sections of the road to be repaired, as well as the overseers of the work itself, were readily bribed. In fact some of these officials were in such powerful positions that their dealings with the Petrovskoe commune appear to be little short of extortionate. "By order of the Borisoglebsk district chief of police, 407 male workers should be sent to level the steep slope of a mountain on the Kirsanov road near the ravine called 'Bare,' but at the request of bailiff Ivan Ivanov indulgences were made in this, for which forty-two rubles is given to him, Gospodin chief of police, as a gift.''. . . Threatening other estates and communes with having to level the same slope of the mountain probably provided the district chief with a considerable income. Payments were also made to district officials for assigning tracts of road that were close to the estate and for extending the deadline when the work was to be completed. Finally, the overseers of the actual labor were often bribed to allow the commune to send fewer than the mandated number of men.

There were numerous other instances of extortion or bribery. Twenty rubles were paid to the rural assessor so that troops would not be quartered on the estate, and it is hard to believe this official did not make the rounds of neighboring villages. When two counterfeit notes were discovered among those paid as taxes in March 1816, fifty rubles were given to the treasurer "so that this would not lead to further trouble." Forty-two rubles were given to the court assessor when an undocumented person was found residing in Kanin, "for releasing the managers of the estate and other residents of the village of Kanin from major responsibility and judicial investigation.''. . .

The only other items of significance in the commune's budget went to cover some of the expenses of the two parish churches at Petrovskoe. As was required by law, the estate provided the clergy with a total of sixty-three agricultural desiatinas (227 acres) of arable land, which the church servitors and their families worked themselves. There is no evidence that the bailiff, the central estate office, or even Prince Gagarin himself was at all concerned with the peasants' spiritual well-being, participation in religious rites, or church attendance. This again may suggest substantial community autonomy, though it more likely testifies to the weakness of Russian Orthodoxy as a religion without content or theology. The serfs themselves did not even care a great deal about maintaining the church. In the village of Petrovskoe, the iconostasis in the church had long since become faded and discolored. There was a bell tower but no bells. The fence around the churchyard had fallen down. The priest and other clerics lived over a mile away

from the church, and their household structures were "very dilapidated.''. . .

Neither the estate nor the commune had particularly good relations with the parish clergy. The estate was often unwilling to supply the materials and labor needed to keep the churches and the clergy's household structures in repair, and the commune felt quite free to complain to clerical authorities about excessive requisitions and fees asked by the parish priests. For almost five years, from August 1821 until May 1826, the Petrovskoe commune was involved in legal proceedings against one of its priests, Aleksei Polikarpov, who according to the parishioners charged too much for performing occasional religious rites. What began as an argument between Polikarpov and the church elder concluded with the commune's filing a sixty-six page list of grievances against the priest in the Borisoglebsk clerical board and the Tambov clerical consistory. Eventually a new priest was assigned. In 1838 the peasants of the parish of Kanin began similar proceedings against their priest "for various offenses committed by him.''. . .

There is little information about the administration of justice and the resolution of disputes among the serfs by the commune. The elders had the right to punish an individual by flogging, though the punishment was supposed to be supervised by the bailiff. A serf bringing a complaint to the elders generally had to accuse someone specifically. Only then would the commune investigate the matter, and only as related to the accused. Guilt was most often established by confession. Falsely accusing someone—that is, casting aspersions on a serf's character—and bothering the elders without sufficient cause were also punished by whipping. The reputation of both parties in a conflict was an important consideration in the decisions taken by the elders and greatly influenced the compensation due the injured party or the punishment imposed on the guilty serf, as the following example reveals:

On 31 March last year, 1828, near the end of Holy Week, various property disappeared from the storeroom of stableman Ivan Timofeev Akhriapkin and his wife Pelageia Vasileva, in the theft of which was suspected stableman Iakov Grigor'ev, but at that time he did not confess to it. Last 3 February the above-mentioned Pelageia recognized her lost shawl at the home of Fedos'ia Iunova, a soldier's wife from Kanin, and upon investigation it turned out that she had received this shawl from the above-mentioned stableman Grigor'ev for weaving for him six yards of cloth. The following had disappeared from Pelageia:

A new calico dress worth 9 rubles 20 kopecks; a checked gingham dress, 7 rubles 20 kopecks . . . [a long list of stolen items follows] for which Iakov Grigor'ev was beaten with a birch rod and had half his head shaved, and to compensate Pelageia it was ordered to take from him livestock of equal value; and although Grigor'ev ought to pay for the stolen items with livestock of twice the value, since the above-mentioned Pelageia had fornicated with Grigor'ev, for her debauched behavior only equal value was paid up in punishment.

Distributing land and tiaglos, collecting taxes, electing peasant functionaries, cultivating the arable land for the emergency stores and the needy, bribing officials, and determining the calendar of field labor seem to have been fairly routine matters for the commune to administer. Neither the bailiffs' weekly reports nor other documents relating to the commune cite any instances of serious disputes over these issues. Obviously the elders were governed by agricultural traditions and were committed to economic equality among households. In addition, they were in agreement that local bureaucrats should be kept both distant and content.

In contrast, determining who would be sent into the army to fill draft quotas was a highly divisive issue. For a household, the economic costs of losing an adult male laborer were considerable. A household not only lost a work team and an allotment of arable land, it still had a daughter-in-law and possibly infant children to support. Patriarchs saw their security in old age diminished, and if recruitment occurred within a year or two of marriage, they would not even have recovered the brideprice.

Young males viewed conscription as comparable to a sentence of death. At Petrovskoe, some cut off an index finger to avoid recruitment; others drank poison or acid hoping to damage their internal organs. Often those fearing they would be recruited simply took flight. Others tried to escape en route to induction centers. In response, communal assemblies were held in secret, and once a serf was designated for conscription he was placed in leg irons and kept under constant guard. It usually took as many men to transport the recruits to Tambov as there were peasants to be inducted. The commune often bribed army doctors to declare serfs who maimed themselves fit for military service. . . .

Recruitment priorities at Petrovskoe were first to rid the estate of undesirables, and then for households to draw lots if draft quotas were still not filled. "Because of the proclamation of a recruit levy, it has been ordered to elect elders from each village to make according to form a priority list of suspected or known troublemakers," the bailiff wrote in his report of 22 October 1834. In August 1837 the bailiff informed the Moscow office that persons "discovered stealing, remiss in domestic matters, and especially those lazy and without horses" would be given as recruits. This was common practice on many estates. . . .

It was important for patriarchs to be able to coerce younger males dissatisfied with their family situations to work. The heads of households, therefore, also used the threat of recruitment to control laziness, disobedience, and failure to fulfill household obligations. After theft, these were the most common reasons the patriarchs selected individuals for military service. A son or nephew disgruntled about his lack of authority, status, or economic position in the household faced conscription and with it the dispossession of property, disinheritance, and the loss of all future rights and benefits that came with age. Young male serfs were thus under great pressure to conform to the will of their ascendants and to adhere to the norms that patriarchy implied at Petrovskoe. . . .

The commune saw in recruitment a way to rid itself of poorer and less productive households, especially those that were likely to default on taxes and dues. The target of the commune was primarily poorer, smaller households with only one tiaglo, called *odinokie*, especially those in which the head of household was young and inexperienced.

Elderly male peasant with handmade pitch fork, Orel Province, 1860s. From *Neskol'ko narodnykh tipov Rossii*, a collection of photographs by J. X. Raoult, Odessa. Courtesy of The New York Public Library, Slavic and Baltic Division.

Such households did not conform to the patriarchal three-generation, multiple family ideal and had virtually no margin of safety against accident or illness. In these households any mismanagement of household affairs could easily result in destitution. In 1837 the bailiff wrote that frequently "the mir has to pay all the taxes and dues for one- tiaglo households and to fulfill their estate and state corvée obligations." Putting a greater share of military obligations on these households served the interests of the village elders in many ways. It reduced the number of males who would be conscripted from their households, and it reduced the number of young heads of house-

hold who might have been a source of envy for other serfs of the same age. Moreover, according to the bailiff, conscription from smaller households did not foster division that undermined patriarchal authority. If anything, at this level, the threat of recruitment induced mergers. For the commune, such a policy provided an alternative for dealing with the poor, reduced the number of households that required communal assistance, and was yet another means of limiting economic differentiation.

In contrast to the commune, the estate was at times reluctant to have the sole male of a household recruited. Such households had often been the recipients of financial assistance from the estate, which would have no way of recovering its investment if these serfs were now conscripted. In 1837, however, after a three-year effort by the estate to reduce the number of households without horses, the bailiff concluded that those still lacking draft animals had only themselves to blame. He asserted that "from obvious laziness they have not come by a horse, regardless of being odinokie." He therefore decided that it would be "useful that the peasants be convinced that recruits will be taken from one-tiaglo households, and thus those without horses would make a greater effort to acquire a horse for themselves." Furthermore, the bailiff noted that by instituting this policy the pressure for larger households to divide would be reduced, and so in time would be the number of one-tiaglo households. All these sentiments were identical to the interests of the serf patriarch. . . .

By providing tax relief or giving over cultivated lands to the needy, the commune did much to ensure the survival of all its members, including the economically weak. The basic approach of the commune, however, was to control access to productive resources. Communal repartitions of arable land and the assigning of labor obligations by tiaglo limited economic differentiation, and they seem to have aroused little controversy among the patriarchs, that is, between households. Institutional forms of assistance to the needy were not used, and direct grants or exemptions to the poor were limited to a very small percentage of the population.

While communal life was certainly not harmonious, in most instances the mir had the serfs' common well-being at heart. The commune served the general good and used its funds to attain freedom from internal deviants and bureaucratic interference, acts the estate found desirable as well. But this does not mean that the commune did not uphold exploitative relationships, only that exploitation did not imply competition between households to subsist or survive. The commune was the instrument of the elders, and they held the power

to regulate household division and determine recruitment priorities, decisions that greatly affected the lives of those a generation younger. Even with conscription, where the interests of the estate and the elders were somewhat at odds, the patriarchs at times were successful in getting the bailiff to rid the estate of smaller and economically less viable households. This policy not only reduced socioeconomic stratification but preserved the wealth of the patriarchs. Most often, however, communal actions were of benefit to the estate. But as successful as the patriarchs seem to have been in working with the bailiff for their common advantage, both were in fact confronted by an enormous amount of resistance and noncooperation, which reflect how deep generational status differences were at Petrovskoe.

SOURCE: Steven L. Hoch, *Serfdom and Social Control in Russia: Petrovskoe, A Village in Tambov* (Chicago, IL: University of Chicago Press, 1986), chapter 4: "Communal Function and Control," pp. 133–59 (excerpted). Copyright © by the University of Chicago Press. Reprinted by permission of the publisher. (The original includes a great many terms in Russian, most of which have been translated here.)

PETER KOLCHIN
Peasant Patterns of Resistance

By the beginning of the nineteenth century peasant bondage had disappeared from all but a handful of large states. Two of the most glaring exceptions to this pattern were the United States of America and the Russian Empire. In this essay Peter Kolchin describes the contrasting ways in which Russian serfs and American slaves tried to resist their bondage, and he makes some interesting observations about similarities and differences. This excerpt concentrates mostly on the Russian side, but the complete article, as well as the book that followed it, gave equal attention to both nations.

Adult male peasants from Poltava Province (southern Russia) in the late 1860s. From *Neskol'ko narodnykh tipov Rossii*, a collection of photographs by J. X. Raoult, Odessa. Courtesy of The New York Public Library, Slavic and Baltic Division.

I

Recent historians of unfree peoples have developed a fascination with the subject of resistance. Conscious of the unjust plight of slaves and serfs and convinced that "love of freedom is hard to crush," scholars have celebrated the attempts of the downtrodden to combat their oppressors and have eagerly searched for evidence demonstrating the existence of such resistance. Special accolades have gone to the participants and leaders of organized rebellions: . . . the Nat Turner insurrection, the quilombos of 17th-century Brazil, the peasant wars of 17th- and 18th-century Russia . . .

Despite their historical importance and dramatic appeal, however, such rebellions were clearly unusual occurrences that did not typify the behavior of most bondsmen. There were only three or four Russian peasant wars, the last of which occurred in 1773–74, over 85 years before the abolition of serfdom. In the United States, larger uprisings were even rarer: of the handful of "major" slave rebellions, none involved more than a few hundred slaves or encompassed more than a local geographic area. Nineteenth-century Russia, like the 19th-century United States South, was largely devoid of massive uprisings.

Historians have developed two common methods of dealing with this absence of rebellion. One has been to argue that slavery, by its very nature, created docile beings who were ill-suited to rebel against their thralldom. This line of argument was most highly developed in the United States, where it culminated in Stanley Elkins's famous Sambo thesis that the rigid system of American slavery infantilized the slaves and rendered them psychologically as well as physically dependent on their masters. Such theories have not, however, proved entirely convincing; as numerous scholars have pointed out, there is little evidence that most slaves became childlike Sambos who internalized the values of their owners.

More common has been the emphasis on small, day-to-day forms of resistance to bondage. Historians have seen practically every act—of either commission or omission—as an effort to sabotage the routine of agricultural operations. Theft, lying, feigning illness, sullen behavior, and shoddy work were thus all signs of the continuing class struggle. . . . Unfortunately, however, it is practically impossible to prove that less than perfect work or behavior usually constituted deliberate resistance to oppression; as two historians have cogently suggested, "malingering may have reflected no more than a disinclination to work, especially when the rewards were so meager. Likewise, what is taken for sabotage may have originated in apathy and indifference."

In this article I shall examine forms of behavior that fell in between these two extremes and might best be termed small-scale confrontations. These local conflicts were by no means the only important forms of resistance; neglect of work, theft, flight, arson, murder, and re-

bellion must all be considered in any complete treatment of responses to servitude. But the small-scale confrontations are especially useful for analytical purposes, because they possess the advantages of both rebellions and invisible sabotage without the major drawbacks of either: they occurred often enough to be significant and subject to generalization, and they clearly involved deliberate, conscious defiance on the part of the bondsmen.

Something should be said by way of preface about the comparability of American slavery and Russian serfdom. Both were systems of unfree labor that emerged on the periphery of a modernizing Europe in the 16th and 17th centuries in areas of intense labor shortage, where there was an abundance of land and relatively few people to work it. Both evolved over the centuries, reaching maturity in the late 18th and first half of the 19th centuries; both were abolished in the 1860s.

There were also major differences. Russian serfdom, unlike American slavery, was a non-racial system of bondage, in which master and laborer were of the same race and national origin. In the United States, slave ownership was spread out among a broad segment of the southern white population, while in Russia, serf ownership was highly concentrated in a small caste of noblemen; as a result, whereas less than half the slaves were held in units larger than thirty each, almost half the serfs were held in units over 1,000. In the United States, most slaves received food, clothes, and housing from their owners, and in return owed them virtually all of their labor, while in Russia the serfs (except for house servants) supported themselves, and consequently worked only part time for their owners. . . . In both countries, the owners were entirely free to determine the nature of the bondsmen's obligations.

Finally, serfdom was juridically not precisely the same institution as slavery: originally, unlike slaves, the serfs were tied to the land, supporting their owners so these noblemen could in turn be free to perform service to the state. Unlike slaves, they were not outsiders plunged into an alien society, but the bottom rank within that society. By the second half of the eighteenth century, however, when noblemen were freed from obligatory state service, Russian serfdom had evolved into a system of labor and social relations in most respects far closer to American chattel slavery than to classical serfdom of the medieval western European variety. Peasants could be bought and sold on the open market, and a Russian nobleman's power over his serfs was just as unlimited as a southern planter's over his slaves. In short, for all practical purposes, during its last hundred years Russian serfdom was a variety of slavery.

II

The typical Russian confrontation is described by the word " *volnenie*," a term without precise equivalent in English, used by both contemporaries and historians to denote something smaller than a revolt or rebellion. . . .

The typical *volnenie* began when the serfs on a given estate, dissatisfied for some reason, banded together and decided on collective action. They might number anywhere from a handful to thousands of souls, but groups in the hundreds were most common: most serfs lived on large estates, and the usual unit of action was either the village, a major village . . . and surrounding hamlets . . . , or several villages and hamlets belonging to the same estate . . . . The initial cause of the serfs' discontent might be anything from an increase in the burdens imposed upon them to oppressive treatment by a steward or sale to a new owner, but almost always involved either a change in their actual condition or a dashing of somehow aroused hopes.

The serfs frequently began their protest by sending a petition either to their owner, a local official, the provincial governor, or the tsar himself. Since the great majority of peasants were illiterate, the petitions were written for them in appropriately humble language by a priest or scribe—or sometimes a literate serf who served as a bookkeeper or clerk—listing the names of all the (male) petitioners. The peasants then chose one or two walkers to carry the petition to the designated recipient, and levied a small tax on themselves to pay the walkers' expenses.

The results of such efforts were usually disappointing to serfs convinced they had legitimate grievances that only had to be revealed in order to be remedied. Occasionally, specific requests to owners met with favorable responses; for example in 1833, after a crop failure, Prince Vorontsov's central administration awarded 1,662 rubles to 5,372 serfs from the Volga region who had complained to their owner of their destitution. But, with the exception of humble appeals for small favors, petitions were usually ignored, and not infrequently the walkers were severely punished for their troubles. Such was especially the case when petitions were directed to the tsar, . . . [since] as late as 1845 the law provided for punishment of up to fifty strokes with birch switches, and petitioners could never be sure of their reception. Appeals to the tsar were routinely forwarded to provincial authorities for consideration; although such complaints occasionally prompted serious investigations of abuses, usually they were simply declared "unfounded," or were lost in the shuffle of official reports, inquiries, and memoranda. . . .

The next step was for the serfs to refuse to recognize their owner's authority over them, or stop working for him—in short, to go on strike. If they had sent a petition to the tsar or governor, they might refuse to work until they received a reply, but they sometimes took such action independently of any petitioning. The serfs' behavior was highly organized, and often included the replacement of seigneurial stewards or loyal *starosty* by new, insurgent leaders. Peasants were usually careful to refrain from major violence against their owners or the owners' highest representatives, although peasants who remained loyal to their masters, and even stewards, sometimes received beatings. Most serfs must have realized, however, that assaulting authorities would bring down upon themselves certain retribution. The *volneniia*, although containing elements of spontaneity, were less expressions of wild fury by serfs seeking vengeance on their owners than organized, collective endeavors by peasants who retained some hope that in the end their efforts would be successful.

In response to such disobedience, the *pomeshchik*—or if, as was often the case, he was an absentee steward—invariably sent for the *ispravnik*, a minor official who in every *uezd* (district, equivalent to a U.S. county) served as a combination of sheriff and magistrate, and headed a three-man board known as the lower land court. . . . He would come to the estate, either alone or with other members of the court, and talk to the recalcitrant peasants, typically alternating between dire threats of punishment should the serfs continue their disobediences and promises that if they relented they would be spared serious harm and their complaints be investigated. No doubt in many cases such urgings were sufficient to restore order, but in the great majority of those for which records have survived—which naturally tend to be the most serious cases— the peasants ignored the *ispravnik*'s pleas, sometimes threatening him with bodily injury if he did not leave the estate. The frightened official would then return to the district capital, although sometimes he would try more than once to convince the peasants to yield, and write a report to the provincial governor, who in turn reported to higher authorities in St. Petersburg.

The governor, upon receiving the *ispravnik*'s report, usually ordered other officials to the scene. . . . These officials, usually accompanied by a small military guard, would repeat in succession the efforts of the *ispravnik*, striving through threats and promises to put down the *volnenie* with a minimum of force. This was so not only because governors preferred not to use soldiers unless necessary, but also because even when they were readily available—which was not always the case—the balance of forces was often such that a full-scale battle would entail serious casualties on both sides. . . .

Ultimately, soldiers were needed to crush the most stubborn *volneniia*. In the worst clashes, dozens of serfs and smaller numbers of soldiers were killed and wounded, although casualties were usually few; almost all the poorly armed and untrained peasants suffered a far higher toll than the military. Following the end of the *volnenie*, its ringleaders received harsh punishments: savage beatings with birch switches, whips, and worst of all the knout, followed by exile to penal servitude were routine inflictions, and under Nicholas I running the gauntlet was a common sentence imposed by the military courts set up to deal with the leaders of the worst *volneniia*. Often the bulk of peasants, however, suffered little or no immediate hardship, and in some cases the serfs won real advantages even in their defeat.

[Two] examples of serf *volneniia* should make clearer many of the points suggested in the above schematization. None of [them] conforms in all details to the model presented—indeed, few did—but together they typify the broad range of possible actions and responses that characterized the peasant outbreaks. . . .

The first example begins with a petition from 25 serfs in Moscow province to the provincial governor, on behalf of themselves and thousands of other peasants living in 8 villages and 43 hamlets. Dated 1823 and written for the illiterate serfs by a servant of a neighboring nobleman, the petition related that before their owner E. A. Golovkina died in 1821 they had been managed by her steward Petr Ivanovich Lapirev. The peasants complained that even though Golovkina had been dead for two years, steward Lapirev continued to have 26 rubles *obrok* [cash dues paid by the serfs to the landlords] collected from each of 3,840 male souls, and begged for governmental intervention against the steward's gathering money for a nonexistent owner. Meanwhile, the district *ispravnik* reported his version of the story to the governor. He wrote that steward Lapirev had told him that over 4,300 souls, led by *starosta* Timofei Fedorov and three other peasants, were refusing to pay their *obrok* obligations. According to the *ispravnik*, the peasants were told that they now had two new owners, the underaged Counts Shuvalov, and had to obey their guardian collegial assessor Vasil'evskii, Lapirev, and the head *starosta* of the area; at this they "in one voice announced that they, not personally seeing the *pomeshchiki*, would not obey the steward and *starosta* or pay the *obrok.*"

In an effort to restore order, the *ispravnik* went to the village of Vishegorod, where steward Lapirev kept his headquarters, together with a noble assessor and four invalid soldiers, and called for representatives from each peasant village to assemble and hear that they must obey their new owners. Instead, over 2,000 serfs descended on the seigneurial house and shouted to the *ispravnik* that they wanted to replace Lapirev with a *burmistr* (bailiff, manager) of their own choosing, and to elect new *starosty*. Then they proceeded to choose one of their own leaders as *burmistr*, selected two *starosty* to assist him, and sent for two local priests to administer oaths to the new peasant officials. The *ispravnik*, however, sent the priests away and then, unable to persuade the serfs to desist, returned to the *uezd* capital. Soon thereafter, he received a letter from the steward that the new *burmistr* had gone to the neighboring *uezd* to collect peasant reinforcements for a new gathering. The *ispravnik* summoned a guard to protect the seigneurial house and requested assistance from the Moscow governor.

It was not until a month later, however, that a punitive expedition headed by a major arrived to suppress the *volnenie*. After futile efforts by the *ispravnik*, a noble assessor, and an adjutant to the governor-general of Moscow province to convince the serfs to yield, the soldiers went into action. In each village, in succession, they assembled the peasants, quartered some troops, arrested the ringleaders, and subdued the remaining serfs. Despite threats of resistance, the peasants yielded without a struggle. Nine of their leaders were jailed for a year and then transported to Siberia. . . .

The third *volnenie* involved a far more protracted and bitter struggle of serfs for what they considered their rights. If in the previous episode an apparent peasant defeat turned into a partial victory, in this case what at first seemed likely to result in a quick redress of grievances led in the end only to bloody repression. Early in 1852 Savelii Matveev, chosen representative of some 575 souls in Tver province, petitioned Nicholas I on their behalf. He

explained that until 1840 they had belonged to Admiral A. S. Shishkov, whose will leaving them to his wife stipulated that the estate could not be mortgaged, sold, or rented out and that the peasants should not be charged more than 12,000 rubles per year in *obrok* dues. Madame Shishkova observed these conditions, but in 1848 she died, leaving the estate to her niece, N. D. Shishkova, who immediately increased the serfs' *obrok* obligations and was now planning to impose on them *barshchina* [labor obligations] dues as well. Matveev implored the "merciful sovereign" to order that the owner not impose *barshchina* or excessive *obrok* levies, refrain from cutting down the peasants' timber, and "in general adhere to the will of her deceased uncle." The tsar forwarded the petition to the governor of Tver province for consideration.

The governor reported back one-half year later that before seeing the petition he had received a complaint from the new owner that the serfs, "for an unknown reason," were seeking their freedom and refusing to pay their *obrok*. The governor ordered the *uezd ispravnik* "to take measures to restore peace to the estate of *pomeshchitsa* Shishkova, and also make an investigation of the causes of the disorders," but learned from him that the peasants' complaints were well founded. The serfs were not seeking their freedom, the *ispravnik* reported, and insisted they were not being disobedient; they merely objected to paying 21,275 rubles *obrok* rather than the prescribed maximum of 12,000, and to the refusal of two agents sent by Shishkova to count the money in front of priests and other witnesses or give the peasants receipts for it. The governor concluded that the owner's behavior "aroused the dissatisfaction of the peasants and gave them cause to make complaints about her action." Moreover, in a private meeting with the governor she "showed an extremely resistant character." He decided, nevertheless, to pursue a cautious policy. Unwilling flatly to take the side of the serfs in a dispute with their owner, he decreed the peasants' petition "unfounded," and ordered the marshal of the nobility to explain to them that "it is much more advantageous" to have their *obrok* payments increased once than to have other forms of obligations—namely *barshchina*—introduced as well. At the same time, he would order the *ispravnik* to be on the lookout for abuses of power by Shishkova, and to report any such misbehavior to the marshal of the nobility.

The peasants, however, were not satisfied with this arrangement, and refused to perform any labor not stipulated in the will until they received a reply to their petition. "One should not suppose," noted the *ispravnik* after a visit to the estate, "that without special severe measures they will be obedient to their *pomeshchitsa* and carry out her demands." Despairing of a voluntary return to order, provincial authorities jailed the original petitioner, Matveev, together with two other troublesome serfs, and, in July, 1853, the governor reported that a punitive expedition had brought the peasants back into obedience. In August and December, however, another serf presented petitions to Nicholas I and to the head of the Third Department. The Minister of Internal Affairs ordered the governor to determine whether outsiders were inciting the peasants, and the *ispravnik* informed the governor that they were once again refusing to pay the increased *obrok*, having promised to do so earlier only out of fear. Angered by the continued agitation, the governor told Shishkova not to make excessive demands on her serfs and instructed the *ispravnik* to take down the names of unruly peasants.

The tsar too was annoyed with this long-festering unrest, which was now of two years' duration, and sent aide-de-campe N. T. Baranov to Tver province to handle the matter. He personally told the peasants that Nicholas I deemed their complaint unfounded, but they remained skeptical and still refused to pay more than 12,000 rubles *obrok*. When Baranov ordered a military command to the scene, the 200 soldiers proved insufficient to keep the serfs from the nine villages comprising the estate from hiding in the woods, and 300 more soldiers had to be sent. The exasperated tsar ordered that the *volnenie*'s ringleaders be forced to run a gauntlet of 1,000 men three times and then be sent to penal servitude in Siberia, but such orders proved easier to give than to execute. While the two chief culprits underwent the prescribed treatment and many others received public chastisement with birch switches, 157 of the 576 male serfs disappeared into the woods, and Baranov had to be content with leaving a list of names of the missing with an adjutant-general, with instructions that upon capture they be sent to the governor for punishment.

Although the *volnenie* seemed to be over, as soon as the troops were removed the serfs resumed their objections to the excessive *obrok* levy. Soldiers were soon once again needed to restore order—in the process 78 peasants were jailed—but this action in turn led to renewed protest. In December, 1854, another peasant representative, Aleksei Vasil'ev, petitioned the head of the Corps of Gendarmes, repeating the whole story of the unjust *obrok* levy and complaining of cruel treatment by police and soldiers. Fifty-four peasants remained in jail, he asserted, nine had been drafted into the army, two—including Kuz'ma Mikhailov, a church *starosta* for nine years and "an honest and sober person"—had run the gauntlet of 3,003 blows and had been resettled in Siberia, others had died in irons, and six more remained to be exiled to Siberia. "And we must now spend our lives worse than unthinking cattle," he asserted poetically, "and suffer frost and hardship, cold and hunger."

This petition was forwarded to the Minister of Internal Affairs, who pronounced it "undeserved of any consideration," but the unrest continued during the following months. After the *pomeshchitsa* once again begged authorities for help, in August, 1856, the Minister of Internal Affairs ordered the governor to take "the most stringent measures for the restoration of order on the estate."

Having determined that Osip Fedorov was now one of the peasant leaders, the *ispravnik* recruited a retired soldier to make friends with Fedorov in order to capture him by stealth. The ensuing ambush was successful, despite the efforts of other serfs to rescue the prisoner, and the exultant governor assured the new Minister of Internal Affairs that calm would now return to the estate. Almost a year later, however, the governor's successor had to order 250 soldiers to the scene to catch fugitives and restore order. "The fugitive peasants...voluntarily began to appear in their houses," reported the delighted governor, "giving their special promises to be in complete obedience to the *pomeshchitsa.*" Finally only one serf remained missing, but the *ispravnik* was certain he would soon return. The *volnenie* was at last over, some five-and-a-half years after it had begun. . . .

The Russian *volnenie* was by its very nature a group enterprise, an action taken by decision of the communal gathering and sustained by the common efforts of the peasants, who showed an extraordinary solidarity in defying owners and officials. Time after time authorities attempting to talk the rebels into submission reported that they "all in one voice announced that they would not obey any authorities," or that they "all in one voice shouted, that they did not want to and would not submit." When officials tried to arrest troublemakers, the mass of peasants often interceded in their behalf. In one typical case, when an *ispravnik* selected a serf for punishment with birch switches, a crowd rushed up shouting "we are all guilty and will not give him over to be beaten," in another, when a staff officer of the Corps of Gendarmes ordered an *ispravnik* to record the names of two peasant leaders, "the whole crowd in one voice repeated, 'write down all of us, we all speak as one.'" Numerous examples could be added but the point is clear: collective behavior characterized the peasant challenge to authority.

At the heart of this group response was the peasant *mir* or *obshchina* (community), an institution of great complexity that has generally been underestimated by both Soviet and western historians. Peasant communal officials, headed by the *starosta*, were often the masterminds of *volneniia*, and when they were not, the assembled serfs frequently began their in-

subordination by replacing a loyalist *starosta* with a new one of their own choosing. In any case, the legitimacy of the *volneniia*, in the eyes of their participants, stemmed from the origins in the *mir* gathering. When Major-General P. E. Zavaritskii's serfs decided to seek their freedom because he had not allotted them sufficient land, their first act was to choose a new *starosta*, "who announced not only to the *pomeshchik* but also to the *zemskii* police that he, elected *starosta* by the *mir*, would not recognize any authority except the will of the *mir.*" Reproached by Zavaritskii for his disobedience, the new *starosta* replied, "I am just as much a general as you, since the *mir* elected me." In short, once the decision to resist was made, the peasant community stood as a group in opposition to owner and officials. . . .

This cooperative element was not totally absent in the resistance of American blacks. Occasionally a group of slaves, surprised in a forbidden act, combined to resist capture or punishment, although this was usually a spontaneous response to an emergency rather than a planned and coordinated undertaking. In both large-scale and small-scale forms of resistance, slaves sometimes acted together to achieve their goals. . . .

But even in these forms of resistance other than local confrontations, lack of collective endeavor was characteristic. The few organized rebellions mounted by American blacks— small affairs by any standards—were plagued by serious organizational problems and a notable lack of slave solidarity . . . . Whatever rebellions existed in the antebellum South were small, isolated movements undertaken by a few brave individuals; nowhere did whole plantations go into revolt. . . .

One should not suppose, of course, that this contrast stemmed from some innate difference in the character of American blacks and Russian peasants: there were concrete reasons for varying patterns of resistance. In part, these involved intrinsic differences between the institutions of slavery and serfdom: while serfs occupied the lowest level of Russian society, slaves were considered—by both black and white—to be largely outside of American society. There was no equivalent among the slaves to the naive monarchism that encouraged serfs to believe their collective protests might be successful—until after emancipation, with the proliferation of the myth of Father Abraham Lincoln. But there were also specific features of American slavery and Russian serfdom that help account for the contrast in forms of resistance, features that included basic differences in demographic patterns, cultural traditions, racial attitudes, and the character and policies of the master classes in the two countries. Slaves and serfs in other times and places have not always responded in precisely the same way that 19th-century American slaves and Russian serfs did. In this sense, it is more useful to see Russian and American bondage as two ends of a broad spectrum of unfreedom, against which subject people could struggle in various ways, rather than as two distinct if kindred institutions of serfdom and slavery. . . .

The American response indicated an individualistic society in which local initiative was widespread, whereas the Russian reaction was that of a bureaucratic organization that had to proceed with extreme caution, checking with higher authority every step of the way, and ducking any decision that could be avoided or postponed. It is inconceivable that, had the slaves on a southern plantation got together and decided to stage the kind of general strike that was so common in Russia, either slaveowners or governmental authorities would have tolerated a situation in which the confrontation remained unresolved for months.

Here, two differences between imperial Russia and the Old South suggest themselves as crucial. Most obvious was the contrast between the highly stratified Russian society in which everyone's place was legally defined, and the democratic but racially oriented environment in which American slaveowners lived. What-

ever the relationship between racial prejudice and the development of American slavery, by the 19th century, southerners had created a politico-juridical system that replaced overt class by racial discrimination. Because this racial barrier was so essential in a society in which all free white men were theoretically equal, antebellum white southerners would never have allowed themselves to engage in the kind of protracted negotiations with insubordinate blacks that occurred on a regular basis in Russia between noble and peasant, where there was no threat of social or political inequality.

Just as important was the basic difference in the character of the two societies created by the master classes. Large Russian *pomeshchiki* had few roots in the countryside, exercised at best a tenuous control over society, and maintained a largely absentee mentality even when they resided on one of their estates; as a recent historian has noted, the Russian village "was a peasant world; the pomeshchik was almost an outsider even on his own ancestral estate." American planters on the other hand, formed with a few exceptions a resident ruling class who created a distinctive sectional culture of their own. There were two consequences. First, the slaves were far more apt to adopt the values of their owners than were the serfs. Second, slaveholders reacted in a more uncompromising manner than *pomeshchiki* when challenged from below because they had more at stake: while serf unrest affected the economic interest—and pride—of the Russian nobility, slave insubordination threatened the very way of life of the southern planter class.

SOURCE: Peter Kolchin, "The Process of Confrontation: Patterns of Resistance to Bondage in Nineteenth-Century Russia and the United States," *Journal of Social History* 11 (Summer, 1978): 457–65, 470–3 (excerpted). Reprinted with the permission of the editors of *The Journal of Social History*.

B. Merchants, Artisans, and Townsfolk

DOCUMENTS

Ivan Pososhkov on Merchants and Artisans in the Early Eighteenth Century (1727)

Pososhkov's famous tract *The Book of Poverty and Wealth*, first appeared in 1727. Written as a series of recommendations and concerns to the emperor about the organization of the economy and regulation of society, the text contains vivid and occasionally fanciful depictions of numerous social groups, native and foreign, both as he thought and wished them to be. As we read his reflections on merchants and artisans, we should pay special attention to how intricately Pososhkov interweaves economics, national pride, and the sanctity of faith into a single narrative. How does he classify and assess the situations of these important urban groups and their importance to Russia?

"OF THE MERCHANTS"

The merchants must not be treated as if they were of no account since no country, whether great or small, can subsist without them. The merchants and the military work in partnership: the military wage war, the merchants support them and furnish them with everything necessary. . . .

If our Russian merchants were given freedom in their trade so that they suffered no kind of interference at the hands of either men of other callings or the foreigner, then His Majesty's revenue from trade would be of quite another order. I am convinced that this revenue would be doubled or trebled since, as things are now, a good half is lost through the actions of interlopers from other countries. . . .

Each estate must conduct itself fittingly so as not to fall into sin before God or commit a fault in the eyes of the Sovereign. Let every man be known for what he really is: if a warrior, then a true warior; if of some other calling, then let him devote himself wholly to that.

The Lord God Himself said: 'No man can serve two masters.' Hence a warrior (or indeed a person in any walk of life) must conduct himself as befits that calling and not intrude into some other sphere; for if a warrior insinuates himself among the merchants he must needs be false to his profession of arms. Moreover Our Savior Himself said: 'For where your treasure is there will your heart be also.' And St. Paul the Apostle says: 'No man that warreth entangleth himself with the affairs of this life; that he may please him who hath chosen him to be a soldier.' Even among the common people there is current a very similar saying: choose one or the other—either to trade or to make war. . . .

At present there are boyars, noblemen and their dependents, officers, soldiers and peasants all engaged in trade which thus escapes tax; moreover, under the name of such people even the merchants do much business which also evades tax. It is my belief that at present less than half the true amount of toll is in fact collected; nor will the full amount ever be collected unless landowners and all those in His Majesty's service are forbidden to trade altogether, since many prominent people have a hand in trade and ordinary folk who do the same are outside the authority of the Board of Civic Administration.

I know for certain that in the district of Novgorod alone there are something like a couple of hundred peasants engaged in trade who do not pay a single farthing in toll. And if the taxgatherers attempt to collect such dues the

"Wagons Drawing Ice for Sale from the Neva River, St. Petersburg" (early nineteenth century). From *Souvenirs de S. Peterbourg: Costumes russes* (St. Petersburg, 1825). Plate 6. Reprinted courtesy of The New York Public Library, Slavic and Baltic Division.

peasants' masters take their part and use force so that these officials go in fear of their lives and dare not come near these peasants. Some of them are so rich that they have in their possession goods worth five or six hundred roubles but do not pay a single farthing to His Majesty. So if all these improvements were to be put into effect the merchant estate would, as it were, be aroused from sleep.

Most wrong too is the inveterate lack of probity of merchants among themselves, for foreigners and Russians alike cheat one another and display wares which appear to be of good quality but are bad below the surface. To some goods of the worst quality they give a spurious look of excellence and thus sell them at a higher price than is right. By such deceitful practices they cause great loss to gullible customers, cheating them as they do over weight and measure and price. But they do not con-

sider such cheating a sin; their honest ways do great harm to the innocent.

In the long run these dishonest merchants come to grief through their dishonesty and fall into greater poverty, and so everyone suffers. Whereas if the honesty which befits Christians were to prevail among our merchants, wares of good quality would be sold as such, and similarly those of moderate or bad quality as such, and the true and proper price asked according to the quality of the goods, as determined for any particular article. Far from receiving an excessive price for anything no merchant would even ask it; he would cheat neither the old nor the young nor the ignorant but always act with perfect honesty in all matters. If this were so God's grace would shine forth on the merchant estate and His blessing would be upon them and their trade be hallowed. . . .

Every customer, whoever he may be—rich

or poor, informed or ignorant— is entitled to the same fair dealing. Merchants must not accept, still less demand, a single kopeck in excess whether the sum in question is one or ten roubles. . . .

No quantity of goods, great or small, should be sold to foreigners at fairs without permission from the official charged with the supervision of trade. If any dare to sell to foreigners any article whatsoever, even if its value is only one rouble, without the permission of the said supervisor, he shall be fined a hundredfold . . . and suffer as many strokes of the knout as shall be laid down, so that he may remember not to do the same again in future.

No one, be he rich or poor, should be allowed to send Russian goods abroad by sea or by land until a price has been set upon them with the permission of such supervisor and by common consent of the merchants concerned, thus ensuring that no one is treated unfairly.

When a foreigner agrees to buy a large or small quantity of Russian goods all the Russian merchants, whether rich or poor, should contribute to the quantity to be supplied, in proportion to their stock-in-trade, in such a way that no one shall be treated unfairly, be he rich or poor. But if any person does not desire to part with some of his stock when the sale of only a small quantity is in view, he may be allowed to do as he pleases. In this way all merchants will act together in amicable agreement and none will be able to offer a lower price than the rest. If a certain price is set upon an article by common consent foreigners will have to buy at that price, however unwillingly. But if the foreigners do not agree to buy our merchandise at the fixed price and try to have it reduced, then our rich merchants should themselves buy up all these goods from their fellows of smaller means. . . .

Should the foreigners later relent and bring us their merchandise as before and bid for ours, nothing whatever shall be taken off the increased prices of our goods: they must be offered thenceforth at the higher price since the increase is entirely due to the foreigners' stubbornness. If they are unwilling to pay more for our goods they will remain with their own

goods on their hands, whereas we, thanks be to God, are able to survive without theirs. But I believe that, for all their ingenuity in commercial and all other civil matters, once they are aware of our merchants' inflexible rule on the matter of increased prices, they will not allow the price to double itself but agree to trade every year. Seeing our inflexibility they will abandon, however unwillingly, their habitual obstinacy and arrogance; for 'necessity knows no law'. As for us, even if they did not offer us any of their goods at all we could still survive, whereas they cannot last even for ten years without ours. That is why we must keep the whip hand over them, and they will have to be our obedient servants and treat us in all matters with deference instead of arrogance. Is it not then strange that they should come here with their trash and try to put a low price on our commodities which are essential to them, but for theirs charge double what they are worth and sometimes more?

Nor is this all: they even presume to decide the value of our great Monarch's money, which should not concern them in any way. Let them rather decide the value of the money of their own monarchs, seeing that they exercise rule over their own rulers! Whereas our Emperor is his own master and if he so order in his own realm that a one-kopeck piece shall count as a ten-kopeck piece, it shall be so. In this country His Majesty's authority empowers us to determine the price of imported merchandise. If the foreigners do not like it they need not sell at that price. A foreign merchant is free to agree to sell or not; we shall not take away his goods by force. But we can insist on refusing storage on shore for unsold goods; let them be taken back or kept on board.

It is high time that they gave up the arrogance which they have shown up to now. It was bad enough treating us in a high-handed manner in the days when our rulers did not personally concern themselves with trade but all was left in the hands of the boyars. In those times the foreigners who came here would slip a present of a couple of hundred roubles to persons of influence and make a profit of a million on a hundred roubles, since the boyars did not care a straw about the merchants and were quite ready to exchange the whole lot of them for a brass farthing. But now, thanks be to God, our Sovereign has looked into all this; foreigners can no longer use such underhand means for having things all their own way and to their own advantage. . . .

Here is another thing very wrong with our merchants. If any person builds a fine residence for the use of himself and his family and runs into debt in doing so, his neighbors and associates take it amiss and procure the imposition of all sorts of heavy taxes and services on him instead of being the more well-disposed and grateful towards him for erecting a barrier to their advantage against the spread of fire and at the same time adding to the adornment of our country; this can only be called diabolical hatred. Rather should such a man be granted exemptions because he has stretched himself too far in building his house; yet instead of lightening his burden his neighbors do their best to ruin him. . . .

Nor is it right, in my view, that many artisans and traders should dress in a style above their degree and their wives and children even more elaborately, wasting their substance through such ostentation. Here too I believe it would be wise to decree that each calling should have its own distinctive dress. . . .

Members of the highest rank—those with property valued at between a thousand and ten thousand roubles—should wear coats of the crimson cloth . . . and vests of various silk brocades but excluding any that are figured or spangled. Such people shall not be permitted to dress even their children in figured brocades. They should wear silver-gilt buttons. Gold and silver braid and piping, and fabric-covered buttons should on no account be permitted on their children's dress. . . .

The middle ranks who own property worth between a hundred and a thousand rubles should wear coats of English cloth . . . vests of cotton or woollen cloth with buttons of solid silver or silvered copper. In the summer they should wear straight-brimmed hats, in winter caps of fox and beaver fur but of a shape distinct from that of the superior rank, and be shod with boots. . . .

Though such regulation of dress may seem to some a trivial matter I think it is important. In the first place it makes each calling distinct and so each person will know his station; secondly, it will prevent any undue expense among persons of each calling; thirdly, our country will benefit no little from it. . . .

If all these things are so arranged for our merchants they will never be impoverished but year by year will prosper in their affairs and God in blessing will bless them for such brotherly love and will give them abundance in all things and salvation for their souls.

"OF THE CRAFTSMEN"

Up to now apprentices have been in the habit of binding themselves to a master for five or six years but, after serving a year or two and learning very little, going away and setting up on their own. By charging lower prices they deprive their former masters of work and make them go hungry while still incapable of making a living for themselves. And so they drag out a wretched existence, being neither masters nor workmen.

I am told that in foreign countries there is a strict ordinance on this matter providing that if a man fails to complete the term of his apprenticeship by even a single day and goes away he can never be accepted as worthy. Further, if he serves his full term but fails to get a certificate from his master, no one (it is said) will take him on as a journeyman or again as an apprentice. Hence all their master craftsmen are worthy and admirable. But we have no such law forbidding apprentices to leave their masters before an agreed date and before they have fully learned their trade. That is why we can never have worthy craftsmen here.

Likewise, foreign laws lay it down that if a man invents a new method of his own or learns it from someone else and begins to make use of it (such work not having been produced by anyone before), the inventor has the sole right to it for his lifetime and others are not permitted to have any part in it until after his death. If the same were done in Russia we should surely have as many inventors as there are abroad. Many ingenious men would of their own accord set about inventing new

Popular handicrafts: the blade of a distaff (A tool used for spinning wool), early nineteenth century. Note the high degree of carved and painted ornamentation for a tool that was meant for constant use.

things which would be profitable to them. As things are much talent goes to waste owing to the deficiencies of our civil laws. Surely an ordinance should be enacted providing that no one shall be allowed to share in any invention or method whatever as long as the inventor is alive. . . .

Similarly we need an ordinance for the regulation of all crafts enacting that each of them must have overseers, in particular that of icon painter. A director should be set over all the crafts whose task it should be to keep a close watch on all the master craftsmen and overseers. He should be given quarters in which to carry on this work, which will be to ensure that every craftsman may exercise his craft with all the skill and care of which he is capable.

A strict ordinance on apprenticeship is needed to the effect that if any person is indentured to a master to learn a craft but leaves his master without a certificate (even if he has been a good pupil) he must be punished and sent into the army. . . .

Every recognized master craftsman shall keep a close eye on all his apprentices and journeymen to see that they do not bring any disrepute on his craft since these wares will all bear his mark. If any fault, either of material or workmanship, is found in an object the master whose mark it bears shall incur a fine. The fine levied shall be ten times the value of the object sold, except in the case of armourers. But if an armourer makes any kind of gun of iron that is too brittle or too soft and badly tempered, so that it explodes when fired, the master whose mark it bears shall be fined a hundred times the value of the piece and shall receive physical punishment. However, if a gun is strong and of good workmanship yet does not shoot true, the fine shall be only ten fold. If anyone makes a gun with a bad firelock so that it will not fire, or a sword or sabre or lance or other side-arm without using the best natural steel for the edge, or of brittle metal, he shall be fined twentyfold. In the case of all other kinds of iron objects made for household use, if any are made of brittle metal, a fine of ten times the value shall be imposed. If a shopkeeper buys such articles for sale without observing their defects and sells them as sound, he too shall pay the fine as shall be laid down by regulations in the matter of the sale of inferior wares. . . .

If a foreign craftsman renowned in some important craft which is new to us comes to Russia, let him be given a workshop and a dozen or more apprentices to teach on the clear understanding that he will teach those pupils diligently and without keeping back any of his knowledge. If he instructs them with diligence so that they attain a skill comparable with his own, he shall be paid whatever sum was agreed upon and a premium to boot for having initiated them fully and taught them rapidly. He may then be allowed to return home with all honour so that other master craftsmen, on learning how well he has been rewarded, may be encouraged to journey hither and so promote all kinds of crafts in Russia.

But if any such foreigner wastes his time in idleness (as is the long-standing habit of foreigners), neglecting to teach his pupils—since he has come here merely to wheedle money out of us and then make off home again—and such deceitful intentions and conduct can be proved within six months of his arrival, let him be sent home with dishonour, taking no more than what he arrived with. We do not want him to spend his time here in idleness, nor do we want others, in the knowledge of this, to come to Russia in future with intent to deceive us.

Such pupils of theirs as prove apt and acquire mastery of a new craft, so that their work is as good as the foreign work, shall be declared master craftsmen and granted emoluments enough to ensure their prosperity. . . .

Above all other craftsmen the icon painters are most in need of careful instructions in their art; they must know to perfection the canon of proportions for persons of all ages and the appropriate representation of every kind of figure.

The icon painters too must have overseers set over them, the wisest and most experienced possible, to ensure that no incompetent person is admitted to their number. Any icon painters who are not fully competent must work under a master and must paint what he orders them to paint; and when they have acquired the requisite skill they may become masters in their turn. In my opinion it should be strictly forbidden for any icon painters to paint sacred icons without having been certified as masters and received a license to exercise their craft.

Holy Writ says: Cursed be he who doeth the work of the Lord negligently. Icon painting is eminently the work of God himself since icons are made for the worship of God and that worship ascends to God himself.

But many paint so carelessly that some icons are terrible to behold. Some painters through their incompetence portray certain figures in such a way that living men with those proportions would be monsters. For instance, when drawing the Virgin they make the nose long and very thin, the neck long and slender, the fingers also long and very slender and the fingertips pointed such as no person ever had. You will not find that any part of the figure conforms to the proportions of a real person. Such drawing in a sacred image cannot but be an offence. . . .

All peasants in the countryside and other uneducated people (whether living in town or country) should be strictly forbidden from now on to paint icons without obtaining a license. Daubers are to be found in the countryside who sell icons at three, two or even one kopeck a piece and paint them so badly that the figures have neither arms nor legs, just a trunk and head and with mere points for the eyes and mouth—and that is accepted as an icon. Hence it behooves us to exercise strict control over this craft above all other crafts.

The following matter also needs careful attention. We ought to introduce into Russia the manufacture of various fabrics made of flax and hemp . . . which can be produced from our own raw materials. It is most necessary that such materials should be put to use here where they are grown. For if instead of exporting our raw flax and hemp we were to make them up here where they are grown, the fabrics would be two or three times cheaper than those manufactured abroad and thus our own people would benefit.

Therefore, to promote such manufactures an ordinance should be issued that all young and middle-aged vagrants be seized, inscribed on a register and put to work. Young children of both sexes should be taught the craft of spinning, adolescents that of weaving or bleaching or calendaring, so that they may in due course become master craftsmen. I believe one could collect something between ten and twenty thousand such vagrants and, having built the necessary workshops, teach these good-for-nothings so as to extract a great deal of work from them. Rather than having to import fabric made of our own materials it is we who should export manufactured fabrics abroad. Even if it appears unprofitable in the first few years and our products turn out to be more expensive than the foreign ones, we should not lose heart but persevere. Should it take five or six years to make such people into good craftsmen this need not cause despondency; for when they have become fully skilled the cost of teaching them will be recouped in a year or two. . . .

If then such things were set in train in Russia what point would there be in our selling raw flax and hemp to foreigners? Better to sell them the finished products—sailcloth and cordage and cambrics and calicoes, and receive in return rix-dollars and other things that we lack.

I believe we could produce enough of such fabrics to supply the whole of Europe and moreover offer them at prices much more attractive than those now prevailing. So rather than let foreigners enrich themselves by using our commodities it were better for us here in Russia to make a profitable living from our own products. Admittedly it will not be easy to establish the manufactories and set these industries in train but as soon as Russians have acquired the necessary skills and work has begun we shall assuredly be able to put such merchandise on the market at half the present price. . . .

If any person sets up any such works (so useful to the realm) by his own origination and at his own expense, he should receive permission to seize vagrant children of either sex to teach them his craft and once taught they shall remain with him in perpetuity; regardless of whom they may have belonged to formerly,

whether they were peasants or household serfs, they shall remain with him in perpetuity. In this way there will be an end to beggars, vagrants and idlers; instead of loitering about in the streets they will all be turned into craftsmen. And when they have been fully taught and have become prosperous master craftsmen themselves our realm will benefit from their work and grow in renown.

SOURCE: Ivan Pososhkov, "Of the Merchants" and "Of the Craftsmen," in *The Book of Poverty and Wealth*. Edited and translated by A. P. Vlasto and L. R. Lewitter. Introduction and commentary by L. R. Lewitter (London: The Athlone Press, 1987), pp. 253–69 and 279–87 (excerpted). Reprinted by permission of the publisher.

Fedor Karzhavin on the Moscow Plague Riots (1771)

Fedor Karzhavin was a prolific writer of the Catherinean period who, at the time of these events, happened to be serving as part of a team overseeing renovations taking place at the Kremlin Palace. He says very little about who the rioters were, but he does make several interesting observations concerning their state of mind, the objects of their anger, and the results of their actions. Popular protests, including violent riots, were a recurring part of urban life in Russia, and they frequently erupted when events undercut the normal course of life and social order. Plagues and epidemics provided an ideal atmosphere for this kind of social eruption.

———

The night of the 15th to the 16th of September a fight broke out at the Varvarskie Gates of Kitai-gorod [a section of Moscow next to the Kremlin] because Amvrosii, bishop of Moscow and Kaluga, had sent thither to seal the money chest, in order that it not be stolen; the fight was in the 9th hour after midday, and in the 11th they came to the Kremlin, pillaged the archbishop's house that is in the Chudov Monastery. In that house tonsured tsars had lived.

"A Moscow Arms Factory in the Early Nineteenth Century." From *Borodino, 1812,* p. 20. Reprinted courtesy of The New York Public Library, Slavic and Baltic Division.

The archbishop drove off to the Don Monastery: the pillage continued all night and the following day till the 7th hour after midday. This day, the 16th of September in the morning, a party of rioters set out to find the archbishop and to open the quarantine houses and release the convicts held in the jail of the Investigation Bureau. Those who entered the monastery beat and interrogated many, asking whether the archbishop was there; they found him, he had been making his confession and, taking Holy Communion, celebrated the mass. After which he dressed himself in a gray muzhik's caftan and hid himself in the church behind the iconostasis [the panel of icons that, in Orthodox cathedrals, usually stands in front of the altar] in the choir loft. From there the miscreants dragged him out, yet at his request they allowed him to kiss the icons. Then, having dragged him into the courtyard, one miscreant struck him in the back with a stake, from which he sat down, but suddenly the others cried out: "Do not beat him in the monastery so that the holy place not be defiled with his blood." And so they hustled him behind the monastery, where the leaders—one assessor, the other a servant of Mr. Raevskii—struck him with stakes on the head, and the others started beating him; they pierced the eyes, cut up the face, tore out the beard, stabbed the chest, broke the bones. In a word, all his body was one wound. Meanwhile in the Kremlin the breakage and pillage in the Chudov Monastery continued: the windows were all broken out, the paintings were ripped, the furniture was all broken and torn; the library, consisting of selected church books and others that relate to all sorts of sciences and arts, in different languages, and of rare manuscript books, everything was utterly destroyed and pillaged; in the stables the coaches and carriages were broken to pieces. And when the monastery servants said to them, the brigands, that those [conveyances] were not the archbishop's but the miracle-makers', then the brigands answered them that miracle-makers do not ride in them. In the chapel the holy icons were ripped, all the metal icon-covers were pillaged;

the gospel was left on the altar, but the Books of the Apostles were torn off and carried away, the communion cloth was torn up, all the vessels were pillaged, the painted icons were defaced by piercing the eyes. They got into the cellar, and finally to the winestores and storerooms in the monastery that belong to the merchant Ptitsin. At that time all the streets were filled with people running home with plunder, some with drink, some with books, some with clothes, some even with fine leather; vodkas from French wine were then for sale by the rioters for ten, twenty, and thirty (kopecks); Hungarian champagne for the same price; English beer for five. Inside and outside the monastery they broke open barrels of wine, dipping it out with hats and caps. They ravaged the consistory, plundered the monastery servants and removed all the property; they got into the brothers' cells, yet their incursion was in vain. Along the streets the rioters went in parties and teams, openly and fearlessly cursing the archbishop, inciting every sort of rabble, threatening the officers and all townspeople loyal to their fatherland. They emptied the Danilov quarantine, they were about to advance on the other quarantines, and on the jail too, but from there they were driven off.

Meanwhile Mr. General Petr Dmitrievich Eropkin had quietly collected a detachment from a variety of volunteers, both cavalry and infantry, because by reason of the sicknesses that were consuming all the people, the detachment in the city was very small; . . . then [after considerable effort], having opened the gates, the detachment set out between the palace and the dark passage that is near the Senate; it came out at the Red Staircase, where after waiting a little while in formation, Eropkin cried out: "Cavalry, cut down without mercy everyone that runs." Suddenly the cavalry split into two columns, one between the Synod and the Church of Ivan the Great, the other between Ivan the Great and the Archangel Cathedral. They began to slash the drunken people, who had broken open barrels and were carousing on the Ivanov Square in front of the Chudov Monastery. And meanwhile the rioters locked the Chudov gates, the

drunken people ran, some downhill toward the Taininskie Gates, some toward the Konstantinovskii Dungeon. Just then the infantry fired a fusillade from muskets at them along the hillside toward the Taininskie Gates, and toward the aforementioned dungeon from a cannon loaded with grapeshot (and there were two cannon in all, which had been found unexpectedly with the necessary at the regimental courtyard on the Presnia). Just then Eropkin set out with the cavalry to the Nikol'skie Gates, cleared the way with one cannon, and the other was pulled to the Spasskie Gates. In the meantime someone from inside the Chudov opened the gates, before which all the Senate company already stood. From thence stones flew upon it, and from it flew back lead bullets; then, having entered the monastery, it set to work with the bayonet. Inside the monastery were put down as many as seventy dead persons; on the square and in all the Kremlin with these seventy persons they estimate as many as six hundred persons, and as many as four hundred persons are estimated to have been killed outside the Kremlin. . . . The rioters sounded the tocsin [the alarm bell] in all the churches for an assembly: at St. Egor, between the Tverskaia and the Nikitskaia, at St. Nikola on the Troitskii Bridge, at S. Nikola Streletskii and at the other churches around the Kremlin. The most powerful assault was at the Voskresenskie Gates and at the Spasskie; here the commanding officers were about to admonish the people that they should go home, cease rioting and perturbing society, but like riotous people, not heeding any suggestions, they swarmed up the hill en masse with stones, stakes cudgels, and axes against the soldiers' battlefront, so it was ordered to fire from empty cannon to frighten them, which was done, and then a round of grapeshot was loaded immediately. The rioters, seeing that none of them had been hit, were even more infuriated and, hurling themselves upon the battlefront, succeeded in overpowering a cannon and turning it upon the Spasskie Gates. But fortunately the cannoneers rushed behind the battlefront, and the rioters had no fire, and so there was nothing for them to fire with. The battlefront, noticing such disarray, set to work with the bayonet and covered all the bridge with corpses; then with cannonfire they drove them downhill and escorted them thither with grapeshot to the very bottom, to Iablonnyi Row. There the rioters scattered, some to the Varvarka, some went off across the Moskvoretskoi Bridge to the other side of the river. In the meantime, on the other side of the Kremlin, that is along the Mokhovaia, the rioters were running about with terrible shouts and calling to each other; but the noise quieted in the 11th hour. And so, having begun in the 7th hour, the battle had continued close to four hours. In going home the rioters shouted along the streets: "We're drunk now, but tomorrow we'll see." One said to his comrade: "If our masters had not left for the vil2lage, then I would have slashed my master, and you would have fixed yours." Another shouted to the servants of private persons sitting on the roofs: "What are you sitting there for, come with us." Many houses they plundered, others in a frenzy hurled themselves bodily at the arms, shrieking: "Rabble, stand for the faith, beat the soldiers to death" and so forth. That night a merchant fighter, one of the brave, hurled himself at a cannon with only his bare fists, but was suddenly repelled by grapeshot. Another, named Kobyla, fell upon three bayonets and, having torn himself away, still possessed enough strength to succeed in striking one noncommissioned officer, but run through by a fourth bayonet he fell at the feet of his victor. . . . The next day, that is, the 17th of September in the morning, the riotous people thronged to the Spasskie Gates from the hill below with bricks, but their attempts were in vain, for the military detachment was everywhere on the alert. However, many of the rioters, coming from the battlefront, dared to offer conditions for peace on the points: that people should be buried at the churches, not taken to quarantines; that the quarantine houses be destroyed; that the field surgeons and doctors not treat people; that the public baths be unsealed; that captives and the wounded be handed over to them and pardoned for the riot; all the conditions were to be signed by field marshal Count P. S. Saltykov, as well as that Eropkin be handed over to them to tear into bits. The officers, coming before the battlefront, listened to these proposals and tried to dissuade them, yet in the meantime Eropkin, from whom they had demanded Eropkin himself, set out with the cavalry . . . and began to slash the people on the square from behind; then the officers, observing from the bridge that Eropkin was slashing from behind, seized by the neck each rioter who stood before them. And so they dragged into the battlefront almost all those who had proposed the conditions; there were schismatics, manufactory workers, clerks, merchants, and serfs. Dragging them into the battlefront, they tried to sober them thenceforth with bronze hilts, then tied their arms behind their backs and threw them into the dungeons appointed for them in the Kremlin.

Finally, everything became peaceful around the Kremlin, a small number of rioters showed themselves for spying and for the most part fell into the hands of the soldiers.

SOURCE: Fedor Karzhavin, "Notes of an Eyewitness of the Plague Riot in Moscow in 1771," *Soviet Studies in History* (Spring, 1987): 82–7 (excerpted). Reprinted by permission of M. E. Sharpe Inc. Publisher.

The Charter to the Towns (1785)

During the 1780s Catherine the Great endeavored to clarify the status of several social groups, to define their privileges and responsibilities to the state, and to give a formal identity to their corporate existence. The Charter to the Towns constitutes one of the major laws to come from this endeavor. We should not imagine that urban life and administration automatically changed in response to, or in the spirit of, this charter. Nevertheless, the text is important, first, because it did carry the power of law; and second, because it elucidates very clearly the direction in which the Empress *wished* the towns to evolve. Those seeking more information should consult the translation of the complete text in Griffiths and Munro.

––––––––––––

From the very foundation of society, all peoples have perceived the advantages and benefits emanating from the ordering of towns, not just for the citizens of those towns but for the inhabitants of surrounding areas. . . .

From earliest times, the Autocrats of All the Russias, with the expansion of the boundaries of their rule and with the increase of the populace, have likewise multiplied the number of towns, providing in them secure refuge for trade and the handicrafts. The breadth of the State, the abundance of vegetation not only on the surface of the earth but also hidden in its womb, the ease of communication by land or by water, the assiduousness and enterprise of the Slavonic Russian people, could yield nothing other than good success. We have endeavored to emulate such beneficial ordinances of Our ancestors with respect to the increase of the population and the expansion of its wealth, to which bear witness the towns, two hundred sixteen in number during Our twenty-three year reign. . .

2. To a town belong the lands, gardens, fields, pastureland, meadowland, rivers, fishing places, woods, groves, scrubland, uninhabited places, watermills, and windmills appertaining thereto. . .

4. Those living in a town are to guard and protect their property and possessions, both moveable and immoveable, which belong to them by right and by law.

6. Whoever settles in a town is to make written acknowledgement, in lieu of an oath, that he accepts the civil law and binds himself to bear the burdens placed upon the townsmen. . . .

10. Everyone carrying on the trade, craft, or industry of an urban dweller in a town is obligated to bear the townsmen's taxes, services and burdens, both personal and material, and on an equal footing with the townspeople, unless emancipated from them by special article.

11. Whoever is not registered among the townsmen in a town does not engage in urban economic activity, under [pain of] the penalty prescribed for that law. . . .

13. Nobles who have their houses, or gardens, or land, or lots, in a town or in its outskirts, whether they live there themselves or rent them to others, are not free from the townsmen's burdens; rather, for such houses. . . , they are responsible for bearing civic burdens equal to those of other townsmen. Owing to their dignity as nobles, the well-born are emancipated from personal taxes and services. . . .

19. A town is permitted to build and maintain, and to lease out, chop-houses, pot-houses, or inns, or taverns on town land along roads.

20. Townsmen are free to own or to build, or to administer, a *gostinyi dvor* [commercial district] in town for storing or selling goods, or to maintain shops and storage areas in their houses for selling and loading goods. . . .

24. Residents of rural districts shall be able to bring their produce, handicrafts, and wares freely and securely to town, and to carry out from town without hindrance whatever is necessary for them: and in pestilence-free times no display or registration of passports is to be required from rural residents when they bring their produce, handicrafts, and wares to town, or take from town that which they need. . . .

CONCERNING URBAN INHABITANTS
AND THE ESTABLISHMENT OF THE URBAN
CORPORATION, AND CONCERNING THE BENEFITS
OF THE URBAN CORPORATION

29. The inhabitants of each town are granted permission to assemble in that town and to form an urban corporation and to avail themselves of the rights and benefits set forth below.

30. The town inhabitants assemble, every three years in the winter time, by order and permission of the Governor-General or Governor, both for the elections permitted the inhabitants and for hearing the proposals of the Governor-General or Governor. . . .

37. The urban corporation is forbidden to

make regulations contrary to the laws, or demands in violation of legislation, under penalty . . . of a fine of two hundred rubles.

42. The urban corporation is permitted to establish a special treasury with its own voluntary contributions, and to use this treasury by common consent. . . .

55. The given name and family name of every citizen in the town owning a house or other structure, or land, or registered in a guild or craft corporation, or engaging in an economic activity appropriate to a townsman, are to be inscribed in the book of town inhabitants. . . .

77. Town inhabitants are comprehended to be all those who either are long-time residents, or were born, or settled in that town, or own houses or other structure, or lots or land, or are registered in a guild or craft corporation, or performed municipal service, or are listed in the tax-bearing category and bear service obligations or burdens in that town. . . .

CONCERNING THE PERSONAL
BENEFITS OF TOWN INHABITANTS,
OF THE MIDDLE SORT OF PEOPLE,
OR OF THE TOWNSMEN IN GENERAL

82. The townsman imparts his station as townsman to his wife, if she is of equal or lower birth.

83. The children of townsmen receive the station of townsman by inheritance.

84. The townsman shall not be deprived of [his] good name, or life, or property without trial. . . .

88. The townsman is free to give away, or to bequeath, or to confer as dowry, or to transfer, or to sell to whomsoever he deems fit, whatever property appropriate to his station he is the first to acquire. But inherited property may be disposed of only in the manner prescribed by law. . . .

90. The townsman is free to set up workbenches of every kind, and to produce every sort of handicraft on them without any permission or order to do so; for this article permits each and every one to set up (and to maintain) every sort of workbench and to produce handicrafts, without requiring any per-

mission to do so from a higher or lower instance. . . .

CONCERNING THE GUILDS
AND GUILD BENEFITS IN GENERAL

92. Anyone, whatever his sex, or age, or birth, or line, or family, or station, or commerce, or business, or handicraft, or trade, who by his own declaration has wealth in excess of one thousand rubles up to fifty thousand rubles, is permitted to be registered in a guild.

93. The term of registration in a guild shall be from 1 December to 1 January; this term is also designated for the annual payment by those registered in a guild of one per cent of the wealth they have declared in good conscience; but the soul tax is not to be collected from them. . . .

102. In the first guild are to be inscribed those of either sex and any age who declare wealth in excess of ten thousand rubles and up to fifty thousand rubles. . . .

104. [Members of] the first guild are not just permitted but also encouraged to conduct all kinds of trade within and beyond the Empire, to order goods and send them overseas, to sell, exchange, and buy them wholesale or retail, on the basis of the laws. . . .

106. [Members of] the first guild are permitted to travel about town in carriage and pair.

107. The first guild is freed from corporal punishment.

108. In the second guild are to be inscribed those of either sex and any age who declare wealth in excess of five thousand rubles and up to ten thousand rubles. . . .

110. [Members of] the second guild are not just permitted but also encouraged to conduct all kinds of trade within the Empire, and convey goods by water and land routes to towns and fairs, and in them to sell, to trade, and to buy what is necessary for their trade, wholesale or retail, on the basis of the laws. . . .

112. [Members of] the second guild are permitted to travel about town in light carriage and pair.

113. The second guild is freed from corporal punishment.

114. In the third guild are to be inscribed those of either sex and any age who declare wealth in excess of one thousand rubles and up to five thousand rubles. . . .

116. [Members of] the third guild are not just permitted but also encouraged to conduct retail petty trade in town and around the country; to sell goods retail in town and district; and to convey petty wares by water and land routes around the villages, settlements, and village marketplaces; and in those marketplaces to sell, trade, and but whatever is necessary for their petty trade, wholesale or retail, in town or district. . . .

118. [Members of] the third guild are permitted to own taverns, inns, commercial baths, and lodgings for those people travelling through on foot or by conveyance.

119. [Members of] the third guild are forbidden to travel around in carriages, and to harness more than a single horse in winter and summer.

120. Each one who wishes to carry on a trade or a handicraft in a town, and who according to the Municipal Regulation is eligible to join the townsmen's corporation, is to be inscribed in a craft corporation or artisan Board. . . .

123. Artisan Regulations

1. The Town Magistracy or Town Court is to divide the trades into craft corporations or Artisan Boards.

2. The Boards or craft corporations are to submit to the Town Magistracy or Town Court, and are obligated to live peacefully in the town and preserve tranquility and good conduct among themselves.

43. Each Board is obligated to contribute five rubles each year into the town's church treasury from the artisan treasury for the maintenance of churches and ecclesiastics. . . .

49. Each master has the right of a pro-

prietor in his own house over his own journeymen as well as over the apprentices and all others of his household. . . .

50. (1) The master is to treat journeyman and apprentices with justice and gentleness. (2) The journeymen and apprentices are to be loyal, obedient and respectful toward the master and his family. . . .

54. All masters, and especially journeymen are forbidden while drunk, to beat apprentices without reason, through malice and stupidity or to treat them evilly. Those venturing to do so must pay a fine to the artisan Board. . . .

66. If an artisan . . . becomes impoverished or falls ill, and neither drunkenness nor extravagance, nor other of his personal faults is the cause of his poverty: in such a case aid must be given him from the artisan treasury. . . .

67. The widow of a master registered in the Board is permitted to continue her husband's trade, and to maintain journeymen and apprentices. . . .

77. Artisan masters must pay their journeymen a real and contracted wage at the designated time . . . On the other hand no journeyman may cease working for his master without legitimate reason . . .

103. There are six working days in the week for artisans; on Sundays and the twelve holidays they do not work except when absolutely necessary. . . .

105. The working hours of the day for the artisans are from six o'clock in the morning until six o'clock in the evening, excluding a half hour for breakfast and an hour and a half for dinner and rest.

SOURCE: David Griffiths and George Munro (translators and editors), *Catherine II's Charters of 1785 to the Nobility and the Towns* (Bakersfield, CA: Charles Schlacks, Jr.:1991), pp. 22–7, 33, 35–9, 44–8, 51 (excerpted). Reprinted by permission of the editors and publisher.

LITERATURE

WALLACE DANIEL

The Merchants' View of the Social Order in Russia

In a society dominated by landlords and peasants Russia's merchants constituted one of the more neglected, politically passive, and least understood elements of the Imperial Russian demographic landscape. Yet their numbers and economic significance were growing rather rapidly during the eighteenth century, and, as Wallace Daniel argues, their sense of a collective identity and collective interests was at least beginning to take shape. How does his characterization of their views compare to Pososhkov's impressions (see under documents, this section)?

In the imperial manifesto of 14 December 1766 that defined the procedure for elections to the Legislative Commission, Catherine II ordered the people of each town in the Russian Empire to prepare for their representative a *nakaz,* a document describing "local needs and deficiencies." The composition of the *nakaz* was to be entirely the work of local people, whom Catherine instructed to elect a committee of five persons for this purpose. She asked the committee members to avoid giving detailed accounts of "private matters." Their task primarily involved treatment of general urban problems and demanded as well statements that attempted to justify legislative reform. In essence, preparation of the *nakaz* required a description of social and economic conditions. . . .

This essay focuses on the merchants' conceptions of themselves as presented in the *nakazy* they helped to prepare. It deals primarily with social rights and responsibilities and the social values and self-perceptions that the materials of the Commission exhibited. . . .

BACKGROUND

In attempting to construct a more harmonious and dynamic economy and society, Catherine's electoral rules to the Legislative Commission aimed to broaden the social structure of town society. In the first half of the eighteenth century the term "townsperson" had a very specific and narrow meaning, a usage that directly related to the townsperson's role in the national economy—as a merchant, craftsman, laborer, and, above all, one who through the payment of taxes increased the state's wealth. Catherine's electoral materials to the Commission imparted a different definition of town society than community of merchants and craftsmen. She established two qualifications for participating in the urban elections, "ownership of a house or a house and trade" within the geographical limits of the town. She thus urged the elected representatives to think consciously of the entire community in composing their *nakaz* to the Commission. . . .

THE TOWN *NAKAZY*: THE MERCHANTRY AND THE CONCEPTION OF THE SOCIAL ORDER

In interpreting the social structure of the Russian state, merchants referred to the historical changes that had occurred during the last century. The description of the past and attempts to justify the merchants' role in the state appeared in many urban *nakazy,* although they expressed their ideas in diverse ways. In its use of language the Suzdal' *nakaz* provided the most eloquent treatment of historical change. It glorified the military and economic reforms of Peter I. It favorably recalled Peter's willingness to borrow from Western Europe, his edicts to establish manufactures, his awards of treasury funds to conduct these enterprises, and his use of laws to provide commands and new instructions to the merchants. . . .

In referring to the past the merchants were also . . . [arguing] that the term "merchant" no longer had any functional meaning. A century ago, in the zemskii sobor of 1649, merchants had expressed very clearly . . . their status, occupation, and position: "we, your slaves, are merchants, . . . and we obtain our livelihood from our crafts and have neither estates held in service tenure nor hereditary estates." Judicially, in Petrine legislation the term "merchant" referred to a member of a trade or craft guild, registered in the Town Hall . . . , and subject to urban taxes and levies on goods in which he dealt. But in the 1767 *nakazy*, merchants described their trading privileges as virtually meaningless, in practice and in law. There were traders who were peasants and peasants who were traders and some persons, formally registered as merchants, never fulfilled merchant "duties.". . . [M]erchants argued that Russian society ought to function as an organic unit in which every person had his proper sphere. They found this order disturbed and their place in it threatened by the problem stressed in nearly every town *nakaz* from [Moscow province], that of peasant trade. . . .

In the 1767 town *nakazy* criticism of illegal trade was even more pronounced, as evidenced by the detailed descriptions of peasant commerce and the size to which it had expanded. *Nakazy* submitted from towns in the northern region of [Moscow province] [for example] mentioned the leather, furs, and wood crafts peasants sold in local markets. . . . Merchants described the organization of this trade, sometimes intentionally exaggerating its scale but always asserting how rapidly peasant commerce had increased. Buying cheaply, peasants sold their goods illegally at retail prices in town markets, the merchants argued. Almost all town *nakazy*, and especially those to the northeast of Moscow, portrayed peasant traders as threats to the merchants' status and livelihood.

The materials of the Commission also revealed the local conditions that generated this conflict over economic privileges. That controversy had its origins in the entire sphere of social relations that had developed in the countryside. There merchants demanded the prohibition of all peasant commerce, from every kind of grain to village crafts, unless they were sold to merchants and at wholesale prices. The merchants also asked that the laws forbid people in the villages from buying an item, including household articles, from anyone other than Russian merchants. Some manufacturers went even further and expressed the opinion that all factory and industrial production should be conducted exclusively by registrants in the merchantry.

Commenting on the conflict over peasant trade, the Russian historian Ditiatin argued that merchants supported the concept of a closed economy in which merchants had exclusive trading privileges that neither nobles nor peasants would have the opportunity to share. These generalizations about social conflict have occurred repeatedly in the historical literature on the Russian merchantry. As noted above, some urban *nakazy* did favor monopolistic rights in industrial production. But a close examination of the town *nakazy* and other contemporary literature reveals a different view. In regard to economic needs, many provincial merchants and peasants were interdependent. Peasants often had become "silent partners" in merchant-owned enterprises, contributing both entrepreneurial skills and financial support. In addition, merchant petitions to the central government had asked permission to accept promissory notes from peasant traders. These reports bore witness to the close ties between peasant commerce and many provincial merchants. The actual operation of the economy had obscured the social functions each group was intended, by law, to function. . . .

In general, the provincial merchants wanted the government to require peasant traders to register in the merchant estate and share the social obligations that merchants had to bear.

In contrast to peasant traders, who often made most of their living from agriculture and remained in the villages, merchants had their homes and families in towns, where there were few other alternatives to trade. Peasants had to pay taxes and fulfill duties, but the legal obligations of the merchants were especially onerous, since they included not only a much higher state tax but service duties required of merchants as well. Perhaps most important, townspeople had urban responsibilities—police and cleaning duties—and they fell with heavy weight on the lives of most persons registered in towns.

Despite Peter I's efforts to transform commerce and make it contribute to the national economy as trade served the economies of France and Holland, the Russian merchants developed different features from their Western counterparts. The authors of several town *nakazy* were aware of these peculiarities. Russian merchants lacked the technical training and skills they had seen among Western traders. But more important, they also pointed out that Russian merchants did not have the "freedom". . . enjoyed by townspeople in the West. The author of the Mosal'sk *nakaz* argued that Russian merchants were "found in great oppression" in comparison with townspeople in other European countries. This difference lay in the heavy duties and treasury burdens demanded by the Russian state. . . .

The urban *nakazy*, however, did not propose to remove social duties, or to acquire the political rights they attributed to Western merchants. Repeatedly describing the burden of their service to the state, they asked the government to lighten most of the responsibilities. The *nakazy*'s statements claiming the necessity of freedom for merchants has a very narrow and practical meaning in the Russian context. They referred to liberation from arbitrary administrative oppressions; they appealed for symbols of status that distinguished merchants from people of lesser rank; and, above all, they expressed the need for sufficient privileges to enable merchants to perform the services assigned to them by the laws.

In short, freedom meant the absence of social and economic obstacles to carrying out state responsibilities.

THE TOWN *NAKAZY:*
THE PROBLEM OF INSECURITY

. . . In 1767 the urban *nakazy* revealed that most provincial merchants were not wealthy traders, but consisted of persons whose lives bordered constantly on the brink of ruin. Deeply affected by price changes, the hazards of travel in the countryside, and the discontinuities of economic activity that resulted from their service duties to the state, these provincial merchants knew at first hand that commerce involved enormous risks. Unlike peasant traders who sometimes had the protection of their lords, they failed or succeeded entirely on their own account, usually without recourse to any other authority. It was only natural that, to them, significant social reforms meant changes that would bring security to their life.

While discussing the uncertainties of town life, merchants offered their only criticism of the actions taken by Peter I. The 1721 Charter of Municipal Institutions, reorganizing the administrative powers of urban government, had referred to the police as the "soul of the citizenry" and the guardian of security and well-being among town inhabitants. Reflecting on the earlier statute, the 1767 town *nakazy* exhibited considerable skepticism towards this description of the police. Rather than extending protection to townspeople, the police, according to many *nakazy*, were often the very source of oppression. . . .

To a remarkable degree, local officials forced from townspeople the funds and services used to support the administrative and military structure. The description of illegal requisitions, seizures of animals, and oppressive levies on goods occurred in nearly every town *nakaz*, regardless of geographical location. As noted above, the term "freedom" in the town *nakazy* had a specific definition, meaning liberation from arbitrary restrictions and oppressions. The merchants' need for statutes limiting such extortionate actions was presented with the same passion and force as problems relating directly to commercial exchange. . . .

In discussing Russian business mentalities in the eighteenth century, both Russian and Western historians have repeatedly pointed out the lack of a capitalist ethic with its emphasis on honesty, reliability, and thrift. Russian merchants were notorious for their cunning and fraudulent practices. The familiar adage "he who does not cheat does not sell" described a system in which standards of honesty were so low that merchants regarded deception and commercial activities as inseparable. But many authors of the urban *nakazy* were aware at least of this problem and saw the need for protection against unreliable persons in commercial transactions. . . .

The desire to gain certainty was finally evidenced by the merchants' discussion of education. While many *nakazy* did not mention the need for formal training, several of them did recognize the merchants' lack of technical skills and inability to keep records of account and wanted the government to establish schools which would make such training available. The merchant V. V. Krestinin, one of the best educated persons of his times . . . emphasized the illiteracy and especially the ignorance of commercial techniques that, he argued, distinguished local merchants from European traders. Several *nakazy* . . . stressed that the state ought to provide compulsory education for Russian merchants and thereby force them to gain skills they did not otherwise seek to acquire. In making these proposals the authors of the town *nakazy* linked them with the achievement of security. . . . On the one hand, knowledge of laws led to awareness of social duties. On the other, such knowledge enabled the individual to seek redress of acts violating his person or property. Law instructed, but it also gave protection, and to the merchants this educational function was crucial to the maintenance of social order.

CONCLUSION

. . . If there is one central theme included in all the urban *nakazy*, it is the reliance on the laws to overcome weaknesses in commerce. The proposal in the Tula *nakaz* to establish minimum standards assigned this task to the government rather than to the trade guilds. The existence of such standards in Central Europe with its history of strong craft guilds undoubtedly contributed to greater decentralization. But Russia lacked a tradition of urban autonomy and the government itself had to provide the standards of reliability and control. . . .

To restore trade privileges to their rightful domain, the town *nakazy* asked the Commission to prohibit all persons who had not registered in the merchantry from participating in commerce. In making these demands . . . , the *nakazy* thus displayed a static view of the merchants' role in the state that aimed to deal with disorder by reasserting previous laws . . . . Seeking to restore social harmony, the town *nakazy* looked to the past, and the methods giving clarity and order to the national economy.

SOURCE: Wallace Daniel, "The Merchants' View of the Social Order in Russia As Revealed in the Town *Nakazy* from Moskovskaia *Guberniia* to Catherine's Legislative Commission," *Canadian-American Slavic Studies*, 11, 4 (Winter 1977): 503–504, 508–22 (excerpted). Reprinted by permission of Charles J. Schlacks, Jr.

ALFRED J. RIEBER
The Merchants' Way of Life

In the previous essay, Wallace Daniel focused on the merchants' relationship to the state and their attitudes toward law as a way of explaining their wounded sense of status and their fears about unfair competition from other groups. Alfred Rieber agrees that the Russian merchants suffered from a stunted development and a sense of inferiority, but he centers his explanation around what he terms "the merchants' way of life" to help understand their failure to emerge as a powerful and self-confident class.

The reluctance of the merchantry to promote social and political change cannot be attributed solely to the inhibiting influence of the government. Nor can it be explained as a consequence of economic stagnation, for the growth and expansion of commerce and industry in Russia throughout the eighteenth century has been clearly established. The merchants' unwillingness to alter traditional patterns of behavior under favorable economic conditions suggests that beneath the maze of legal and bureaucratic restraints lay an even tougher layer of resistance to social and political change. At this deeper level of cultural values and social structure, the essential characteristics of merchant life were patriarchal authority, religious piety, and insecurity of status. In combination the three elements paralyzed independent action and retarded the development of a political consciousness.

Although the merchants perceived that many of their difficulties could be traced to the government's policy, their patriarchal attitudes toward legitimate authority discouraged them from organizing against it. In merchant families child rearing, religious and educational practices, and business mores centered on the father, who commanded almost complete obedience. The family was the school, and the father was the teacher of both ethical norms and practical lessons. Well into the nineteenth century the traditional pre-Petrine values were instilled in generation after generation by . . . the development of an "automatic conscience."

Success in maintaining the old forms depended upon raising children at home, sealing them off from the outside world in the tightly knit, isolated life of the family, and preserving the formal, highly stylized etiquette that hindered social intercourse with anyone outside the narrow circle of relations. In this atmosphere, so vividly portrayed in merchant memoirs, the business was safe. Whatever specialized knowledge the merchant possessed about his trade he passed on to his son. To be sure, it was important to be literate, to master the fundamentals of arithmetic, to draw up bills of exchange, and perhaps even to read a few "good books." After all, respect for the well-read, God-fearing man had many precedents in Old Russian culture. But the practical lessons of buying and selling took precedence over book learning, for "knowledge nourishes badly.". . .

What particularly worried the merchants about schooling was that excessive or indiscriminate reading might spawn pretensions to high culture that could find no outlet in merchant society and would certainly lead to efforts to escape from it. Once removed from their parents and exposed to the harsh environment of church or secular schools, the merchants reasoned, their sons would lose the emotional component of their instruction and training. Thus, obedience and filial piety would rest on the uncertain foundation of punishment; new allegiances would be formed and new aspirations cherished; and the family as the basic economic unit would be doomed. As long as the father maintained a monopoly over the son's education, he could protect the sanctity of the family firm—the main defense against loss or ruin with its inevitable consequence of decline in social status. Thus, he was apt to resist innovation, no matter how efficient and profitable, if it threatened to weaken the primary loyalty to the family. . . .

For many merchants the family meant not just blood relatives and relatives by marriage but also dependent people. These began to play an increasingly important role as a few of the wealthiest merchants yielded to the temptation to give their sons a formal education in order to allow them to compete with foreigners in the export trade or even to move into the nobility. When the better-educated scion of the merchant began, predictably, to "take on airs," abandon commerce, and desert his soslovie [social estate], the head of the household relied more and more on the faithful "servitor" in his shop to carry on the business. An orphan or the child of an impoverished family, he would have been brought into the household and the shop as a ward and errand boy, slowly making his way up by dint of hard work, total subservience, and complete honesty to become a clerk or assistant. Then, frequently, the merchant would command either during his lifetime or in his will that his daughter marry the tried and tested young man, thus rewarding business acumen and submission to authority with adoption into the family. In these cases, social origin meant little to the merchant in comparison with the advantages of having personally supervised the teaching and training of someone whose utter dependence on him was in many ways greater than that of his own son.

The reluctance to employ new business techniques was also rooted in the close identification of firm, family, and membership in the merchant guilds. Subscription in the guilds was not individual but collective. By declaring its common capital all members of the family shared equally in the privileges and the obligations of whichever guild its stated wealth entitled it to belong to. This regulation not only reinforced the authority of the father but strengthened the interdependency among other members of the family as well. Long after double bookkeeping was introduced into Russia in 1780, merchant account books made no distinction between personal and business expenses. . . . Trust in anyone outside the family was bound to be misplaced. The lesson was clear enough from the histories of trading companies in the eighteenth century. Most were short-lived because of the clashes between merchant and noble members and family feuds among the participating merchants.

The rampant suspicion of the merchants toward outsiders confounded public officials and private citizens who sought to gather information on their commercial activities. While travelling in 1854 through the market towns of southern Russia collecting information for a book, Ivan Aksakov soon discovered that the merchants' secretiveness prevented them from acquiring the insights necessary to their taking full advantage of prevailing market conditions. Confronted with conflicting answers on the most fundamental questions, he began "to lose respect for the much vaunted Russian common sense; yes and truly each one has his own pet notion, so that if I talk to ten merchants a day, I do not know from lack of information whom to believe."

One incident reveals the extremes to which a merchant might go to maintain his family as an economic unit. On his death bed, P. M. Vishniakov extracted an oath from all the members of his extended family to live in one house and conduct his business affairs as a group for a period of six years after his death. The ties between family ideology and business practice cushioned the shock of economic change and enabled the merchantry to resist the introduction of new forms of business organization. Merchants felt no compelling need to demand from the state the economic and social reforms that were an integral part of capitalist development elsewhere in Europe.

Attitudes toward authority within the family were transferred automatically into public life. In society, as in the home, life was governed by "mysterious and arbitrary acts from above." Outside the family the prevailing code of behavior was that of Solomon: "The wise see misfortune and seek cover; the naive march forward and are punished." Children were taught that "it was necessary to be afraid, to be quiet, to hold one's tongue as if one knew nothing." In the long run God's will would triumph. . . . The only area in Russian public life in which the merchantry made a significant voluntary contribution was in the charities, where service to the throne and Christian living found a happy union. Even here the state set limits upon the range of choices. Merchants were required to obtain imperial approval for the establishment of any new charitable organization and were forbidden to support any outside their own soslovie. The main beneficiaries of merchant giving were the institutions that exemplified Christian virtues—hospitals, shelters for the poor, orphanages, and the church.

In the family, the firm, the church, and the school, the merchantry clung more tenaciously to the older forms of Russian life than did the nobles, petty officials, and professional cadres emerging from the raznochintsy. . . . [T]he unavoidable conclusion is that the overwhelming majority of the merchantry . . . were cut off from the intellectual currents and social contacts that might have enriched their meager larder of ideas and supplied them with alternative explanations of their place in the social and political order.

The merchants' way of life resembled that of the meshchanstvo [the artisans and petty traders] and the peasantry at the other end of the social scale, with their patriarchal attitudes, religious piety, and social isolation. The crucial difference was that the merchants had more of a stake in preserving the status quo. His ownership of property, his hard-won but shaky "social honor", his petty office holding made him far more cautious than the lower orders of the population in challenging state authority, even during periods of deep social and economic crisis.

SOCIAL INSTABILITY AND STATUS ANXIETY

Insecurity of status was another characteristic of the merchantry which warped its social role in the urban community. The merchantry had become by the early nineteenth century the most internally unstable of all the sosloviia. What distinguished it from every other soslovie was that economic factors alone determined membership. Any free citizen could petition to enroll in one of the three merchant guilds. It was only necessary to declare that he possessed a specific sum of capital, fixed by law but varying in size over the period 1775–1863, and to be approved by the elected representatives of the merchant estate. A heavy financial loss, a large fine, or even a sharp tax increase could wipe out a merchant's capital and drop him precipitously into a lower guild or into the meshchanstvo. Heavy penalties accompanied loss of status. Economically, each guild enjoyed advantages denied the lower guilds and the meshchanstvo and trading peasantry. More important, however, were the social privileges that the merchants shared with the no-

bility and clergy. All merchants were exempt from military service, and those of the first two guilds had immunity from corporal punishment as well. To spare their sons from serving in the army—a living death in Nicholaen Russia—an entire stratum of "fictional" third-guild merchants came into existence. Falsely declaring more capital than they possessed, small tradesmen with sons eligible for military service struggled for years to pay guild taxes. When their sons passed the age limit, they lapsed back into the meshchanstvo. . . For the merchantry downward mobility was a constant and far greater hazard than it was for any other soslovie. Much evidence suggests that the turnover was significant, and the fear of losing status was persistent and deep seated. . . .

The merchants were particularly vulnerable to the destructive impact of wars and natural calamities, from which they found it painfully difficult to recover. In the wake of the Napoleonic Wars and the subsequent economic dislocation, their numbers and wealth fell sharply. . . . By 1824 the guild population fell under fifty thousand, representing a loss of almost two-thirds of the population of 1808. During the same period merchant capital shrank from over twenty million to just over thirteen million rubles. The decline was fairly uniform in all regions of the empire. Although Moscow province was not hit hardest, its merchant population was halved between 1808 and 1824, and its capital decreased by one-third. . . .

These dramatic losses demonstrated on a massive scale the ever-present danger that faced the individual merchant throughout the eighteenth and early-nineteenth centuries. Intimidated by the state and riddled with status anxieties, he was incapable of joining with others to check the erosion of the entire soslovie. Even if he cast off his reverence for the state, he could ill afford to take the further risk of jeopardizing his own social standing and that of his family by diverting his energies away from his enterprise into the uncharted waters of public life. Therefore, it was safer and more profitable in the short run to compete more vigorously against his fellow merchants. In that competition he might hope to amass sufficient capital to secure him against all but the greatest catastrophes.

Still, even the wealthiest merchant might acknowledge that the only means of obtaining absolute security for his family was to enter the hereditary nobility. There, status if not wealth could never be lost short of lese majeste. In the meantime, he could only petition the government to keep his competitors at bay lest they destroy him. . . .

Long before Catherine's reforms a small oligarchy of big merchants emerged as the dominant force in the towns. Using their wealth, status, and official positions in the town administrations they exploited the less affluent guild members and lorded over the rest of the town populations. . . . The tax system, based on joint responsibility and graduated rates, enabled the rich merchants to reduce the town populations to economic dependence on them. Although the rich were in a small minority in the town assemblies, which apportioned the taxes, the smaller merchants were too intimidated and debt ridden to organize resistance. No wonder, then, that the big merchants' only form of political action was to smash the opposition of their rivals, and often their heads as well, to secure control of the top offices in the town administrations. The most famous case in the eighteenth century was that of Grigorii Ochapov, president of the town council of Arkhangel'sk, who tyrannized the merchants with the help of his accomplices . . . Ochapov had his rivals beaten, publicly humiliated, and put in irons for years before his victims organized to replace him. . . .

If some wealthy merchants chose to protect their interests and defend their status through terror and extortion, many more preferred the more genteel method of ennoblement. In either case the natural leaders of the merchantry abdicated their responsibilities to the urban community and further undermined the structure of their own soslovie. Originally, three ways were open to the merchants seeking entry into the nobility: by imperial favor, normally in return for some outstanding public service to the state; by promotion in rank . . . , for

those merchants who served as town officials or tax collectors; and by imperial decoration . . . of the first class. Merchants sought honors, decorations, promotions, and the right to own serfs not as ends in themselves but as the means to obtain security of status that only a patent of nobility could guarantee. Even after the government prohibited the majority of newly ennobled merchant industrialists from buying serfs, the merchants continued their pursuit of noble status, thus demonstrating their real motives. . . .

The merchantry pressed so hard, in fact, that the nobility stiffened its resistance. At the turn of the nineteenth century the government found it necessary to declare again that merchants could not become nobles simply by achieving a certain rank. Only service in the specific civil and military offices designated in the Table of Ranks could bring about an automatic promotion into the noble soslovie. All other cases had to be approved by the emperor himself. Although the pill was sweetened for some individual merchants by confirming their special privileges to buy land and peasants, the law solemnly affirmed that these privileges could not be transmitted to their descendants; "in this way the rights secured eternally to the nobility and their descendants are preserved inviolate."

In addition to providing security noble status also translated social prestige into concrete economic advantages. In metallurgy and the farming out of the state vodka tax the close relationship between private enterprise and the government placed the ennobled industrialist in a more favorable position relative to that of the socially inferior merchant in dealing with state bureaucrats, who were themselves noble. The most striking case here is that of the legendary Tula blacksmith Nikita Demidov, who rose to become one of the greatest iron and coal magnates in Russia under Peter the Great. Even before he was ennobled in 1720, Demidov was not afraid to tangle with imperial officials ranking as high as a voevoda [military governor]. But after he became a noble, it was far easier and less costly for him to take on a man of such stature as the famous historian V. N. Tatishchev, who was the head of all the state mining enterprises. . . .

By the end of the nineteenth century all but one of the great merchant families who played a leading role at the time of Peter the Great had moved out of their estate, having been either raised to the nobility, which appears most probable given their wealth and high status to begin with, or dropped into the lower orders . . . Even in Siberia, where the nobility had no local roots, the big merchants scrambled for hereditary ennoblement. . . .

This striving for ennoblement also sharpened and transformed the naturally competitive economic relations among merchants into a bitter social struggle with victory going to those who could invoke the authority of the state on their side. The circle was fully drawn: the insecurity of the merchants not only sapped their will to organize and impelled them whenever possible to abandon their soslovie but also forced them into greater reliance upon the state.

This dependence was tested in the late eighteenth and early nineteenth centuries by the subversive power of a capitalist transformation of Russia. Merchants shifted from commerce, with its passive turnover of capital, to industry with its dynamic investment capital, as the markets expanded and the hiring of free labor grew rapidly. Under similar circumstances at an earlier period, the commercial and indus-

trial leaders of Western Europe had sought to break down the administrative and social constraints that blocked their drive for greater profits and economic power. A comparable response by Russian merchants was seriously hampered by the peculiarities of the soslovie system. Peter the Great's weak successors allowed a succession of economic competitors to challenge the merchants' control over trade and industry without freeing the merchants from their obligations to the state so that they could compete on equal terms.

To be sure, the merchants themselves did little to rise to the challenge. In their patriarchal fashion it was easier for them to perceive these alien social groups, rather than the state of their own inertia, as constituting the main threat to their preeminent position in commerce and manufacturing. Moreover, unless the merchantry could hold on to its natural leaders, who were themselves tempted by new openings for upward mobility, and to generate a political consciousness, it would be forced to continue to appeal to an unresponsive state for protection. Hostile feelings toward social outsiders would feed the merchants' growing sense of isolation. Under these circumstances, the merchant soslovie could easily adopt the mentality of a besieged camp.

SOURCE: Alfred J. Rieber, *Merchants and Entrepreneurs in Imperial Russia* (University of North Carolina Press: Chapel Hill, 1982), 24–39 (excerpted). Reprinted by permission of the author and the publisher.

C. The Clergy and Religious Communities

DOCUMENTS

The Responsibilities of the Parish Priest:
The Spiritual Regulation of Peter the Great (1721)

In 1721 Peter the Great abolished the patriarchate of the Russian Orthodox Church, and he replaced it with a Holy Synod, roughly comparable to his civil collegia, that would consist of lay and ecclesiastical officials who would report to a chief, or procurator, appointed by the Emperor. This reorganization effectively integrated the hierarchy of the Russian church into the administrative structure of the state.

The Spiritual Regulation, published in 1722 and very widely circulated, explained the functions and responsibilities that inhered in this new arrangement. A supplement to it, from which the passages below are taken, discussed the status and responsibilities of parish priests, monks, and nuns. As we read these sections we should pay attention to the low esteem in which this law holds parish priests, and its prescriptions for elevating them as a group. Pay heed also to the ways in which *The Spiritual Regulation* proposed connecting the clergyman's religious and new administrative responsibilities.

------

1. Many do insinuate themselves into the priesthood for no other reason than only for greater freedom and subsistence, and they do not possess any requisite aptitude for their vocation. Accordingly no one shall be installed as a priest or deacon who has not been instructed in a bishop's household. . . .

2. An arriving candidate shall have, in a deposition, authentic testimony from his parishioners that they know him to be a good person: namely, not a drunkard, not an idler, in the maintenance of his household, not a scandalmonger, not a querulous grumbler, not a fornicator, not a brawler, and not accused demonstrably in deception and fraud. . . .

7. Priests must especially know these things: in confession, if they encounter someone who is cold and without emotion, how to terrify with God's judgment him who is confessing; if they see someone who is skeptical and inclined to despair, how to restore such a one, and how to strengthen him with the hope of God's mercy and kindness; how to instruct one in the breaking of a sinful habit; how to visit and comfort a sick person; how to sustain and administer to the passing of a dying person with words; and how, especially, to support those who have been sentenced and are being led to death, and reassure them of God's mercy. These are truly the most necessary duties of priests.

But since these cannot be expected from a priesthood that is little educated, for that reason (until God grants to see in Russia complete education), it is fitting to write out the parts serving the aforementioned needs. Then a priest, after having committed them to memory, should either say them or read them to a sick person, a dying person, to one being led to death, and in rendering all his other ministration.

8. To those who come to him for confession, a priest shall not be oppressive. He becomes oppressive when, either at the time of confession, he prides himself and appears stern to him who is confessing, whom he ought to comfort with all humility, or at other times, when

he impudently asks for something from his spiritual sons, or as it were, importunes with authority. . . .

11. If someone in confession informs his spiritual father of some illegality that has not been committed, but that he yet intends to commit, especially treason or mutiny against the Sovereign or against the state, or evil designs upon the honor or well-being of the Sovereign and upon His Majesty's family, and in informing of such a great intended evil, he reveals himself as not repenting but considers himself in the right . . . —what can be concluded therefrom is this: When the spiritual father, in God's name, enjoins him to abandon completely his evil intention, and he, silently, as though undecided or justifying himself, does not appear to have changed his mind, then the confessor must not only not honor as valid the forgiveness and remission of the confessed sins, for it is not a regular confession if someone does not repent of all his transgressions, but he must expeditiously report concerning them, where it is fitting, pursuant to His Imperial Majesty's personal [edict], promulgated on the twenty-eighth day of April of the present year, 1722, which was published in printed form with reference to these misdeeds . . . However, in that report, the salient points of what has transpired in confession shall not be disclosed. . . .

21. Priests should not make a commercial enterprise from the performance of their ministry: for example, baptisms, marriages, funerals, etc., but should be satisfied with the remuneration willingly given them. This shall be especially watched with respect to the requiem service on the fortieth day after death, for which priests demand great prices even if they are not asked about it. They themselves often do not think of conducting a requiem service on the fortieth day after death, but forcibly extort payments as though they were a duty on death. This is one evil which, if a bishop neglects to suppress it, shall furnish sufficient reason for him to be summoned to the Most Holy Ruling Synod for judgment.

22. Whereas it is His Imperial Majesty's intention to arrange the churches in such a way that a sufficient number of parishioners shall be registered at each one, and to determine what every parishioner shall owe the clergy of his church annually, so that, from their donation, all the clergy may have adequate subsistence, accordingly, in compliance with His Imperial Majesty's ukase [or *ukaz*], the Most Holy Ruling Synod, concurring with upstanding lay authorities, shall convene a council and enact the intended decree. When this has been accomplished, then priests must not thereafter seek even the smallest remuneration for the religious services that have been assigned to them unless someone should, of his own free will, wish to present some gift. But even that is not to be offered at the time when the priest is fulfilling some requirement, but after the passage of several weeks. . . .

27. In many churches a priest does not accept outsiders among the churchmen, but fills the vacancies of that office with his sons and kinsmen, sometimes even exceeding the need, heedless of whether they are suitable or proficient in reading and writing. This, over and above other sufficient reasons, is especially harmful because it is thereby easier for a priest to act unrestrainedly, to be unconcerned with church ritual and order, and to conceal schismatics. . . . Accordingly bishops must most zealously eliminate this evil and severely punish the priests who act in violation, except that, in accordance with the decision of the parishioners and with the permission of his particular bishop, a priest may install one, and only one, of his sons, who is capable of singing and reading, as a sexton or sacristan, and the rest, who have been well educated, shall be placed in other churches or in some other honest occupation.

29. Henceforth all priests shall personally be in possession of books that are customarily called *metriki*, that is, parish registry books, in which are recorded the births and baptisms of the children in their parish, designating the year and day, and naming the parents and godparents. Likewise, when children died without receiving baptism, together with an additional statement of the reason why the child was deprived of Holy Baptism. They shall also record

in those books the persons of their parish who are united in matrimony. Likewise, those who die and are buried . . . These books shall be declared to the Episcopal Chancery annually; how many are born and die shall be reported to the Episcopal Chanceries every four months, and written notification concerning that shall be made from the Episcopal Chanceries to the Synod.

SOURCE: Alexander V. Muller (translator and editor), *The Spiritual Regulation of Peter the Great* (Seattle WA: University of Washington Press, 1972), pp. 58–63, 68–71 (excerpted). Reprinted with the permission of the University of Washington Press.

I. S. Belliustrin's Description of the Clergy in Rural Russia (1858)

I. S. Belliustrin, a nineteenth-century Russian priest, was so scandalized by what he maintained were the abysmally low standards of his fellow clergy, and by their debased standing in Russian society, that he wrote this diatribe to draw public attention to the issue. It is interesting to compare his impressions with the hopeful projections that we just read from the *Spiritual Regulation* of 1722. How are we to account for such diametrically opposed characterizations of the condition of the Russian parish priest?

———

It is sad and painful to see how degraded and demoralized the rural clergy has become. It is even sadder, and even more painful to see that the clergy itself is partly responsible for this state of affairs, and does not even have the right to console itself by saying that we suffer everything for Christ's sake. It does not behave in a manner that would arouse in others the veneration that is always vital for its service, warm feeling—the kind of undying love that would indissolubly bind priest and parish together in a common quest for the celestial calling.

What has caused this unsatisfactory condition of the clergy? Wherein lies the evil?

To answer these questions, we shall follow the life of a rural priest from the years of his childhood . . .

APPOINTMENT

The best student—that is—the best according to seminary records—need not dream of receiving a good position in the diocese. Such positions are usually given out to the bishop's relatives; if he has none, then the swine who surround the bishop will get them. "Swine" is strong language; but what else can you call the bishop's lackeys, servants, secretaries, and choirboys? What kind of people are they? The lackey is always someone driven from the district school or seminary because of dissolute conduct; it is the same pupil who was a watchman somewhere for several years, then a novice, and came to the bishop's residence; somehow or other, he then wormed himself into the position of lackey there. If he shows special ability in service, he rises to the rank of personal servant, enjoying the broadest trust. The secretary is the most brazen, unscrupulous, merciless clerk; compared to him, the clerks who work in secular courts are mere lambs . . . And the choirboys are nothing but a nest of drunkenness, debauchery, violent uproar; incredibly unscrupulous, they are forever plundering churches, monasteries, and the entire clergy; and nothing ever satisfies them. They accompany the bishop on visitations to villages in the diocese, where they rage at the priests and church elders, brazenly demand vodka and money, and curse (if sober) or permit themselves still worse (if drunk). And they do all this without the slightest fear of punishment, because they are protected by the prelate's mantle. . . They are always joined by archdeacons and subdeacons, who are distinguished from the choirboys only in their dress; in all other respects they are identical to each other. Can this contemptible gang be called anything but swine?. . .

The student can receive a mediocre position, but under one condition: that he pay for it. Twenty years ago this evil was not so wide-spread, but of late it has become incredibly common. The reason is that the number of seminary graduates has sharply increased, and as a result, up to ten people (sometimes more) apply for the same position. However, the position is not given to the person with the best seminary record, but to the one who pays the most. It is sold either by the bishop's personal secretary, who always has great influence, or by his servant, or sometimes by the two together. The better the position, the higher the price; it sometimes rises to as much as 200 rubles. But it is not all over when you pay these gentlemen, for you must also pay off the consistory: it must review the documents and compile an "opinion," and such things are not done gratis. . . . What are the thoughts of the future priest? He has no time now to reflect upon what he is entering into, or to prepare his mind and heart for a miraculous paradise: all his thoughts, concerns, and contemplation are focused on one thing—money! money! . . .

Now where is a seminary pupil or graduate, who is invariably poor, to obtain so much money? Having no particular place in mind, he usually seeks a fiancee for himself—not just any fiancee, but one who has a bagful of money. Hence he is not concerned to choose a friend for life, but to find as much money as possible. After he has bargained for a few potential fiancees, he decides in favor of the one that can pay the most, although she may have every kind of failing, moral and even physical. The bargain struck, he receives both money and a position. . . .

FAMILY LIFE

So now the former seminarian is a rural priest. He has joined a home or assumed a vacant position. Let's look at the family life in both situations. I should note that I am describing the majority, but certainly not all. One can find better, more lofty cases than the ones I shall describe; because they occur so rarely, however, I shall not discuss them in this or the following section.

The seminarian enters a household. Dire necessity, not free will, dictated this decision on both sides—the original household and the seminarian who enters it. On the one hand, the girl's advanced age or the priest's loss of his position for misdeeds prevent the priest from being too discriminating in the choice of a fiancee, from seeking the one who is intellectually and morally best, and oblige him to take the cheapest he can find. On the other hand, the need for food and shelter forces the seminarian to agree to the most onerous terms on joining a family with many members (and sometimes with open disorders), and moreover to take as his wife some sort of monster, in a moral if not physical sense. The consequences of such fatal deals become apparent all too soon. The cheapest candidate hardly manages to become a priest when he proves the truth of the proverb: "If it's cheap, it's no good." And from the very first he does not know how to conceal his moral decadence. The conflict always starts with the terms of the contract: the former cleric demands literal compliance, while the new priest at first cannot, then does not want to comply. His noncompliance gives rise to quarrels, which are morally harmful for parishioners when they see two priests (indeed, closely related ones) quarreling; these quarrels turn into irreconcilable hostility, then into lawsuits and a division of property. . . .

In general, the practice of bringing the new priest into his predecessor's home while the girl's father and mother are still alive is an evil that should have been brought to the government's attention long ago. We may assume something that is exceedingly rare (perhaps true in just 5 percent of the cases)—that the fiance and fiancee like each other; that, having become man and wife, they fall in love with each other; and that even the contractual terms are bearable. Yet the very fact that the household has two masters leads to mutual dissatisfaction: one is accustomed to living in the old way (that is, in filth and simplicity), the other to live more cleanly; one performed all the work himself, the other does not want or even know how to do so; the one loves raucous holidays, the other cannot stand them, etc. Conflict between the old priest and the new one, however well intentioned their aims may have been, is inescapable. In a word, feuds are inevitable. . . .

MEANS OF SUPPORT

It is difficult to imagine who has less support, who is more vulnerable to mere chance in his material support than the rural clergyman. How are these uncertain means of support acquired? What is their relation to the priest's service? Oh, how much evil lies in these means of support!! They consist of *agriculture* and *emoluments*.

EMOLUMENTS

If you gave a prize for inventing a way to inflict the maximum humiliation and disgrace, to convert a lofty and miraculous calling into a trade, then surely one could not find a better means to do so than those unfortunate exactions from parishioners known among clergy as "revenues." The priest administers a short prayer service, and thrusts out his hand for a reward; he accompanies a deceased person to his eternal resting place, and again he holds out his hand; a wedding ceremony has to be performed, and he even bargains over his fee; and on holidays he goes about the parish with the sole purpose of collecting money. In a word, no matter what he does, he has a single aim: to obtain money. . . . And how must the parishioners look upon him? Walk across Russia from end to end and listen to how they revile the clergy because of these accursed emoluments. . . . After all this, what benefit is to be gained from the priest's service? What moral influence can he exert on the parishioners when they understand perfectly the primary goal of all his actions? And, lacking in authority, what kind of pastor can he be? Given this order of things, what is the point of a pastorate anyway?. . .

But one cannot cast stones at the priest for making these dishonorable exactions. He can do nothing else, because he simply has no other means at his disposal. However much these abuses may outrage the soul, to some degree you have to forgive him if you examine his material condition. The priest lives with a family that rarely has fewer than ten members and sometimes include as many as twelve to fifteen persons. How much does he need each year to support his family? Let us suggest a minimum, that is, the amount required by a peasant (who needs no cassock or similar things) with a family of ten: 120 to 180 rubles. In addition, the priest has one, two, and sometimes three sons at the district school or seminary . . . In addition, the priest has unmarried daughters, so he has to set something aside for them, too. . . . What would you have him do in such circumstances? You will say: "Pray and rely upon divine providence." But he was not taught to do this before he became a priest; on the contrary, they took from him and robbed him; from childhood to ordination he has been used to regarding exactions as something ordinary, even inevitable. So calmly, without troubling his conscience, he does the same thing that everyone else does . . .

The very same thing that earlier existed among the Chuvash is found in the villages all across Russia: people detest the priest precisely because of his levies. Despising the priest, they are ill disposed toward his very service and look with hostility upon religion itself. Here is the origin of that profound ignorance among our Orthodox people about everything that concerns their faith. Our *Orthodox* folk, and I say this without the slightest exaggeration, do not have *the remotest conception of anything spiritual.*

Do the authorities wish to correct this deplorable state of affairs? There is but one means: provide the clergy with proper material support. . . . But our bishops—who bear primary responsibility for taking care of Christ's flock—do not want to recognize these facts. I did not say "cannot" but "do not want." That is precisely the situation: they do not *want* to know.

Where the land is good and the priest tills it with his own two hands, he enjoys good support. The priest and his family are not only sated but, when God blesses him with a good harvest, he also is able to sell some of it. But look closely at such a priest: is there even the slightest hint that he is a priest? Look, here he is hauling manure: can you go up and ask for a blessing from someone steeped in nitrogen and filthy from head to toe? Or there he is, drying out the barn for grain storage: can you possibly suspect that this monster, covered with soot and draped in rags, is a servitor of the Heavenly Lord?. . .

In a word, the farmer-priest is just a peasant, distinguished only by his literacy; otherwise he has a cast of thought, desires, aspirations, and even a way of life that are strictly peasant. After about ten years of such a life, he has so thoroughly assimilated this coarse and dirty way of living that it is sheer torture for him to spend two or three hours in good society. Indeed, he even finds it onerous to dress decently. For him, the epitome of pleasure is to fraternize with the peasants in noisy, wild drinking bouts; with joy he sets off to the tavern, drinking

house, whatever—just so he is invited. . . .

No, a farmer priest cannot be a true priest or even vaguely resemble one. . . The priest, for the most part, lives by his spirit, that is, it is of great importance that he develop his own spiritual life. But how can he do that?. . . A life so overwhelmingly physical invariably destroys the spiritual life; that is why the farmer-priest has no thoughts or ideas of anything beyond his daily life, not even the desire to liberate himself from this dirty rut in which he is so completely mired.

Source: I. S. Belliustrin, *Description of the Clergy in Rural Russia: The Memoir of a Nineteenth-century Parish Priest.* Translated with an interpretive essay by Gregory L. Freeze (Ithaca, N.Y.: Cornell University Press, 1985), pp. 65, 109–15, 122–8 (excerpted). Originally published as *Opisanie sel'skogo dukhovenstva* (Paris, 1858). Reprinted by permission of the publisher, Cornell University Press.

LITERATURE

GREGORY L. FREEZE
The Disintegrating Parish in Eighteenth-Century Russia

Although religious faith occupied a central and pervasive place in Russian culture, both popular and elite, the role of the Orthodox Church in the everyday life of the Russian people was more ambiguous. The official literature—laws, sermons, etc.—prescribed what its authors imagined were ideal relationships between Orthodoxy and laity, or between parish priest and community. But these texts acknowledged that the actual situation was often far from ideal. Gregory Freeze suggests in this essay that these acknowledgements were, if anything, understated.

The eighteenth century brought fundamental changes in Russian society and culture, and

perhaps no institution was affected more profoundly than the Russian Orthodox Church. Most dramatically, the Church came under a direct assault by the secular state, which replaced the patriarchate with a more tractable Synod in 1721 and sequestered church lands and peasants in 1764. But even more significantly, the church suffered a silent erosion of its essential substructure—the parish, its key institutional link to lay society. In medieval Russia, the parish had been much more than simply an administrative unit of the Church; it was also identical with an autonomous local community, thus fusing secular society and religious organization into a single unit. But this traditional parish community changed markedly in the eighteenth century, acquiring a different structure and set of functions. . . .

The scope [of this essay] is limited to the central provinces of Great Russia, for only there did the transformation of the parish reach full development in the eighteenth century. An analysis of this transformation involves two interrelated questions: how did the parish change as a *social* organization and what impact did this have upon its operation as a *religious* organization? A careful reexamination of the Church's social foundations should yield a fresh insight into the processes of "secularization" and how it actually operated in Russian society and culture.

The [old] parish performed essentially three . . . functions for the laity. First, it was the administrative center of the community. Because the state had only a skeletal administration in the provinces, the community assumed routine functions of self-government and made the parish church its administrative center. The laity convened at the church to make collective decisions, to hold court in minor matters, and to draw up legal documents. This explains why many vital dates in medieval law—such as Saint George's Day in serf relations—coincided with religious holidays. The administrative function of the church even affected the clergy's role: one sacristan acted as village clerk, and the term for his clerical rank (*diachok*) was derived from the word for clerk (*diak*). Second, the parish church held much economic importance for its members. It was the commercial center of the community, which used the occasion of Sunday services to conduct a lively trade. The great trade fairs of medieval Russia were also held on the chief religious holidays. The parish church itself sometimes became an enterprise: it acquired land and valuables, operated businesses, and extended loans to parishioners. Third, the parish was the cultural center for the community. While secular tastes and interests became increasingly evident in the seventeenth century, religious celebration still provided the main focus of the parishioners' cultural experience. The church and clergy usually provided such education as there was through the informal parish schools: some churches could even boast of sizable libraries. The simple parishioners also used the church for entertainment and merrymaking. . . .

The parishioners wielded complete control over their local church. This broad local autonomy resulted primarily from the adminis-

trative weakness of the Church: because of the vast size of each diocese and poor communications, close hierarchical control was impossible in medieval Russia. The laity alone built and maintained the parish church; they provided the land and revenues to support the resident clergy. Probably the most impressive display of their power was the right to select clergy: the parish (either community or landlord) chose candidates, who were then routinely ordained by the bishop. To oversee "their" church, the parishioners elected a layman as church elder . . . who managed church revenues and enjoyed considerable esteem, even official recognition. This broad parochial authority and independence provoked one frustrated bishop in the late seventeenth century to complain that "not the hierarchs but the peasants are running the churches." Indeed they were.

This traditional integrity and cohesion of parish and community began to disappear in the eighteenth century. While rate and form varied depending upon the surrounding social environment, the parish everywhere experienced basic changes in its structure and functions. Two processes were at work: the parish underwent basic structural changes and, more important, it gave up the traditional "extrareligious" functions.

One important structural change was the forced reorganization of parishes. Arbitrarily altering parish boundaries, the authorities destroyed the traditional identity of parish and community. . . . Before Peter the Great, hierarchs regularly complained of redundant churches and clergy. Sometimes from a false sense of piety, sometimes from a more worldly desire to win divine favor in an effort to ward off plague, the laity built new churches, often without any serious possibility of supporting the clergy they required. The result was a proliferation of dilapidated churches and impoverished, vagrant priests. Peter the Great actively sought to remedy this problem: he imposed limits on the number of allowable clergy, set 100 households as the norm for parish size, and issued stringent rules against "superfluous churches and clergy." After its establishment in 1721, the Synod obediently enforced these rules and maintained close scrutiny over the subordinate hierarchs. Hence external authority intruded to the lowest levels for the first time, seeking to determine arbitrarily the structure and composition of a local parish. . . .

The city of Moscow was particularly in need of parish reorganization. A list of 100 churches, compiled in 1771–72, shows that many had fewer than ten households—far below the legal minimum of twenty. The plague of 1771 provided a convenient opportunity to reorganize parishes: following the plague the authorities eliminated many parish churches and arbitrarily redistributed parish households. . . .

[T]hroughout most of central Russia the average size of city parishes increased steadily, and by the 1780s they far exceeded the minimum size of twenty households. The hierarchs thus achieved their primary goal: the elimination of uneconomical parishes. One indicator that urban parishes were more economically viable was the appearance of expensive stone churches, even in provincial towns: by the late eighteenth century most city churches were no longer wooden but of stone—and virtually the only stone structures in most towns. In Riazan, a traveller reported, the buildings and houses were uniformly wooden and ugly, but twenty-three of the twenty-five churches were of stone. . . .

In rural areas, however, the bishop found parish reorganization much more difficult. Above all, he faced almost insurmountable obstacles of nature—forests, marsh, rivers, and spring flooding. Rural Russia was broken down into many scattered villages, hamlets, and tiny settlements that were combined to support the parish churches in the countryside. A bishop, however, could not heedlessly merge units, disregarding natural barriers, for he would deprive parishioners of sacred rites—in particular, baptism and extreme unction. For such vital services, the parishioners required immediate and sure access to the church and priest. . . .

Bishops nevertheless managed to force

through many reorganizations, disrupting the cohesion of parish communities. If circumstances permitted, they closed and divided parishes. In 1793 a bishop transferred thirty-six households from one parish to another solely in order to create adequate support for the latter. . . . Furthermore, the bishops carefully reviewed applications to repair or rebuild churches and often rejected them. Bids to create a new parish came under especially close scrutiny. These efforts to reorganize rural parishes gradually took effect. One index of their effectiveness is the sharp increase in the average size of the parishes. While the natural increase in population was only 26 percent in central Russia during this period, the average parish increased by 50 percent to 85 percent. Data on clerical staffing also indicate that parish reorganization was successful: clerical vacancies (found mainly in small undersized parishes) were consistently reported as late as the 1750s, but they had virtually disappeared by the 1780s. . . .

A second structural change was due to the internal disintegration of the parish community, a process that inevitably accompanied the ever-quickening pace of social and economic development. This pattern was most pronounced in the cities. Under the impact of the Petrine reforms, the city collective. . .began to disintegrate; a merchant oligarchy emerged to rule the city, its economy, and its churches. Moreover, the cities were inundated with peasants and other migrants, despite legal obstacles and the townsmen's opposition. . . .

The functions of the parish as an administrative, cultural, and economic unit were also eroded in the eighteenth century. Its administrative role, once so important, declined rapidly as the state administration expanded and gradually took over parochial responsibilities. It was, however, a gradual process. Although Peter the Great refused to incorporate the parish into the structure of provincial administration, he could not resist using the parish as an auxiliary link to rural communities. He required priests to collect vital statistics, to inform authorities of "evil-intentioned thoughts" revealed in confession, to read state laws aloud in church, and to perform a host of other services to the state. After mid-century, however, a nervous government came to regard the parish as an unreliable institution and likely to aid in organizing peasant rebellions or disturbances. . . . After a series of preliminary measures by Catherine the Great, the parish was finally dealt a crippling blow in 1797: Paul outlawed the right of the parish to issue collective petitions on secular and religious matters.

The parish also surrendered its claim to economic significance. Instead of taking place on Sunday around the parish church, commerce in the cities was now centered around regular market days. Provincial towns had two or three days a week specifically designated for trade when the merchants came in with food stuffs, firewood, and handicrafts. Moreover, parishioners even came into economic conflict with their local church. . . . [T]he most serious conflict arose in the countryside in 1754 when the state ordered each parish community to apportion its church and clergy a share of the land. With good land already in short supply, the nobility and peasantry firmly opposed this new requirement. After encountering stiff resistance from the laity, the Senate in 1767 reaffirmed the law on apportionment and rebuked landlords who refused to comply. Nevertheless, lay opposition remained, and repeated government decrees failed to smooth over the seething discontent of the parishioners.

Finally, the parish church began to lose its former monopoly over social and cultural life in the community. To a considerable degree, this was due to the enhanced vigilance and intervention of church authorities in defense of sanctity in the churches. As Russian culture became ever more secular, church authorities acted vigorously to secure at least formal signs of piety and decorum. Leading this fight was the Synod, which issued many pertinent decrees and prodded the subordinate bishops to do likewise. In the 1740s, for instance, the Synod demanded that the taverns which traditionally crowded around the parish church

be relocated at a respectable distance. . . . At the diocesan level, the bishops took similar measures. The bishop of Pereslavl' diocese was horrified to learn that "the parishioners . . . on the occasion of a wedding in the churches, bring beer and wine along from home and then drink it inside the churches after the services." He therefore ordered the parish clergy to eliminate the custom or "suffer merciless punishment" themselves for tolerating such improprieties. . . .

The parish gave up its extrareligious functions, and the identity of parish and secular community slowly dissolved. But this does not mean that the parish vanished as a *religious* organization, with its power suddenly shifting into the outstretched hands of diocesan authorities. On the contrary, the laity—whether community or noble landlord—continued to claim and exercise their traditional right to manage and rule the local parish church.

The crucial test was the right of the parish to determine clerical appointments. The bishops had long expressed displeasure with the custom of parish election of clergy, and, as the new seminaries began to produce educated candidates, the hierarchs were predictably eager to reward these students with worthy positions. Yet few bishops dared to violate parish electoral rights, and even fewer succeeded in imposing their candidates upon parishes. . . .

[T]he stiffest resistance to episcopal pretensions came from the outlying village churches. One of the first bishops to violate the parish electoral prerogative was Metropolitan Arsenii Matseevich of Rostov. Arsenii ordinarily did not try to impose seminarians as candidates, since his seminary in fact was one of the smallest; yet he claimed the *right* to appoint clergy and jealously asserted his authority. But to his boundless consternation and fury, he found that the parishioners abused, starved, and unceremoniously evicted the candidates he had ordained without their permission. . . .

The parishioners had good reason to oppose such encroachments. They feared the presence of an alien cleric, who would be inclined to inform the authorities of any spiritual or other irregularities in the parish. And the parishioners often had much to conceal: clandestine practice of the Old Belief, violation of canon law (especially on minimum ages for marriage), or evasion of state law (such as the concealment of peasants from the poll-tax registry). To protect its traditional insularity, the parish preferred to have its own dependent, elected priest who could be relied upon not to expose his parishioners' misdeeds. Moreover, noble landlords viewed episcopal appointment as a violation of their authority and steadfastly opposed such encroachments. The local priest or sacristan often was instrumental in reinforcing parish resolve. Seeking to reserve positions for their own sons, the parish clergy lobbied vigorously against outsiders who came bearing episcopal support; as long as the cleric enjoyed village respect, his solicitation was usually successful.

Thus, in spite of the disintegration occurring within the parish, its traditional authority over the local church remained largely intact. The parishioners' ability to resist episcopal authority derived from several sources. First, the parishioners were laymen belonging to the "secular command" or state authority; because they were outside the jurisdiction of the Church, even an imperious hierarch like Arsenii Matseevich was at a loss to deal with them. Although in extraordinary cases a bishop could excommunicate a stubborn layman or submit a formal appeal through civil authorities, neither measure provided an effective or sure means for asserting regular control over the laity. Second, the parishioners still held the power of the purse. Since they provided voluntary economic support to the clergy through incidental fees (for example, for baptism or wedding), a hostile parish could easily—and legally—drive off an unwanted appointee simply by withholding such emoluments. If the cleric still insisted upon his fees or withheld services until properly remunerated, he was liable to charges of extortion, which guaranteed swift and harsh punishment. Finally, the noble reigned supreme on his estate and felt free to abuse and maltreat

his clergy. Since bishops found that they could do little to protect their clergy from beatings or expulsion, most hierarchs had the good sense not to violate a landlord's right to select candidates.

It is therefore not surprising that, to the very end of the eighteenth century, bishops continued to recognize the right of parish or landlord selection. . . .

In the absence of a cohesive parish community, bishops came to rely increasingly upon the "better parishioners" when dealing with the parish. Whereas the entire parish had once participated in decision making, authority tended to gravitate into the hands of the more prosperous, respectable parishioners. This development was partly spontaneous; parish petitions usually carried the signatures of literate parishioners and sometimes included the self-description of "the better parishioners." It also stemmed from the special privileges long accorded church patrons. . ., who bore primary responsibility for constructing or maintaining the church. But the dominance of "better parishioners" was also deliberately encouraged by the hierarchy. In Moscow, for example, Metropolitan Timofei decreed that the clergy could construct personal houses on parish-owned land only with the consent of the "main parishioners." Similarly, in his instructions to the ecclesiastical superintendents in 1775, Metropolitan Platon specifically ordered them to make certain that "the better parishioners" were present at the election of clerical candidates. . . .

To help fill this gap created by a weakened parish institution, the bishops increasingly emphasized the role of the church elder. The post was, however, falling into disuse, and in the first half of the eighteenth century many parishes ceased to elect church elders. Orders to elect the elder began to appear as early as 1705 and rapidly multiplied thereafter. Yet many churches ignored these instructions or simply authorized their clergy to perform the tasks of church elder. After much effort the authorities finally succeeded in reestablishing the position in Moscow churches by the 1760s. But in provincial dioceses the bishops were still castigating parishioners at the end of the century for their failure to elect elders. Altogether it is a revealing episode: parishioners had come to disdain the position of church elder as a burdensome responsibility, while the bishops sought to utilize the elder in establishing firmer control over the parish.

In conclusion, the identity of parish and secular community in medieval Russia began to dissolve in the eighteenth century: the parish was split off from the parallel secular society. The process was most advanced in the cities. Although the parish still served as a popular point of reference . . . , the urban parish inexorably lost its former cohesion. Somewhat less dramatically, the rural parish also began to break down as a unified, cohesive unit. It underwent basic structural changes and gave up extrareligious functions that were once so important. The parish also lost its identity in a juridical sense, ceasing to belong completely either to the Synod or the secular command. . . .The key dynamic behind this disorganization was secularization in the subculture of the Church: a growing split between the parish and secular community.

SOURCE: Gregory L. Freeze, "The Disintegration of Traditional Communities: the Parish in Eighteenth-Century Russia," *Journal of Modern History* 48, 1 (March 1976): 32–50 (excerpted). Copyright © 1976 by the University of Chicago Press, and reprinted by permission of the publisher.

ROBERT CRUMMEY

Vyg, An Old Believer Community

If, as Gregory Freeze maintains, the parish ceased to be an organizing center of Russian rural society, the same cannot be said about the fraction of the population that broke with the official church in the late seventeenth century to form the religious communities that were collectively known as the Old Believers (or Old Ritualists). For the Old Belief, adherence to the "true" faith and rituals, tenets that

from their perspective the Official Church had rejected in the seventeenth century, constituted the central fact of their lives and the basis upon which they fashioned a community. It is precisely the unbreakable oneness of faith and the organization of everyday life that Robert Crummey discusses in his book on the Old Believer community of Vyg in the forests far north of Moscow. In this selection he compares the Vyg community with other forms of religious community, in particular the monastery. We might also profitably pose comparisons with peasant communities in general, as described by other contributions to this text.

Andrei Denisov and the other leaders of the Vyg community envisioned the scattered Old Believers of Russia as a complete society, standing apart from the citizens of the empire who were loyal to the state church. In their writings, the Vyg fathers used every opportunity to point out that Old Belief had drawn its supporters from every class—the nobility, the merchants, and the peasants. The defenders of the old faith could therefore consider themselves the continuation of pre-Nikonian Russian society. To make their vision of an Old Believer counter-society a reality, however, the movement's leaders had to create institutions that would coordinate the efforts of their followers and provide them with the educational and cultural benefits they would otherwise lack. . . .

Andrei Denisov left no doubt about the institutional form and religious role which he wanted the Vyg community to take. His writings, and those of its other leaders, frequently state flatly that the Vygovskaia Pustyn' was, in every sense, a monastery—the legitimate successor of the renowned Solovetskii Monastery whose monks had died in defense of the old faith. . . .

The most obvious feature of Vyg, its appearance, graphically expressed the intentions of the men who built it. By the 1730s, the settlement on the Vyg River had grown from a cluster of small huts into a replica of a traditional Russian monastery. A tent-shaped bell tower

"The Barber Wishes to Cut Off the Dissenter's [Old Believer's] Beard." A famous picture depicting Peter the Great's assault on the Old Believers, including ordering the cutting off of beards. Woodcut from the first quarter of the eighteenth century.

and the tower of the chapel stood over the buildings where the men of the community lived and worked. Close by was another fenced-in settlement in which lived the sisters who worked in the Vyg monastery. The main women's community, similar in appearance, was located about twelve miles away on the river Leksa, a tributary of the Vyg. At its greatest, the total population of the two communities was approximately one thousand, of whom about seventy-five per cent were women. Together with the small hermitages that surrounded them, the two settlements constituted a self-contained world, isolated in the northern forests. . . .

The community's success as a rallying-point of Old Belief soon undermined its informal organization. A flood of new members brought with them new and trying problems. The arrival of women in the settlement, for example, forced the Vyg fathers to take elaborate measures to preserve monastic propriety against the temptations of the flesh. In a small settlement, the task was not easy. In other respects as well, the members' freedom to govern their own lives by the dictates of their own consciences produced chaos when practiced in a community of one hundred rather than of ten. In many of the other centers of the Old Belief—Vetka and Starodub, the Nizhnii-Novgorod area, and the Urals, for example—the adherents of the old faith solved the problem of rising population by founding an ever-increasing number of new skity [settlements]. In Vyg, however, the community drifted in another direction, toward a showdown.

In the late summer of 1702, Daniil Vikulich stepped down from his position as leader of Vyg. Apparently its members had become convinced that, in spite of his saintly qualities, his was not the strong personality needed to lead the community under its new conditions. They turned instead to . . . Denisov. . . .

The contrast between Vikulich and Denisov reflects, in part, the differences between the two generations of Old Believers. . . . In the final analysis Denisov was as willing as his older colleague to face martyrdom. He realized, however, that intransigent courage alone might do the cause of the old faith more harm than good. If the end of the world was not at hand, the Old Believers had to be prepared to organize their forces and systematize their religious practices so that islands of salvation would flourish in the ocean of Antichrist's power. And if Antichrist's agents were prepared to be flexible, then the guardians of Old Belief should adjust their tactics accordingly and make a small concession or offer a bribe if such a step would do more for the cause than a grand gesture of defiance. . .

The conditions on which he accepted the leadership of the Vyg community left no doubt about the direction of his policies. At his demand, the members of Vyg solemnly swore to obey their new nastoiatel' [leader] in the faithful practice of the liturgy and in strict adherence to the rules of monastic conduct which he should lay down. They swore also to accept the authority of their leader to mete out punishments of beating, imprisonment, or ejection from the community for extreme cases of disobedience. For his part, Denisov agreed not to make any major decisions without the consent of a council of all the members of the community. The document embodying this agreement was signed on September 17, 1702, in the presence of seventy-seven brothers.

The terms of the agreement were remarkably consistent with Denisov's oft-stated desire to recreate the Solovetskii Monastery. As the practices of the community evolved under his leadership, the administrative structure of Vyg took on all of the main features of its model. At the head of the community was an abbot, known in the case of Vyg' as the nastoiatel' or *bol'shak*. By tradition, the monks of Solovki had chosen their own leader and the Vyg community, which recognized no institutionalized authority outside itself, followed its example. In both cases, the members also chose the other main officers, the cellarer . . . , the treasurer . . . , and the . . . overseer of the community's agriculture and other economic enterprises. The holders of these offices were usually members of the council of elders which, in both instances, assisted the abbot in his functions as spiritual leader and as manager of the practical affairs of the community. In theory, at least, both Vyg and its predecessor recognized the right of all full members of the community to have a voice in the most important decisions affecting their common life. In the Solovetskii Monastery, the elders admittedly became a self-perpetuating aristocracy, but the tradition of deciding the most important questions by a vote of the general council was never forgotten and underwent a dramatic revival during the revolt against the Nikonian reforms. Moreover, like its model and other important Russian monasteries, the Vyg community had officers who conducted its foreign affairs—agents . . . who, from time to time, lived in important centers of Russia and were in charge of the community's economic operations in that area, and . . . a judicial agent or "fixer" who represented the community in legal disputes and lobbied with representatives of the government. . . .

At the same time, Denisov's authority was

never absolute. In routine matters of discipline, he usually legislated with the aid of the inner circle of advisers, made up of the elders of the community and the chief administrative officers. The elders were older members who were respected for their piety. Because they were the spiritual fathers of other members, including the other leaders, they had considerable influence in matters of doctrine and ritual observance. Very often they were assigned to positions of authority in situations in which it was difficult to enforce discipline. Sometimes, for example, they were sent to oversee projects in which men and women worked closely together in order to make sure that monastic proprieties were observed.

Even at the height of its development, moreover, the Vyg community never entirely lost the elements of voluntary association which had characterized its first years. In times of crisis, the council of the members of Vyg together with representatives of the surrounding communities decided the policy to be followed. Sometimes there was a sharp division of opinion which produced lively debate. When Peter the Great came near the settlement in 1702, the members of the community were divided on questions of tactics, one group favoring self-immolation, the other a limited accommodation with the government. There was also sharp debate on the future location of the women's settlement after the fire of 1727. Andrei Denisov and others inspected the old site carefully and decided that a better location had to be found. They met sharp opposition from many of the brothers who felt that the old location should be used because the rebuilding program in that case would be cheaper and less trouble to carry out. The impasse was broken by one member who saw a vision in which the community was enjoined to choose a new site.

The authority of the general assembly of Vyg exceeded that of the Solovetskii Monastery in that it decided the community's stand on questions of dogma, ritual, and political principle. . . . The consensus of opinion in the community decided the most important issue of all—whether or not to pray for the tsar. In the mid-1720s, the leaders of the community dropped plans to begin prayers for Peter II when faced with determined opposition from among the followers. Later, when the very life of the community was at stake, a majority of its members accepted prayers for the imperial family only after bitter debate at the end of which the defeated party of intransigents withdrew from Vyg to form their own sect. . . .

The presence of women among their followers was the cause both of pride and of deep concern to the early leaders of the Vyg community. In the first years the women had, of necessity, lived in the same compound as the men, but even with . . . stringent precautions . . . , the arrangement was as canonically dubious as it was risky. . . . As the community's population continued to grow, its leaders found a way out of their dilemma, by founding the separate women's settlement on the Leksa River . . . The sisters administered their own enterprises, applied their own discipline, and made the decisions on matters of immediate concern to them, but were subordinate to Vyg in all questions which touched on the total life of the community. The [father superior] of Vyg laid down the rules by which the sisters were to live. In all administrative questions, the officers of Leksa were under the supervision of the corresponding officers in Vyg. For example, the [father superior's assistant] of Vyg was responsible for the distribution of clothing in both settlements. It is difficult to determine how much influence the sisters exerted on the formation of general policy. There is no record that the women of the community participated in the meetings of the general council.

The relation of the Leksa settlement to Vyg is an excellent example of a pattern unique to Old Belief—the combining of a monastery and a convent, discreetly separated yet in close cooperation. The tactic was repeated elsewhere, for example, in the Irgiz Old Believer communities in the early nineteenth century.

The Leksa convent illustrates yet another unusual feature of Old Belief. Over the years, the Vyg community attracted far more women postulants than men: the community's report to Catherine II's legislative commission in 1767, for example, gives the population of the Vyg complex as 279 men and 757 women. . . . [T]he Leksa convent gradually eclipsed the monastery and, in the last days of the community in the mid-nineteenth century, was its undisputed center.

Explanations for the community's greater success in recruiting women might be sought in several directions. The simplest reason, perhaps, is to be found in the conditions of life in the northern peasantry. The basic economic unit among the peasants was the family, often consisting of grandparents, married sons and daughters-in-law, and grandchildren. Early marriage was the order of the day, if only because a single adult could hardly farm by himself and was of less value to the larger family unit than his married brother. If a man failed to marry and found a family, it was often for a special reason: he might, for example, be drafted for what was, in effect, a lifetime of military service or go off to become an itinerant laborer. On the other hand, a woman for whom a husband could not be found occupied a marginal position economically and socially. If she were an adherent of Old Belief, however, she could enter a convent like Leksa where she would receive a modicum of education, live a comfortable, if not easy, life, and achieve a position of respect and equality with the men of the community. In this light, it was almost to be expected that, when the first crusading fire of Old Belief died down, the monastic communities of the movement would find it easier to attract women than men.

At the same time, however, the Old Believers did not deviate in essence from the patriarchal patterns of Russian peasant life. Although, on the whole, male Old Believers probably treated their female coreligionists with greater respect than was customary among the peasantry or, for that matter, the urban population, the leaders of the movement, with the exception of the most radical sects, were almost always men. Even when the Leksa convent had become far larger and richer than the Vyg monastery, the acknowledged head of the whole complex was a man. . . .

Because there were no ordained priests in the community, it was canonically impossible to celebrate the Eucharist and other sacraments in the usual manner. Despite this, the inhabitants of Vyg observed an exhausting schedule of devotions. Every day there was a three-hour morning service and evening prayers. On Sundays, there was a night service which lasted five hours. Special religious festivals were observed in an all-night service and hours, celebrated every second hour throughout the day. Every member of the community was obligated to attend all of the services unless he was seriously ill or unavoidably absent from Vyg. . . .

The rule of the community forbade personal property. In accord with monastic tradition, the members of Vyg gave all they had to the common treasury. In Vyg the treasurer was responsible for the maintenance of all of the community's property. It was his duty to take in all of the belongings of new members. He was required to keep careful records of everything he received so that a member could get back his valuables if he were to leave the community by mutual consent. During any member's life in Vyg, his possessions were completely at the disposal of the community. If, for example, a new member brought with him a suitable icon, the treasurer could hand it over for use in one of the chapels.

The officers of the community distributed the basic necessities of life from community supplies. The members of the two main settlements wore a special monastic habit. Each one received a stipulated amount of clothing and could get a new issue only in exchange for worn-out garments. . . . The distribution of food was organized in a similar way. The members ate all their meals in common dining-halls unless they were excused because of illness. The diet was monotonous but satisfying. . . . If the members were not content with the normal menu, they could not do anything about it. They were strictly forbidden to keep food in their cells. . . .

Except for the leaders of the community, no man was ever allowed to enter the compounds where the women lived. Even in case of an emergency, ordinary brothers could come in only when the sisters had left and when the supervisor of the sisters had given her approval. If, in the course of official business, a brother should have dealings with a woman who was not a member of the community, he was to carry out his errand as quickly and decorously as possible. For their part, the sisters were forbidden to have any contact with the men of the community. They were not allowed to leave the settlement except under supervision. If one of the leaders were to order a sister to carry out a certain errand, she was to take one or two other sisters with her when she went outside of the walls. The rules forbade the sisters to write anything on the grounds that they might maintain secret contacts by letter.

Only for men and women of the same family was an exception made. Members of the same immediate family were allowed to meet for an hour once every two weeks. . . . The community assigned chaperons who were to be present at all meetings of second and third degree relatives to make sure that the conversation was decent and limited to urgent personal matters. While the whole community still lived together on the Vyg, such meetings took place in a special cell which formed part of the wall separating the men's and women's sections. The inside of the cell was divided into three compartments, two for the participants and the third for the chaperon. . . .

Andrei Denisov and his colleagues seem to have believed that sexual relations of any kind were intrinsically evil and consequently that a Christian could achieve his full potential as a witness to the faith only if he remained chaste. This conviction, by no means uniquely theirs, shaped their whole lives. The Denisov brothers fled to the hermitage while still in their teens and lived out their lives as members of a monastic community. Their experience could not but strengthen their conviction that the monastic life was the only path toward Christian perfection. Even though both brothers and the other leaders had frequent contact with the world outside the cloister, they seem never to have seen the image of a sanctified lay life that was both of this world and above it. . . .

The only virtue which the early leaders of Vyg prized more highly than chastity was complete obedience to the community. Its members were obliged to obey the elders in all questions and those who were disobedient were subject to a punishment appropriate to their crime. . . . In the eyes of the leaders, the most serious offenses were those which demonstrated that the culprit was not totally devoted to the community. Newcomers were tested by a long period of fasting before they were admitted as full members. Once they were admitted, any sign of lack of loyalty was punished. The members were expected to inform on any of their followers who broke the rule. They were, above all, prohibited from maintaining any traces of a personal life outside the bounds of the community. All members were forbidden writing materials and unofficial personal contacts. For example, if any sister maintained secret contacts, she was to be kept in chains and questioned closely about those with whom she had been in communication. . . .

As a religious and cultural center, the Vyg community made a contribution to Old Belief far out of proportion to its size and resources. The writings of the Vyg fathers, transcribed by its copyists and distributed throughout Russia by its missionaries, soon enjoyed an authority almost as great as the Scriptures and achieved a popularity rivalled only by the works of the first martyrs of the faith, such as Avvakum and Fedor the Deacon. In the long run, moreover, the contribution of the Vygovskaia Pustyn' to the religious and cultural life of the inhabitants of the areas of its greatest influence perhaps surpassed that of all of the other centers. The peasantry of north Russia—stable, industrious, and often isolated from the outside world—was most fruitful soil on which to plant the seeds of the faith and the traditionalist culture of Old Belief. . . .

The Vygovskaia Pustyn' could not have achieved its well-ordered communal life, its economic prosperity, or its remarkable cultural attainments, if it had not been permitted to exist for more than a century and a half in comparative tranquility. In large measure, then, it owed its accomplishments to its special relations with the state. The leaders of Vyg were not content to rest on the original agreement of 1705. On the contrary, they made great efforts to win the favorable attention of the successive rulers and of others in positions of power. Whenever Peter the Great visited Petrozavodsk and the mineral baths nearby, the community sent him profuse greetings and gifts. Over the years, they presented him with reindeer, game birds, a pair of gray horses, and some bulls. According to tradition, the emperor was pleased with the gifts and remained favorably disposed toward the community. . . .

The founders of the Vygovskaia Pustyn' wanted to create a monastic community that would be the cornerstone of Old Belief. When they applied this ideal to reality, they had to make many adjustments in order to cope with the demands of their environment. Nevertheless, the community, to a remarkable degree, remained true to its monastic ideal and to its role as an outpost of faith in the world of Antichrist.

SOURCE: Robert O. Crummey, *The Old Believers and the World of Antichrist: The Vyg Community and the Russian State, 1694–1855* (Madison: University of Wisconsin Press, 1970), Chapter 6: "A Community Apart," pp. 101, 103–16, 120, 122, 131–4 (excerpted). Copyright ©1970 by the University of Wisconsin Press and reprinted by permission of the publisher.

17

Everyday Life in Imperial Russia

For the great majority of Russian subjects, the family or clan constituted the primary social institution, or framework, within which they lived their daily lives, and through which they negotiated their relationships with their communities, and ultimately with the entire society. We have seen in earlier chapters just how central the family system was to the distribution of property, inheritance, marriage agreements, and economic activity. Such remained the case in the eighteenth and most of the nineteenth century. The family rather than the individual tended to negotiate with other families and with the larger community in determining how individual lives were lived and organized. But, once again, there are obvious limits to this line of reasoning, as the memoir of the militantly independent Nadezhda Durova, the "cavalry maiden," so poignantly reveals.

It is difficult to speak of change in discussing family structure or relations between the Muscovite and Imperial periods. Even though the state and landlords did get somewhat more involved in the domestic world of common people, custom and relevant legislation, so far as is known, did not undergo major transformations. Thus, family relations, unlike the bureaucracy and service system, did not undergo massive reorganization during most of the imperial period. The major exception to this rule was the landed nobility. As we see from Marc Raeff's reconstruction of noble home life, the demands of service, education, and city life had a profound bearing on the upbringing and outlook of noble boys. The memoirs of Durova and Labzina suggest that something comparable may well have been taking place among noble girls, even though they were not reared for state service or public life. But we still have much to learn about women's lives, and more generally about the changing contours of gender relations, within the noble household.

For the lower classes, changes in child rearing or domestic relations were far more subtle. The most obvious distinction between Muscovy and Imperial Russia in family history is the relative abundance of sources for the later period. Thanks to censuses and estate records it is possible to sketch fairly detailed pictures of the constitution of urban and peasant families and of their relationships with the community and the state. As a result, it is possible for historians to speak with some authority about the distinctions between urban and rural family size and patterns. As Peter Czap tells us, peasants invested a great deal of effort in keeping households together, and they determined that a large and multi-generational family was the best means to do so. By contrast, in M. G. Rabinovich's view, urban families who were less concerned with farming and inheriting land, tended to be fairly small.

The literature on gender, or on women's roles and images is unfortunately less extensive, not just for the nobility but for every stratum of Russian society. One of the odd paradoxes of Russian women's history has been the relative dearth of recent research in the first century and a half of the Imperial period, when compared both to Muscovy and to the late nineteenth and twentieth centuries. Brenda Meehan-Waters has been one of a very few modern scholars to explore women's history for this period, both in this essay on women rulers and in subsequent studies of women's religious communities. Still, as the passages from the memoirs demonstrate, some women were acutely conscious of the ways in which Imperial Russian society employed gender as an instrument of authority, and as a mechanism for excluding women from access to public life. For male constructions of women read the relevant passages in S. T. Aksakov's *A Family Chronicle*, confirm the importance of gender as a tool of both classification and the exercise of authority within a noble clan. For an extreme example of gender segregation as an expression of a religious ideal, students may also wish to reread Robert Crummey's selection which describes the physical segragation of men and women in Vyg.

A. Family

D O C U M E N T S

The Noble Head of the Household: The Memoirs of Sergei Aksakov (Nineteenth Century)

This memoir originally was published in several installments over many years during the middle of the nineteenth century. It describes three generations in the lives of the Aksakov family, going back to the mid-eighteenth century. The brief passage included in this volume focuses on the character of Aksakov's grandfather, Stepan Mikhailovich Bagrov, who had moved the family in the eighteenth century from Simbirsk province on the Volga River to the relatively unsettled territory of Ufa on the eastern border of European Russia. As Aksakov tells us, this move brought them into intimate contact with several non-Russian, non-European ethnic groups, a reminder of the complex assemblage of peoples who occupied the "Russian" Empire.

The character of Stepan Mikhailovich provides a vivid example of the extremes of patriarchal behavior among the land-owning nobility. In an instant, the head of the household, whose unchallenged moral authority permeated the entire family, his serfs, and even other families in the outlying district, could switch from a benevolent and paternal generosity to a raging and uncontrolled violence. This passage also provides some insights into status, alliances, and tensions that shaped the relationships among members of the household beyond the immediate orbit of the patriarch.

———————

Scarcely had my grandfather established himself in his new surroundings than, with his characteristic energy, and perseverance, he set himself to work on agriculture and cattle breeding. The peasants, encouraged by his example, developed into willing and skillful labourers, and soon nothing remained to be done in the building or carpentering line. The threshing floor of New-Bagrovo occupied an area three times the size of the village itself; and the magnificent herds of horses, cattle, swine, and flocks of sheep bore striking witness to the wealth of the new settler. It really seems as if Stepan Michailovitsch had set the fashion of emigration; for a stream of folks flowed into Ufa and Orenburg. From all sides came the Steppe Mordvins, Tscheremisses, Tschuvasches, Tartars, and Meschtcheriaks: nor was there any lack of Russian emigrants, of Crown Peasants from various districts, and of more or less well-to-do owners of serfs. My grandfather soon had neighbours. His brother-in-law, Ivan Vasilievich Neklyudov, purchased a tract of land twenty versts [a verst is about two-thirds of a mile] distant from New-Bagrovo, transferred his serfs to this estate, built a wooden church, called the place Neklyudovo, and established himself there with his family—a circumstance by no means pleasing to my grandfather. For he detested all his wife's relations—the whole Neklyudovery, as he called them. A landed proprietor—Bachmetev—bought an estate still nearer at hand, only about ten versts from Bagrovo, near the source of the Sovruscha [River], which flows parallel with the Buguruslan in the South-East. He brought along his serfs, and called his place Bachmetevka. On the other side, on the banks of the Nasjagai (or Motschagai, as the natives now call this river) lay the demesne of Polibino, which is now the property of the Karainzins. . . .

In the end, quite a little Mordvin village grew up under the name of Kiwazkoie, only two versts away from Bagrovo, but farther towards Buguruslan. Stepan Michailovitsch at first was somewhat inclined to pull a long face at such near neighbours, who reminded him of the old days at Troizkoie. But the case was different here. These were decent, quiet folk, who never caused the slightest trouble to my grandfather in his capacity of District Inspector. In a few years my grandfather had gained the love and respect of the whole countryside. He was a true benefactor to all, far and near; old and new neighbors; especially to the latest comers, who, as is so frequently the case with emigrants, came poor and empty-handed into a strange land; frequently unprovided with seed, corn, and with no money to buy any. To all such my grandfather's bursting granaries lay open. "Take all you need; and if the first harvest yields enough and to spare, you can repay me. If not—accept it as a gift in God's name." With such words as these my grandfather shared his store generously with those who lacked corn or bread. And here let me add that, with all this, he was so clear-sighted,

so charitable, and sympathised so heartily with all in need and want; and kept his plighted word and promise so faithfully and constantly—that he came to be a veritable oracle in those parts. And not only a friend in the day of distress was he; but an adviser and a prudent guide to all who needed advice. Only tell him the plain truth, and his assistance might be reckoned upon. But those who had lied to him to excite his compassion, were well advised never to show themselves on his land again. They would get nothing more, and well for them if they escaped with their whole skins. Many a family quarrel was healed by him—many a lawsuit nipped in the bud. From every part of the country people sought him out for advice and arbitration: and his decision was respected, and observed to the utmost degree. I have known grandsons and even great-grandsons of that bygone generation, who have testified their gratitude and indebtedness to the firm and just decisions of Stepan Michailovitsch, as handed down to them by their fathers and grandfathers. To many a simple, but strangely moving story have I listened, and the narrator at the end would cross himself, and pray for the repose of the soul of Stepan Michailovitsch. Small wonder, then, that the peasants had a genuine affection for such a master; but this affection was equally shared by the house servants, who frequently had to bear the brunt of his ungovernable outbursts of passion. In years to come, many an ancient servitor of my grandfather ended his days under my roof; and often have these old men—while tears rained down their cheeks—spoken lovingly to me of their choleric, but generous old master.

And this noble, magnanimous, often self-restrained man—whose actual character presented an image of the loftiest human nature—was subject to fits of rage in which he was capable of most barbarous cruelty. I recollect having seen him in one of these mad fits in my earliest childhood [at a much later date than that of the foregoing narrative]. I see him now. He was angry with one of his daughters, who had lied to him, and persisted in the lie. There he stood, supported between two servants, for his legs refused their office; I could hardly recognise him as my grandfather: he trembled in every limb, his features were distorted, and the frenzy of rage glared from his enraged eyes. "Give her to me!" he howled in a strangled voice. (All this remains clearly in my memory; what came later has often been related to me). My grandmother threw herself at his feet, beseeching him to have pity and forbearance, but the next instant off flew her kerchief and cap, and Stepan Michailovitsch seized his corpulent and already aged better half by the hair of her head. Meanwhile, the culprit as well as all her sisters—and even her brother, with his young wife and little son— had fled into the woods behind the house; and there they remained all night: only the young daughter-in-law crept home with the child, fearing he might take cold, and slept with him in the servants' quarters. My grandfather raved and stormed about the empty house to his heart's content. At last he grew too tired to drag his poor Arina Vasilevna about by her plaits, and fell exhausted upon his bed, where a deep sleep overpowered him, which lasted until the following morning. He awoke calm, and in a good humour, and called to his Arischa in a cheery tone. My grandmother immediately ran to him from the adjoining chamber, just as if nothing had happened the day before. "Give me some tea! Where are the children? Where are Alexei and his wife? Bring little Sergei to me!" said this erstwhile lunatic, now that he had slept off his rage; and everyone—with the exception of the daughter-in-law and her son—made their appearance with bright and serene countenances. This daughter-in-law was a woman of strong character, and no entreaties would induce her to betake herself so promptly to the madman of yesterday and greet him civilly: and the children kept crying: "I won't go near my grandfather! I'm afraid of him!"

As she really was not very well, she pleaded indisposition, and kept her son with her in her own apartments. All held a terrified council, and awaited a fresh storm. But the man had conquered the wild beast of the previous evening. After Stepan Michailovitsch had drunk

his tea, and chatted amicably with his children, he went himself to visit the young wife, who was in fact in a very shattered condition, and lay, pale and exhausted, on her bed. The old man seated himself beside her, kissed and embraced her, called her dear, beautiful little girl; caressed his little grandson, and at last left the room saying he felt lonely without his beloved daughter-in-law. Half an hour later the door of my grandfather's room was gently opened, and in walked his daughter-in-law, elegantly dressed in a gown which the old gentleman had once declared became her better than anything else in her wardrobe. My grandfather was much touched. "What's this?" he said tenderly, "My poor, sick little daughter has got up and dressed in spite of her illness, and come to cheer up the old man!" The mother-in-law and her daughters, who could not endure the young wife, cast down their eyes, and bit their lips, while she responded gaily and respectfully to the friendly greeting of her father-in-law, and cast a glance of sly triumph at her malevolent relations. . . .

But enough of the darker side of my grandfather's character. I prefer to describe one of his cheery happy days, of which I have heard so much.

SOURCE: S. T. Aksakov, *The Family Chronicle*. Translated by M. C. Beverley. Introduction by Ralph E, Matlaw (New York: E. P. Dutton, 1961), pp. 18–22 (excerpted). Reprinted by permission of Routledge Chapman and Hall, Publishers.

The Dowry of Avdot'ia Bogdanova, A Nobleman's Daughter (1787)

Marriages were almost invariably arranged and negotiated by the heads of the respective households. Irrespective of social standing, the families involved recognized that marriage involved the transfer of property, the transfer of the bride from her paternal home to that of her husband, and, eventually, the creation of a new household. Consequently, the arrangements of these property transfers had to be

"A Russian Wedding Feast." Although highly stylized, this nineteenth-century engraving shows a wealthy family in traditional attire celebrating a wedding. Compare the demeanors of the men and women, especially those of the bride and groom. From The Oleg I. Pantuhoff Collection, courtesy of The New York Public Library, Slavic and Baltic Division.

worked out in detail before the wedding could take place. Terms varied enormously across time and social class, and among peasants the practices of a ritualized bride theft and, more commonly, bride price (in which the groom's family paid a price for the bride) were as widespread as were dowries. This dowry contract constitutes a particularly formalized variant of marriage arrangements, and, as is obvious from the property included, it involved an unusually wealthy household.

On the 8th day of March, 1787 army lieutenant Ivan Iakov's son Bogdanov composed this dowry in regard to the fact that I gave over my daughter, the maiden Avdot'ia, in July 1785, to marry guard's captain Petr Vlasov, the son of

Mikhail. For her I have bestowed as payment a blessing of sacred images, first, of Christ the Divine Savior, a silver and gilded crown, and an icon case with silver ornament. The second image, of the Holy Mother of God of Akhtyr, also a silver and gilded crown, a pearl orb, and, in payment of a dowry of diamonds and silver valued at 3,214 rubles; dresses, bed linens, miscellaneous items worth 2,786 rubles. In all, the dowry is valued at 6,000 rubles.

And, of the immovable property in my inheritance. . . [I bequeath] the following: peasants, in the villages on the Large Island, 55 males, 48 females; in Beletovo 69 males, 80 females; in Derbyshi 30 males, 22 females, in Malakhovo 88 males, also 88 females; in Zhabino 69 males, also 69 females; in Vvanfimy 36 males and 38 females; [all] to be brought to the village of Zhabino from the village of Nerozhino, along with the peasant Ivan Andreev and his wife. In all, in these villages there are currently 348 males on hand, and 346 females. And both the arable and non-arable land in these villages along with the woods and . . . everything that goes with it, amounting to 8,000 desiatinas [one desiatina 2.7 acres]. All this I grant to my daughter willingly to have as her own property without any question.

And, beyond these [I give over] the following of what was left to me by my late wife, her mother Anna Sergeevna . . . : [there follows a list of villages, peasants and household servants. The dowry is witnessed by fifteen fellow officers and it is certified by the Company Secretary.]

SOURCE: "Riadnaia Avdot'i Ivanovny Vlasovoi rozhd. Bogdanovoi 1787 goda," in *Letopis' Istoriko-rodoslovnogo obshchestva v Moskve* Vol. 4, No. 3 (1908), pp. 14–18. Translated by Gary Marker.

LITERATURE

PETER CZAP JR.
A Large Family: The Peasant's Greatest Wealth

One of the great truisms of Imperial Russia is that it consisted overwhelmingly of peasants. This abiding fact, so fundamental to understanding Russian culture and institutions, has sparked an outpouring of scholarship on peasant life, economics, and institutions. Many issues remain hotly contested, but nearly everyone recognizes that the primary institution of Russian peasant life, upon which all others were overlaid, was the family or household. In this article Peter Czap takes a microscopic look at peasant families in four villages of central Russia on the Mishino estate, in order to reconstruct the structure and inner dynamics of family life among the peasantry during the first half of the nineteenth century.

––––––––––

'Nowhere is a large family a greater blessing than among the Russian peasants. Sons always mean additional shares of land for the head of the family . . . In western Europe a large family is an immense burden and nuisance for the lower classes; in Russia a large family represents the peasant's greatest wealth.' So observed the German political economist August von Haxthausen of the peasantry of the central provinces of European Russia in the 1840s. . . . Haxthausen attributed the large and complex households of central Russia to a unique cultural configuration and a peculiar Russian need for 'secure family ties.' Frederick Le Play, travelling in the province of Orenburg in 1853, was also struck by the large size and complexity of serf households, which he attributed to the implacable authority of the peasant family patriarch.

These descriptions of the peasant family by two eminent western European observers, while arresting the attention of Russians and non-Russians alike, were not, however, the first to be written. One of the earliest published descriptions of serf peasant households appeared in Russia in 1829. It signaled growing awareness by gentry landlords that to improve rural estates something must be known about their basic units of labour and taxation—the serf/family household. This and other early descriptions refer to a certain proportion of peasants living in 'family communes' of 30 to 40 individuals under the rule of a stern patriarch. None of these accounts provides a statistical basis for generalization, and all are at best impressionistic. At worst they may be nothing more than the wishful thinking of seigneurs, who favoured 'strong households' . . . among the peasants. . . .

LOCATION

The data employed for this study have been drawn from the province of Riazan in an area approximately 170 kilometres south-east of Moscow ... Here the central black-earth begins to give way to the forests and the thinner soils of the north. Natural conditions favoured agriculture, which dominated the region's economy. Rye was the principal crop. In 1858 Riazan was the seventh most densely settled province of the Empire. The region was originally opened to settlement in the early seventeenth century as a buffer zone between Moscow and the Tatars, who still mounted desultory raids against the older population centres to the north. By the end of the eighteenth century in-migration ceased to be a significant factor in the region's population growth. The area's population has always been predominantly Great Russian. Peasants made up nine-tenths of the population of the province. Approximately 65% were proprietary serfs; state peasants, servile agriculturalists living on state-owned land, accounted for the bulk of the remaining peasantry. . . .

The estate of Mishino consisted of four villages, in two of which parish churches were located. It was a larger than average proprietary estate, carefully managed and prosperous. In 1800 the majority of peasants settled in the villages of Mishino performed labour services . . . for their seigneur, Prince Nikolai Sergeevich Gagarin, a magnate and government office-holder who owned approximately 27,000 serfs on various estates at the time of his death in 1842. Between 1830 and 1849, the seigneurial obligations of the peasants of Mishino were gradually converted to quit rent . . . , with only incidental labour services remaining. . . .

Records indicate a water mill, several windmills, fish ponds, orchards and gardens, and a stud located among the four villages making up the estate. The economic mainstay of the estate was the production of rye, oats, and buckwheat in that order of importance. The production of small amounts of other commodities rendered the estate largely self-sufficient in foodstuffs. Cattle raising was an important part of the seigneurial economy.

In addition to their agricultural labour, a number of peasants engaged in trade or were artisans. One-third of the households contained one or more members engaged in some kind of non-agricultural work. Carpenter and cooper were the most frequently listed crafts and the inventory included blacksmith, bricklayer, felt-maker, miller, pitch-boiler, sawyer, stonecutter, stove-maker, tailor, wheelwright, etc. Trade was carried on by the peasants in charcoal, bast, rope, harnesses, and pitch. The fleeting presence of non-peasants in the villages is marked in records of the estate, which carry notations about grain dealers, merchants, and occasional government officials inquiring about anomalies appearing in reports compiled by the estate administration on behalf of the central government.

THE PEASANT HOUSEHOLD

The first problem in describing Russian serf households is to understand just what is being described. The Russian term 'dvor' had two complementary meanings in the nineteenth century. First, it referred to a distinct, usually enclosed, space which encompassed all the structures and appurtenances of a single economy: dwelling, barns, sheds, threshing floor, haycocks, gardens—in short a farmstead. Second, it described a group of individuals, or perhaps more accurately a collective, whose members were connected by a unity of material interests and usually (but not exclusively) by ties of kinship, and residing in a single farmstead. The unit excluded from membership hired workers and servants, i.e. all those who may have worked about the farmstead but who did not contribute their earnings to and did not draw upon the common purse. . . .

Russian peasant farmsteads were constructed according to well-defined conventions, with regional variations dictated by weather conditions and available building materials. In the province of Riazan a farmstead was usually square in shape, its limits formed by the walls of the dwelling and outbuildings, which enclosed an inner court. The entire complex was set on a parcel of land, an acre or more, called the *usadba*, which in addition to the farmstead included space for a kitchen garden, fruit trees, and summer enclosures for domestic animals. Construction of the dwellings and more substantial outbuildings was of hewn, unpainted logs, and the roofs were of straw.

The dwelling . . . sided on the street and in its simplest form consisted of a single room dominated by a large earthenware stove . . . which was used for cooking and heating. . . . Different corners of the room were used for cooking, dining, entertaining guests, and sleeping. More elaborate dwellings included open or enclosed porches and unheated storage areas. . . .

POPULATION

The serfs of Mishino are an example of a nearly closed, but not necessarily immobile, population. Between 1814 and 1858 permanent outmigration among males was confined largely to military recruits, who served in the army for 25 years. In addition, occasional solitaries and orphans, when they were not relocated among the villages of Mishino, were transferred to one or another Gagarin estate. The listings also refer to fugitives, but they number no more than six in 40 years. Because women appeared on a list only if they were present—unlike males, whose names were 'cleared' after their disappearance with a notation about their recruitment, transfer, or death—it is not possible to speak about their movements with the same certainty. Women disappearing from the lists are assumed to have married off the estate, died, or perhaps been transferred to work in a cloth mill Gagarin built in 1817 on an estate elsewhere in Riazan province. However, the rate of female endogamy within the estate was over 90%, so the number of women who disappeared and cannot be accounted for directly or indirectly is low. . . .

Some of the male population could be expected to be temporarily absent from the estate at any given time, more in winter than in summer. On the order or with the permission of the estate administration, peasants could leave their homes for periods of weeks or months. They hauled the lord's grain to market, delivered produce to or fetched manufactured goods from Moscow, or travelled about the countryside as itinerant craftsmen. The names of such travellers always appeared in the soul revisions, which were lists of official inscription. Yet in Mishino the difference between *de jure* and *de facto* residence was not great. Moscow, at a distance of 170 kilometres, did not exert a strong attraction for peasants seeking additional earnings. The Riazan region itself did not offer many alternatives to agriculture. Even after the peasants' obligations had been largely transformed into quit rent, most peasants remained on the estate to till the land.

The serfs of Mishino were of two types—*krestiane* (peasants or agricultural serfs) and *dvorovye liudi* (household people). Agricultural serfs, who constituted the overwhelming majority of the estate's population, lived in family groups in their own farmsteads. In addition to their own obligations to their lord, they had to maintain themselves, their animals, and their equipment, including their dwellings and outbuildings. The peasants of each village were organized in a *mir*—the traditional Russian agrarian commune which bore collective responsibility for the lord's obligations andthe annual soul tax levied by the central government and collected by the lord. . . .

With the manor house of Mishino almost never visited by the lord, the household people living on the estate were assigned tasks connected with supervising and maintaining the seigneurial economy. Household people filled the offices of steward . . . , foreman. . . , clerk . . . , and scribe. . . . The estate steward was also described as 'architect'. The estate's gardeners, driver, stableman, and stockyard man were likewise household people. . . .

MARRIAGE

Among the important factors contributing to the household size and composition of the household serfs of Mishino was the particular marriage pattern that prevailed among them. . . . The dynamics of peasant nuptiality are by no means fully understood, but the data for Mishino make it clear that they worked to produce a consistent pattern of early and nearly universal marriage for both sexes. . . . A unique feature of the Russian peasant marriage pattern . . . is the small age difference between spouses. This is uncharacteristic in a marriage pattern in which women consistently married on average below the age of 20. A comparison of spouses' ages appearing in the Mishino listings shows a minimum of 33% and a maximum of 46% of wives older than their husbands. . . . In circumstances where the peasant arable was periodically redistributed to take account of changes in the household labour force, the probable reason for the high proportion of older wives lay in the advantage that accrued to a household which could import an able-bodied worker. The advantage could be hastened if a match were concluded between a 15-year-old groom and an 18-year-old bride. Any economic disadvantage the bride's household might suffer was compensated by a bride price. Furthermore, peasant wisdom held that a good match must not be passed up lightly, for the longer a young woman remained unmarried the greater the chance she would be dishonoured and bring shame on her family. . . .

In addition to the expected role taken by parents in the marriage of their offspring, in Mishino, as in many proprietary estates, the peasant community and the seigneur or his agents also took part in shaping nuptial behavior. An order . . . written in December 1817, which informed the overseer of Mishino of the opening of a cloth mill on the Gagarin estate of Petrovskaia in Riazan province, is one dramatic example of seigneurial interference in the nuptial process. The order indicated a need at the mill for young female operators who would be drawn from among unmarried females 15 years and older and young widows living on Mishino and other Gagarin estates in the province. The estate administration was instructed to compile a special register of all females falling into the germane categories and to convene a meeting of their parents to explain the situation. Parents were given the option of arranging marriages for their daughters before the arrival in Mishino of an agent of the prince or risk the loss of their daughters to the mill in Petrovskaia. An annotated copy of the special register, dated February 1818, documents the impact on the peasant community of the prince's order. Two 16-year-olds, two 17-year-olds, and an 18-year-old were shown to have wed since the issuing of the order. Parents of a majority of the remaining young women appearing on the list made firm promises to have their daughters wed by the end of the first week after Easter. A number of women appearing on the register were indicated by the overseer as unsuitable for marriage by reason of physical handicaps, and six 15-year-olds and one 16-year-old were indicated as 'immature'. . . .

HOUSEHOLD SIZE

It became commonplace at the end of the eighteenth century and beginning of the nineteenth century for Russian seigneurs to issue instructions forbidding, or at least controlling, household fission among their peasants. . . . Prince Gagarin was one of those serf owners who attempted to control his peasants' domestic arrangements. His 'instruction' concerning household divisions, if one was ever issued, has not been found. But the reports of his overseer carry references to the prince's 'firm wish' that peasant households in Mishino be allowed to divide only for urgent reasons. The prince's direct interest in this question is reflected by his order that a special register be compiled at the end of 1816 summarizing household divisions among the peasants of Mishino for the preceding four years. His concern to preserve households that could suitably be described as 'economically viable' . . . , along with the peasants' natural inclination to regard their own domestic arrangements at least in part from an economic point of view, combined to produce a family system in Mishino unlike any found by investigators of western societies. . . .

Household size is the first variable in which households in Mishino deviate from the western standard. At the upper limit of their range, households in the period 1814–58 fluctuated between a maximum size of 18 and 25, although households of 20 persons or more were rare. Households of 1 or 2 persons were equally rare and invariably a fleeting phenomenon—households of this small size captured in one listing failing to appear in thenext.

Mean household size fluctuated between 8.0 and 9.7, but the much steadier median size of 9 . . . is a more accurate indication of the relative stability in household size over the whole period. . . .

As an example of a household with 9 persons, let us consider the household of Dmitri Fedorov. A widower aged 53, he headed a farmstead composed of married brother and sister-in-law and their children and his own married daughter, widowed son, and granddaughter. . . .

[O]n average 65% of the population lived in households of 9 or more persons. An example of a household at the upper limit of the size range was that of 58-year-old Tikhon Ignatev, composed of his wife and their 2 married sons plus 5 unmarried grandchildren, an unmarried son, and a married brother with 5 children. In addition the household contained Tikhon's widowed sister-in-law, her married son, and unmarried daughter.

HOUSEHOLD TYPE

. . . . A look behind the numbers . . . will reveal some of the dynamics of household formation in Mishino. . . . There was no accommodation in Mishino for able-bodied males or females to live alone, and ageing widows or widowers ending their days alone in a hut at the end of the village were also unknown. Provision was made, usually but not always, for kin to provide shelter for the aged and likewise the orphaned young. . . .

The proportion of 'Simple-family households' was small by comparison with western societies but nevertheless formed a significant proportion of the domestic groups in Mishino. Here simple families were typically not composed of a newly married couple with or without children. The formation generally was linked to other phases of the family life cycle. . . . One arose from the hiving off of a married brother from a household consisting of 3 married brothers and their offspring. Another simple household formed when one of two married brothers sharing a household died and the widow remarried and left with her offspring. . . . Conspicuously absent from this category in Mishino are households consisting of newly married couples or couples with very young children. . . .

Extended-family households, numbering 14 in 1814, included 6 stem families, e.g. a widowed representative of the parental generation living with one married son, or daughter and son-in-law, and their unmarried children. The remaining 8 extended households included other extensions, such as uncle, grandparent, or mother-in-law. Whether the stem families . . . were the result of conscious planning or whether they took shape as the result of random demographic events cannot be answered with certainty. . . . However, it would appear that the system of land partibility commonly practised by Russian peasants, periodic redistribution of arable to reflect changes in unit work-force, would have made the calculated formation of stem families, from a purely economic point of view, counterproductive. . . . The peasants were not free to establish new farmsteads as their population grew nor to divide households at their pleasure. The serfs of Mishino moved from one set of premises to another only with the agreement of the head of their household, their community, and their seigneur or his agents. Unable to move about freely, the peasants, when resources were available to them, added on to their premises to create the phenomenon we are discussing.

GENERATIONAL COMPOSITION

Despite a mean life expectancy at birth no greater than 31 years for males and 33 for females, households of three or more generations represented a majority of all households for the entire period under examination. This was the result of large household size, the short interval between generations, and the peculiar features of the family process common to Mishino peasants.

Just as we do not find newly married couples living apart from their parents or other representatives of the parental generation, we also do not find a significant proportion of the elderly living apart from their children or kin in the offspring generation. Those peasants about to start families and those who had completed theirs lived together in large households, headed usually by representatives of the older generations. This residence pattern was the pre-condition for the large percentage of three-and four-generational households. . . .

The early age at marriage reduced the time interval between generations to a little over 20 years. . . . [I]t was possible for peasants and their offspring fortunate enough to elude accident, recruitment, and death, to become parents at age 18–20, grandparents at age 38–40, and great grandparents at age 55. . . . In terms of cross-cultural comparisons, the proportion of households in Mishino with three or more generations, on average 65%, is greater than any that has so far come to light.

FAMILY LIFE PROCESS

. . . In Mishino the flow of births and deaths, and the exchange of household members through marriage and to a lesser extent adoption, constantly changed the size and composition of households and simultaneously marked stages in their evolution. The centrifugal forces which conventionally seem to strain the coherence of large households in most societies studied to date (disputes between brothers, mother-in-law/daughter-in-law strife, and miscellaneous, diffuse animosities), or various moments of passage such as the death of the head or the marriage of the eldest or youngest son which resulted in household fission, met strong countervailing forces in the circumstances of life in Mishino. The authority of the seigneur to inhibit household fission wherever possible could not be resisted, at least not directly. The peasant commune, which bore corporate responsibility for the performance of peasant labour services and the payment of quit rent, also looked upon requests for household division with a sceptical eye. Finally, the household head, who could usually, but not always under all circumstances, depend on the community to uphold his authority, could prevent members of his household from hiving off. . . .

Between 1812 and 1816, 9 households, out of approximately 130 on the estate, underwent partial or complete fission. . . . [i.e.,] the removal of one or more conjugal family units from the household of orientation. With the exception of brides, a single individual rarely moved to another household and never established one of his own. . . .

'Constant fighting' was the explanation given to 6 of the 9 household fissions in Mishino between 1812 and 1816. In these instances division served to relieve potentially disruptive social pressures. The case of a 57-year-old widower living with his granddaughter who was joined by his married nephew, whose family included three unmarried children, illustrates a different purpose served by household division. Here the process of fission/fusion transformed a marginal household into one more closely approaching a size and generational composition typical of the estate. . . . Although marriage and parenthood came early to the peasants of Mishino, household headship, in most societies one of the important indicators of full social maturity, came late. The family system being described here was hostile to the free formation of new households and thus denied to many males, perhaps a majority of those who survived to marry, the opportunity to become household heads. . . .

CONCLUSIONS

Analysis of the Mishino revisions and household lists leaves the overwhelming impression of a stable family system, preserving its fundamental characteristics over a period of 40 years. The large, multi-generational families/households prevalent in Mishino appear to be like those encountered in the world of Russian folklore and literature. Individual members were susceptible to early death and conjugal family units to sudden dissolution, but the larger entities which contained them were remarkably durable and offered refuge and continuity to survivors, young and old. It is difficult to conceive how any peasant born in Mishino would not have passed a significant part of his life, certainly his earliest years, in crowded physical proximity with kin other than members of his biological family. Whether the family system which prevailed in Mishino realized a peasant ideal or whether it was a burden to him we do not know. Certainly partial responsibility for it must go to the peasant community . . . and the seigneur. Until an individual became a head of household, he was perforce responsible, as a worker and as a member of a household, to three levels of authority—the household head, the community, and the seigneur. Not until he succeeded to headship—on average in his late 30s or early 40s—could he partially change that situation.

SOURCE: Peter Czap, Jr., " 'A Large Family: The Peasant's Greatest Wealth': Serf Households in Mishino, Russia, 1814–1858," in Richard Wall (ed.), *Family Forms in Historic Europe* (Cambridge: Cambridge University Press, 1983), pp. 105–51 (excerpted). Copyright © 1983 by Cambridge University Press. Reprinted with the permission of Cambridge University Press.

M. G. RABINOVICH

The Russian Urban Family at the Beginning of the Eighteenth Century

Peasant families, as we learned from Peter Czap, tended to be large and multi-generational. We also have seen how the family functioned as a social system in the village commune, and how the distribution of resources and authority were critical issues of everyday life. In this essay M. G. Rabinovich raises comparable questions for urban families but arrives at somewhat different conclusions about the size and organization of the household. How does his view compare with other images of the Russian towns and their inhabitants that have been given earlier?

Disputes continue to this day in the learned literature over whether the [urban] family . . . was nuclear or extended, and what its numbers and structure were. For an immense span of years, nearly a millennium (from the ninth to the eighteenth centuries), one must content oneself only with indirect evidence in manuscripts and documents. The most valuable source . . . [does] not provide a complete notion of the family, because not all elements of the urban population were entered. . . . Moreover, it was usually only the male half of the family that was recorded—the head of the house, his sons, and at best, his grandsons. . . . Thus, a family having only daughters may be regarded as childless. Widows who did not own homes were not counted at all. A family that included the householder's mother-in-law, his married son, and granddaughters, i.e., consisting of four generations, would be recorded as having two generations, and so forth.

Therefore special value attaches to those few sources in which the family is described in full, both the women and the men being listed. One such source, the *Landrat* census of the town of Ustiuzhna Zheleznopol'skaia was compiled in 1713, when Ustiuzhna was already declining because its iron ore resources were becoming exhausted. Soon thereafter the main operations were shut down, the master craftsmen were transferred to other works, and many of the townsfolk were transferred to other towns. But the census of 1713 still reflected the condition of the town at the close of the seventeenth century and the beginning of the eighteenth, when Ustiuzhna was flourishing and was a rather populous industrial town, in which master craftsmen from other towns, Tula for example, were resettled.

The census-takers identified among the population: townsfolk as such (only 43 families), landless peasants ... (both those who were subject to taxation, like the townsmen, 103 families, and those who were tax-exempt due to poverty, 67 families), workers at cannon foundries (66 families, including 13 recently transferred from Tula), state servitor master craftsmen (8 families), and 20 families of soldiers and paupers. The clergy (56 families) and civil officials of the Moscow government (9 families) occupied a special place in the census. Nobility and rich merchants were not subject to the census, but the stewards who occupied their households (chiefly townsfolk and landless peasants, 10 families each, less often peasants and personal servitors, 14) were listed.

The book recorded 413 homesteads (408 inhabited and only 5 abandoned), and eight estate compounds. The total population of all these homesteads was 2,288 persons (1,144 men and the identical number of women). This was not the entire population of the town, of course, inasmuch as there also dwelt in it ... people who did not belong to the taxable castes, and these were not recorded. It would appear that the total population of Ustiuzhna Zheleznopol'skaia might have reached approximately 2,500. What we have before us is a small industrial town, typical of the Russia of that day.

The 408 inhabited homesteads were the residences of 419 families, i.e., each homestead had an average of 1.2 families (5.6 persons), giving us an idea of average family size—about five (5.04). However, this concealed wide differences. It was highest among the civil officials (nine families averaging eight persons each, in nine homesteads). ... while the figure was lowest among soldiers and paupers—1.8. These computations agree in general outline with the results of prior studies, which found the families of townsfolk to average six or seven ..., landless peasants five ..., and drafted master craftsmen four. ..

[I]n Ustiuzhna as in other Russian towns of that day, two-generation families consisting of parents and children prevailed. Such families comprised nearly three-quarters of the whole. ... Among landless peasants this percentage was somewhat higher, while among townsfolk, gunsmiths, and clergy it was lower. Among the most prosperous stratum—government officials—the two-generation family alone existed, and among the poorest—soldiers and paupers—it accounted for 90%. Three-generation families, with parents, children, and grandchildren, ranked second. They comprised nearly one-fifth ... of the total number of families. ... Nonetheless, the tendency for nuclear families, including two-generation families, to develop among urban people is quite clear.

Only one genuine four-generation family was found in Ustiuzhna, in the ranks of the taxable landless peasants: "The landless peasant Matvei, son of Aleksei Kitaev, aged 52, his wife Fevron'ia aged 30, his son Avram aged 32, the latter's wife Efim'ia aged 32, and his (Avram's) children Afinogen aged two, daughter Avdot'ia aged 12, Natal'ia aged six [?]; his sister-in-law the widow Anna Il'inskaia, a woman of 30, with a son, Pavel 10; also living with him is his cousin Leontei Anufriev aged 47, with wife Ustin'ia aged 42, their cousin Artemii,11, Anufrei, 10, Ivan, 4; as well as his uncle Ivan Ivanov, 42, with wife Anis'ia, 40, and their son, Fadei, 11 years old." In that family, numbering 17 persons, one can distinguish the remnants of the large fraternal family of Aleksei, Anufrii, and Ivan Ivanovich Kitaev, headed by the son of the eldest brother, who was older, as was often the case in those days, than his "third uncle," and was now married for the second time. Only two members of the first generation remained ... ; of the second generation there were six. ... The third generation consisted of the married son from the first marriage (he was older than his stepmother), and four minor children. ... The fourth generation comprised the head's three grandchildren (in the same age group as the children of the prior generation). In this instance we use the term "household head" arbitrarily, because the homestead was listed under his name. The character of the entry as

THE IMPERIAL PERIOD

such does not make it possible to judge the real relationships within the family, although it is quite possible that the head of household actually was the "big man" in the family.

There were relatively few single-generation families (i.e., without children) in Ustiuzhna: only 36, or 8.6%. But among the clergy this figure was over thrice as high as average (28.5%) which is probably to be explained by the particular circumstances of that social group. . . .

The information on the persons listed as heads of family is interesting. . .

As a rule, it was a man, father of the family and owner of the homestead (this was true in more than two-thirds of families . . .). In the majority of cases the head of the family was married . . . but rarely it was a widower or an unmarried man. . . Quite often (20%) the head of the family and possessor of the homestead was the widowed mother. . . .

Families headed by a brother, and those in which there were several brothers and the head was not indicated are of great interest (in all they were one-tenth of all families . . .). In the former instance it was the older brother who headed the family, while the younger—married or single—were rank-and-file members. In the latter case the homestead was jointly held by two or more brothers. This could constitute either an undivided fraternal family or simply a family of brothers joined solely by their joint possession of the homestead. . . .

The two-generation family . . . , most typical of the townsfolk, accounted for about three-fifths of all the people of Ustiuzhna. The 303 such families totaled 1,506 persons, for an average of five . . . per family. These 303 families included 375 sons, 339 daughters, 42 brothers, 21 sisters, 25 sisters-in-law, 21 nephews, 23 nieces, and 36 daughters-in-law. Thus, a complete two-generation family consisted of the parents and two or three children . . . Fairly often brothers (sometimes married) and sisters of the head also resided in such families. Less often, his nieces and nephews also did so. The presence of married brothers and married sons either testified to a forthcoming di-

vision or indicated that the family had become an extended one. . . .

Here is how the census-takers described a family of traders: "Townsfolk Andrei, Fedot, and Ivan, the children of Plotnikov Deev. Andrei, 55, has a wife, Mar'ia, 22, childless, and a daughter, Anna, 17; Fedot, 47, has a wife Marem'iana, 42, with their daughter Tat'iana, 10; Ivan, 42, has a wife, Tat'iana, 36, with their daughters Akilina, 4, and Afrosin'ia, 3." The three married brothers had apparently kept undivided not only their homestead but their business, which was often the case in sixteenth- to eighteenth-century towns. But it cannot be stated with confidence that this was a genuine extended family, for whether or not a common household was maintained is unknown.

Approximately one quarter of the Ustiuzhna people belonged to three-generation families. Such families, numbering 80, totalled 633 persons, the average number per family being about 8. . . . The eldest generation survived in full in about half the families—10 were headed by widowers and 31 by widows. There were 160 sons, 48 daughters, 106 daughters-in-law, 101 grandsons, and 89 granddaughters in these families. Brothers, sisters, sisters-in-law, and nephews were present in but one family each, which, in our opinion, points to the gradual dying out of patronymies. In the third generation members by direct line of descent predominated. Brothers, nephews, and grand-nephews had divided off, or in one way or another abandoned the family. . . . The numerical relationship of daughters-in-law and daughters is interesting: together they numbered as many as did sons. This is indirect evidence that people married into other families in town: the number of daughters lost in certain families equalled the number of daughters-in-law in others. Family size varied quite considerably, from four to 17, but families of seven were most common.

Thus far we have not dealt with families of household servants, because that category . . . usually did not maintain operations of its own, but was part of the family of its owners and was totally dependent upon them. But within the holdings of that kind of extended family . . .

there might also be small units consisting of families of the servants. Our source records only 25 household servants in Ustiuzhna, or about 1% of the town's population. Of these, 13 were unmarried, while 12 formed five families. . . . The household servants included 13 males (of whom five were boys aged 10 and less), and 12 women (aged 15 and over). Over half the household servants . . . belonged to government officials, three to clergy, two to a noblewoman, and seven to townsfolk (six to merchants, and in a single case, a woman belonging to a craftsman). . . .

Now let us pause briefly for consideration of some questions associated with marriage, above all the relationship between the ages of the spouse.

We find a total of 449 married couples in the Ustiuzhna census. . . . Among them there is a considerable number in which both spouses are the same age (21%. . .). If to this one adds spouses whose ages differ by only one or two years (that is, also of the same age for all practical purposes), the total is 34%, and among taxpaying people even 37%. . . However, in the overwhelming majority of cases (70%) the husband is older than the wife. It was apparently regarded as preferable that the bride be from three to five or even as much as ten years younger than the groom (the situation obtaining in nearly half the marriages . . .) . . . In only 9% of marriages was the wife older than the husband, and in these cases the difference was most often a year or two, never exceeding 10 years. But it is important to note that this kind of unequal marriage was twice as frequent among the clergy (18%). This may be explained by the long-standing practice of having parishes served by sons-in-law taken into the home of the father-in-law. When one married "into a parish" the age of the bride was not of particular significance.

Finally, let us attempt to derive from our sources some information on the age of townsfolk at marriage. This is quite difficult, due to the absence of direct information, but it is possible to derive indirect data by comparing the ages of mothers and children living in the family. . . .

[O]ne can . . . say that in Ustiuzhna it was comparatively rare for girls to be married off at less than 15, that marriage occurred most often between the ages of 19 and 24, but there were also cases in the 30–35 range. If we recall that it was apparently preferred that the groom be three to five years older than the bride, the probable ages of men at marriage turn out approximately as follows: rarely under the ages of 18 to 20, and most often between 24 and 27. . . .

The notion held by foreign travelers that Russians married extremely young, boys being married off even at age 12, is something of an exaggeration even for the mid-seventeenth century, at least as far as townsfolk are concerned.

All in all, analysis of the data of the *Landrat* census of the town of Ustiuzhna Zheleznopol'skaia leads us to the conclusion that the urban family at the beginning of the eighteenth century was in many respects similar to the family in other Russian towns of an earlier period, and that its principal features of structure, which apparently became established back in the seventeenth century, persisted into later times, the eighteenth and nineteenth centuries. Here we had primarily the nuclear paternal family, which was also observed in other Russian regions, particularly along the Volga and in Siberia.

The extended patriarchal family that had existed at one time had not persisted in Ustiuzhna, where there was but a small number of undivided fraternal families. The tendency for an extended family of this kind to arise was stronger among townsfolk possessing some property that heirs did not wish to fragment, be this a merchant business or a pottery. . . . But there was a relatively smaller number of such families. Neither property nor fiscal considerations (which were essentially the same) could preserve the extended family, that had retreated into the past.

SOURCE: M. G. Rabinovich, "The Russian Urban Family at the Beginning of the Eighteenth Century," *Soviet Studies in History* XXI, 2 (Fall, 1982): 63–69, 76, 80–81, 83–86 (excerpted). Originally published as "Russkaia gorodskaia sem'ia v nachale XVIII v.," *Sovetskaia etnografiia* (1978) 5: 96–108. Copyright © 1982 by M. E. Sharpe Inc. Reprinted by permission of the publisher.

MARC RAEFF
The Home and School Life of a Young Nobleman

These excerpts from Marc Raeff's provocative essay on the eighteenth-century nobility pays little attention to the demographic or economic organization of the family, unlike the previous two essays. But they do make a number of valuable—and at times surprising—suggestions about the upbringing of noble boys, the organization of authority within the household, the complex inequalities of relations across the boundaries of social status, and the differences between male and female spheres. We should keep in mind that the life which this selection describes required a considerable income, far more than even most noble families could hope to accumulate. Still, one cannot help but notice the many differences that distinguished a noble family from the other family systems that we have observed. Less visible, perhaps, are the similarities, but they, too, deserve our attention.

The Russian nobility of the 18th century played a major role in their country's development not only as its leading class in the 18th century but also as the seedbed of its cultural elite and intelligentsia in the 19th century. . . . The material available on some of the important aspects of childhood in 18th century Russia is unfortunately limited. But it still reveals certain interesting facts. Most members of the Russian nobility born toward the middle of the 18th century were born on the estates of their fathers. Their early years would be spent in the rural environment of these estates, though the winter months would often be passed in the city. The family was still predominantly patri-archal. But most of the time the father would be away on service. Even after 1762 it was only the invalid or extremely poor nobles who failed to spend a good part of their active life in service. As countless memoirs show, a nobleman on service was unable to visit his estate and family very often, and sometimes he stayed away for years. His children and particularly his sons thus grew up in an alternation of almost anarchical freedom and shorter periods of very strict discipline and control. It is true, as the examples of the families of Sergey Aksakov and Ivan Turgenev show, that the authority of a mother and grandmother might sometimes be greater than that of a father. But it was no adequate substitute for the father's authority, especially a father endowed with an officially and socially sanctioned authority as an officer or government official.

Not all the nobles on service left their families behind on the estate. Some would have their immediate family with them in the place where their service was carried out. But in spite of the father's presence there was little feeling of permanency even here. Service needs forced families to move frequently from one town or garrison to another. Residence in a town also meant separation from the larger family and the estate, and attachment to family and estate was an important aspect of a nobleman's life both emotionally and economically. Except among the few members of the most 'aristocratic' families of dignitaries, the feeling prevailed throughout the 18th century that residence in the city or town was only temporary, and that the nobleman's place was in the countryside, on an estate.

The practice of dividing the estate among all the children . . . continued to flourish in spite of Peter the Great's efforts to change it in his decree of 1714 on single inheritance; and to the extent that the inheritance had to be divided as fairly as possible each heir would receive lots in several estates or possibly one of these several estates if this proved more convenient. As the original property was split up and the size of the estates decreased, noblemen found it necessary, or at least desirable, to acquire new property. This could be done in a variety of ways such as purchase, marriage, and exchange. But as often as not the new property was not assembled around the nucleus of the old estate. Instead the old estate tended to be sold or exchanged, and the family moved to a new area. Resettlement of this kind was particularly dramatic in new areas like the Ukraine and middle Volga, as Sergey Aksakov's unforgettable picture shows. Alternatively the separate bits of property would be retained, and the family would live on them in turn. This meant that it would move from one province to another every few years or possibly oftener.

The general result was that the Russian nobleman of the 18th century normally lacked strong roots in any particular area and had no real feeling of attachment to a specific locality and to a family estate on which his ancestors had lived for generations. The estate was simply a piece of property; the value placed on it was limited by its economic worth; and it was easily interchangeable with another estate of equal economic worth. There is little evidence of the attachment to and ties with the ancestral home which characterised the mentality of western noblemen. On the contrary the Russian nobleman tended to feel 'at home' whichever estate he moved to. This feeling was fostered by the country's geographical uniformity and the identity of basic social conditions such as serfdom, which also strengthened the idea that every estate in Russia was interchangeable with any other. When a nobleman settled on another estate he had no impression that he was moving into a different environment, all the more so if he followed the example of the Aksakovs and had his serf families move with him. . . .

The absence of deep local roots and the overwhelming feeling of the uniformity of the Russian land and of the universal sameness of the social environment were undoubtedly among the important and permanent experiences of the Russian nobleman. They were also experiences acquired from childhood onwards and may go far towards explaining the nobleman's detachment from the soil and easy adaptability to the capitals and to foreign lands. They may also help to explain why the Russian nobleman often thought of his country, his nation, Russian in short, as a sort of complete entity, a general category, even an abstraction. . . .

Another very important element in the early experiences of the Russian nobleman which is too often overlooked is that as a child he was in the care and under the supervision of serf nursemaids, tutors, and servants. These serfs had no rights and very rarely any powers of discipline. When clashes and conflicts occurred it was always the young master who prevailed and the serf nurses or tutors who had to give away and see their authority undermined by parents who seldom sided against their children. These children must also have been quick to sense from the bad example which their parents set them that the serfs need not be much considered or respected and were a kind of second-rate adult who had to be guided and supervised and were obliged to comply with their own wishes and caprices. The young nobleman thus suffered little from the authority and controls and had his whims easily gratified. He was able to give orders to grown-ups who had him under their care and was able to make use of other human beings to gratify his wishes. This meant that he could exercise his will on others even from an early age. Evidence is available to show that once the young *barchuk* had acquired some western knowledge he would try to transform his serf nurse, tutor, or playmates according to the idea of human nature which he had formed for himself. The general results were well described by a contemporary in the following words: "[serf-nurses] accustom the child to believe that his will must be executed without question; he gets used to this, and when he grows up this passion increases and the consequence is that the child entrusted to their care often becomes a slave to his passions, for without the approval of the nurse he could not have let his passions manifest themselves so easily and with such success."

After the carefree years on the estate came the time to go to school and learn. Education for nobles was made compulsory by Peter the

Great who needed men with at least a rudimentary education for his modernised armies and administration. The obligation to learn, go to school, and pass examinations in order to be considered legally of age did not at first suit the average nobleman who strongly resisted it. . . . But education nevertheless took hold of the majority of noblemen as the century progressed.

It became a matter of pride as well as a requirement for a satisfactory career in the state service to possess whatever was considered the minimum of education at the time. It was their higher level of education, greater degree of culture, and more sophisticated style of life, which distinguished the nobility from other classes of society. In the absence of a clear legal definition of nobility, which resulted from the confusion caused by the conflicting claims of service and birth as the basis for noble status, participation in a cultured way of life came to be regarded as the real criterion. The very poor and uneducated nobleman. . .was hardly considered to belong to the nobility and became assimilated to the peasantry in the course of the century.

The obligation to undertake education involved attendance at school. . . . Boys were sent to school at an early age, which might vary from about six or seven to twelve or thirteen. As schools were not very numerous, distances great, transport difficult, and families often on the move, the pupils lived and spent nearly all their time in school and remained separated from their families throughout the year and often for several years at a stretch. Special family circumstances might sometimes even keep a child at school and away from his home and family for the whole duration of his studies, and it was only when he finished school that he would revisit his family, almost as a stranger, on his way to his service appointment. Whatever the circumstances, the break with the previous way of life and environment was undoubtedly radical and often caused a psychological shock. . . .

To appreciate the element of psychological shock it should be remembered that to go to school meant not only to leave home but also to come under discipline and into a new and almost artificial atmosphere after years of capricious and virtually anarchic freedom on the estate. Prevailing pedagogical practices and the need for preparing the boys for a state service which was primarily military meant that discipline in schools was strict and military in character. The nature of the education provided also added greatly to the feeling of isolation, bewilderment, and disorientation. Since Peter the Great's time the main function of education in Russia had been to help in the country's modernization and westernization and in the creation of a new type of Russian who would be European-minded and modern and capable of actively serving a modern and power-directed state. The aim of all Russian educators like the Cadet Corps and the boarding schools connected with Moscow University and the Academy of Sciences was to remove and isolate the pupils from their traditional environment, from the 'barbarous' and uneducated serf tutors, and from the insufficiently westernised families, in order to be better able to fashion them according to their own very different lights. Hence the attempts to keep them in school as long as possible without allowing them to return to the family. Betskoy's project, for example, advocated a period of twelve years.

It is not surprising in these circumstances that school took the place of home, and that fellow students and the more popular teachers became the real family. The boys developed a feeling of closeness and a strong spiritual bond with one another. . . . As most of the friendships made at school were continued within the framework of state service and social and intellectual contacts in the capitals, a group solidarity was formed which rested not on family relationships (though these often existed in some circles) or on regional connections, but rather on a common educational experience. Those involved had shared the important and powerful experiences of discovering the worlds of ideas and emotions during adolescence, while cut off from their families and childhood environment and kept apart from the outside world by the cold discipline of an impersonal institution. At the same time their experiences isolated them from the lives and problems of those who had never shared these experiences with them. It thus became easier for them to conceive the outside world and those belonging to it as objects to be acted upon in the light of their experience than to think of them as something of which they themselves were part and with which they would have to share the future. . . .

In school the young Russian nobleman received a completely western education which had practically submerged the Muscovite traditions of learning and education by the middle of the 18th century. . . . The infatuation with foreign languages and the western content of Russian education in the 18th century are too well known from literature and the reports of foreign travellers to need elaboration. What is more important to remember is that the education had no ties with the traditional culture of pre-Petrine Russia. The schools barely mentioned old Russian literature and history, and the repeated calls for a better knowledge of the Russian language indicate that even this was a rather neglected subject. . . .

It is also important to realise that the content of this western-oriented education gave it a special dynamic function in Russia. In the west itself education never isolated children from their natural environment and the realities of their country however strictly they may have been treated in institutions such as Jesuit establishments and the later English public schools. The reason why it had the opposite effect in Russia is not far to seek. Peter the Great's reforms had produced a sharp break in the historical continuity of the Russian nobility's consciousness, and the traditional values and ways of thought and action of the Muscovite boyars had all been pushed out and discarded within one or at the most two generations. Among what was abandoned were prejudices and much that was antiquated and useless. But spiritual and moral traditions were rejected as well, and their place was taken by the western ideas and models acquired at school. These were not felt to be merely substitutes. On the contrary, like all newly acquired values they were regarded as absolutes. In the west they were counter-balanced by traditional customs and habits or conflicting norms. In Russia by contrast they became imperatives to be applied as closely and completely as possible. . . .

The reign of Peter the Great had produced a break in Russian historical consciousness, or more accurately in the feeling for historical continuity. The members of the Russian *elite* felt themselves to be new men (as many were in practice), dedicated to the task of radical transformation. In Max Weber's sense, their whole frame of mind was 'rationalistic' rather than 'traditionalistic'. For this reason they were particularly receptive to the rationalist, geometric, absolutist, uniformity-oriented, and universal ideas and attitudes amounted to Utopianism which they were able to derive from the west. Their 'rationalistic' frame of mind in its turn grew out of their psychological experiences within the framework of Russia's basic institutions of family, school, and service.

SOURCE: Marc Raeff, "Home, School, and Service in the Life of the 18th-Century Russian Nobleman," *Slavonic and East European Review* 40 (1962): 295–303 (excerpted). Reprinted by permission of the editors of *Slavonic and East European Review*.

B. Women's Lives

D O C U M E N T S

The Memoirs of Anna Evdokimovna Labzina, An Eighteenth-Century Noblewoman (1810)

Anna Labzina came from a reasonably prosperous and—as the passage below vividly shows—extremely devout family which divided its time between provincial residences and the capital. After being given away in marriage at age fifteen she spent most of her adult life in the company of her husband's companions, several of whom helped to organize the Imperial Russian Bible Society during the reign of Alexander I, an organization that was dedicated to disseminating the Russian-language Bible to a lay audience.

Labzina herself had been educated at home, and she spent a good deal of time during the latter stages of her life penning her own impressions of the life that she lived. The *Memoirs* were composed in 1810 and they cover a wide range of experiences. Written in a sentimental style that was popular in its day but that is somewhat grating to a modern reader, they demonstrate a remarkable, and in some ways very modern, sensitivity to questions of gender, authority, and the powerlessness of young noblewomen. As she presents it, her adolescence was completely dominated by a variety of figures—her mother, her husband, and then the heads of the various households in which she lived—whose authority she felt compelled to accept. This passage, describing her life shortly before her fourteenth birthday, reflects on her betrothal and marriage.

Passion Week arrived, and on Friday evening I went to the prisons with my nanny, and behind us the horses carried all the wares that we were to hand out. But everything was twice its normal quantity. It was as if my mother had foreseen that this was to be the last time that we would do this. We entered the prison quickly, and then all those unfortunate people began to weep and asked whether my mother was still alive and whether there was any hope for her recovery.

I too was weeping, and I told them that my mother was in danger. "Pray, my friends, that God will save her!"

They all grew silent and bowed their heads. One said with a groan: "God Our Lord, do You truly want to take her away from us and leave us orphans and without any help?" And, turning to me, he asked: " Kind child, will you be like your mother and not leave us when she is gone?"

With tears in my eyes I said that I would respect her instructions and her will as if it were the law and I would come to visit them with my friend as my mother had.

They all said: "God bless you and grant you happiness now and forever."

Easter Sunday arrived and my mother appeared to be somewhat stronger. All the relatives had dinner at our house, and Alexander Matveevich [Labzin, her future husband] said: "Treat me as a relative and allow me to spend a day with you."

All of Holy Week was passed grimly in contemplation of my mother's illness; I never left her side, and I read to her from Scripture. At night I slept beside her bed, but even sleep eluded me. And when I would fall asleep, horrible dreams disturbed me, and I would awaken once more. In the week after Easter his sister arrived and asked to have a word with

Popular images of women: "The Milkmaids." From *Pushkinskii Peterburg* (Leningrad, 1972).

mama. And when I had gone out she conveyed Alexander Matveevich's proposal to be accepted as a son. My mother demurred due to my youth, but his sister said that my youth would be protected from everything. "She shall have another mother who shall love her and shall hold her to any charge that might be given to her."

But knowing that she did not have long to live, the thought of being separated from me frightened my mother even more. So on that day she didn't say anything decisive. Left by herself, she called to my nanny who stayed with her for some time. When she finally emerged she was all in tears.

Seeing her in this state, I threw myself upon

ЧЕТЫРЕ ЛЮБАЧИ СЕРДЕЦЪ, ВЫІГРАХЪ ІЗЗАБАВАХЪ БРЕМА ПРОВОДАЮ
ІЗДРАВЫЕ ЛЮБЕЗНЫХЪ, ПОПОЛНОИ ІСПОЧТЕНИЕМЪ ВЫПИВАЮТЪ,
ХОТА БЫЛИ РАЗГОВОРЫ, НЕНАВИРША ХЪ Ѧ ЛЮБЕЗНЫ ІПЛЕН НЫ:
ІОТВЗГЛАѦОВЪ ѦРУГЪ КОѦРУГУ, ВЛЮБОВНОИ СТРАСТІ РАСПАЛЕННЫ
ЗГОВОРІВШІСЪ БУѦЕТЪ КОЗЫРЬ, ТОМУ ВСЛЮБЕЗНО ПОПОЦАЛУЮ Ѧ ѦТЬ
ІСТАЛІ ТАКЪ МОЛЧАЛВО, ЧТО КОМПАНІА СКУЧНА БУѦЕМЪ ЛУТЧЕ ВРѦ
ОѦІНЪ ОТВЕРНУЛСѦ, ЗѦРУГОИ УЛЫБНУЛСѦ, ѦРУГОИ ѦѦЕТЪ ЗНѦКЪ
КАКУЮ КАРТУ ѦѦТЬ. ВЕНЕРѦ ОТБАХУСѦ ПРИСЛАНА УГОѰѦЕТЪ
СКОРО ИХЪ ИГРУ ѦРУГОИ ИГРОИ ОКОНЧѦЕТЪ ,

Popular images of women: "Four Loving Hearts," a stylized view of society women idly chatting and playing cards. Woodblock print from the late eighteenth century.

her and asked: "I can see that we are going to lose her; do you, too, honestly think that she is at death's door?"

My nanny simply said, "Pray, dear mother, and ask God for his mercy."

I again went to see my mother, who appeared upset. And she gave the order to send for my uncle and aunt. And when they arrived she spoke with them for a long time. My heart was pounding, I don't know from what, and it was saddened by all these secret negotiations. I had no idea what any of this meant. When the conversation was over my aunt and uncle emerged in tears. And all of this surprised and frightened me, but out of respect I did not make so bold as to ask anything.

And, so, the matter was resolved without me. Alexander Mikhailovich got word of it three days later, but no one said anything to me. . . .

At last the day which had been fixed for our wedding arrived. Early in the morning my mother sat me down and began to speak: "Now, my friend, this is the day on which you

Popular images of women: "Baba Iaga [The Witch-Baby] and the Bald Old Man." Baba Iaga is a well-known female figure of supernatural evildoing in Russian folklore. Woodcut from the first quarter of the eighteenth century.

begin a completely new life, one you know nothing about. You shall no longer be dependent upon me, but upon your husband and your mother-in-law, to whom you should show unbounded obedience and true love. You shall no longer take orders from me, but from them. My authority over you has come to an end, and what remains is love alone and friendly advice. Love your husband with a pure and fervent love, obey him in everything: you shall not be submitting to him but to God, for God has given him to you and made him your master. If he is cruel to you, then you shall bear it all patiently and oblige him. Don't complain to anyone. People will not come to your assistance, and all you will do is expose his weaknesses, and through this you shall bring him and yourself to shame. Always conduct yourself in such a manner that your conscience will be forever clear. Do not favor another man over him, even if he wears a crown. Do not pay any attention to the flirtations of men, they are never sincere. He who loves you directly will not attempt to flatter. Conduct yourself so that no man would be so bold as to say something

indecent, and do not have any close contact with any man of whom your husband does not approve. But be careful about this too. In your choice of friends don't rely on yourself, but defer to the choices of your new mother, who, out of her love for her son and for you, will provide you with kind and worldly friends from whom you shall learn. Hide nothing from her that is in your heart, and in that way you shall be spared many misfortunes that might otherwise befall you. Don't even conceal whom you speak with, for she will know those people and will show you with whom you can carry on relations and with whom you can't. Your own sincerity will spare you from a great deal. If, in your youthfulness, you commit some indiscretion, don't be ashamed to reveal it, for in revealing it you avoid doing it again. Love your husband's mother, for she is your own. She is another me. Will you promise me, as your friend, that you will do all of this?"

I threw myself at her knees and wept. "I shall do exactly as you say, even if they become my enemies and tormentors." . . .

So, a week after the wedding we moved to the country, but my mother's illness got worse, and we had to take her to town, not a great distance, only about sixty miles away. But she was so weak that every little movement caused her great suffering. And here began my first source of grief when my husband refused to let me sit with her in the carriage, and I obeyed him with grief-stricken tears, but without uttering a word. This journey was sheer torture for me; all gladness inside me died, and I felt nothing except a profound grief, and my thoughts were constantly with the sick one. Who will comfort her now? She is used to me, and I have eased her pain. This cruel man is depriving her of her only remaining comfort in her final days. Those were my very thoughts. In these depths only tears eased the burden.

My husband became enraged over these tears and he said to me: "Now your love should be all mine and you should give no thought to anything but how to please me. You now live for me and for no others."

I asked: "What could possibly diminish my love for her who is more precious to me than anything else in the world? Do you love your mother any less now that you are married? I'll do anything in the world for you, except this!"

He answered me: "You still don't understand the great obligations that you have toward a husband. So I will teach you!"

And he said this in a voice that made my heart stop with fear. I grew silent, but I could not stop crying.

His favorite niece was sitting with us, and she laughed at my grief, saying to him: "I'm amazed that you don't make her stop. I'm sick of seeing these useless tears!"

He said: "Just you wait, my friend, there's still time. I don't want to start anything while we're travelling."

What was I to expect after these words? But my mother had placed in my heart [the vow] not to say anything and not to complain. Even more, I didn't want my mother to witness my grief. At last we arrived at the first station. I leapt out of the carriage to see whether or not my mother was still alive. I found her in such a weakened state that she couldn't speak or even give me her hand. I gave her some wine to drink and rubbed her with some vinegar, after which she got a bit stronger and asked me: "Are you well, my friend? Isn't your face unusually pale?"

"I am well, but your illness frightens me."

"What are you so scared of? Of course, I feel that I am rapidly approaching eternity."

I saw that we must not move her without letting her rest. I asked to be permitted to spend the night in the station. But my husband said to me: "You are not spending the night here. You're coming with me."

Beg as I might to be allowed the pleasure of being at my mother's side: "At least I'll be able to see how she is doing and whether she can be moved."

He answered: "They'll do all of that without you."

I went to see my mother-in-law, who, seeing my pale complexion and my swollen eyes, embraced me and asked: "What has happened to you?"

I responded that we were leaving at once, and my sick mother was being left behind, that I was afraid that she might die. I then fell to my knees: "Do me this first kindness. Stay with her and I shall be much more at ease!"

She began to weep and said even if I had not asked that she would not leave her alone, and she would keep her as peaceful as she could. My nanny was not with us since she had been sent ahead to town to make the necessary preparations for us. And so we went to town, leaving mother behind. It seemed to me that I would never see her again, and I barely remember how the trip ended. We arrived in town around supper time. Nanny met us and prepared supper. I couldn't eat a thing since I had been crying so much. And my bitter tears caused my niece to laugh all the more, when she should have been crying along with me. You see, my mother had been her benefactress. . . .

We arrived in St. Petersburg and went straight to Mikhail Matveevich's [Kheraskov, a very well-known writer and journalist] house, who was at that time the vice president of the

College of Mining. . . . And thus began a completely new way of life. My benefactors, upon seeing how young I was, took me as a daughter and began to provide me with an upbringing. My lessons began, and they advised me to stay busy all the time, and they even set out a schedule of when to get up and when to start to work. Getting up so early was burdensome to me at the outset, because my husband had taught me to get up late and drink tea in bed before washing. I had even begun to neglect my prayers to God because they considered them unnecessary. I rarely went to church, and all those rules that my mother had given me were now utterly forgotten. When I did recall the poor and misfortunate, there weren't any opportunities to do anything about it.

Now that I was living with my honored benefactors all of this was renewed. I got up early, I prayed to God, in the morning I occupied myself with a good book which they would choose for me. I still had never had the misfortune of reading a novel [*roman* in Russian], and I hadn't even heard the word. One time they began to discuss some books that had just come out, and they happened to mention a novel which I had already heard about several times. Finally I asked Elisaveta Vasil'evna [Kheraskova] about who this 'Roman' was she kept talking about, and why I had never seen him. At that point it was said to me that they were not discussing a person but books with that name; "but it is not a good idea for you to read them so soon."

And, seeing my childhood innocence and great ignorance of everything, especially the customs of polite society, they started keeping me out of the way. When they were entertaining a large number of guests I was to sit with my benefactor and father even though this saddened me at first. I must never be taken by anyone to the theater or out walking. My husband at that point had no authority over me, and he was spending entire days over at the Corps of Cadets. Since he had been newly installed, there was a lot for him to do.

This sort of upbringing was altogether new to me. They told me that I didn't have to say everything that I was thinking. Not to put much stock in flatterers; to pay no heed to flirtatious men, and not to develop any close friendships with men; not to select my acquaintances according to my own taste; to love most of all those who tell me my shortcomings, and to be grateful. "Such straightforward people are your friends (said Kheraskov). While you are here you have no one besides us, and we are your friends. And, seeing that you have been raised with good manners—your manners it seems are tender and soft—then I am sure that you will love me and open up to me all your thoughts, intentions, and even the slightest motions of your heart, your conversations with others, especially with men. Don't be frightened of my strictness. You will find me to be an indulgent father and friend, and if I do anything unpleasant to you, then it is only for your own good and future happiness. I'm not going to say anything about being civil and warm to people, because you already are."

He asked me how I had been raised and what rules I had been given, how I spent my time and how the time was organized. I told him everything. He embraced me and said: "Give thanks to your kind and honorable tutoresses, pray for them, and never forget their instructions. Strive to say your prayers faithfully every morning, ask Him for His mercy, and every evening give thanks for the day you have spent. Begin every activity asking your Maker for assistance. Your journey in the world is just beginning, and the path along which you will travel is very slippery. Without a guide you will fall, my friend. And now I am your guide, given to you by God. That person is happy who does not journey alone in youth, but has a guide. Will you select me to be among your friends, and will you trust me to be your indulgent father?" I wept and took his hand, which I clasped firmly to my heart: "So long as this keeps beating I shall not stop loving you and calling you dear father and instructor of my youth!"

At that time I was fourteen, and from that very day I was under his complete authority. I was told that they would demand direct and complete obedience, submissiveness, humility, meekness, and patience from me, so that I would not take any independent actions, but simply listen, stay silent, and obey. I promised everything. . . .

When we arrived they were staying at the summer cottage. They had a large family, but the harmony among them was such as I had never seen,—never even heard of. The eldest in the family was the one whom I called father. I was in good spirits at the cottage. They hadn't yet begun their real work with me, but instead they acquainted me with their relatives and friends. This state of affairs continued for three months, and I became everyone's favorite. My own relations could not have been more loving, and I felt nothing but happiness. I sent word to my mother-in-law about where I was and what was happening, and I set it all out in detail. She was immensely pleased, and she wrote the most heart-felt letter to my benefactors and she gave me over to their protection. "I am now content," she said: "my circumstances, perhaps, shall keep me separate from her for some time, but I know that she shall be in good hands."

At last we arrived in town where my upbringing commenced at once. That was extraordinarily tough for me, and I wished I could have just stopped it. My benefactor saw this, but he never lost hope, and just kept on correcting me. Guests would often drop by and it was very jolly, but I was never allowed into their presence. I only saw them at dinner and supper. Occasionally, on someone's nameday, or at a dinner-party ball, they would let me in, but only until midnight. And even that was late for me; when I offered my good-bys to everyone, they were all sorry to see me go, and feeling chagrined, I left as quickly as I could. At times like those I was so angry that I wanted my benefactor just to die. I could not love him any more, but fear and shame led me to do as he wanted. He often would shame me in front of everyone, regaling them with my stupidities. But within about seven or eight months I began to feel love toward him, and day-by-day my affection and open-heartedness returned.

SOURCE: *Vospominaniia Anny Evdokimovny Labzinoi, 1758–1828* (St. Petersburg, 1914), pp. 18–24, 47–50 (excerpted). Translated by Gary Marker.

Nadezhda Durova,
The Cavalry Maiden (1836)

Nadezhda Andreevna Durova (1783–1866) lived a most extraordinary life as a young noblewoman who, in rebellion against what she saw as the suffocating bounds of female identity, masqueraded as a man and joined the Russian Imperial cavalry during the Napoleonic wars. Her complete memoir is now available in English with full annotations, thanks to Mary Zirin's capable translation. This brief selection comes from Durova's memories of her childhood home, and, with hindsight, reflects her own sense of self-discovery and her observations on male and female spheres in the world of the nobility. How would you compare her outlook to Labzina's?

With each passing day I grew more bold and enterprising, afraid of nothing on earth except my mother's wrath. It seemed quite odd to me that other girls of my age were frightened of being left alone in the dark; on the contrary, I was prepared in the dead of night to go into a graveyard, a forest, a deserted house, a cave, or a dungeon. In short, there was nowhere I would not have gone as boldly at night as in the daytime. Although I, like other children, had been told tales of ghosts, corpses, wood goblins, robbers, and water nymphs who tickled people to death, and although I believed this nonsense with all my heart, none of it frightened me. On the contrary, I thirsted for dangers and longed to be surrounded by them. If I had had the least freedom, I would have gone looking for them, but my mother's vigilant eye followed my every step and impulse.

One day Mama and some ladies went for an outing into the dense pine forest on the far side of the Kama. She took me with her, as she put it, to keep me from breaking my neck alone at home. This was the very first time in my life that I had been taken out into the open where I could see dense forest and vast fields and the wide river! I could barely catch my breath for joy, and we no sooner came into the forest than I, out of my mind with rapture, immediately ran off and kept running until the voices of the company were no longer audible. Then my joy was complete and perfect: I ran, frisked, picked flowers, and climbed to the tips of tall trees to see farther. I climbed slender birches and, holding tight to the crown, leaped off; the sapling set me down lightly on the ground. Two hours flew like two minutes! In the meantime they were searching for me and calling me in chorus. I heard them, but how could I part with such captivating freedom? At last, completely exhausted, I returned to the company. I had no trouble locating them, because the voices had never stopped calling me. I found my mother and the other ladies in a terrible state of anxiety. They cried out in joy when they caught sight of me, but Mama, who guessed from my contented face that I had not strayed, but gone off of my own volition, flew into a violent rage. She poked my back and called me a damned pest of a girl, sworn to anger her always and everywhere!

We returned home. Mama pulled me by the ear all the way from the parlor to her bedroom. She took me over to the lace pillow and ordered me to get to work without straightening up or looking around. "Just you wait, you wretch, I'll tie you on a rope and give you nothing but bread to eat!" With these words she went to tell Papa about what she called my monstrous act, and I was left to sort bobbins, set pins, and think about the glories of nature which I had just seen for the first time in all their majesty and beauty. From that day, although my mother's supervision and strictness became even more unremitting, they could no longer either frighten or restrain me.

From morning to night I sat over work which, I must confess, was the vilest imaginable because, unlike other girls, I could not, would not, and did not want to acquire the skill, but ripped, ruined, and tangled it until before me lay a canvas ball with a repulsive, snarled strip stretching across it—my bobbin-lace. I sat patiently over it all day, patiently because my plan

was prepared and my intentions resolute. At nightfall, when the house quieted down, the doors were locked, and the light in Mama's room went out, I got up, dressed stealthily, sneaked out across the back porch, and ran straight to the stable. There I took Alcides [her horse], led him through the garden to the cattleyard, mounted him, and rode out down a narrow lane straight to the riverbank and Startsev mountain. Then I dismounted him again and led Alcides uphill, holding him by the halter because I didn't know how to bridle him and had no way of getting him to climb the mountain of his own volition. I led him by the halter across the precipitous slope until I reached a level spot, where I looked for a stump or hillock from which to remount. Then I slapped Alcides' neck and clicked my tongue until the good steed broke into a gallop, a run, and even a breakneck dash.

At the first hint of dawn I returned home, put the horse in the stable, and went to sleep without undressing. This was what led at last to the discovery of my nocturnal excursions. The maid who took care of me kept finding me fully clothed in bed every morning and told my mother, who undertook to find out how and why this came about. She herself saw me going out at midnight fully clothed and, to her inexpressible horror, leading the wicked stallion out of the stable! She thought I must be sleepwalking and did not dare stop me or call out for fear of alarming me. She ordered the manservant and Efim to keep an eye on me, and she herself went to Papa's room, roused him, and told him what had happened. My father, astonished, got up hastily to go and see this singular occurrence for himself. But it all ended sooner than they expected: Alcides and I were led back in triumph, each to his proper place. The servant whom Mother had ordered to follow me saw me trying to mount the horse and, unlike Mama, decided that I was no sleepwalker. He came out of ambush and asked me, "And where are you going, miss?"

After this affair my mother wanted without fail to rid herself of my presence at any cost and decided to take me to my old grandmother Aleksandrovicheva in Little Russia. I had entered my fourteenth year by then. I was tall, slim, and shapely, but my martial spirit was sketched on my features and, although I had white skin, bright rosy cheeks, sparkling eyes and black brows, every day my mirror and Mama told me that I was very ugly. My face was pitted from smallpox, my features irregular, and Mother's continual repression of my freedom, her strict and at times even cruel treatment of me, had marked my countenance with an expression of fear and sadness. Perhaps I would at last have forgotten all my hussar mannerisms and become an ordinary girl like the rest if my mother had not kept depicting woman's lot in such a dismal way. In my presence she would describe the fate of that sex in the most prejudicial terms: woman, in her opinion, must be born, live, and die in slavery; eternal bondage, painful dependence, and repression of every sort were her destiny from the cradle to the grave; she was full of weaknesses, devoid of accomplishments, and capable of nothing. In short, woman was the most unhappy, worthless, and contemptible creature on earth! This description made my head reel. I resolved, even at the cost of my life, to part company from the sex I thought to be under God's curse. Papa, too, often said, "If I had a son instead of Nadezhda, I shouldn't have to worry about my old age; he would be my staff in the evening of my days." I would be ready to weep at these words from the father I loved so extravagantly. These two contradictory emotions—love for my father and aversion to my own sex—troubled my own soul with equal force. With a resolve and constancy rare in one so young I set about working out a plan to escape the sphere prescribed by nature and custom to the female sex.

Such was my frame of mind and spirit at the beginning of my fourteenth year when my mother delivered me to my grandmother in Little Russia and left me there. My grandfather was no longer alive. The family consisted of my eighty-year-old grandmother, an intelligent and pious woman who had once been a beauty and was known for her unusually gentle dis-

position; her son, my uncle, a man in his middle years, comely, kind, sensitive, and insufferably capricious, who was married to a young woman of rare beauty from the Lizogub family of Chernigov; and, finally, my aunt, a spinster about forty-five years old. I liked my uncle's young and lovely wife best, but I never remained willingly in the company of my relations; they were so grand, so devout, such implacable foes of martial propensities in a girl that in their presence I was afraid even to think about my cherished intentions. Although my freedom was in no way restricted and I could roam wherever I wanted from morning to night without fear of rebuke, I think they would have condemned me to ecclesiastic penance if I had even dared to hint at riding horseback, so unreserved was my relations' horror at the mere idea of such illicit and unnatural, to their mind, pursuits for women, and particularly girls. . . .

My mother, who no longer took any pleasure in society, led a reclusive life. I took advantage of this circumstance to win permission from my father to ride horseback. Papa ordered a Cossack *chekmen* tailored for me and gave me his Alcides. From that time on I was always my father's companion on his excursions outside the city. He took pleasure in teaching me to ride handsomely, keeping a firm seat in the saddle and managing the horse skillfully. I was a quick student. Papa admired my ease, skill, and fearlessness. He said that I was the living image of him as a youth and that, had I been born a boy, I would have been the staff of his old age and an honor to his name. This set my head a whirl, and this time for good! I was no child; I had turned sixteen. The seductive pleasures of society [and] life in Little Russia. . .faded from my memory like a dream; brightly colored scenes from my childhood in camp among the hussars were sketched in my imagination instead. It all revived in my soul. I could not understand why I had not thought of my plan for nearly two years. My grief-stricken mother now described woman's lot in even more horrific colors. Martial ardor flared in my soul with incredible force; my mind swarmed with dreams, and I began searching actively for means to realize my previous intention: to become a warrior and a son to my father and to part company forever from the sex whose sad lot and eternal dependence had begun to terrify me. . . .

At last the decisive time came to act according to the plan as I had worked it out. The Cossacks received the order to move out, and they left on September 15, 1806. Their first full day's halt would be some fifty versts from the city. The seventeenth was my name day, and the day on which, through fate, coincidence of circumstance, or invincible propensity, it was fixed for me to quit my father's house and take up an entirely new way of life. On September 17, I awoke before dawn and sat by my window to await its appearance; it might well be the last I ever saw in my own land. What awaited me in the turbulent world? Would not my mother's curse and my father's grief pursue me? Would they survive? Could they await the realization of my colossal scheme? How horrible it would be if their death took from me the goal of my actions! These thoughts now clustered and now passed one after another through my head. My heart constricted and tears glistened on my lashes. Just then dawn broke. Its scarlet glow quickly flooded the sky, and its beautiful light, flowing into my room, lit up the objects there: my father's saber, hanging on the wall directly opposite the window, seemed to catch fire. My spirits revived. I took the saber off the wall, unsheathed it, and looked at it, deep in thought. This saber had been my toy when I was still in swaddling-clothes, the comfort and exercise of my adolescent years; why should it not now be my defense and glory in the military sphere? "I will wear you with honor," I said, kissed the blade, and returned it to its scabbard. The sun rose. That day Mama presented me with a gold chain, and Papa, three hundred rubles; even my little brother gave me his gold watch. As I accepted my parents' gifts, I thought sorrowfully that they had no idea that they were outfitting me for a distant and dangerous road.

I spent the day with my girl friends. At eleven o'clock in the evening I came to say good-night to Mama as I usually did before going to bed. Unable to suppress my emotions, I kissed her hands several times and clasped them to my heart, something I had never done before nor dared to do. Although Mama didn't love me, she was moved by these extraordinary effusions of childlike affection and obedience; kissing me on the head, she said, "Go with God!" These words held a great significance for me, who had never before heard a single affectionate word from my mother. I took them as a blessing, kissed her hand for the last time, and left.

Source: Nadezhda Durova, *The Cavalry Maiden. Journals of a Russian Officer in the Napoleonic Wars.* Translated, Introduction, and Notes by Mary Fleming Zirin (Bloomington: Indiana University Press, 1988), pp. 6–9, 14–16 (excerpted). Reprinted by permission of Indiana University Press.

LITERATURE

BRENDA MEEHAN-WATERS
Catherine the Great and the Problem of Female Rule

Imperial Russia, like most other societies, tended to distribute authority along a few fundamental matrixes, such as social standing, generations, and gender. Nowhere were the assumed virtues of patriarchy more transparent than within politics: government and formal rulership were deemed to be a male preserve, and political authority was thought to descend in a patrilinear line from God the father, to the Tsar-father, and from him to the ruling institutions. During the seven decades between 1725 and 1796, however, Russia was ruled by a woman for all but about three and a half years. In this selection Brenda Meehan-Waters discusses how Russian thinkers confronted this anomaly.

Power is a magnet, alternately attracting and repelling people. When power is held by a woman, the ambivalence and complexities become heightened. Such ambivalence is found in the character descriptions of Catherine the Great written during her lifetime. These character descriptions reveal both the reactions of the authors towards a woman who exercised power and their underlying attitudes toward women in general. The voluminous literature on Catherine the Great contains gratuitous remarks and asides on the nature of women and the problem of female rule, although these occur more frequently in the works of West European writers than of Russians.

The memoirs of foreign ambassadors to the Russian court offer particularly striking insights into the attitudes of Catherine's Western contemporaries toward women. James Harris, First Earl of Malmesbury, clearly indicates this tendency. Speaking of Catherine, he says:

Her majesty has a masculine force of mind, obstinacy in adhering to a plan, and intrepidity in the execution of it; but she wants the more manly virtues of deliberation, forbearance in prosperity and accuracy of judgment, while she possesses in a high degree the weaknesses vulgarly attributed to her sex—love of flattery, and its inseparable companion, vanity; an inattention to unpleasant but salutary advice; and a propensity to voluptuousness which leads to excesses that would debase a female character in any sphere of life.

Even Voltaire and Diderot, Catherine's most distinguished public relations agents abroad, were continuously conscious of her gender. Voltaire took a delight in the fact that the Moslem Turks were being humiliated by a woman. His correspondence with Catherine is always witty and flirtatious. . . . Diderot was willing to exempt Catherine from the double standard

of morality, distinguished between "the decencies and the virtues, the worn-out rags of your sex," and the "large views and masculine patriotic designs, which are the proper concern of monarchs."

Russian descriptions of Catherine less often betray this tendency to generalize Catherine's individual characteristics into female ones and to dwell on the exceptionalness of a woman in power. Catherine had her critics in Russia, but they were less likely to pinpoint her faults as those of a woman, just as her idolators seldom saw the source of her greatness in her femininity.

The character sketches of Catherine II drawn by Prince M. M. Shcherbatov and N. M. Karamzin provide two notable exceptions. Shcherbatov's famous . . . On the Corruption of Morals in Russia indicted Catherine's reign. Despite grave misgivings about Catherine's moral character, however, Shcherbatov grudgingly acknowledges her abilities:

It cannot be said that she is unqualified to rule so great an empire, if indeed a woman can support this yoke, and if human qualities alone are sufficient for this supreme office.

This aside on women parallels his statement that "generally speaking, women are more prone to despotism than men, and as far as she is concerned, it can justly be averred that she is in this particular a woman among women."

In his . . . Historical Eulogy to Empress Catherine II, Karamzin assumes unique masculine and feminine characteristics that carry into styles of rule. Contrasting the achievements of Peter the Great and Catherine the Great, Karamzin argues that the work of Catherine completed and complemented the work of Peter:

Two souls, two characters, with so many differences between them, nevertheless worked in astonishing harmony for the well-being of the Russian people. In order to confirm the glory of the bold, masculine, awesome Peter, it was necessary that forty years later Catherine should reign. In order to foresee the glory of the gentle, philanthropic, enlightened Catherine, it was necessary that a woman reign.

In the . . . Memoir on Ancient and Modern Russia, Karamzin affirms that the main achievement of "this unforgettable queen was to soften autocracy without emasculating it." Karamzin, falling into the habit common to many foreign contemporaries of Catherine, describes positive characteristics as masculine ones. For example, "Catherine's spirit was firm, masculine and truly heroic." On the other hand, her negative traits become characteristic of her sex:

Catherine—a great statesman at principal states assemblies—proved a woman in the minutiae of royal activity. She slumbered on a bed of roses, she was deceived or else deceived herself.

Pavel Sumarokov, in ... *Characteristics of Catherine the Great*, provides a more typical example of Russian perceptions of Catherine. He relies heavily on foreign sources and quotes extensively from them. As a result, the contrast between his own frame of reference and that of his foreign sources becomes all the more delineated. In the citation of passages from such authors De Ligne, Segur, Tannenburg, etc., characteristics such as deception and vanity appear as female traits, such virtues as strength and intelligence masculine. By contrast, in his own character sketch of Catherine II, Sumarokov never mentions the word "woman." He argues that history has shown that rulers are either distinguished by their conquests or by their concern for their subjects. Unlike Karamzin, however, he does not make this into a male-female dichotomy. Frederick the Great is his example of an outstanding conqueror; King Alfred, the concerned ruler. According to him, Catherine's strength consists in her balance between these two styles of rulership.

The treatment of Catherine's individual personality traits reveals much about a writer's implicit assumptions about women, and the treatment of the problem of favorites reveals both underlying attitudes toward female rule and toward the basic power relationship between men and women. Here too a difference in tone distinguishes Western discussion from Russian. . . .

A secret agent of Louis XV to the court of St. Petersburg, Jean Charles Thibault de Lav-

eaux, painted a . . . complicated picture of the relationship between Catherine and Potemkin.

According to him, Catherine deluded herself and tried to delude others into believing that she made the controlling decisions. Laveaux dismissed this as vanity on Catherine's part, admiring Potemkin's cleverness in getting around Catherine. Potemkin supposedly kept others, such as Grigorii Orlov, her earlier lover and conspirator in the coup d'etat of 1762, and Nikita Panin, statesman and supporter of the coup, from having undue influence over Catherine by insinuating to her that they were trying to dominate her:

Since Potemkin had noticed that Catherine had the vanity to make the world believe that she governed alone, and without the help of ministers, he did not miss any opportunity to present these men as ambitious people to her, who, not content to partition among themselves the government of the Empire, wished to have all Europe see that they were the principal source of state affairs, and that the reign of Catherine derived all its sparkle from them.

According to this view, Potemkin had first gained influence over Catherine as lover and favorite, but though he was no longer favorite, "he was still the master.". . .

But Laveaux, believing that Potemkin dominated Catherine, criticized her as a ruler yet remained tolerant of her as a woman. In a slightly different version of the same tale, Catherine appears as the quintessential woman, representing all the weaknesses and foibles of women writ large. Hence, no particular man (superman or superego) dominates Catherine the woman—only her own sensuality, the sensuality of all women given a unique opportunity to express itself fully through the permissive power of the throne.

In this case, Catherine, having surrendered to sensuality, has lost mastery over herself. . . . Catherine was ruining Russia by her morals and extravagance and in the end would be judged "a weak and romantic woman."

According to such reasoning, female rule stands condemned by the presumed weakness of women and their propensity to fall under the domination of powerful lovers and advisors. Women, by nature highly emotional, cannot separate their sex lives from their jobs. But Catherine's demonstrable ability to do precisely that proved even more disturbing to several of her contemporaries. Rather than condemning Catherine for losing control of herself, some attacked her self-mastery, her coldness, and her propensity to use people. . . .

Open in his support of Grand Duke Paul, Kaspar von Saldern habitually spoke of Catherine as "une femme ambitieuse et denaturee" ["an ambitious and unnatural woman"] as though there were something inherently perverse in female ambition. He maintained that she "degraded the throne by making it an altar on which she sacrificed a great number of victims to her dangerous passions." The levity with which she chose and disposed of favorites indicated her lack of "the tenderness proper to her sex."

The wide range of Western European attitudes and opinions cannot be forced into a single mold, but the idea of a woman ruler clearly threatened many contemporaries, who responded in two ways. Some denied that the problem existed by denying that Catherine actually exercised power. For them, the question of favorites and the domination of Potemkin became a central theme. Others faced Catherine's power squarely, exaggerated it, and emphasized her ambition, manipulative characteristics and her depravity. . . .

How did the Russians handle the relationship between Catherine and her favorites, and especially that between Catherine and Potemkin? Shcherbatov does not dwell on it, mentioning Potemkin in passing as Catherine's "former lover who has remained her all-powerful friend" and bemoaning the cost "to the tune of millions of rubles" of the empress's favorite. Although he has nothing but contempt for favorites, he recognizes that Peter II and Peter III also had their minions and remarks that Empress Elizabeth maintained "regal authority" over her favorites.

In [The Memoir on Ancient and Modern Russia] Karamzin insists that Catherine was "firm, unshakable in her declared purposes. Constitut-

ing the sole spirit of all the political movements in Russia," she held "firmly in her hands the reins of power.". . .

The eighteenth-century phenomenon of female rulers did not become an issue or a special problem for Russians. Evidence from the Russian sources is overwhelming. Even writers as hostile to Catherine as G. S. Vinsky, a Ukrainian malcontent, never focuses on Catherine's femininity. I. V. Lopukhin, one of the leaders of the Moscow Free Masons, does not attribute his difficulties to the sex of the autocrat. The polemics of the famous satirist Novikov are free of misogynist statements, and Radishchev's tyrant is a male. The writings of Engel'gart and Bolotov remain strikingly silent on the subject. . . .

Since Catherine II was the last and not the first of the Russian sovereign empresses, one would not judge Russian attitudes toward female rule simply on the basis of opinions expressed about her. Four women autocrats ruled Russia during the eighteenth century. How and why the long Muscovite tradition of male tsars was broken remains unclear; little discussion of this issue took place. Unlike the long and heated debate on female rule in sixteenth-century England, signaled by John Knox's First Blast of the Trumpet Against the Monstrous Regiment of Women (1558), no similar ideological battle occurred in eighteenth-century Russia. Catherine I, wife of Peter the Great, was the first female sovereign in modern Russia—Sophia having been a regent. Her supporters justified her selection in a manifesto which argued that Peter had demonstrated his intention to make her his successor by formally crowning her two years before his death. In a manner suggestive of Western views, Peter's decree had praised his wife for her "manly courage and deeds," for her assistance to him on the battlefield during the long Northern War, and in general for her ability to "throw off the weakness of a woman."

The next logical time to discuss the issue of female rulers should have occurred during the political crisis of 1730. Of all the conditions, projects, and petitions written during that period of political exploration, the only one mentioning the subject of a woman ruler is that of Tatishchev, a student of Western political theory. One of his justifications for the need for a senate and a governing body is the proposed elevation of a woman:

Concerning the Sovereign Empress, although we are sufficiently convinced of her wisdom, good conduct and orderly government in Courland, nevertheless, since she is a female person, and thus awkward about much work, and moreover, since her knowledge of the law is inadequate, therefore, until the time when we have a Most High Person of male sex on the throne, it will be necessary to establish something to help Her Highness.

These are the only references in eighteenth-century Russian political sources to female rule. In contrast, a rich elegiac literature celebrates individual women rulers.

Much Russian poetry and prose mentions the several Russian empresses. As some of the better known panegyric verses of the century show, emphasis falls upon the exalted position and rank of the empress. Anna and Elizabeth were at times described as great military warriors, and in Tred'iakovsky's "Solemn Ode on the Surrender of the City of Danzig [Gdansk, both in the original title and the contemporary name of the city], 1734" the frequent epithet is "brave Anna," she who wields a sword and is "more august than Augustus." Lomonosov also saw no difficulty in fitting a woman into the model of the imperator, the warrior, the wrathful, the awesome. In a stanza which suggests the unity of masculine and feminine attributes, he advises the defeated Hagarites:

Come kiss the hand that showed you dread,
with sword all bloodied from the battle.
The dreadful gaze of mighty Anna
is quick to comfort those who ask.

Tred'iakovsky speaks of Anna as *imperatrix*, *tsaritsa*, and *imperatritsa* and succinctly states the reason why she deserved respect:

Everyone must esteem our Anna,
An autocrat bestowed by God.

Religious ritual, particularly the coronation ceremony, exalted the image of the autocrat. The Russian imperial coronation rite evolved during the eighteenth century, reflecting as did so many other aspects of Russian life changes introduced by Peter the Great. The Petrine imperial coronation ceremony was first performed in 1723 for the crowning of Peter's second wife, Catherine. It differed from the pre-Petrine ceremony, also based on the imperial Byzantine form, in its diminution of the role of the church and exaltation of the autocrat. Christian coronation ceremonies usually include symbolic reminders of the priestly function of the ruler. Thus, the coronation of a woman presents a problem since she is ineligible for priesthood. However, the coronation of the Empress Anna in 1730 set important precedents in the religious symbols of the ceremony. Empress Anna was the first Russian sovereign to walk up into the holy altar—the altar set aside for the clergy—for her anointing. She was also the first monarch to take Holy Communion, according to the rite of the clergy rather than the laity. In 1742, Empress Elizabeth followed these precedents while starting an important one of her own. She was the first Russian ruler to place the crown and the imperial mantle on herself, without the assistance and symbolic approval of the metropolitan. Catherine the Great followed the same ceremonial order, which became in the nineteenth century the fixed ritual for the Russian coronation rite. Thus the imperial coronation ceremony which evolved during the eighteenth century and symbolically attested to the increased power of the ruler had its origins in ceremonies designed to glorify Russia's female rulers.

But after 1797 no women ruled Russia. . . .

In sum, there is no philosophical confrontation of the issue of female rule among most Russian writers; this was not an important problem. In this respect, the Russian opinion of Catherine II and of female rule in general seems to differ from that of West European contemporaries of Catherine. On the whole, Russian writers viewed her more positively and

"Sirin the Bird Woman," a late eighteenth-century popular print. Although the text places the action in "The land of the Indians," the picture portrays a bird-like female warrior/ruler who looks suspiciously like Catherine the Great, thus popularizing her image.

displayed much less agitation over the female issue. Catherine is desexualized to the extent that she is treated as an individual rather than as a woman. A woman holding power poses few discernible psychic threats to the Russian men writing about her. . . .

The question persists as to why there should be this difference between Russian and West European perception. For the moment, I should like to suggest some possible lines of inquiry. In a provocative article entitled "Royalty and Sexual Ambiguity," Dean Miller argued that the early European and Byzantine concept is of a hermaphroditic being, uniting masculine and feminine principles, and has implied that the concentration on masculinity is a modern phenomenon. In this sense, the Russians, with their neutral attitude toward female rule suggest a premodern concept of rule and power. In a different vein, these Russians may have been demonstrating a respect for power per se regardless of the person in whom it is manifested. Or again, is it that the Russian image of the sovereign emperor had become such an abstraction that it could be held by a German princess bereft of dynastic ties?

Alternatively, are we following the most fruitful road in suggesting that it is the Russian attitude that must be examined and explained? Why not take their silence on the question of female rule as a normal and valid acceptance of the varied potentialities of women and focus instead on the West European emphasis on masculinity and the concomitant unease with a woman who is not subordinate to a man?

SOURCE: Brenda Meehan-Waters, "Catherine the Great and the Problem of Female Rule," *The Russian Review* 34, 3 (July, 1975):293–307 (excerpted). Copyright © 1975 by *The Russian Review*. Reprinted by permission of the editors of the journal.

18

Culture

The swirling winds that buffeted Russian culture during the imperial period do not lend themselves to easy characterization, except perhaps to say that the culture became much more literary, heterogeneous, and even fragmented. Muscovite Russia, as we have seen, had generated a rich and multi-dimensional culture of its own, replete with saints' lives, pagan rituals, religious poetry, heroic tales, chronicles, minstrels, holy fools, beautiful cathedrals and icons, and much more. In spite of its *apparently* low level of literacy, old Russian culture did produce an extensive manuscript tradition that found audiences at all levels of society. But for all of its complexity and dynamism, virtually everything that we know about Muscovite culture, at least as it became written down or performed, points to the centrality of spirituality and religious faith. Certainly, popular expressions and rituals often reflected confusion or out-and-out invention as to the actual teachings of Russian Orthodoxy. The true meaning of faith could also generate furious disagreements among lettered religious figures, as well, as the violent church schism of the seventeenth century graphically showed. But none of these contestations cast doubt about the centrality of faith itself.

Beginning in the late seventeenth century, and with gathering momentum in the eighteenth, the hegemony of religious faith was challenged by the advent and subsequent blossoming of an alternative outlook that we commonly term "secularization." The concept of secularization recurs frequently in historical writing, and it refers to many different phenomena. In this context "secularization" describes a shift from religious authorities, ideas, and symbols to nonreligious ones. In Russia, as elsewhere, this shift involved the emergence of large numbers of lay (i.e., not from the clergy) writers and artists, most of whose works gave precedence to improving life on earth over the pursuit of grace. Along the way it came to include new conceptions and forms of architecture, writing, language, art, and political ideology.

As with so many areas of change, the reign of Peter the Great marks a convenient point of origin. In 1707 Peter instituted a revision in the alphabet and written language, with the new "civil" script formally denoting this-worldly affairs (state, law, modern literature) and the old script, now termed "church" or "Slavonic," signifying faith or religious texts. This division between secular language and sacred language came to reflect a much more fundamental dualism in Imperial Russia between the culture of religion and the culture of secularity. The former came to be associated with tradition, antiquity, Muscovy, Tsar, and sometimes, the lower classes, backwardness, and superstition. The latter, over the course of several generations, came to be linked with the new European-styled capital of St. Petersburg, cosmopolitanism, and modernity. Even iconography, the most religious of all art, reflected the change, as some court painters dared to place the face of the ruler in paintings where Russians had been attuned to see God, Christ, or a Holy Saint.

From the middle of the eighteenth century onward, it was this cosmopolitan secular culture that gave rise to modern Russian literature—novels, short stories, literary essays—and to journalism, and ultimately the profession of letters. The famous figures of the Russian Enlighten-ment—Mikhail Lomonosov, Denis Fon Vizin, Nikolai Novikov, and a host of others—were all products of this new secularity. And in the nineteenth century, this secular world provided a fruitful environment for the salons, or "polite society" as William Todd describes it, in which a generation of brilliant writers, actors, and artists circulated, such as Alexander Pushkin, Nikolai Gogol, and Fedor Dostoevsky. During the "marvelous decade" of the 1840s, secular urban culture gave rise to a corps of critical thinkers, such as Alexander Herzen and Ivan Kireevskii, whom we refer to as the first wave of the Russian intelligentsia, and who are described by Nicholas Riasanovsky's and P. V. Annenkov's selections in this chapter.

This new world of literature, journalism, and lonely intellectual circles proved to be remark-ably creative, and its leading lights produced texts that inspired educated contemporaries and later generations as well. (Not so long ago, albeit before MTV and Bart Simpson, legions of American college students found themselves enraptured by the "passion" and "moral" com-mitment of nineteenth-century Russian writers.) Largely as a result of the rise of secular culture, Russian publishing grew from a mere handful of titles per year in the beginning of the eigh-teenth century to several hundred per year by the end of the eighteenth. On the eve of the Great Reforms, well over 1,000 Russian-language titles were being produced annually. Little wonder that Nicholas Karamzin chose to celebrate Russia's publishers and readers in his essay, "On the Book Trade and the Love for Reading in Russia," that is reproduced in this chapter.

We should not, however, be misled into thinking that the "sacred" culture that had endured for centuries somehow disappeared, or that the mass of people who were not a part of cosmo-politan society somehow lacked "culture." Literature and journals very much reflected an exclu-sive, largely noble, and generally male preserve in which the vast majority of Russians did not in any way participate. Barriers of literacy, education, social standing, and gender precluded active engagement by all but a small, mostly privileged minority of Russian subjects. By contrast, oral culture, folk tales, carnivals, puppet theater, and religious ritual remained as vital elements in the lives of common people. M. M. Gromyko's selection gives a clear synopsis of the vivacity and sophistication of peasant culture in this period, even though much of it did not call for reading and writing.

When Soviet ethnographers began compiling inventories about four decades ago of the books and artifacts kept by Russian peasants, they discovered that prayer books and religious almanacs, read over and over again and kept as heirlooms within single families from one generation to the next, remained the texts of choice for virtually all literate populations outside of secular "society." Until the latter decades of the nineteenth century, most people who learned to read, learned and preferred books of hours and saints' lives to novels. Clearly, then, imperial Russian culture was sufficiently rich to be able to accommodate the dualisms of sacred and secular, literate and aural, old and new, without one being sacrificed for the other.

A. Oral Traditions and Popular Culture

Historians nowadays are very interested in the outlooks, traditions, and expressions of the lower classes, a subject that is often termed "popular culture." In most cases, however, the sources that we use to understand how common people thought (such as fairy tales, songs, investigations of protests) were written down by—or for the benefit of—outsiders such as governmental officials and intellectuals. Such transcriptions involved selectivity, interpretation, and even outright invention. Often there is no simple means of determining where a "popular voice" ends and an elite one begins.

The documents presented in this section offer a good example of this vexing process. Popular prints, copper engravings, and chap books are collectively known as *lubki*, named for the bast fiber (*lub*) on which many of them were printed. Hundreds of these reproductions were made in Russia during the eighteenth and nineteenth centuries. Most preferred pictures to words, so that one need not have been literate to understand them, and they typically depicted scenes and themes that we presume were familiar to the peasants (what specialists call folklore). However, the majority of the *lubki* apparently were produced in urban workshops and presses, frequently on private commission from well-to-do nobles or merchants, and few traces exist of their having circulated among the peasantry.

Similarly, the fables and stories that are included in this section came into print via two very different routes. The eighteenth-century ones were actually composed by a well-known writer, Fedor Emin (1735–1770), and first published in a collection entitled *Moral Fables (Nravouchitel'nye basni)* by the Academy of Sciences Press in 1764. Although Emin's collection of fables went through three editions during the eighteenth century, they certainly never reached a wide audience, and there is no basis for imagining that they circulated, either in printed or in spoken form, among the peasants. Their language was simple and colorful, but they contained none of the local expressions and imagery that would have been employed by peasant storytellers. Hence, in what ways can either the prints or the fables be considered "popular"?

The answer to this vexing question must be conditional and tentative. We cannot reasonably argue that these texts were widely known outside of an educated urban public, or that the specific moral or ideological messages that they conveyed were derived in any sense from popular mentality. Research suggests, however, that much of their imagery, subject matter, and modes of expressions did contain extensive traces of an oral culture that was very widespread.

The other tale, "The Blacksmith and the Devil", had a more direct link to oral traditions in that it appeared as part of an anthology that the famous mid-nineteenth century folklorist Aleksandr Nikolaevich Afanas'ev published from stories that had been collected by other nineteenth-century ethnographers and linguists on their travels in the Russian countryside. Even in this case we have to depend upon the transcriptions of outsiders and on the particular versions which these outsiders heard. But we can, at least, be confident that something like these tales were told by Russian peasants during the mid-nineteenth century, and that the figures and characters from these particular tales most likely had been circulating in peasant lore for generations. We can then profitably compare the tales that Afanas'ev collected with Emin's more original reworking of similar themes and with the visual representations in the *lubki*.

D O C U M E N T S

Selections from Fedor Emin's **Moral Fables** *(1764)*

THE PEACOCK AND THE ROOSTER

The peacock, seeing a certain rooster fanning his tail, said to him, "Rooster, you're wasting your time fanning your tail like that! Believe me, no one's going to compliment you on it."

To this the rooster responded, "It's true that you have a good tail, but that's the only good thing you have. Your voice is terrible, and it's very boring to listen to. I, however, rouse hard working people to their labors every day with my singing, and they are very pleased with me. Your legs"—continued the rooster—"are really ugly, and they don't have any meat on them at all. But as for me, I am always useful to people, even when I'm dead: for they buy my meat for even more money than when I was alive. For your meat, however, no one will pay even a quarter of a kopeck. Instead they toss it out, whereas they place mine in a silver, and often even in a golden dish. So you have no reason to act so stuck-up, when all of your beauty is in your tail, and the rest of you is worth nothing at all."

The greatest and most praiseworthy virtues are not on the surface, but are within.

THE NIGHTINGALE AND THE ROSE

The nightingale, bursting with pride over his lovely singing, flew to Jupiter with a petition that Jupiter rate him first after the eagle. And, upon seeing that Jupiter was not responding to this request, the nightingale said the following, "O King of kings! You know that I sing the best of all the birds. Therefore I truly am worthy of a top rank."

To this Jupiter responded, "So, you think that you sing better than all of the other birds! It's true that many rate you higher than the other birds on this score, but the Africans like the canary's voice better than yours, and the Egyptians prefer the lark's voice to yours. And the Africans have good reason to hold such an opinion about you. They know that you do most of your singing when people are asleep. What's more, you sing for only a short time, and you remain quiet much longer. For three quarters of the year you are mute, and for only one quarter do you sing, and in the one when you do sing, it's often inappropriate."

But none of these facts could dissuade the nightingale from his demand. So, with such a stubborn bird, Jupiter was forced to use some ingenuity. He said to him, "Go, nightingale, and bring me news of how the rose produces its flower from a green twig, and how it spreads itself open, and then I shall grant your request."

The nightingale, quick as he could, flew to the rose and sang there all spring, wishing to watch it flower. But, being so preoccupied with his desire for recognition, he never did catch sight of the rose opening up. Because of this, or so the storytellers think, the nightingale became enraptured with the rose, and is forever unrequited in his love.

Those who hope for everything while they live, end up dying with nothing.

THE PEASANT AND THE DOG

A peasant had to go see his neighbor on some business. But knowing that the neighbor owned a very nasty dog, he brought a big loaf of bread with him.

When he arrived at the neighbor's house he tossed a hunk of bread to the dog, who grabbed it and ate it up. Meanwhile the peasant went into the hut.

He chatted for a while, and then, bidding the neighbor farewell, he set off for home, when the dog set upon the peasant once again. Just as before, the peasant threw him a piece of bread. The dog swallowed it at once and

Popular print: "The Bear and the Nanny-Goat at Play." Woodcut, first half of the eighteenth century.

then lunged at the poor peasant, who threw yet another piece of bread to the dog, which the dog gobbled up and went after the peasant once more. Finally, he ran out of bread, and the dog gave him a very bad bite on the leg. It's possible that he would have done him worse harm if the peasant hadn't grabbed a rock and given the dog a sharp blow to the head with it. In this way he was able to drive the dog off.

You cannot save yourself from wickedness with kindness.

THE PEASANT AND THE HORSE

A peasant was riding in the woods gathering firewood, bemoaning that fate had made him a peasant. "How am I so guilty in your eyes, O Fate," said the peasant, "that you have made me so base? Oh, woe to us, the poor peasants, who are the saddest folk on earth! We work for our lord like donkeys, we feed him, we bring him firewood and provisions, and still he punishes us for that. And if some noble friend of his happens to annoy him, then instead of dealing with him he punishes us for that as well."

Thinking about it gets the peasant so worked up that he whips his horse hard five times or more, and, what's more, the horse has to listen to all of his complaints. At that point the animal says to the poor peasant, "You complain about your lord, but you're even worse than he is. You get angry at the lord, and then

ДА ЕТИНА НЕБОГАТОН ДИ МЕЮНОС ЗГ ОРЕДПОН
СОБОЮ ВЕСТА ВА ЖЕ ВА ПОН ЗОБУПЗ МЕНА
ѲАРНОСЪ КРАСНОН НОСЪ ? ТРИАПИ
НДА ХВАЛСА ? КАКЪ ВТАНЦАЕ
АЛНЫЕ ВАШМАПН ОБХВАЛСА ?
АКОЛПАКЪ СПЕРОМЪ НАДЕЛЪ
ПОЛНЫ ШТАНЫ НАБЗАЕЛЪ ? СОВ
СЕМЪ ОБОЛОКСА ? НАВИНОХОД
НОН СВИНЬЕ ПОВОЛОКСА ? ДС
ВИНЬА МОА ХРЮКАЕКЪ ? Л
АКОМСТВА СВОЕГО НЮ
ХАСТЪ ?

Popular print: "Farnos the Jester [or "Red Nose"] Riding a Pig," woodcut from the mid-eighteenth century. The text and picture emphasizes the jester's odd and misshapen appearance, his meager assets, and his contentment.

you beat me, even though I do more good for you than you do for him. For without me you would be of no use to him at all. You make me plow the grain, which you eat yourself and also provide to the lord. You use me to carry the firewood both for the lord and for yourself. Yet you never acknowledge all the things I must bear on your behalf. Instead, you foolishly and shamelessly beat me. So if I have to put up with all of this abuse from you without uttering a word, then you have no business complaining about the lord. Our fates are practically the same. He who is unlucky is guilty, and he who has power is right."

Misery cannot pacify anyone else, and it brings more harm to others than it demands of you.

SOURCE: Fedor Emin, *Nravouchitel'nye basni* (St. Petersburg: The Academy of Sciences Press, 1764). Translated by Gary Marker.

From the A. N. Afanas'ev Collection of Popular Legends (1859)

THE BLACKSMITH AND THE DEVIL

Once upon a time there was a blacksmith and he had a son, a smart and clever lad, who was about six years old. One time the old man went to church and stood before an image of The

Popular print: "The Supper of the Pious and the Impious," woodcut from the first half of the eighteenth century. In this picture Sinfulness, below, is accompanied by devils and musicians; Piety, above, is looked upon approvingly by angels. Otherwise, the differences are rather subtle.

Last Judgment, and he sees a picture of the devil, and such a frightful one—black with horns and a tail. "Would you look at that!" he thought, "I ought to paint a copy of this for myself back in the shop." So he found himself a painter and told him to draw the devil's likeness on the doors of his smith shop, just as he had seen it in church. The painter drew. From that time on, whenever the old man entered his workshop he would always glance up at the devil and say: "Your health, my countryman!" And after that he would go over to the hearth and get to work.

The blacksmith lived like this in harmony with the devil for about ten years. But then he became ill and died. His son took over the smithy in his place, but he didn't wish to honor the devil the way his old man had done. When he came to work in the morning he would never exchange greetings with him. In place of these endearing words he would grab hold of his hammer and smash it into the devil's forehead three times, and then he would start to work. And on every religious holiday he would go to church and place a candle before each saint, but when he came to the devil he would spit in his eye.

Three whole years passed, and every morning he would entertain the devil in this fashion, first with the hammer, then with the spitting. The devil put up with it again and again, until finally he lost patience. He just couldn't stand it any more. "He thinks that I'm prepared to put up with such profane abuse from him! Well, I'm a crafty one, and I'll get him back somehow."

So the devil decides to turn himself into an ordinary fellow and he goes to the smithy. "Hello, uncle!" he said heartily. "Listen, uncle, would you be willing to take me on as an apprentice? I'd bring in the coal for you if you like, or I'd blow on the bellows."

This pleased the blacksmith: "Why not take him on? Everything will go twice as fast . . ."

The devil started in on his apprenticeship. After a month he had come to know blacksmithing better than the master himself: when the master didn't know how to do something, then he would do it himself. It was a sight to see! Words cannot express how the blacksmith loved him, or how pleased he was with him. Sometimes he didn't even go to the smithy at all, but just relied upon his worker to run the whole show.

Once, the smith was away from home for some reason, and the worker was left alone in the shop. He sees an old noblewoman riding past, and he sticks his head out the door and shouts: " Hey, M'lords, let me invite you in. We have a new kind of work here, we make old people young again!"

The noblewoman right away gets out of the carriage and comes into the shop. "What are you boasting about? Is this really true? Can you really do this?" asks the lady.

"We're not just green horns," answered the unclean one. "If I didn't know how I wouldn't have called you in."

"So, what's it cost?" asks the noblewoman.

" A mere 500 rubles."

" Well, O.K., here's the money, now make me young."

The dishonest one takes the money and sends a driver to the village: "Go," he says, "and bring back two tubs of milk." He himself grabbed onto the lady's legs with some tongs and tossed her into the hearth and burned her clean. Only her bones were left. When they returned with the tubs of milk he poured them out into a vat. He gathered up all the bones and tossed them into the milk. Observe, in three minutes the noblewoman emerges from the milk alive, young, and beautiful!

She got in her carriage and rode home. She walks up to the nobleman who looks her straight in the eye and does not recognize his own wife! "What are you staring at," says the noblewoman. "You see how young and stately I am. I don't want my husband to be old! Come on, let's go straight to the smithy, so that he can make you young, too. Otherwise I don't want anything to do with you!" There was nothing to be done about it, so off the nobleman went.

By this time the blacksmith had returned home and he went into his work shop. He looks around, and sees that his worker is nowhere to be found. He searched and searched, called and called—nothing, not a trace! So he got down to work all alone, first knocking with his hammer. In walks the nobleman, and he goes straight up to the blacksmith:

"Make me young," he says.

"What are you thinking of, my lord? How am I supposed to make you young?"

"You're the one who knows that!"

"I don't know any such thing."

"You're lying, you swindler! You managed to transform my old wife, now do it to me too. Else she won't give me a moment's rest . . ."

"I've never even laid eyes on your wife."

"Then your assistant did. If he could manage it, so can you, as the old master, and you should know it even better. So, turn back the clock of my life. Get to it quickly, or watch out—you'll get a taste of my birch bath."

There was nothing to be done. The blacksmith somehow had to transform the lord. On the sly, he asked the driver how the worker had managed it with the noblewoman. How could he?" he thinks to himself. "I just have to do it. If I get it right—fine. If not—I'm done for anyway!" He immediately stripped the nobleman naked and grabbed onto his legs with tongs. He shoved him into the hearth and set to blowing on it with the bellows. Toasted him to a crisp. Then he pulled out the bones, bathed them in milk, and waits—soon he'll find out whether or not a young nobleman will emerge from all of this. He waits an hour . . . then another. Nothing. He looks into the vat, and sees nothing but bones floating around, and they are all burnt. . . . Then the noblewoman sends to the smithy to ask: Will the nobleman be ready soon? The poor blacksmith answers that the nobleman ordered to make sure that he live a long time. Kiss him good bye! When the lady realizes that the blacksmith had only toasted her husband, and had not made him young, she grew furious, and she summoned her loyal servants and ordered them to drag the smith off to the gallows. No sooner said than done.

The servants rushed at the blacksmith, grabbed him, bound him and dragged him to the gallows. Suddenly, the very young man who had been working for the blacksmith came upon them and asks: "Where are they taking you, master?"

"They want to string me up," answered the blacksmith, and he recounted everything that had happened.

"Well, uncle," said the unclean one, "Swear that you will never again hit me with your hammer, and that you will show me the same respect that your father did, then the nobleman will at once return to life and be young."

The blacksmith swore, and made a pledge that he would never raise his hammer against the devil, and would grant him all the respect that was due him. Then the worker rushed to the shop, and quickly brought the nobleman back with him: "Stop!" he called to the servants, "Don't hang him! Here is your lord!" At once they untied the ropes and set the blacksmith loose.

From that time on the blacksmith stopped spitting on the devil and beating him with his hammer. The assistant disappeared and never was seen again, and the nobleman and lady lived happily ever after. In fact they are still alive, if, that is, they haven't died yet.

SOURCE: A. N. Afanas'ev, *Narodnyia russkiia legendy* (Moscow: Grachev, 1859), pp. 104-07. Translated by Gary Marker.

LITERATURE

M. M. GROMYKO
Peasant Culture in the Eighteenth and Nineteenth Centuries

Until recently, Russian peasant culture had not received very much attention from the historical profession, a sad fact that Marina Gromyko rightly laments. Even now, most of what we know about celebration, folklore, writing, and oral transmission among the peasantry has come from the diligent work of a small number of cultural anthropologists and musicologists, the result of whose expeditions and analyses are summarized in this essay.

Gromyko has a number of interesting observations about peasant mentalities, their sense of justice, their understanding of history, and their hopes for the future. Her comments on the quality of peasant memory are especially interesting. You might want to compare her understanding of the peasantry's use of literacy and their deployment of written texts with Karamzin's impressions of city folk during the same period, or with the earlier discussions of literacy in Kievan and Muscovite times.

For about the last decade and a half, ethnography (both abroad and in our own historical research) has tended when studying popular culture to concentrate primarily, and even exclusively, on rituals. This has mainly involved studying the most archaic elements and strata of rituals by analyzing their origins and their semantic structures. . . .

By itself, this tendency . . . can be very fruitful in reconstructing ancient rituals and faiths. But it is not uncommon for research projects to cross over into other fields of expertise when studying the spiritual life of the peasantry at a specific historical stage. Research areas then get mixed up, and phenomena which are reconstructed from rare and isolated archaic remnants, having lost their original functions, are [nevertheless] interpreted as *the* essential facts of peasant culture of the 18th and 19th centuries.

To overly dramatize one side of spiritual life, in the absence of research from other areas, generally paints a picture which does not correspond to historical reality. Such an approach [typically] leads to a body of theory which articulates a stark contrast between an intellectual elite and the inert masses, who are then deemed to be possessed of a static mentality, [a construction] which amounts to an unformulated and virtually unsubstantiated roster of stereotypes of beliefs, symbols, and taboos. As a result of approaches of this type, the characteristic features of popular culture, which have always served as a life-giving source of the best achievements of world culture, are reduced to primitive forms. . . .

The task of the present article is to (re)define the basic components of Russian peasant culture for the 18th and 19th centuries, and to point out some of the possibilities in this respect that have been put forth in previous work on various problems. . . .

For a peasant, custom served as a source of definitions in resolving many social problems.

In documents of various types one often finds peasants referring to the actions or rights of their forefathers, grandfathers, and fathers as the basis for their own actions or rights. This is true for the commune as well as for individuals. In the peasants' sense of things there existed a link with preceding generations which served as a source of support in the burdensome life of the toiler. Nevertheless, peasant protest often recognized and acknowledged the constraints of tradition. Taking part in a movement to abolish obligations that had been long standing and were sanctioned by custom, fleeing, and presenting individual petitions which opposed the established order in the community—these forms of social protest, in fact, confronted tradition.

When resisting the feudal lords' assault on their rights, the peasants employed their knowledge of the law. Sometimes the peasants imposed their own interpretations on the Law Code of 1649, and on Petrine and other pieces of legislation. In the daily life of the commune peasants often availed themselves of various forms of written law for composing petitions, communal remonstrances, and trusts. . . .

An assumption may naturally arise that the peasants relied upon the assistance of scribes or clerks when making reference to the laws in composing petitions. In fact, such instances have emerged from the sources. But, as D. I. Raskin, who specifically studied the subject, has remarked, "the role of those who helped the peasants write petitions should not be exaggerated." The ways in which the peasants acquired an understanding of laws and specific legislative texts varied. Many decrees were printed on individual sheets of paper which were accessible to the peasants. Others were transcribed by the peasants from scribes' copies; and peasants received some information about the law from scribes and clerks. Still other information was gleaned through conversation and rumors, about which inaccuracies in the texts and mistaken dates bear witness. Having penetrated the peasant environment one way or another, the law, if it interested the peasantry (whether through their own interpretations or in its actual meaning), became an integral part of peasant social consciousness for a long time. . . .

In the beginning of the 18th century the figure of Peter the Great—his wide-ranging activities, personal relations within the Tsar's family, and the character of life at court—attracted the peasantry's interest. Rumors of the Tsar's conflict with his son, Aleksei, spread simultaneously with the events themselves right up to the execution of the tsarevich. Stories came to the peasantry directly from participants and from eye-witnesses about the construction in 1702 of "the Tsar's road" through the swamps and the impassable forests of the North which a four thousand man army passed through and took Notheborg. In contrast to the rumors about the Tsar's conflict with Aleksei, where the peasants' conception of events clearly evoked their discontent with Peter's domestic policies, the stories about the northern road manifested a sympathy which arose from direct contact with his fascinating and vivid personality, from the simplicity of his demeanor, his diligence, his physical strength and resourcefulness, all of which responded to the peasants' notions of the ideal monarch.

The palace revolts of the post-Petrine era generated an endless stream of rumors and gossip, which shows how the peasants were interested in all the basic facts surrounding the struggle for the throne. It is noteworthy that even the surnames of several influential aristocrats who actively participated in the palace struggles in only a short time found their way into the tales which circulated widely among the people. From the 1740s to the 1760s a great many rumors and much gossip circulated within the peasant milieu concerning the unusual fate of Ivan Antonovich [the infant who reigned as Tsar Ivan VI for eighteen months in 1740–41], his imprisonment and struggle for the throne.

When interpreting the rumors, the peasants would often speak out critically about the authorities and express their own views of several social problems. Thus, rumors got reworked into "a cacophony of popular publicism in its spoken and hence most accessible form for the broad masses." The rumors and peasant discourse reached a particularly critical tone during the reign of Anna Ivanovna. The peasant war of 1773–1775 provided for a broad wave of rumors and a relatively high level of informed-ness among the peasantry. In the first half of the 19th century, as is well known, rumors and gossip about freedom and about the abolition of payments played a large role in the mood of the peasantry. Notable in this respect is the extent to which the peasants had become well informed on the eve of the reforms of 1861. Within the framework of research into the peasants' interest in the affairs of state, and the degree and means of information about them, a question arises concerning the relationship between spontaneous and consciously-circulated rumors. . . .

Social-utopian attitudes about society occupied a defining place in the representations of the Russian peasants during the 18th and 19th centuries. These were expressed in the rumors about the Promised Land, on the basis of which legends began to appear as did related texts. Some peasants migrated in search of these lands and they even established peasant communes in which life was organized in an attempt to realize these utopian ideals. The existence of such communities in turn fed the stories and legends about lands and settlements with an ideal social structure, with exceptional natural wealth and economic prosperity. . . .

One organic feature of the peasants' representations of their social utopia was the ideal of the just monarch who could bring order to earth through divine right. These representations of good Tsars created the conditions for the phenomenon of pretenders. This phenomenon was possible because of a complex of ideas which circulated widely among the peasantry in connection with awaiting the arrival (or return) to power of a sovereign who, in their opinion, was unjustly driven from the throne, and who possessed the ideal qualities of a ruler, including an inclination to take the peoples' interests into consideration. . . .

Studying songs about history through folkloric sources shows that these songs reflected reality rather faithfully. The elements of fantasy were, as a rule, absent; significant events were chosen, and they were then described without embellishment, and historical figures were portrayed at the most important and socially significant moments of their lives. Because of the breadth of historical events that the songs reflected, folklorists consider the 18th century as a period of "a genuine flowering of the culture of popular songs, which rested on the traditions of the past". Historical songs which were a part of the peasant milieu (possibly originating not just from the peasants, but from soldiers, cossacks, and city-dwellers as well) served as a form of reaction to recent events, a means of preserving the memories of bygone epochs. Not infrequently, these songs named the precise battlefields, replete with specific geographic locations. They also cited the exact names of military leaders, strategic positions, and the personal relationships of real historical figures. . . .

During the post-Reform period the themes of newly-composed historical songs became less vivid, and folklorists have noticed a decline in this genre during the second half of the 19th century. However, the broad circulation of heroic tales and songs continued, and these made reference both to their times of origin and to events from earlier periods of history (from ancient Rus' to the 19th century). The overwhelming number of songs that have been transcribed date particularly from the second half of the nineteenth century. . . .

The depth of popular memory is measured by many centuries. When studying these issues one must keep in mind the possibility of the penetration of historical information from chronicles and literature, coming from towns, the village clergy, teachers, minor clerks, and directly from literate peasants who may have served as one of the sources for a part of the stories that occurred in the peasant milieu. But some peasant story tellers also make specific references to their grandparents in describing a process whereby historical information was passed on orally from one generation to another.

In spite of the unevenness and selectivity of the peasants' knowledge of history, there ex-

isted a distinct sense of chronology in the depiction of historical personages and their surroundings. Even with all the uncertainty about the time in which the epic took place, none of the peasant narrators would have situated Prince Vladimir in the recent past. In the 18th century the masses of peasants had a completely accurate understanding that the Mongol-Tatar invasion had taken place before Ivan the Terrible, and that Pugachev appeared a hundred years after the Razin campaign. In folklore about history one can distinguish even specific spans of time within a given epoch, the chronology of which was fully understood by the peasantry. So, in the tales, Ermak was connected with Ivan the Terrible and the Stroganovs, and Sheremetev, Menshikov, and Demidov figured in the stories about Peter the Great and his battles. And everyone, both the narrators and the listeners, knew that the first came earlier than the second, and in earlier times. . . .

[In addition to oral expression] the written and printed word played a substantial role in the spiritual life of the Russian peasantry during the 18th and 19th centuries. The word entered into the spiritual world of the peasant not only obliquely, through various types of folklore, but also directly, on account of the literacy of a part of the peasantry, and the practice of reading aloud both within the family and in a larger social setting. Various kinds of sources point to literacy among a section of the peasantry, and, over the past few years, the circle of such sources has widened extraordinarily. Among these are signatures in the peasants' own hand in census records of households and souls, and documents relating to work.

The present state of research does not yet allow us to establish the percentages of such signatures in documents which describe the popular masses. Only in certain regions have there been attempts at selective calculations. It now seems that state peasants had a larger proportion of literate people than did serfs. But the percentage of literacy among the landowners' peasants varied greatly by district and by the particular property. All of these quantitative constructs which are based upon the presence or absence of signatures in the peasants' own hand, or according to data from official inquiries, can be accepted only conditionally because some peasants hid their literacy from the authorities or did not want to put their signatures on official documents for religious or other reasons. Moreover, among the peasants who refused to write were those who knew how to read ("I know how to read correctly but don't know how to write in cursive and was never taught").

As the research of the past few years shows, a significant portion of petitions from the eighteenth century was composed in final form in the peasants' own hand. Moreover, scribes would often merely copy the rough draft which had been composed by the peasants themselves. Among the peasants one even finds occasional masters of the scribal hand and signatures of various types. They were employed, in particular, during revolts.

Several peasant families preserved significant collections of laws concerning the land during the 18th and 19th centuries as a way of verifying their rights to various spots of land. Some of these documents dated from the sixteenth and seventeenth centuries. In certain peasant families, which were linked to trade and craft, family archives of work-related documents were filled in the eighteenth and nineteenth centuries with documentation of business deals, agreements with contractors, and the personal correspondence of family members. . . .

The wide circulation of handwritten texts of the most varied types within the peasant milieu offers convincing evidence of the spread of literacy. Among such texts are: manuscript books and collections of religious and secular contents; peasant compositions; copies of decrees from central and local establishments which were of interest to the peasants who used them in their petitions and complaints; counterfeit decrees written in the interests of peasants, and copies of them; manuscripts of prayers, spiritual verses, important records; collections of songs; medical (herbal) handbooks, or individual recipes from them; calendars and extracts from them. . . .

A solid tradition of peasant book culture and writing from the eighteenth and nineteenth centuries emerged out of the Russian North. In the Pushkin House [an archive in St. Petersburg] [numerous] collections . . . consist entirely of manuscript materials which were discovered in the peasant milieu. Inscriptions on several manuscripts attest to their belonging to peasants even in the 16th and 17th centuries; and more than a few peasant ancestral libraries have been uncovered, the origins of which date to the seventeenth and eighteenth centuries. Other inscriptions refer to a form of joint ownership of expensive books. Of particular interest are inscriptions on copies of Psalters which directly reveal their use as school books. . . .

The peasant book culture of the northern and southwestern regions served as important sources for their spread into Siberia. This was connected both to patterns of migration (both free and governmental colonization), and also to the preservation and establishment of ties after resettling. Among the collection of peasant Old-Believer literature from the Urals and Siberia are original works of various genres: historical narratives about Old-Believer centers and their leaders, their tracts concerning basic polemic questions of priestly or priestless elements, their homilies, and their biographies.

Old-Believer centers and entire regions of peasant written culture were not simply preserving an archaic layer of culture. The sixteenth-and seventeenth-century traditions of writing and printing were reworked in the 18th century peasant milieu in ways that were closely tied to the special characteristics of the spiritual and material lives of the peasants. . . .

For Orthodox peasants who did not break with the official church there was no need to rewrite liturgical literature. However, even here one finds copiers of spiritual and moral works. In the literate culture of the nonschismatics secular literature occupies a larger place than among the Old Believers. Chronicles, accounts of the battle of Kulikovo, the Time of Troubles, the capture of Narva in 1704, and other historical texts were actively recopied. Belles lettres, fables, and works of popular satire also entered into the domain of reading, and copying (made both for themselves and for sale). The fact that various collections within the country include handwritten books of a secular nature with notations of peasant owners and peasant transcribers attests to the relatively wide distribution of readings of this type. The appearance of peasant editors of several works belonging to this genre also says something about the extent to which secular works had become an organic part of the circle of peasant reading by the end of the eighteenth century. . . .

[Nevertheless] folklore remained by far the major form of artistic creativity and satisfaction of the peasants' aesthetic demands for the entire period. Its basic genres from the seventeenth century—ceremonial poetry built around the calendar and the clan, epics, historical and lyrical songs, stories, legends, and proverbs—were preserved in the eighteenth and nineteenth centuries but they underwent fundamental changes in composition and form. In its profound sense of traditional, folklore is connected most intimately to everyday life, and then later it comes to be defined by its flexibility and sense of immediacy. Peasant conversation was full of proverbs and sayings, as were their letters and petitions, and their descriptions of domestic life and labor. . . .

The majority of folklore genres provided a kind of duality of words and melodies. Music had entered into the spiritual life of the peasant quite naturally, and it interacted with local written traditions. Contemporary ethnographic surveys have managed to collect numerous manuscripts with *kriuk* or *znamennyi*

[forms of musical notation indicating techniques of chanting], sheet music belonging to peasants from the seventeenth through the nineteenth centuries. Manuscripts of music were often artistically embellished with large painted initials, borders, ornamentations, and sometimes even with miniatures which reflected local traditions of applied art. Singing "by kriuk" was learned from childhood from the local "literate" singers. If the tradition of singing by kriuk was absent or had been lost, then they taught service singing orally, creating groups of ten to twenty children for that purpose. The peasant custom during the period under consideration included "ABC's"—practical guides which contained the basic rules for kriuk singing. . . .

The last of the basic components which we are describing (the last within the structure of this article, but by no means the last in terms of its significance in the spiritual life of the peasantry) is the culture of celebrations, a multifarious . . . fusion of oral, musical, dramatic, and choreographed creativity involving complex ethical representations and ethical norms, rites, and superstitions. It is within the culture of celebration that the unity and wholeness of various sides of peasant spiritual life come together and receive their maximum expression.

SOURCE: M. M. Gromyko, "Kul'tura russkogo krest'ianstva XVIII–XIX vekov kak predmet istoricheskogo issledovaniia" ["The Culture of the Russian Peasantry during the Eighteenth and Nineteenth Centuries as a Subject of Historical Research"], *Istoriia SSSR* 31 (May/June, 1986): 40–41, 44, 46–9, 51–3, 55–8 (excerpted). Translated by Darrin Mendlove and Gary Marker. Reprinted by permission of the author.

B. Elite Culture and Educated Society: Eighteenth Century

DOCUMENT

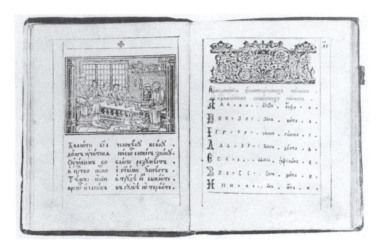

Engraved pictures and exercises from Fedor Polikarpov's *Primer of Slavonic, Greek, and Latin* (Moscow, 1701). Although Polikarpov's *Primer* was far too complex to be widely used, it provides a good example of Slavonic letters and syllables as they often appeared in Russian primers. Also, the school scenes engraved on these pages say a good deal about late seventeenth-century notions of teachers, pupils, and discipline.

M. M. Kheraskov, "The Rossiad," an Epic Poem (1779)

Much of the published literature that was made available to the public in eighteenth-century Russia was, as Karamzin says in a subsequent selection, translated, or at least extensively adapted from non-Russian originals. Poetry, however, tended to be penned by native writers. Odes and epics, like Kheraskov's "Rossiad," enabled Russian writers to explore themes of national identity by praising rulers, or bemoaning past enemies and cruel fate, all in an effort to situate Russia in the modern world as a deserving—if misunderstood—participant in European civilization. In Kheraskov's case (incidentally, this is the same Kheraskov whom Labzina described in an earlier selection), the wish to define Russia's virtue as a nation (simultaneously conceived as a "fatherland" and as a woman who "made move to bare her bosom, faint and wounded. . .") led to a fanciful celebration of Ivan the Terrible, the moral avenger against the "barbarian" Tatars and evil magnates. Pay particular attention to the highly emotional imagery to see what, according to Kheraskov, constituted the attributes of virtue and greatness, what marked nations as civilized and worthy, and what identified them as barbaric. It is also illuminating to observe the ways in which Kheraskov employs male and female imagery and characteristics in depicting nations, races, states and cities. Students, then, may want to pay as much attention to Kheraskov's images as to his narrative.

HISTORICAL INTRODUCTION

In the most remote times that the ancient historians have made familiar to us, the Russian state was powerful. It was dreaded by its neighbors and esteemed by many nations. In glory, strength, abundance, and victories, according to the position of states at the time, it did not take second place to any European power,

while in the expanse of its territory, then as now, it surpassed all others. But after the death of Grand Prince Vladimir the fragmentation of Russia into different parts, into separate principalities; the internal dissension, disorders, and the ambition of the now greatly multiplied princes began gradually to sap its strength. The result was that finally they succumbed to the calamitous yoke of the plundering Tatar hordes. From that time on, the former glory of Russia was extinguished and was hardly known throughout the world. Thus it lay for nearly three centuries in oblivion beneath its ruins. This lamentable and shameful situation in which the Tatar invasions and power had submerged Russia; the wresting of many of its principalities plundered by her other neighbors; the disorder caused by internal sedition—which was completely exhausting the fatherland—brought Russia to its complete and utter collapse.

This evil endured to the time of the Tsar Ioann Vasil'evich the First [Ivan III, who ruled from 1462–1505], who on a sudden built Russia anew, prepared it for its autocratical course, boldly and courageously removed the yoke of the Tatar khans, and restored peace within the bosom of his state. But in his time the kingdom of Kazan' was not yet destroyed; the Novgorodians had not yet been entirely subdued; neighboring states did not yet manifest the necessary esteem for Russia. This great change from which this nation passed from weakness to strength, from humiliation to glory, from subservience to domination, this important and extreme change transpired in the time of the grandson of Ioann, Ioann Vasil'evich the Second [Ivan the Terrible] who is the hero of this poem.

Should not, then, the reign of Ioann Vasil'evich the Second represent the middle level to which Russia, after reaching a disastrous position, began to come to life again, to grow and to regain its former brilliance, which it had lost for nearly three hundred years? When we imagine a state in complete disarray, oppressed by its neighbors, torn asunder by internal dissension, agitated by the disharmony of its polyarchy, subjugated by infidels, plundered by its own magnates, when we imagine

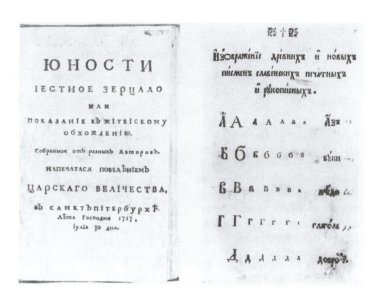

A Mirror of Honor for Youth, title page and first leaf (St. Petersburg, 1717). Ordered into production by Peter the Great, this was the first major primer to teach the new "civil" alphabet along with modern rules of etiquette for what Peter hoped would be his newly cultured service elite. Note the difference in appearance between this book (and the letters) and Polikarpov's. Although highly celebrated, the book had a relatively limited audience.

all this and picture to ourselves a young monarch accepting the power of autocracy, rooting out the confusion in his Fatherland, restraining the strong and terrible enemies of his authority, bridling the polyarchy, pacifying rebellious insurgents within the bosom of the state, returning the cities wrested by neighbors and adding whole states to his scepter, quelling the pride and disharmony of his boyars, granting wise laws, organizing his army in the most efficient manner, do we not feel esteem for a sovereign of so great a spirit?. . . Such a monarch was Ioann Vasil'evich!. . .

CANTO THE FIRST

I sing of Russia freed from the barbarians,
The rule of Tatars overthrown and their
  pride humbled;

Movement of ancient arms, travail, and
  bloody battles,
Russia triumphant and Kazan' reduced to
  ruins.
The years of peace from these times had
  their true beginning,
Which like a bright dawn came to shine over
  all Russia.
O Thou, that soar higher than all the stars of
  heaven,
Spirit of poetry, come from those heavenly
  places,
And pour your rays, O Art, and your
  illumination
Upon this frail and dark creation I now
  offer. . . .

By insolent Trans-Volga hordes' despotic
  power

The eastern part of ancient Russia still was
  burdened
And on our prisoners the fetters rattled
  loudly.
Revolts were brewing and new crimes began
  arising;
Through villages and towns pale fear itself
  extended;
Woe followed woe and evil made pursuit of
  evil.
The altars in the churches had no incense
  smoking;
Church singing came to cease and winds
  alone there howled;
Beneath thorns in the field the plow lay idly
  quiet,
And to the dark woods from their flocks went
  shepherds running.
When daylight cast its bright glance and the
  North illumined,
It found a prostrate Russia suffering and
  groaning.
Kazan', which drew the breath of life in its
  embrace,
Ignoble tribute from her weary hands was
  taking.
This city, thrown up by the enemies of
  Russia,
Like some proud mountain to the north was
  elevated,
And when it raised its head it stood beside
  two rivers
From where it looked upon the shores of
  raging Volga. . . .

When it saw Moscow fall asleep, its swords
  abandoned,
The trembling moon did dare to peek out
  from the clouds;
It raised its open eyes then smoldering with
  hatred
From River Volga like some dreadful storm
  erupted.
Having disturbed the peace the horde tore
  off its fetters
And moved by anger stirred itself, incited
  riot,
And there began its head and shoulders to
  raise up,
And Russia to oppress as it had done before.

Again this dreadful beast did enter Russian
  cities,
In his train bringing murder, violence, and
  plunder.
One hand a sword held, but the other—
  clanking irons;
Walls crumbled all around and steppe and
  forest suffered.
On the command of the perfidious Sumbeka
The rivers of Kazan' flowed rich with blood
  of Russians.
Bearing a torch the scourge of evil now
  unleashed
In fury put the flame to Moscow's
  settlements.
Chastisement, blade in hand, did enter
  Christian dwellings
And martyrs' blood soon cried out to the
  heavens.
The sadness, cries, and groans of orphans
  but remained;
Their fatherland turned just to dream this
  lamentation. . . .

Sad was the capital, fair Moscow bent her
  head,
And sadness like the night had shaded her
  face over
Grief crept into her heart and sorrow found
  her lips;
The splendid places which surrounded her
  mourned also;
And letting loose her hair misfortune strolled
  the city,
Her eyes cast downward all into despair
  conducted.
In agony she beat her chest and cried
  profusely.
The streets knew triumph not nor did the
  dwellings peace;
In grassy vales just grief, in groves reigned
  naught but moaning.
Among the city's throngs no wedding songs
  were heard;
All were arrayed in garb of sadness and as
  orphans;
Inside God's temples all that could be heard
  was wailing.
Consumed by a disease to which there was no
  end,

Moscow then bore resemblance unto
    stagnant water
Which, suddenly deprived of movement or of
    freshness,
Turns dull, grows fetid, and breeds poison of
    itself.
Its people cast into despair, pursued, and
    wearied,
Were like volcanic fire in Aetna blazing
    suddenly
Which tosses up thick clumps of trees and
    wooded hillocks
From mountain summit to the very heavens.
The people have bestirred!. . . Then in their
    violent fury
From just a spark a brazen rising burst to
    blazing.
It swept right through the streets and burned
    in marketplaces,
And Moscow saw the glow of woeful
    consequences.

Those in rebellion rose against the evil
    magnates
Who had endeavored to increase the
    monarch's sternness
And tried to keep his soul in constant
    agitation,
So they could plunder Russia bare during the
    tempest.
The princes Glin'skii were both victims of
    this rising;
One of them was slain by the
    insurrectionaries,
The other managed to escape through
    cunningness
And from the throne began to rage with a
    new thundering.
Extending o'er the tsar's bright house the
    cloud of vengeance
This power implacable did arm itself with
    lightning
And levied its blows at those men and at
    those places
Where Truth did dare its mouth to open and
    speak plainly.
To champions of games did go just
    compensation,

ЖИЗНЬ

и

ПРИКЛЮЧЕНІЯ

РОБИНЗОНА КРУЗА

ПРИРОДНАГО АГЛИЧАНИНА.

переведена сь Французсскаго

Я. Т.

ЧАСТЬ ВТОРАЯ.

ВЪ САНКТПЕТЕРЬУРГѢ
при Императорской Академіи Наукъ
1764 года.

Title page to the first Russian edition of *The Adventures of Robinson Crusoe,* translated from a French edition (rather than from the English original) and published by the Academy of Sciences Press, St. Petersburg, 1764.

While loyal sons, their eyes tear-filled, fell
    into silence.

Losing the loveliness which once it could be
    proud of,
And seeing all around it desolation, conflict,
Grief everywhere and in the breast of
    Moscow illness,
Its borders jeopardized by bold hordes'
    frequent raiding,
A throne unsteady 'neath a shade of pomp
    and splendor,

'Neath foreign rule the Don, the Dniepr,
  Dvina, Volga,
And now expecting the approach of night
  eternal—Russia her tear-filled eyes raised
  to the very heavens,
She raised her arms outstretched unto the
  Heavenly Father,
And kneeling humbly did petition the
  Creator.
She then made move to bare her bosom,
  faint and wounded,
And with one hand did indicate all Moscow
  bloodied,
The sea of evil poured about it—with the
  other.
She then commenced to sob, and not a word
  could utter.

On rainbowed dawns above the stars there
  sat supremely
The mighty God who roars in thunders and
  in tempests;
Before Whom light of day is like the very
  darkness;
Who animates all things and sets worlds into
  motion;
Who from the heavens looks upon all
  equally,
Forgives, treats tenderly, becalms yet fears
  not to chastise.
Of fire and water King—He knew the voice
  of Russia

And seeing the last hour of His children's
  glory
In one brief moment the days of their sorrow
  reckoned;
And then determined to extend a hand of
  sustenance.

The heavens up above suddenly grew
  brighter;
A dew with power of restoration then
  descended,
Besprinkled lightly her unhappy breast and
  countenance,
And in a moment's time the weary Russia
  strengthened.
Upon this suddenly a red dawn cloaked the
  Northland,
And angels, peering at the earth through
  crystal doors,
Did then compose upon their lyres celestial
  concert
And sang of the beneficence now crowning
  Russia.

SOURCE: Mikhail M. Kheraskov, "The Rossiad," in Harold
B. Segel (translator and editor) *The Literature of Eighteenth-
Century Russia.* Vol. II (New York, NY: E. P. Dutton, 1967),
pp. 110–11, 115–22 (excerpted). Originally published in
Russian in 1779. Translation copyright © 1967 by Harold B.
Segel. Used by permission of the publisher, Dutton, an im-
print of New American Library, a division of Penguin Books
USA.

LITERATURE

STEPHEN L. BAEHR

Rebirth, Renewal, and Renovatio *in Eighteenth-Century Russia*

The spirit of optimism and national revival constituted one of the most pervasive themes of the Russian Enlightenment, at least for the educated elites who saw themselves as participants in this improvement. In this essay Stephen Baehr explores some of the most prominent expressions of this optimism in the political propaganda of the eighteenth century.

———————

When Prince Antiokh Kantemir announced that because of the Petrine reforms "we suddenly (are) a new people", he was stating a theme that would echo throughout much eighteenth-century official culture and political propaganda—the idea of a Russian cultural rebirth and of new beginnings for Russia. The images of new birth, beginnings, spring, and resurrection which inundate eighteenth-century Russian culture often reflect this perception (and official ideology) of a Russian renewal—a belief in an apocalyptic re-beginning of history in Russia which often assumed mythic forms and became part of a highly rhetorical utopian vision depicting Russia as paradise-on-earth in the second and third quarters of the eighteenth century.

I

During the eighteenth century, Russian courtly panegyrics [orations in praise of a ruler] frequently took Biblical passages and substituted the name of the monarch on the throne for the name of the Virgin, God, or Christ—a style directly befitting the Russian tsar's position as the "viceroy of God" on earth. So just as the monarch was variously described as "the resurrection and the life",

"the beginning and the end of all things", and "blessed . . . among women", so was he or she also depicted as the cosmogonic God of Genesis who created the world "in the beginning".

The image of the Tsar as creator *ex nihilo . . .* appeared particularly frequently in the literature praising Peter the Great. When, for example, Chancellor P. A. Golovkin wrote in a 1721 speech celebrating the Treaty of Nystadt that through Peter the Russian people "were created . . . from the darkness of ignorance to the theatre of glory of the entire world and, so to speak, from non-existence to existence. . .", he was implicitly embodying the myth of the tsar as re-creator of his people. In a similar . . . vein, Peter's contemporary apologist P. N. Krekshin used this same image to praise "Our father, Peter the Great, [who] led us from non-existence to existence". . . . Russian panegyric literature frequently implied that in re-creating Russia, Peter was re-creating not only man but also the world as a whole. . . . Peter himself contributed to this myth by calling Petersburg "paradise" in his letters and descriptions—the beautiful earthly dwelling place resulting from the creation of light out of darkness, cosmos out of chaos, and dry land out of swampy waters.

Instead of depicting the monarch as the cosmogonic God, one variant strategy portrayed God himself as re-creating the universe and restoring time to its beginnings at some event or celebration connected with the life of the current monarch on the throne. This 'cosmogonic strategy' most often used (or transformed) the words of *Genesis* 1—especially the words "let there be light". . . ; it appeared most often in odes dedicated to a monarch's accession, coronation, or birthday or in New Year's odes—in short in works which actually *did* mark some new beginning or the anniversary of that beginning. The logic of these odes is somewhat like that of our own contemporary New Year's celebration where we "ring out the old and ring in the new". Indeed, the pattern of optimism at these "new beginnings" is very

САНКТЪПЕТЕРЗБУРХЪ,

ВѢДОМОСТИ.

Полученные Сего Іюня вь 28 день, 1711.

Изъ ЛАГАРУ изъ волоскои земли, изъ заднестра за мілю, 31 дня маіа.

Его Царское Величество ізволіль сюда прітишпи изъ яворова 22 дня, тогожъ маіа, котораго дня и королев-

Title sheet to the first Russian newspaper, *Vedomosti [The News]* for June 28, 1711, showing a very active St. Petersburg harbor.

much like that in most primitive calendar rituals, where the beginning of a new time period is connected with the beginning of a new life and the end of sin, sorrow, and suffering.

II
THE STRATEGY OF 'ETERNAL RETURN'

Despite the frequent emphasis on the Biblical book of *Genesis* to depict the Russian recreation of the world, the myth of Russian rebirth frequently owed more to pagan than to Biblical sources. Indeed, the very idea of a return to a perfect world-beginning contradicts the Judeo-Christian theory of history as linear and goal-directed, which allows only one world-creation; it reflects instead the classical or pagan theory of history as cyclical—the idea that events regularly repeat themselves at certain intervals. . . .

Associated with this strategy of 'eternal recurrence' was the return of great world heroes and the recapitulation of great world events in eighteenth-century Russia. Although, under the influence of Byzantine rhetoric, Russian panegyric literature had for centuries praised Grand Princes as "new Constantines", "new Alexanders", and the like, during the eighteenth century not only heroes but also events were "born again" in Russia. Throughout the century adjectives like . . . 'new' and . . . 'second', nouns like . . . 'the return' and 'the dawn' . . . multiplied to describe repetitions of historical or mythological events or personalities. Thus Russia was often described as the "new Rome" or "new Athens" and its citizens were depicted through such epithets as "the second Columbus", "the new Pindar", or "the new Horace"; courtly festivals were given such titles as . . . 'The Return of Happiness', . . . 'Russia Again Rejoicing After Her Sadness', . . . and 'The Return of the Golden Age'. . . .

III
THE STRATEGY OF RESURRECTION

Closely connected with the strategy of 'eternal recurrence' was a strategy which depicted Russia as reborn from the dead. This resurrection of Russia was often attributed to Peter the Great. Feofan Prokopovich, for example, in his 1725. . . 'Funeral Oration for Peter the Great' portrayed Peter as "resurrecting . . . Russia from the dead . . . or even more significantly . . . giving birth to and raising her like a true father of his country. . .". During the reigns of Elizabeth Petrovna and Peter Fedorovich this image of a resurrected Russia became particularly frequent and was often accompanied by the image of a resurrected Peter the Great, reflecting the Old Testament idea that a person achieves resurrection through his descendants (here his daughter and grandson). The image of Peter the Great's resurrection is quite frequently played during the reign of Peter III and often . . . impl(ies) that *a* Peter must be

ОПЫТЪ

ИСТОРИЧЕСКАГО

СЛОВАРЯ

О РОССІЙСКИХЪ

ПИСАТЕЛЯХЪ.

Изъ разныхъ печатныхъ и рукопис-
ныхъ книгъ, сообщенныхъ извѣстій,
и словесныхъ преданій

Собралъ

Николай Новиковъ.

ВЪ САНКТПЕТЕРБУРГѢ 1772 ГОДА.

Title page to *The Historical Dictionary of Russian Writers,* (St. Petersburg, 1772), compiled by Nikolai Novikov, the great eighteenth-century man of letters and publisher. This book represents one of the earliest efforts to celebrate the secular literary world of the eighteenth century. Simultaneously, it emphasized the fact that these writers were *Russian,* and not just translators of European literature.

which were perceived as raising Russia to a level of equality with the major powers of western Europe—the theme gradually came to propagandize the ideal of a Russian *renovatio*—the idea of restoring a universal Christian empire led by "holy Russia". In principle, the Russian symbolism of *renovatio*—which has distinct ties to the theory of Moscow as Third Rome—can be traced back to the reign of Vasilii III (ruled 1505–33) when the imperial orb . . . was added to the regalia of the Muscovite ruler. This orb, which took the form of a golden apple . . . symbolized the rebirth of the Roman empire under a Christian. . .ruler, who, in the image and likeness of Christ, was to reverse the consequences of the apple-caused Fall of man and restore the world to the Edenic state of its beginnings. In practice the symbolism of *renovatio* became widely popular only in the panegyric literature of the eighteenth century. . .

[I]t is not coincidental that the theme of rebirth parallels the theme of *translatio imperii* (and especially the idea of Russia as "new Rome") throughout the eighteenth century, that the imagery of re-beginning often appears in the imagery of a world empire (especially images like the "seven seas", "vast territories", and "entire world"), or that these themes reached their apogee during the reign of Catherine the Great—one of the greatest periods of imperial expansion in Russian history. . . .

SOURCE: Stephen L. Baehr, "In the Re-Beginning: Rebirth, Renewal, and Renovatio in Eighteenth-Century Russia," (Originally Published in A. G. Cross (ed.), *Russia and the West in the Eighteenth Century* (Oriental Research Partners: Newtownville, Mass., 1984), 152–161 (excerpted). Reprinted by permission of Oriental Research Partners.

the Peter. As I. F. Bogdanovich wrote in his 1762 ode on the accession of Peter III: "Again great Peter has arisen.". . .

In conclusion, then, I would suggest that while the general theme of re-birth and re-beginnings arose in Russia in response to the optimism generated in many circles by the westernizing, scientific, and military reforms begun by Peter the Great and continuing throughout much of the century—reforms

RICHARD WORTMAN

The Development of a Russian Legal Consciousness

Enlightenment, Isabel de Madariaga demonstrated in a previous selection, constituted a real, if elusive, goal of Russian despotism under Catherine the Great. For the servitor-in-

tellectuals in St. Petersburg and Moscow, Enlightenment was a defining passion. One of several areas in which the reasoning of enlightened officialdom and intellectuals overlapped was in a shared concern for the law and for pursuing the rule of law in a juridical system which they viewed as a tangled jungle of disorder and arbitrariness. This selection by Richard Wortman provides an evocative glimpse into the language which eighteenth-century Russian writers used when discussing the role of law in improving Russian society.

Catherine's most active spokesman for legal enlightenment was S. E. Desnitskii, the first Russian professor of law. Desnitskii, the son of a petty burgher, . . . completed his studies at Edinburgh and on returning to Russia, received a teaching position at Moscow University. A disciple and translator of Blackstone, he championed the cause of university education in the law in Russia. But there were few noblemen enrolled at Moscow University in the eighteenth century and few of them wanted to devote themselves to the law. Desnitskii's public speeches exhorted the nobility to change their attitude to the law. His address to the ceremonial assembly of Moscow University in 1770 developed a theme set forth in Catherine's *Nakaz*; it praised the achievements of Russian arms, but insisted that the arts of peace were as worthy as those of war:

To capture and subdue many peoples and spread one's power is only to prove military art and its excelling force; but to maintain limitless conquests in single-minded obedience and universal satisfaction is the type of work that proves human wisdom and the happy gift of the governing to achieve great deeds.

Previous generations had distinguished themselves on the field of battle; it should be the task of contemporaries to provide effective civil institutions. The true unity of the empire depended on "proper legal statutes," and Desnitskii went on to enumerate reasons for studying "legal art". . . .

In an address of 1778, Desnitskii tried to dispel the moral stigma attached to the study of law. "We should not disparage and call chicanery a science which defends the sacredness of the property, the possessions and the life of those living under the nation's laws." He assured Russians eager to study the law that no one at the university was so corrupt as to teach under this science "the chicaner's eloquence." Noblemen, as property owners, needed to study the law "for the defense of one's life and estate, for the compliance of one's acts with the general rules prescribed by the regime, and for the knowledge of the mutual obligations of society, without whose execution society cannot defend the tranquil life of its members." The law would show the nobleman how to effect sales and mortgages of his estates, how to fulfill his role as a judge over the peasants, and how to conduct suits against his neighbors.

But Desnitskii hoped that the knowledge of the law would . . . also permit them to serve in administrative and, particularly, chancellery positions. Peter, he recalled, had reserved secretarial posts for members of the nobility and Catherine had urged chancellery positions in the new provincial governments upon them. Desnitskii . . . tried to convince noblemen of the honor of serving in clerical posts, and the benefits of such work for civil government.

This office in Russia . . . is, without doubt, of great importance and may justly be honored for the refinement of theoretical reason in practical legal process and the most reliable preparation of noblemen as skillful judges. By despatching this office, he [the nobleman] can learn not only how to know the law well, but how to apply it in actual legal process.

Desnitskii well understood that his high words on the office of clerk were in conflict with the nobility's own attitudes. "The inattentiveness of many to both their own and the general welfare has left this essentially noble position, that has been so exalted by monarchs, to chancellery people."

Vasilii Novikov, a nineteen-year-old Kaluga nobleman, expressed similar ideas in a speech he prepared for the Kaluga nobility in 1786. Like Desnitskii, Novikov responded to Catherine's reform by urging the nobility to participate in the new institutions and assume a civil role. Their forefathers had undertaken the defense of the fatherland and the extension of its borders. Now, with the borders of the empire ensured, they should turn their attention to internal well-being. They should combat ignorance and strive to improve the lot of their peasants. He called upon them to elect the best and the most experienced to serve as judges.

To assist the nobility, Novikov compiled the first Russian guide to being a judge: *Theater of Court Conduct or Reading for Judges and All Lovers [Amateurs] of Jurisprudence, Containing Remarkable and Interesting Court Cases, the Judicial Investigations of Famous Practitioners of the Law and Other Events of This Type Able to Enlighten, to Touch, to Move to Virtue, and to Furnish a Useful and Pleasant Pastime.* The *Theater* was a collection of cases, most of them from a recent French compendium. It instructed future judges how to determine the truth in court cases, advising "caution in conclusions, perspicacity in the investigations of crimes, and respect for humanity."

Law for Novikov played much the same instrumental and didactic role as did literature in the eighteenth century. Culture and study had the goal of teaching and spreading virtue. Novikov considered it would be a great triumph of his labors "if this book took the place of card playing and other empty wastes of time so unbecoming to the judicial calling." His good judge would be able to correct human vices so that in the future courts would be less necessary. . . .

Similar didactic motifs ran through the literature of eighteenth-century Russia. Theater and verse strove to correct and cultivate—to uplift the Russian nobleman to the level of European culture. . . . Alexander Sumarokov, the court playwright of Elizabeth and Catherine, declared that learning, or science—*nauka*—was the only grounds of nobility. *Nauka* enabled the nobleman to promote the good of his country and attain a genuine rather than a specious glory. Knowledge was most necessary for the nobleman who would serve as judge. . . .

In his "satire," *On Bad Judges* . . . , Sumarokov wrote with contempt of judges who slept through the hearing of cases, weary from the previous night of card playing. They unthinkingly signed decisions prepared for them by clerks. "An illiterate judge," he wrote, "should not be in charge of a court."

The ignorant and irresponsible judge appears frequently in the satirical literature of the eighteenth and early nineteenth centuries. *Chicanery* of Kapnist, the works of Gogol and Sukhovo-Kobylin, [well-known satirists of the early and mid-nineteenth century] all followed a tradition of describing the hypocrisy of legal justice that had originated with Aristophanes' *The Asses*. It was the conviction of eighteenth-century writers that such satire could lead to moral improvement and impel the Russian nobleman to educate himself to assume his new civil role. Perhaps the most striking example of the bad judge is the character of the counselor in Denis Fonvizin's *Brigadier*. The counselor declares,

In my day, every person with a just or unjust case went to the department and could, once he got friendly with a judge, receive a favorable resolution. In my day you didn't poke your nose any further. We used to have a saying: To God it is high, to the tsar far.

His notion of justice was simple. When asked why an innocent person should be declared guilty, he replies,

Because all people are sinners. I myself was a judge. It used to be that the guilty paid for his guilt and the innocent for his innocence. In my time everyone was satisfied that way: the judge, the plaintiff and the defendant.

Fonvizin . . . gave his answer to the problem in the letters from his character, Starodum (old thought)—the fount of traditional wisdom. In Starodum's letters, Mr. Zdravomysl' (Mr. Common Sense) says that sometimes judges could not understand cases because they lacked practice and the ability to understand. The ability could only be acquired by reading and study.

I do not ask for learned judges, but I think a judge should definitely be enlightened and able to read and write, that is he should at least know spelling, which I notice few here do.

An appeal directed more sharply at the provincial nobleman was a satirical dialogue written by Mikhail Khrapovitskii, "A Conversation of District Noblemen about Elections to the Courts." In the conversation, Mr. Zdravomyslov (Mr. Common Sense) is appalled to hear the description of local elections given by Mr. Prostiakov (Mr. Simpleton). Mr. Prostiakov tells how all the candidates for positions were chosen at a special meeting of important noblemen at the house of a powerful landlord of the district. Mr. Nevezhin (Mr. Ignorant) had been selected district judge, because, Prostiakov argues, he is too poor and stupid to engage in chicanery. Mr. Nevezhin has read nothing but the Bible. Zdravomyslov replies that the secretary will lead Nevezhin by the nose, take bribes, and very quickly relieve him of his entire salary. He proposes Mr. Den'gov (Mr. Money). Prostiakov objects that a rich man would not take such a post. "And is it lowly to serve as a judge?" asks Zdravomyslov. "What a strange notion! The judge is appointed to be the preserver of sacred justice, the basis of all prosperity. He is entrusted with the security of our property and therefore his position becomes important and respected." Prostiakov pleads that not he, but Mr. Naglov (Mr. Impudent) had proposed Nevezhin to be judge and he was helpless to object. Other local positions were also filled with incompetents and drunkards, for, Prostiakov explains, landlords at the meeting would not put up with brainy people. . . .

But if the nobility was to heed the sovereign's call and develop a practical knowledge of the law, there would have to be books of laws for them to consult, and such books were not available. Without books, one could learn about the law only in the chancellery. Desnitskii himself admitted that clerical work was poor preparation for legal officials. He pointed out that clerks never progressed beyond the mechanical tasks of assembling and transferring legal citations. "No one, not only of wealthy background, but even a student, would wish to subject himself to the yoke of work and the endless copying of mountains of paper." As a result, the law had turned from "a lord's" into "a slave's" science.

Catherine's own commitment to the spread of legal enlightenment helped to moderate misgivings about publications on the law, and law books began to appear in her reign. The first description of Russian laws for practical use was Professor Dilthei's *Juridical Exploration of the Rightful Place of the Court, on Juridical Authority, on the Juridical Office, on the Juridical Petition and Proof* . . . , published at the press of Moscow University in 1779. The book's preface gave eloquent testimony as to why such a study was so long in coming. The learned Austrian felt he was writing in a hostile atmosphere and tried to defend his effort. "This book has experienced the cruelest enemy, who has charged the author with the greatest guilt— that he has dared to write laws." He argued that he wrote not laws, which only the sovereign could issue, but commentaries on them for the benefit of students. Other enemies charged that his book might take the place of the laws in the courts. He rejected this contention by declaring most emphatically his intention to remain within the bounds of his discipline. "What teachers of the law assert about the reason and interpretation of the laws and their application to cases represents only an opinion and it is forbidden to transfer it from school to court. For one is School Jurisprudence, and the other Court." Another objection denied the need for instruction in the laws. This criticism, which he received more tolerantly than the others, held that a good mind and a good heart were sufficient to perform the obligations of the judge. He replied that they were not, "for cases should be decided according to laws and not according to one's own reason." The final objection, that the book contained nothing that was not already known, was more to the point, for Dilthei, careful not to press his claims to interpretation too far, kept his exploration as vague and abstract as possible. His description of types of courts and their obligations, types of suits, and proofs was based on Roman law with an occasional reference to Russian legislation, mostly to decrees of Peter the Great and Catherine the Great. . . .

The first guide to Russian laws, Chulkov's *Juridical Dictionary*, came out in 1788, and was followed by several others in the 1790s. The best known of these was Fedor Pravikov's *Memorial from the Law . . .*, which began to appear in 1798, and received several editions and numerous supplements. Pravikov set forth laws issued since the Code of 1649 by category, then beginning with 1798, presented them year by year. The *Memorial* was a published version of a clerk's notebook. Himself a clerk, and the son of a rural priest, Pravikov had attended Moscow University, and entered the Senate as a copyist in 1766 at the age of fifteen. He had learned about the laws in the Senate chancellery, where he served all his life, reaching the position of secretary in 1797.

Pravikov's compilation was followed by others, such as Maksimovich's widely used *Guide to the Laws. . . .* The numerous works of this kind, published at the beginning of the nineteenth century and often in several editions, attest to the quickening demand for legal guides. But though answering a need, these were individual efforts and could not in themselves make order out of the chaos of Russian legislation.

At the end of the reign of Alexander I, it was still difficult to locate particular laws. This was the experience of Przheslavskii, who spent long hours in Petersburg chancelleries trying to protect a relative's estate from confiscation. He searched through all the compilations and made inquiries among friends but could find no law concerning the confiscation of estates. Then he learned from an old man who worked as a representative in the courts that it could be found in the statute of the Treasury College, an institution which had been finally abolished by Alexander in 1802. But no one in Petersburg seemed to be able to locate a copy of the statute. Przheslavskii tried the Senate bookstore, but he was assured that no such law existed. Requests everywhere were equally fruitless. Finally, an appeal to the management of the Senate bookstore brought a search of the premises, which revealed the statute in a dusty corner of the shop, at the bottom of a large heap of rubbish.

SOURCE: Richard S. Wortman, *The Development of a Russian Legal Consciousness* (Chicago: University of Chicago Press) 1976, pp. 26–33 (excerpted). Copyright © 1976 by the University of Chicago Press, and reprinted by permission of the publisher.

C. Elite Culture and Educated Society: The Nineteenth Century

DOCUMENTS

Nikolai M. Karamzin, "On the Book Trade and the Love for Reading in Russia" (1802)

Part and parcel of the secularization of Russian intellectual life was the advent of a reading public, however small, for this new literature and medium. Some writers worried that this new public was getting drawn away by frivolous and merely entertaining literature, and thereby lost to the moral improvement of individual and nation that many writers wished to foster. In this essay, Nikolai Karamzin, one of the most prominent essayists and historians of the late eighteenth and early nineteenth centuries, expresses a more optimistic perspective. Pay particular attention to the con-

nection that Karamzin seems to be drawing between reading and writing, on one hand, and
national progress on the other.

———————

Twenty-five years ago there were two bookstores in Moscow; they had a turnover of not
more than ten thousand rubles a year. Now
there are twenty such stores, and all told they
take in about 200,000 rubles a year. By how
much, then, has the number of readers in Russia increased? It is a most pleasant development for everyone who desires the success of
intellectuality and knows that love for reading
helps it most of all. . . .

Since 1797 newspapers have become important for Russia because of the highest imperial
orders and other governmental information
they have included. At the present time there
are about 6,000 copies of Moscow newspapers
distributed—undoubtedly still a small number, considering the vastness of the country,
but large in comparison to the past. And, indeed, the number of curious people has never
grown so fast in any other country as it has in
Russia. It is true that many wealthy noblemen,
as well as many comfortably situated people,
do not touch newspapers; on the other hand,
however, merchants and townsmen already
have grown to love reading them. The poorest
people subscribe, and the most illiterate want
to know *what is happening in foreign countries!*
One of my acquaintances happened to see a
few bakers who crowded around a reader and
listened with great interest to the description
of an encounter between the French and the
Austrians. He asked them and found out that
the five of them pool their money for Moscow
papers, even though four do not know how to
read; the fifth, however, knows the letters, and
the others listen to him.

Our book trade cannot yet rival either the
German, the French, or the English; but judging by the yearly successes, what can one not
expect in time? Almost every provincial capital
has bookstores. To every fair, along with other
merchandise, the richness of our literature is
also brought. Thus, for example, noblewomen

at the St. Macarius fair not only stock up on
bonnets but on books as well. Before, travelling salesmen would go through the villages
offering ribbons and rings; nowadays they
travel with learned merchandise, even though
in most cases they themselves do not know how
to read, but in their wish to stimulate interest
they retell the contents of novels and come-
dies, usually in their own way, and quite hu-
morously. I know some noblemen who have a
yearly income of no more than 500 rubles, but
they collect, according to their own words, *little
libraries*, take pleasure in having them, and
while we abuse our expensive editions of Voltaire and Buffon, they do not allow a speck of
dust to fall on *Miramond*. They read every book
a few times and then reread them with renewed pleasure.

The curious would perhaps like to know
what kind of book proves most popular? I put
that question to many of our booksellers, and
without thinking all of them replied "novels"!
And it is not surprising: the majority of the
people are captivated by this type of literature
because it entertains the heart and imagination, presenting, as it does, a picture of the
world and of people like us in curious situations, and depicting the strongest as well as the
most ordinary passion in all the variety of its
action. Not everyone can philosophize or put
himself in the place of the heroes of the story;
but everyone loves, loved, or wanted to love,
and seems to see himself in the character of
the romantic hero. The reader imagines that
the author talks to him in the language of his
own heart; in one novel he nourishes hope
and in another—a pleasant reminiscence. This
type of literature in Russia, as we know, is dominated by translations, and therefore foreign
authors take fame away from the Russians. . . .

I do not know how others feel but I am
happy as long as people read! Even the most
mediocre novels written without any talent in
some way aid the cause of enlightenment.
Whoever is captivated by *Nikanor the Unfortunate Nobleman* stands lower on the staircase of
intellectual development than the author, but
it is good that he is reading the novel because
he will undoubtedly learn something from the

ideas expressed or in the manner of expression. If the distance between the author and the reader is great, the former cannot have an influence on the latter, no matter how intelligent the latter may be. Everyone needs something on a par with himself: for some it is Jean-Jacques, for others *Nikanor*. As our physical taste informs us of the concord of a food with our need, so the spiritual taste discloses to man a true analogy of a subject with his soul. But this soul can elevate itself gradually—and he who begins with the *Unfortunate Nobleman* very often graduates to *Grandison*. The novel *Sir Charles Grandison* written by the English novelist Samuel Richardson in 1753].

Every pleasant bit of reading has an influence on the intellect, without which neither the heart is able to feel nor the imagination to create. In the worst of novels there is already some kind of logic and rhetoric: whoever reads them will speak better and more coherently than a complete ignoramus who has never opened a book in his life. Besides, today's novels are rich in all kinds of knowledge. An author who decides to write a three-or four-volume book resorts to all methods to fill them and even to all the sciences: he may describe some American island ... or he may explain the nature of the plant life there ... In this way, the reader becomes acquainted both with geography and natural history. ...

In short, it is good that our public reads even novels!

SOURCE: Nikolai Karamzin, "On the Book Trade and the Love for Reading in Russia," in Harold B. Segel (translator and editor), *The Literature of Eighteenth-Century Russia*, Vol. 1 (New York: E. P. Dutton, 1967), pp. 449–53 (excerpted). Originally published in Russian in *Vestnik Evropy* no. 9 (1802). Translation copyright © 1967 by Harold B. Segel. Used by permission of the publisher, Dutton, an imprint of the New American Library, a division of Penguin Books USA.

P. V. Annenkov,
The Extraordinary Decade:
Literary Memoirs *(1840s)*

P. V. Annenkov was a familiar figure in the literary life of polite society during the 1840s, a time in which that small universe was polarized into two warring ideological camps: Westernizers and Slavophiles. Although he wrote relatively little, he knew everyone, and his renowned memoir offers a lively and insightful window onto the social and personal sides of some of the most famous figures in the Russian intelligentsia. These passages vividly portray the personal intimacy and social exclusivity that characterized the literary life of their day, a point that William Mills Todd develops in the discussion that follows.

Not being a permanent resident of Moscow and my visits there being chance occurrences with fairly long intervals of time between them, I was not fortunate enough to become acquainted with the Elagin household, ... the favorite meeting place of the celebrities of the learned and literary world of Moscow; its reigning tone of temperateness, decency, and kind attention made it into something like a neutral territory where conflicting opinions could be expressed freely without fear of ambushes, sallies, or personal insults. This venerable house had a very marked influence on Granovsky [Timofei Granovsky, a historian at Moscow University, and a leading influence on the young Westernizers], Herzen [Alexander Herzen, a leading Westernizer and radical, often termed the father of Russian socialism] and many other Westernizers who were its assiduous visitors; and they spoke of it with great respect. Perhaps it is to that house they owed a certain moderation in their judgments on questions of folkways and folk beliefs, a moderation which Belinsky, who stood and acted in seclusion, did not know and which he curtly called tea-table affability. That the Westernizers, in turn, had an effect on the Moscow Slavophiles, who made up the majority of the company at the Elagin house, is also beyond any doubt. All this taken together gives the house the right to an honorary page in the history of Russian literature equally with other, similar oases where Russian thought remained in sequester during those periods when organs for its expression were still lacking.

I myself had a chance to see an example of the effect on Herzen of conversations with people whose attitudes differed from his own. . . . On one of my morning visits to Herzen in the garret of his house in Sivtsev-Vrazhek, where his study was located, he began talking of the scorn Belinsky had expressed for peasant life in general, calling it *"bast-shoe and sackcloth reality."* The term was used in an analysis of some silly book of stories taken from folk life, which the author had crudely and comically idealized. "The book is one thing," said Herzen, "but the review is irresponsible both in itself and for the fact that it eggs the journal on to consider itself a great lord before the people." Why despise bast-shoes and sackcloth? They are, after all, nothing more than a sign of extreme poverty and crying need. . . .

Generally speaking, Belinsky was, if the expression can be used, the disturber of the peace of Moscow life: were it not for his provoking words, Moscow could, perhaps, have kept for a longer time the mien of refined difference of opinion, not unconducive to easy and genial relations between disputants, which comprised its distinctive feature during the first period of great literary debate that had begun in Russia. With his peremptory aphorisms and the progressively greater boldness of his conclusions, Belinsky kept sending his Moscow friends every minute to the barricades, so to speak, against his enemies in Moscow.

The first person to sense the absurdity of this situation where people went out of their way to be as polite and considerate as possible in inflicting on one another, if not fatal, in any case very serious wounds, was the exceedingly decent and exceedingly consistent Konstantin

Sergeevich Aksakov. It is quite true that Slavism and Russian national life constituted for him something more than a doctrine or set of ideas that one was honor-bound to defend: Slavism and the Russian national mode of life became the vital basic motive of his existence and his very life's blood. In his memoirs, Herzen relates the story of how K. S. Aksakov, meeting him on the street, movingly bid him farewell forever since he could no longer consider him a companion on the road of life. This was even more impressive in Granovsky's case. K. S. Aksakov came to him late at night, woke him up, threw his arms about his neck, and, pressing him tightly in his embrace, announced that he had come to him to perform one of the most grievous and onerous duties of his life—to break off relations with him and to bid him a last adieu, as one does a lost friend, despite the deep respect and love he felt for his person and personality. Granovsky urged him to look on their differences of opinion with greater dispassion, but to no avail; he said that, apart from ideas of Slavdom and nationality, they had other ties and moral beliefs between them which were not subject to the peril of a rupture, but K. S. Aksakov remained unwavering and departed from him very upset and in tears. That was a time in Russia when doctrine and opinions could still cause inner, intimate dramas.

Also at Madame Elagin's house, Herzen would meet his perpetual opponent, A. S. Khomyakov, in whom he regarded with extreme respect his very own ability to discern the inherent negative side, the diseases and distempers, in ideas and facts, and for that reason would seek out occasions for debates and confrontations with an opponent of such power, erudition, and cleverness. . . . On first meeting with A. S. Khomyakov, Herzen came up against, in opposition to his own philosophical radicalism, another, similarly unqualified radicalism, but of a completely different kind.

Herzen himself reported, in one of his publications abroad, a part of the run-ins he had with Khomyakov having to do primarily with the tenor, spirit, and basic principles of German philosophy. From these reports it becomes clear that Khomyakov's main argument against the Hegelian system was provided by the proposition that no philosophy worthy of the name could be deduced from an analysis of the properties and phenomena of *Reason* alone, with all other, no less important, moral forces of mankind excluded. . . .

The basic reason, though not yet clearly formulated as such, responsible for the second part of their disputes was A. S. Khomyakov's attempted rehabilitation of Byzantium, so much an object of opprobrium among scholars in the West. The manner in which Byzantinism had been understood and applied by its proper and natural defenders in Russia—the preceptors at our theological seminaries and academies—had had the effect of further increasing aversion for it. With the appearance of Chaadayev's famous letter in 1836, however, where Byzantium was declared to be the source of the intellectual and spiritual stagnation of all Russia and was all but consigned to the damnation of history, Byzantium became an issue which no one who wanted his beliefs and convictions to have the aspect of something critically reasoned out and scrutinized could circumvent. A. S. Khomyakov not only did not circumvent the issue, he persistently worked it into everything in life, including spheres of human activity where its presence was least to be expected, everything providing him a convenient device for measuring truth, good, and beauty. The key to an understanding of many of the Khomyakov school's extravagantly original opinions and verdicts, which went counter to all known facts and ideas, lies precisely in its invention and manipulation of this new criterion for evaluating historical phenomena. . . .

[B]y declaring Byzantinism a great and still not fully appreciated phenomenon in mankind, A. S. Khomyakov thereby negated and wiped out the enormous mass of Western historical, critical, and theological works hostile to Eastern civilization and degraded the West's self-esteem as well as many of the things on which it prided itself, the eras of the Reformation and the Renaissance, for instance, to

the level of secondary and even pathological phenomena of human thought. For him, the Reformation was a sorry attempt on the part of Western peoples to rectify their religion, its direct sources having been clogged with Catholicism, and the era of the Renaissance, which preceded it, was a desperate appeal, on the part of these same people, to the pagan world for help in creating for themselves something at least resembling science, art, and civilization.

The positive side of his defense of the all-saving grace of Byzantinism Khomyakov grounded in a conception and understanding of the Eastern church doctrine as one allowing complete freedom of thought under the unlimited authority of political or ecclesiastical dogma. A. S. Khomyakov was not the least bit embarrassed by the history of the Byzantine Empire, which could have contradicted his position. . . .

Eastern Christianity [he believed], even in company with and in spite of the Asian despotism which sometimes stood at its head, retained the notion of the congregation of the faithful as a prototype of a state where each man depends on the other and where each man is at once both subject to and exerciser of authority. It allowed in practice, but did not recognize in principle, divisions of people into those who instruct and those who are instructed, into those responsible to command and those responsible to carry out commands, because all people had the same mission—to serve the *church*— and the least of them could stand side by side with an exalted member in the course of this unceasing service and as suited its needs. . . .

Summoned to the great task of renewing the, morally speaking, deteriorated life of Europe was the nationality which, by the workings of history and Providence, had become heir to and representative of Byzantinism in the world, no matter, be it added, how poor, humble, and lowly a lot this chosen nationality might have had for the time being.

No more abstract and radical a kind of thinking could have been put in opposition to Herzen's philosophical radicalism. . . . Everything our "Westerners" then enthused over, from the novels of G. Sand, which had great success with them owing to the social questions they raised, to the new attempts at formulating the political and social life of states. . .— all these were dismissed by the Khomyakov school as things unworthy of attention. Europe was declared untenable ground for a vigorous art, for the satisfaction of the highest needs of human nature, for the gratification of the religious cravings of peoples and for the establishment among them of justice, law and order and love. . . . It was condemned for the development of comfort, luxury, and riches when it went about amassing in measureless quantity. Europe's well-being, unprecedented in history, continued to grow even greater in detriment to its ever more deteriorating moral significance. It even closed its eyes to the doom rising up before it in the form of the proletariat, which was multiplying under its custody and threatening to bring on a return of the age of barbarism. . . . According to the testimony of all who heard him, Khomyakov conducted his criticism of the social and intellectual situation in Europe with particular skill, brilliance and wit, although also within the bounds of decency and decorum, which were inherent properties of his keen intellect. However Herzen, on his part, might have tried to ward off and cool Khomyakov's critical enthusiasm, he himself was not exempt from the effect of that criticism. Khomyakov's words, in our opinion, left marks on Herzen's mind and heart, against his own will, perhaps, and were reflected in his later avowals of the insubstantiality and bankruptcy of Western life in general. . . .

In the press, in the then modest field of pub-

licistics, all this, needless to say, appeared toned down and was expressed less graphically and less frankly. People came out on stage somewhat dressed up—with a few, well-known exceptions. Nevertheless, traces of the turbulence behind the scenes were bound to be reflected in journalism and were, in fact, reflected there. The *Muscovite*, which had become the echo of the Slavophile school, went to the extreme of monomania in the defense of its basic stands—about the richness of the Russian national spirit, about its religious essence, about the elements of humility, meekness, endurance, and wisdom which made it unique—going so far as to assert, for instance, that the Russian land was fertilized for history with the tears of its inhabitants, not, as was true of the lands of Western nations, with their blood. *Notes of the Fatherland,* the rallying center for Westerners from 1840 on, in promulgating universal human development, the laws of which, it argued, were the same for all countries, very often carried its denial of national distinctions to such a pitch of incomprehension that it seemed deliberately put on. Both journals conducted furious polemics and, of course, neither lacked its complement of crackbrains, its *enfants perdus*, whom the editors sent out as skirmishers; and it was these people who produced the eccentricities and absurdities of which one can harvest a fair collection from both the one and the other side. . .

SOURCE: P. V. Annenkov, *The Extraordinary Decade. Literary Memoirs.* Edited by Arthur P. Mendel; translated by Irwin R. Titunik (Ann Arbor: University of Michigan Press, 1968), pp. 92–101 (excerpted). Reprinted by permission of the publisher.

LITERATURE

WILLIAM MILLS TODD III
The Literary World of Polite Society

The two selections on nineteenth-century intellectual history adopt widely divergent approaches to their topic. In the subsequent essay, Nicholas Riasanovsky provides a synopsis of the leading currents of social and political thought that defined the great debates that captivated the journals and the salons of the mid-nineteenth century. In the process it puts forth a number of explanations for the split or "parting of ways" that took the newly-termed "intelligentsia" and the government into separate directions. William Todd's essay, by comparison, focuses more on the internal life and cultural dynamics of the still very small and intimate polite society within which these debates took place, its manners, forms of expression, and behavior. He suggests that these manners carried with them a powerful political and ideological component of their own that at times ran entirely counter to the stated beliefs of the thinkers involved. How does Todd's interpretation compare with the on-sight observations of Annenkov from the 1840s?

————————

A Russian gentleman was generally an Orthodox Christian, however unenthusiastic or swayed by fashionable foreign faiths, and a subject of the autocrat, holding officerial rank in the military or civil service. Nevertheless, the special languages associated with these aspects of his being, Church Slavonic and the chancellery language, were generally barred from the intercourse of polite society, or were permitted to enter it under special circumstances. . . . This linguistic program could make social gatherings seem a place of relative liberty—from the restrictions of rank, from the ritual piety of the Church, and from financial concerns—a place for wit, fantasy, brilliant ex-

aggeration, and verbal improvization. It could make the literature devoted to and inspired by these gatherings remarkable for its attentiveness to the emotions and to fine points of social interaction. But it also permitted its members to exclude those whose experience bound them to less acceptable linguistic practices. . . .

THE AMELIORATION OF MANNERS

Language and literature are not merely means of mass enlightenment, they are the *principal* means. (N. M. Karamzin, "Speech Delivered at the Solemn Assembly of the Imperial Russian Academy," 5 December 1818)

Literature—understood as the active process of letters— was assigned an important role in this process of social harmonization, through comedy and satire and, indirectly, through the infectious civility of its manners. To inspire civility and to inculcate good taste became the moral purpose of literature and literary criticism. Consequently, such writers as Karamzin and Zhukovsky took pains to avoid the slightest offensiveness in their criticism. . . .

Perhaps no work of the time pays greater tribute to the ameliorating role than does an essay by the Decembrist Aleksandr Kornilovich, "On the First Balls in Russia". . . An army officer who would later bravely try to rally the rebels on Senate Square, Kornilovich couched his celebration of balls in a form ideologically consistent with his refined topic, an elegantly conversational letter to a young lady. His epistle presents an all-inclusive vision of ritualistic conjunction. Social distinctions, economic status, civil service ranks, even differences of sex and nationality disappear or undergo transformation, as the eighteenth-century balls join their participants in harmonious community. Commoners dance with the imperial family, forgetting their rank; Russians, taught to dance by Swedish prisoners of war, later invite captured French officers to join them on the dance floor; the Empresses dance both the

Western minuet and Russian folk dances; women disguise themselves as men and vice versa. Competitive games, such as cards or draughts, figure in the festivities, but the division into winners and losers that these produced did not (at least in Kornilovich's idealization) undermine the sense of universal pleasure and harmony.

Such balls, instituted in Russia by Peter the Great as instruments of his Westernizing policy, appear less and less subject to official regulation as Kornilovich's chronicle advances and increasingly overcome hierarchical distinctions in a carnivalesque manner, especially when the balls began to be given privately. . . .

REBELLION IN SOCIETY

The inclusion of Kornilovich's article in an almanac of two no less prominent members of the period's most important political conspiracy, A. A. Bestuzhev and K. F. Ryleev, demands mention of that complex movement's proximity to the everyday life and ideology of polite society. In geographical and architectural terms nothing reveals this proximity more strikingly than the magnificent Laval mansion, where the Decembrists gathered. The interrelationship between their political activities and their other social commitments during the decade that ended with the failure of the uprising in December 1825 was from all accounts a fluid one, and one on which there was no unanimity within the movement. To the extent that members of the conspiracy and its sympathizers were scattered from the Baltic to the Caucasus, held a variety of political opinions ranging from republican to constitutional monarchist, adhered to a spectrum of Enlightenment and Romantic literary views, advocated in turn such disparate tactics as open propaganda and regicide, and represented both the impoverished provincial gentry and the enlightened Westernized gentry that I have been calling "society," such a fluid relationship to the daily life of polite society is not surprising. However, the Northern Society, headquartered in St. Petersburg, was more aristocratic in composition, more restrained in its program for political transformation, and more involved in the social-aesthetic life of the fashionable world than was the Southern Society. Consequently, the Northern group's dynamism depended more upon a relationship with society. Its members, descended from the best families, belonged to important literary groups . . . ; frequented the theater, salons, and balls; conversed on such fashionable topics as political economy and history; and with few exceptions belonged to prestigious regiments or branches of the civil service. The Constitution of the Union of Welfare . . . , which preceded the Northern Society (1822–1825), committed its members to public involvement in spheres familiar to society and its notions of enlightenment: philanthropy, education, justice, and the national economy. These legal activities did not merely screen clandestine work—as would be their primary function with subsequent revolutionary organizations—but were considered generally conducive to social improvement. As such, public action (or at least talking about it) was one role that a gentleman's ideology would license him to play. Indeed, the Northern Society's commitment to ameliorating governmental harshness, limiting the power of the autocrat, and educating the broader public at relatively little expense to the status of the gentry expressed the same independence *vis-à-vis* the government that marked the very language of polite society.

At times the logic of this independence swept the Decembrists and those close to them beyond the conventions of polite social interaction. Speaking bluntly (instead of using polite periphrasis), cultivating mild scabrousness and later obscenity (in Arzamas and in the Green Lamp), sacrificing the company of women for serious study, or refusing to play cards and dance at balls were some of the ways in which the Decembrists chose to challenge the status quo and to make changes beyond those involving the gradual amelioration of manners. . . .

Yet the Decembrists in the capital needed the social conventions and ideology of polite society in order to mount challenges through this process of cultural estrangement. . . . After all, they had to appear at balls in order not to dance at them, take cognizance of social fashions in order to oppose them diametrically, and, ultimately, contribute to the theatricality of society's behavior by staging scenes of latter-day Roman virtue in ways that did more to intensify the *honnete homme's* image of Stoic virtue and self-control than to contradict it. . . .

The legends that soon enveloped the captured Decembrists have generally passed over their behavior under interrogation, the point at which their vulnerability as members of society became most evident. The five executions, the ruthless sentences to hard labor and suicidal military missions, and the behavior of the exiled Decembrists in Siberia—their mingling with and service to the people of that region—have earned them the title of "martyrs," both in the popular consciousness and from historians of the movement. To the extent that the Christian martyrs were often depicted as young patricians with seemingly everything to lose by adhering to their faith, this term has considerable appeal.

But the title "martyr"—which Russians have so generously bestowed throughout their history—should not obscure the extent to which the Decembrists embodied the ideology of polite society with its vision of independence and social amelioration. An English traveler who met a group of Decembrists after they had endured decades of hard labor, physical privation, and psychological harassment paid the following tribute to the polite society that they had raised along the banks of the Angara:

At the time of my visit to Irkutsk there were six of the exiles still living in town. . . .These formed the best society in Irkutsk, and some of the most agreeable days which I spent in Siberia were in enjoying the intercourse with them. They are now living in comfort, mixing in society, and gathering around them all the best that Irkutsk afforded. . . .

Here, on the brink of death . . . , insanity, and suicide . . . , and three thousand miles from the Laval mansion, the Decembrists kept alive the conversation, cosmopolitanism, and educational ideals of polite society.

The Decembrist uprising represents the most intense and principled political manifestation of society's ideology, an expression so direct that many other members of society recoiled from it, shocked by the bloodshed and talk of regicide. Karamzin's wife, an important salon hostess, voiced this shock and revulsion most vividly. . . . Nevertheless, the connections, social and intellectual, between polite society and the crushed conspiracy continued to excite the suspicion of Nicholas I and his subordinates during the decades following the uprising. The religious experimentation, political speculation, and cosmopolitanism made possible by society's discourse found direct and conscious opposition in the ideology of "official nationality" ("Orthodoxy, Autocracy, Nationalism") that the advisors of Nicholas I would formulate during the years that Pushkin, Lermontov, and Gogol were writing their novels.

At the same time, the ideology of polite society would be challenged even more powerfully on other fronts, as it failed to answer the cultural needs of a new generation of Russian intellectuals: aspiring professional writers, university students, low-ranking civil servants, and children of the clergy—most of whom had been barred from full participation in society. Nevertheless, the ideology embedded in the language, behavior, self-image, art, and ethics of Russia's cultural elite could not be eradicated overnight. For the negative forms of government control—censorship, restriction of academic freedom—made a cultural life oriented toward talk, salons, and familiar circles even more of a necessity. Russian literature would still be bound, even in the 1830s, to the ideology of polite society, and this did much to shape the institutions of literature through which, and in opposition to which, the literature was produced.

SOURCE: William Mills Todd, *Fiction and Society in the Age of Pushkin: Ideology, Institutions, and Narrative* (Cambridge: Harvard University Press, 1986) Chapter 1: "A Russian Ideology", pp. 20, 37–44 (excerpted). Copyright © 1986 by the President and Fellows of Harvard College. Reprinted by permission of the publisher.

NICHOLAS N. RIASANOVSKY

The Split between the Government and the Educated Public

The ebullient expressions of rebirth and renewal that had been so emblematic of the Russian Enlightenment came to a rather abrupt halt, as William Todd alluded to, in the wake of the Decembrist revolt in 1825. Certainly the polite society of 1830s expressed far less confidence in institutions and the course of progress than their parents had. But their disillusionment rarely took on an overtly political tone. By the middle 1840s a critically thinking, politically independent cadre of intellectuals, or intelligentsia, had come to define progress and intellectual life as a realm that was separate from and in many ways hostile to the autocratic state and to the going concerns of Russian society. Here Nicholas Riasanovsky traces the change of heart and ideology of Russia's leading thinkers from the 1840s and offers a variety of possible explanations as to why the "parting of ways" took place.

The modern Russian educated public was created by the reforms of Peter the Great. Throughout the eighteenth century and well into the nineteenth it co-operated most closely with the government for the sake of what both parties, inspired by the ideas and the hopes of the Age of Reason, considered to be the interests of Russia. When enlightened despotism failed in the task of enlightenment, the Decembrists tried to take matters into their own hands through military rebellion. Yet that daring step implied no basic intellectual change: reason and progress were to be imposed upon the Russians by their rulers, who would utilize the political form of a constitutional monarchy or a Jacobin republic or a dictatorship, rather than of the old autocracy. . . .

Although . . . Nicholas I and his associates were greatly worried by the possibilities of sub-

version . . . the years from 1826 to 1840 were . . . a remarkably calm and quiet period in Russia. . . .

The mood began to change around 1840. The gendarme report for that year warned:

and, therefore, it should not be passed over in silence that, although there are as yet no complaints against the person of the Sovereign, there is hidden everywhere a certain general dissatisfaction, which can be expressed in a statement written to the Chief of Gendarmes from Moscow: 'I do not know, exactly, but something is wrong', and this expression we now hear often from the most gentle, the most well-intentioned people. . . .

How can one account for all these developments? What were the reasons which terminated, or at least so greatly impaired, the more than century-old intimate alliance between the government and the educated public in Russia, transforming the apparently monolithic image of the 1830s, with the government in virtually complete control, into a picture of alienation and opposition?

Most pre-revolutionary Russian scholars blamed directly the government itself, and more specifically Nicholas I. With a characteristically liberal, and occasionally radical, bias they saw the educated public, in particular its intellectual leaders, as bearers of light and the conscience of Russia. These leaders naturally supported progressive Petrine reforms, and they offered their strong backing to the activities of Catherine the Great and the projects of Alexander I, although in these last two instances they might have been misled and mistaken to some considerable extent. But with Nicholas I co-operation ceased. The new emperor refused to solve the pressing problems of the country. Notably, he would not abolish serfdom, and he established a regime of unbearable reaction, oppression, and militarism. The last harrowing years of his rule, which followed the revolutions of 1848 in many European countries, raised oppression to an insane pitch and made a fundamental break between the state and all aware and self-respecting Russians inevitable. . . .

Oppression can indeed produce alienation and opposition. And yet . . . the liberal view fails to carry conviction. For one thing . . . the

Salon society in the 1830s. From *Pushkinskii Peterburg* (Leningrad, 1972).

last years of Nicholas I's rule were probably more painful than decisive in the relationship between the government and the educated public in Russia because the split between the two had preceded their onset. More importantly, the emperor's beliefs, aims, and policies remained essentially the same in the 1820s, 1830s, 1840s, and 1850s. It was the educated public that changed. . . .

The educated Russian public was affected . . . by many factors of diverse kinds and potency. Among the most persistent and important was the course of Russian foreign relations and the role which Russia played on the world stage in an increasingly nationalistic age. . . . In respect to foreign policy and public opinion, Nicholas was much less fortunate than Catherine the Great, whose enormous acquisitions

could satisfy almost any appetite, or Alexander I who had striking ups and downs but saved Russia, triumphed over Napoleon, and became Agamemnon, the king of kings, 'the monarch of Europe'. The Crimean fiasco at the end of the reign constituted a terrible disaster for Russians in general, but especially for the nationalists among them. The government looked so strikingly isolated in 1855 precisely because it had lost all nationalist support.

In another respect too, in regard to the West the decades of Nicholas I's rule proved to be on the whole highly disastrous as well as, once again, highly significant for Russian public opinion. . . . [T]hroughout the eighteenth century and the reign of Alexander I Russia enjoyed, so to speak, a good press, everything considered, in other European countries. . . .

Most importantly, the cosmopolitan European Enlightenment welcomed Russia as a promising, as well as enthusiastic, disciple. . . .

It was in the years following. . .that the image of Russia changed. The change was determined by the increasing polarization of European politics and by the logical alliance of the Russian empire with the Right. Nicholas I's personal devotion to the conservative cause and his directness and rudeness probably accelerated and sharpened the process. In any event, whereas Alexander I had been hailed as the liberator of Europe, Nicholas I came to be known as its gendarme. Consequently, whereas Catherine the Great had been eulogized by Voltaire, Diderot, and d'Alembert, among others, and whereas Alexander I had received praise, e.g., from Jefferson, all liberals and radicals denounced Nicholas I, his system, and his country. . . .

Russian intellectuals could and did react in a variety of ways to this massive Western criticism and condemnation of their government and their country. Those on the Right frequently chose defiance, which is so prominent in the political writings of Tiutchev or of Pogodin. It was Tiutchev, a diplomat with some twenty years of residence in Germany, who composed the remarkable lines:

> One cannot understand Russia by reason,
> Cannot measure her with a common measure:
> Cannot measure her with a common measure:
> She is under a special dispensation—
> One can only believe in Russia.

The Slavophiles . . . constructed an entire ideology to demonstrate that Russia and the West were activated by different and incompatible principles, and that, therefore, they could not be comprehended in the same way.

Most educated Russians, however, drew comparisons and suffered accordingly. The entire argument of the Westernizers, for example, implied trying to catch up with the West. To be sure, seeing and admitting Russian deficiencies did not have to imply being blind to those found abroad, and some progressive Russian intellectuals, such as Herzen, criticized the West with a vengeance after they

had left their native land. Like Chaadaev, they were to discover hope for Russia in its very youth and even in its historical backwardness. Yet in trying to understand the Russian intellectuals of the 1840s the salient point is to realize that the integrative framework of the Age of Reason was gone. Defiance, counter-attack, Utopian hopes, or an emphasis on separateness, could not restore the harmonious vision of the enlightened despot leading his people ever farther along the universal road of progress, a vision of their country once shared by the educated Russians with other enlightened Europeans. The new Western rejection of Russia thus cut deep to the fundamental intellectual assumptions of the epoch. . . .

Russian intellectuals in the reign of Nicholas I were, of course, deeply concerned with serfdom. Very broadly speaking, it might be suggested that such Westernizers as Belinskii and Herzen saw it . . . as a direct exploitation of men by men past all bearing. By contrast, the Slavophiles, . . . stressed the social disorientation, and especially their conviction that serfdom represented compulsion and division in what should have been a free, united, and harmonious nation-wide commune of Russian Orthodox believers. In any case: "By the middle of the nineteenth century, educated, or 'enlightened' public opinion was, almost by definition, abolitionist opinion. . . ."

Serfdom, to be sure, was not only a moral scandal, but also a fundamental economic reality of Russia. Gentry fortunes, linked intimately to that institution, could well worry members of the possessing class quite apart from any ethical implications of their situation. As the enormous indebtedness of the landlords to the state on the eve of the emancipation indicate, landlord agriculture was in a condition of crisis in the mid-nineteenth century. . . . Again, economic dissatisfaction and criticism, like moral awareness, grew in Russia, apparently at an accelerating rate, providing a more explosive setting for the intellectual evolution in the decades immediately preceding the emancipation than had existed earlier.

Service ranked with land and serfs in its importance for the gentry. Although obligatory service had been abolished by Peter III in 1762 ... many landlords had to serve to support themselves and their families. Besides, state service, especially in the army, remained an established pattern of the upper-class way of life. . . . [The bureaucracy] held the gigantic country firmly together and governed it with considerable success. . . . It remains very difficult, however, to estimate the efficiency of this bureaucracy, although most estimates have rated it as very low. . .

The last point is illumined in part by extensive, and frequently extremely negative, comments on state service scattered throughout gentry memoirs. The reactionary policies of the government in the reign of Nicholas I made joining the bureaucracy particularly unattractive. As Boris Chicherin, certainly no radical, presented the matter, reflecting the climate of the last years of the autocrat's rule:

And how could I, in the political conditions of the time, be enticed by service? To become a direct tool of the government, which was repressing mercilessly every thought and all enlightenment, and which I hated for that from the bottom of my soul; to crawl slavishly up the service ladder, pleasing superiors, never expressing my convictions, often doing what seemed to me to be the greatest evil—such was the service perspective which opened in front of me. I turned away from it in indignation, but there was no other solution in sight.

Yet simply blaming the government, much as it deserved the blame, does not tell the whole story. Apparently there were failings also on the side of the gentry. In fact a clear distinction between the two is more than a little artificial, because it was the landlords who in their capacities as officials ran the state machine. . . . Of the various explanations of the general difficulties experienced by the gentry in the service, most suggestive is the emphasis on the rather archaic character and traditions of the landlord class and its inability to adjust effectively to modern trends. Life on an estate was very different from life in the St. Petersburg bureaucracy, and as government service became more professional and more exacting the gap between the two worlds widened. . . . Little kings at home, admired by their family

and relatives, mostly women, and confident that they were superior in kind to their serf servitors and playmates, gentry children frequently lacked the presence of even the one obvious authority, their father, whose service obligations had taken him elsewhere. They ruled the roost. The awakening, whether in a military school or government office, was bound to be rude. And some of the bitterness must have remained to feed feelings of alienation and opposition in the Russian educated public. . . .

The *raznochintsy*, people of mixed background below the gentry, [certainly] had their role and their stake in the Russian Age of Reason. Moreover, the growth of precisely that group has been presented as a main motif of the intellectual and cultural evolution of Russia in the 1840s and 1850s. . . .

But . . . the gentry continued to be the dominant class. . . . More to the point, there is no substantial evidence that the emerging split between the government and the educated public in the reign of Nicholas I was connected with a democratization of that public. . . .

Whereas social composition per se is of little help in explaining the emerging split . . . , the evolving structure of intellectual life in the country might offer more promising leads. Although the number of universities did not alter in the reign of Nicholas I, at least they developed their work and became better established in Russian society and culture. . . .

It is not at all surprising, therefore, that much significant thought in Russia had its starting-point at university lectures, whether those of Pavlov discussing the philosophy of Schelling at the University of Moscow or those of Poroshin explaining the views of Fourier at the University of St. Petersburg. Not only knowledge but inspiration too came from the universities, especially from the University of Moscow during its 'golden age', or at least so reads the testimony of intellectuals as different as Herzen and Constantine Aksakov. . . .

The periodical press developed in the reign of Nicholas I much more strikingly than did higher education, and it reflected in a number of ways the remarkable evolution and growth of the Russian educated public. The history of journalism in Russia in the first half of the nineteenth century might be divided into two periods. The first spanned the years 1801 to 1838. It witnessed a full recovery from the repression under Paul I, with a journalistic activity far surpassing the highest levels attained at the time of Catherine the Great. Numbers, circulation rates, and the durability of journals all increased markedly. But it was the second period, from 1838 to 1855, that constituted a virtual journalistic explosion. . .

Active and successful publishers such as Andrew Kraevskii . . . became significant figures in Russian intellectual life. Others acquired popularity and occasionally fame writing for the journals; indeed their appeal sometimes determined the success of a particular periodical. They included not only the irrepressible and vacuous Senkovskii . . . but also serious writers like Nicholas Polevoi and especially Belinskii. . . . Because periodicals had to support themselves to survive in a limited and insecure market, publishers developed sensitivity, adaptability, and business sense. In fact, it has been suggested that journalism was the only industry in Russia in the second quarter of the nineteenth century which operated along sophisticated capitalist lines and responded promptly and effectively to market conditions.

A student of Russian intellectual history cannot fail to note that Russian journals were expounding increasingly pronounced and varied ideological positions. . . . [T]he government doctrine of Official Nationality, championed in journalism in particular by the notorious trio of Bulgarin, Grech and Senkovskii, found massive support in such publications as Bulgarin and Grech's newspaper . . . *Northern Bee*, Grech's periodical . . . *A Son of the Fatherland*, and Senkovskii's immensely popular but intellectually insignificant . . . *The Reader's Library*. . . . But the vast and varied array of Right-wing publications was losing ground in the 1840s and 1850s to the generally more moderate or liberal, occasionally covertly radical, press, exemplified best by the two journals with which Belinskii came to be associated, . . . *Notes of the Fatherland* and . . . *The Contemporary*. Al-

though, to be sure, Bakunin could not preach anarchism openly, and although even the Slavophiles found it very difficult to propagate their word in print, Russian journalism in the reign of Nicholas I came to express to some considerable extent the buoyant and contentious thought of Russian intellectuals.

Some figures might be in order to substantiate this insufficiently appreciated point of the great growth of the Russian periodical press by the middle of the nineteenth century. During the last year of Paul I's reign, 1801, eleven periodical publications existed in Russia. . . . By 1807 . . . , thirty-nine periodicals were being published in the empire. One obvious reason for this growth was the repeal of the Pauline laws, and the enactment of much milder censorship regulations which, among other things, again allowed private individuals to operate printing-presses. There was little or no progress between 1807 and 1822, followed by a spurt during the remaining years of the decade, when the number of journals reached the annual average of forty-two. Steady growth continued in the eighteen-thirties, so that forty-six periodicals were published on the average annually between 1831 and 1837. . . .

Circulation rates are of special interest to historians, because they remain the best index available of readership, although, needless to say, that index lacks precision. . . [T]he circulation of Russian periodicals was rising steadily in the first decades of the nineteenth century. In published literature, figures exist for seventeen separate general periodicals which came out between 1801 and 1837. Almost all of them started with printings of between 300 and 600 copies. The more successful ones quickly increased the number to between 1,000 and 1,500. . . . Still larger figures were reached in the 1830s. In particular, Bulgarin and Grech's newspaper, . . . *The Northern Bee*, acquired 4,000 subscriptions early in the decade, while *The Reader's Library* reached an unprecedented figure of 5,000 subscribers in 1835, and of 7,000 two years later. Senkovskii especially catered frantically to the undiscriminating taste for entertainment of a public that was beginning to read the periodical press for the first time. . . .

Circulation of the periodicals also apparently rose markedly in the 1840s. . . . *The Russian Messenger*, for example, rose early in the decade from printings of between 1,000 and 1,200 copies to printings of 2,000, although it quickly went down after the departure of Nicholas Polevoi. . . . *The Contemporary* and . . . *Notes of the Fatherland* proved to be especially popular. The former printed 2,000 copies per issue in 1847, and as many as 3,100 a year later. [The latter] made in the course of the decade the still more striking jump from about 1,200 to some 4,000 copies. . . .

Most studies of Russian intellectual life in the second quarter of the nineteenth century [also] give some consideration to *kruzhki*, or circles, . . . [which] served frequently as the main vehicle for the formulation and dissemination of thought in Russia . . . Aronson and Reiser in their book which focuses on the same period as my present work, refer to '400 circles, salons, and other forms of association'. . . . Suffice it to state here that for the period the basic form was a relatively small, intimate group of young men devoted to a particular, although at times rapidly evolving, teaching. . . . Youth, enthusiasm, togetherness, intellectual and emotional discovery all gave the circles their unforgettable appeal. . . .

Yet the circles had their critics too. To quote the most famous instance of such criticism, mounted by Ivan Turgenev, who had a full personal knowledge of the matter, in his story 'Hamlet of the Shchigry District':

What do I find horrible [in a circle]?—he exclaimed.—That is what: a circle is a destruction of all autonomous development; a circle is a disgusting substitution for society, women, life; a circle . . . oh, just wait, I shall tell you what a circle is! A circle is an indolent and sluggish existence together and next to one another, which is given the appearance of a reasonable undertaking; a circle replaces conversation with ratiocinations, accustoms you to fruitless talk, diverts you from solitary beneficial work, inoculates you with the literary itch; finally, it deprives you of the freshness and the virgin strength of your soul . . . in a circle people adore an empty rhetoritician, a selfish smart alec, a man old before his time; they carry in their arms a versifier who has

no talent but possesses 'hidden' thoughts; in a circle young, seventeen-year-old fellows discuss cunningly and in an involved manner women and love, while in front of women they remain silent, or they talk to them as if they were talking to a book. . . .

Still, this ferocious condemnation of the circles did not tell the full story, even as far as Turgenev was concerned, let alone other Russian intellectuals. Chicherin wrote in his memoirs:

On one occasion I told Ivan Sergeevich Turgenev that he had no business attacking so hard Muscovite circles in his 'Hamlet of the Shchigry district'. The stifling atmosphere of a closed circle had, without doubt, its disadvantages; but what was one to do, when people were not allowed into the open air? These were the lungs with which at that time Russian thought, pressed on all sides, could breathe. And how many fresh forces these circles contained, what lively intellectual interests, how well they brought people together, how much they had of what was supportive, encouraging, exciting! The exclusiveness itself disappeared when at a general tournament gathered people who had opposite views but who valued and respected one another. Turgenev agreed with my remarks. . . .

The period of the circles leading to the emergence of the Russian intelligentsia corresponded to a certain level in the growth of the Russian educated public. Larger and more independent, differentiated, and divided than it had been in the eighteenth century, or in the first decades of the nineteenth, that public remained a small and circumscribed elite. Russia was still far from general education and modern mass culture.

Russian foreign relations and the internal development of the country, the opinion of Russia in the Western world and the changing structure of Russian intellectual life, in particular its increasing professionalization, all affected Russian thought, and indeed contributed to its turn against the government. In the end, it is necessary to revisit briefly the thought itself. . . . Russia experienced two intellectual transformations in the second quarter of the nineteenth century: the change from the ideology of the Age of Reason to romanticism and idealism, and the disintegration of the new world view, or rather views. . . .

The philosophy of the Enlightenment was probably the last truly unifying ideology of the Western world. In Russia, as elsewhere, it was followed by division and fragmentation, the common language of the rulers and the educated public by a babel of tongues. The poignancy and the special tragedy of the Radishchev episode was due precisely to the fact that the critic and Catherine the Great belonged to essentially the same intellectual camp. . . . But there was no way for Benckendorff [the head of Nicholas I's Third Department, or political police] to understand the Slavophiles. . . . The connection was no more. At the same time the thought of Russian intellectuals, and to a certain extent of the government too, was becoming, so to speak, increasingly unreal. The point is not that Enlightenment is health and romanticism sickness—both certainly can be sick and perhaps both can be healthy—but rather that in the particular historical experience of Russia the ideas of the intellectuals of the 1830s and the 1840s were much further removed from any actual or possible reality than those of their counterparts in the preceding generations . . . : what was collapsing was not only the concept of enlightened despotism, or of autocracy, but an entire intellectual order.

SOURCE: Nicholas V. Riasanovsky, *A Parting of Ways: Government and the Educated Public in Russia 1801–1855* (New York, NY: Oxford University Press, 1976), 248–97 (excerpted). Reprinted by permission of Oxford University Press.

19

The Great Reforms

The "era of the Great Reforms" refers to a remarkable ten-year period beginning in the late 1850s, during which time the Russian government generated an enormous corpus of legislative reform, some of which touched upon the most fundamental institutional underpinnings of Russian society. These laws were drafted by a series of legislative committees (the so-called "Secret Committee," then the "Main Committee" succeeded by the "Editing Committee" and numerous other such committees), most of which convened in nominal secrecy in the capital after being given specific mandates by the new ruler, Alexander II (1855–81). But the political atmosphere within which these major reorganizations were discussed was anything but secret.

As Bruce Lincoln has already noted, the leading members of all of these committees came from the corps of "enlightened bureaucrats" who had privately been urging major changes for years in the drawing rooms and salons of polite society. Sanctioned or otherwise, petitions, supplications, and formal recommendations emerged from strikingly frank and heated discussions that went on all over the empire, and among numerous social groups. The nobility, in particular, was roused to unprecedented attention, and they met in the tens of thousands to debate and generally oppose the reforms, and then to send on the "instructions" to the committees that the Tsar had requested of them. Thus, "the era of the Great Reforms" refers as much to the politics and discourse of reform as it does to the legislation itself. Indeed, the extensive encouragements to speak publicly ("glasnost' ") constituted one of the major departures from the political repression of the reign of Nicholas I.

By the late 1860s major reform legislation had modified taxation, secondary and higher education, the officer corps, finance, the judicial system, and local government. All of these had a marked bearing on the way the state governed and intervened in the relationships among various social groups. However, the most fundamental legislative change came in March 1861, when Alexander II issued the manifesto that emancipated the serfs from the legal bondage that had tied them to their landlords for well over two centuries.

The emancipation decrees freeing the serfs and a comparable one freeing state peasants in 1864 made freedom partial and conditional, and it did not come cheap. Clearly the autocracy was not about to undermine the stability of the Russian countryside or impoverish the landed nobility upon which it continued to rely very heavily for service. Peasants could not move of their own free will, and, by a complex set of formulas, they gained only a portion of the land that they had formerly worked. They incurred large 49-year indemnity payments (a form of mortgage owed by the entire village community to the state in exchange for the land that they received), and they still paid the soul tax. This was not the "true freedom" (*volia*) that was inscribed in so much peasant lore, and most scholars of the period have concluded that the peasants expressed disappointment and disbelief when they understood how much the emancipation decrees fell short of their prayed-for deliverance unto freedom.

The peasantry also learned that emancipation did not free them from financial dealings with the landlord. Land poor and in need of more cash, the communes were obliged to negotiate from a position of relative weakness with their former masters for access to their land, via share-cropping, rent, or wage labor. Emancipation, therefore, did not undermine landlord–peasant society as such, at least not initially and not by design. Still, the great reforms did bring about visible and important changes in the relations between landlords, peasants, and government. Landlords had forever lost their source of free labor, about which they expressed the most profound bitterness. As a majority of landlords saw it, emancipation deprived them not just of their source of free labor; it constituted an assault on the patriarchal authority that stood at the core of their outlook on the world. No longer could they look upon the peasantry and the entire countryside as extensions of their domain; or presume to intervene in the lives of the peasant villagers. They lost their standing as the primary source of rural authority, and in their place there arose a network of formal institutional arrangements between commune, local govern-ment (the new *zemstvos*) and the central government. Thus, from the perspective of provincial landlords, the emancipation amounted to an attack on their whole way of life.

The documents in this chapter provide a glimpse into some of these outlooks, as well as offering a perspective of the reform process from the inside, mostly in the speeches and remi-niscences of the tsar and participants of the committees. This chapter also includes a sampling of the major pieces of legislation, some of which are connected only generally to freeing the serfs. The selections by Larissa Zakharova and Terence Emmons represent just two of the many ways that have been offered by historians of making sense of the Great Reforms. At the same time, these selections raise what undoubtedly loom as the most compelling questions that the reforms pose: Why did the autocracy feel compelled to introduce these basic changes? And what impact did they have on the dynamics of Russian life?

Had we been compiling this reader a couple of generations ago, we would have presented a somewhat different picture of the state of the historical literature. At that point, most scholars treated the reforms as the deliberate onset of a change in Russia's social system. For most Soviet historians, the circumstances that produced the Great Reforms were captured by the concept of "The First Revolutionary Situation" that obliged the Russian state and ruling class to abandon its feudal economy and society and enter the era of capitalism. Few non-Soviet scholars endorsed the concept of a revolutionary situation, but they, too, tended to argue that Russia underwent a systemic crisis in the 1850s. For most of them, the crisis was brought on by the loss of the Crimean War, the first such loss in about 150 years, which forced Russian officialdom to confront anew Russia's "backwardness." Some historians have seen this confrontation as a moral dilemma, or crisis of confidence, rather than a breakdown of the system as such. Others have argued that it was specifically the military failure in the Crimea, and the desire to provide a more dependable social underpinning to the armed forces, that set the Great Reforms in motion. The most widely held view, though, conceived of the era as one in which the autocracy (described variously as "liberal," "conservative," "the great liberator,") was facing a crisis of "modernization," in which numerous institutions suddenly appeared to be in need of urgent renovation. Once again, emphases varied, but most adherents to the modernization approach stressed the incompatibility of serfdom and the dawning state-sponsored course of industrial development.

Recently, scholars have edged away from these images of a systemic crisis leading inexorably to reform, without explicitly rejecting them. Current writing pays attention to the complexity and fluidity of the reform process itself, and to the experiences of landlords and peasants, men and women, administrators and engaged reformers, during and after emancipation. Implicitly, this discourse makes the reforms appear less determined or inexorable, and more subject to the ambiguities, reluctance, contradictions, and even backward-looking sentiments that character-ized many of the negotiations that gave the legislation their final cast. As of this writing, no new overarching theories are looming on the horizon.

The texts that follow provide a general understanding of the deliberations that led to the Great Reforms and that shaped them, as well as present the main terms of the most important new laws. The range of institutions that this tidal wave of legislation affected was immense, and it would be impossible to reproduce here every facet of legislative reform of this era. Clearly, the central change was the emancipation of the serfs (1861) and state peasants (1866); the creation of the *zemstvos*, or agencies of local government (1864), and the various reforms of education, the judiciary, and the military.

As you read the documents, pay attention to the concerns expressed by the speakers, and to the changes that the laws proposed bringing about in the lives of Russia's peasant majority.

DOCUMENTS

The Political Debates (1856–61)

TSAR ALEXANDER II'S SPEECH TO REPRESENTATIVES OF THE MOSCOW NOBILITY (MARCH 30, 1856)

I have learned, gentlemen, that rumors have spread among you of my intention to abolish serfdom. To refute any groundless gossip on so important a subject I consider it necessary to inform you that I have no intention of doing so immediately. But, of course, and you your-selves realize it, the existing system of serf own-ing cannot remain unchanged. It is better to begin abolishing serfdom from above than to wait for it to begin to abolish itself from below. I ask you, gentlemen, to think of ways of doing this. Pass on my words to the nobles for con-sideration. [p. 589]

REMINISCENCES OF IA. A. SOLOV'EV ON THE EDITORIAL COMMISSIONS (1870s)

From the moment that the sovereign an-nounced to the Moscow nobility his intention to free the serfs, there began a struggle be-tween the liberal and the conservative ele-ments. The regulator of the preponderance of one or the other of these parties was the will of the sovereign emperor. Only this autocratic power, moved by a deep love for Russia and a passionate desire for her good, could support the numerically small and socially weak pro-gressive party, which otherwise could have been destroyed by the strong and influential representatives of the estate-owners' inter-ests. . . .

Immediately after the publication of the first rescript, a reactionary movement started in the committee itself . . . supported and nourished by the obvious sympathy of the society of the time. . . . The aims of this group were either to block the reform completely or, if that proved impossible, to free the serfs without land and to receive compensation for having granted them personal freedom. As a means of attain-ing one of these aims they launched a scare campaign threatening peasant unrest and democratic revolution and also a general eco-nomic upheaval in the state. . . .

A significant majority of estate owners either did not sympathize at all with the enterprise that had begun or at least objected to giving the serfs land along with their freedom. The provincial opposition movement fed the Petersburg movement, which in turn supported the provincial movement. In Petersburg drawing rooms, at court functions, at parades and inspections of the troops, behind the walls of the State Council and the Senate, and in the offices of the ministers and members of the State Council were heard more or less energetic protests against the intentions of the government. These protests expressed in vigorous terms more or less the same idea—that the emancipation of the serfs was premature; the result of the change, said the numerous enemies of the proposed reform, would be that the estate owners would remain without working hands, the peasants because of their natural indolence would not work even for themselves, the productivity of the state would decrease, causing general inflation, famine, disease, and nationwide misery. At the same time would come insubordination on the part of the peasants, local disorders followed by widespread rioting—in a word, they predicted another Pugachev rebellion with all its horrors and with the addition of a "deeply plotted" democratic revolution. [pp. 590–91]

GENERAL IA. I. ROSTOVTSEV ON THE ROLE OF THE EDITORIAL COMMISSIONS (1859)

1. The problem before us of eliminating serfdom and improving the welfare of the peasants must be solved with strict fairness and impartiality for both parties, and in such a way as to prevent any grounds at all for hostility between the two classes; in other words, in such a way that Russia may find in the peaceful solution of this problem a true, long-term guarantee against upheaval in the state.

2. Along with individual freedom the peasants must receive full opportunity to acquire enough land of their own to provide for their everyday needs . . . , for without this the life of the peasants would improve merely in word and not in deed. . . .

7. The land to be redeemed by the peasant should consist of a farmstead and a sufficient allotment of land in a plot that is separate from the remaining land possessed by the owner.

8. For the land they cede, estate owners must be remunerated justly and as far as possible without loss and impoverishment.

9. The peasants' yearly payment of both interest and redemption dues must not exceed the average amount of their present obligations, or else there will be no improvement in their living conditions. [p.593]

THE COMPLAINT OF THE COMMITTEES OF THE PROVINCIAL NOBILITY (1859)

Having distorted in the guberniia committees the deeds of the tsar and the people, and having distorted for so many years the tsar's best thoughts and trampled on his most noble feelings, could the bureaucracy tolerate a situation in which the tsar would hear the voice of his people other than through its own untruthful lips! . . .

The deputies who arrived in Saint Petersburg were completely neglected. The minister of internal affairs did not bother to present them to Your Majesty, nor even to the Main Committee. Then they were suddenly sent an unsigned invitation to visit the Editorial Commission, and there Adjutant General Rostovtsev issued written instructions signed by Butkov, head clerk of the Main Committee, in which, without any regard for the normal system of announcing imperial commands, Your Majesty's orders were countermanded and the deputies were obliged to answer questions which the Editorial Commission considered necessary. . . .

Our grief, Sire, cannot be expressed! More than once in the course of the present matter we have seen the bureaucracy either counterpose one imperial command against another or violate them, but their effrontery had never reached this point before.

Throughout the course of this matter the administrative authorities have continually scorned legality and justice; but they did so out in the provinces in the obscurity of office correspondence, whereas now they are doing it in front of the sovereign and Russia, in plain sight of everyone.

The records of the Editorial Commission and all its administrative actions are filled with harmful and ruinous ideas; we can see them but we are powerless to expose them. [pp. 593–94]

ROSTOVTSEV'S VERSION OF THE PROVINCIAL NOBILITY'S COMPLAINTS (1859)

YOUR IMPERIAL MAJESTY!

At our last meeting you expressed a desire to know how our sacred cause was proceeding.

With some of the deputies . . . we have not yet reached agreement on details, but we expect to do so more or less. With others of them we have been unable to agree on fundamentals, and there will be no possibility of coming to terms.

The main divergence is that the Commissions and certain deputies proceed from different premises. The commissions proceed from state necessity and state law, while the deputies base themselves on civil law and private interests. They are right from their viewpoint, and we from ours.

From the standpoint of civil law the entire reform we have undertaken is unjust from beginning to end, since it is a violation of the right to private ownership; but as a state necessity and on the basis of state law, the reform is legitimate, sacred, and essential.

A large number of enemies of the reform who are unable to see its urgency accuse the Editorial Commissions both verbally and in writing of a desire to fleece the nobles, and others even call some of the members of the commissions ''Reds'' and accuse them of wanting to cause anarchy. . . .

The efforts of the commissions have been and are still:

First, to *save* Russia. If eleven million people who have been consoled for two years by the hope of freedom and an improvement in their position are disappointed, they will become despondent and lose their faith in and love for the supreme power; they will attribute the failure of their hopes to the estate owners, and Russia will not be saved. . . .[pp. 595–96]

ALEXANDER II'S SPEECH TO THE STATE COUNCIL (1861)

The matter of the liberation of the serfs . . . I consider to be a vital question for Russia, upon which will depend the development of her strength and power. I am sure that all of you, gentlemen, are just as convinced as I am of the benefits and necessity of this measure. I have another conviction, which is that this matter cannot be postponed . . . I repeat—and this is my absolute will—that this matter should be finished right away.

For four years now it has dragged on and has been arousing various fears and anticipations among both the estate owners and the peasants. Any further delay could be disastrous to the state. . . . I hope, gentlemen, that on inspection of the drafts presented to the State Council, you will assure yourselves that all that can be done for the protection of the interests of the nobility has been done; if on the other hand you find it necessary in any way to alter or to add to the presented work, then I am ready to receive your comments; but I ask you only not to forget that the basis of the whole work must be the improvement of the life of the peasants—an improvement not in words alone or on paper but in actual fact. [pp. 599–600]

The Reform Statutes (1861–66)

THE GENERAL STATUTE ON THE EMANCIPATION OF THE SERFS (1861)

1. The serfdom of peasants settled on estate owners' landed properties, and of household serfs, is abolished forever. . . .

2. Peasants and household serfs who have emerged from serfdom are accorded both the personal and the property rights accompanying the legal status of free village dwellers. . . .

3. Estate owners, retaining the right of ownership to all land belonging to them, accord the peasants . . . the permanent utilization of their homesteads and in addition, in order to provide for their livelihood and the performance of their duties to the government and the estate owner, that amount of fields and other landed resources which is determined according to the principles set forth in the local statutes.

4. In return for the allotment assigned to them . . . , the peasants are obliged to discharge to the estate owners, in labor or in money, the obligations defined in the local statutes.

CHAPTER II.

CONCERNING THE ADMINISTRATION OF
THE VILLAGE COMMUNITY

46. The administration of the village community is composed of:

a. The village assembly.

b. The village elder.

In addition, those communities that deem it necessary may have: special tax-gatherers; overseers of the granaries, schools, and infirmaries; forest and field wardens; village clerks, and so forth.

47. The "village assembly" is composed of the peasant-householders belonging to the village community and, in addition, all elected village officials.

51. Under the jurisdiction of the village assembly are:

a. The election of village officials and the appointment of delegates to the volost' [rural district] assembly. . . .

c. The release of members from the community and the acceptance of new ones. . . .

e. The settlement of family divisions (of property).

f. Matters relating to communal utilization of land belonging to the commune, that is: the redistribution of land, the imposition and re-

moval of work obligations, the final distribution of communal land into permanent plots, and so forth. . . .

k. The apportionment of all fiscal taxes, land, and communal monetary levies, and likewise the land and communal obligations in kind imposed upon the peasants; and the systematic keeping of accounts for the aforesaid taxes and levies. . . .

q. The bestowal of power of attorney for representing the community in legal matters. . .

69. The volost' administration is composed of:

a. The volost' assembly.

b. The volost' elder with the volost' executive board.

c. The volost' peasant court. . . .

71. The volost' assembly is composed of village and volost' officials who hold office through election . . . and of peasants elected from each settlement or hamlet. . . .

78. Under the jurisdiction of the volost' assembly are:

a. The election of volost' officials and judges of the volost' courts.

b. Decisions on all subjects in general that relate to the economic and public affairs of the entire volost'.

c. Measures of public care for the poor; the establishment of volost' schools. . . .

g. The verification of the recruiting lists and the apportionment of recruit obligations. . . .
[pp. 600–602]

FROM THE STATUTES ON LOCAL GOVERNMENT (ZEMSTVO) (1864)

1. For the management of affairs relating to the local economic welfare and needs of each uezd, guberniia and uezd zemstvo institutions are to be formed. . . .

2. The matters that are subject to the jurisdiction of zemstvo institutions . . . are:

i. The management of the property, capital, and monetary levies of the zemstvo.

ii. The organization and maintenance of buildings belonging to the zemstvo, other equipment, and roads maintained at the expense of the zemstvo. . . .

"Three Generations of Peasants," Orel Province, late 1860s. Observe the peasants' attire and tools that they are holding. Some machine-made textile implements (such as the spinning wheel) are intermingled with handmade farming implements, an indication of the growing diversity of the rural economy in the mid-nineteenth century. From *Neskol'ko narodnykh tipov Rossii,* a collection of photographs by J. X. Raoult, Odessa. Courtesy of The New York Public Library, Slavic and Baltic Division.

iv. The management of zemstvo charitable institutions and other measures of care for the poor; methods of eliminating poverty; looking after the building of churches. . . .

vii. Participation, primarily in an economic capacity and within the limits defined by the law, in looking after public education, public health, and prisons. . . .

ix. The execution of the demands that the military and civil administrations place upon the zemstvo. . . .

xiii. The holding of elections for membership and for other positions in zemstvo institutions, and the allocation of money for the maintenance of these institutions. . . .

6. Zemstvo institutions function independently within the sphere of activity entrusted to them. . . .

9. The guberniia head has the right to suspend the execution of any disposition of the zemstvo institutions that is contrary to the laws, or to the general welfare of the state. . . .

13. The uezd zemstvo institutions are: the uezd zemstvo assembly and the zemstvo executive board.

14. The uezd zemstvo assembly is composed of zemstvo members, elected: (a) by the landed proprietors of the uezd; (b) by the urban communities; and (c) by the village communities. . .

43. The uezd zemstvo assembly is under the chairmanship of the uezd marshal of the nobility. . . .

50. The guberniia zemstvo institutions are: the guberniia zemstvo assembly and the guberniia zemstvo executive board.

53. The guberniia zemstvo assembly. . . is under the chairmanship of the guberniia marshal of the nobility. [pp. 613–14]

FROM THE JUDICIAL REFORM (1864)

THE ESTABLISHMENT
OF JUDICIAL INSTITUTIONS

1. Judicial authority belongs to: Justices of the peace; Sessions of the Justices of the peace; Circuit courts; Judicial tribunals; The Governing Senate, in the capacity of a supreme court of appeal.

2. The judicial authority of the[se] extends to persons of all classes and to all cases, both civil and criminal. . . .

6. Examining magistrates are attached [to the courts] for conducting investigations in cases involving crimes and offenses.

7. For determining the guilt or innocence of the accused in criminal cases, jurors are added to the composition of the court, in instances designated in the statute on criminal procedure.

8. Chief prosecutors, prosecutors, and their assistants are attached to the courts for supervising prosecutions. . . .

19. To the post of justice of the peace may be elected those local residents who: first, are at least twenty-five years of age; second, have received a higher or secondary education, or have passed an examination equivalent to it, or have served for not fewer than three years in a post the duties of which could enable them to acquire a practical knowledge of judicial procedure; and third, if in addition they themselves, or their parents or wives, own . . . real estate with a value of not less than fifteen thousand rubles. . . .

24. Election of justices of the peace are held at uezd zemstvo assemblies. . . .

81. Jurors are elected from among all classes of local inhabitants. . . .

202. The posts of chairmen, assistant chairmen, and of (other) members of the judiciary . . . may be filled . . . only by persons who have a certificate from a university or other institution of higher education, testifying to the completion of a course in jurisprudence, or who have passed an examination in this science, or who have demonstrated their knowledge of judicial procedure in some official capacity. [pp. 614–16]

FROM THE DECREE ON STATE PEASANTS (1866)

1. The village communities of state peasants retain all the land and landed resources reserved to them as allotments and which they are utilizing. In those communities where the land in peasant utilization is not demarcated from the land remaining at the immediate disposal of the treasury, the area of the peasant allotment is determined in proportion to existing utilization. . . .

3. State peasants who own, on the basis of this decree, the land reserved to them in accordance with the aforesaid deeds are obliged to make the treasury a yearly payment as determined by law, which is called the "state obrok tax"; this tax was not to exceed by more than 15 percent the amount the state peasants had been assessed by the government before this time. . . . [pp. 620–21]

SOURCE: Unless otherwise noted, these documents come from the superb collection and translation of materials in George Vernadsky et al. (eds), *A Source Book for Russian History from Early Times to 1917*. Vol. 3 *Alexander II to the February Revolution* (New Haven, CT, and London: Yale University Press, 1972), pp. 589–621. These selections are reprinted by permission of Yale University Press. Students wishing a more extensive rendering of the reform legislation may wish to consult the Vernadsky source book. (The relevant pages from which the translated texts come are given in brackets at the end of each selection.)

LITERATURE

LARISSA ZAKHAROVA
The Government and the Great Reforms of the 1860s

For decades, most Soviet scholars insisted that the emancipation of the serfs in 1861, and more generally the entire enterprise of the "Great Reforms," arose because a "revolutionary situation" threatened to undermine autocracy and the political authority of the nobility. If the government did not agree to reform from above, the argument had it, it was risking an imminent popular rebellion from below. This line of reasoning never won many adherents outside of the Soviet Union, and, more recently, post-Soviet historians have begun to articulate alternative readings of the reform era. Larissa Zakharova, a leading specialist from Moscow, attempts in this essay to bring together a great many issues and several traditions of historical explanation as a way of bringing new understanding to this important transition in Russian history.

The abolition of serfdom in Russia in 1861 and the ensuing reforms (in local self-government, the courts, the military, education, censorship, etc.) are events of vital importance, a break and turning point in our country's history. The reformers themselves, their contemporaries, researchers, the classics of Russian literature, and the founders of Marxism all agree with this appraisal. Interest in the history of the reforms, which were called "great" in prerevolutionary historiography and "bourgeois" in Soviet historiography, has been particularly intense and has assumed political overtones at certain times, as, for example, during the Revolution of 1905–1907. Nowadays, it might be said, such interest has reached the highest

point it has known during the entire 125 years that separate us from the event itself. . . .

WHAT WAS SIGNIFICANT ABOUT 1856?

Alexander II ascended to the throne in February 1855. On the 18th, the day Nicholas I died, the manifesto concerning his accession was issued and on the 19th the State Council took an oath to the new emperor and his successor. Unlike 1825, the transfer of power was smooth. The death of Nicholas I coincided with and laid bare the crisis of the military-police system that had lasted thirty years and had been created to counter the ideas of the Decembrists and progress.

The first powerful blow to Nicholas's system came from without. The defeat suffered in the Crimean War (1853–1856) had shown the real state of Russia. The country not only emerged defeated from the war but also found itself isolated internationally. . . .

Is it really by accident that the government's first proclamation concerning the future reforms, obscure and vague as it was, appeared in the Manifesto of March 19, 1856, which announced the terms of the Treaty of Paris that brought Russia no glory? "Let good internal order be affirmed and achieved (in Russia); let truth and mercy reign in her courts; let a longing for education and every useful activity develop everywhere with fresh vigor and let each and every person with justice for all be protected under the rule of law and universal justice, and let the fruits of the labor of the innocent be enjoyed in peace." A few days later, responding to widespread rumors and fears among the gentry that had been aroused precisely by these words of the manifesto, Alexander II uttered his famous pronouncement before marshals of the nobility in Moscow on March 30, 1856, in which he spoke of the liberation of the serfs: "It is far better that this come from above than from below."

Dissatisfaction gripped every level in society; it provoked a stream of hand-written accusatory communications and plans for reform, a regular underground literature. It seemed as though the whole of thinking Russia had started writing. A passionate, uncontrollable demand for society to express itself swept away the prohibition Nicholas I had imposed on the printed word, which had led from 1848 to 1855 to a "terror of censorship." M. E. Saltykov-Shchedrin, who returned from exile at this time and landed in Moscow before proceeding to St. Petersburg (for service in the Ministry of Internal Affairs), was astounded how freely everybody was expressing his opinion everywhere and on everything. Ordinary people, officials, the intelligentsia, and the leadership were talking on the streets, in homes, in taverns, and in salons. . . .

This openness ["glasnost'" in Russian] sprang spontaneously from below. The government lagged behind events; it renounced the worst forms of censorship but continued to eye openness askance. Keenly sensing his country's demand for truth after such a long period of silence and lies, A. I. Herzen began to publish *Poliarnaia zvezda* [*Polar Star*] (1855), *Golosa iz Rossii* [*Voices from Russia*] (1856), and lastly *Kolokol* [*The Bell*] (1857), which were known to everyone who could read, from the tsar and his highest officials down to provincial gentry and clergy in the most remote areas, to say nothing of students. In Russia proper, publications that reflected the thaw began to appear "like mushrooms after a rain" (to use the expression of Tolstoi upon his return from Sevastopol').

Openness is yet another word that symbolizes the unique year of 1856. Openness unmasked, but its pathos lay in creation. It brought a wave of optimism and bright hope; it aroused government and society to action and curbed the fear that had nurtured Nicholas's system. The release of society's spiritual force preceded the reforms and constituted a prerequisite for them. . . .

As early as January 1857 the ruling elite and Alexander II learned the true financial position, which was extremely bad and ominous.

During the war years, from 1853 to 1856, ordinary expenditures increased the budget deficit almost sevenfold, from nine million to almost sixty-one million silver rubles and the total deficit went up sixfold from fifty-two million to 307 million rubles. . . .

At first, particularly in 1856, innovation in domestic policy expressed itself in the removal of numerous prohibitions. This involved abolishing the restrictions that had been imposed on universities after 1848, eliminating the military settlements and the governor-generalships in Khar'kov and Vitebsk, reaching the decision freely to issue passports for travel abroad (which increased from 6,000 to 26,000 persons, more than fourfold, from 1856 to 1859), easing censorship, offering opportunities "to establish trading links with foreign countries and to import the latest European scientific achievements from them," shrinking the army, forgiving arrears, and freeing for three years taxpaying estates from army impressment, as well as other measures. Of special importance was a proclamation issued during the coronation ceremonies in August 1856, freeing political prisoners. . . . Nine thousand were released from administrative and police surveillance. . . .

CHOOSING THE WAY: OVERCOMING OLD MODELS AND DEVISING A NEW ONE

Preparation for the reform began in a purely traditional manner, when the regular Secret Committee assembled in the Winter Palace in January 1857. But because of the "thaw" old traditions suddenly produced new effects. As early as the second session, the statesmen of Nicholas's era decided that the government should publish an edict on the peasant question for general consumption, print it, frame it in glass and circulate it in all provinces, districts, and remote outposts of the empire in order to "calm turbulent minds." Even the chief of police expressed himself in favor of this move. The edict was not issued, but this episode reveals how unexpectedly life had intruded upon the "holy of holies" in the government mechanism. Another ten months had to pass before secrecy was removed from this committee and from the peasant question. . . .

The rescripts [instructions approved and signed by the emperor in November and December, 1857] were not at all radical. They still had nothing to say about "liberating the peasantry," only about "an improvement in life," but the documents accompanying them made it clear that this phrase meant abolition of peasants' personal dependency. The rescripts formulated the chief question, involving the land, in an even more vague and contradictory way. Landlords were to keep their property and peasants could anticipate no more than a right to redeem small plots and to occupy their allotments. But the terms under which they could use them, how long an allotment might be kept and its size, and, above all, what the ultimate goal was—"perpetual" use, like the case of agricultural implements in the southwestern provinces or freedom without land as in the northwestern ones—remained open.

The rescripts had come down "from above," which meant they had to be acted upon. The gentry obtained the right to form local provincial committees to draft reforms for each province following the rescripts. It was assumed that each would devise its own plan and rules, which would be introduced gradually from west to east.

Shaken by the publicity given to the peasant question and the firm commitment to reform, the bulk of the gentry failed to respond to the government's initiatives calling upon them to take action. The Nizhegorod nobility alone sent an "all-embracing" request to obtain the rescript, which was done immediately. . . . The stand-off lasted two months and was only broken with difficulty on January 16, 1858.

After this, one group after another among the local gentry took up the task, set to work on rescripts in reply, and formed provincial gentry committees. Their "initiatives" were apparent. In 1858 and early 1859 forty-six provincial committees, comprising 1,500 persons, were established in European Russia. Elected to those committees, which composed re-

sponses addressed to Alexander II, were some 44,000 gentry, forty percent of the total number who possessed serfs. This is the way the techniques for reform began to come into existence. In every provincial committee two "members of the government" were designated in order to control the actions of the gentry, whom the government had summoned into public life.

After a delay of three months since its activities had become known, the Secret Committee came out in the open and was renamed the Main Committee. Although its composition stayed the same, the scope of its activity, tempo, and style of work underwent a change. . . . The Main Committee was involved in a struggle that had exploded among the gentry in various places over the question of what concrete steps had to be taken and how many concessions would have to be made to the peasantry. . . . In addition to those who supported or opposed the abolition of serfdom, there were others who advocated different ways for the country to develop variations on the reform. The Main Committee found itself caught up in the maelstrom of events, to which it was forced to react. Telegrams poured into St. Petersburg, couriers arrived from the "majorities" and "minorities" on the gentry committees: so-and-so needs support; so-and-so must be turned down; and inquiries came in concerning the obscure programmatic positions found in the rescripts.

At the same time, provincial committees on their own initiative held public meetings in the field. There were stormy scenes of uncensored fighting and brawling. Leaders of the group had bodyguards; Iu. F. Samarin carried a revolver. The committees began to forge links among themselves. They learned how to discuss and resolve matters of state; they learned methods of political struggle and the rudiments of constitutionalism. . . .

This openness assumed forms the government had not anticipated and brought about unexpected consequences. The press grew bold and temporarily forgot the limits the rescript had imposed, and the censorship could not cope with events. But the government followed the situation in the country with great care. . . .

Government policy fluctuated between the reactionaries and the liberal bureaucrats. In the spring of 1858, the Main Committee was inclined to free the peasants without land and also to a scheme that would establish everywhere a military administration based on governors general. At that particular time, the journal *Sovremennik* was harassed. It was withdrawn from circulation and the April number, containing an article by K. D. Kavelin which spelled out that the ultimate goal of the reform was to force the peasantry to redeem fertile land as property, was banned. Kavelin fell into disfavor, was deprived of his post as tutor to the heir, and was denied any direct participation in the peasant reform. In addition, on April 15 and 22, a circular was issued in the department of the censorship that forbade any discussion of the peasant question in the press. . . .

A new concept had made its way into the realm of official government policy and become prevalent: the ultimate goal of the reform was to transform former serfs into proprietors of their own allotments, eliminate the patrimonial power of the landlords, and legally involve the peasantry in the life of the state. This switch in government policy, which took place during October and November 1858, was due to the activities of Adjutant General Ia. I. Rostovtsev, a member of the Main Committee, whom Alexander II trusted completely. After six months of intensive work on the social and political situation, Rostovtsev, who had thought and agonized much, rejected the variant that freed the peasants without land and for all practical purposes accepted liberal notions and reform goals, which the government as early as April 1858 had forbidden and persecuted. . . .

Rostovtsev expounded his views on the goals of the peasant reform in four letters to the tsar in August and September 1858. Alexander instructed the Main Committee to discuss them.

Two questions of principle collided in its stormy sessions: either leave all property under the control of landlords and create a strong landlord economy after emancipation or allot land to the peasants as their own property, which they would redeem. After the reform, two kinds of agriculture would then exist in the countryside—large landlord holdings and small peasant properties. First, Lanskoi succeeded in negotiating with the liberal fraction on the Tver' Provincial Committee to expand the redemption to include fields for the peasants, not merely plots. Next, with pressure from Alexander II, who agreed with Rostovtsev, the government adopted a peasant reform program that differed from the rescripts, and the monarch ratified it on December 4, 1858. It would allow peasants to redeem land and form a class of peasant property owners. Most Main Committee members were violently opposed but the tsar cut off debate and declared the question closed. . . .

While the reform was being drawn up, the move from secrecy to openness begun at the end of 1857 intensified late in 1858 when the government dropped its opposition to having the peasants redeem the land and admitted the fundamental purpose of the reform was to create a class of peasant proprietors while still preserving manorial agriculture. This led to a regrouping of forces among the "authorities," and the liberal bureaucracy now took on the leading role in the peasant question.

THE MECHANISM OF CREATION AND THE MECHANISM OF DELAY; THE DIE IS CAST; THE REFORMS

[O]n February 17, 1859, Alexander II sanctioned the formation of a special commission, with the sole proviso that Rostovtsev serve as its chairman. Its modest title of Editing Commissions fully corresponded with the ideas of the members of the Main Committee, who thought it was formed as a kind of subcommission. . . .

The new institution was primarily nontraditional in that most of its members were liberal activists. Naturally the commissions contained serf-owners, but they constituted a minority. P. A. Valuev, a savage opponent of the commissions, had every reason to say: "they were set up in such a way so that no one could oppose the majority.". . . The fact that a liberal majority had formed on the commissions took on exceptional significance due to the disposition of forces among the provincial committees and the gentry at large, the bureaucracy and officialdom, the higher and central power entities and local administrations, where liberals constituted a minority. Thus the Editing Commissions became very anxious to support liberal minorities on provincial committees. . . .

Openness as a policy tool of the autocracy assumed a vital role in the activities of the Editorial Commissions. On fixed days after their meetings 3,000 copies of their journals, or protocols, were published and distributed to senior officials, provincial headquarters, marshals of the nobility, and various important men and officeholders, and they also went where they were not supposed to go, as, for example, to Herzen and Chernyshevskii. But such openness had not yet become part of the bourgeois order. The liberal majority on the Editing Commissions restricted the principles of openness and publicity as far as statements made by the conservative and reactionary opposition were concerned.

The fate of the peasantry and the country was not decided in open political contest or in class struggles. The new nontraditional institution functioned within the serf monarchy and had not shaken off the traditions of feudal organization and political culture. "All minds" were obliged to use the works produced by the commissions. Their leaders deliberately used publicity to rally the liberal forces, disseminate and make known their reform program, and prevent any possibility of its being revised or of the government's going back on its word. . . .

The liberal majority on the Editing Commissions conceived of the peasant reform as a revolution embodied in a single legal act. The first stage would be to free landlord serfs from personal dependency; the final one to convert all of them into petty property owners while still preserving a substantial part of gentry land and large landlord estates. They planned to

achieve their goal peacefully and avoid the revolutionary upheavals that had shaken countries in Western and Central Europe. This would be a distinctive characteristic of the reform and Russia's future agricultural development. . . .

Specifically, this meant constructing the reform on the basis of "existing reality," that is, the gentry would keep its lands for large-scale agriculture while allowing the peasants to keep their pre-reform plots, initially rented on payment of imposts, and subsequently as their own property in return for redemption payments. . . . Redemption payments lay at the heart of the reform. They were not required of landlords. Alexander II stated: "As long as even a single member of the gentry opposes redemption of peasant allotments I shall not permit compulsory redemption." Forced to reckon with this insurmountable obstacle, the Editing Commissions devised an internal mechanism for the reform to ensure the movement would not be interrupted or take on a life of its own. Permanent tenure and unalterable taxes would literally force landlords to accept redemption. . . .

The peasants likewise really had no choice. Determined to avoid the growth of a proletariat, as had happened in Europe, but also aware that the economic circumstances surrounding the liberation of the peasantry were harsh and landlords would do anything in their power to make them worse, the framers of the programs inserted a clause into the law that forbade peasants from alienating an allotment for nine years. When the law went into force this period was extended. This was the main reason why the commune was preserved to hold the land. . . .

The change in the legal position of the peasantry was even more thoroughgoing and decisive. Abolishing personal dependency and depriving landlords of patrimonial power thrust many millions of peasants into the life of society, although they all remained a taxpaying estate. Peasants now could regulate themselves through regional and rural societies (based on the commune) with officials elected at meetings conducted by the peasantry. Under the control of local administrations and performing financial tasks, such entities also looked out for peasant interests against the landlords, yesterday's serf-owners. They were instrumental in involving peasants in other reforms, such as the zemstvos, and serving on juries. It was assumed that in time it would be easier to leave the commune, mutual guarantees would be abolished, and the commune would gradually lose its hold over the individual peasant. Social estates would be replaced by universal citizenship, and the inevitable land shortage experienced by some peasants would be mitigated by grants of state land.

The initiative displayed by the monarchy was a symbol of faith in the liberal bureaucracy and the fact that constitutional change was not at the moment on the agenda of the liberal-bureaucratic group made the program acceptable. The initiative the monarchy demonstrated was a special guarantee of the reforms caused by the abolition of serfdom. This was the weakest link in the liberal bureaucracy's political conception, but another was the related notion that it would be possible to achieve equality between peasants and other social estates without real freedom for the "favored." This was why they were prohibited from leaving the land, had to give mutual guarantees, experienced difficulties in quitting the commune, and corporal punishment continued. . . .

The abolition of serfdom was a watershed in Russia's history. Serfdom as a system of social relationships had ceased to exist, although many of its characteristics survived until 1917. Describing the countryside after the reform, Tolstoi used Konstantin Levin in *Anna Karenina* as his spokesman: "Among us now, when everything has changed and is in the process of settling down, the one important question in Russia is how to arrange matters." These words moved Lenin to observe: "It is difficult to imagine a more apt characterization of Russia from 1861 to 1905." In his opinion, the most vital question was "how to establish this structure, the bourgeois structure, in Russia."

SOURCE: L.G. Zakharova, "Autocracy, Bureaucracy, and the Reforms of the 1860s in Russia," *Soviet Studies in History* (Spring 1991), pp. 6–33 (excerpted). Originally published as "Samoderzhavie, biurokratiia, i reformi 60-kh godov XIX v. v Rossii," *Voprosy istorii* 10 (1989): 3–22. Reprinted with the permission of M. E. Sharpe Inc.

TERENCE EMMONS

The Emancipation and the Nobility

In the previous essay, Larissa Zakharova wrote about the background to the Great Reforms, the political circumstances that brought them about, as well as the motivations of the people involved. In this selection, Terence Emmons returns to the question of motivations mostly in terms of the long-term meaning that emancipating the peasants had for Russian politics, ideology, and government.

Russia provides ample confirmation of Tocqueville's classic observation that 'the most perilous moment for a bad government is one when it seeks to mend its ways.' The emancipation was probably the greatest single piece of state-directed social engineering in modern European history before the twentieth century. Its ultimate aim was to fortify social and political stability; in fact it produced serious stresses and strains, of both a short- and a long-term character, in the social and political fabric.

The political ferment resulting from the raising of the emancipation issue makes it clear, in retrospect, why Nicholas I had so feared taking that step: He rightly foresaw that it would give rise to a political challenge to the autocracy. . . . Totally unaccustomed to taking directives from without, the government assumed the initiative in preparing the emancipation and a series of related reforms, with no intention of allowing public interference in its deliberations. In order, however, to prepare the gentry for emancipation and to acquire their cooperation in its preparation and implementation, the government was compelled to invite the gentry, and to some extent the public at large, to discuss the impending changes.

The government itself provoked the challenge, for it sought the unattainable: acquiescence and cooperation without a share of responsibility. Confronted with a confused and noisy response to its November 1857 invitation to the gentry, the government, in reflex action, began to circumscribe the terms of its invitation. This in turn provoked opposition, which led the government, in a series of moves in 1858–9, to withdraw entirely its invitation to gentry and public discussion: The gentry assemblies were forbidden to further discuss the 'peasant question', and the vise of censorship was once again tightened on the press. The government's retreat further stimulated the opposition and led to the raising of political demands in the gentry assemblies of 1859–60. But the government held fast and promulgated its emancipation with only minimal recognition of the gentry's criticisms.

In the tense atmosphere surrounding the proclamation and initial implementation of the reform, the gentry, in a state of outrage and fear for the future, set underway their 'constitutionalist campaign' in the assemblies of 1861–2. The government responded with a number of concessions to gentry complaints about the terms of emancipation, and some recognition of public opinion was reflected in the further reforms already under preparation. But it also ceased experimenting with public discussion of its reform plans. These concessions, time, and some fortuitous circumstances allowed the government to weather the crisis, which was clearly over with the outbreak of the Polish insurrection in January 1863.

It is only in terms of this pattern of events that the much-debated question of gentry attitudes toward the emancipation can be resolved. Generalizations about static group or regional interests, about the black soil—non-black soil dichotomy, are plainly insufficient. The only adequate approach to the problem is through analysis of the dynamics of gentry attitudes; and the key to this analysis is to be found in the development of government–gentry relations in the preparation of the reform. . . .

Another observation which can be made about periods of reform is that they afford particularly good vantage points for studying the structure and functioning of social and political systems. . . . [S]everal points worth stressing in conclusion can be discussed within the context of three problems, which will be called: (1) the autocracy; (2) Russian liberalism; (3) the gentry.

1. *The autocracy.* The Russian autocracy had come by the mid-nineteenth century to a political crossroads, and the turn it chose there determined, to a great extent, the subsequent character of internal state politics.

The day had passed when a Peter the Great could institute sweeping reforms in the life of the state with only sporadic reactions from a fragmented and inarticulate society. By the reign of Alexander II it had become clear— abundantly so in the years 1857–62—that there had come into existence in Russia a 'public opinion', ultimately the product of the expansion of education and the means of communication, and that the autocracy, if it were to undertake significant changes, would henceforth be confronted by this 'public opinion' in one way or another. The government, by announcing its intention to emancipate the serfs, opened the door to a wide-ranging movement for the liberalization of the autocratic system, a movement in which the gentry played the leading role. The autocracy learned from the confrontation in this period that attempts at reform give rise to demands for public participation in affairs of state. Having no intention of relinquishing undivided political authority, the autocracy drew a profoundly conservative conclusion; namely, that all change is dangerous. At the same time, for good or ill, it received a brief education in the politics of minimal compromise, and this lesson was not forgotten.

The opposition movement of the 1860s did not wring a 'constitution' from the autocracy, but it did win concessions. As Witte [Sergei Witte, the future Minister of Finance and Prime Minister during the reign of Nicholas II] later argued in his pamphlet *Autocracy and the Zemstvo*, the *zemstvo* reform, as devised, was a concession to gentry opinion. Reform of local administration, to be sure, was made necessary by the emancipation, but it was pressure from the gentry which brought the government to admit an element of popular representation into the reorganized administration, instead of proceeding, as it had originally intended, with a simple extension of the bureaucratic apparatus. It is similarly noteworthy that the most radical and best-organized of the reforms—the judicial—embodied most of the principles of judicial organization which had been repeatedly and universally demanded by all the gentry and Russian 'society' at large. Thus, the reforming activities of the autocracy in this period were to some extent the 'logic of things', dictated by the initial step of emancipation and the concerns that had led to that step. They bore, however, the stamp of political concession and were carried through by the momentum of the opposition movement. The attrition to which these reforms, especially the *zemstvo* reform, were subsequently subjected is indicative of the extent to which the political atmosphere of the early 1860s was responsible for their original character.

The politics of emancipation show clearly that the government of the 'bureaucratized' autocracy was far from being a genuine bureaucratic system of the type described by Max Weber. The autocrat retained undivided political authority and intervened systematically in the workings of the government administration—by disallowing effective inter-ministerial communications; by appointing personal favorites to higher administrative offices; by handling such important affairs of state as the emancipation outside the regular bureaucratic channels; by playing various elements of society off against the bureaucracy and vice versa. The 'personal character of political authority' remained very strong in Russia in the middle of the nineteenth century. Ironically, this was indicated by the very insistence of the gentry

—conservatives and liberals alike—that this was no longer so, that the monarch was the slave of a sovereign bureaucracy.

2. *Russian liberalism.* The 'union of tsar and people' was in fact a notion that pervaded Russian political thought from right to left, reflecting both the survival of pre-modern political conceptions (often nestled among the latest western doctrines) and prevailing political conditions. This fact, together with the broadly voiced demand for the *Rechtstaat* [government based on the rule of law] which was raised in the reform period, provokes numerous questions about the nature and history of Russian liberalism.

Paul Miliukov distinguished two periods in the history of Russian liberalism. In the first period, according to him, the history of liberalism had been the history of 'public opinion' (in the sense that it was essentially an intellectual movement, possessing neither a clearly-defined class orientation nor an organized political party). Its practical goal was emancipation, and the social milieu in which the struggle for emancipation developed was the educated gentry. . . . The second period, which began after the goal of the first period—emancipation—had been achieved, was the history of a political party and its goal was political liberty, a constitutional order. The heroes of the second period were the *zemstvo* liberals and, increasingly as time passed, people of non-noble origin, men of the 'liberal professions'. In the second period, Miliukov observed, it was in the *zemstva* that the liberal 'political party' elaborated its system of practical politics and organized itself.

It is apparently true that in Russia the emancipation was a prerequisite for the development of political parties in general. Before that event, the elaboration of practical programs by different segments of political opinion had been subordinated to the common goal of emancipation. . . . [H]owever, . . . it was even before emancipation, specifically in the period of its preparation, that the practical program and further goals of political liberalism began to be defined. That is to say, these goals were initially elaborated not in the *zemstva*, but by the gentry assemblies in their confrontation with the government in the period 1857–62. The platform of *zemstvo* constitutionalism was initially formulated then, and most explicitly by the Tver gentry in their 1862 assembly.

If it is, nevertheless, clear that the political-constitutionalist phase of Russian liberalism belongs essentially to the post-emancipation period, what can be said about liberalism in the pre-emancipation period beyond noting that it was a set of values very broadly shared in educated society? In so far as it aimed at eliminating administrative arbitrariness and establishing certain fundamental 'civil' rights for the individual, the entire anti-bureaucratic opposition of the immediate pre-emancipation years could be called liberal. Within this opposition, however, there were elements which, in almost any other context, could not be called liberal—the 'aristocratic' party and the proto-Populist radicals, to mention the two most obvious cases. The conflict between the government and the gentry over the peasant emancipation revealed, sociologically and intellectually speaking, who the direct antecedents of the *zemstvo* liberals were: The people who made up the liberal gentry opposition. . . .

Probably the single most important political result of the struggle between the government and the gentry over emancipation was the disintegration of [faith in enlightened despotism] and the turn by many to the belief that the desired reforms could come only through popular participation in government. More often than not, this belief was expressed in traditional Russian terminology, but its aim was constitutional monarchy. Russian liberals turned in 1861 from civil rights to political rights, from *Rechtstaat* liberalism to constitutional liberalism. . . .

3. *The gentry*. The epoch of the great reforms was a decisive moment in the history of the Russian landed gentry.

It may be said that in this brief span of time there occurred both the birth and death of the provincial gentry as a political force in the state. . . . [I]t was only in the 1850s, when the provincial gentry were called upon to participate in the preparation of emancipation, that their provincial institutions were given the breath of political life on a significant scale, and the gentry began to utilize them for clearly political purposes. Some of the provincial assemblies then rose to demand a role for the gentry in affairs of state. But it was an ironical fact in the history of that class that its provincial institutions were also politicized for the first time for the express purpose of demanding the abolition of gentry privileges and the elimination of these institutions themselves. The liberal gentry, who had no interest in the organs of gentry administration for their own sake, utilized them because they were the only available means of bringing political pressure to bear on the central government.

The emancipation and accompanying administrative changes—in particular the creation of the exclusively peasant communes and *volosti*—served to destroy such bonds of common interest as had existed between landlord and peasant, and the *zemstvo* reform, which was in large part a concession to the gentry demand for political participation, at the same time destroyed the exclusive significance of the local gentry institutions.

The emancipation dealt the gentry class an economic blow from which it never recovered. The glowing promises of the liberal abolitionists about the future of the gentry as commercial farmers was never realized for most of them. The economic plight in which the gentry found themselves immediately after emancipation—mainly their lack of capital to adapt to the 'new order of things'—was not solved by their wholesale turn to redemption. Most *pomeshchiki* had been living on credit since long before the emancipation, maintained by loans from the state and the availability of 'free' labor. The emancipation brought them to a reckoning with their debts—preliminarily deducted from the redemption payments made to them—which left few of them with enough capital to set up farming on a hired-labor basis. (By 1881, these deductions amounted to about 303,000,000 rubles out of a total sum of about 750,000,000 paid for redemption.) And those credit certificates which were received after deduction of debts were subjected to rapid and drastic devaluation (a process itself reflecting the gentry's dire need for cash). The gentry thus turned to renting the lands left them, and increasingly to selling them—an alternative which became progressively more attractive as land prices rose (under the pressure of peasant land-hunger) but grain prices declined throughout the last third of the nineteenth century. . . .

The reform produced no immediate, dramatic changes in the social and economic order—the peasants were released from their state of thralldom in a highly cautious and incomplete fashion, in accordance with the government's essentially conservative aims. But in a negative way—for what it failed to do—the emancipation was largely responsible for the social and economic crisis that resulted in the Russian Revolution. To the extent that it was the relatively undifferentiated peasant masses, goaded on by the pressure of rapid population growth and the burden of state-directed industrialization and war, which provided the elemental force for the destruction of the old regime, the emancipation contributed heavily to the Revolution's coming. By retention of the commune and various other restrictions, it hindered the creation of conditions that could have led to the social and technological modernization of rural Russia. The emancipation also removed the possibility that the impetus for such change might have come from the landed gentry.

SOURCE: Terence Emmons, *The Russian Landed Gentry and the Peasant Emacipation of 1861* (Cambridge: Cambridge University Press, 1968), 414–23 (excerpted). Copyright © 1968 by Cambridge University Press. Reprinted by permission of the publisher.